Creative Resources
for Infants and Toddlers

Dedication

THIS BOOK IS DEDICATED TO:

My grandchildren, Jeffrey and Eva Herr.

J. H.

My son, Randy, and my nieces and nephews.

T. S.

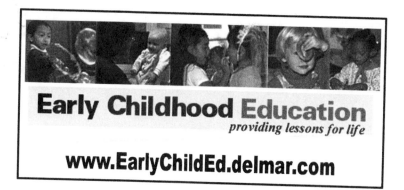

Creative Resources
for Infants and Toddlers

by

Judy Herr ♡ Terri Swim

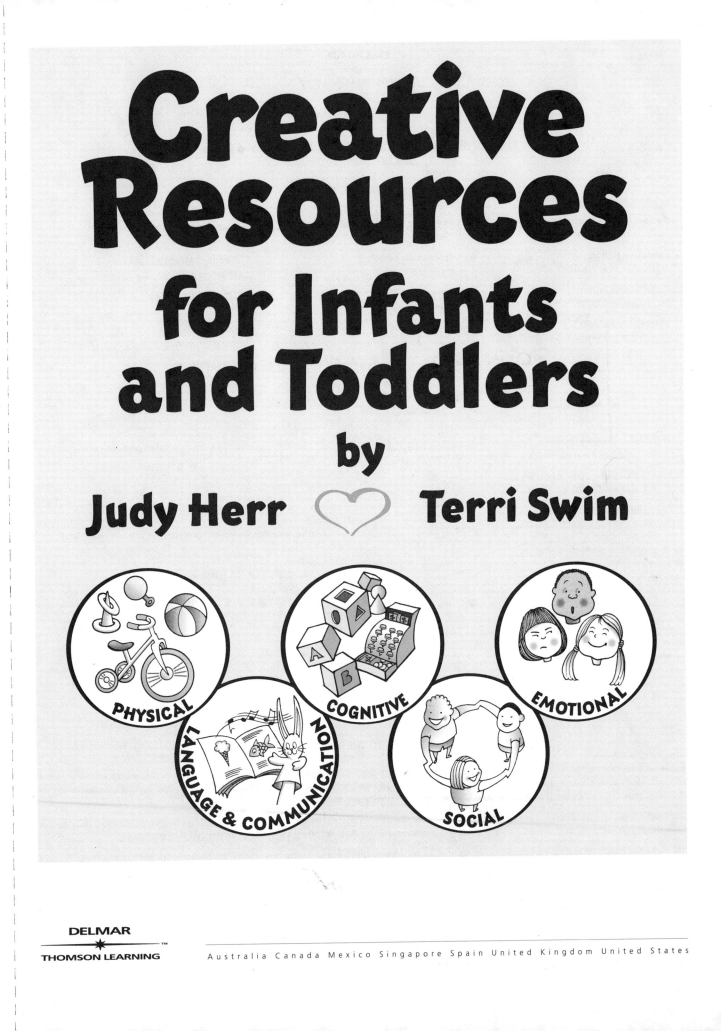

PHYSICAL

COGNITIVE

EMOTIONAL

LANGUAGE & COMMUNICATION

SOCIAL

DELMAR

THOMSON LEARNING™

Australia Canada Mexico Singapore Spain United Kingdom United States

DELMAR

THOMSON LEARNING

Creative Resources for Infants and Toddlers, Second Edition
Judy Herr and Terri Swim

Business Unit Director:
Susan L. Simpfenderfer

Executive Editor:
Marlene McHugh Pratt

Acquisitions Editor:
Erin O'Connor Traylor

Editorial Assistant:
Alexis Ferraro

Executive Production Manager:
Wendy A. Troeger

Production Editor:
Joy Kocsis

Technology Project Manager:
James Considine

Executive Marketing Manager:
Donna J. Lewis

Channel Manager:
Nigar Hale

Cover Illustrations:
Jeanne Benas

Cover Design:
Joseph Villanova

Composition:
Publisher's Studio

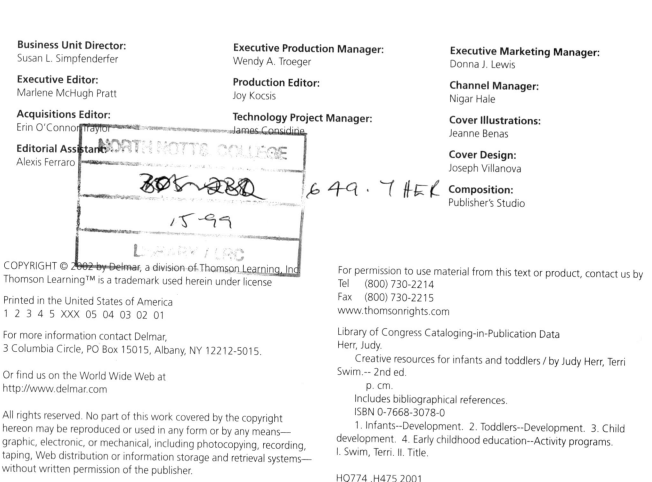
COPYRIGHT © 2002 by Delmar, a division of Thomson Learning, Inc.
Thomson Learning™ is a trademark used herein under license

Printed in the United States of America
1 2 3 4 5 XXX 05 04 03 02 01

For more information contact Delmar,
3 Columbia Circle, PO Box 15015, Albany, NY 12212-5015.

Or find us on the World Wide Web at
http://www.delmar.com

For permission to use material from this text or product, contact us by
Tel   (800) 730-2214
Fax   (800) 730-2215
www.thomsonrights.com

Library of Congress Cataloging-in-Publication Data
Herr, Judy.
    Creative resources for infants and toddlers / by Judy Herr, Terri Swim.-- 2nd ed.
        p. cm.
    Includes bibliographical references.
    ISBN 0-7668-3078-0
    1. Infants--Development. 2. Toddlers--Development. 3. Child development. 4. Early childhood education--Activity programs. I. Swim, Terri. II. Title.

HQ774 .H475 2001
305.232--dc21   2001047514

NOTICE TO THE READER

Contents

Thirty-One to Thirty-Six Months 397

References 457

Appendices 459

Preface

Responding in a warm, loving, and responsive manner to a crying infant or playing patty-cake with a young toddler both exemplify ways that caregivers and families promote healthy brain development. In fact, recent research on brain development emphasizes the importance of the environment and relationships during the child's first three years of life (Shore, 1997). With this in mind, the second edition of *Creative Resources for Infants and Toddlers* was written for you, the caregivers and families. The ultimate goal of this book is to assist in promoting healthy development of our youngest children. Thus, it should be part of all parents' and caregivers' libraries.

The book focuses on the growth of the whole child by including norms for physical, language and communication, cognitive, social, and emotional development. To support, enhance, and promote the child's development in all of these areas, this unique book includes specially designed activities for infants and toddlers. Note that the book has five main sections. The first section includes information for understanding, assessing, and promoting development, as well as suggestions for interacting with young children. The next two sections include 380 innovative activities to promote development for infants and toddlers, respectively. The fourth section includes references for the material cited in the text. The final section's appendices are a rich resource including, but not limited to, lists of recipes, songs, finger plays, chants, and books. It also contains a list of toys and equipment, as well as criteria for making selections.

To assist you, the experiences are grouped by age ranges and developmental areas. Each of these activities is designed to illustrate the connection between a broad area of development and specific goals for children. For example, physical development may be the primary area and eye-hand coordination may be one specific goal. The materials, preparation, and nurturing strategies for the activities are designed for easy and effective implementation. Moreover, variations and additional information have been incorporated to enrich the experience for both you and the child. Highlighting Development boxes provide valuable information for fostering an understanding of young children's development. Collectively, the information and experiences provided in this book will enhance your ability to meet the developmental needs of infants and toddlers, fostering optimal development of the whole child. Furthermore, these early experiences will create a strong foundation for children's subsequent thinking, interacting with others, and learning.

ONLINE RESOURCES™

The Online Resources™ to accompany *Creative Resources for Infants and Toddlers, Second Edition* is your link to early childhood education on the Internet. The Online Resources™ contains many features to help focus your understanding of the learning and teaching process.

♡ Sample Activities and Preface
♡ Developmental Milestones
♡ Books for Infants and Toddlers
♡ Books for Two-Year-Olds
♡ Criteria for Selecting Materials and Equipment for Children
♡ Materials and Equipment for Promoting Optimal Development
♡ Movement Activities for Children from Thirteen to Thirty-Six Months
♡ Favorite Finger Plays, Nursery Rhymes, and Chants
♡ Songs
♡ Rhythm Instruments
♡ Recipes
♡ Resources Related to Infants and Toddlers
♡ Developmental Checklist
♡ Anecdotal Record
♡ Sample Running Record
♡ Panel Documentation
♡ Lesson Plan
♡ Daily Communications
♡ A Summarized list of Web links is provided for your reference.
♡ On-line Early Education Survey – This survey gives you the opportunity to let us know what features you want to see improved on the Online Resources™.

The authors and Delmar make every effort to ensure that all Internet resources are accurate at the time of printing. However, due to the fluid, time-sensitive nature of the Internet, we cannot guarantee that all URLs and Web site addresses will remain current for the duration of this edition.

> Online Resources
>
> You can find the Online Resources™ at <www.EarlyChildEd.delmar.com>.
> username: s7w9m5i8
> password: 8i5m9w7s

ACKNOWLEDGMENTS

We would like to thank many people. First, our husbands, Dr. James Herr and James Daniel Swim, who supported us during this process.

To our families, who have continuously provided encouragement and facilitated our personal and professional development.

Furthermore, this book would not have been possible without the inspiration of the numerous young children who have touched and influenced our lives in so many meaningful ways. The children we have met in university laboratories and child care settings and their teachers and parents have all demonstrated the importance of the early years of life.

We want to acknowledge the contributions of the numerous colleges, universities, colleagues, and students that have fostered our professional growth and development:

College of William and Mary, Norfolk, Virginia; University of Akron, Ohio; Harvard University, Cambridge, Massachusetts; Purdue University, West Lafayette, Indiana; University of Minnesota, Minneapolis, Minnesota; University of Missouri, Columbia, Missouri; University of Texas, Austin, Texas; and University of Wisconsin-Stout, Menomonie, Wisconsin.

Specifically we would like to thank Carla Ahman, Carol Armga, Michelle Batchelder, Chalandra Bryant, Mary Jane Burson-Polston, Bill Carver, Linda Conner, Kay Cutler, Sandi Dillon, Loraine Dunn, Nancy File, Nancy Hazen-Swann, Debra Hughes, Susan Jacquet, Elizabeth Johnson, Joan Jurich, Susan Kontos, Gary Ladd, Julia Lorenz, Pat Morris, Linda Norton-Smith, Barbara O'Donnel, Diana Peyton, Douglas R. Powell, Kathy Pruesse, Julie Rand, Karin Samii, Jen Shields, Cathy Surra, Adriana Umana, Chris Upchurch, Lisa West, and Rhonda Whitman for their encouragement and support.

Also, special thanks to Carol Hagness, University of Wisconsin-Stout Educational Materials Collection Librarian, and Ann Salt, Children's Librarian at the Menomonie Public Library, who developed the list of books for infants and toddlers that is located in Appendix A; Erin O'Connor Traylor, our editor from Delmar who provided continuous encouragement, support, and creative ideas; and Deb Hass and Vicki Weber, who typed the manuscript.

The authors and publisher would like to thank the following reviewers for their constructive suggestions and recommendations:

Davia Allen
Western Carolina University
Cullowhee, NC

Alice Beyrent
Hesser College
Manchester, NH

Billie Coffman
Pennsylvania College of Technology
Williamsport, PA

Irene Cook
Taft College Children's Center
Taft, CA

Linda Estes
St. Charles County Community College
St. Peters, MO

Jody Martin
Children's World Learning Centers
Golden, CO

Introduction

Smiling, crying, bicycling with their legs, and laughing at caregivers are all signals infants use to gain and maintain attention. Watching them is exciting. They are amazing. Each infant has an individual style; no two are alike. Differences in temperament are apparent from birth. Some infants are quiet, while others are active. Each is unique. However, all infants grow and develop in predictable patterns, even though the exact rate varies from infant to infant.

Development can be defined as change over time. According to Bentzen (2001), development refers to any "change in the structure, thought, or behavior of an individual that comes from biological and environmental influences" (p. 15). Human development occurs in two distinct patterns. First, development proceeds from the top of the body to the bottom. For example, control of the head develops before control of the torso or the legs. The second pattern is for development to proceed from the center of the body outward. To illustrate, the arm muscles develop before those of the hands or fingers.

UNDERSTANDING THEORIES OF DEVELOPMENT

Searching the literature, you will find numerous beliefs about or theories of child growth and development. Some beliefs are in direct opposition to each other. There are theories that state children are biologically programmed at birth. These theories purport that children develop according to their own individual timetable, regardless of environmental influences. In contrast, there are nurture-based theories that emphasize the importance of environmental factors. These theories assume that children enter the world as blank slates. According to these theories, the children's environment is instrumental in molding their abilities. A third set of theories incorporates aspects from both of these two extremes, nature and nurture. These interactional theories are based on the premise that biology and environment work in concert to account for children's development.

While reading this book, you will note that it celebrates interactional theories. Current research on brain development supports the belief that human development hinges on the dynamic interplay between nature and nurture (Shore, 1997). At birth, the development of the child's brain is unfinished. Through early experiences, the brain matures and connections are made for wiring its various parts. Repeated experiences result in the wiring becoming permanent, thereby creating the foundation for the brain's organization and functioning throughout life.

Your role is critical because early experiences significantly affect how each child's brain is wired. The child's relationships with parents, caregivers, and significant others will all influence how the brain becomes wired. Therefore, loving encounters and positive social, emotional, language and communication, cognitive, and physical experiences all influence the development of a healthy brain.

However, this influence is far from unidirectional. Children, for example, are born with different temperaments. Research has shown that children's dispositions influence their involvement with both people and materials in their environment. To illustrate, Quincy is a quiet, slow-to-warm-up child. He initially holds back and observes. Moreover, he becomes very distressed in new situations. To prevent Quincy from feeling distressed, his caregivers and parents sometimes respond by minimizing the introduction of new experiences or situations. Consequently, his physical, language and communication, emotional, social, and cognitive development are shaped by his characteristics and his caregivers' and parents' responses to these characteristics.

USING DEVELOPMENTAL NORMS

Research on human development provides evidence that infants and toddlers grow and develop in predictable sequences or patterns. Such predictable, or universal, patterns of development occur in all domains—physical, cognitive, language and communication, social, and emotional. The specific components of these universal patterns are called developmental norms. Norms provide evidence of when a large group of children, on average, accomplishes a given task. Because norms are averages, they must be interpreted with caution. There are differences from child to child in the timing for reaching developmental milestones within one specific domain and across different domains. For example, a child may reach all developmental milestones as expected in the cognitive domain but develop on a later timetable in the language domain. Hence, each child has a unique pattern of timing of growth and development that must be taken into account.

Notwithstanding their limitations, developmental norms are useful to caregivers and parents for three main reasons. First, they allow for judgments and evaluations of the relative normalcy of a child's developmental progression. If a child is lagging behind in one developmental task, generally there should be little concern. But if a child is behind on numerous tasks, human development specialists should be consulted for further evaluations.

Second, developmental norms are useful in making broad generalizations about the timing of particular skills and behaviors. Understanding the child's current level of development in relation to the norms allows predictions about upcoming tasks. For example, a child who can easily find a toy that is partially hidden is ready to begin searching for a toy that is completely out of view.

This knowledge of future development ties into the third reason why developmental norms are helpful. Developmental norms allow caregivers and parents to create and implement experiences that support and enhance the child's current level of development. Following the example just given, an adult playing a hide-and-seek game could begin by partially hiding a toy with a towel and then add the challenge of completely covering the toy.

The following table includes a list of developmental norms for infants and toddlers, highlighting significant tasks. Norms are grouped by areas of development, and within each area the specific tasks have been arranged sequentially. When using this table, please remember that it represents universal patterns of development. You will need to be cognizant of each child's unique patterns.

Developmental Milestones*

PHYSICAL DEVELOPMENT

Birth to Three Months	Four to Six Months	Seven to Nine Months	Ten to Twelve Months	Thirteen to Eighteen Months	Nineteen to Twenty-Four Months	Twenty-Five to Thirty-Six Months
Acts reflexively—sucking, stepping, rooting	Holds cube in hand	Sits independently	Supports entire body weight on legs	Builds tower of two cubes	Walks up stairs independently, one step at a time	Maneuvers around obstacles in a pathway
Swipes at objects in front of body, uncoordinated	Reaches for objects with one hand	Stepping reflex returns, so that child bounces when held on a surface in a standing position	Walks when hands are held	Turns the pages of a cardboard book two or three at a time	Jumps in place	Runs in a more adult-like fashion; knees are slightly bent, arms move in the opposite direction
Holds head erect and steady when lying on stomach	Rolls from back to side	Leans over and reaches when in a sitting position	Cruises along furniture or steady objects	Scribbles vigorously	Kicks a ball	Walks down stairs independently
Lifts head and shoulders	Reaches for objects in front of body, coordinated	Gets on hands and knees but may fall forward	Stands independently	Walks proficiently	Runs in a modified fashion	Marches to music
Rolls from side to back	Sits with support	Crawls	Walks independently	Walks while carrying or pulling a toy	Shows a decided preference for one hand	Uses feet to propel wheeled riding toys
Follow moving objects with eyes	Transfers objects from hand to hand	Pulls to standing position	Crawls up stairs or steps	Walks up stairs with assistance	Completes a three-piece puzzle with knobs	Rides a tricycle
	Grabs objects with either hand	Stands with adult's assistance	Voluntarily releases objects held in hands		Builds a tower of six cubes	Usually uses whole arm movements to paint or color
	Sits in tripod position using arms for support	Claps hands together	Has good balance when sitting; can shift positions without falling			Throws ball forward, where intended
		Learns pincer grasp, using thumb with forefinger to pick up objects	Takes off shoes and socks			Builds tower using eight or more blocks
		Uses finger and thumb to pick up objects				Imitates drawing circles and vertical and horizontal lines
		Brings objects together with banging noises				Turns pages in book one by one
						Fingers work together to scoop up small objects
						Strings large beads on a shoelace

*The developmental milestones listed are based on universal patterns of when various traits emerge. Because each child is unique certain traits may develop at an earlier or later age.

Developmental Milestones* (continued)

LANGUAGE AND COMMUNICATION DEVELOPMENT

Birth to Three Months	Four to Six Months	Seven to Nine Months	Ten to Twelve Months	Thirteen to Eighteen Months	Nineteen to Twenty-Four Months	Twenty-Five to Thirty-Six Months
Communicates with cries, grunts, and facial expressions	Babbles spontaneously	Varies babble in loudness, pitch, and rhythm	Uses preverbal gestures to influence the behavior of others	Has expressive vocabulary of 10 to 20 words	Continues using telegraphic speech	Continues using telegraphic speech combining three or four words
Prefers human voices	Acquires sounds of native language in babble	Adds *d, t, n,* and *w* to repertoire of babbling sounds	Demonstrates word comprehension skills	Engages in "jargon talk"	Able to combine three words	Speaks in complete sentences following word order of native language
Coos	Canonical, systematic consonant-vowel pairings; babbling occurs	Produces gestures to communicate, often by pointing	Waves good-bye	Engages in telegraphic speech by combining two words together	Talks, 25 percent of words being understandable	Displays effective conversational skills
Laughs	Participates in interactive games initiated by adults	May say *mama* or *dada* but does not connect words with parents	Speaks recognizable first word	Experiences a burst of language development	Refers to self by name	Refers to self as *me* or *I* rather than by name
Smiles and coos to initiate and sustain interactions with caregiver	Takes turns while interacting		Initiates familiar games with adults	Comprehends approximately 50 words	Joins three or four words into a sentence	Talks about objects and events not immediately present
					Comprehends approximately 300 words	Uses grammatical markers and some plurals
					Expressive language includes a vocabulary of approximately 250 words	Vocabulary increases rapidly, up to 300 words
						Enjoys being read to if allowed to participate by pointing, talking, and turning pages

*The developmental milestones listed are based on universal patterns of when various traits emerge. Because each child is unique certain traits may develop at an earlier or later age.

Developmental Milestones * (continued)

COGNITIVE DEVELOPMENT

Birth to Three Months	Four to Six Months	Seven to Nine Months	Ten to Twelve Months	Thirteen to Eighteen Months	Nineteen to Twenty-Four Months	Twenty-Five to Thirty-Six Months
Cries for assistance	Recognizes people by their voice	Enjoys looking at books with familiar objects	Solves sensorimotor problems by deliberately using schemas, such as shaking a container to empty its contents	Explores properties of objects by acting on them in novel ways	Points to and identifies objects on request, such as when reading a book, touring, etc.	Uses objects for purposes other than intended
Acts reflexively	Enjoys repeating acts, such as shaking a rattle, that produce results in the external world	Distinguishes familiar from unfamiliar faces		Solves problems through trial and error	Sorts by shapes and colors	Uses private speech while working
Prefers to look at patterned objects, bull's-eye, horizontal stripes, and the human face	Searches with eyes for source of sounds	Engages in goal-directed behavior	Points to body parts upon request	Experiments with cause-and-effect relationships such as turning on televisions, banging on drums, etc.	Recognizes self in photographs and mirror	Classifies objects based on one dimension, such as toy cars versus blocks
Imitates adults' facial expressions	Enjoys watching hands and feet	Anticipates events	Drops toys intentionally and repeatedly looks in the direction of the fallen object		Demonstrates deferred imitation	Follows two-step directions
Searches with eyes for sources of sounds	Searches for a partially hidden object	Finds objects that are totally hidden		Plays body identification games	Engages in functional play	Concentrates or attends to self-selected activities for longer periods of time
Begins to recognize familiar people at a distance	Uses toys in a purposeful manner	Imitates behaviors that are slightly different than those usually performed	Waves good-bye	Imitates novel behaviors of others	Finds objects that have been moved while out of sight	Points to and labels objects spontaneously, such as when reading a book
Discovers and repeats bodily actions such as sucking, swiping, and grasping	Imitates simple actions	Begins to show interest in filling and dumping containers	Shows evidence of stronger memory capabilities	Identifies family members in photographs	Solves problems with internal representation	Coordinates pretend play with other children
Discovers hands and feet as extension of self	Explores toys using existing schemas such as sucking, banging, grasping, shaking, etc.		Follows simple, one-step directions		Categorizes self and others by gender, race, hair color, etc.	Gains a nominal sense of numbers through counting and labeling objects in a set
			Categorizes objects by appearance			Begins developing concepts about opposites such as big and small, tall and short, in and out
			Looks for objects hidden in a second location			Begins developing concepts about time such as today, tomorrow, and yesterday

*The developmental milestones listed are based on universal patterns of when various traits emerge. Because each child is unique certain traits may develop at an earlier or later age.

Developmental Milestones* (continued)

Birth to Three Months	Four to Six Months	Seven to Nine Months	Ten to Twelve Months	Thirteen to Eighteen Months	Nineteen to Twenty-Four Months	Twenty-Five to Thirty-Six Months
Turns head toward a speaking voice	Seeks out adults for play by crying, cooing, or smiling	Becomes upset when separated from a favorite adult	Shows a decided preference for one or two caregivers	Demands personal attention	Shows enthusiasm for company of others	Observes others to see how they do things
Recognizes primary caregiver	Responds with entire body to familiar face by looking at the person, smiling, kicking legs, and waving arms	Acts deliberately to maintain the presence of a favorite adult by clinging or crying	Plays parallel to other children	Imitates behaviors of others	Views the world only from own, egocentric perspective	Engages primarily in solitary or parallel play
Bonds to primary caregiver	Participates actively in interactions with others by vocalizing in response to adult speech	Uses adults as a base for exploration, typically	Enjoys playing with siblings	Becomes increasingly aware of the self as a separate being	Plays contently alone or near adults	Sometimes offers toys to other children
Finds comfort in the human face	Smiles at familiar faces and stares solemnly at strangers	Looks to others who are exhibiting signs of distress	Begins asserting self	Shares affection with people other than primary caregiver	Engages in functional play	Begins to play cooperatively with other children
Displays a social smile	Distinguishes between familiar and unfamiliar adults and surroundings	Enjoys observing and interacting briefly with other children	Begins developing a sense of humor	Shows ownership of possessions	Defends possessions	Engages in sociodramatic play
Is quieted by a voice		Likes to play and responds to games such as patty-cake and peekaboo	Develops a sense of self-identity through the identification of body parts	Begins developing a view of self as autonomous when completing tasks independently	Recognizes self in photographs or mirrors	Wants to do things independently
Begins to differentiate self from caregiver		Engages in solitary play	Begins distinguishing boys from girls		Refers to self with pronouns such as I or me	Asserts independence by using "no" a lot
		Develops preferences for particular people and objects			Categorizes people by using salient characteristics such as race or hair color	Develops a rudimentary awareness that others have wants or feelings that may be different than their own
		Shows distress when in the presence of a stranger			Shows less fear of strangers	Makes demands of or "bosses" parents, guardians, and caregivers
						Uses physical aggression less and uses words to solve problems
						Engages in gender sterotypical behavior

*The developmental milestones listed are based on universal patterns of when various traits emerge. Because each child is unique certain traits may develop at an earlier or later age.

Developmental Milestones* (continued)

EMOTIONAL DEVELOPMENT

Birth to Three Months	Four to Six Months	Seven to Nine Months	Ten to Twelve Months	Thirteen to Eighteen Months	Nineteen to Twenty-Four Months	Twenty-Five to Thirty-Six Months
Feels and expresses three basic emotions: interest, distress, and disgust	Expresses delight	Responds to social events by using the face, gaze, voice, and posture to form coherent emotional patterns	Continues to exhibit delight, happiness, discomfort, anger, and sadness	Exhibits autonomy by frequently saying "no"	Expresses affection to others spontaneously	Experiences increase in number of fears
Cries to signal a need	Responds to the emotions of caregivers	Expresses fear and anger more often	Expresses anger when goals are blocked	Labels several emotions	Acts to comfort others in distress	Begins to understand the consequences of basic emotions
Quiets in response to being held, typically	Begins to distinguish familiar from unfamiliar people	Begins to regulate emotions through moving into or out of experiences	Expresses anger at the source of frustration	Connects feelings with social behaviors	Shows the emotions of pride and embarrassment	Learns skills for coping with strong emotions
Feels and expresses enjoyment	Shows a preference for being held by a familiar person	Begins to detect the meaning of others' emotional expressions	Begins to show compliance to caregivers' requests	Begins to understand complicated patterns of behavior	Uses emotion words spontaneously in conversations or play	Seeks to communicate more feelings with specific words
Shares a social smile	Begins to assist with holding a bottle	Looks to others for cues on how to react	Often objects to having playtime stopped	Demonstrates the ability to communicate needs	Begins to show sympathy to another child or adult	Shows signs of empathy and caring
Reads and distinguishes adults' facial expressions	Expresses happiness selectively by laughing and smiling more with familiar people	Shows fear of strangers	Begins eating with a spoon	May say "no" to something they want	Becomes easily hurt by criticism	Loses control of emotions and throws temper tantrums
Begins to self-regulate emotional expressions			Assists in dressing and undressing	May lose emotional control and have temper tantrums	Experiences a temper tantrum when goals are blocked, on occasion	Able to recover from temper tantrums
Laughs aloud			Acts in loving, caring ways toward dolls or stuffed animals, typically	Shows self-conscious emotions such as shame, guilt, and shyness	Associates facial expressions with simple emotional labels	Enjoys helping with chores such as cleaning up toys or carrying grocery bags
Quiets self by using techniques such as sucking a thumb or pacifier			Feeds self a complete meal when served finger foods	Becomes frustrated easily		Begins to show signs of being ready for toileting
			Claps when successfully completes a task			Desires that routines be carried out exactly as has been done in the past

*The developmental milestones listed are based on universal patterns of when various traits emerge. Because each child is unique certain traits may develop at an earlier or later age.

"All children have the potential, albeit in different ways, to learn and to develop their own ideas, theories, and strategies. All children also have the right to be supported in these endeavors by adults. Teachers and parents, therefore, should observe and listen to them" (Gandini & Goldhaber, 2001, p. 125).

Assessment is the process of observing, listening, recording, and documenting behavior in order to make decisions about a child's developmental and, thus, educational needs. This process is applicable for an individual child, a small group, or an entire group of children. Your observation skills are the main tools needed for assessing development. By observing and listening, you will discover much about children's needs, interests, and abilities.

This is a simple process. Your eyes and ears are like a video camera capturing children's behaviors, language, attitudes, and preferences. Most of the time you should be examining the children's abilities on worthy and meaningful tasks that you have created. Thus, your assessments will be directly tied to the curriculum that you have planned and implemented. For example, you do this when interacting with an infant or when assisting a toddler who is busy "working" at an experience. In other words, this is a spontaneous process that is continuously occurring. Authentic assessment requires your focused attention and some additional time for documenting your observation. To assist you in this process, a checklist has been included in Appendix K. If you are caring for more than one child, reproduce a copy for each. Appendix L is a form for recording anecdotal records. This form will allow you to document behaviors and incidents not represented on the checklist.

Appendix M provides a sample running record. This method of assessment allows you to continuously observe and record, in narrative form, behaviors over a specific period of time. Notice the similarities between the anecdotal and running records. The main difference involves the amount of time covered during the observation. An anecdotal record involves one event whereas a running record covers all of the various behaviors that were exhibited within a specified time period. Therefore, a running record provides a complete view of a particular time period or behavior.

You can also collect artifacts that represent the children's abilities. For example, collect samples of artwork, writing (scribbling), or sculptures. To record the children's performance during an activity that does not result in a product, use a camera to document behavior and abilities.

There are several reasons why caregivers and parents need to assess the development of young children. First, assessment tracks growth and development, noting progress and change over time, thereby providing evidence of learning and maturation. Each observation conducted by a parent or caregiver provides a "snapshot" of the child's development. Combining several snapshots over time provides a comprehensive composite of the changes in the child's growth and development. These changes can be in one of three directions. Typically, children's growth and development follow a predictable sequence. That is, infants coo before they babble. Likewise, they produce a social smile before they are able to wave good-bye. Children can also continue working on the same skills. For example, they may spend several weeks or even months working on picking up objects with their thumbs and fingers. Finally, children can regress in their development. Although this happens infrequently, it can occur in times of great stress. For example, a toddler who had demonstrated proficiency at using a spoon at mealtime may revert back to using fingers to eat nonfinger foods.

Second, assessment provides insight to children's styles, interests, and dispositions. This information is invaluable in determining the correct level of responsiveness by parents and caregivers. It is much easier to meet a child's needs when you understand, for example, that the infant has difficulty transitioning from one activity to another. Knowing this assists you in preparing the infant for the next component of your daily routine, such as eating lunch.

Third, assessment data provides you with information regarding the normalcy of children's growth and development. This information directly impacts the experiences you create for the children. You should plan a balance of activities that support, enhance, and foster all areas of development. Some activities should be repetitious and represent developmental tasks that a child has accomplished yet still shows interest in and enjoys. Other activities should be a continuation of developmental tasks that the child is currently mastering. Still other activities should stimulate the child's development by requiring a higher skill level, thereby providing a challenge. At these times, children may need more adult support and assistance for scaffolding their learning as well as building their confidence as competent learners.

Fourth, developmental data must be gathered for effectively communicating the child's development with others. For example, if you are caring for children other than your own, you could discuss their progress with their parents or guardians. Likewise, if you are a parent, you will want to share this information with your child's caregiver, your significant other, or your child's pediatrician. Then, too, you may want to compile a portfolio or scrapbook containing a developmental checklist, photographs, videotapes, artwork, and other documents representing the child's growth and development.

Finally, assessment must be conducted to ensure that data is gathered for all areas of development. People have different biases and values. As a result, they may overlook or slight one area of development because of selective attention. If all areas are not assessed, experiences, toys, and equipment provided for children may not meet their developmental needs.

To undertake effective assessment, you will want to compile the data you collect into a meaningful form. The format you choose will depend on how you intend to use the data (Helm, Beneke, & Steinheimer, 1998). For example, if you wish to communicate with others about learning that occurred during a specific activity, you could display the artifacts collected, the photographs taken, and the dialogue transcribed while the children were working. If working in an early childhood program, this information could be displayed on a two-dimensional panel (see Appendix N) or a three-dimensional "Look at What I Did Table." Moreover, to communicate about one child's current level of development, you might want to create a portfolio containing significant artifacts, such as a developmental checklist, anecdotal records, running records, photographs, videotapes, and artwork that represents the child's growth and development.

RESPECTING INFANTS AND TODDLERS

Respect. Regard. Honor. Value. These words are seldom used to describe very young children. Yet, these are traits or characteristics that are desired and valued in older children and adults. How better to teach such traits than to model them to infants and toddlers from the very beginning? Respect must be demonstrated in your behaviors. More importantly, respect for infants and toddlers must be something that emanates from inside of you. You have to believe that infants and toddlers are worthy of your time and attention as individuals, because a respectful relationship is vital to all aspects of child development. For example, when infants are respected, they learn to trust that adults can be counted on to meet their needs. This foundation of trust allows them to actively explore their environment during toddlerhood. Hence, trust leads to learning about the world and the toddler's place in it.

It may seem hard to demonstrate respect to infants and toddlers because we are unaccustomed to thinking about very young children in this manner. However, it is not difficult. Respect means believing in the children's abilities to explore, solve problems, or cause events to happen in their world. It also means setting and enforcing clear boundaries for behavior. This is not always easy to do as toddlers are gaining a sense of autonomy and want to do things by themselves. We think that this is the most important time to demonstrate respect. Watch them for cues on how to help. Monitor your own behaviors to avoid doing too much or too little. Toddlers need help that is "appropriate" to support their development and learning.

Furthermore, employing positive guidance techniques promotes a sense of autonomy and self-efficacy. To illustrate, when a toddler is exploring her body in space by climbing and jumping, ensure that she has a safe place for these behaviors. If the spot she has selected is not appropriate, guide her toward a safer location by saying, "If you want to jump, jump from this step onto the mat. It is safe to jump over here." This redirection technique recognizes the child's underlying desire for activity and finds a more acceptable, safer substitution (Marion, 1999). Moreover, setting clear limits allows toddlers to make decisions within a framework of boundaries. Demonstrating respect does not mean that the infants and toddlers have control over the adult. In fact, it is just the opposite. Adults who are respectful of young children have established clear rules and enforce them. These adults also explain the rules to children. Making rules explicit and clear has been found to assist toddlers with adhering to rules and developing a sense of morality (Charlesworth, 2000).

A great deal has been written for parents/guardians and teachers about toddlerhood. Unfortunately, much of the focus is on the "terrible twos." It is easy to see how this could happen. On one hand, toddlers can be challenging to be around because they want to do so many things on their own that they actively resist help, even when help is clearly warranted. They are also continuing to learn about emotions and ways to control them. Unfortunately, they do lose control, but we all have at some point in our lives. On the other hand, a two-year-old can be an absolute delight, full of humor and self-confidence, and a remarkable source of pleasure for adults. Within a framework of respect, both "hands" of toddlerhood are valued and cherished for what they are at any given moment and for what they can be in the future. Respectful caregivers of toddlers realize that important life lessons and foundations for future life lessons are being learned now.

Take the time to look through the eyes of toddlers. From their perspective, there is so much to see and the world is absolutely fascinating. No wonder they are so enthusiastic, energetic, and inquisitive. With this mindset, you will come to share their never-ending curiosity.

COMMUNICATING WITH INFANTS AND TODDLERS

Parents and caregivers play a vital role in helping children master communication and language skills. Listen to the infant-directed speech people use while interacting with and speaking to infants. Originally, this speech was referred to as "motherese"; now it is called "parentese." This type of speech involves speaking slowly and exaggerating changes both in intonation and pitch.

When people use parentese while speaking to an infant, the higher pitch and slower pace capture the child's attention. Then, too, the careful enunciation and simplified style and meanings make the speech easier for the child to understand. By emphasizing one word in a sentence, the adult helps to provide a focal point for the child. When speaking parentese, adults consciously reinforce the infant's role in the conversation by encouraging turn taking and responding to the child's utterances. The following example illustrates the components of parentese:

Caregiver: *"Look at the kitteeee."*
Infant responds by cooing: *"Ahhhhh."*
Caregiver: *"The kitty is black."*
Infant responds by cooing: *"Ahhhh."*
Caregiver: *"The cat is eating now."*
Infant responds by cooing: *"Ohhhh."*
Caregiver: *"Yes, you knew the cat was hungry."*

Common features of parentese are highlighted in the following table:

Common Features of "Parentese"

Producing Sounds

♡ Exaggerates intonation and uses higher pitch

♡ Moves frequently between high and low pitches, occasionally whispers

♡ Enunciates more clearly

♡ Emphasizes one or two words in a sentence

♡ Parrots a child's pronunciation, correct or incorrect

Simplifying Meanings

♡ Substitutes simple words for more complicated ones: moo moo for cow

♡ Uses diminutives: doggy for dog

♡ Labels objects according to simplest category: bird for parrot

♡ Repeats words invented by child: baba for bottle

Modifying Grammar

♡ Simplifies sentences grammatically to use short sentences: daddy go

♡ Uses nouns in lieu of pronouns: mommy helping Jeffrey

♡ Uses plural pronouns, if spoken: We drink our bottle

Interacting with a Child

♡ Focuses on naming objects, sounds, or events in the immediate environment

♡ Asks and answers own questions

♡ Uses questions more than statements or commands

♡ Pauses to allow for turn taking

♡ Repeats own utterances

♡ Responds to the child's utterances through repeating, expanding, and recasting

(Baron, 1992; Snow, 1998; Zigler & Stevenson, 1993)

Once young children begin understanding language, they begin using it. Language comprehension occurs before production. In the beginning, new words emerge slowly, then suddenly there is a burst. Nouns are acquired more rapidly than verbs. Children's first words focus on their body parts, toys, clothing, and words for social interaction such as *bye-bye* and *hello*. After developing and expressing a repertoire of single words, between 18 months and 2 years of age, children begin to combine words to make two-word phrases for communicating.

Toddlers' attention spans during the third year of life are increasing in small increments and their language and cognitive development is fascinating. During this stage of development, they make tremendous strides in understanding their world. Children now produce three-word phrases for communicating. Then, at about 30 months, toddlers begin using private speech. By talking to themselves, they are beginning to use language to regulate their own behavior without the intention of social communication (Fogel, 2001).

Environments are powerful for facilitating toddlers' language development. One of the primary roles of the adult is to provide a literacy rich environment to encourage exploration and keep toddlers interested in listening and communicating. Toddlers need unlimited opportunities for conversing, reading stories, engaging in finger plays, singing, and pretend play where they construct their own version of reality. Therefore, provide them with toys and household items to stimulate their language development. Then, too, it is important to talk often to help them learn that talking is communication.

Because language is learned in authentic interactions, talk to toddlers in meaningful contexts as well as in social situations. Whenever possible, get down to their level and give them your full attention to reinforce the importance of the spoken word. Nonverbal cues, voice tones, and facial expressions convey important information. While communicating, provide the children with labels for objects, feelings, and ideas. To engage them, use prompting techniques by either asking a question or creating a situation that requires a response.

Kratcoski and Katz (1998) offer some guiding principles that can be used to support the children's language growth including:

♡ Use simple sentences.

♡ Speak slowly and clearly.

♡ Vary your tone/expression to emphasize key words.

♡ Use concrete vocabulary.

♡ Build from the child's utterance/phrase.

♡ Follow the child's topic of interest.

♡ Try to "comment" more than question. (p. 31)

Likewise, you need to:

♡ Provide the child with labels for objects, feelings, ideas, colors, and shapes.

INFANT BEHAVIORAL STATES AND APPROPRIATE ADULT RESPONSES

State	Facial Expression	Action	Adult Response
Regular Sleep	Eyes closed and still; face relaxed	Little movement; fingers slightly curled, thumbs extended	Do not disturb
Irregular Sleep	Eyes closed, occasional rapid eye movement; smiles and grimaces	Gentle movement	Do not disturb
Periodic Sleep/ Drowsiness	Alternates between regular and irregular sleep; eyes open and close or remain halfway open; eyes dull/glazed	Less movement than in irregular sleep; hands open and relaxed, fingers extended	Do not disturb; Pick up if drowsiness follows sleeping; do not disturb if drowsiness follows awake periods
Quiet Alert	Bright eyes, fully open; face relaxed; eyes focused	Slight activity; hands open, fingers extended, arms bent at elbow; stares	Talk to infant; present objects; perform any assessment
Waking Activity	Face flushed; less able to focus eyes than in quiet alert state	Extremities and body move; vocalizes, makes noises	Interact with infant; provide basic care
Crying	Red skin; facial grimaces; eyes partially or fully open	Vigorous activity; crying vocalizations; fists are clenched	Pick up immediately; try to identify source of discomfort and remedy it; soothe infant

Adapted from Kostelnik et al. (2002)

♡ Give the child an opportunity to learn vocabulary in meaningful ways, and provide new objects and experiences to expand the child's language.

♡ Expose the child to a variety of books, catchy rhymes, and music.

♡ Connect the child's actions, ideas, and emotions with words.

♡ Engage in verbal interactions focusing on the child's interest. Prompt the child either by asking questions or creating a situation that requires a response.

♡ Engage the child in problem solving.

♡ Provide toys and household items that stimulate the child to talk.

RESPONDING TO INFANT BEHAVIORAL STATES

An infant's cues are important. Infants experience seven different behavioral states that caregivers need to recognize. Each behavioral state is characterized by differences in facial expressions, muscle tone, and alertness. Following birth, the newborn has irregular states. Predictable patterns, however, emerge within a few weeks. Additionally, newborns spend the majority of their day, between 16 and 20 hours, sleeping. As the baby grows and develops, the amount of sleep time decreases. Accordingly, the amount of time the infant is awake begins increasing. When this occurs, you will need to spend more time interacting with the child. The table above provides valuable information for recognizing the seven behavioral states. Study it carefully to be able to respond to the infant's cues.

Providing stimulation and the timing of interactions is important. Infants should not be interrupted or stimulated during regular, irregular, or periodic sleep or drowsiness. Rather, caregivers should observe for quiet alert periods. During this state, the infant exhibits a relaxed face and bright, focused eyes that are fully open. The child's activities are slight. Typically, the infant's hands will be open, with arms bent at the elbows and fingers extended.

SOOTHING INFANTS

When infants are crying, the caregiver should respond immediately. This reaction is important because children need to experience predictable and consistent care. Such care results in learning to trust, which is the foundation for later social-emotional development. Furthermore, responding promptly to the cries of infants is vital to the development of language and communication skills. This teaches children that through communication their needs will be met.

Many caregivers worry that promptly responding to infants' cries will result in spoiling them. Current research suggests this is not true. In fact, some studies found that promptly responding to the cries of very young infants results in less crying at later stages of development (Zigler & Stevenson, 1993). The infants, in essence, have learned to trust that their communication results in signaling their caregivers.

The following table provides suggestions for soothing infants, including reasons for their effectiveness:

Soothing Crying Infants: Techniques and Reasons for Effectiveness

Technique	Reasons for Effectiveness
Lift baby to your shoulder and rock or walk	Provides a combination of physical contact, upright posture, and motion

Technique	Reasons for Effectiveness
Wrap tightly in a blanket	Restricts movement while increasing warmth
Offer a fist or pacifier	Provides pleasurable oral stimulation
Talk softly or provide a rhythmic sound such as a ticking clock or whirling fan	Reminds child of mother's heart-beat heard while in the uterus
Provide gentle rhythmic motions such as a short walk in a stroller or a ride in a swing	Lulls an infant to sleep
Massage the infant's body with continuous, gentle strokes	Relaxes the infant's muscles

INTERPRETING NONVERBAL CUES

Developing a social relationship with children is paramount and dependent on your ability to interpret their behaviors. This requires careful observation. You will study children's nonverbal behavioral cues. To illustrate, if the child is looking at you face-to-face, this behavior can be interpreted as being fully engaged. When this occurs, continue the interaction. However, if the child lowers the head, it is time to stop. The following table will provide you with some ways to interpret infants' behaviors and facial expressions:

Infant Gaze and Social Meaning to Caregivers

Position and Expression	Typical Interpretation
Face-to-face, sober	Fully engaged, intent
Face-to-face, smiling	Pleased, interested
Head turned slightly away	Maintaining interest; interaction too fast or too slow
Complete head rotation	Uninterested; stop for a while
Head lowered	Stop
Rapid head rotation	Dislikes something
Glances away, tilts head up; partial head aversion	Stop or change strategy
Head lowered, body limp	Has given up fighting off overstimulation

Source: Kostelnik et al. (2002)

If you fail to recognize the child's cues, the infant may become overstimulated. Overstimulation can result from interactions that are too intense. Noises or voices that are too loud can also contribute to overstimulation. When overstimulation occurs, infants protect themselves by changing from one state to another. Because there can be a rapid fluctuation between states, the goodness of fit between the child's state, the caregiver, and the environment is important. When children signal changes in state, alter your behavior immediately. Cease the interaction even without completing the activity. Of course, when the child signals readiness, the activity can be reintroduced.

While toddlers do not change states, their level of interest can fluctuate rapidly. At times, they quickly move from one activity to another. In contrast, another activity or new toy can completely captivate them for upwards of 15 to 20 minutes.

APPLYING THIS BOOK

This book can be a wonderful companion when working with infants and toddlers. To use it effectively, you will need to begin by reviewing the developmental norms and assessments. After this, you can use the checklist in Appendix K to begin gathering and documenting data. Once you have collected this developmental data, evaluate it to determine each child's needs, interests, and abilities. At this point, you are ready to begin searching for activities in this book that provide a balance of experiences to support, enhance, and foster all developmental areas.

When undertaking this process, you will need to narrow your selection of activities to prevent overstimulating the child(ren) in your care. This minimizes your preparation time and the amount of materials and equipment required; hence, you will have more energy to expend while interacting with the child(ren) in your care.

While working with infants and toddlers, questions often arise. To support you, a list of resources related to infants and toddlers has been included in Appendix J. You may discover these resources can be very useful in supporting your role as a caregiver.

We hope you enjoy reading and implementing the activities in this book as much as we did developing them. We leave you with this thought:

For a baby, those early weeks and months of growth, understanding, and reasoning can never be brought back to do over again. This is not the rehearsal. This is the main show. (Irving Harris)

Promoting Optimal Development in Infants

BIRTH to THREE MONTHS

FOUR to SIX MONTHS

SEVEN to NINE MONTHS

TEN to TWELVE MONTHS

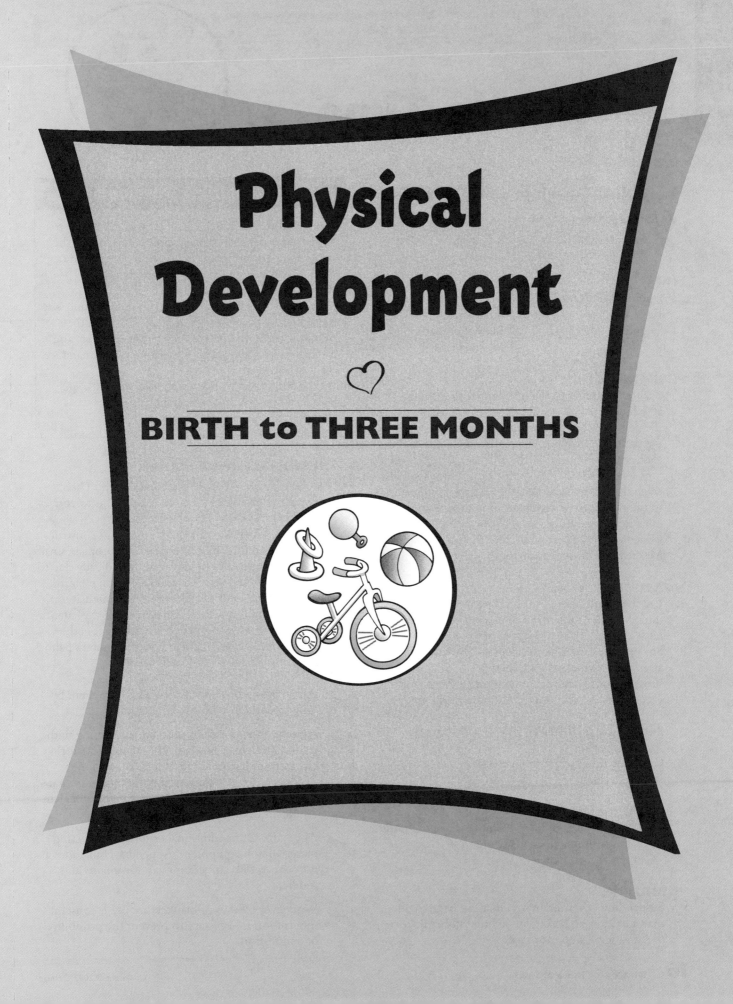

Physical Development

♡

BIRTH to THREE MONTHS

DEVELOPMENTAL AREA: **Physical**

Rattle Time

Child's Developmental Goals

✓ To practice the grasping reflexes

✓ To refine eye-hand coordination skills

MATERIALS:

- ❏ 3 rattles of different sizes and sounds
- ❏ 3 eighteen-inch strips of elastic
- ❏ 6 diaper pins
- ❏ Infant crib
- ❏ Blanket or mat
- ❏ Masking tape

PREPARATION:

♡ Secure the rattles to the infant's crib. Begin by attaching one end of each piece of elastic around the center of each rattle with a diaper pin. After the rattles are attached, secure the other ends of the elastics to the bottom of the infant's crib with diaper pins. Adjust the elastics so that the infant can easily reach the rattles. Make sure the elastic is long enough so the rattle can be brought to the infant's mouth once it is "caught."

♡ Place the blanket halfway under the crib.

♡ Make sure you can continuously view the infant.

NURTURING STRATEGIES:

1. Lay the infant faceup on the blanket with the legs directly under the crib to allow easy viewing of the rattles.

2. Shaking the rattles may encourage the infant to attempt to swipe and grab them.

3. Provide positive reinforcement when the infant successfully makes contact with one of the rattles. For example, say:
   "Olivia, you did it! You are playing with the rattle. Listen to the rattle."

4. Continue the interaction by making such comments as:
   "Do it again!"
   "Olivia, touch this rattle."

5. Continue encouraging the infant to shake the rattle by making comments such as:
   "Can you shake the rattle?"

VARIATION:

♡ Suspending other infant toys that can be grasped may add interest. Examples include rubber floating toys and small stuffed animals.

Highlighting Development

The newborn's distance vision is blurred. It is 10 to 30 times poorer than that of most adults. Thus, the visual acuity of an infant is about the same as adults who wear corrective glasses or contact lenses (Feldman, 1998).

An infant's visual system will not develop unless it is exercised. Babies can see at birth, although they cannot focus both eyes on a single object. Focusing distance is 8 to 10 inches. Therefore, the human face is a newborn's favorite "toy."

The ability to see, however, improves with age. By about one year of age, babies can see about as clearly as adults.

ADDITIONAL INFORMATION:

♡ Whenever possible, use the child's name. Then, too, use your voice and facial expressions to convey your enthusiasm.

♡ Checking the rattles for sharp edges and construction defects is important. Because rattles contain small pieces, they need to be replaced periodically due to normal wear and tear. To avoid a choking hazard, dispose of worn or defective rattles immediately.

♡ Rattle games foster the coordination of the infant's senses; the eyes and ears begin working together.

♡ When a rattle is placed in a newborn infant's palm, an automatic grasp reflex will occur.

 After closing diaper pins, always secure them by wrapping them with masking tape.

 Closely observe infants who are interacting with rattles. To help consumers choose safe toys for children under age three, the U.S. Consumer Product Safety Commission has set part-size standards. The ends of the rattle must be greater than 1⅜ inches in diameter to be safe for infants.

 Appendix C has additional criteria for selecting materials and equipment. Appendix D includes a list of materials and equipment for infants and toddlers.

 Whenever pillows or blankets are used, constant supervision is necessary to prevent the possibility of suffocation.

Lift Up and See

Child's Developmental Goals

✓ To strengthen upper-body muscles

✓ To practice lifting head

MATERIALS:

❑ 1 or 2 interesting infant toys

❑ Blanket or mat

PREPARATION:

♡ Select an area that you can constantly supervise. Spread the blanket out.

NURTURING STRATEGIES:

1. Lay the infant facedown on the blanket.
2. Talk about each toy as you place it in front of the infant. For example, say:
   "Taye, you like rattles. Here is a blue rattle. Look at it."
3. Pause. Observe the infant's efforts in lifting the head and shoulders.
4. Periodically observe the infant's attempts, accomplishments, and interests. Provide encouragement or positive reinforcement as necessary. Say, for example:
   "Look at the stuffed bunny, Taye."
   "You are looking at the bunny."

VARIATION:

♡ Propping open a favorite book, shaking a rattle, moving a puppet, or snapping your fingers to gain the infant's attention can provide variety. Encourage infants to raise their upper body; by doing so, they can have a better look at their surroundings.

☀ Highlighting Development

Crying is a form of communication for the infant. It is a reflexive reaction to discomfort. Infants may cry because of pain, hunger, restlessness, boredom, and overstimulation.

Observe infants closely while interacting for signs of overstimulation since they cannot physically remove themselves from the situation. When this occurs, they may cry, withdraw, tune out, or drop off to sleep. If the child exhibits any of these behaviors, it is time to stop the activity.

ADDITIONAL INFORMATION:

♡ Trying new motor skills is not only strenuous, it can also be frustrating for infants. You might need to remain close to the infant. This will help prevent the infant from becoming upset or even distressed. In addition to becoming frustrated, infants tire easily.

♡ Readily respond to the child's cues or signals. When children receive responsive care, they are more likely to feel secure with their caregiver and in their environment.

♡ Babies also get bored when repeatedly shown the same thing. For this reason, you periodically need to change their visual stimulation to prevent boredom.

♡ The critical window of opportunity for developing vision is from birth to six months of age.

 Ensure the child's safety. Check the U.S. Consumer Safety Commission's Web site located at www.cpsc.gov to make sure that no toys you are using have been recalled.

 Whenever pillows or blankets are used, constant supervision is necessary to prevent the possibility of suffocation.

Wind Chime Stretch

PHYSICAL

Child's Developmental Goals

✓ To practice reaching and stretching the arm muscles

✓ To develop eye-hand coordination skills

MATERIALS:

❑ Wind chimes producing soft noise

❑ Tree or support structure

❑ Wool yarn

❑ Blanket or mat

PREPARATION:

♡ Select a flat, grassy area under a tree or support structure. Secure the wind chime from the structure with the yarn so that it is approximately ½ to ¾ feet from the ground. Adjust the height of the wind chime so that the infant has to stretch to reach it while lying on her back.

NURTURING STRATEGIES:

1. Lay the infant faceup on the blanket.

2. Encourage the infant to move the wind chime by saying:
   "Maya, look at me. I'm moving the chime. Can you move the chime?"

3. Reinforcing your words with actions may be necessary. If so, take the child's arm and move the chimes. Explain what is happening by saying, *"You moved the chime, Maya."*

4. Continue providing positive reinforcement and encouragement for the infant by saying:
   "You did it! You moved the chime. You made a pretty sound. Listen. Do it again, Maya."

☀ Highlighting Development

At birth, infants lie in a curled-up position similar to that of lying in the womb. They move their limbs in an uncontrolled, jerky manner. Over time, the brain refines the child's circuits, and motor skill development moves from gross to fine in two distinct patterns. First, motor control of the head comes before control of the arms, trunk, and legs. This developmental pattern is referred to as cephalo-caudal. Second, control of the head, trunk, and arms precedes control of fingers and feet. That is, growth occurs on a proximodestal pattern. Because of this, an infant's arms are small in proportion to the body trunk. Likewise, the hands and fingers are small in proportion to the arm.

VARIATIONS:

♡ Exercising leg muscles is important. Placing the wind chime over the infant's legs can promote the development of leg muscles.

♡ This activity can be adapted for use indoors.

ADDITIONAL INFORMATION:

♡ Choosing the wind chime is important to the success of this activity. Select a chime that makes soft, gentle noises; the infant may be more likely to engage in the activity.

 Carefully inspect the wind chime to ensure the small parts are securely attached.

 Whenever pillows or blankets are used, constant supervision is necessary to prevent the possibility of suffocation.

PHYSICAL

Outside Tummy Time

Child's Developmental Goals

✓ To practice the grasping reflex

✓ To develop muscle coordination skills

MATERIALS:

❑ Blanket or mat

❑ Pillow that is at least 1 foot square

❑ 2 or 3 toys of interest

PREPARATION:

♡ Select a flat area and spread out the blanket.

♡ Place the pillow in the center of the blanket.

NURTURING STRATEGIES:

1. Lay the infant facedown on top of the pillow so that the upper body is supported by the pillow. This will free up the infant's arms and hands for exploration.

2. While placing each toy in front of the infant within reach, describe it for the child. Say, for example:
    "Here is your favorite toy, Peter. The black and white zebra is right here."

3. Encourage the infant to play with the toys. For example, say:
    "Reach out and grab it."
    "You can play with it."

4. Provide positive reinforcement when the infant attempts to or actually does play with a toy. Make such comments as:
    "Peter, you are holding the zebra."

☀ Highlighting Development

During the first three months, expect rapid development in hand and arm movements. The hand is clenched into a fist. Typically, the thumb is curled inside the fingers. When the hand comes in contact with the mouth, the child will typically suck it. This is comforting.

If you open the fingers and place a rattle in the palm, the infant will automatically grasp it. At two months of age, an infant can grasp a rattle briefly. By three months, an infant begins swiping at objects in the line of vision, but frequently misses.

In addition, infants grasp objects differently than toddlers, older children, or adults. First, infants look at objects, look at the hands, look back at the object, and proceed to move their hand to meet the object.

VARIATION:

♡ Suspending sun catchers will provide something interesting to look at when the infant raises up.

ADDITIONAL INFORMATION:

♡ This activity is good for infants who are just learning to lift their heads because it provides them with a break from this task. They are then able to use their energy to explore objects with their hands and mouths.

♡ At birth, touch is one of the most highly developed sensory systems. Touch is one of the ways infants gain information about their world.

CAUTION Whenever pillows or blankets are used, constant supervision is necessary to prevent the possibility of suffocation.

DEVELOPMENTAL AREA: **Physical**

Textured Mat

PHYSICAL

Child's Developmental Goals

✓ To explore different textures

✓ To strengthen upper-body muscles

MATERIALS:

❏ 4 identical-size pieces of carpet of different textures such as Berber or shag (include something soft, bumpy, smooth, and cushiony)

❏ Carpet thread, fishing line, or duct tape

❏ Upholstery needle

PREPARATION:

♡ Sew or tape together four pieces of carpet to make one large block.

♡ Select an area that you can constantly supervise. Clear this area, if needed, and spread out the textured mat.

NURTURING STRATEGIES:

1. While touching the infant's hand to each section, describe how the mat feels. For example, say:
   "Kenya, this part is soft."
   "This part is rough."
2. Lay the infant facedown on the textured mat.
3. Encourage the infant to explore the mat by making comments such as:
   "Kenya, you're touching the soft part."
   "Your hand is on the rough part."
4. Periodically reposition the mat so that all of the different textures are under the infant's hands.

☀ Highlighting Development

An infant's brain is unfinished at birth. Hence, infants need environmental stimulation. Frequent repetition of physical, intellectual, and emotional experiences helps promote the growth of a healthy brain. Through these experiences, the infant's brain becomes "wired."

VARIATION:

♡ Use mats that are commercially available. Some of these are see-through vinyl mats in which different objects float when the mat is filled with water. Because these mats can be filled with cold water, they are especially nice to use on hot summer days.

ADDITIONAL INFORMATION:

♡ Closely observe infants' reactions to the mat. They might not like the feeling of all the different textures. Move them around as needed.

♡ As infants develop the coordination to raise their heads and shoulders, you will observe the emergence of grabbing at the carpet or material under their hands. Hence, this experience provides practice for the grasping reflexes.

PHYSICAL

Lovin' Rubbin'

Child's Developmental Goals

✓ To develop awareness of body parts

✓ To coordinate seeing and touching

MATERIALS:

❑ Baby lotion
❑ Bath towel
❑ Changing table

PREPARATION:

♡ Check the changing table to ensure baby lotion is readily available.

NURTURING STRATEGIES:

1. This experience can be introduced after changing a diaper while the infant is lying on the changing table.
2. Place a quarter-size dab of lotion on one of your hands. Warm the lotion by rubbing your hands together before applying it on the infant.
3. Rub lotion on infant's chest, back, belly, arms, legs, hands, feet, fingers, toes, etc.
4. While rubbing on the lotion, talk about the body part you are touching. For example, say:
   "I'm putting lotion on Juan's feet and toes. How many toes do you have? 1, 2, 3, . . . 10. Yes, Juan has 10 toes!"
   In this situation, counting fosters the development of rhythm. This is important for language development.
5. When you are finished applying the lotion, dress the child.

☼ Highlighting Development

Infants need exposure to warm and positive relationships with their world. Through their senses—touching, smelling, hearing, seeing, and tasting—children experience relationships. These relationships affect how the infant's brain is wired, thereby shaping subsequent learning and behavior (Shore, 1997).

VARIATION:

♡ Doing this activity before nap time may help the infant to relax.

ADDITIONAL INFORMATION:

♡ When applying the lotion, use soft, gentle strokes. This type of stroking helps the infant to focus on the body part that is being touched at that time.

♡ If the child makes a sound like a gurgle or coo, move closer to the infant. Place your face close to the infant's so that you are seen. While smiling, repeat the infant's sound, thereby promoting language development.

I'm Gonna Get Your Tummy!

PHYSICAL

Child's Developmental Goals

✓ To develop awareness of body parts

✓ To explore using the sense of touch

MATERIALS:

❑ Blanket, mat, or infant seat

PREPARATION:

♡ Select an area that you can constantly supervise. If needed, clear this area, and then place a blanket, mat, or infant seat there.

NURTURING STRATEGIES:

1. Lay the infant faceup on the blanket or mat. If using an infant seat, securely restrain the infant in the seat with the safety strap.
2. Begin the game by "walking" your index and pointer fingers up the infant's legs toward the abdomen while saying:
   "I'm gonna get your tummy, Adriana."
   Smile while playing this game. Because infants imitate, your expression should elicit a smile from the child.
3. When you get to the infant's tummy, tickle it! Hopefully, the infant will be showing signs of enjoying the activity such as smiling at this point.
4. Talk about the infant's reactions to the game. For example, comment:
   "Adriana, you like this game. You smiled when I got your tummy."
   "You're having fun!"
5. Repeat the activity as long as the infant shows signs of enjoying it, such as maintaining eye contact or smiling.

Highlighting Development

The infant's physical development is rapid during this period. Changes in shape, size, and body proportions are occurring almost on a daily basis (Zigler & Stevenson, 1993). To illustrate, observe the infant's legs. They are becoming stronger and more active. Also, they are moving from the newborn position of curling inward to a straightened position.

VARIATION:

♡ Pretending to get different body parts, such as the infant's chin or toes, provides further information about the body.

ADDITIONAL INFORMATION:

♡ Pay close attention to the infants' cues. When infants are overstimulated or finished with the activity, they will let you know by doing things such as averting their eyes or even turning their entire head away from you. Often, infants will even cry when wanting to avoid activities they dislike such as dressing or undressing.

 Whenever pillows or blankets are used, constant supervision is necessary to prevent the possibility of suffocation.

Language and Communication Development

♡

BIRTH to THREE MONTHS

Reciting Nursery Rhymes

Child's Developmental Goals

✓ To develop expressive language skills

✓ To hear native language patterns

MATERIALS:

☐ Select a nursery rhyme for this activity. See the list of nursery rhymes in Appendix F. Consider a short, nonfantasy rhyme with familiar words. In addition, always choose rhymes with nonviolent themes.

PREPARATION:

♡ If you have memorized the words to your favorite nursery rhymes, no materials are needed. However, if you need a prompt, create a poster with the words to your favorite nursery rhyme and hang it up or place it by your side for quick reference. This teaching tool may also be an aid for other adults to reinforce this activity.

NURTURING STRATEGIES:

1. Hold the infant in a position allowing you to visually connect.
2. Recite the nursery rhyme. Use your voice and facial expressions as tools for communicating enthusiasm.
3. Observe the infant for signs of interest. Some signs are eye contact, vocalizations, or smiles. If the child is interested, try repeating the nursery rhyme or reciting a different one.

☼ Highlighting Development

The word *infant* is derived from Latin. It means "without speech" (Junn & Boyatzis, 1998). An infant's first cry is the beginning of language development. One-month-old infants may respond with small, throaty sounds and cries. By three months of age, infants begin communicating by chuckling, squealing, and cooing.

Infants have much they want to tell people in their world. At first, communication focuses on hunger, pain, or being wet. Gradually, language learning emerges out of duet or social exchange between the adult and infant.

VARIATION:

♡ Reciting your favorite story or fable is another way to promote language development.

ADDITIONAL INFORMATION:

♡ Repeated exposure to their native language is important for infants learning to speak. One way to do this is by reciting nursery rhymes and stories. These language facilitation experiences are especially useful activities when infants have not developed the muscles for holding up their own heads. While holding the infant and verbally interacting, you are fostering the development of language skills.

♡ The infant enjoys the closeness and warmth of being held.

Infant-Picture Stories

Child's Developmental Goals

✓ To develop expressive language skills

✓ To practice vocalizing

MATERIALS:

❑ Pictures or posters of infants

❑ Blanket or mat (optional)

❑ Pillow

PREPARATION:

♡ Hang the pictures or posters at the infant's eye level.

♡ Clear the area on the floor next to the pictures for the blanket. If desired, spread out the blanket and place a pillow on the blanket.

NURTURING STRATEGIES:

1. Prop the infant up on one side on a blanket using the pillow for support.

2. Gain the infant's attention by pointing to a picture. For example, say:

   "Clint, look at this picture of a baby."

3. Create a story about the picture. Paralleling the story with the life or daily routines of the infant you are talking to makes this task easier. For instance, say:

   "This is Erin. She loves to play with rattles. She shakes the rattles."

4. Reinforce any vocalizations the infant makes during the story. Make comments such as:

   "Wow! That's true. You also like rattles, Clint."

   Doing this will encourage the infant to take part in the "conversation."

☀ Highlighting Development

An infant can perceive and produce sounds from the moment of birth. Speak and observe the infant's behavior. The infant will move to the rhythm of your speech. When your speech becomes faster, the infant will move his legs and arms faster. Likewise, if your speech slows, the infant's motions also will slow down. Hint: When you want the child to relax or even sleep, speak quietly and slowly.

Infants between one and three months will begin cooing. These sounds are open, vowel-like, gurgling sounds. Listen. You will hear "oooh" and "aaah." While crying is a signal of distress, cooing signals happiness and contentment (Snow, 1998).

VARIATION:

♡ Post pictures on the wall at your eye level. Hold the infant and walk around the room while looking, commenting, and telling stories about the pictures.

ADDITIONAL INFORMATION:

♡ Infants are particularly interested in stories and pictures of other infants. Therefore, this activity can be used to foster the development of social skills in older infants.

 Whenever pillows or blankets are used, constant supervision is necessary to prevent the possibility of suffocation.

Rockin' the Day Away

LANGUAGE & COMMUNICATION

Child's Developmental Goals

✓ To develop receptive language skills

✓ To practice communication skills

MATERIALS:

❑ Outside rocker or glider

PREPARATION:

♡ Observe the child to make sure she is in a responsive state.

NURTURING STRATEGIES:

1. While sitting in the rocker or glider, hold the infant in your lap so you both are facing the same direction.
2. While rocking, talk about the surrounding environment. You can discuss different objects as well as people that you can see. When talking, use as many descriptive words as possible. Comments might include:
   "Look at the little, red bird. It is sitting in the green pine tree."
3. Reinforce any vocalizations the infant makes. To illustrate, say:
   "Yes, the bird flew away."
   "Tell me more about the red bird."
   Doing this may encourage the infant to continue to take part in the "conversation."

☼ Highlighting Development

Adopt a parentese style to help the infant learn. This type of speech attracts babies' attention. To do this when speaking, place your face very close to the infant so that she is able to see you. To capture the infant's attention, use a high-pitched, rhythmic style and short utterances. Speak slowly and with careful enunciation. The parentese style will make it easier for the baby to hear individual sounds.

VARIATIONS:

♡ Repeat this activity inside before nap time. It may help the infant to relax.

♡ Singing rather than talking to the infant may be enjoyable for everyone.

ADDITIONAL INFORMATION:

♡ Periodically moving the rocker or glider to different locations will provide a new view of the world. As a result, there will be "new" things to look at and talk about.

Picture Book Time

Child's Developmental Goals

✓ To develop expressive language skills

✓ To engage in taking turns

MATERIALS:

❏ Black and white picture book

❏ Blanket or mat

PREPARATION:

♡ Clear an area and then spread out the mat or blanket.

♡ Prop open the book on the blanket or mat.

NURTURING STRATEGIES:

1. Place the infant faceup on the blanket.
2. Gain the infant's attention by looking in the child's eyes and saying:
   "Ridi, look at what I have. A book. Let's read it together."
3. "Read" the picture book to the infant. Pointing to the pictures and verbally identifying the object will assist the infant in connecting words with objects. While saying the word or describing what is on the page, "converse" with the infant.
4. To promote turn taking, ask questions such as:
   "Ridi, what is this?"
   Wait for a response.
5. Encourage the infant to continue responding by providing positive reinforcement to the vocalizations. Make comments such as:
   "You are right! It is a baby."
6. Closely observe the infant for signs of interest. When the infant begins to lose interest, stop reading. However, read the book a second or third time if the infant maintains interest.

☀ Highlighting Development

When selecting pictures or toys, remember babies prefer patterns over solids. At birth, they prefer looking at black and white in a vertical stripe. Watch them search pictures and toys. Because fewer eye muscles are needed for scanning patterns horizontally, newborns use this method.

VARIATIONS:

♡ Allow the infant to "read" the book when you are finished. An infant will "read" the book by holding and mouthing it. Vinyl, cloth, or plastic books are especially good for this reason.

♡ Select a picture book with only colored pictures and no words. Create a story for the child about the objects in the book.

ADDITIONAL INFORMATION:

♡ Just like infants' play with other toys, they need the opportunity to explore books with their hands and mouths. Having several vinyl or plastic books available will allow you to substitute a clean book for a soiled book. To promote a healthy environment, infant toys should be sanitized as often as necessary, usually several times throughout the day.

 Avoid letting toys sit in the sun. They can become hot enough to burn the child.

 Whenever pillows or blankets are used, constant supervision is necessary to prevent the possibility of suffocation.

The Lullaby Rub

Child's Developmental Goals

✓ To develop expressive language skills

✓ To hear native language patterns

MATERIALS:

☐ Select a short lullaby for this activity.

☐ If you have memorized the words to your favorite lullaby, no materials are needed. However, if you need a prompt, create a poster or "crib sheet" with the words to hang in the crib area for quick reference. This teaching tool may also be an aid for others who interact with the child.

PREPARATION:

♡ Observe the infant to determine the best time for introducing the lullaby rub.

NURTURING STRATEGIES:

1. Place the infant faceup in the crib.
2. While rubbing the infant's abdomen, look into the child's eyes and sing the lullaby you selected. Use your voice as a tool to soothe and communicate that it is time to sleep.
3. Repeat the lullaby as many times as necessary. Rubbing the infant's abdomen and singing the lullaby may help the infant to relax and, hopefully, promote sleep.

☀ Highlighting Development

The number of words children hear will affect their language development. The language children experience needs to be related to ongoing events in their lives. Consequently, the television will not produce the language-boosting effects for infants and toddlers that caregivers, siblings, or other adults can provide. For variety, you may supplement your voice with music recorded on compact discs or tapes.

VARIATION:

♡ Softly recite your favorite finger play or sing a song.

ADDITIONAL INFORMATION:

♡ Infants, like adults, sometimes need help relaxing before falling asleep. Singing, rubbing, or rocking are often soothing activities for infants.

 Given the threat of Sudden Infant Death Syndrome, infants should be placed on their backs to sleep.

What Am I Doing?

Child's Developmental Goals

✓ To develop receptive language skills

✓ To engage in a conversation

MATERIALS:

None

PREPARATION:

♡ Observe the infant for times of alertness.

NURTURING STRATEGIES:

1. This activity works best during routine care times such as feeding.
2. Hold the infant so that you can visually connect with the child while preparing a bottle.
3. Talk about what you are doing. For example, say: *"Carrie, I'm warming your bottle. You like warm bottles. Milk tastes good when it's warm."*
4. Respond to the vocalizations or cries of the infant with conversation. To illustrate, comment: *"You are very hungry. I'm warming the bottle for you. The milk will taste so good. It is almost done. You are so hungry!"*

☀ Highlighting Development

Reading an infant's subtle signs is an important tool for assessing behavior. When the child lies still with bright and wide eyes, the infant is probably in a state of enjoyment and is ready to interact. When this occurs, sing, look, talk, and read to the child. These interactions will stimulate the child's brain to make connections that are important to growth and later learning.

VARIATION:

♡ Talk about what the other people in the infant's environment are doing. This technique is most effective if another person is locating something for the infant you are working with. For example, say: *"Barbara is bringing your blanket. I forgot it. You need your blanket to sleep."*

ADDITIONAL INFORMATION:

♡ Infants learn by repetition. By hearing caregivers talk about routine care or tasks, infants associate particular words with actions. This contributes to the development of their receptive language skills.

♡ The acquisition of language is one of the most remarkable accomplishments of early childhood. The beginnings of language focus on the interaction between caregiver and infant.

What Are You Doing?

Child's Developmental Goals

✓ To develop receptive language skills

✓ To participate in a conversation

MATERIALS:

None

PREPARATION:

♡ Observe the child's state of readiness. If the child is alert, introduce the activity.

NURTURING STRATEGIES:

1. This activity works best during routine care times such as preparation for napping.
2. Hold the infant so you can visually connect with the child while preparing the crib.
3. Talk about what the infant is experiencing. For example, say:
   "Logan, it's time for your nap. You are very tired. You keep rubbing your eyes. That tells me you need to sleep."
4. Respond to the vocalizations or cries of the infant with conversation. To illustrate, comment:
   "Logan, you are very sleepy. Your crib is ready now. You can enjoy a nice nap."

☼ Highlighting Development

Infants have a range of preferences, which may vary from child to child. Discover their likes and dislikes by observing them and experimenting. Like adults, children desire variety. Sometimes an energetic baby may prefer quiet and soothing interactions while a quiet baby may prefer more dramatic interactions.

VARIATION:

♡ Talk about what other children or people are doing.

ADDITIONAL INFORMATION:

♡ Talking about the routine care or tasks that are being experienced on a daily basis will help the infant to associate words with actions. Hence, describing the routine tasks can greatly increase the infant's receptive language skills.

♡ This activity can help soothe a child, as well as provide language stimulation.

Cognitive Development

♡

BIRTH to THREE MONTHS

DEVELOPMENTAL AREA: Cognitive

Tugging the Towel

COGNITIVE

Child's Developmental Goals

✓ To practice the grasping reflex

✓ To gain voluntary control over reflexes

MATERIALS:

❏ Hand towel

❏ Blanket or mat

PREPARATION:

♡ Spread out the blanket or mat in an area that can be constantly supervised.

NURTURING STRATEGIES:

1. Lay the infant faceup on the blanket. Sitting in an upward position, move your legs into a "V" formation. You should be facing the infant. In addition, you should be able to comfortably bend over.
2. Roll the towel. Then gently pick up and place each of the infant's hands on to the towel. This will help to stimulate the infant's palmar grasp reflex. Hold on to the towel so that your hands are on the outside of both of the infant's hands.
3. Slowly pull your hands toward your body and gently raise the infant's shoulders from the blanket.
4. As you raise the infant, engage the child by talking. Describe what is happening. For example, say: *"Kayla, you pulled yourself up. What a strong baby!"*

5. Then lower the infant to the blanket or mat. Make sure to gently lay the infant's head down.
6. Repeat this activity until the infant signals a lack of interest.

☀ Highlighting Development

Infants make contact by signaling. Attentiveness is shown through visual tracking and looking into another's face (Kostelnik et al., 1998). Infants will also signal you when they finish an activity. They will cry, fuss, turn their heads away, or otherwise signal that they have completed this activity. By closely observing an infant, you will know when to stop. To soothe the child, cuddle, rock, pat, or provide something for sucking.

VARIATION:

♡ Substitute your index fingers for the infant to hold on to instead of the towel.

ADDITIONAL INFORMATION:

♡ When selecting a towel, blanket, or mat, consider infants' preferences. Typically, they prefer bright colors and unusual, soft textures.

 Whenever pillows or blankets are used, constant supervision is necessary to prevent the possibility of suffocation.

Reach for It!

Child's Developmental Goals

✔ To practice eye-hand coordination skills
✔ To imitate a caregiver's behavior

MATERIALS:

❑ Mobile

PREPARATION:

♡ Suspend the mobile from the ceiling at a height that is comfortable for an adult to reach while holding an infant.

NURTURING STRATEGIES:

1. Carry the infant over to the mobile.
2. Touch the mobile with your hand and describe what is happening. Comments might include:
   "I moved the mobile. I used my hand. Watch me."
3. Invite the infant to imitate your actions by saying:
   "Rashad, can you make the mobile move? Touch it with your hand. Push it. Swipe at it. Watch."
4. Raise the infant up so that the swiping motions result in moving the mobile.
5. Praising the infant for moving the mobile, you might say:
   "Rashad, good for you. You did it. You moved the mobile. You used your hand."
6. Invite the infant to move the mobile again. Increase the challenge by positioning the infant so that the mobile is a little farther away.
7. Encourage the infant to move the mobile again. Comments might include:
   "Rashad, reach. You can do it."
   If the child moves the mobile, praise the accomplishment. If the infant's swipe misses the mobile, provide further encouragement.
8. If the infant continues swiping without touching the mobile, adjust your position by moving closer.

☀ Highlighting Development

Studies show infants usually look longer at a novel object than at a familiar object (Baillargeon, 1994). They need to be stimulated with things to look at such as other people, mobiles, stuffed toys, nonglass mirrors, etc. When stimulated, watch the infant's face freeze with intense interest. Observe. It is amazing how much interest infants can invest in a toy that appeals to their senses.

VARIATION:

♡ Suspending the mobile from a counter or table will encourage the infant to move it while lying on the floor. Increasing the distance between the mobile and the floor, once the infant has experienced success in moving the mobile, will provide a new challenge.

ADDITIONAL INFORMATION:

♡ Provide infants with positive reinforcement when they are engaging in activities. Also, use infants' names during activities. By doing so, they will learn to recognize it.

 For safety purposes, the string attaching the mobile to the ceiling must be strong enough to support the infant's weight.

Touring in the Stroller

COGNITIVE

Child's Developmental Goals

✓ To enhance existing cognitive structures

✓ To integrate the senses of seeing and hearing

MATERIALS:

❑ Infant stroller

PREPARATION:

♡ This tour can be scheduled indoors or outdoors, depending on the weather and available space. If going outside, dress the infant appropriately for the weather. Remember, infants need outdoor stimulation as much as older children or adults.

NURTURING STRATEGIES:

1. Place the infant securely in the stroller using safety restraints.
2. Begin the tour by pushing the stroller and talking about what you see. For example, say:
   "Olga, there goes a car. It is moving fast."
   "Here is a flower. It is yellow."
   Continue communicating with the child by commenting on what you are seeing. Remember to focus on pointing out objects only at the infant's eye level.
3. Kneel down occasionally, look in the child's eyes to gain attention, and point out objects in the environment.

☼ Highlighting Development

A stimulating environment promotes growth of the infant's cognitive structures. For this to happen, caring, responsible adults need to introduce variations in the environment. The infant needs stimulation and responsiveness. In fact, the way parents, families, and other caregivers relate, respond, and mediate the infant's contact with the environment directly affects brain development (Shore, 1997).

VARIATIONS:

♡ Increase the number of children on the tour to add variety.

♡ If possible, take tours to various locations such as parks, grocery stores, zoos, etc. Invite older children to join you since they provide different types of stimulation.

ADDITIONAL INFORMATION:

♡ Always look at the tour through the eyes of an infant. There are so many new things to see! Be as descriptive as you can when talking. The sound of surprise in your voice when discovering something novel will assist in gaining the infant's attention.

♡ The rhythm, pattern, and sound of your voice contribute to the child's language development.

Bell Ringing

Child's Developmental Goals

✓ To experience the principle of cause and effect

✓ To develop existing cognitive structures

MATERIALS:

- ❑ Elastic band (length depends upon the size of the infant's hands)
- ❑ Large bell, a minimum of 2 inches in diameter
- ❑ Fishing line
- ❑ Blanket or infant seat

PREPARATION:

♡ Cut a piece of elastic band large enough so that it comfortably fits over the infant's hand. Once placed on the infant's arm, it should not leave a mark on the skin. Sew the elastic ends together using a piece of fishing line. Then tightly secure the bell to the elastic band. Pull on the bell to ensure that it remains attached to the elastic.

NURTURING STRATEGIES:

1. Place the infant faceup on the blanket. Otherwise, secure the infant into the seat, fastening the safety restraint.
2. Place the elastic band with the bell on the infant's arm.
3. Gently shake the infant's arm, acting surprised when the bell makes a sound.
   "Andre, what was that? Listen. Can you make that sound again?"
4. Wait to see if infant repeats the movement. If it is repeated, provide positive reinforcement by making comments such as:
   "Andre, you are making a sound."
   If a noise is not made, shake the infant's arm again. Wait to see if the movement is repeated.

5. If there's no response, the infant probably is interested in something else right now. Try this experience again later.

☀ Highlighting Development

Infants gradually are beginning to note their effect on the world. Therefore, they need interactive experiences and some structure to their playtime. At this stage of development, the child loves people most of all. He enjoys responding to their facial expressions, listening to their voices, and being cuddled. In fact, the infant's preference for a toy is a human face.

VARIATION:

♡ Make an elastic band with a bell attached to fit the infant's leg.

ADDITIONAL INFORMATION:

♡ Whenever possible, reinforce words with actions. To illustrate, when saying the word *shake,* perform the action.

♡ Continue the activity as long as the infant is showing interest. Promptly remove the band if the infant appears frightened by the sound of the bell or the feel of the band.

 For safety purposes, use the paper core of a toilet paper roll to check the bell size. If the bell falls through, it is considered a choking hazard for infants.

 Whenever pillows or blankets are used, constant supervision is necessary to prevent the possibility of suffocation.

Infant Imitation

COGNITIVE

Child's Developmental Goals

✓ To imitate a caregiver's action

✓ To experience repetition of an action

MATERIALS:

None

PREPARATION:

♡ Observe the infant to note alertness.

NURTURING STRATEGIES:

1. This activity can occur any time when you are interacting with the infant throughout the day. However, an ideal time to introduce the activity would be during the diapering routine.
2. Closely listen to any sounds the infant makes (e.g., ooooo).
3. Imitate that sound by repeating what the infant said (e.g., ooooo).
4. Usually, the infant will repeat the sound again to continue the "conversation." When this happens, provide positive reinforcement in the form of praising or smiling. You could comment, for example:
   "We are talking to each other."

Highlighting Development

According to new brain research, infants' brains rapidly develop from the moment of birth. Infants' optimal development is dependent on the experiences provided for them during the first three years of life. At birth, the brain stem, which controls vital wiring for breathing and the heartbeat, is completed. The connections in other parts of the brain's circuit are weak. These circuits govern emotions, language, math, music, and language. The circuits for governing emotions are some of the first circuits constructed. Therefore, the right kind of emotional stimulation is important (Shore, 1997).

VARIATIONS:

♡ Imitate an infant's facial expression, such as a frown or smile.

♡ Performing an action such as sticking out your tongue or saying "ahhh" with exaggerated movements while looking at the infant may also result in an "imitative" conversation. Sticking out the tongue is one of the first actions a child can imitate.

ADDITIONAL INFORMATION:

♡ Infants will tell you through their behavior when they have finished with an activity. They will cry, fuss, turn their heads away, fall asleep, or otherwise signal that they have had enough stimulation. To prevent the frustration of overstimulation, show sensitivity by closely observing and responding to an infant's signal.

Can You Follow Me?

Child's Developmental Goals

✓ To practice coordinating the senses of hearing and seeing

✓ To develop existing cognitive structures

MATERIALS:

☐ Blanket, mat, or infant seat

PREPARATION:

♡ Select an area that you can constantly supervise. Clear this area and spread out the blanket, mat, or infant seat.

NURTURING STRATEGIES:

1. Lay the infant faceup on the blanket or mat; otherwise, secure the infant in the seat with the safety restraint.
2. Gain the infant's attention by talking about what the infant can see. For example, say:
   "Maha, you are looking at me. Can you follow me? I'm going to move."
3. While continuing to talk, move your body out of the visual path to a different location near the infant such as to the side of the child.
4. Observe the infant's behavior. Did the infant move any part of her body to visually locate you again? If movement was detected, provide positive reinforcement. Comment by saying:
   "Maha, you can still see me. You moved your head to find me."
   If the infant did not respond, move back into her visual path to regain her attention.
5. Repeat steps 3 and 4 as long as the infant is interested in the activity.

☼ Highlighting Development

It is important to exercise both sides of the infant's body. Using a rattle, move the location of the sound equally to both the left and right side. Avoid moving the rattle behind the infant's head, which makes it difficult for the infant to experience success in locating you. Once infants have developed control of their neck and head muscles, the rattle can be moved behind their head.

VARIATION:

♡ Use a soft bell, drum, rattle, or musical instrument instead of your voice.

ADDITIONAL INFORMATION:

♡ Infants are learning to track and follow objects. As a result, they need experiences and interactions for practice to promote their optimum development.

♡ At birth, the auditory system is fairly well developed. This is not surprising because infants have had some practice in hearing before birth (Feldman, 1998).

 Whenever pillows or blankets are used, constant supervision is necessary to prevent the possibility of suffocation.

Get Me If You Can!

COGNITIVE

Child's Developmental Goals

✓ To enhance coordination of the arm muscles

✓ To practice the grasping and sucking reflexes

MATERIALS:

❑ Blanket or mat

❑ 2 to 3 plastic, rubber, or fabric infant toys

❑ Pillow at least 1 foot square

PREPARATION:

♡ Select an area that you can constantly supervise. Clear this area and spread out the blanket or mat.

NURTURING STRATEGIES:

1. Lay the infant facedown on the blanket if he has acquired the skill of lifting the head and shoulders up from the surface. Lay the infant on one side and support the back with pillows if this skill is undeveloped.

2. Show the toys by placing them in the infant's visual track. Then begin verbally describing them. Say, for example:
   "Here is a rubber duck. You see the eyes. You can squeeze this."

3. Place these toys in the infant's visual path, but just beyond his reach.

4. Verbally encourage the infant to reach for the toys. For example, say:
   "Sean, get it. Stretch. You can do it. Reach for the duck."

5. When the infant touches a toy, provide positive reinforcement, such as:
   "You did it. You stretched and touched the rattle."
   Use your voice to share your enthusiasm.

6. Encourage the infant to grasp and suck the toy. To illustrate, say:
   "Sean, grab the rattle."
   "Put it in your mouth."

7. If the infant becomes upset or distressed because the toys are out of reach, move them closer.

☀ Highlighting Development

Infants can become frustrated, upset, and even distressed when they cannot reach something within their visual path. Some frustration can be a positive experience because it encourages them to think and explore different ways to solve their problems. However, pay close attention to the sound of their voice. Intervening and moving the toys closer may prevent infants from becoming too upset or distressed.

VARIATION:

♡ Use a ball or small, soft teddy bear to encourage the child's grasping behavior.

ADDITIONAL INFORMATION:

♡ Collect a variety of toys. If the infant does not show interest in one toy, try introducing another.

 Whenever pillows or blankets are used, constant supervision is necessary to prevent the possibility of suffocation.

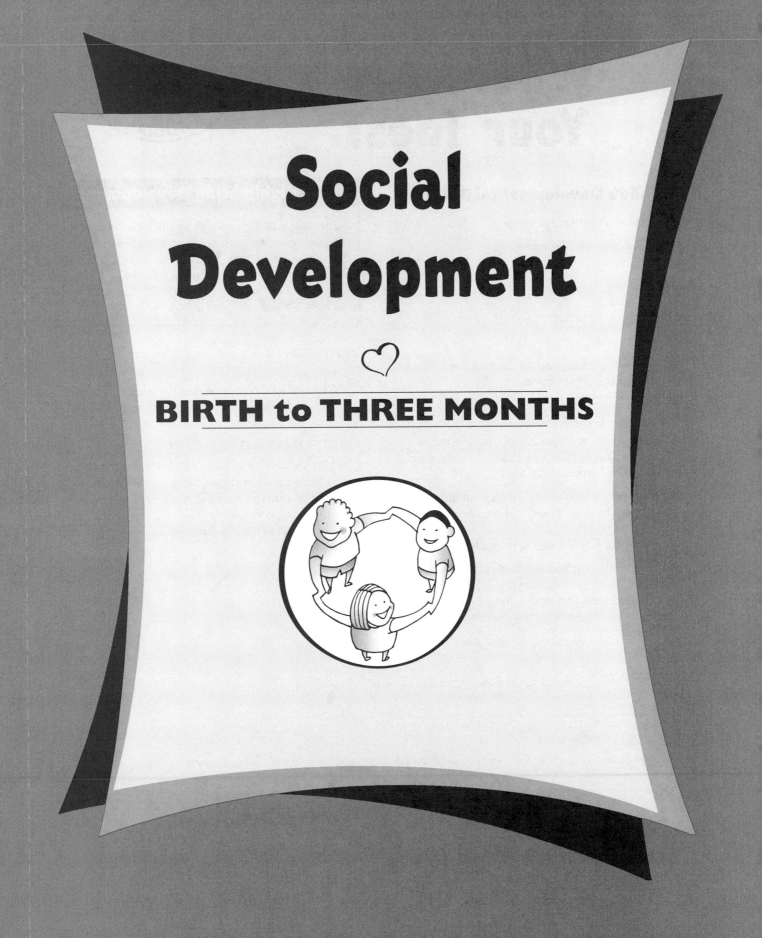

Social Development

BIRTH to THREE MONTHS

Where Are Your Toes?

SOCIAL

Child's Developmental Goals

✓ To develop a positive self-image
✓ To experience social interactions

MATERIALS:

None

PREPARATION:

♡ Select a song to sing, such as the one that follows, containing the child's name.

NURTURING STRATEGIES:

1. After diapering and before removing the infant from the changing table, sing the following song: (Tune: "The Farmer in the Dell")

    ♫ Where are *Rosa*'s toes? (shrug shoulders)
    ♫ Where are *Rosa*'s toes? (shrug shoulders)
    ♫ Hi Ho Hi Ho
    ♫ Here are *Rosa*'s toes. (point to toes)

2. Substitute different body parts such as arms, hands, ears, legs, and fingers in the verse.
3. Continue singing this song as long as the infant shows interest by maintaining eye contact, smiling, etc.

☼ **Highlighting Development**

Babies can read your moods by the look on your face, the sound of your voice, and your interaction style. In addition, they imitate your moods. Therefore, if you appear sad, the baby will be sad. Likewise, if you are happy and energetic, chances are the baby will imitate your mood.

VARIATIONS:

♡ Sing about and point to your own body parts.
♡ Change the word *are* to *is* in the song. Then use the words *mouth*, *nose*, *hair*, *thumb*, and *knee*.

ADDITIONAL INFORMATION:

♡ This activity is most successful when the infant is in the quiet-alert stage of wakefulness. During this time, infants are most responsive and enjoy interacting with others.
♡ The most fascinating thing for an infant to observe is your face.

SOCIAL

Where Are You?

Child's Developmental Goals

✓ To form a positive self-image

✓ To develop self-identity

MATERIALS:

❑ Blanket, mat, or infant seat

PREPARATION:

♡ Select an area of the room that can be easily supervised. Spread out the blanket or place the infant seat in this area.

NURTURING STRATEGIES:

1. Lay the infant faceup on the blanket. Otherwise, securely place the child in an infant seat, fastening the safety restraint.

2. Gain the infant's attention by singing the following song:
(Tune: "Where Is Thumbkin?")

   ♫ Where is *Marcus*? Where is *Marcus*?
   ♫ There she is. There she is.   (point to infant)
   ♫ How are you today, *Marcus*?
   ♫ Very well we hope so.
   ♫ Want to play? Want to play?

3. Stimulate the infant by talking about reactions to the song. For example, say:
   "What a smile! You liked that song, Marcus. Should we sing it again?"

4. Repeat the song as long as the infant seems interested and enjoys it. Check for signs of interest such as maintaining eye contact, smiling, or cooing.

☼ Highlighting Development

By three months of age, most infants will track sounds by turning their heads and gazing toward the source. Their brains are stimulated by hearing a variety of sounds. From this stimulation, new connections called "learning pathways" are formed. At the same time, existing connections are strengthened (Shore, 1997).

VARIATION:

♡ Move away from the infant to another part of the room. Repeat the song. Observe the infant's ability to track your voice.

ADDITIONAL INFORMATION:

♡ Infants love to hear songs, especially ones that include their names. Continue this activity as long as the infants' behaviors indicate pleasure or enjoyment. Infants convey disinterest by looking away, fussing, or crying when they are finished with an activity.

 Whenever pillows or blankets are used, constant supervision is necessary to prevent the possibility of suffocation.

0 to 3 months

Singing Good-Bye

SOCIAL

Child's Developmental Goals

✓ To develop self-identity
✓ To develop social interaction skills

MATERIALS:

None

PREPARATION:

♡ Observe the infant's state of consciousness to determine the level of responsiveness.

NURTURING STRATEGIES:

1. When a guest, sibling, or a child is departing, sing the following song:

   ♫ Good-bye *Terri*.
   ♫ Good-bye *Terri*.
   ♫ Good-bye *Terri*.
   ♫ We'll see you another day.

   (Rhonda Whitman, Infant-Toddler Specialist University of Wisconsin–Stout)

2. Foster social development by showing the infant how to wave good-bye. You could say, for example:
   "Watch me wave good-bye, Terri."
   Whenever necessary, reinforce your words with actions.

☀ Highlighting Development

Infants prefer an orderly, consistent, and predictable environment. They also become familiar with, like, and need routines. Routines help them develop a sense of security. Infants, like other children, are reassured when routines are associated with rituals and pleasurable feelings.

VARIATION:

♡ Sing this song to family members before they leave for the day.

ADDITIONAL INFORMATION:

♡ Singing this song consistently is important for both infants and adults.

What's Everyone Doing?

Child's Developmental Goals

✓ To develop social interaction skills

✓ To develop a self-identity

MATERIALS:

❑ Blanket, mat, or infant seat

PREPARATION:

♡ Select an area that you can constantly supervise. Clear this area and spread out the blanket or mat. If preferred, use the infant seat.

NURTURING STRATEGIES:

1. Lay the infant faceup on a blanket or mat. Otherwise, secure the child in the infant seat using the safety restraint.
2. Talk to the infant about where you are going to be working and what you will be doing. For example, comment:
   "Emilio, I'm by the sink. I'm making a bottle. You are hungry."
3. Observe the infant's interests and behavior. Talk about what the infant is looking at. For example, say:
   "Emilio, that is a poster of a baby. That baby is in the snow. The snow is cold."
4. If necessary, encourage the infant to look at other objects or people in the immediate environment. To illustrate, comment:
   "Look at Tommy push the balls. He is using his hands."

5. Provide positive reinforcement to acknowledge what the infant is looking at. For example, say:
   "Emilio, you are watching me. I am heating your bottle."

 Highlighting Development

Infants regulate their level of stimulation verbally and nonverbally. Observe them. Play with them in a way that lets you follow their lead. Move in when children want to play and pull back when they seem to have had enough stimulation. By following their lead, you are respecting their needs (Shore, 1997).

VARIATION:

♡ Provide a toy for the infant to hold while looking around the room. When people are not in sight, this will give the infant something to play with.

ADDITIONAL INFORMATION:

♡ Infants need constant supervision to promote their health and safety. However, this does not mean you have to be beside the infant the entire day. Observing and talking to the infant from another part of the room will meet his needs for security and safety.

 Whenever pillows or blankets are used, constant supervision is necessary to prevent the possibility of suffocation.

Welcome Song

SOCIAL

Child's Developmental Goals

✓ To begin the day positively

✓ To develop self-identity

MATERIALS:

None

PREPARATION:

♡ Observe the infant's state of consciousness to determine the level of responsiveness.

NURTURING STRATEGIES:

1. When a guest, family member, or child arrives, greet her by saying her name. For example, say: *"Good morning Ramona. How are you today?"*

2. Look at the child and sing the following song while waving:

   ♬ Hello *Ramon*a.
   ♬ Hello *Ramon*a.
   ♬ Hello *Ramon*a.
   ♬ We're so glad you're here.

   (Rhonda Whitman, Infant-Toddler Specialist University of Wisconsin–Stout)

☀ Highlighting Development

During this stage, infants enjoy being held and drawn into social interactions with people in their environment. Unlike in subsequent stages, they do not discriminate their primary caregiver from other people they might interact with.

VARIATION:

♡ Sing the song in the Singing Good-Bye activity in this section.

ADDITIONAL INFORMATION:

♡ Infants love to hear songs, especially ones that include their names.

♡ Singing this song is important for infants. They become familiar with, like, and need routines. Routines help them develop a sense of security.

Waking Up

Child's Developmental Goals

✓ To develop a sense of trust

✓ To acquire a positive sense of self

MATERIALS:

None

PREPARATION:

♡ Listen for the infant's cries or movements that indicate wakefulness.

NURTURING STRATEGIES:

1. After waking from a nap, promptly remove the infant from the crib.

2. Talking about the nap will provide the infant with information about his behavior. Comments might include:

   "Lakota, you must be so rested. You slept a long time."

3. Begin to investigate whether other basic needs require your attention. For example, check to see if the infant is wet or hungry. Comments to make include:

   "Lakota, let's check your diaper. You might be wet after that long nap."

   "Are you hungry? It's been a long time since you ate."

4. Respond to the vocalizations of the infant with conversation. To illustrate, comment:

   "Lakota, you are wet. I'll change you."

☀ Highlighting Development

After birth, infants may sleep 16 or more hours per day. Gradually, their need for sleep decreases, while the need for stimulation increases.

VARIATION:

♡ Repeat this activity during eating. Always hold the infant while feeding and look into his eyes. Be warm and loving. Smile, coo, and talk to the child.

ADDITIONAL INFORMATION:

♡ Promptly meeting infants' basic needs fosters a sense of trust. They quickly learn they can depend on you for help during periods of discomfort or distress.

I'll Help

SOCIAL

Child's Developmental Goals

✓ To develop a sense of trust

✓ To experience social interactions

MATERIALS:

None

PREPARATION:

♡ Observe the infant's signals for signs of readiness.

NURTURING STRATEGIES:

1. When an infant signals you, move to the child's side immediately while verbally describing what you can see or hear. Say, for example:
   "Midori is crying. She sounds very upset. I'm coming, Midori. I'm here to help."
2. Using your knowledge of the infant, provide comfort.
3. Use your voice as a tool to communicate calmness and reassurance.
4. Verbally describe what you are doing for the infant while you are performing the action. For example, state:
   "I'm wrapping you tightly in a blanket. Midori, you like to be warm."

5. Continue the social interaction once the child is calm if the infant signals she wants to interact by smiling or gazing at you.

☼ Highlighting Development

The relationship between infants and adults is believed to be the foundation for later relationships with adults and peers. If infants learn to trust adults, they tend to have more positive relationships with peers later in life (Cassidy, Scolton, Kirsh, & Parke, 1996; Park & Waters, 1989).

VARIATION:

♡ Try other techniques for soothing a crying infant described in the Introduction (see pp. 11–12).

ADDITIONAL INFORMATION:

♡ Paying close attention to an infant's signals is vital for developing a positive relationship. Infants need to know that you can be counted on to meet their needs.

Emotional Development

♡

BIRTH to THREE MONTHS

Labeling Emotions

EMOTIONAL

Child's Developmental Goals

✓ To express the basic emotions of distress, disgust, and interest

✓ To learn self-soothing techniques

MATERIALS:

None

PREPARATION:

♡ Constantly observe the infant. When an infant is displaying an emotion such as distress, disgust, or interest, respond immediately.

NURTURING STRATEGIES:

1. Using your observation skills and knowledge of the situation, describe and label the infant's emotions. Comments include:
   "Tunde, you are crying. You must be hungry. You need to eat. Let's warm a bottle. It is hard to wait."
   "You are angry. You don't enjoy having your diaper changed. We're almost done. I'm pulling up your pants."
2. Assist the infant in developing self-soothing techniques. For example, providing a pacifier or rattle to suck on can sooth a distressed infant.
3. Describe how the self-soothing technique was beneficial to the infant. Say, for example:
   "The rattle is helping. You are calming down."

☼ Highlighting Development

During the first few months, babies appear to cry more frequently as a means of communication. They may cry for many reasons other than anger, sadness, or fear. They also cry because they are hungry, cold, or have a wet diaper. Moreover, they may also cry if they want company because they are lonely or bored.

VARIATION:

♡ Try using other techniques for reducing stress: changing the diaper, feeding, holding, moving to a new position, covering with a blanket, etc.

ADDITIONAL INFORMATION:

♡ For infants, crying is a way of communicating. Therefore, infants cry for a variety of reasons, including anger, sadness, or fear. Careful observation of infants is necessary to accurately label their emotions and needs.

♡ Each infant has a unique emotion rhythm. Observe carefully and make mental notes. Then respond accordingly.

Finding Your Fist

Child's Developmental Goals

✓ To recognize basic emotions—distress, disgust, and interest

✓ To learn self-soothing techniques

MATERIALS:

None

PREPARATION:

None

NURTURING STRATEGIES:

1. During nap time when the infant is fussy, provide verbal encouragement for sucking on a fist. Say, for example:
   "Tara, you are fussy. Sucking on your fist may help."
   "Put your fist in your mouth."
2. If more than verbal encouragement is needed, physically guide the infant's fist to the mouth. Encourage the infant to suck the fist. Make comments such as:
   "Tara, that's better. You are soothing yourself."
3. Speaking in a quiet, soft voice also assists in soothing the infant.

☀ Highlighting Development

Infants crave tactile stimulation, which plays an important part in their emotional development. Through tactile stimulation from being held and caressed by their caregivers, infants develop attachment behaviors. When they have healthy interactions with nurturing caregivers, infants become better prepared to learn from and deal with the stressors of everyday life (Shore, 1997).

VARIATION:

♡ Sucking on a pacifier or infant toy can also be self-soothing.

ADDITIONAL INFORMATION:

♡ Infants enjoy sucking for its sheer pleasure. Fists are preferable over pacifiers because the infant is in control. The tool is immediately available. Moreover, teaching infants to suck on their fists should not promote thumb sucking.

 Exercise caution and sanitize toys before giving them to an infant. A bleach solution to sanitize an infant's toys can be prepared by mixing 1 tablespoon of household bleach with 1 gallon of water. After immersing the toys in the bleach solution, let them air dry.

"Hickory, Dickory, Dock"

EMOTIONAL

Child's Developmental Goals

✓ To express basic emotions—distress, disgust, enjoyment, and interest

✓ To respond to the emotional expressions of others

✓ To practice responding with a smile during social interactions

MATERIALS:

None

PREPARATION:

♡ Observe the child's state of alertness to determine when the rhyme should be introduced. If the infant is sleepy, delay this activity.

NURTURING STRATEGIES:

1. After diapering the child and before removing the child from the changing table, chant the nursery rhyme "Hickory, Dickory, Dock."

2. While chanting the nursery rhyme, walk your fingers up and down the infant's body.

3. During this interaction, respond to the infant's display of emotions by labeling his feelings. Make comments such as:
   "Umberto, you are laughing. What a happy baby."
   "What a big smile. Umberto, does this tickle?"

4. During this interaction, smile. Because infants imitate, your expression should elicit a smile.

5. Continue chanting the nursery rhyme as long as the infant appears interested. Check to see that the child is maintaining eye contact or smiling.

☀ Highlighting Development

An emotion is a feeling that motivates, organizes, and guides perception, thought, and action (Izard, 1991). For healthy well-being, the emotional expression of all feelings is important to develop. Therefore, infants need to learn self-soothing techniques for coping with sadness, anger, or frustration. Coping with these emotions is more difficult than coping with happiness.

VARIATIONS:

♡ While singing a song about emotions, move the infant to the rhythm.

♡ Finger plays may be substituted for songs. See Appendix F for a list of finger plays to use with infants.

ADDITIONAL INFORMATION:

♡ Infants will learn appropriate emotional expression and regulation through close, sensitive contact with adults.

♡ In the beginning, emotional reactions for the infant are involuntary and cannot be controlled.

EMOTIONAL

Who's That in the Mirror?

Child's Developmental Goals

✓ To show different emotions, such as enjoyment, interest, or disgust

✓ To regulate self-expression of emotions

MATERIALS:

❑ Blanket or mat
❑ Nonbreakable mirror

PREPARATION:

♡ Select an area that can be constantly supervised. Clear a space for the mirror and blanket or mat.

NURTURING STRATEGIES:

1. Lay the infant facedown on the blanket or mat.

2. Tapping lightly on the mirror typically gains the infant's attention. If the infant looks into the mirror, say, for example:
   "Who's that in the mirror? There is Christina."
   If the infant doesn't look into the mirror, providing more verbal cues may be necessary. Comments include:
   "Christina, push yourself up."
   "Raise up your head."
   "Look here, there's a baby."
   You may also try moving the mirror to attract the infant's attention.

3. While the infant is looking in the mirror, describe your observations, focusing on emotions. For example, remark:
   "Christina, you are smiling. What a happy baby."
   "You raised your head. You must be proud."

4. Provide positive reinforcement or encouragement as needed. Statements such as the following could be made:
   "Christina, it is hard to keep your head raised."
   "You are working hard."

☀ Highlighting Development

Infants show facial expressions that appear to convey their emotional states. They smile when they appear happy. They show anger when frustrated. When they are unhappy, they look sad (Feldman, 1998). Respond to children's cues and clues. Their rhythms and moods are evident even during the first days and weeks of life. Respond to them when they are upset, as well as when they are happy. Try to understand what children are feeling, what they are communicating to you, and what they are trying to do (Shore, 1997).

VARIATION:

♡ Holding a small mirror while the infant is sitting in your lap will reduce the physical exertion of this activity for the infant, yet still provide an outlet for emotional talk.

ADDITIONAL INFORMATION:

♡ Surrounding the infant with "emotional talk" will assist her in learning how to recognize and label emotions. These are very important skills for young children to develop.

CAUTION Whenever pillows or blankets are used, constant supervision is necessary to prevent the possibility of suffocation.

DEVELOPMENTAL AREA: Emotional

Resting with Lullabies

Child's Developmental Goals

✔ To relax by listening to music
✔ To develop self-soothing skills

MATERIALS:

❑ Crib
❑ Tape or compact disc of lullabies
❑ Tape or compact disc player

PREPARATION:

♡ Select a lullaby, place the tape or compact disc in the player, and set the player in a safe place.

NURTURING STRATEGIES:

1. Lay the infant faceup in the crib.
2. Rubbing the infant's abdomen using soft, gentle strokes while humming or singing to the music will help the child relax.
3. With music playing in the background, comment:
   "What soft music. It helps you calm down."
   "This music makes you sleepy."
   "Listen to the music."
4. Walking away before the infant falls asleep will support the development of self-regulation skills by providing the opportunity to finish calming down.

Highlighting Development

During this stage, infants express emotions not only through facial expressions or vocalizations but also with their entire bodies. For example, when interested in objects, infants may gaze at them while moving their arms and legs in anticipation.

VARIATION:

♡ By using different types of music such as nature tapes or classical music, the development of appreciation for a wide variety of sounds and sound patterns will be fostered.

ADDITIONAL INFORMATION:

♡ The role of the caregiver cannot be overemphasized for this activity. For this experience to be effective, the caregiver must be calm and soothing. Consequently, rushing while rubbing the infant's abdomen may cause the infant to be overstimulated rather than relaxed.

 Given the threat of Sudden Infant Death Syndrome, always lay infants faceup in cribs.

Friends Have Feelings Too

Child's Developmental Goals

✓ To identify the emotions of interest, enjoyment, disgust, and distress

✓ To become aware that other people have emotions

MATERIALS:

None

PREPARATION:

♡ Observe the infant for a "teachable moment." Watch to see what is captivating the child, then interact.

NURTURING STRATEGIES:

1. When an infant turns toward another person who is displaying an emotion, reinforce this behavior by discussing feelings. Comment by saying:
   "You are looking at Zach. He is sad. He is crying. Zach wants his mommy."
   "You are watching Simone. She is laughing. She is exploring the rattle. Listen to Simone shake it."

2. Continue the conversation by connecting an emotional display of the other person to the life experiences of the infant to whom you are talking. To illustrate, you might say:
   "When you are hungry, you sometimes cry."
   "You like rattles. They are fun to shake."

☀ Highlighting Development

By three months, infants show interest in sounds by turning their heads toward the source. When this happens, explaining the sound is imperative to their cognitive, language, and emotional development.

VARIATION:

♡ Using emotional talk, speak to infants by describing their emotional expressions.

ADDITIONAL INFORMATION:

♡ Infants are interested in an assortment of sounds, especially those made by humans. Therefore, it is important to introduce them to a variety of sounds.

♡ Observe. Most infants will begin to coo between five and eight weeks of age. Cooing can be interpreted as an expression of comfort, enjoyment, satisfaction, or interest.

"This Little Piggy"

EMOTIONAL

Child's Developmental Goals

✓ To share the emotions of interest and enjoyment

✓ To respond to the emotional expressions of others

MATERIALS:

None

PREPARATION:

♡ Observe the infant's signal for interaction.

NURTURING STRATEGIES:

1. If the infant's toes are exposed during the diaper-changing procedure, recite the nursery rhyme "This Little Piggy." If the infant's toes are covered, remove clothing to expose the toes.

2. While reciting the nursery rhyme, lightly shake the infant's toes.

3. Look into the baby's face and respond to his expression. Your expressions will provide cues to the infant as to how to respond. Therefore, while lightly shaking the infant's toes, you should share a smile.

4. Describing the infant's reactions to this game will provide meaningful information about emotional content and expression. Comments might include: *"Look at that smile. Hemant, you like this game." "Hemant, now you are laughing."*

5. Observing the infant's cues will allow you to stop this game before it becomes overwhelming. When the infant is frowning or avoiding eye contact, it is time to end the interaction.

☼ Highlighting Development

Infants actively participate in their own brain development by signaling their needs to caregivers and by responding selectively to different kinds of stimulation (Shore, 1997). For example, when children become bored, they may cry to elicit being picked up and moved to another location.

VARIATION:

♡ Recite a different nursery rhyme that also encourages touching. See Appendix F for a list of nursery rhymes.

ADDITIONAL INFORMATION:

♡ Caregivers must observe and monitor the level of infant stimulation. Even though infants can signal overstimulation, they are unable to completely remove themselves from the situation because of their lack of mobility. Therefore, you must pay close attention and quickly respond to the body and vocal signals given by infants.

♡ Observe. The infant will respond to the drama of your body language such as the brightening of your eyes and playfulness of your voice.

Physical Development

♡

FOUR to SIX MONTHS

Fluttering Tree

PHYSICAL

Child's Developmental Goals

✓ To refine eye-hand coordination skills

✓ To practice reaching and strengthening arm muscles

MATERIALS:

❑ Wool yarn cut in an 18-inch section for each toy

❑ 2 or 3 interesting infant toys

PREPARATION:

♡ Attach one end of the yarn to each of the toys. Then tie the other end of the yarn around the structure allowing the toy to hang. Adjust the yarn so that the infant can easily reach the toys while being held.

NURTURING STRATEGIES:

1. Carry the infant over to the suspended toys.
2. Touch the toys with your hands and describe what is happening. Comment by saying:
   "Antonia, I touched the toys. Watch me. I used my hand."
3. Invite the infant to touch the toys using the hands by saying:
   "Can you touch the toys? Grab them. Use your hands."
4. Raise the infant up so that the toys will easily move with a swipe of a hand.
5. Praise the infant for touching/moving the toys. Examples might include saying:
   "Antonia, you did it. You moved the toys!"
6. Position the infant so that the toys are a little farther away. Then invite the infant to move the toys again.
7. Encourage the infant to try by saying:
   "Reach, Antonia, reach. You can do it! Grab the toy."
   If the toys move or are caught, praise the infant's accomplishment. If the infant misses, provide further encouragement.
8. If the infant swipes but continues to miss, move him closer to the toys so that he experiences success.

☀ Highlighting Development

Hand-eye coordination is improving. At three months of age, the infant is swiping at objects in an uncoordinated fashion. Among the movement milestones accomplished during this stage, the infant will reach with one hand to obtain desired objects. Using a raking motion, she will be able to pick up the objects.

By six months of age, most infants have a sophisticated way of reaching for and grasping objects. They can focus on an object at a distance and direct their hands straight to it. Moreover, they can adjust their hand to fit the size of the object they are grasping. At this time, they may manipulate, bang, or bring the objects to their mouths in a coordinated manner (Bentzen, 2001).

VARIATION:

♡ Use a longer string so that the infant can reach for the toys while lying on a blanket.

ADDITIONAL INFORMATION:

♡ Observe how young children love to pull on yarn strings. Repeated practice in pulling the strings will help teach them problem-solving skills in obtaining desired objects.

 For safety purposes, use wool yarn because it breaks easily. To prevent strangulation, constant supervision is always necessary when using yarn. Toys with cords, ribbons, string, rope, or ties should be avoided with young children. They could become wrapped around the infant's neck or wrists.

Rolling Over

Child's Developmental Goals

✓ To practice rolling from side to back

✓ To practice visually tracking an object

MATERIALS:

❑ 1 or 2 interesting infant toys

❑ Blanket or mat

PREPARATION:

♡ Select an area that can be constantly supervised. Clear this area and spread out the blanket or mat.

NURTURING STRATEGIES:

1. Lay the infant on a side on the blanket.
2. Gain the infant's attention by showing and describing the toys one at a time. Comment by saying:
   "Nikko, this is an elephant. It has a long nose."
3. Move the toys out of the infant's line of sight. Encourage the infant to search for the toys. Say, for example:
   "Where did the elephant go? Look for it. Roll over."
4. If the infant rolls or attempts to do so, provide positive reinforcement. To illustrate, say:
   "Nikko, you are working hard."
   "You rolled over!"
5. If the infant does not visually search for the toy, move the toy back into the infant's line of vision. Slowly move the toy while the infant tracks it visually. Continue to move the toy until the infant rolls from the side to back. Provide encouragement and reinforcement as needed.

☀ Highlighting Development

An infant's vision is improving at this stage of development. Everything he does he watches closely. Vision now is playing an important role in his physical development. Color recognition skills are emerging. Chances are the infant will recognize blue, green, red, and yellow compared to other colors (Berk, 1997).

VARIATIONS:

♡ When developmentally ready, begin to practice rolling from back to side.

♡ Use soft, textured balls that make pleasant sounds when moved.

ADDITIONAL INFORMATION:

♡ Hiding toys on both the left and right sides of the infant's body will promote the uniform development of the child's muscles.

 Consider safety precautions when selecting toys for infants. Beware of toys containing removable small parts. If removed, these can become lodged in nostrils, ears, or windpipes.

 Always check mouthable toys for safety. Make sure they are at least two inches in diameter. Use the core of a toilet paper roll to measure; if a toy can fit inside the cardboard core, it is too small for an infant.

 Whenever pillows or blankets are used, constant supervision is necessary to prevent the possibility of suffocation.

4 to 6 months

All Propped Up!

PHYSICAL

Child's Developmental Goals

✓ To strengthen lower back muscles

✓ To sit in an upright "tripod" position with assistance

MATERIALS:

❏ Blanket or mat

❏ Pillows or rolled quilt

❏ Toy

PREPARATION:

♡ Observe the infant. Once she is strong enough to raise her chest off the floor when in a facedown position, you can help her practice sitting up.

♡ Select an area that you can constantly supervise. Clear this area and spread out the blanket or mat.

♡ Lay out the pillows or rolled quilt on the blanket for support and a safe fall zone.

NURTURING STRATEGIES:

1. Sit the infant upright on the blanket. To assist the infant in balancing, spread the legs apart to create a wide base. If necessary, rearrange the pillows or rolled quilt so the infant is securely supported.

2. Once the infant is steady and sitting without your assistance, provide positive reinforcement. Make comments such as:
    "Look at Imani. You are sitting up."
    "What a strong baby!"

3. Encourage the infant to visually explore the room. Say, for example:
    "Look around, Imani. What can you see?"
    "Look at the toy clown."

4. Constant supervision is always necessary to protect the child from bodily harm and suffocation.

 Highlighting Development

When infants are able to raise their chest from the floor, they are ready to begin sitting with assistance. Although infants desire to sit, they are unable to do this alone. They need help getting into the sitting position and balancing once there.

VARIATION:

♡ Provide a toy for the infant to explore with both hands and mouth while sitting up. Note that the infant may attempt to transfer items from one hand to the other.

CAUTION Constant supervision is necessary.

CAUTION Infants often topple over while learning to sit. To promote their safety, create a fall zone by surrounding them with cushioning materials, such as pillows or blankets.

CAUTION Whenever pillows or blankets are used, constant supervision is necessary to prevent the possibility of suffocation.

PHYSICAL

Holding On

Child's Developmental Goals

✔ To practice the ulnar grasp

✔ To develop the lower back muscles

✔ To practice transferring objects from one hand to the other

MATERIALS:

❑ Cube at least 3 inches in diameter

❑ Blanket or mat

❑ Pillows or rolled quilt

PREPARATION:

♡ Select an area that you can constantly supervise. Clear this area and spread out the blanket or mat.

♡ Because most infants this age will be unable to sit without assistance, lay out the pillows or the rolled quilt on the blanket for support and to create a fall zone.

NURTURING STRATEGIES:

1. Sit the infant upright on the blanket. To help promote balance, spread the infant's legs in a tripod position to create a wide base of support.

2. Once the infant is steady, offer the cube while talking about it. Comments might include: *"Forrest, look. Here is a cube. It is red. The cube is smooth."*

3. Encourage the infant to explore the cube with both hands and mouth. Foster these skills by saying: *"Forrest, touch it with your other hand." "Put it in your left hand."*

☀ Highlighting Development

When the reflexive grasp of the newborn weakens, it is replaced by the ulnar grasp, a clumsy motion in which the fingers close against the palm (Berk, 1997). Objects are held by all four fingers, which is why it is sometimes referred to as the mitten grasp. Eventually, objects will be held by only one or two fingers against the palm.

VARIATION:

♡ Provide other stimulating toys for the infant to observe, hold, or explore in a sitting position.

ADDITIONAL INFORMATION:

♡ Labeling the hands left and right serves only to alert the infant that there are two hands and they are slightly different. Infants will be unable to accurately demonstrate understanding of which hand is the right one and which hand is the left one.

♡ Select toys carefully to avoid safety hazards and promote development. See Appendix C for a list of criteria to aid in your selection.

 Whenever pillows or blankets are used, constant supervision is necessary to prevent the possibility of suffocation.

Activity Gym

4 to 6 months

Child's Developmental Goals

✓ To develop eye-hand coordination skills

✓ To practice using the ulnar grasp

MATERIALS:

❑ Blanket

❑ Activity gym

PREPARATION:

♡ Select an area that can be constantly supervised. Clear this area and spread out the blanket.

♡ Place the activity gym on the blanket.

NURTURING STRATEGIES:

1. Lay the infant faceup on the blanket under the activity gym.

2. Gain the infant's attention by shaking the toys hanging from the activity gym. Describe the objects while touching them. Comment, for example:

   "Darcy, look at the black bear. It makes a noise."

3. Encourage the infant to reach for or grab the toys by saying:

   "Darcy, reach. Stretch. Touch the bear."
   "You touched it! Now grab it."

4. Reinforce the infant's attempts and accomplishments. To illustrate, state:

   "You grabbed the bear. It is soft."
   "Darcy, you are shaking the toy. You are working hard."

☀ Highlighting Development

After infants are able to bring objects to their mouth, they will begin using their fingers and palm in a raking motion. This type of hand development can be stimulated by placing objects within reach. Furthermore, infants are learning the importance of using their hands.

VARIATION:

♡ Make your own activity gym by suspending toys with wool yarn from a table.

ADDITIONAL INFORMATION:

♡ Infants need responsive toys to learn about cause and effect. They need toys to bat, hit, bang, and shake.

 Be proactive by checking the stability of the activity gym. If the activity gym is on an uneven surface, it might not be able to support the child's weight and, therefore, it could be a risk to the child's safety.

 Carefully observe the infant working with the activity gym. Make sure the infant's body is not pulled off the ground or floor.

 Suspended toys can become dangerous if used too long. Once infants begin sitting or getting on their hands or knees, these toys should be removed (Abrams & Kaufman, 1990).

 Whenever pillows or blankets are used, constant supervision is necessary to prevent the possibility of suffocation.

Grabbing and Pulling

Child's Developmental Goals

✓ To practice the ulnar grasp

✓ To strengthen the upper and lower arm muscles

MATERIALS:

❑ Blanket or mat
❑ Wooden spool
❑ 12-inch piece of elastic
❑ Diaper pin
❑ Masking tape

PREPARATION:

♡ Prepare this game by securing the wooden spool to the elastic. Attach one end of the elastic around the center of the spool with the diaper pin.

♡ Select an area that you can constantly supervise. Clear this area for the blanket or mat.

NURTURING STRATEGIES:

1. Lay the infant faceup on the blanket.
2. Gain the infant's attention by lowering the spool into the child's line of vision, pointing to the spool, and saying:
   "Parker, look at this spool. Grab it."
3. Reinforce any attempts to grab the spool by commenting:
   "You touched it. Now grab it."
   "You are holding the spool, Parker."
4. When the infant has grasped the spool, say:
   "Hold on tight. I'm going to pull the spool."
   While saying this, begin gently tugging on the elastic.

5. Encourage the infant to exercise arm muscles by explaining:
   "Now, you pull it, Parker."
   "Pull. You are pulling the spool."
6. Providing positive reinforcement may help to sustain the interaction. Comments might include:
   "What a strong baby."
   "Keep pulling. Wow, you have strong arms."

☀ Highlighting Development

Infants' hands are becoming more functional now. As their hand-eye coordination improves, they will begin grabbing their feet and bringing them to their mouth. They may also clap their hands against the thighs. Through these physical activities, they are also discovering new sensorimotor sensations.

VARIATION:

♡ Attach any favorite toy to the piece of elastic.

ADDITIONAL INFORMATION:

♡ The strength of the infant may surprise you. Keeping a tight grasp on the elastic will prevent the infant from being injured by the spool. If the elastic snaps, the child could be hit by the spool.

 After closing diaper pins, always secure them by wrapping with masking tape.

 Whenever pillows or blankets are used, constant supervision is necessary to prevent the possibility of suffocation.

Pulling Up to Sit

4 to 6 months

Child's Developmental Goals

✓ To strengthen the lower back muscles

✓ To gain balance in a sitting position

MATERIALS:

❑ Blanket or mat

PREPARATION:

♡ Select an area that can be constantly supervised. Clear the area and spread out the blanket or mat.

NURTURING STRATEGIES:

1. Lay the infant faceup on the blanket.
2. Talk to the infant about what is going to happen by commenting:
   "Amanda, give me your hands. Hold them out."
   "I'm going to help you sit up."
3. Reinforcing your words with actions may be necessary. If this is the case, repeat the words:
   "Give me your hands."
   While speaking, take the infant's hands.
4. Gently pull the infant into a sitting position. If necessary, spread the infant's legs in a tripod position to create a wide base of support.
5. Continue to support the infant in the sitting position.

6. Provide positive reinforcement so that the infant begins to understand what is happening. Say, for example:
   "Amanda, you pulled yourself up. You are sitting now."
   "What a strong baby. You can sit up."

☀ Highlighting Development

By leaning forward and extending their arms in a tripod position, infants learn to balance their upper bodies. This position is used to avoid falling when attempting to sit up. Eventually, infants will be able to sit using just their legs to support their body weight.

VARIATION:

♡ Whenever the child is lying flat and needs to be picked up, help the infant move into a sitting position first.

ADDITIONAL INFORMATION:

♡ Often infants enjoy repetition; therefore, repeat the activity until the infant signals a lack of interest.

 Whenever pillows or blankets are used, constant supervision is necessary to prevent the possibility of suffocation.

Language and Communication Development

♡

FOUR to SIX MONTHS

4 to 6 months

"Pat-A-Cake"

Child's Developmental Goals

✓ To hear native language patterns

✓ To associate words with actions

MATERIALS:

❑ Blanket or mat

PREPARATION:

♡ Select an area that can be constantly supervised. Clear this area and spread out the blanket or mat.

NURTURING STRATEGIES:

1. Lay the infant faceup on a blanket or mat.
2. Gain the infant's attention by chanting (clap to rhythm) "Pat-A-Cake" while performing the actions:

Pat-a-cake, pat-a-cake	(clap to the rhythm)
Baker's man.	(clap to the rhythm)
Bake me a cake	(clap to the rhythm)
As fast as you can.	(clap to the rhythm)
Roll it	(roll hands)
And pat it	(pat belly)
And mark it with a *J*	(insert first letter of child's name)
And put it in the oven	
For *Jamal* and me	(point to infant and then self)

3. Stimulate the infant by talking about reactions to the song. For example, say:
   "Jamal, you are smiling. Did you like it when I patted your belly?"

4. Repeat the song as long as the infant shows interest. Signs of interest include smiling, cooing, and maintaining eye contact.

☀ Highlighting Development

Because of increased control over their vocal mechanisms, infants begin to babble during this stage, typically between 6 and 10 months of age. Listen carefully to them. You should hear infants beginning to combine consonants and vowels in alternating sequences heard in their native language. While cooing focused on vowels, babbling shifts toward a focus on consonants. Typical combinations include "ma ma ma," "da da da," and "ba ba ba" (Snow, 1998).

VARIATION:

♡ Hold the infant in a position that allows you to visually connect while reciting the chant.

ADDITIONAL INFORMATION:

♡ Infants need to engage in one-on-one, face- to-face interactions with adults. During this time, they learn trust, security, and language skills.

♡ Repeat any recognizable sounds the infant makes by parroting them.

 Whenever pillows or blankets are used, constant supervision is necessary to prevent the possibility of suffocation.

Babble Time

Child's Developmental Goals

✓ To practice producing babbling sounds

✓ To develop language skills

MATERIALS:

None

PREPARATION:

♡ Observe the infant. Is the child babbling spontaneously? Does the child appear to be seeking social interaction? For example, is the infant looking around the room or gazing toward you?

NURTURING STRATEGIES:

1. If the infant appears to want interaction, move closer to the infant. Position yourself so that you can visually connect with the infant. If desired, hold the child.

2. Listen to the vocalizations made by the infant. When the infant pauses, imitate the child's vocalizations. Pause. Your pausing will encourage the infant to vocalize again.

3. To add a twist to the conversation, create a new string of babble during your turn. Observe closely to see if the infant imitates your vocalizations.

4. Providing positive reinforcement may encourage the infant to continue babbling. For example, say:
   "Mahala, we are talking."
   "You are talking a lot today, Mahala. Tell me more."

Highlighting Development

Talkativeness by young children partly depends on the stimulation they receive from adults around them. Therefore, you need to frequently talk and converse with infants (Leach, 1992).

Infants respond to sounds by making sounds. The ease, fluency, and complexity with which infants babble is closely related to the ease and speed with which they will later learn to use expressive language.

Note that before they can see differences between facial expressions, infants can detect different emotions in the voice. By five months of age, infants will listen longer to a voice expressing approval than one expressing disapproval (Fogel, 2001).

VARIATIONS:

♡ When a recognizable sound is made, parrot it back to the infant.

♡ Introduce new syllables.

ADDITIONAL INFORMATION:

♡ Many infants engage in private "conversations" as a way of improving their language skills. Therefore, infants also need time to practice babbling in private.

♡ Listen to the infant voice for signs of pleasure and displeasure. This will be a clue to continue or discontinue the activity.

What's Coming Up?

Child's Developmental Goals

✓ To develop receptive language skills

✓ To hear native language patterns

MATERIALS:

None

PREPARATION:

♡ Observe the infant's level of alertness to determine the appropriate time to introduce the experience.

NURTURING STRATEGIES:

1. This activity can be introduced any time you are transitioning the child from one activity or routine to another. Prepare the infant for the upcoming event by verbally describing it.

2. Let the infant know what the transition will include. Examples of comments include:
   "After I wash your hands, we can go for a stroller ride. You like being outside."
   "After I wash your hands, I will lay you in your crib. You are so sleepy. Would you like to hear a song?"
   "Before you eat, your hands need to be washed."
   "I'll read you a book before you take your nap."

☼ Highlighting Development

Routines create an environment of predictability and consistency for infants by providing a pattern. Preparing the infant for the next step in the routine is necessary to foster a sense of security.

VARIATION:

♡ Infants also enjoy songs. Therefore, to add variety try communicating the change of routines by singing. (For a variety of finger plays and songs, see Appendix F and Appendix G, respectively.)

ADDITIONAL INFORMATION:

♡ Discussing what will happen creates a context for future events and promotes the development of auditory memory skills.

"Bumping Up and Down"

Child's Developmental Goals

✓ To associate words with actions

✓ To develop receptive language skills

MATERIALS:

❑ Song, "Bumping Up and Down"

❑ Tagboard or index card and felt-tip marker

PREPARATION:

♡ If you have memorized the words to the song "Bumping Up and Down," no preparation is needed. However, if you need a prompt, create a poster or note card with the words and actions.

NURTURING STRATEGIES:

1. In a sitting position, hold the infant on your knees so that you can visually connect and gently bounce.

2. Sing the following song:

   ♫ Bumping up and down in a little red wagon (bounce child on knee)

   ♫ Bumping up and down in a little red wagon (bounce child on knee)

   ♫ Bumping up and down in a little red wagon (bounce child on knee)

   ♫ Won't you be my darling?

   ♫ One wheel's gone and the axle's broken (bounce child on knee)

   ♫ One wheel's gone and the axle's broken (bounce child on knee)

   ♫ One wheel's gone and the axle's broken (bounce child on knee)

   ♫ Won't you be my darling?

   ♫ Josiah gonna fix it with his hammer (make motion of tool)

   ♫ Josiah gonna fix it with his hammer (make motion of tool)

   ♫ Josiah gonna fix it with his hammer (make motion of tool)

   ♫ Won't you be my darling?

3. Substitute different people such as a parent, sibling, or friend in the song. Tools such as hammers, pliers, and rulers can also be substituted in subsequent verses.

4. Continue singing this song as long as the infant shows interest by maintaining eye contact and smiling.

☀ Highlighting Development

Children learn the sounds of their native language through repeated exposure. During this stage, the children's babbling imitates the rhythm and sounds they have been exposed to. Listen carefully. You will observe that infants drop their voice as when making a statement. They also raise their voice as when asking a question.

VARIATION:

♡ Recite a nursery rhyme while performing accompanying actions.

ADDITIONAL INFORMATION:

♡ This is a very long song. You may want to sing only the first verse, pause, and then sing the second verse if the child is interested.

4 to 6 months

Telling Picture Book Stories

Child's Developmental Goals

✓ To develop receptive language skills
✓ To produce babbling sounds

MATERIALS:

❑ Picture book

PREPARATION:

♡ Observe the child's state of alertness to determine the most appropriate timing of the experience.
♡ Place the book in an accessible location.

NURTURING STRATEGIES:

1. Hold the infant in your lap so that both of you can view the book.
2. Gain the infant's attention by saying:
   "Esme, I have a book. It is about kittens. You like kittens. Let's look at it together."
3. Begin "reading" the book. Describe the pictures while pointing to them.
4. Engage the infant in conversation by pointing to the picture and asking questions such as:
   "Esme, what is this kitten doing?"
   "What is this?"
5. Pause to allow the infant the opportunity to respond by babbling.
6. Reinforce the infant's response through comments like:
   "That's right, Esme. The kitten is pushing a ball."
7. If the infant maintains interest through such actions as smiling and babbling, consider reading the book again.

☼ Highlighting Development

Infants learn turn-taking skills when adults model this behavior. To illustrate, adults first should ask a question. Then they need to pause, allowing the infant an opportunity to respond by babbling. After the infant produces a recognizable syllable, it needs to be responded to or echoed back.

VARIATION:

♡ Prepare a picture book based upon the infant's interests. Pictures can be obtained through magazines or actual photographs of the child, family, and the immediate environment.

ADDITIONAL INFORMATION:

♡ Choose picture books that are sturdy and have one large picture per page. Preferably, the pictures should reflect items in the child's immediate environment. At this stage of development, infants are unable to follow story lines, making print unnecessary.
♡ Cardboard picture books are easier for you and the infant to handle. In addition, these books are more durable.

"One, Two, Buckle . . ."

Child's Developmental Goals

✓ To hear native language patterns
✓ To develop rhythm

MATERIALS:

❑ Infant seat
❑ Index card and felt-tip marker

PREPARATION:

♡ If needed, write out the words to the nursery rhyme "One, Two, Buckle My Shoe" on an index card. Carry this in your pocket for quick reference.
♡ Select and clear an area to place the infant seat.

NURTURING STRATEGIES:

1. Secure the infant in the seat using the safety restraint.
2. Position your body so that you can visually connect with the infant and any other children in your care.
3. Gain the infant's attention by reciting the following nursery rhyme:

   One, two, buckle my shoe
   Three, four, shut the door
   Five, six, pick up sticks
   Seven, eight, lay them straight
   Nine, ten a big tall hen.

4. While reciting the nursery rhyme, lightly tap the infant's leg with your hand to the rhythm of the rhyme.
5. Continue reciting this nursery rhyme as long as the infant shows interest through vocalizing, smiling, making body movements, or maintaining eye contact.

☀ Highlighting Development

An infant's first exposure to rhythm is through listening to his mother's heartbeat while in the womb. Rhythms such as a whirling fan or ticking clock help an infant to block external or internal discomforts. Thus, communication through rhythms plays an important part in the infant's development.

VARIATION:

♡ Sing songs or do finger plays that have steady, easy rhythms. See Appendix F for finger plays and Appendix G for songs.

ADDITIONAL INFORMATION:

♡ At this stage of development, counting is used to develop rhythm rather than for promoting the understanding of numerical concepts.

Conversing

Child's Developmental Goals

✓ To practice turn-taking skills

✓ To develop expressive language skills

MATERIALS:

None

PREPARATION:

♡ Gathering all diapering supplies may facilitate the activity and allow you to focus on the child.

NURTURING STRATEGIES:

1. While diapering the child, talk about what you are doing. Comments include:
   "Anika, I'm putting on my gloves. They keep me safe."
   "This might be cold. I'm going to clean your bottom with the wipe."
2. Engage the infant in conversation by asking questions such as:
   "What happens next?"
3. Pause to provide the infant time to respond by babbling.
4. Reinforce the infant's response. Use comments such as:
   "Anika, yes. I need to sanitize the table."
   "Well, I need to put on the clean diaper first."

☀ Highlighting Development

Modeling language plays an important role in the child's development. Only through exposure do infants learn to make more complicated sounds. Consequently, an environment rich in language usually results in the infant generating more speech.

VARIATIONS:

♡ Talk about what the infant is looking at.
♡ Repeat this activity during other routine care times such as feeding.

ADDITIONAL INFORMATION:

♡ Infants learn important language and communication skills while conversing with adults. Therefore, repeating this activity frequently will promote this area of development.
♡ There is similarity in the babbling of infants from all language backgrounds. Even deaf children babble. Because they lack auditory feedback, their babbling tends to stop earlier (Snow, 1998).
♡ If an infant does not respond by babbling at this stage, the child may be having difficulty hearing. A child with frequent ear infections may often experience difficulty hearing. If this occurs, it is advisable to seek medical attention.

Cognitive
Development

♡

FOUR to SIX MONTHS

4 to 6 months

Shaking the Rattle

COGNITIVE

Child's Developmental Goals

✓ To repeatedly engage in purposeful behaviors

✓ To imitate a caregiver's actions

MATERIALS:

❑ 3 rattles of different sizes and sounds
❑ Blanket or mat

PREPARATION:

♡ Select an area that can be constantly supervised. Clear this area and spread out the blanket.

NURTURING STRATEGIES:

1. Lay the infant faceup on a blanket or mat.
2. Gain the infant's attention by shaking and describing the rattles. Make comments such as: *"Camden, I have three rattles. They all sound different. Listen to them."*
3. Lay all three rattles within the infant's reach. Direct the infant to pick one up by saying: *"Touch a rattle. That's it."* *"Use your hand to pick one up."*
4. If necessary, reinforce your words with actions by gently placing the infant's hand on the rattle while repeating: *"Camden, use your hand to pick one up."*
5. Discuss the sound of the chosen rattle. Examples of comments include: *"That rattle makes a soft sound."* *"That rattle is noisy. It sounds loud."*
6. Reinforcing the infant's actions may lead to repetition. Comments include: *"Shake, shake, shake."* *"Camden, do it again."* *"I want to hear the rattle. Keep shaking."* *"You like shaking the rattle."*

☀ Highlighting Development

Infants need to perform actions or behaviors repeatedly in order to add information to their cognitive structures. Therefore, when an infant tires of the activity, stop and repeat it again at a later time.

VARIATIONS:

♡ Supporting the infant in a sitting position gives him a different view while he shakes the rattles.
♡ With the child in a sitting position, repeat the activity using a ball that produces soft music.

ADDITIONAL INFORMATION:

♡ Providing a variety of rattles may gain and sustain the child's interest. See-through rattles that show colors and make noises are particularly attractive.
♡ Change the infant's rattle and toys, allowing the child to have new as well as familiar ones.

 Closely observe infants who are interacting with rattles. To help consumers choose safe toys for children under age three, the U.S. Consumer Product Safety Commission has set part-size standards. The ends of the rattle must be greater than 1⅜ inches in diameter to be safe for infants.

 Appendix C has additional criteria for selecting materials and equipment. Appendix D includes a list of materials and equipment for infants and toddlers.

 Whenever pillows or blankets are used, constant supervision is necessary to prevent the possibility of suffocation.

Dropping It over the Edge

Child's Developmental Goals

✓ To develop an understanding of object permanence

✓ To develop problem-solving skills

MATERIALS:

❑ High chair

❑ Interesting infant squeeze toys such as a rubber foot

PREPARATION:

♡ Gather the toys and prepare the high chair for the infant.

NURTURING STRATEGIES:

1. Introduce this activity right before lunch when the food or bottle is not quite ready.
2. Securely fasten the infant in the high chair using the safety restraint. Lock the tray in place.
3. Placing the toy foot on the tray may gain the infant's attention. If necessary, comments include:
   "Shannon, look at the toy. Here is the foot. The toes are good for chewing."
4. Observe the infant playing with the toy. Eventually, the infant will drop the toy over the side of the tray. Ask questions to help the infant learn that the object exists even when it can't be seen. For example, ask:
   "Where did the toys go Shannon?"
   "Should we look for the toy?"
5. Provide suggestions of what the infant could do to find the toy. To illustrate, say:
   "Look on the floor."
   "Look around."

6. Reinforce any attempts or accomplishments in looking for the toy by commenting:
   "You are looking for the toy, Shannon!"
7. It may be necessary to reinforce your words with actions. Make comments such as:
   "Here is the toy—it was on the floor," while picking up the toy and handing it back to the infant.

☀ Highlighting Development

Between four and five months, infants refine the principle of cause and effect. By dropping toys on the floor, they learn of their personal ability to influence their environment as they notice a chain of reactions. As a result, they will purposefully continue dropping items.

VARIATIONS:

♡ Repeat this activity, especially steps 4 to 7, any time during the day when a toy has been dropped and forgotten.

♡ Sit the child in an infant seat rather than in a high chair.

ADDITIONAL INFORMATION:

♡ Infants drop objects when the grasping reflex relaxes. At this stage, it is not intentional behavior. This activity helps to teach them to look for the dropped objects.

♡ Use the child's name while engaging in the activity. During this stage, children begin responding to their own names.

Where Is It?

COGNITIVE

4 to 6 months

Child's Developmental Goals

✓ To develop an understanding of object permanence

✓ To develop problem-solving skills

MATERIALS:

❑ An interesting infant toy such as a small stuffed animal

❑ Lightweight blanket

PREPARATION:

♡ If available, clear off a child-size table for this activity. Otherwise, a coffee table may be used. Place the stuffed animal on the table.

NURTURING STRATEGIES:

1. Sit down at the table, crossing your legs in a pretzel style. Next, sit the infant in your lap to provide necessary support. Position yourself so that the infant is close to the table.

2. Gain the infant's attention by pointing to, verbally identifying, and describing the toy on the table. To illustrate, say:
   "Tamarron, look at the puppy. It is black and white."
   "See this pig? A pig says 'oink.'"

3. While you have the infant's attention, partially cover the toy with the blanket.

4. Ask the infant:
   "Where did it go? Where is the puppy?"

5. If the infant does not search for the toy, provide hints or suggestions to encourage such behavior:
   "Tamarron, look for the toy."
   "Lift the blanket."

6. Provide positive reinforcement for attempts and accomplishments.
   "Tamarron, you looked. You found the puppy!"
   "You moved the blanket. The pig was hiding!"

☼ Highlighting Development

The infant is now learning a principle called "object permanence." This is the understanding that objects exist even when they are out of view. During this stage, when objects are partially out of sight, the infant typically will search and find the object.

VARIATION:

♡ To increase the difficulty of this activity, partially hide the toy while the infant is attending to other things.

ADDITIONAL INFORMATION:

♡ Encouraging the child to look for the hidden object will assist in the development of an understanding of object permanence.

♡ Infants need different objects with diverse textures (e.g., hard, soft, rough, etc.) They learn through grasping, patting, mouthing, and touching objects. So, give them the toy to explore once the activity is over.

 Whenever pillows or blankets are used, constant supervision is necessary to prevent the possibility of suffocation.

Where Did You Go?

Child's Developmental Goals

✓ To develop an understanding of object permanence

✓ To develop cause-and-effect skills

MATERIALS:

❑ Lightweight blanket

❑ Diapering supplies

PREPARATION:

♡ Gathering all the materials and placing them near the changing table may help facilitate the success of this activity.

NURTURING STRATEGIES:

1. Introduce this activity during and after the diapering routine.
2. Wad the blanket into a small ball and hand it to the infant encouraging her to grasp it with both hands.
3. As the infant raises the blanket to her mouth, the child's face may be blocked from your view. In an excited voice, ask:
   "Where did Stephanie go?"
4. The infant will probably lower her arms to look at you. When this happens, comment:
   "Oh, there you are. Stephanie, you didn't leave!"
5. To foster the development of cause and effect, show interest in the infant's efforts to create movement. For example, say:
   "Stephanie, when you cover your face, I can't see you."

☀ Highlighting Development

Now infants are more purposeful when engaging with people and items in their immediate environment. Watch. They shake rattles to hear sounds or explore to see what happens. Prior to this stage, infants focus on motor activity while shaking rattles. Now, infants use babbling as a strategy to gain your attention.

VARIATION:

♡ Cover your face with your hands and then ask, *"Where's Stephanie?"*

ADDITIONAL INFORMATION:

♡ Hide-and-seek and peekaboo are favorite games for children from this age to approximately 24 months. Therefore, it is important to repeat these games frequently. Repetition promotes learning and security.

 Whenever pillows or blankets are used, constant supervision is necessary to prevent the possibility of suffocation.

Going Fishing

Child's Developmental Goals

✓ To experience the principle of cause and effect

✓ To develop an understanding of object permanence

MATERIALS:

❑ 1 piece of wool yarn

❑ Lightweight toy in the shape of fish

PREPARATION:

♡ Tie one end of the string to the toy fish.

NURTURING STRATEGIES:

1. Sit the infant in a high chair and fasten the safety restraint.
2. While showing the infant the fish, say:
   "Miguel, here is a fish. Look at it. It is on a string."
3. Hanging the fish over the edge of the high chair tray will allow the string to be easily grasped. Encourage the infant to find the fish. Comments include:
   "Find the fish. Where did it go?"
   "Pull the string to find the fish, Miguel."
4. If the infant fails to look for the fish, reinforcing your words with actions may be necessary. To illustrate, while touching the string, say:
   "Pick up the string. Pull it. The fish will come."
5. Providing positive reinforcement may help the infant to continue this game. For example, comment by saying:
   "Miguel, you did it. You pulled the string. The fish came up!"
   "You found the fish."

☀ Highlighting Development

At this stage of development, infants' memory and attention span are increasing. When they move or hit a rattle, it will make a noise. Likewise, after dropping a spoon, they notice a reaction occurs. Someone may pick it up, make a face, or even comment. As a result, infants may repeat these behaviors to get a reaction. This is how they learn about the principle of cause and effect.

VARIATION:

♡ Provide three pieces of wool yarn. Attach the fish to only one piece of yarn. Encourage the infant to find the fish.

ADDITIONAL INFORMATION:

♡ At first, infants may not look for the fish because "out of sight" means "out of mind." Encouraging them to look for the fish will assist in their developing understanding of object permanence.

 At this stage of development, infants need constant supervision when involved with any toy or activity, including yarn. This is because infants have "object hunger" and typically place everything in their mouth for exploration.

What Do I Do with This?

Child's Developmental Goals

✓ To use existing cognitive schemas

✓ To develop new cognitive schemas

✓ To experience the principle of cause and effect

MATERIALS:

❑ A toy the infant has never seen before

❑ Blanket

❑ 3 or 4 pillows

PREPARATION:

♡ Select an area that you can constantly supervise. Clear this area and spread out the blanket.

♡ Place the pillows in a small semicircle on the blanket.

NURTURING STRATEGIES:

1. Sit the infant in the center of the pillows. Adjust the pillows as necessary to securely support the infant.

2. Gain the infant's attention by holding the toy in the line of vision and saying:
   "Gillian, here is a new toy. What can you do with it?"

3. Observe the infant exploring the object. Note what cognitive schemas are being used to explore the object. For example, observe to see if the object is being sucked, grasped, dropped, shaken, banged, etc.

4. To assist the infant in developing new cognitive schemas, suggest that she explore the object in a new way. For example, if the infant is sucking and grasping the object, suggest and demonstrate how it can be shaken.
   "Shake it, Gillian. Shake, shake, shake."

5. Whenever necessary, reinforce your words with actions. While gently moving the infant's arm, say:
   "Shake, shake, shake."

☀ Highlighting Development

Infants need objects and opportunities to explore the principle of cause and effect. At this stage of development they have developed a surprisingly large number of ways to explore objects using their senses: looking, tasting, touching, hearing, and smelling. Encourage them to continue adding new schemas to this existing repertoire as they explore objects.

VARIATION:

♡ Reintroduce a favorite toy. Observe the infant's exploratory behavior. How has it changed?

ADDITIONAL INFORMATION:

♡ Unless provided with new or unusual toys, the child may lose some interest; however, toys need not be expensive. Substitute boxes, wooden spoons, measuring spoons on a ring, unbreakable glasses, and cups.

♡ By manipulating objects, the infant gets to look at them from different perspectives.

 To promote safety, the objects you give to infants need to be large enough that they cannot be swallowed. They also need to be lightweight and unbreakable.

 Whenever pillows or blankets are used, constant supervision is necessary to prevent the possibility of suffocation.

4 to 6 months

Moving the Ducky

COGNITIVE

Child's Developmental Goals

✓ To use one's body for obtaining a desired effect

✓ To develop problem-solving skills

MATERIALS:

❑ Lightweight blanket

❑ Interesting infant toy such as a rubber duck

❑ Child-size table or coffee table

PREPARATION:

♡ Clear off a small table for this activity. Spread out the blanket on the table 5 to 6 inches from the edge of the place where you and the infant will be sitting.

♡ Place the toy in the middle of the blanket.

NURTURING STRATEGIES:

1. Sit down at the table and adjust your legs in a pretzel position. Next, sit the infant on your lap to provide the necessary physical support. Readjust your position as necessary, allowing the infant to sit close to the table.

2. Gain the infant's attention by pointing at the toy and describing it. Comment by saying:
   "Hector, look at the duck. You like to squeeze the duck. It makes a noise."

3. Encourage the infant to get the duck by saying:
   "Grab the blanket. Pull on the blanket. Pull. Move the duck."

4. Reinforcing your words with actions may be necessary. If so, gently place the infant's hand on the blanket while saying:
   "Touch it, Hector. Grab the blanket."
   "Now, pull it."

5. Continue providing positive reinforcement throughout the experience to maintain the infant's attention. To illustrate, say:
   "Hector, you grabbed the blanket."
   "You moved the blanket."
   "You know how to get the duck."
   "Look at you! You are squeezing the duck."

☼ Highlighting Development

Children during this stage are rapidly learning. Their development hinges on the interplay of nature and nurture. To thrive, they need stimulation, and they benefit from early interactions with parents and caregivers.

VARIATION:

♡ Repeat this activity while the infant is lying facedown on the floor. This will encourage the child to support the weight on one hand or side of his body. Moreover, in this position, the infant will be strengthening his upper body.

ADDITIONAL INFORMATION:

♡ This activity promotes high-level cognitive problem-solving skills. Infants can successfully engage in this activity with your assistance. In several months, they may be able to repeat it independently.

 Whenever pillows or blankets are used, constant supervision is necessary to prevent the possibility of suffocation.

Social Development

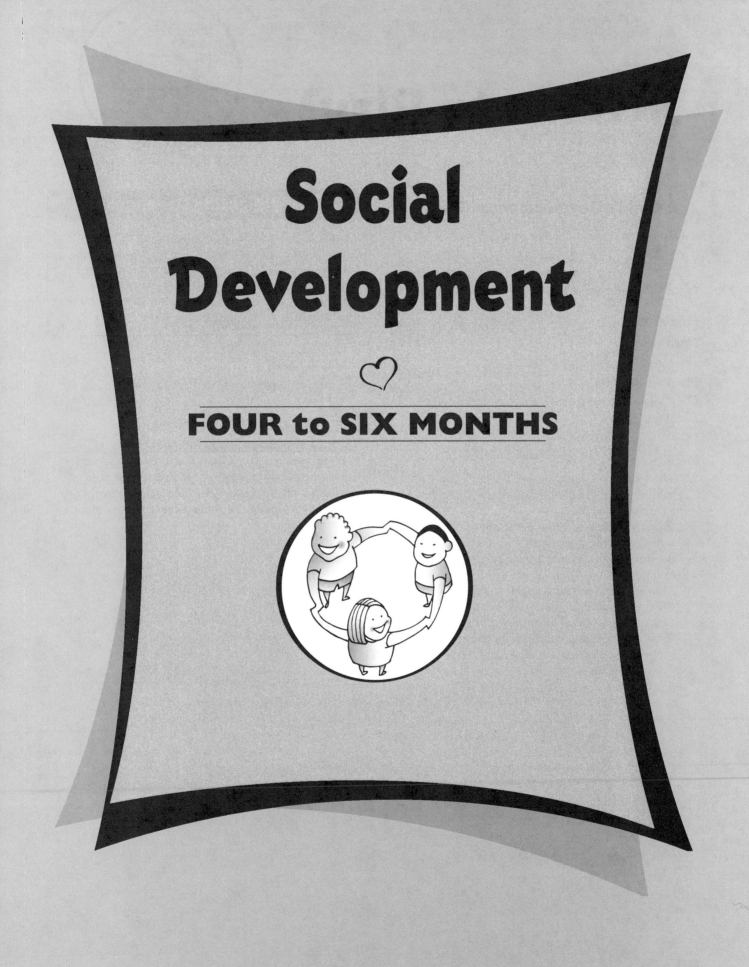

FOUR to SIX MONTHS

Want to Play?

SOCIAL

Child's Developmental Goals

✓ To interact with a familiar adult

✓ To gain an adult's attention

✓ To develop a sense of trust

MATERIALS:

None

PREPARATION:

♡ Closely observe the infant for signs of interest and alertness.

NURTURING STRATEGIES:

1. The infant will signal a desire for interacting by babbling or smiling while looking for or gazing at a familiar individual.
2. When you observe these signals, position yourself so you can visually connect with the child.
3. Respond to the infant's signals by saying, for example:
   "You are telling me that you want to play."
   "You got my attention. Let's play."
   "I heard you babbling. Tell me more."
4. Continue engaging the infant by describing what is happening or by imitating the child's babble.

☀ Highlighting Development

During this stage of development, infants will usually seek out a familiar caregiver for interacting. They also enjoy social play and responding to the emotional expression of others. In fact, by five months of age, they are able to discriminate between sad and happy vocal expressions (Feldman, 1998).

VARIATION:

♡ Engage in playing by sharing a favorite toy.

ADDITIONAL INFORMATION:

♡ Infants often enjoy babbling to themselves. To gain the caregiver's attention, they may signal by smiling or squealing and using body language such as kicking their legs. This helps to further the development of their communication skills.

Making Music

Child's Developmental Goals

✓ To imitate a caregiver's behavior

✓ To continue developing a relationship with a familiar adult

MATERIALS:

❑ Blanket or mat

❑ 4 pillows or a quilt

❑ 2 wooden spoons

❑ 2 aluminum pie pans

PREPARATION:

♡ Select an area that can be constantly supervised. Clear this area and place the blanket or mat on it.

♡ If the infant can sit unassisted, the preparation is complete. If this skill has yet to be mastered, arrange the pillows in a semicircle or roll the quilt in a semicircle on the blanket or mat.

NURTURING STRATEGIES:

1. Sit the infant on the blanket or mat. Spreading the infant's legs apart into a tripod position creates a wide base of support. Adjust the pillows or quilt to ensure that the infant is securely supported in the sitting position.

2. Place the aluminum pie pan between the infant's legs while handing the child a wooden spoon.

3. Position yourself so that you can visually connect with the infant. In addition, place an aluminum pie pan in your lap.

4. Observe the infant exploring the new tools.

5. Encourage the infant to make some music with the tools you have provided. For example, say:
   "Molly, bang the spoon on the plate."
   "Hit them together."

6. Providing further assistance may be necessary. Reinforce your words with actions by saying:
   "Molly, watch me hit them together."
   "I'm banging the spoon on the plate."

7. Providing positive reinforcement usually results in a continuation of the desired behavior. For example, say enthusiastically:
   "Molly, you are making music."
   "You are banging the spoon on the plate."

8. Asking the infant to play will continue this interaction. Use your voice to communicate enthusiasm. For example, say:
   "Let's make music together."
   "Can I make music with you?"
   Wait for the infant's affirmative response such as smiling or gazing at you and then join in.

☀ Highlighting Development

During this stage of development, infants will show affection for their caregivers. They will smile, laugh, babble, wiggle, and make frequent eye contact. Moreover, they will enjoy being in close proximity to you.

VARIATION:

♡ See Appendix H for a list of rhythm instruments to use with young children.

ADDITIONAL INFORMATION:

♡ Infants will be delighted in the response they receive from their actions. Therefore, this activity also fosters the development of cause and effect, which is a cognitive skill.

 Whenever pillows or blankets are used, constant supervision is necessary to prevent the possibility of suffocation.

Face to Face

SOCIAL

4 to 6 months

Child's Developmental Goals

✓ To continue developing a relationship with a familiar adult

✓ To develop a sense of trust

MATERIALS:

❑ Pillow at least 1 foot square
❑ Blanket or mat

PREPARATION:

♡ Select an area from which you can easily supervise the infant. Clear this area and lay out the blanket or mat.

♡ Place the pillow in the center of the blanket.

NURTURING STRATEGIES:

1. Lay the infant facedown on the pillow allowing his hands freedom for exploration.

2. Lie down in a prone position, placing your face 8 to 12 inches away from the infant's face.

3. Gain the infant's attention by enthusiastically saying:
   "Judd, look up. What do you see?"
   "Raise your head up."

4. When the infant looks up at you, smile to reinforce the behavior. In addition, you could say:
   "Judd, I see you looking at me."
   "You raised your head. I can see you now."

5. Continue this interaction by talking about past or future events as long as the infant communicates an interest.

☼ Highlighting Development

The best way to help very young children grow into curious, confident, able learners is to give them warm, consistent care. Such care needs to be responsive to the infants' own needs. This will help them to form positive relationships with those who care for them (Shore, 1997).

VARIATIONS:

♡ Repeat this activity outdoors.
♡ Lie beside the infant so that you can describe and discuss items you both are looking at.

ADDITIONAL INFORMATION:

♡ Brief interactions are important since the length of an interaction should never reflect the quality. Brief, intense, one-on-one contacts can greatly assist the infant in the development of trust.

CAUTION Whenever pillows or blankets are used, constant supervision is necessary to prevent the possibility of suffocation.

SOCIAL

Floating Ball Exploration

Child's Developmental Goals

✔ To develop skills in gaining an adult's attention

✔ To develop a sense of trust

MATERIALS:

❑ Blanket or mat

❑ 4 pillows or 1 quilt

❑ 1 clear ball containing a suspended object

PREPARATION:

♡ Select and clear an area that can be constantly supervised and spread out the blanket or mat.

♡ If the infant can sit unassisted, the preparation is complete. Otherwise, arrange the pillows in a semicircle or roll the quilt and shape it in a semi-circle on the blanket or mat.

NURTURING STRATEGIES:

1. Sit the infant on the blanket or mat. Spread the infant's legs apart in a tripod position to create a wide base of support. If necessary, adjusting the pillows or quilt will ensure that the infant is securely supported in the sitting position.

2. Hand the infant the floating ball while describing it. For example, say:
   "Tisha, here is a ball. It is round."

3. Observe the infant's behaviors while exploring the ball.

4. Be alert to the infant's signals of pleasure or dis-pleasure. Balls can easily roll out of reach and frustrate the infant. Focusing on the infant's signals will allow you to quickly respond.

5. Responding to the infant's sounds of pleasure such as babbling and laughing may reinforce these behaviors and extend the time spent exploring the floating ball. Comments include:
   "Tisha, you are watching the ball roll."
   "You are making the clown move."

☀ Highlighting Development

Balls have a lasting play value. Up to four months of age, a child will track a colorful, moving ball if it is within close proximity. From four to eight months of age, the child interacts by reaching. Moreover, the child's hands will come together in an effort to play with the ball. Through the sense of touch, the child will begin to integrate the feeling of roundness (Abrams & Kaufman, 1990).

VARIATION:

♡ Provide a favorite toy for exploring.

ADDITIONAL INFORMATION:

♡ A sense of trust is developed when caregivers are responsive to infants. Quickly responding to signals of distress and enjoyment will equally reinforce the sense of trust.

♡ If the ball rolls away, the child may become frustrated.

 Whenever pillows or blankets are used, constant supervision is necessary to prevent the possibility of suffocation.

4 to 6 months

Acting-Reacting

SOCIAL

Child's Developmental Goals

✓ To develop a self-identity

✓ To become aware of other people

MATERIALS:

❑ Large blanket or mat

❑ Activity gym

PREPARATION:

♡ Select and clear an area that can be constantly supervised. Then spread out the blanket or mat.

NURTURING STRATEGIES:

1. Lay the infant faceup under the activity gym.
2. Observe the infant exploring and interacting with the toy.
3. Describe the child's interactions. For example, say:
   "Awan, you are swatting at the bear."
   "Now you are grasping the bear."
4. Encourage the infant to explore in new ways. Suggest, for example:
   "Awan, can you move the toys like me? Watch me. I am swatting at them."
   "Now can you try swatting the toy? Good, you hit it."
5. Reinforce all attempts as well as accomplishments to foster the continuation of these behaviors.

☀ Highlighting Development

When uncomfortable or under stress, infants are quick to show signs of strain because they lack effective coping skills (Morrison, 1996). Adults must assume responsibility for exposing infants to other people and new experiences gradually. Otherwise, these new sources of stimulation may cause tension. This tension may result in the child crying. If this occurs, the child needs to be comforted.

VARIATION:

♡ Lay the infant facedown on the blanket. Then position the gym in front of the infant, allowing a new perspective. Movements required for this activity will strengthen the infant's upper arm and body muscles.

ADDITIONAL INFORMATION:

♡ The infant will probably spend more time grasping the toys hanging from the activity gym than paying attention to you. This is normal behavior for children this age. If other children or siblings are present, encourage them to interact with the child and the gym.

 Whenever pillows or blankets are used, constant supervision is necessary to prevent the possibility of suffocation.

Playing with a Friend

Child's Developmental Goals

✓ To develop a self-identity

✓ To continue developing a trusting relationship with a familiar adult

MATERIALS:

❑ Large blanket or mat

❑ 4 pillows or 1 quilt

❑ Infant toy

PREPARATION:

♡ Select an area that can be constantly supervised, clear it, and spread out the blanket or mat.

♡ If the infant can sit unassisted, the preparation is complete. Otherwise, arrange the pillows in a semicircle or roll a quilt and shape it in a semicircle on the blanket or mat.

NURTURING STRATEGIES:

1. Sit the infant on the blanket or mat. Spreading the infant's legs apart into a tripod position will create a wide base for support. Adjusting the pillows or quilt will ensure that the infant is securely supported in the sitting position. Sit next to the child in a position that will allow you to visually connect.

2. Hand the infant one of the toys while describing it. Say, for example:
   "Jing-Mei, I have an elephant for you."
   "Look at this long nose."

3. Describe what the child is doing. To illustrate, say:
   "Jing-Mei, you are holding the elephant. You are touching the trunk."

4. Continue by discussing the infant's behavior. Comments include:
   "Jing-Mei, you are playing with an elephant. You are sucking on the trunk."

5. Encourage the infant to explore the toy in new ways. Suggest, for example:
   "Jing-Mei, shake the elephant. Listen. The elephant is making a noise."

☀ Highlighting Development

When infants are born, they do not view themselves as separate from their primary caregivers. During the first year or year and a half of life, they are working on developing their self-identity. One way to foster this development is to frequently call the child by name. In addition, identifying yourself by name demonstrates that two separate and distinct people are interacting.

VARIATION:

♡ Introduce the activity in an outdoor environment, providing it is appropriate.

ADDITIONAL INFORMATION:

♡ Infants often spend more time exploring toys than gazing at you. This is normal behavior for children this age. However, if you have other children in your care, foster their involvement. This will eventually lead to development of important social skills.

 Whenever pillows or blankets are used, constant supervision is necessary to prevent the possibility of suffocation.

Riding a Blanket

SOCIAL

Child's Developmental Goals

✓ To interact with a familiar adult

✓ To develop a sense of trust

MATERIALS:

❑ Blanket

PREPARATION:

♡ Select an area that is flat and soft. Clear the area and spread out the blanket.

NURTURING STRATEGIES:

1. Lay the infant facedown on the blanket.
2. Explain to the infant what is going to happen during this activity. Say, for example:
   "Luka, let's take a ride in the blanket. You hold on. I'll pull you."
3. It may be necessary to reinforce your words with actions by helping the infant grasp the blanket.
4. Slowly begin to pull the blanket while walking backward. Respond to the infant's expressions by saying:
   "Luka, wow! You're moving!"
   "What fun! I'm pulling you on the blanket."
   "Oh, did that startle you? Should we go slower?"
5. Talk about how it feels to move in this manner. To illustrate, say:
   "Luka, what a bumpy ride."
   "It feels funny to move like this!"

Highlighting Development

Exposing the child to the outdoors or a new environment is an important experience for the infant. Through outdoor activities and stroller rides, the infant is exposed to and becomes comfortable in the larger world.

VARIATIONS:

♡ Taking a stroller ride is another way to experience movement.

♡ Introduce this activity outside in a grassy area.

ADDITIONAL INFORMATION:

♡ Adjust this game to the infant's temperament. To do this, pay close attention and respond to the infant's signals. If the infant appears frightened or upset by the activity, stop immediately and soothe the child.

 CAUTION Whenever pillows or blankets are used, constant supervision is necessary to prevent the possibility of suffocation.

4 to 6 months

Emotional Development

♡

FOUR to SIX MONTHS

4 to 6 months

Holding On

EMOTIONAL

Child's Developmental Goals

✓ To develop self-help skills

✓ To develop independence

✓ To refine a sense of self

MATERIALS:

❏ Bottle

❏ Adult-size rocking chair

PREPARATION:

♡ Heat bottle, as needed.

NURTURING STRATEGIES:

1. Sit in the rocking chair. Hold the infant in an upright position so you can visually connect.
2. Offer the infant the bottle.
3. Talk about what is happening. Comment by saying, for example:
   "Cheyenne, it's lunchtime. Time for your bottle."
   "You are hungry. You are drinking fast."
4. Encourage the infant to hold the bottle. Examples of comments to make include:
   "Cheyenne, help me. Hold your bottle."
   "Touch it with your hands."
5. It may be necessary to reinforce your words with actions. To illustrate, while moving the infant's hands to the bottle, say:
   "Cheyenne, touch the bottle. Hold it with your hands."
6. Providing positive reinforcement may encourage the infant to continue this behavior. Comments might include:
   "Cheyenne, you are doing it! You are holding your bottle."
   "What a big child!"
   "You are feeding yourself."

☼ Highlighting Development

Infants are often eager to participate in their own care. One of the first ways in which they assist is through attempting to hold the bottle during feedings. Typically, infants begin to hold the bottle independently around five to seven months of age.

VARIATION:

♡ Provide toys for the infant to grasp.

ADDITIONAL INFORMATION:

♡ By the fifth or sixth month, an infant can be provided a teething biscuit.

♡ While feeding an infant, cradle the baby in the crook of your arm so that her well-supported head is above the level of her stomach. This allows air bubbles to rise to the top of the stomach for easy burping. In addition, this may prevent earaches from milk flowing backward into the ear canal.

♡ Intimacy and trust with primary caregivers is developed during routines such as diapering and feeding.

Mirror, Mirror on the Wall

Child's Developmental Goals

✓ To express the basic emotions of interest, disgust, distress, and enjoyment

✓ To respond to the emotions of others

MATERIALS:

❑ Nonbreakable mirror

PREPARATION:

♡ Attach the mirror to the wall at a comfortable height for an adult.

NURTURING STRATEGIES:

1. Ask the infant to play by saying, for example:
   "Oded, do you want to play?"
2. If the infant indicates a desire to interact by making eye contact or smiling, pick the child up. Hold the infant so that you are facing the same way.
3. Walk over to the mirror.
4. Gain the infant's attention by gently tapping on the mirror. Say, for example:
   "I see Oded in the mirror."
   "Oded is looking at me."
5. Observe and describe the emotions being displayed by the infant. To illustrate, say:
   "You are smiling. You must be happy, Oded."
   "You are frowning. Are you sad?"

6. Display an emotional expression that the child has not shared. Verbally describe your emotional expression.

☀ Highlighting Development

Infants are interested in mirror images. However, they lack the cognitive structures to recognize the image as themselves (Berk, 1997). Observe. Often they will stop crying and focus on their image when held in front of the mirror.

VARIATION:

♡ While holding the child and looking in the mirror, describe each of your expressions.

ADDITIONAL INFORMATION:

♡ Infants are learning to express and regulate their emotions. They need to learn how to properly express negative emotions as well as positive emotions.

♡ The way you deal with and express your own emotions teaches the infant. Infants read and respond to your body language, tone of voice, and words. They pick up on incongruencies! Therefore, think about the emotional messages you send to infants.

I'll Help You

EMOTIONAL

Child's Developmental Goals

✓ To respond to soothing or calming behaviors of adults

✓ To learn self-soothing techniques

MATERIALS:

❑ Favorite infant toy

PREPARATION:

♡ Observe the infant for signs of distress.

NURTURING STRATEGIES:

1. When the infant displays distress, respond immediately.

2. Using your knowledge of the infant's likes and dislikes, decide on and enact behaviors that you think will be soothing or calming. For example, picking up the infant and rocking, gently bouncing, or walking may produce a calming effect.

3. Talk to the infant about feelings and emotions. To illustrate, say:
   "Frida, you are frightened. That was a loud noise."
   "You are angry."
   "You are upset."
   To accurately label the infant's emotions, you need to carefully observe the child and the environment.

4. When the infant has calmed down, provide a favorite toy. Suggest sucking, banging, or grasping the toy. All of these behaviors may have a calming effect.

5. Reinforce the infant's behavior with the toy. Say, for example:
   "Frida, you are sucking the toy. Sucking helps you calm down."

☀ Highlighting Development

The expression of happiness becomes selective around six months of age. Infants will laugh and smile more when interacting with familiar people. This is believed to be one method the infant uses for maintaining the presence of caregivers to whom they are attached.

VARIATION:

♡ Provide infants with a security item such as a blanket or pacifier to help calm them. Refer back to the Introduction (see pp. 11–12) for ways to soothe a crying child.

ADDITIONAL INFORMATION:

♡ During this time period, infants are becoming most responsive and expressive with familiar adults. Observe them and their reactions.

4 to 6 months

That's Funny!

Child's Developmental Goals

✓ To laugh aloud in response to caregiver's behavior

✓ To express the emotion of enjoyment

MATERIALS:

❑ Blanket, mat, or infant seat

PREPARATION:

♡ Select an area that can be constantly supervised. Clear this area for the blanket, mat, or infant seat.

NURTURING STRATEGIES:

1. Lay the infant faceup on the blanket or mat or securely restrain the infant in the seat using the safety strap.

2. Say the following finger play while making the motions:

Here is the beehive	(make fist)
But where are the bees?	(look in fist and shrug shoulders)
Hidden inside where nobody sees Here they come out of the hive	
One, two, three, four, five.	(bring out one finger at a time until reaching the number five; then tickle the infant's abdomen)

3. Smiling provides the infant with the social cue that this interaction is enjoyable. Hopefully, the infant will imitate your expression.

4. Discuss the infant's reaction to the interaction. Comments might include:
   "Mark, you are smiling. What a fun game."
   "What a laugh, Mark! You must like this game."

5. Continue this interaction as long as the infant demonstrates interest by maintaining eye contact or smiling.

☀ Highlighting Development

Infants laugh aloud or have a belly laugh around five months of age. You can respond positively to these laughs by providing lots of reinforcement such as smiling or laughing.

VARIATION:

♡ Sing a favorite song. See Appendix F for a list of additional finger plays or Appendix G for songs.

ADDITIONAL INFORMATION:

♡ Infants will imitate your expressions. Therefore, model smiling and laughing for them.

 Whenever pillows or blankets are used, constant supervision is necessary to prevent the possibility of suffocation.

That Hurts!

EMOTIONAL

Child's Developmental Goals

✓ To communicate emotions such as pain

✓ To learn techniques for controlling emotions

MATERIALS:

☐ Cold teething rings

PREPARATION:

♡ Placing sanitized teething rings in a refrigerator will keep them cool.

NURTURING STRATEGIES:

1. When an infant is crying, respond immediately. Using your knowledge of the child and the situation will help you begin to understand why the infant is crying.

2. In a calm and soothing voice, talk with the infant about her feelings. Comments include:
   "Eva, you are upset because you are wet. Let's get you changed."
   "You are in pain. You are getting a tooth."

3. If the pain is from teething, provide the infant with a cold teething ring. Discuss how this will make her mouth feel better. Say, for example:
   "Eva, chewing on this will help. It's cold."
   "New teeth hurt. Chew on this."

4. Suggest ways to deal with his emotions. Make comments such as:
   "Chewing will help the pain."
   "Crying will make you feel better, Eva."

☀ Highlighting Development

Although infants vary on the timing of tooth development, by six months of age most infants will be getting the lower front teeth. During the eruption of teeth, the child may be uncomfortable. The eruption usually causes an irritation and swelling of the gums, resulting in crankiness and fussiness. During the teething process, infants will try to bite on objects. To reduce the pain, infants may also rub at their gums. You can help them by rubbing their gums with your finger. Usually, this will help to relieve the pain.

VARIATION:

♡ Provide other sanitized infant toys for chewing.

ADDITIONAL INFORMATION:

♡ The first sound most infants make is likely to be a cry. However, infants cry for a variety of reasons. During the first six months, there typically are four types of crying. A hunger cry occurs the most frequently. Other types of cries include a cry caused by pain, a boredom cry, and an angry cry. Close observation will help you to better understand why an infant might be crying.

4 to 6 months

Helping to Undress

Child's Developmental Goals

✓ To develop self–help skills
✓ To develop independence

MATERIALS:

None

PREPARATION:

♡ Gather diapering supplies and place them on or near a changing table.

NURTURING STRATEGIES:

1. After placing the infant on the changing table, elicit the infant's assistance in undressing. For example, say:
   "Darius, I have to take off your shoes. Give me a foot."
   "I have to take off your bib overalls. Raise up."

2. You might need to reinforce your words with actions. For example, gently tap the infant's foot while saying:
   "Darius, give me your foot."

3. Praise the infant's attempts and accomplishments by commenting:
   "Darius, thank you for raising up."
   "You really helped to undress yourself."

☀ Highlighting Development

Infants find pleasure in exploring their own bodies. Watch. They may explore their ears. Over and over again, they will feel or pull on them. They also may develop an interest in exploring their nose, navel, feet, hair, and genitals.

VARIATION:

♡ Continue eliciting the infant's help when dressing and undressing before going out and after coming in from the outdoors. Emphasize different body parts such as arms, hands, legs, and feet.

ADDITIONAL INFORMATION:

♡ This activity, with repeated experience, promotes emotional as well as physical development. Infants learn body parts and can demonstrate this knowledge.

Counting

Child's Developmental Goals

✓ To laugh aloud in response to caregiver's behaviors

✓ To express the emotion of enjoyment

MATERIALS:

None

PREPARATION:

♡ Gathering diapering supplies and placing them near the changing table will free you for interacting with the child.

NURTURING STRATEGIES:

1. After diapering the child, invest quality time by interacting with the infant.
2. Ask the infant to play a counting game by saying:
   "Skye, can we play a game?"
3. If the infant indicates a desire to continue the interaction by gazing at you or smiling, begin the game. Say to the child:
   "Skye, let's see how many fingers and hands you have. Let's count."
4. Count hands first. As you count, reinforce your words with actions by touching each hand. If possible, develop a rhyme while counting.
5. Smile to convey your interest in the activity. Chances are the infant will imitate your facial expression.
6. Continue the game by counting the infant's fingers. Again, touch each finger while saying a number.

7. If this is an enjoyable activity, it may result in the infant laughing.
8. Reinforce the emotions expressed by the infant. Say, for example:
   "Skye, you like this game."
   "What a laugh. You are having fun!"

☀ Highlighting Development

Infants typically begin laughing between two and four months of age. Laughter at first is elicited only in response to stimulation such as loud sounds or tickling. Social and visual stimuli based on cognitive interpretation beginning at six months of age will foster laughter in the infants. Action book games and toys such as a jack-in-the-box will also promote laughter (Snow, 1998).

VARIATION:

♡ Reinforce the names of body parts by counting the infant's feet, toes, ears, and nose.

ADDITIONAL INFORMATION:

♡ Share your enthusiasm. The success of this activity greatly depends on your facial expressions. Infants will look to you for cues for reacting.

♡ In this situation, counting promotes the development of rhythm rather than the development of numerical skills.

Physical Development

♡

SEVEN to NINE MONTHS

Clapping

Child's Developmental Goals

✓ To practice clapping hands

✓ To practice coordinating hand movements

MATERIALS:

None

PREPARATION:

♡ Observe the child's level of alertness.

NURTURING STRATEGIES:

1. If the child is alert, this activity can be introduced any time throughout the day. It is especially good to do after diapering.

2. While you are changing the diaper, gain the infant's attention by slowly singing:

   ♪ Clap, clap, clap your hands
   ♪ Clap your hands together.
   ♪ Clap, clap, clap your hands
   ♪ Clap your hands together.

3. Reinforcing your words with actions may assist the child in developing association skills. Infants this age can easily imitate your behaviors when they are slightly different than usually performed. If your modeling fails to result in imitation, you can physically move the infant's hand for encouragement while singing the song.

4. Infants show their enjoyment through clapping. Therefore, they continue smiling and clapping even when the song is over.

5. Continue singing the song as long as the infant shows interest by smiling and maintaining eye contact.

☀ Highlighting Development

Clapping is a difficult skill for infants to master because it requires eye-hand coordination and bilateral coordination of arms and hands. Bilateral coordination is the ability of infants to cross the midline of their bodies with their hands. Infants first demonstrate this ability when they transfer objects from one hand to the other around four to six months of age. To be successful at clapping, several muscles must work together. Moreover, the timing of the movements is important in order for the hands to meet.

VARIATION:

♡ Recite your favorite nursery rhyme, sharing your enthusiasm and clapping to the rhythm.

ADDITIONAL INFORMATION:

♡ Infants at this stage of development are unable to maintain a steady rhythm because of a lack of coordination. Continued exposure to this type of activity fosters development.

Splashing

Child's Developmental Goals

✓ To refine eye-hand coordination skills

✓ To continue developing balance by sitting unassisted

MATERIALS:

❑ Warm water

❑ Large, nonbreakable mixing bowl

❑ Vinyl tablecloth

PREPARATION:

♡ Exercise caution when selecting an area for this experience. To protect the flooring, spread out a vinyl tablecloth.

♡ Fill a bowl with warm water and place it on the middle of the tablecloth.

♡ If the room is warm and not drafty, remove the infant's outer clothing. However, if the room is drafty or cool, put a large, waterproof bib on the infant and roll up his sleeves, if necessary.

NURTURING STRATEGIES:

1. Sit the infant on the mat, close to the bowl.

2. Gain the infant's attention by moving the water with your hand while saying:
   "Joben, here is some warm water. Touch it! Feel it!"
   "Splash like me."

3. Reinforcing your words with actions may be necessary. If needed, using your wet hand, touch the child's hand and say:
   "Joben, see. It is warm water."
   If the child does touch the water, gently guide the infant's hand to the bowl while saying:
   "Joben, let's splash together."

4. Providing positive reinforcement may encourage the child to repeat the behavior. Say, for example:
   "Joben, you are splashing the water."
   "What a smile! You must like splashing."

☀ Highlighting Development

Toward the end of this developmental stage, infants have made milestones in motor development. They will be able to sit alone steadily, raise themselves to a sitting position, stand up by furniture, and cruise along the crib rail. They also are able to successfully reach and grasp with their hands. Observe them. They can transfer objects from one hand to another (Black & Puckett, 1996). Even though they use both hands, they are developing a preference for one hand. Dominance of one side of the body usually is not stable until about 24 months of age.

VARIATIONS:

♡ Repeat this activity outside if weather permits.

♡ Add one tool to the bowl such as a measuring cup.

ADDITIONAL INFORMATION:

♡ Periodically check the water to make sure it is the right temperature. If necessary, add warm water.

 To prevent accidentally burning the child's hand, test the water in the bowl. It should be about the temperature of a warmed bottle.

7 to 9 months

Walking Together

PHYSICAL

7 to 9 months

Child's Developmental Goals

✓ To practice the stepping reflex
✓ To develop balancing skills

MATERIALS:

None

PREPARATION:

♡ To reduce safety hazards, clear pathways.

NURTURING STRATEGIES:

1. Respond to the infant's desire to walk. The infant, for example, may be attempting unsuccessfully to walk. Observe and intervene before the infant becomes frustrated.

2. Provide positive reinforcement by commenting to the child, for example:
   "Jamila, you are working hard."
   "Walking takes practice."
   "Good work. You're getting it!"

3. Volunteer to assist the infant. To illustrate, say:
   "Jamila, can I help you walk?"
   "Can we walk together?"

4. If the child responds positively to your question, hold out your hands while saying:
   "Jamila, take my hands. Let's practice walking together."

5. If the infant responds negatively to your question, allow independent work while continuing to provide positive reinforcement (see step 2).

6. If a child becomes distressed because of unsuccessful attempts while refusing your assistance, it is time to stop the activity. Say to the infant, for example:
   "Jamila, walking is hard. We'll practice again later."

☀ Highlighting Development

What motivates infants to stand is not fully understood. One of their motivations may be to obtain attractive objects at eye level. The stepping reflex is present at birth but vanishes in a few days or weeks. At about seven months of age, standing is really a reflex stiffening of the body. Usually infants begin standing by pulling themselves up. Typically, infants enjoy standing and walking with assistance. As a result, these actions are repeated. They also gain skill in cruising by holding on to furniture and walking around. Before infants can walk, they need to master standing in an erect position. Infants also need to have enough confidence to let go and stand without support (Snow, 1998).

VARIATION:

♡ Assist the infant in walking whenever you need her to change locations. Your physical support will guide her direction.

ADDITIONAL INFORMATION:

♡ Infants have different temperaments. Some infants will easily give up on a task while others will continue to the point of becoming distressed. Your knowledge of the child will assist you in providing the right amount of reinforcement and in intervening at the proper time.

Stepping Up

Child's Developmental Goals

✓ To practice the stepping reflex

✓ To practice balancing skills

MATERIALS:

❑ Flat surface, such as floor

PREPARATION:

♡ Select an area that can be constantly supervised. Make sure you can monitor other children who may be present.

♡ Clear this area of toys and other obstacles that could present a safety hazard.

NURTURING STRATEGIES:

1. While carrying the infant to the cleared area, talk about what is going to happen. For example, comment:
   "Liam, let's work over here. You can stand up on the floor."

2. Sit down, placing your legs in front of your body. Shape them in a "V." To visually connect with the infant, stand the child between your legs facing you.

3. Because the standing position practices a reflex, the child's legs will begin to move as soon as the feet touch the floor.

4. Hold the infant securely under the arms. Avoid holding the child's hands or arms, which could result in an injury to his shoulder if balance is lost.

5. Be cautioned: Infants are typically "wild" during this activity. They become excited by the movements and then the jumping or dancing increases.

6. Providing positive reinforcement may be unnecessary because of the intense pleasure of the activity. However, commenting on the child's expressions will foster emotional development. Say, for example:
   "Liam, what a laugh! You like moving your legs."
   "You are really enjoying this activity."

☀ Highlighting Development

When infants practice the stepping reflex, their knees and elbows may produce crackling sounds. This noise signals how loosely supported the joints are at this period of development. This noise will disappear as the muscles become stronger.

VARIATION:

♡ Hold the infant in a standing position on your legs while you are sitting on a chair.

ADDITIONAL INFORMATION:

♡ In preparation for walking, the stepping reflex returns. The reflex will develop from a jumping motion such as bending and straightening knees at the same time to a dancing motion, alternatively lifting and placing the feet. Walking with assistance can begin after the infant's reflex has reached the "dancing" stage of development.

Come and Get It

PHYSICAL

Child's Developmental Goals

✓ To strengthen and coordinate muscles by developing crawling skills

✓ To move one's body to obtain a desired object

MATERIALS:

❑ Favorite stuffed infant toy

❑ Blanket

PREPARATION:

♡ Select and clear an area that you can constantly supervise. Spread out the blanket in the area.

♡ Place the favorite toy near the edge of the blanket.

NURTURING STRATEGIES:

1. While carrying the infant to the blanket, talk about the activity. To illustrate, say:
   "Bria, you can practice crawling on this blanket. See if you can crawl over to the bunny."
2. Lay the infant facedown on the blanket.
3. Move over by the infant toy. Gain the infant's attention by moving the toy and saying:
   "Bria, crawl over here. Come get the bunny."
4. Providing positive reinforcement may encourage the infant to continue the desired behaviors. Comments might include:
   "Bria, you are crawling. Keep going."
   "You are almost there."
   "Come get the bunny."
5. Encourage the infant to explore the toy once it is reached. Say, for example:
   "Bria, shake it."
   "Touch it. Use your fingers."

☼ Highlighting Development

Frequently, the definitions of crawling and creeping in common usage are reversed. Crawling occurs when the infant's abdomen is on the ground. Infants use the hands to slide the body forward or backward. When crawling, their legs usually drag behind. Creeping differs. As muscle strength increases in the legs, the child advances toward creeping (Snow, 1998; Bukato & Daehler, 1995). When infants can get up on bent knees and elbows, they are able to creep. Most infants creep backward before they creep forward. When infants first learn to creep, they raise up on their hands and knees and rock back and forth (Herr, 1998). During this process, they often lose their balance, falling forward or backward.

VARIATION:

♡ Encourage the infant to crawl to you.

ADDITIONAL INFORMATION:

♡ Use your knowledge of each child's crawling abilities in deciding how far away to place the toy.

 Whenever pillows or blankets are used, constant supervision is necessary to prevent the possibility of suffocation.

PHYSICAL

Ramping It

7 to 9 months

Child's Developmental Goals

✓ To practice creeping skills

✓ To refine balancing skills

MATERIALS:

❑ Foam ramp

❑ Foam pads or mats

❑ Interesting infant toys that roll

PREPARATION:

♡ Select an area that you can constantly supervise.

♡ Arrange the foam ramp so that it is surrounded by the other mats. Carefully check that a safe fall zone has been created.

♡ Place the infant toy at the top of the ramp.

NURTURING STRATEGIES:

1. Allow the infant to select this activity. As soon as an infant creeps near the area, provide assistance or support.

2. Describe the activity for the infant. For example, say:
   "Toshi, creep to the top of the ramp."
   "Creep up the ramp and get the ball."

3. Providing positive reinforcement may result in the infant continuing the desired behaviors. Comments might include:
   "Toshi, you are working hard."
   "Keep creeping. You are almost to the top."
   "Toshi, you did it. You got the ball."

☀ Highlighting Development

At this stage of development, children move from one place to another in a variety of ways. Some children crawl by pulling themselves on their bellies; some infants creep on their hands and knees; still others use their hands and feet. Hitching is another movement infants make, occurring after they are able to sit without support. By moving their arms and legs, infants will slide their buttocks across the floor (Herr, 1998).

VARIATION:

♡ Encourage the infant to roll the toys down the ramp.

ADDITIONAL INFORMATION:

♡ After infants can roll onto their stomach and sit alone, crawling will appear.

♡ Locomotion against gravity is a much more difficult task. Therefore, introduce this activity only after the child has experienced some success creeping.

 For safety reasons, never leave an infant unattended during this activity.

Pulling It Around

PHYSICAL

Child's Developmental Goals

✓ To develop a pincer grasp

✓ To refine eye-hand coordination skills

MATERIALS:

❑ 2 pull toys

PREPARATION:

♡ Clear a space for this activity in a noncarpeted area so that the toys will easily roll.

♡ Place the pull toys in an open area of the identified space.

NURTURING STRATEGIES:

1. While carrying the infant to the area, talk about the upcoming activity. Say, for example:
   "Darlene, I have a toy for you to play with. You pull the string and it moves."

2. Sit the infant on the floor.

3. Encourage the child to grasp the string.
   To illustrate, say:
   "Darlene, pick up the string."

4. Observe how the infant picks up the string.
   Did she use a pincer grasp?
   If so, reinforce that behavior by saying:
   "Wow. You used your thumb."
   If the child has not demonstrated the pincer grasp, encourage that behavior by commenting:
   "Use your thumb and finger. Let me show you."

5. Reinforcing your words with actions may be necessary. If so, model the pincer grasp while explaining:
   "Watch me. Look, Darlene. I'm picking up the string with my thumb and finger."

6. Once the infant has picked up the string, observe her actions and exploration of the toy.

7. Encourage the infant to move the pull toy by suggesting:
   "Darlene, move your hand."
   "Pull the string."

8. Reinforce the infant's play with the toy.
   To illustrate, say:
   "Darlene, look at the wheels move."
   "You are pulling the toy."

☀ Highlighting Development

Infants are learning to use just their hands. Observe. At this stage of development, waving is becoming more sophisticated. They can wave now by turning their hand and wrist. Up to this point, waving occurred by moving the entire arm.

VARIATION:

♡ Encourage the infant to pull the toy while crawling. When the child has mastered walking, introduce the pull toy again.

ADDITIONAL INFORMATION:

♡ Infants are gaining control of their separate fingers. This allows them to point as well as perform a pincer grasp.

♡ To encourage forward movement, put toys just beyond arm's reach in front of crawlers.

7 to 9 months

Language and Communication Development

♡

SEVEN to NINE MONTHS

Making Sounds

7 to 9 months

Child's Developmental Goals

✔ To practice producing babbling sounds
✔ To add new sounds to babbling

MATERIALS:

None

PREPARATION:

♡ Closely observe the infant's babbling. Conduct an assessment by asking yourself, "What sounds am I hearing?"

NURTURING STRATEGIES:

1. Join in a conversation with the infant. To do this, wait until the infant pauses, then imitate the same sounds the child was producing.
2. When your turn to talk arrives again in the conversation, introduce one new sound for infant to imitate. For example, say:
   "Wo wo wo."
   "Nu nu nu."
3. Providing positive reinforcement may result in the infant repeatedly making the new sound. For example, say:
   "You can do it. Wowowowowo. Keep trying."
   "That's right. Nununu. You've got it."
4. Listen. If the infant repeats your sounds, echo them again.

☼ Highlighting Development

Babbling begins at about four months of age and may continue into the second year. During babbling, the infant will keep repeating the same vowels and consonants. However, the pitch will change from high to low. Babbling will progress from simple to complex. Infants typically add the sounds of *d*, *t*, *n*, and *w* to their babbling at about seven months (Feldman, 1998).

At seven or eight months of age, babies around the world typically make four basic sounds: "ba ba," "da da," "ma ma," and "wa wa." These sounds are considered a universal first step toward speaking.

VARIATION:

♡ To provide a challenge, add two new sounds at once.

ADDITIONAL INFORMATION:

♡ Try to reduce interference from other sources of stimulation such as the television or stereo while verbally encouraging the child to babble.
♡ Communicating with children is important. They learn they are loved and worthwhile through praise and smiles from caregivers.

Talking to Toys

Child's Developmental Goals

✓ To practice producing babbling sounds

✓ To listen to native language patterns

MATERIALS:

❑ 2 or 3 stuffed animal toys

PREPARATION:

♡ Select an area that can be constantly supervised. Clear this area and lay out the toys you gathered for the activity.

NURTURING STRATEGIES:

1. If the infant is unable to crawl, carry the child to the carpeted area. If the infant can crawl, encourage the child to do so. One way to do this is to hold up one of the toys while commenting:
    "Edwardo, come and get the pig. The pig wants to play."
    "Here is your favorite toy. It is a bear."
2. Observe the infant interacting with or exploring with the toy.
3. Reinforce the infant's spontaneous babbles. Comments might include:
    "Edwardo, you are talking to the bear."
    "Tell the pig more about that."

☀ Highlighting Development

While babbling, infants will begin to experiment with both rhythm and loudness. Often the sound of the infant's changing voice will attract your attention. Providing reinforcement for these variations may result in more experimentation.

VARIATION:

♡ Move the infant toy while "talking" for it.

ADDITIONAL INFORMATION:

♡ For some children, the act of remembering will give them pleasure. When they recognize a favorite toy, they will squeal with delight and make small gurgling sounds of joy.

♡ For behaviors you want infants to repeat, praise them. Use eye contact and speak in a soft voice.

♡ Use the "feeding in" technique while interacting with the child. This technique involves introducing simple words to describe the child's actions. To illustrate, you might say:
"Edwardo, you are banging the block."

Looking at Books

Child's Developmental Goals

✓ To listen to native language patterns

✓ To engage in conversational turn taking

MATERIALS:

☐ 3 to 4 cardboard books with simple pictures

PREPARATION:

♡ Select an area for interaction that will not distract the infant. Set the books upright and slightly open on the floor in that area.

NURTURING STRATEGIES:

1. When an infant crawls over to the books, move closer to the child.
2. Observe the infant's interaction with the book.
3. Offer to read the book to the infant by asking, for example:
   "Lucinda, would you like me to read the book?"
   "May I read to you?"
4. If the infant shows interest, begin reading the book. If the infant does not appear interested, continue to observe her.
5. Verbally label each picture while pointing to it.
6. While reading the book, periodically ask questions about the pictures to engage the infant in conversation. Pause after each question, allowing time for the infant to respond. Then provide positive reinforcement for any vocalizations or gestures.
   For example:
   "Lucinda, what is this?" Pause. *"That's right; it is a baby who is eating."*
   "Lucinda, what animal is this?" Pause. *"Yes, you pointed to the monkey."*

☼ Highlighting Development

Children between seven and nine months of age are capable of producing a variety of sounds. Listen. You will hear *m*, *b*, and *p* sounds. They are also beginning to imitate your intonation and speech sounds. Infants must have this understanding before they are able to produce words themselves.

VARIATION:

♡ Provide vinyl or cloth books for the infant to explore unassisted.

ADDITIONAL INFORMATION:

♡ Given their improved fine motor skills, infants at this stage are ready to begin reading books unassisted. Books with thick pages are easier for infants to page through. Children this age often engage in "mouthing" books, so vinyl books are also a good choice because they can be washed or easily sanitized.

Turning Pages

Child's Developmental Goals

✓ To practice producing babbling sounds

✓ To "read" a book by independently turning the pages

MATERIALS:

❑ 2 or 3 books

PREPARATION:

♡ Prop the books upright and slightly open on the floor to gain the infant's attention.

NURTURING STRATEGIES:

1. When the infant crawls near the books, move closer to the child.
2. Observe what the infant does with the book. Note, for example, how he turns the pages or how he verbally labels the pictures. While turning the pages and looking at the pictures, the infant may point and babble.
3. Providing positive reinforcement may encourage repetition of the desired behavior. Reinforce the behaviors that you want to see continued. Say, for example:
   "Isaiah, you are turning the pages by yourself."
4. If a desired behavior was not observed, encouraging the infant may result in the behavior being performed. Suggest, for example:
   "Isaiah, point to the bunny. Talk to the bunny."

5. If the infant attempts or accomplishes the encouraged behavior, provide positive reinforcement by saying, for example:
   "Isaiah, you pointed to the bunny."
   "You are talking to the bunny."

Highlighting Development

According to recent research, the most important year for brain development is the first (Shore, 1997). The results of these studies have major implications for understanding the needs of young children. Talking, singing, cuddling while reading a book, and rocking are all important experiences for infants and toddlers.

VARIATION:

♡ Read the book together. Point to the pictures and verbally label the objects. The infant can also participate by turning the pages and babbling.

ADDITIONAL INFORMATION:

♡ Some books are designed especially for infants such as those in which the next page raises slightly when the top page is turned. This allows the infants to easily grasp and turn the page using their thumb and forefinger, which is called a pincer grasp.

♡ To prevent them from tuning out, infants also need periods of quiet. These times will encourage the infant to look at things and to practice making sounds with their own voices (Abrams & Kaufman 1990).

Reading Nursery Rhymes

Child's Developmental Goals

✓ To listen to native language patterns

✓ To "read" a book by independently turning the pages

✓ To engage in a conversation

MATERIALS:

❑ 1 or 2 cardboard books of nursery rhymes such as "Jack and Jill"

PREPARATION:

♡ Prop the books in a standing position and leave them slightly open. Displaying the book should help capture the child's attention.

NURTURING STRATEGIES:

1. When a child crawls near the books, move closer.
2. Observe the infant's interactions with the book.
3. Talk about the book the infant is looking at. Comment, for example:
   "That story is about Jack and Jill. Jack and Jill walk up a hill."
   "Victoria, that story is about pigs. The pigs go to the market."
4. Ask the infant:
   "May I read the book to you?"
   If the infant responds affirmatively, begin to read the book. If the infant responds negatively, allow the child to explore the book uninterrupted.
5. Using your voice as a tool to communicate enthusiasm may gain and sustain the infant's attention.
6. While reading the book, encourage the infant to turn the pages. Say, for example:
   "Victoria, turn the page. We've read these words."
   "What's going to happen next? Turn the page so we can read more."

7. Asking questions while reading may prompt the infant to babble. For example, while pointing to the picture, ask:
   "Victoria, who is that?"
   "What are they carrying?"
8. Providing positive reinforcement may result in the infant holding longer conversations. To illustrate, say:
   "That's right. Jill has a bucket."

☀ Highlighting Development

Repeated exposure to words and labeling people and objects will help foster language development in infants. The infants may accidentally begin stumbling on words. They may say "mama" for one of two reasons. Infants may be practicing the sounds by repeating the word over and over. On the other hand, some infants may have made the connection that words gain the attention of people who are important to them.

VARIATION:

♡ Introduce a book to a child if a quiet, calming activity is needed.

ADDITIONAL INFORMATION:

♡ Reading books of nursery rhymes is important because you have been reciting them for the past seven to eight months. The familiar words easily gain the infant's attention.

Goodnight

Child's Developmental Goals

✓ To listen to native language patterns

✓ To use books for relaxing

MATERIALS:

❑ *Goodnight Moon* board book by Margaret Wise Brown

❑ Rocking chair

❑ Security items needed for sleeping such as blanket, teddy bear, etc.

PREPARATION:

♡ Gather the security items and the book and position the rocking chair so that you are comfortable.

NURTURING STRATEGIES:

1. Pick up the infant and sit in the rocking chair.
2. Provide the infant with the security items. Talk in a quiet, soothing voice about nap time, while slowly rocking. Say, for example:
   "Jimmy, it is time to rest. You played hard today. You need to rest."
3. Once the child is relaxed, introduce the story by saying:
   "Jimmy, I picked out a story for us to read today. It is about going to sleep."
4. In a quiet, soothing voice, read the story.
5. Respond if the infant babbles, points, or otherwise attempts to communicate.
6. Avoid asking questions to engage the infant in babble or conversation because you are using the book as a calming tool.
7. If the infant is still awake, you may want to repeat the story.

☀ Highlighting Development

Books can be used to excite children or calm them down. In fact, one book can be used for both purposes. Use your voice as a tool to communicate your intentions to the infant. Encourage the infant to assist in reading the book. Listen. Chances are the infant's babbling is following the intonation pattern of your reading.

VARIATION:

♡ Choose other books the infant enjoys. Refer to Appendix A for a list of books.

ADDITIONAL INFORMATION:

♡ Observe the children's reactions. They may have favorite books. Reading the same book over and over may be an enjoyable experience. Other hints for helping foster children's development of listening skills include:

  🦋 talking directly to the infant while making eye contact.

  🦋 using labels to help the infant associate names with objects and people in his environment.

  🦋 providing the infant an opportunity to touch objects while talking about them.

♡ When choosing books for children this age, look for those that are wrinkleproof, droolproof, and chewproof.

Look Who Walked In

7 to 9 months

Child's Developmental Goals

✔ To begin to associate words with people

✔ To reproduce the words "mama" and "dada"

MATERIALS:

None

PREPARATION:

♡ Prepare the child by talking about who will be coming.

NURTURING STRATEGIES:

1. Talk about who will be coming to visit the infant. Comment, for example:
   "Mama will be coming soon."
   "Dada is coming in the door."
2. Gain the infant's attention when the individual walks in the room by saying:
   "Kawanna, look who just walked in."
3. Reinforce the infant's babbles or vocalizations by stating:
   "You are excited to see Mama."
   "Yes, Dada is here to play with you."
4. Welcome the individual by singing the following song when the visitor enters:

   ♫ Hello, *Mama,*
   ♫ Hello, *Mama,*
   ♫ Hello, *Mama,*
   ♫ We're so glad you are here.

Highlighting Development

Attachment is the development of a bond between adults and children. The first and primary attachment is usually parents and children. Attachments are noticeable during separations and reunions. For example, when an important person is visible to the infant during a reunion, the infant may smile, babble, and, if able, move closer to that person.

VARIATION:

♡ When a person leaves, sing the song from the Singing Good-Bye activity (see p. 42).

ADDITIONAL INFORMATION:

♡ When interacting, provide the infant ample time to respond. Repeat people's names over so that the infant will understand that everybody has a name.

Cognitive
Development

♡

SEVEN to NINE MONTHS

Go Find It

Child's Developmental Goals

✓ To develop object permanence

✓ To engage in intentional behaviors

MATERIALS:

❑ Favorite infant toy

❑ Lightweight blanket

PREPARATIONS:

♡ Select an area that can be constantly supervised. Clear this area for the activity.

♡ Place the infant toy on the surface. Partially cover the toy with the blanket.

NURTURING STRATEGIES:

1. Encourage the infant to find a favorite toy. Say, for example:
   "Levi, go find Pooh bear. Look. Pooh is on the floor."
   "Crawl over by the blanket. Look."

2. Reinforce the infant's movement toward the blanket. For example, comments may include:
   "Levi, keep crawling."
   "You're almost there. Keep going."

3. Observe the infant's behaviors once he is near the blanket. If the infant moves the blanket, wait until the toy is uncovered. React with enthusiasm to the infant's discovery.

4. If the infant doesn't move the blanket, suggest that. Say, for example:
   "Levi, grab the blanket with your hands."
   "Move the blanket with your hands."

5. Reinforcing your words with actions may be necessary. For example, while gently placing the infant's hands on the blanket, say:
   "Levi, grab it." Pause. "Now pull the blanket."

6. Provide reinforcement for the infant's attempts and accomplishments. To illustrate, state:
   "Levi, that's it. Move the blanket."
   "Keep pulling! Almost there."

7. When the infant discovers the toy, react with enthusiasm. Say, for example:
   "You did it! You found Pooh."
   "Pooh was hiding from you!"

☀ Highlighting Development

Infants engage in goal-directed or intentional behaviors during this stage. In other words, when faced with a problem, they choose a particular way to solve the dilemma. For example, if a toy is hidden under a blanket, the infant may move the blanket aside to view the object.

VARIATIONS:

♡ Completely cover the toy with the blanket.

♡ Substitute blocks, small pots, or pans for the toy.

ADDITIONAL INFORMATION:

♡ This is a difficult activity. Providing plenty of reinforcement may keep the infant interested in the activity. Use your voice to convey your enthusiasm.

 Whenever pillows or blankets are used, constant supervision is necessary to prevent the possibility of suffocation.

7 to 9 months

Where Is It?

Child's Developmental Goals

✓ To develop an understanding of object permanence

✓ To engage in intentional behavior to solve a problem

MATERIALS:

❑ Piece of cardboard or shoe box lid
❑ Favorite infant toy
❑ Child-size table or low coffee table

PREPARATION:

♡ Clear an area for working at the table. Place the piece of cardboard and the infant toy in that work space.

NURTURING STRATEGIES:

1. Carry the infant to the table while talking about the activity. To illustrate, say:
    "Shalini, I have a special game just for you."
    "Let's play hide the giraffe."
2. Sit with pretzel legs at the table. Sit the infant in your lap. Move your body so that the infant is close to the table.
3. Gain the infant's attention by moving the toy and saying:
    "Shalini, here is your favorite toy. It is a giraffe."
4. Introduce the game by saying:
    "Shalini, I'm going to hide the giraffe. You find it."
5. Place the giraffe on the table and hold the cardboard with one hand in front of it. Encourage the infant to find the toy by commenting:
    "Find the giraffe. Look for it."
6. The infant may need suggestions on how to look for the toy. Comments to make include:
    "Shalini, move the cardboard."
    "Push the cardboard with your hand."
7. Reinforcing your words with actions may be necessary. If so, gently move the infant's hand while repeating:
    "Shalini, push the cardboard with your hand."
8. Provide positive reinforcement for all attempts and accomplishments. Enthusiastically state, for example:
    "Shalini, you did it! You found the giraffe."

☀ Highlighting Development

For infants a developmental task is the understanding that objects exist even when out of sight. In the beginning, infants can find objects that are partially hidden. During this stage, infants can find an object that is totally hidden from sight. However, the development of object permanence remains incomplete until the infant searches for the object when it is hidden in a second location.

Note the infant's behavior once objects are in hand. *Object hunger* is the term that describes the play behavior of infants at this stage of development. Infants orally examine objects by mouthing them, gaining physical knowledge about the objects.

VARIATION:

♡ Use a pillow or your body for hiding the toy. Encourage the infant to crawl or creep to find the toy.

ADDITIONAL INFORMATION:

♡ If the infants show more interest in pushing the cardboard than finding the object, this is acceptable. They will be practicing an important skill for locating desired objects.

♡ To gain understanding, infants perform similar experiences repeatedly.

Exploring Balls

7 to 9 months

Child's Developmental Goals:

✓ To engage in intentional behaviors

✓ To experience the principle of cause and effect

MATERIALS:

❑ 2 to 3 balls at least 6 inches in diameter

PREPARATION:

♡ Select an area that can be constantly supervised. Clear this area for the activity.

♡ Place the balls on the floor in this area.

NURTURING STRATEGIES:

1. Carry the infant to the selected area while talking about the activity. Say, for example:
   "Xui, I have some balls for you to play with."
   "Here are some balls. What can you do with them?"

2. Sit the infant on the floor while moving the balls within reach.

3. Observe the infant interacting with the balls.

4. Describe how the infant is exploring the balls. For example, comment:
   "Xui, you're touching the bumps with your fingertips."
   "That ball is smooth. You touched it with your tongue."

5. Reinforcing infant behaviors that accidentally occur may result in those behaviors being repeated. Comments include:
   "Xui, you pushed the ball. Do it again."
   "You're rolling the ball. Roll the ball to me."

6. Be prepared to retrieve the ball when it rolls out of the infant's reach or view.

☀ Highlighting Development

With age, infants' ability to track moving objects improves. Their movements become more coordinated and smooth. Now infants can easily track the path of balls and other moving objects.

VARIATION:

♡ Use a toy with wheels instead of balls.

ADDITIONAL INFORMATION:

♡ Infants learn through repetition. Therefore, repeating this experience several times leads to expanded knowledge about oneself and objects in the environment.

 Be sure to sanitize all toys that are touched by or placed in the infant's mouth.

What Is Inside the Box?

Child's Developmental Goals:

✓ To develop an understanding of object permanence

✓ To solve problems using intentional behaviors

MATERIALS:

❑ Shoe box with lid
❑ Favorite infant toy

PREPARATION:

♡ If desired, cover the shoe box and lid with colored, self-adhesive paper for aesthetic purposes.
♡ Place the toy in the box and replace the lid.

NURTURING STRATEGIES:

1. Gain the infant's attention by saying the child's name, shaking the box, and commenting:
   "Katisha, listen. What could be in the box?"
   "Look at my box. What do you hear?"
2. Encourage the infant to open the box and look inside. Say, for example:
   "Katisha, use your fingers. Pick up the lid."
   "Take off the lid. Look inside the box."
3. Using your voice as a tool to communicate excitement and pleasure may increase the infant's interest in the activity. To illustrate, when the infant removes the lid, say:
   "Katisha, you did it! You took off the lid."
   "Look at what's in the box? It's a ball."
4. If the infant seems interested, play the game again. To maintain interest, find a new toy to place in the box.

Highlighting Development

Infants' attention spans are gradually improving. At the same time, they are differentiating themselves from the world. To illustrate, when discovering or finding a toy, infants may explore it with sucking actions. After this, they may alternate between sucking their thumb and sucking toys. In other words, at this stage of development, infants are learning to differentiate between their bodies and their environments.

7 to 9 months

VARIATIONS:

♡ Show the infant the toy and then place it inside the box. Encourage the infant to find the toy by removing the lid.
♡ Place the toy inside a gift bag and encourage the child to find the toy.

ADDITIONAL INFORMATION:

♡ Infants may spend more time playing with the box than trying to find the toy in the box. Removing and replacing objects are often enjoyable behaviors that infants attempt. These actions also promote the development of intentional behaviors.

Clapping the Lids

Child's Developmental Goals

✓ To repeat a behavior discovered by accident
✓ To practice clapping the hands together

MATERIALS:

❑ 2 lightweight metal saucepan lids

PREPARATION:

♡ Select and clear an area that can be constantly supervised. Place the lids in this area.

NURTURING STRATEGIES:

1. Gain the infant's attention by lightly clapping the lids together.
2. Suggest that the infant come over and play with the lids. To illustrate, say:
   "Ryan, crawl over here. You can bang the lids."
   "The lids are over here. Come play with them."
3. Observe the infant interacting with the lids.
4. If the infant is banging the lids together by using a clapping motion, provide positive reinforcement by saying:
   "Ryan, you're clapping the lids together. You're making music."
5. If the infant is making music in another way, provide time for exploration. Later, you might model how to use the lids.
6. Reinforcing your words with actions and assisting the infant may be necessary. If so, gently place each lid in the infant's hands while saying:
   "Ryan, clap your hands together."

7. Providing positive reinforcement may result in repetition of the behavior. Comments to make include:
   "Ryan, you did it. You're clapping the lids together."
   "Wow! Listen to the music you're making."

☀ Highlighting Development

Between seven and nine months of age, infants will continue repeating a behavior or reaction that was discovered by accident. To illustrate, after accidentally reaching for a bell hanging from an activity gym and obtaining a response, the infants will repeat the kicking motion, thereby learning a new behavior.

VARIATIONS:

♡ Provide a saucepan lid and a wooden spoon for making music.
♡ Repeat this activity in an outdoor area.

ADDITIONAL INFORMATION:

♡ This can be a very noisy activity. The infants will revel in their ability to make music. Therefore, this activity also fosters the development of self-esteem and self-efficacy.
♡ To enhance listening skills and promote auditory discrimination, provide toys that make sounds. Infants especially enjoy toys that make soft musical sounds or noise.

Coin Drop

Child's Developmental Goals

✓ To develop an understanding of object permanence

✓ To solve problems using intentional behaviors

MATERIALS:

❑ Oatmeal container with a plastic lid

❑ 4 to 5 juice can lids

PREPARATION:

♡ Carefully check the perimeter of the lids to make sure there are no sharp edges.

♡ Cut a slot in the top of a plastic oatmeal container lid so juice lids can easily be inserted.

♡ If desired, cover the oatmeal container with colored, self-adhesive paper for aesthetic purposes.

♡ Select an area that can be constantly supervised. Clear this area for the activity and place the oatmeal container and juice lids on the floor.

NURTURING STRATEGIES:

1. If the infant crawls near the materials for the activity, move closer.

2. Observe the infant's exploratory behavior with the materials.

3. If necessary, suggest that the infant put the juice lids into the container by saying:
   "Dakota, pick up the lid. Put it in the slot."
   "Put the lid inside the container."

4. Reinforcing your words with actions may be necessary. If so, point to the metal lids and touch the container while saying:
   "Dakota, put the lids through the slot."

5. Provide positive reinforcement for attempts or accomplishments. Comments to make include:
   "Good work. You put the lid inside the container."
   "Keep trying. You almost did it."

6. To foster the understanding of object permanence, ask the infant:
   "Dakota, where are the lids?"

7. Encourage the infant to turn the container upside down and shake the lids out. If necessary, model these actions.

☀ Highlighting Development

The principle of object permanence continues to develop during this period. Infants are learning that objects continue to exist even when out of sight. Playing games, such as hide-and-seek with toys, will help them practice the developing skills. Watch them. Independently, they will hide and find a wide variety of objects.

VARIATION:

♡ Use objects with different shapes such as plastic cookie cutters. Cut holes in the plastic lid to accommodate the shapes.

ADDITIONAL INFORMATION:

♡ Infants love hiding objects, especially when they are working on the concept of object permanence. Observe them. They will enjoy hiding and locating all types of objects.

Bring It to Me

Child's Developmental Goals

✓ To develop an understanding of object permanence

✓ To engage in intentional behaviors

✓ To obtain a desired object by moving one's body

MATERIALS:

❑ Infant toy that can be held while creeping such as large, plastic keys

PREPARATION:

♡ Place the toy 4 or 5 feet away from the infant. Be sure the toy is highly visible to the infant.

NURTURING STRATEGIES:

1. Gain the infant's attention by pointing to and verbally describing the toy. To illustrate, say:
   "Damon, the keys are on the carpet."
2. Encourage the infant to move closer to the keys. Suggest, for example:
   "Damon, pick up the keys."
   "Crawl over to the keys."
3. Observe the infant exploring the keys.
4. Describe how the infant is exploring the toys. Comments include:
   "Damon, you are touching the keys with your fingers."
   "You're chewing on the keys."

5. Encourage the infant to bring the toys to you. Comment, for example:
   "Damon, bring the toys to me."
   "Come to me. Bring the keys with you."
6. Reinforce the infant's attempts or accomplishments by saying:
   "Damon, you're doing it. Keep crawling. You are almost here."
   "Thank you. You brought me the keys."

☀ Highlighting Development

Infants need private time to play by themselves. They do not need to be constantly entertained. One of the most important skills is to self-entertain. Solitary playing will help lay a foundation for protecting them against boredom and loneliness later in life.

VARIATION:

♡ Ask the infant to pick up and hand you an object that you have dropped.

ADDITIONAL INFORMATION:

♡ Infants enjoy helping. Their new mobility and cognitive skills allow them to assist when given a reasonable, developmentally appropriate task.
♡ Cover the keys with a blanket to provide a challenge.

Social Development

♡

SEVEN to NINE MONTHS

Rolling It Back

SOCIAL

Child's Developmental Goals

✓ To interact with a familiar caregiver

✓ To develop a sense of trust

MATERIALS:

❏ Smooth, flat surface

❏ Clean ball, 6 to 12 inches in diameter

PREPARATION:

♡ Select a smooth, flat surface that will allow the ball to roll.

NURTURING STRATEGIES:

1. While carrying the infant to the designated area, talk about the activity. Comments include:
   "Ariel, let's play ball. We can roll it back and forth."
2. Sit the infant in the designated area. Position your body, allowing about 1 foot between you and the infant. Adjust yourself or the infant as needed.
3. Hand the ball to the infant.
4. Allow time for the infant to explore the ball. Comment on the infant's actions. For example, say:
   "Ariel, you are touching the ball with your fingers. The ball feels smooth."
   "Now you are hitting the ball."
5. Encourage the infant to roll the ball to you. Comments include:
   "Ariel, roll the ball to me. Push it."
   "Let's play a game. Roll the ball to me. Then, I'll roll it back."
6. Reinforce the infant's attempts and accomplishments. To illustrate, you might say:
   "Ariel, you made the ball roll."
   "You pushed the ball to me."
7. As long as the infant shows interest, continue the game by gently pushing the ball back and forth.

☀ Highlighting Development

An infant's smile is reserved for special, familiar faces. This is the way the infant reaches out and rewards them. When the infant smiles, reinforce the importance of your relationship by talking and returning the smile.

VARIATIONS:

♡ As the infant progresses in the development of fine muscle skills, introduce balls that are smaller.

♡ Introduce this activity outdoors if conditions are appropriate.

ADDITIONAL INFORMATION:

♡ Infants learn to trust adults when their cues and signals are answered quickly and in a caring, responsive manner. Therefore, play this game only as long as the infant seems interested. Signs of interest to look for include smiling, maintaining eye contact, and babbling.

 Exercise caution with this activity, particularly if you introduce smaller balls. Never use a ball that could pose a choking hazard.

7 to 9 months

Peekaboo

Child's Developmental Goals

✓ To participate in a game
✓ To engage in social interaction with an adult

MATERIALS:
❑ Usual diapering supplies

PREPARATION:
♡ Prepare the diapering table to ensure the supplies are available.

NURTURING STRATEGIES:

1. While you are removing the child's clothing or the wet/dirty diaper, encourage the infant to hold the clean diaper. Say, for example:
   "Jesus, help me out. Hold your diaper."
2. Usually the infant will raise the diaper so that you can't see his face. When this happens, use your voice as a tool for communicating excitement by saying:
   "Where did Jesus go?"
3. When the infant lowers the diaper, say:
   "Jesus, peekaboo. I see you!"
4. Continue the interaction as long as the infant shows interest by laughing, smiling, or covering his face.
5. When interest in the game ceases, finish diapering the child.

☀ Highlighting Development

Because of their new abilities to anticipate events and engage in intentional behaviors, infants may now purposefully initiate social interactions. For example, watching a parent putting on a coat might result in crawling/creeping over and hugging the parent's legs in an attempt to maintain proximity.

VARIATION:
♡ Cover the infant's face with a favorite blanket and continue the game.

ADDITIONAL INFORMATION:
♡ Infants love to play peekaboo games. Responding to their bids to play the game will foster the development of self-efficacy skills. They will learn that they have some control over interactions with people in their environment.

Where Am I Hiding?

SOCIAL

Child's Developmental Goals

✓ To learn to cope with separation anxiety

✓ To act deliberately to maintain contact with an adult

MATERIALS:

None

PREPARATION:

♡ Observe the infant to determine the level of alertness.

NURTURING STRATEGIES:

1. Introduce the game to the infant. For example, tell the child:
   "Inez, I would like to play a game of hide- and-seek."
2. Ask the child to join in by saying:
   "Will you play with me?"
3. Explain the rules of the game by saying, for example:
   "Inez, I'll hide and you find me."
4. Using your knowledge of the child's development of object permanence, either hide completely or leave a body part easily visible.
5. When the infant finds you, react with enthusiasm. To illustrate, comment:
   "Inez, you found me. You knew exactly where to look."
   "You are good at this game."
6. Continue the game as long as the infant is interested.

Highlighting Development

Hide-and-seek games help infants learn how the world works. They learn things exist even when out of sight. This knowledge will help them gradually develop the understanding that the world has some consistency and dependability.

VARIATION:

♡ When the game is understood, ask the child to hide an object.

ADDITIONAL INFORMATION:

♡ Mini-separations occur throughout the day. For example, you may need to diaper another child. If this occurs, continue talking to the infant to reduce separation anxiety.

♡ Continue playing hiding games and discussing the arrival and departure of people to help reinforce the principle of object permanence.

7 to 9 months

Measuring Water

Child's Developmental Goals

✓ To imitate an adult's action

✓ To engage in social interactions and play

MATERIALS:

❏ 1-cup measuring cup
❏ ½-cup measuring cup
❏ Large, nonbreakable mixing bowl
❏ Water
❏ Vinyl tablecloth
❏ Large bib

PREPARATION:

♡ Select an area that will not be damaged by water. Clear this area and spread out the vinyl tablecloth.

♡ Pour warm water in the bowl. Then place the bowl on the tablecloth.

♡ If the room is warm and free from draft, remove the infant's outer clothing. If these conditions are not present, roll the child's sleeves and put on a large bib.

NURTURING STRATEGIES:

1. Sit the infant close to the bowl on the tablecloth.
2. Encourage the infant to explore the materials. For example, ask:
   "Mike, what can you do with the cups?"
   "How does the water feel?"
3. Observe the infant's interactions with the materials.
4. Modeling new ways to hold the measuring cups may be necessary. For example, if the infant is holding the cup with the entire hand, demonstrate how to hold the handle using a pincer grasp.

5. If the infant continues to hold the cup in the same manner, verbally describe your actions by commenting, for example:
   "Mike, I'm holding the cup with my thumb and finger. Look at me. You try it."
   "Look at me. Try my way."
6. Providing positive reinforcement may encourage the infant to repeat the behavior. To illustrate, say:
   "Mike, you did it! We are holding the cups the same way."
   "Look at you. You're using your thumb."

☼ Highlighting Development

Given the development of motor skills, infants can now imitate the way adults use their hands. Showing them new skills may result in refining fine motor skills as well as adding new information to their self-identity.

VARIATIONS:

♡ Add large spoons to practice scooping the liquids. This may also help to foster the development of self-feeding skills.

♡ If outdoors, use a wading pool for water play to encourage the use of arm and leg movements.

ADDITIONAL INFORMATION:

♡ Infants enjoy the soothing sensation of water play.

 Infants can drown in as little as 1 inch of water; therefore, water play needs constant supervision. An adult should be within an arm's reach of the child.

I Am Here to Help

SOCIAL

Child's Developmental Goals

✓ To use an adult as a secure base

✓ To continue developing a sense of trust

MATERIALS:

None

PREPARATION:

♡ Observe to see when adults or siblings are leaving.

NURTURING STRATEGIES:

1. Prepare the infant for the departure of a family member. Say, for example:
   "Grandpa will be leaving soon. Let's walk to the door and wave good-bye."
   "Aunt Lisa is going to school. Wave good-bye."
2. If the infant becomes upset at a family member's departure, pick up the child while talking in a soothing voice. Identifying the infant's emotions is important to the child understanding how she is feeling. For example, comment:
   "Xia, you are angry because Aunt Lisa left you. You wanted to go with her."
   "You are upset. You didn't want Grandpa to leave. You like spending time with Grandpa."
3. Let the infant know that you are there to help. Say, for example:
   "I'm here to help you."
   "It's okay to be sad. Let's rock for a while."
4. When the infant is ready to begin the day, encourage the child to explore the room. Suggest new things to look for around the room, by saying:
   "Xia, look at the new mirror."
   "I put out some new rattles."

5. Provide a secure base from which the infant can explore. Make comments such as:
   "I'm right here. I'll stay in the room. I'm not leaving."
   "I'll be right here if you need me."
6. As the infant explores the room, provide positive reinforcement. This may encourage the infant to explore for longer periods of time before "checking in" with you. To illustrate, say:
   "Xia, you are looking in the mirror. What can you see?"
   "You found the new rattle. What does it sound like?"

☀ Highlighting Development

During this period of development, infants begin to use familiar adults as secure bases. This means that the infants may leave the adult's side to explore their surroundings, but they frequently look back to check the adult's whereabouts. They also may move closer to the adult to make sure they are safe. Your reaction to their exploration or distance influences those factors. For example, displaying a fearful look may result in the infant moving closer to you.

VARIATION:

♡ Use family members' names when talking to the child. The infant needs to learn that everyone and everything has a name.

ADDITIONAL INFORMATION:

♡ During this time period, infants often experience separation anxiety. This occurs when a parent, guardian, or primary caregiver leaves their sight. Your role is to be supportive of these reactions while encouraging independence at the same time.

Stacking Cups

Child's Developmental Goals

✓ To interact socially with an adult

✓ To develop a sense of trust

MATERIALS:

❑ 1 set of stacking cups

PREPARATION:

♡ Select and clear an area that can be constantly supervised. Place the stacking cups in this area to motivate the infant.

NURTURING STRATEGIES:

1. As soon as an infant crawls near the area, move closer to provide assistance or support as needed.
2. Observe the infant's behaviors with the cups.
3. Describe what the infant is doing with the cups. Say, for example:
   "Jami, you are stacking the little cup on the big cup."
   "You are building a tower."
4. Ask questions or offer suggestions as necessary. Comments may include:
   "Where could you put this little cup?"
   "Stack this cup next."
   If necessary, point to the cup to continue maintaining his attention.
5. Talk about the child's reactions to the stacking cups. Say, for example:
   "Jami, you are smiling. You like stacking the cups."
   "How frustrating, the cups fell over. Try again."

6. Providing positive reinforcement may increase the infant's time at this activity. Say, for example:
   "Jami, keep trying. You've used all of the cups!"
   "You are working hard. You've stacked three cups!"

☀ Highlighting Development

Infants at this age prefer caregivers and parents to others. When familiar people are out of sight, they may cry and become irritable. This may cause you to feel guilty. By crying, the child is testing your behavior. Separation anxiety is more prevalent when infants are hungry, tired, or sick. Therefore, to reduce the effects of separation anxiety, it is important that the child is well rested and fed prior to your leaving.

VARIATION:

♡ For a new challenge, demonstrate how to nest the cups rather than stack them.

ADDITIONAL INFORMATION:

♡ Infants' newfound fine motor skills of pinching and releasing objects make this activity possible and successful. A supportive adult can assist the child in working through frustrations. To illustrate, when the stack tumbles over, you may have to assist the child.

Rolling Together

SOCIAL

Child's Developmental Goals

✓ To demonstrate interest in others

✓ To play a game

MATERIALS:

❏ 2 identical wheeled toys

PREPARATION:

♡ Select and clear an area that can be constantly supervised. Place the toys in this area.

NURTURING STRATEGIES:

1. Carry the infant to the designated area while talking about the planned activity. For example, say:

   "I have some toys for you to roll. You can push the toys back and forth."

2. Sit the infant close so that you are facing each other.

3. Hand the child a toy. Observe the infant exploring the toy.

4. Encourage the child to roll the toy to you. To illustrate, say:

   "Mai, roll your toy to me. Push it."

5. Providing positive reinforcement may encourage the infant to repeat the desired behavior. Comment, for example:

   "You did it Mai. Now I have both toys."

6. When the infant gazes at you or is engaged in the game, provide positive reinforcement. Doing this emphasizes the social interactions that are occurring. For example, state:

   "Mai, you are looking at me."
   "We are playing a game together."
   "We are pushing the toy back and forth. What a fun game."

7. Repeat the game as long as the infant seems interested.

☀ Highlighting Development

Infants are beginning to show interest in engaging in some basic interactions with others. For example, they look to others who are exhibiting signs of distress or happiness. Given their newly developed motor skills of crawling, they can now move toward others when interested.

VARIATION:

♡ Roll balls rather than wheeled toys.

ADDITIONAL INFORMATION:

♡ If the infant rolls the ball three or four times, this will be a highly successful activity.

♡ To encourage reaching, place push toys in front of the child. This will encourage full arm movements and forward motion.

 To promote safety, you should provide careful supervision. Otherwise, hair pulling, poking, and other behaviors can occur.

Emotional Development

SEVEN to NINE MONTHS

Making Music

Child's Developmental Goals

✓ To express the emotions of interest and enjoyment

✓ To express emotions in distinct, meaningful patterns

MATERIALS:

❑ 2 lightweight saucepans of varying sizes with lids

PREPARATION:

♡ Select and clear an area that can be constantly supervised. Place the pans and lids in this area.

NURTURING STRATEGIES:

1. When an infant crawls or creeps over to the pans, move closer to the child.
2. Observe the infant's interactions with the pans and lids.
3. If the child bangs them together to make a sound, provide positive reinforcement by saying:
   "Radi, you're making music!"
   "What a loud sound you make. Do it again!"
4. If the infant is exploring the toys in different ways, verbally encourage the child to bang the pans together. For example, comment:
   "Radi, hit the lid on the pan."
   "Bang the lid and pan together. You are making music that way."

5. Describe the child's reactions to the action. Comments might include:
   "Radi, you are laughing and smiling. You must really enjoy making music."
   "You are working hard to make music."
   "You are enjoying this activity."

☀ Highlighting Development

Infants may be afraid of loud noises such as those from thunder, the vacuum cleaner, car horns, firecrackers, etc. When this occurs, reach out to comfort them by cuddling and providing verbal assurance. Over time, the fears should gradually decrease with increased experiences.

VARIATION:

♡ Substitute nonbreakable, lightweight cereal or mixing bowls and wooden spoons for the saucepans and lids.

ADDITIONAL INFORMATION:

♡ Some infants may be frightened by loud noises. If so, provide tools that make quieter music. Gradually, you may build back up to the loud, noisy tools.

7 to 9 months

Jack-in-the-Box

Child's Developmental Goals

✓ To begin coping with the emotion of fear

✓ To express emotions in distinct, meaningful patterns

MATERIALS:

❏ Jack-in-the-box pop-up toy

PREPARATION:

♡ Select and clear an area that can be constantly supervised. Then place the jack-in-the-box toy in this area.

NURTURING STRATEGIES:

1. When the infant crawls over to the toy, move closer. Begin the activity by asking the infant questions about the toy. To illustrate, ask:
   "Kumiko, what is this?" Pause. "It is a new toy."
   "How does this toy work?"
   "What could you do with this handle?"

2. Observe the infant exploring the toy.

3. Provide suggestions on how to "open" the toy. Say, for example:
   "Kumiko, turn the handle."
   "Grab hold of the handle. Move your arm in a circle."

4. Reinforcing your words with actions may be necessary. If so, point to the handle while saying:
   "Grab and turn the handle."
   "Push the handle in a circle."

5. Describe how to make music using the toy. For example, comment:
   "Kumiko, look and listen. Turning the handle makes music."
   "Oh, listen to the music you're making."

6. Prepare the infant for Jack popping out of the toy by stating:
   "Kumiko, look. Something is going to happen."
   "Jack is going to pop out of the toy."

7. When Jack pops up, describe the infant's reactions. Say, for example:
   "That startled you. You moved your body backward."

8. Encourage the infant to find Jack again. To illustrate, say:
   "Where did Jack go? Let's find him again."
   "Turn the handle to find him."

☼ Highlighting Development

Infants express more fear from this time until about 18 months of age. This rise in fear is believed to be linked to the infant's abilities to distinguish between familiar and unfamiliar faces. This ability results in both stranger and separation anxiety.

VARIATIONS:

♡ Use a musical box or push-up toy.

♡ Introduce the child to other action toys. Infants may squeal in delight watching them move.

ADDITIONAL INFORMATION:

♡ Children may be fearful of this activity when it is first introduced. This is most likely related to their lack of understanding of object permanence. Repeated exposure to action toys such as the jack-in-the-box toy will usually result in enjoyment.

♡ For the first experience, turn and have Jack pop up from a distance to reduce the possibility of fear.

Popping It Up

Child's Developmental Goals

✓ To use the caregiver as a social reference point

✓ To express emotions in distinct, meaningful patterns

MATERIALS:

❑ 2 pop-up boxes

PREPARATION:

♡ Select and clear an area that can be constantly supervised. Place the toys on a child-size shelf or the floor.

NURTURING STRATEGIES:

1. When an infant crawls or creeps into the area, position yourself so you are closer to the child.
2. Describe the toy for the infant. Say, for example:
   "Graham, if you push this button, something will happen."
   "If you turn this knob, something will pop up."
3. Observe the infant interacting with the toy.
4. Reinforcing your words with actions may be necessary. To illustrate, model pushing the button, while saying:
   "When I push the button, something pops up."
5. Reacting with excitement for the infant models how to respond when unexpected things happen. When the infant looks at you, you are being used as a social reference point.
6. Encourage the infant to push the button by saying:
   "Graham, you do it now. Push the button with your hand."
   "You try it. Show me where the Mickey Mouse is hiding."

7. Providing positive reinforcement may result in the infant repeating the behavior independently. Comments might include:
   "You found where it was hiding."
   "You did it! You found the Mickey Mouse."
8. Describing the infant's reactions to this behavior may help the child to better understand emotions. To illustrate, say:
   "Graham, you are excited because you found the Mickey Mouse."
   "You are laughing and smiling. You must like this toy."

☀ Highlighting Development

During this stage, infants begin to anticipate routine activities. To illustrate, when a bottle is filled by the caregiver, the infant may crawl over, sit up, and reach for the bottle. When a doorbell rings, the infant may crawl or creep to the door. Likewise, when playing with action toys, the infant might anticipate the objects popping up.

VARIATION:

♡ Use other pop-up or action toys to stimulate the infant's emotional expressions.

ADDITIONAL INFORMATION:

♡ During this time period, infants will be dependent on you for information on how to react to new or unusual experiences or objects. In other words, the infants use others as social reference points. Therefore, modeling excitement or interest may encourage infants to actively explore their environment and reduce their fears of new experiences.

A Stranger among Us

Child's Developmental Goals

✓ To begin coping with stranger anxiety

✓ To express the emotion of fear

MATERIALS:

None

PREPARATION:

♡ Tell the child that a visitor will be arriving.

NURTURING STRATEGIES:

1. When a stranger enters the room, prepare yourself for the infant's reaction. The infant might cry or move closer to you.

2. Position yourself so you can make eye contact with the infant. Then introduce the infant to the stranger. This will let the infant know that you know who this person is. Say, for example:
   "Elma, this is my friend Houa. He is coming to pick up Vang."
   "This is my friend Tammy. She came to help make snack."

3. Comfort the child by remaining close and talking in a soothing voice. Make comments such as:
   "It's okay to be afraid, Elma."
   "New faces can be scary."

4. Be sure to remind the infant that she is safe. State, for example:
   "I'm here to help. Tammy is my friend."
   "I will hold you while she is here."

☀ Highlighting Development

Prior to this stage of development, infants emoted by using their entire body. Now they are beginning to express emotions in distinct, coherent patterns. They can combine facial expression, gaze, voice, and posture to communicate one message. To illustrate, when a stranger enters a child's visual path, she may respond by crying and looking at and moving closer to you.

7 to 9 months

VARIATIONS:

♡ Introduce the child to all the new faces she comes in contact with.

♡ Alter your language to reflect the relationship between the visitor and the child: mother, father, aunt, uncle, etc.

ADDITIONAL INFORMATION:

♡ Strangers such as neighbors, friends, mail carriers, and delivery people come and go frequently. Your job is to help infants cope with seeing new faces. Warm, caring interactions will help them to know they are safe.

I Found Something New

EMOTIONAL

Child's Developmental Goals

✓ To express the emotion of interest
✓ To self-regulate through mobility

MATERIALS:

❏ Favorite infant toy

PREPARATION:

♡ Select an area that can be constantly supervised. Clear this area and place the toy there.

NURTURING STRATEGIES:

1. Observe the infant's behaviors in the room.
2. When the infant needs something new to play with, encourage the child to find a favorite toy. Say, for example:
   "Where is the drum? Keep looking."
   "Look around. Find the drum, Brian. Move closer so you can play with it."
3. Reinforce the infant's attempts and accomplishments by saying:
   "Brian, you found the drum."
   "You found something new to play with by crawling."
4. The goal is to encourage the infant to find things of interest independently. Reach this long-term goal by saying things such as:
   "You were bored. You found something new and interesting to play with."
   "When you get tired of one toy, look for another."

☀ Highlighting Development

Because most infants can crawl now, they are able to self-regulate. They can leave a situation that is overwhelming, or they can join one that is inviting.

VARIATIONS:

♡ To maintain interest, rotate the infant's toys.
♡ Instead of commercial toys, provide the child with common household items. Examples include cups, saucers, wooden spoons, pots, and pans.

ADDITIONAL INFORMATION:

♡ Once they are mobile, infants often move from one activity to another. The goal is to have toys available that will sustain their interest.
♡ The beginnings of behavior and impulse control typically occur between eight or nine months of age. The infant will respond to caregivers who encourage them to look with their eyes.

A New Friend

Child's Developmental Goals

✓ To begin coping with stranger anxiety

✓ To use an adult as a social reference point

MATERIALS:

❑ Infant stroller

PREPARATION:

♡ Tell the infant that a stroller ride is planned.

♡ Secure the infant in the stroller using the safety restraints.

NURTURING STRATEGIES:

1. Talk to the infant about where you are going and why. Say, for example:
   "We are taking a stroller ride. We are going to Mrs. Nicholson's store. She sells us bread. She is my friend. I want you to meet her."

2. Upon arrival at the bakery, greet your friend. Model excitement or enjoyment by smiling, shaking hands, and maintaining eye contact. When watching you interact, the child is using you as a social reference.

3. Talk with Mrs. Nicholson for two or three minutes to allow the infant time to get comfortable with the stranger.

4. Tell her that you would like to introduce someone. Say, for example:
   "Mrs. Nicholson, this is Jasmine. She likes to take stroller rides."

5. Observe the infant's reactions to the stranger. Provide support as necessary. To illustrate, state:
   "It's okay to be afraid. I'm here to help. Mrs. Nicholson is my friend."

6. Thank Mrs. Nicholson for her time and say to the infant:
   "Let's continue riding in the stroller. Where should we go next?"

☀ Highlighting Development

Strangers and parents often do not understand why infants become upset at the presence of new people. You need to help them understand this is a normal stage that infants go through. Given time and repeated experiences, the infants will gradually reduce their fear of the unknown.

VARIATION:

♡ Take trips to the post office, store, restaurant, shopping malls, etc.

ADDITIONAL INFORMATION:

♡ Infants need to learn skills for coping with strangers. Begin by introducing new people in safe and supportive environments.

7 to 9 months

Jazzing It Up!

EMOTIONAL

Child's Developmental Goals

✓ To experience different types of music
✓ To practice self-soothing techniques

MATERIALS:

☐ Tape or compact disc player
☐ Tape or compact disc of music such as *Lullabies Go Jazz* by Jon Crosse

PREPARATION:

♡ Select an outlet for plugging in the tape or compact disc player. Make sure a high cabinet or shelf is nearby to place the player safely out of the infant's reach.
♡ Put the tape or compact disc in the player and plug it in.

NURTURING STRATEGIES:

1. Dim the lights and turn on the tape player.
2. Lay the infant faceup in the crib.
3. Gently rub the infant's belly.
4. Using a gentle, soothing voice, talk about the music. Say, for example:
   "Listen to the music. The saxophone is soothing."
   "What a pretty lullaby. Relax. Listen to the music."
5. Allow the infant to use the music to relax and fall asleep. Therefore, you should leave before the infant falls asleep.

☀ Highlighting Development

During this time, infants may begin to express anger. This feeling often arises when infants are trying to accomplish a goal and are ineffective. Given their cognitive abilities to engage in intentional behaviors, they may also express anger when their goals are blocked. Adults often block infants' goals when they are unresponsive to their cues. An example would include making them take a nap when their bodies are rested.

VARIATIONS:

♡ Encourage the infant to imitate your humming to the music.
♡ Introduce different types of music such as classical music or nature tapes.

ADDITIONAL INFORMATION:

♡ This tape is useful when infants need quiet, relaxing activities. Refer to the Introduction (see pp. 11–12) for additional suggestions for soothing a crying infant.

7 to 9 months

Physical Development

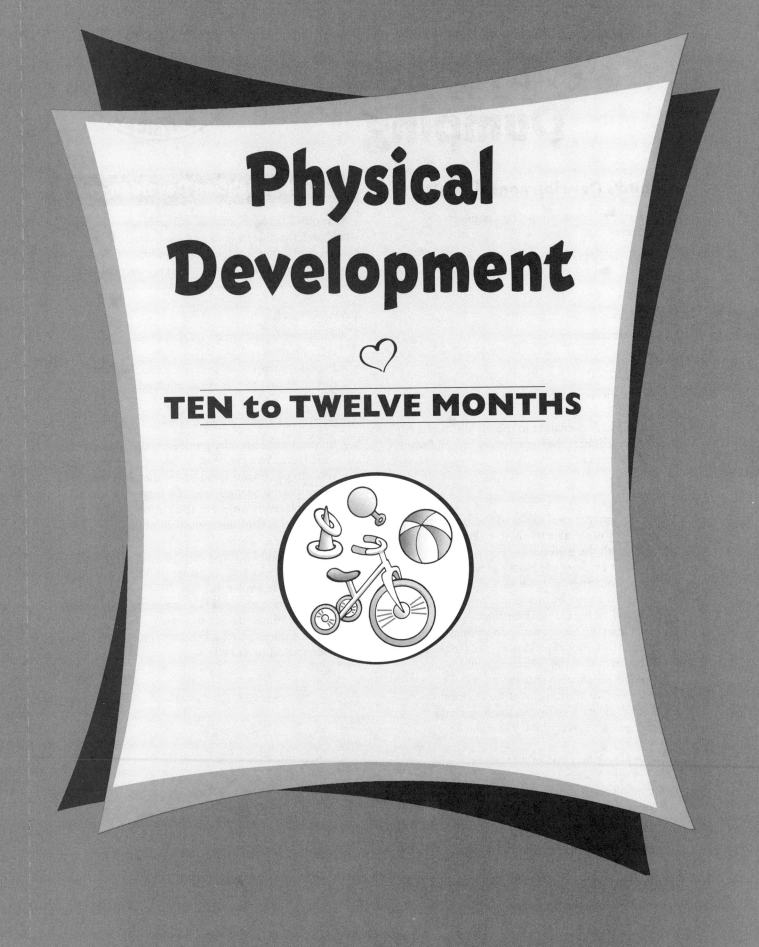

TEN to TWELVE MONTHS

Filling and Dumping

PHYSICAL

Child's Developmental Goals

✓ To practice releasing objects by opening the fingers

✓ To deliberately place an object in a container

MATERIALS:

☐ Foam blocks

☐ Large plastic container

PREPARATION:

♡ Select and clear an area that can be constantly supervised.

♡ Place the plastic container in the middle of the cleared area. Scatter the foam blocks on the floor around the container.

NURTURING STRATEGIES:

1. When the infant moves closer to the area, position yourself so you are able to observe the infant's behavior with the materials.

2. If the infant explores the blocks as opposed to filling the container, watch him. Later, suggest filling the container by saying:
   "Lucien, put the blocks in this container."

3. Reinforcing your words with actions may be necessary. If so, model picking up the blocks and releasing them into the container while saying:
   "Let's fill up the container with the blocks."

4. Provide positive reinforcement for attempts or accomplishments. Comments might include:
   "Lucien, you are working hard. The container is almost full."
   "You are placing the blocks in the container."
   "Look at you! You've picked up all the blocks."

5. If the infant seems interested, dump out the container and begin the game again.

☀ Highlighting Development

At about 10 months of age, infants learn to voluntarily release objects held in their hands. Observe them. They spend a significant amount of time concentrating on picking up and releasing objects.

VARIATIONS:

♡ Enlist the infant's help to fill containers during cleanup time.

♡ Introduce variety by providing the child rubber or plastic toys to put in the container.

ADDITIONAL INFORMATION:

♡ Infants might need help releasing the blocks from their hand. You can assist in one of two ways. First, you can place your hand under the object in the infant's hand. Second, you can suggest that the infant place the object in the bottom of the container. A firm surface usually stimulates infants to open their hands.

♡ Once the child is interested, you can leave him with the blocks and container to repeat and practice independently.

♡ With practice, the child's movements will become more coordinated and efficient.

♡ Blocks are response toys that teach spatial relationships and cause and effect.

Letting Go

Child's Developmental Goals

✓ To develop the voluntary release of hand muscles

✓ To refine the development of fine motor skills

MATERIALS:

❑ Complicated infant toy.

PREPARATION:

♡ Observe the child for times of alertness. Make sure the toy you select has been cleaned and sanitized.

NURTURING STRATEGIES:

1. When the infant needs a toy to explore, provide the toy you selected while saying:
   "Vivaca, here is a new toy for you."
   "Look at this new toy. Feel it with your fingers."
2. Observe the infant exploring the toy. Note the infant's exploration style such as mouthing and touching it with a finger.
3. Provide language stimulation by describing what the infant is doing. Say, for example:
   "You are touching the toy with your pointer finger."
   "You are holding the toy in your left hand."
   "You are touching your tongue to the small circle."
4. Practice voluntary release by asking the infant to hand you the toy while extending your hand.
5. It may be necessary to assist the infant in releasing the toy. If so, place your hand under the object and apply gentle pressure to create a firm surface.

6. Reinforcing the infant's attempts and accomplishments may encourage the behaviors to be repeated. To illustrate, say:
   "Vivaca, you did it! You gave me the toy."
   "You are working hard. Keep trying."
7. If the infant continues to appear interested, hand the toy to the child, thereby repeating the interaction.

☀ Highlighting Development

At this developmental stage, infants are learning to voluntarily release their grasp. When holding a foam block in their hand, for example, they can open their hand, causing the block to be released.

VARIATION:

♡ Introduce a favorite toy from the past.

ADDITIONAL INFORMATION:

♡ Continue to connect behaviors with actions by describing what the child is doing.

♡ When choosing toys for infants, construction is an important consideration. Choose toys that are durable and can withstand enthusiastic handling (Abrams & Kaufman 1990).

10 to 12 months

Dropping Objects

PHYSICAL

Child's Developmental Goals

✓ To practice releasing objects by opening the fingers

✓ To practice problem solving by pulling on a string to get a desired object

MATERIALS:

❑ 3 infant toys

❑ 3 three-foot pieces of wool yarn

PREPARATION:

♡ Select a piece of yarn and tie it to one end of the infant toy. Attach by tying the free end of the yarn to an arm of the high chair. Repeat this procedure with the other pieces of yarn and toys.

♡ Place the infant in the high chair, securing the child with the safety strap. Position and lock the tray in place.

NURTURING STRATEGIES:

1. While placing each toy on the tray, talk about it. Say, for example:
   "Hugh, here is a stuffed dinosaur."
   "You like this toy. It is a cow. Cows say moo."
2. Explain to the child what to do if the toy is dropped over the edge. Comments may include:
   "Hugh, look at the toys. They are on strings. Pull the string."
   "If it falls, pull on this string."
3. Reinforcing your words with actions may be necessary. If so, while touching the toy, say:
   "Watch me pull on the string."
4. Watch the infant exploring and dropping the objects.

5. Respond to the infant's vocalizations. If the infant is interested or excited, comment:
   "Hugh, you found the cow!"
   "You like this game!"
   If the infant becomes frustrated, remind the child what to do using a warm and supportive voice. For example, say:
   "Pull the string."
   "You can do it. Find the cow."

☀ Highlighting Development

Infants are perfecting their skills when they drop objects. These actions teach them cause and effect. Each time an item hits the surface, children see an immediate response as a result of their actions. If the adult immediately picks up the object, the action is likely to be repeated becoming a game. Often this game will be accompanied by expressions of positive emotions such as laughing or squealing with delight.

VARIATION:

♡ Secure a favorite toy to the crib with short pieces of wool yarn.

ADDITIONAL INFORMATION:

♡ Infants naturally drop things from the high chair. Therefore, this activity builds upon this interest.

♡ Whenever possible, admire the child's accomplishments.

 Using wool yarn reduces safety concerns because it will break before it reaches a strangling point.

Basket Throw

Child's Developmental Goals

✓ To practice throwing an object

✓ To refine walking skills

MATERIALS:

❏ Laundry basket with sturdy sides

❏ 6 to 8 tennis or lightweight balls

PREPARATION:

♡ Clear an area for the basket. If indoors, place the basket near a wall for a backboard. If outdoors, place it along a fence or building.

♡ Place the tennis balls on the ground around the basket.

NURTURING STRATEGIES:

1. When the infant walks or crawls over to the area, move closer.

2. Introduce the activity by saying:
   "Dera, this is a game. Throw the balls in the basket. How many balls can you put in the basket?"

3. Demonstrate the activity and then encourage the child to throw the ball in the basket.

4. Count the number of balls that land in the basket.

5. Provide positive reinforcement for attempts or accomplishments. Comments to say include:
   "Dera, you threw the ball into the basket."
   "One. Two. Three. Three balls are in the basket."
   "You've thrown all the balls in the basket."
   "You're helping to pick up the balls."

☼ Highlighting Development

When first learning to throw, children are uncoordinated. They often drop the ball behind them or at arm's length in front of them because they are experimenting with the timing of when to release their grip. This is normal behavior and, with practice, they will learn when to release.

VARIATION:

♡ Introduce bigger balls such as soccer balls or basketballs to promote the development of large muscle skills.

ADDITIONAL INFORMATION:

♡ Young children find throwing exciting. Watch them. Their pleasure is reflected in their facial expressions. Moreover, they are devoted to the activity.

10 to 12 months

Scribble Table

PHYSICAL

Child's Developmental Goals

✓ To refine fine motor skills

✓ To practice standing at a table using one hand for support

MATERIALS:

❑ Piece of newsprint or light-colored butcher paper large enough to cover the entire table

❑ Masking tape

❑ Red, green, blue, and orange chunky crayons

❑ Plastic container

❑ Child-size table or coffee table

PREPARATION:

♡ Cover the table with the paper and secure with masking tape.

♡ Place the crayons in the container and on the table approximately 5 to 6 inches from the edge, allowing the child to conveniently reach them.

NURTURING STRATEGIES:

1. When a child crawls or toddles over to the table, introduce the activity by saying:
   "Mateo, watch me. Use the crayons. Mark on the paper."
2. Encourage the infant to choose a crayon from the container. To illustrate, say:
   "Choose a crayon."
   If necessary, move the container closer.
3. Label the crayon chosen by the infant and say:
   "Mateo, you chose a blue crayon."
4. Observe the infant working. Provide the child time to think about the artwork. Then describe the motions or markings by saying:
   "You are using your arm to draw a circle."
   "You are making long lines. The lines go from side to side."
5. Providing positive reinforcement may extend the infant's participation in the activity. Comments include:
   "Mateo, you are working hard."
   "You've used three different colors: red, blue, and orange."

6. Before interest is lost in the activity, print the infant's name near the markings. Model proper writing skills by capitalizing the first letter of the name and using lowercase letters for the rest. Likewise, because in our culture we write from left to right, place the child's name in the upper left-hand corner. In addition, say each letter as you write it.
7. To boost the child's self-esteem, point to the name and markings, while smiling and saying, for example:
   "Mateo, you made all of these marks! You should be proud."

☀ Highlighting Development

During this stage, infants are perfecting their newly acquired fine muscle skills. The ability to mark with crayon is possible once the pincer grasp is developed. As with other activities, they will enjoy the cause and effect of scribbling. The infants can see that marks are created by using their hands.

VARIATIONS:

♡ After covering the table with newspaper, tape down individual pieces of paper for the child to decorate.

♡ Introduce this activity with the child sitting in the high chair.

ADDITIONAL INFORMATION:

♡ The choice of crayons and paper is important when working with infants. Using dark crayons on light paper increases the chance of infants' light marks being visible. In addition, using fat or chunky crayons is necessary because of the infants' fine motor skills.

♡ Write the date the child completed the artwork on it. By collecting samples of work over time, you will be able to observe the infant's developmental accomplishments.

♡ To prevent scribbling on walls, floors, or furniture, activities with crayons should always be carefully supervised.

10 to 12 months

PHYSICAL

Cruising Time

Child's Developmental Goals

✓ To practice pulling self to a standing position by using a table

✓ To practice "cruising" along the edge of the table

MATERIALS:

❑ Sturdy child-size table or coffee table

PREPARATION:

♡ Clear the table and the area around the table.

NURTURING STRATEGIES:

1. When the infant is attempting to pull up on an unsturdy item, redirect the child by carrying her to the table and saying:
   "Lian, the table is safe. Pull yourself up using the table."
2. Stay close while the child is working because the child may lose her balance and fall backward.
3. Observe the infant's behavior. If necessary, provide a few verbal suggestions to assist the child. Be sure to not overwhelm the infant with suggestions. Infants learn best through trial and error and practice. For example, suggest:
   "Lian, use both hands."
   "Push up with your legs."
4. Provide positive reinforcement for attempts and accomplishments. Comments include:
   "Look at you! You're standing."
   "You're using the table to walk."
   "You can walk fast using the table."
   "You're working hard."
5. When you think the infant is becoming tired or wants to change the activity, help the child return to a sitting position.

6. Close the activity by saying things such as:
   "Lian, you worked hard today pulling up."
   "You are really practicing walking."
7. If needed, help the infant transition to another activity. For example, say:
   "You are tired after that activity. Do you want to look at some books?"

☀ Highlighting Development

A word of caution: Avoid hurrying infants toward independent standing or walking. Positioning an infant into a standing position seldom results in the learned behavior. Infants will pull themselves into a standing position when developmentally ready and given the opportunity. Providing sturdy furniture such as a coffee table or couch will support this development (Leach, 1992).

10 to 12 months

VARIATION:

♡ Help the infant pull up and cruise along a sturdy structure outdoors.

ADDITIONAL INFORMATION:

♡ This is a very strenuous physical activity for infants. Therefore, they may be extra tired or hungry after participating in this activity.

♡ Once infants pull themselves to a standing position, they are unable to sit back down because they need their hands for support. You will often need to help them move back into a sitting position.

♡ Infants should have access to furniture that will assist them in pulling up to a standing position.

Walking during the Snack-Time Routine

PHYSICAL

Child's Developmental Goals

✔ To walk with assistance

✔ To develop balance in an effort to stand or walk unassisted

MATERIALS:

None

PREPARATION:

♡ Warn the infant that snack time will be in a few minutes and it will be necessary to stop playing and wash hands.

NURTURING STRATEGIES:

1. Assist the infant in preparing for snack by saying: *"Kwame, it is snack time. You will need to wash your hands."*
2. Encourage the infant to walk with you to the bathroom or sink by extending your hands and saying:
   "Give me your hands. Let's walk together."
   "We will walk to the sink together, Kwame."
3. Using both hands, gently pull the infant to a standing position and begin walking to the sink.
4. Providing positive reinforcement may make the infant feel good about the newly acquired skills and, thereby, increase self-esteem. To illustrate, say:
   "What a good walker you are."
   "You are working hard."
   "Kwame, you are strong."
5. Wash and dry the infant's hands.
6. Repeat step 4 while walking to the snack area.

☼ Highlighting Development

Motor skills work as a system. More advanced skills are developed when separate systems blend together and cooperate with others. Thus, prior to walking, a child needs to sit and stand.

After crawling, most infants begin walking by supporting themselves on furniture. By 11 months, they can walk when their hand is held and they are led. Most infants can walk on their own by their first birthday (Berk, 1997).

VARIATION:

♡ Help the infant walk during other transitions, such as nap time, outdoor play, etc.

ADDITIONAL INFORMATION:

♡ Infants should be encouraged, but not forced, to practice walking during different routines throughout the day. Crawling or creeping should be encouraged while playing; these types of locomotion are necessary for brain development because they exercise both sides of the body and brain simultaneously.

♡ Children learn lessons about balance and gravity by moving their bodies through space.

 To prevent accidents, paths should be kept clear so that children do not bump into furniture.

10 to 12 months

Language and Communication Development

♡

TEN to TWELVE MONTHS

Dressing to Go Outside

Child's Developmental Goals

✓ To increase receptive language skills

✓ To demonstrate an understanding of words

MATERIALS:

None

PREPARATION:

♡ Make sure the child has the appropriate clothing for outdoor play.

NURTURING STRATEGIES:

1. Warn the child that a change in activities is coming by saying, for example:
   "Ashley, in a few minutes we are going to clean up. Then we will get ready to go outside."

2. After a few minutes, begin singing a cleanup song, such as:

   ♪ Clean up, clean up.
   ♪ Everybody everywhere
   ♪ Clean up, clean up.
   ♪ Everybody do your share.

   Sing this as long as it takes to pick up all of the toys.

3. After the toys are picked up, say, for example:
   "Let's get ready to go outside. What do we need? It is windy today. Get your hat and jacket."

4. Encourage the child to get the necessary items by saying:
   "Ashley, let's go get your hat."
   "Come over here. You need to get your coat."

5. Provide positive reinforcement when the child retrieves an item of clothing. These actions will show the infant's new level of independence. Reinforce their actions by saying:
   "Here is your hat. We found it."

6. Assist the child in putting on the clothes and going outside.

☀ Highlighting Development

An infant begins to point at about 11 months of age. Pointing is used as a communication tool to direct your attention to another object or person at a distance. Observe the infant during this process. Typically, she will look at you while pointing and immediately after. The infant is interested in knowing whether she has redirected your attention. Listen. At this stage, the infant makes prelinguistic speech, which is referred to as echolalia. This begins occurring at about 9 to 10 months of age. The infant will consciously imitate the sounds of others. However, this occurs without understanding (Bentzen, 2001).

Studies show that the earlier an infant begins to point, the more words she knows by two years of age (Butterworth, 1997).

VARIATION:

♡ This activity can be repeated when undressing after coming in from playing outdoors.

ADDITIONAL INFORMATION:

♡ Children need to have warnings that transitions are coming. These warnings will help them finish the activity and start a new one.

♡ Encourage the infants to participate in as much of the dressing and undressing as possible. This promotes feelings of independence.

10 to 12 months

That's What I Want

Child's Developmental Goals

✓ To use gesturing skills to achieve a desired outcome

✓ To add to the repertoire of receptive language skills

MATERIALS:

None

PREPARATION:

♡ Carefully observe the infant.

NURTURING STRATEGIES:

1. When a child points to an object or otherwise gestures a need, respond by elaborating or explaining his need. To illustrate, say:
   "You are pointing at the box of crackers. Cody, are you hungry? Do you want a cracker?"
2. Reinforce the infant's behaviors by saying:
   "This is a cracker. You pointed to the box of crackers."
3. Assist the infant in obtaining the desired outcome by, in this example, handing the infant the cracker.
4. Observe the infant. If still hungry, the child may gesture for a second cracker. If this happens, ask:
   "Cody, do you want another cracker?"

☀ Highlighting Development

Infants show their knowledge of language through the use of preverbal gestures. To illustrate, they may point to an item of interest. These gestures are typically accompanied by babbling. Labeling these gestures assists in the development of receptive and expressive language skills.

VARIATION:

♡ Reinforce your words with gestures when giving instructions to an infant. For example, while saying, "Put the truck on the shelf," place your hand on the shelf.

ADDITIONAL INFORMATION:

♡ Infants will quickly learn that words are more effective than gestures. Therefore, this activity also promotes the development of expressive language skills.

♡ During this stage infants begin deliberately using nonverbal actions to convey meanings. To illustrate, they will shake or turn their head away to indicate no. They may wave bye-bye. Hand gestures are also used with an accompanying "ah ah ah." The "ah ah ah" means they want something such as a toy or cracker. Whenever this occurs, the caregiver should respond with words.

10 to 12 months

More, More, More

10 to 12 months

Child's Developmental Goals

✓ To express desires verbally

✓ To communicate through gestures

MATERIALS:

❑ Nutritious snack on a small plate

❑ Pitcher of juice and cup with lid

PREPARATION:

♡ Prepare the snack and position the high chair next to a table. Sanitize the high chair and wash the child's hands.

NURTURING STRATEGIES:

1. Place the child in a high chair using the safety restraint.
2. Place a small, nonbreakable plastic plate with the snack and cup on the tray of the high chair.
3. Observe the child eating snack.
4. If the child gestures or vocalizes for more food, respond by saying:
   "Lara, what do you want?"
5. Encourage the child to verbally respond. Make comments such as:
   "Tell me what you want."
6. If the infant gestures, verbally label the actions. Comments include:
   "Lara, you are pointing at the pitcher. Do you want more juice?"
   "You are pointing at the crackers. Do you want more crackers?"

7. If necessary, provide the words for the infant. To illustrate, say:
   "More. More juice. You want more juice."
   "More. Crackers. You want more crackers."
8. Of course, provide the infant with the desired item.

☼ Highlighting Development

Infants' first words appear, on average, at about 12 months. These words tend to refer to important people (*mama, grandpa*), actions (*bye-bye, no*), or moving objects (*ball, car*).

VARIATION:

♡ Repeat this activity during breakfast, lunch, or dinner.

ADDITIONAL INFORMATION:

♡ Encourage the child's communication efforts as well as accomplishments by sharing your enthusiasm through your voice and facial expressions.

 Observe to see that the child does not choke.

Animal Sounds

Child's Developmental Goals

✓ To continue developing receptive language skills

✓ To practice responding to questions

MATERIALS:

❑ Cardboard book with familiar animals such as dogs, cats, or farm animals

PREPARATION:

♡ Display the book in an area of the room where the child can easily access it. This allows it to be selected by the infant.

NURTURING STRATEGIES:

1. When the book is chosen, position yourself so you can observe the child exploring the book.
2. Offer to read the book to the infant by saying: *"Oliver, would you like me to read the book to you?"*
3. If the infant responds "no" by shaking the head or saying "no," offer to be available to read. For example, state: *"I'll be over here if you change your mind."*
4. The infant may respond by saying "yes," nodding his head, or handing you the book. When this occurs, sit down beside the infant making sure you can view any other children you are caring for.
5. Begin reading the book.
6. While reading, ask questions about the pictures. For example, ask: *"Oliver, what sound does a cow make?"* *"What animal is this?"*
7. Providing positive reinforcement will assist the infant in developing expressive language skills. For example, comment: *"That's right! A cow says moo."* *"Yes. That is a duck."*
8. Read the book again if the infant seems interested.

☀ Highlighting Development

Asking questions helps to direct the child's attention. Questioning also stimulates the development of language skills. During this time, infants are more likely to respond with gesturing. During the second year of life, a child begins to respond with recognizable words.

VARIATION:

♡ While singing the song "Old MacDonald," encourage infants to make the animal sounds.

ADDITIONAL INFORMATION:

♡ Stimulate the infant's language development by reading to the infant throughout the day. If a book is unavailable, recite a favorite story or nursery rhyme. The value of these activities cannot be overlooked. They expose the infant to his native language and promote the development of both receptive and expressive language skills.

♡ Show the child how to turn the pages of the book. If the child wants to assist, provide encouragement.

♡ The availability of books is important. The child may want to look at them independently. They may view them by holding the book upside down or turning several pages at a time. This is typical behavior.

10 to 12 months

"This Is the Way"

Child's Developmental Goals

✓ To continue developing receptive language skills

✓ To imitate another person's behavior/actions

MATERIALS:

❏ A carpet piece, large towel, blanket, or rug

❏ Picture of items in song, including a toothbrush, hairbrush, and spoon

PREPARATION:

♡ Collect all the materials and place them in an area where they are easily accessible.

NURTURING STRATEGIES:

1. Prepare the room. Then gain the child's attention by sitting on the floor and laying out the objects.
2. Invite the child to sing with you.
3. Introduce the song by saying:
   "Murphy, I have a song for us to sing today."
4. While singing the song, hold up the prop that accompanies the verse.

   ♫ This is the way we brush our teeth,
   ♫ brush our teeth, brush our teeth.
   ♫ This is the way we brush our teeth
   ♫ so early in the morning.

   Additional verses include actions such as:
   Brush our hair (or comb our hair)
   Put on clothes
   Eat our breakfast
   Wash our hands
   Drive to school
   Exercise

5. Encourage the infant to join in the activity by making comments such as:
   "Show me how you brush your teeth."
6. If the child seems interested, introduce the song again later in the day.

☀ Highlighting Development

A child's first word appears usually at about 12 months of age. These words typically are related to actions, people, or objects. Therefore, action songs help the child develop receptive and expressive language skills.

VARIATION:

♡ Continue adding verses such as take a nap, eat our cereal, etc.

ADDITIONAL INFORMATION:

♡ Infants have short attention spans. Consequently, they are able to sit only for short periods of time, usually only a few minutes. Therefore, keep the activities short. If the child likes the activity, repeat it again at a later time.

♡ Songs such as this, if sung in the order of your daily routines, help children develop a sense of time. They learn that one action precedes another.

10 to 12 months

Animal Puppets

Child's Developmental Goals

✓ To continue developing expressive language skills

✓ To continue increasing receptive language skills

MATERIALS:

❏ 2 animal puppets

❏ 2 empty and sanitized liquid soap containers close to the size of the puppets

PREPARATION:

♡ Place the puppets over the top of the sanitized liquid soap containers. Then display the puppets in an area where they will attract the child's attention.

NURTURING STRATEGIES:

1. When you see a child select a puppet from the shelf, move closer and invite yourself to play by saying:
   "Ahmed, can I play puppets with you?"
2. If the child indicates "no" either verbally or with his body language, then say:
   "I'll just watch you play."
3. If the child uses a gesture or word to encourage your participation, then say:
   "Great! I'll play with the duck puppet."
4. If necessary, reinforce your actions with words. Comments to make include:
   "Ahmed, look at me. My hand is inside the puppet."
   "I can move the puppet because my hand is inside it."
5. Encourage the child to make the sound of the animal. Ask, for example:
   "Can you make a cow sound? Moo, moo."
   "What sound does a duck make? Quack, quack."

6. Reinforce the infant's animal noises by saying:
   "Ahmed, you mooed just like a cow!"
   "What a loud quack."
7. Model the animals having a conversation. Do this by having your puppet talk to the infant's puppet. This will foster the development of receptive language skills.

☀ Highlighting Development

A variety of tools such as puppets, stuffed animals, books, and cassettes all can be used to promote language skills in young children. Although children often show preferences for favorite tools, rotating them may introduce novelty, thus stimulating their interest.

VARIATION:

♡ Choose a book or books with the same animals as the puppets to read to the child.

ADDITIONAL INFORMATION:

♡ When purchasing books or puppets, choose those representing different ethnic groups.

♡ Choose puppets carefully. Because young children lack fine motor skills, the puppets need to be easy to manipulate.

♡ Puppets can also be used as a tool to encourage children to label items they touch.

10 to 12 months

Let's Play

Child's Developmental Goals

✓ To initiate a familiar game

✓ To practice using gestures to achieve a desired outcome

MATERIALS:

None

PREPARATION:

♡ Observe the child for her state of alertness.

NURTURING STRATEGIES:

1. While changing the infant's diaper, observe the behavioral cues being displayed such as the infant attempting to grab her toes.

2. Respond to the infant's cues. For example, say: *"Michaela, do you want to sing 'This Little Piggy'?"* Pause. Waiting for the infant to respond will display value and respect for the child.

3. If infant responds by shaking her head "no," bear in mind that children at this age are beginning to show negativity.

4. If infant responds "yes" by nodding, smiling, or otherwise showing interest, begin playing the game.

5. Throughout the interaction, keep smiling and showing interest. This nonverbal behavior will reinforce the infant for initiating the game.

6. When the game is over, reinforce the infant for initiating the game by making comments such as: *"Michaela, you picked a fun game to play." "What a great idea to play this game."*

7. If the infant shows interest by smiling, babbling, or maintaining eye contact, begin the game again.

Highlighting Development

Infants use two forms of preverbal gestures to influence the behavior of others. The first is the proto-declarative, in which the infants touch, hold, or point to objects while looking at you to gain your attention. With the second type, called protoimperative, the infants get other people to do something by pointing, reaching, and often producing sounds at the same time (Bates, 1979; Fenson et al., 1994).

VARIATION:

♡ See Appendix F for a list of finger plays, nursery rhymes, and chants, or play games such as Lovin' Rubbin or Where Are Your Toes (in "Birth to Six Months, Physical Development," and "Social Development," respectively).

ADDITIONAL INFORMATION:

♡ As infants get older, they will begin initiating some of their favorite games with you. Careful observation will assist you in knowing what game they want to play.

♡ Following their lead shows infants that they do have an effect on their environment. In this way, it promotes their sense of self-efficacy.

10 to 12 months

Cognitive Development

♡

TEN to TWELVE MONTHS

Ball and Tube

Child's Developmental Goals

✓ To refine the understanding of object permanence

✓ To continue developing cause-and-effect relationships

MATERIALS:

- ❏ 6 to 8 tennis balls
- ❏ 2 diaper pins
- ❏ 4-foot piece of hollow plastic tubing
- ❏ 2 twelve-inch pieces of elastic band
- ❏ 2 nonbreakable containers
- ❏ Masking tape

PREPARATION:

♡ Sand the ends of the plastic tubing to remove sharp edges.

♡ Choose a smooth area by a chain-link fence for this activity. If necessary, clear this area of debris.

♡ Align the pipe at an angle along the fence. The tip of the pipe should be between 2 and 3 feet from the ground, depending upon the height of the children. Secure the pipe to the fence using the elastic bands and diaper pins. Put one band at the top of the pipe and one at the bottom.

♡ Place one container at each end of the pipe. Put the tennis balls in the container under the tallest end. Adjust the placement of the container at the lower end. Check to ensure that when the tennis balls go through the tube, they land in the container.

NURTURING STRATEGIES:

1. When the activity is chosen, observe the child's behavior.

2. If the child appears to need help understanding the activity, verbally describe the activity. To illustrate, say: *"Seiji, put the ball in the top. It will roll through the tube."*

3. If necessary, reinforce your words with actions by putting the ball at the top of the tube and saying: *"Seiji, put the ball in the tube."*

4. To work on the concept of object permanence, ask the child: *"Where did the ball go?"*

5. Describe what happens after the child releases the tennis ball. Comments to make include: *"Seiji, the ball rolls through the tube." "The ball lands in the container."* These comments are important for assisting in development of cause-and-effect relationships.

6. Providing positive reinforcement may result in the child spending more time at the activity. Examples might include: *"Seiji, you're working hard." "You like this game. You have a big smile on your face."*

☀ Highlighting Development

Children at this stage are continuing to develop an understanding of object permanence. Objects out of sight are out of mind for the three-month-old child. By eight months, children begin searching for items that are covered. Now children's growth is evident. They will track and find toys that are covered.

VARIATION:

♡ Lower the height of the pipe so nonwalkers can do the activity while sitting on a blanket.

ADDITIONAL INFORMATION:

♡ If the children have not mastered the principle of object permanence, this game will have magical appeal.

 After closing diaper pins always secure them by wrapping in masking tape.

Which Are the Same?

Child's Developmental Goals

✓ To begin classifying objects

✓ To practice grouping similar objects

MATERIALS:

❑ 3 toys; 2 identical and 1 different such as 2 cars and 1 truck

PREPARATION:

♡ Select and clear an area that can be constantly supervised. Display the toys.

NURTURING STRATEGIES:

1. When the child selects the activity, observe the infant's behavior. Notice which toys the infant selects.
2. While the infant is playing, move closer and ask:
   "Marya, which two toys are the same?"
3. Reinforce the child's attempts or accomplishments at classifying the toys. Say, for example:
   "That's right! There are two buses."
   "You pointed to a bus and a truck."
4. Encourage the infant to physically separate the toys. To illustrate, while pointing say:
   "Marya, put the buses over here and the truck over there."
5. If necessary, reinforce your words with actions by moving the toys while saying:
   "Put the buses together."
6. Reinforce the child's attempts and accomplishments at separating the toys. Comments to make include:
   "Marya, you put the buses together in one spot."
   "You separated the buses from the truck."

Highlighting Development

Classification is an important skill for young children (Herr, 1998). For infants at this age, classification is the process of physically grouping objects into categories or classes based upon unique features. Simple classification is the ability to group by color, size, or function. Language helps children categorize related objects because it provides the children with cues as to how items are alike and different from each other.

VARIATION:

♡ To challenge the infant, increase the number of objects to classify.

ADDITIONAL INFORMATION:

♡ Infants begin to classify objects very early in life. In fact, you have assisted them in acquiring these skills whenever you have described how toys are alike and different.

♡ The child's memory and visual perceptual skills are increasing. Both of these skills assist in making visual interpretations.

10 to 12 months

Which Box Is It In?

COGNITIVE

10 to 12 months

Child's Developmental Goals

✓ To refine the understanding of object permanence

✓ To remember where an object is hidden

✓ To use existing schemas to search for the hidden objects

MATERIALS:

❑ 2 boxes with lids

❑ 1 favorite toy that will fit inside both boxes

❑ Child-size table or coffee table

PREPARATION:

♡ Clean and sanitize the table. Set the two boxes and the toy on the table.

NURTURING STRATEGIES:

1. Invite the child to play a game with you. To illustrate, say:
   "Paolo, I have a game on the table. Want to play?"

2. When the child arrives at the table, pick up the toy. Explain the game by saying:
   "I'm going to hide the car in one of the boxes. You try to find it."

3. Hide the toy in a box. Say to the infant:
   "Find the car."

4. Provide positive reinforcement for attempts and accomplishments. Comments include:
   "Paolo, you did it; you found the cars."
   "You're looking in the box."
   "You lifted the lid and looked inside."

5. If the infant needs a challenge, hide the toy in one box and then move it to the other box while the infant is watching. Observe where the infant searches for the object.

6. Repeat the game as long as the infant seems interested.

☀ Highlighting Development

Understanding object permanence shows that the child is developing memory skills and goal-oriented thinking. Children at this stage of development typically have good memories. Their search strategies have matured. Watch them. Now they are able to follow the movement of an object from place to place.

VARIATION:

♡ Hide the toy in a gift bag or pillowcase.

ADDITIONAL INFORMATION:

♡ When infants search for the toy in a second hiding place, they are showing their understanding of object permanence.

Where Is It?

Child's Developmental Goals

✓ To search for a desired object

✓ To engage in intentional behaviors

MATERIALS:

❏ Child's security item(s) such as blanket, teddy bear, pacifier, etc.

PREPARATION:

♡ Place the security items in a convenient location.

NURTURING STRATEGIES:

1. When the child is upset, suggest locating a favorite comfort item. To illustrate, say:
   "Rylan, where is your doll? It helps you feel better to hug him."
   "Help me find your blanket. Where did you leave it?"
2. Suggest that the infant look for the item. Comments to say include:
   "Look. Where could it be? Move around the room."
3. Assist the infant in the search by suggesting where to look. Say, for example:
   "Rylan, you had your blanket at rest time. Look by your crib."
   "You were playing with your doll."

4. Provide positive reinforcement for attempts and accomplishments. Make comments such as:
   "Rylan, you remembered where you left your doll."
   "Keep looking. We'll find it soon."

☀ Highlighting Development

The role of the adult is to assist children in tasks beyond their skill level. This assistance can take the form of verbal or physical help. The term describing the adult's behavior when engaged in assisting the child is *scaffolding* (Vygotsky, 1978).

VARIATION:

♡ To promote memory skills, ask the infant to search for a lost toy.

ADDITIONAL INFORMATION:

♡ Assist infants in finding the lost item, especially when they are upset. The inability to remember is just as frustrating for young children as it is for adults.

10 to 12 months

Scavenger Hunt

COGNITIVE

10 to 12 months

Child's Developmental Goals

✓ To refine the understanding of object permanence

✓ To engage in intentional behaviors to solve a problem

MATERIALS:
- 1 set of star builder manipulatives
- Container to hold star builders

PREPARATION:
- Count and record the number of star builders in your set.
- Hide all but one of the star builder manipulatives either indoors or outdoors. See the Highlighting Development box.
- Put the remaining star builder in a pocket to show to the child later.
- Place the container in a central location.

NURTURING STRATEGIES:
1. Introduce the activity to the child. Using a tone that conveys enthusiasm, say:
   "I hid some star builders. Can you help me find them?"
2. Remove the star builder from your pocket while stating:
   "This is a star builder. Let's find them."
3. When the infant finds a hidden toy, either by crawling or walking to it, clap and verbally provide positive reinforcement. This may encourage the child to continue looking for the star builders. Comments include:
   "Benjamin, you found one!"
   "Wow! You are good at this game."
4. Explain the purpose of the container by saying:
   "Here is a special bucket. This bucket is for holding the star builders. Put the star builders in here."

5. If necessary, model putting the toy in the bucket by using the star builder you had in your pocket.
6. The child may need assistance in finding a hidden toy. Walk beside the infant while saying things such as:
   "Where could they be hiding? Let's look here by the chair."
   "Look behind the tree. You found one!"
   "Good work, Benjamin! Now, put the star builder in the bucket."
7. If the infant finds all the hidden toys and still is enjoying the game, you may want to continue by removing some of the star builders from the container and hiding them.

☀ Highlighting Development

Observe to note the child's understanding of object permanence. For some children at this stage, it is developmentally appropriate to completely hide the objects. For others, partially hidden objects are still a challenge to find. Therefore, you need to be aware of the child's developmental level to provide a stimulating, yet challenging, environment.

VARIATIONS:
- Hide items that are related but not identical such as plastic zoo or farm animals.
- Substitute by hiding large plastic blocks for a scavenger hunt.

ADDITIONAL INFORMATION:
- Children often enjoy finding their favorite toys.
- Evaluate the child's level of understanding of object permanence. Use that knowledge for hiding toys.

Sorting Cars

Child's Developmental Goals

✓ To distinguish objects that are different

✓ To categorize objects into two groups

MATERIALS:

❑ 6 red cars
❑ 6 blue cars
❑ Red bowl
❑ Blue bowl
❑ Clear container
❑ Child-size table or coffee table

PREPARATION:

♡ Clear an area on a child-size or coffee table. Place the cars in the clear container. Place one colored bowl on each side of the clear container.

NURTURING STRATEGIES:

1. When a child exhibits interest in the activity, introduce the activity by saying:
   "Tory, look at these cars."
2. Describe the toys to the infant. Comments to make include:
   "Here are red and blue cars."
   If necessary, say:
   "The cars are two different colors."
3. Observe the infant interacting with the toys. Ask yourself, "Is the infant sorting the cars by color?"

4. Suggest that the infant sort the cars. Say, for example:
   "Can you put the blue cars in the blue bowl?"
   "Can you divide the cars by color?"
5. Provide positive reinforcement for attempts or accomplishments. Comments include:
   "Tory, you did it. You put a red car in the red bowl."
   "You are sorting the cars."

☀ Highlighting Development

The development of a child's receptive and expressive language skills occurs at different rates. Receptive language or comprehension skills occur prior to expressive language skills, the ability to speak. Therefore, when describing the child's actions, you are building connections between actions and the spoken word. Infants may be able to sort by category; however, at this time they cannot tell us what they are doing or have done.

VARIATION:

♡ Use other objects for sorting.

ADDITIONAL INFORMATION:

♡ Avoid pushing the infants to sort items, even though they may exhibit this skill very early on. Suggest that they sort, but encourage free exploration of the materials.

10 to 12 months

A Visitor Comes

COGNITIVE

Child's Developmental Goals

✓ To distinguish strangers from familiar caregivers

✓ To cope with stranger anxiety

MATERIALS:

None

PREPARATION:

♡ If you know a visitor is coming, schedule his arrival after the child is well rested and fed.

NURTURING STRATEGIES:

1. When a stranger enters the room, greet the individual by saying:
    "Hello, Tres. How are you?"

2. Move closer to whomever may be experiencing stranger anxiety while saying in a calm, soothing voice:
    "Tres came to visit today."

3. If the child is becoming upset by the visitor's presence, talk about this so that both the visitor and the child understand it. Say, for example:
    "You don't remember Tres, do you? Tres is my friend. He visits us sometimes."

4. Your voice can be a tool for helping the child calm down. In addition, use your knowledge of the child when deciding on soothing techniques. Comments to make include:
    "Would you like to hold your ducky? It helps you to feel better."
    "Would you like me to rub your back? Rubbing helps you to calm down."

5. If the visitor seems upset by the child's reaction, explain that this is normal behavior for children this age.

☀ Highlighting Development

Once children begin grasping the concept of object permanence, they become frightened of unfamiliar faces. Typically this reaction occurs between 9 months and 15 months of age. After this period, the distress gradually weakens. Throughout this process, adults need to model and foster the development of successful coping skills to assist the child.

VARIATION:

♡ Slowly introduce children to adult strangers by taking walks in the community, taking them shopping, etc.

ADDITIONAL INFORMATION:

♡ Anticipate the child's reaction to strangers and be prepared to offer assistance to reduce anxiety.

Social Development

♡

TEN to TWELVE MONTHS

All about Me

SOCIAL

Child's Developmental Goals

✓ To recognize picture of self

✓ To recognize pictures of friends or family members

MATERIALS:

☐ Camera and film

☐ Tape

☐ Piece of paper with tree drawn on it

☐ Pictures of friends and family members, if available

PREPARATION:

♡ Take pictures of the child. If you are caring for more than one child, also take their pictures.

♡ Tape the pictures on the tree figure drawn on the piece of paper. Put the paper on a wall or bulletin board.

NURTURING STRATEGIES:

1. When a child observes the pictures, join the infant.
2. Watch the infant looking at or touching the pictures. It is typical for infants to try to remove the pictures. If you don't want the pictures removed, see the Variations section.
3. Talk to the infant about the pictures. For example, say:
   "Georgia, these are the children and teachers in this class."
4. Encourage the infant to find the picture of herself by asking:
   "Where is Georgia?"

5. Encourage the child to point to the picture by saying:
   "Point to the picture. Show me your picture."
6. Provide positive reinforcement for attempts or accomplishments. Comments might include:
   "Georgia, yes! That's you. You were eating in that picture."
   "You did it! You found your picture."
7. Repeat steps 4 to 6 by asking the child to find pictures of family members, if available.

☀ Highlighting Development

Gradually, children begin to recognize familiar people and objects in their world. When shown a photograph and people or objects are named, they will point to them. They will also use pointing to communicate their interest or to show recognition.

VARIATION:

♡ If desired, cover the paper with clear self-adhesive paper so that the pictures can be touched but not removed or damaged.

ADDITIONAL INFORMATION:

♡ Although infants are unable to recognize themselves in the mirror, they are beginning to recognize themselves in photographs. To develop a positive self-identity, activities like this are important.

10 to 12 months

Playing in the Sand

Child's Developmental Goals

✓ To join a sibling or peer in play

✓ To play beside a sibling or peer

MATERIALS:

❑ A set of sand toys, including a bucket, scoop, and sieve, for each child you may be supervising

PREPARATION:

♡ Display the sand toys so they attract the infants' attention and suggest what materials belong to each child.

NURTURING STRATEGIES:

1. When a child chooses to play with the sand toys, move closer.
2. Observe the infant interacting/experimenting with the toys.
3. If possible, encourage another infant to join the first child in the sandbox by saying:
   "Loren, look at the sand toys. Would you like to dig?"
4. If the second child joins the area, comment on how the children are doing the same thing. To illustrate, say:
   "You two are both playing in the sand. Loren is digging and Jaden is filling the bucket."
   "You are both working in the sand area."
   "Loren is playing in the same area as Jaden."
5. If a sibling or peer is not available, join the activity.

Highlighting Development

Before learning to play with others, infants learn to play beside them. This is called parallel play. When engaged in parallel play, infants use similar materials as their playmates but have no verbal or visual interaction.

VARIATIONS:

♡ Use sand toys indoors in a plastic swimming pool or sensory table.

♡ Moisten the sand slightly to provide the children with another experience.

ADDITIONAL INFORMATION:

♡ Be proactive and introduce identical sets of materials. This reduces the potential for conflicts and makes conflicts that occur easier to solve. To illustrate, if a child takes another's scoop, say, "Here is your scoop."

♡ Sand play provides an opportunity for exploring different textures.

 Check the sand area for hazardous items such as broken glass or animal waste.

10 to 12 months

A Book about Me

SOCIAL

Child's Developmental Goals

✓ To develop a positive self-identity

✓ To recognize self in a photograph

MATERIALS:

❑ Camera and film

❑ Marker

❑ Construction paper

❑ Hole punch

❑ Yarn

❑ Glue

PREPARATION:

♡ Take and develop pictures of the child.

♡ Make a book of the child. To do this, cut the construction paper about 2 inches bigger than the photograph on all sides. To illustrate, if you have a 3-by-5-inch photo, cut the paper into 5-by-7-inch pieces. Cut a piece of paper for each picture. If possible, construct the covers from a heavier stock of paper. Glue one photograph on each page and allow to dry. Collate the pages of the book and the covers. Punch five to seven holes in the left-hand side of the book. Using yarn, lace the holes to bind the book, securing it with knots at both ends. Print "A Book about [child's name]" on the front cover and "The End" in the inside of the back cover.

NURTURING STRATEGIES:

1. Before nap time, place the book near the infant's crib or cot.
2. Read the book to the child before nap time. If the child likes to rock, read while rocking. If lying down is preferred, place the infant in the crib and rub the child's stomach while reading.

3. While reading the story, point to the pictures and say: "Who's this?"
4. Provide positive reinforcement for attempts and accomplishments. For example, say: "Yes, that is a picture of you. That is Corey."
5. Describe the pictures, pointing out activities the infant engages in. To illustrate, you may say: "Here you are pushing a truck. You like to push trucks and say 'voom, voom.'" "It is nap time in this picture. You are hugging your baby and falling asleep. Just like now."
6. If the infant appears interested, read the story again.

☀ Highlighting Development

Infants can recognize pictures of themselves even though they are unable to recognize themselves in a mirror. Self-recognition refers to the perception of being a separate person, distinct from other people and objects in the surrounding environment. This process begins as early as the first few months of life but typically takes two years to fully develop. When provided with pictures or videotapes of their behavior, 9- to 12-month-old infants play peekaboo with their image (Berk, 1997).

VARIATIONS:

♡ Look at books of the infant's family, favorite toys, etc.

♡ Prepare books using pictures from toy catalogs.

ADDITIONAL INFORMATION:

♡ Use large, color photographs whenever possible.

♡ Books can be prepared for "My Favorite Toys," "My Friends," "My First Year of Life," "My Pets," etc.

Washing Babies

Child's Developmental Goals

✓ To begin to distinguish boys from girls

✓ To practice prosocial skills

MATERIALS:

☐ 1 large plastic quilt box

☐ 1 large towel

☐ Vinyl tablecloth

☐ Anatomically correct, multiethnic female and male doll

☐ 1 washcloth

☐ Smock or dry clothes

PREPARATION:

♡ Select and clear an area that can be constantly supervised. Then spread out the tablecloth.

♡ Fill the quilt box with 1 to 2 inches of warm water. Place the container on the tablecloth. Set both baby dolls inside. Place a washcloth on the edge of the container and place the towel on the tablecloth beside the container.

♡ If more than one child participates, individual materials should be provided for each.

NURTURING STRATEGIES:

1. When the child selects the activity, help the infant put on a smock. While introducing the activity, say, for example:
   "Eric, we are going to play in water. You can wash the baby."

2. Observe the infant's behavior with the baby. Encourage the infant to be gentle with the baby by saying:
   "Gently wash her face. She doesn't like water in her eyes."
   "You are washing his toes. Wash gently."

3. Help the child notice the differences in the ways the dolls look. For example, talk about the fact that one doll is female and one is a male. Also, discuss the differences in skin tones. Connect the doll's characteristics with the child's or family members'. To illustrate, say:
   "Eric, you have dark curly hair just like the doll."
   "This doll is a boy. You are also a boy."

4. Once the baby is washed, encourage the infant to dry it using the towel. In addition, you can suggest holding or cuddling the doll.

5. Reinforcing the infant's behaviors may promote the understanding of how to care for another. Comments may include:
   "Eric, you are taking care of the baby."
   "The baby was cold, so you're drying it."

☀ Highlighting Development

Infants this age are beginning to notice some basic biological differences between females and males. Using the correct language to label body parts is important. However, reinforce that there are more similarities than differences between the sexes.

VARIATION:

♡ To assist in developing body awareness, label the doll's parts. Begin with the most obvious such as eyes, arms, toes, legs, mouth, ears, and nose.

ADDITIONAL INFORMATION:

♡ All children need to be taught and reinforced for engaging in positive caregiving behaviors. Caring for others is an important skill children need to acquire.

♡ Children find playing with water a pleasurable sensory experience for learning about their environment.

10 to 12 months

Putting On Lotion

SOCIAL

Child's Developmental Goals

✓ To increase body awareness

✓ To interact with an adult

MATERIALS:

❏ Hand lotion with a pump dispenser

PREPARATION:

♡ Have the lotion in a convenient location, preferably on or near the sink.

NURTURING STRATEGIES:

1. After changing the infant's diaper, you and the infant need to wash your hands.

2. After washing your hands, encourage the infant to apply lotion. Say, for example:
   "Washing makes your hands dry. Would you like some lotion? Lotion keeps our hands soft."
   If the child responds "no," assist her in finding an activity. If the child responds "yes," retrieve the bottle of lotion.

3. Model dispensing the lotion. Connect your actions with words by saying, for example:
   "One push of lotion. Rub, rub, rub. I'm rubbing my hands together."

4. Encourage the infant to hold out her hands while dispensing lotion. Then say:
   "Rub your hands together. Spread out the lotion. Rub your fingers together!"

5. If necessary, reinforce your words with actions by rubbing the lotion on the child's hands while commenting:
   "Rub, rub, rub. I'm rubbing the lotion on your hands."

6. Providing positive reinforcement may encourage the infant to apply the lotion independently the next time. Comments to make include:
   "You rubbed on the lotion. Now your hands are soft."
   "We worked together to put lotion on your hands."

☀ Highlighting Development

An infant at this stage of development should be able to demonstrate knowledge of body parts. Recognition will be typically demonstrated through gestures such as pointing or showing. Labeling body parts throughout the first year of life assists children in developing this skill.

VARIATION:

♡ Encourage the infant to push the lotion lever independently.

ADDITIONAL INFORMATION:

♡ Always purchase nonfragrant, hypoallergenic lotion.

 Observe the infant carefully to make sure the lotion is not consumed orally. Avoid introducing this activity to children who suck their hands or fingers.

10 to 12 months

Caring for Babies

Child's Developmental Goals

✓ To practice prosocial skills

✓ To play beside another child, if possible

MATERIALS:

❑ 2 anatomically correct, multiethnic female and male dolls

❑ 2 bottles

PREPARATION:

♡ Clear space on a child-size shelf for the dolls. Set the dolls on the shelf.

NURTURING STRATEGIES:

1. When a child begins interacting with the doll, observe the infant's behavior. Notice how the infant is caring for the doll.

2. Suggest new or different ways to care for the doll. For example, say:
   "Is the baby hungry? Does he need a bottle?"
   "Maybe the baby would like to rock in the rocking chair."
   "Would the baby like to go for a walk around the room?"

3. If another child is present, encourage playing with the dolls. To illustrate, say:
   "Jonah, would you like to feed this baby? She's hungry."
   "Hector, here is a baby for you."

4. If other children are present, discuss how the two children are playing with similar toys. Comments may include:
   "Charlene and Hector are both playing with dolls."
   "Jonah and Catherine are both feeding the babies."

5. Provide positive reinforcement for engaging in caregiving behaviors. For example, comment:
   "You are hugging the baby gently."
   "You help your baby. Your baby stopped crying."

☀ Highlighting Development

Children need to learn prosocial behavior, which includes acts of kindness toward others. These behaviors include helping, sharing, and cooperating. Examples include verbally and physically comforting others, cooperating at play and cleanup, sharing materials, showing concern, and sharing affection (Herr, 1998). Playing and caring for dolls can foster prosocial behavior.

VARIATION:

♡ Providing stuffed animals or puppets may also encourage caregiving behaviors.

ADDITIONAL INFORMATION:

♡ All children need to be taught how to care for others. These skills are the basis for future social skills such as empathy and perspective taking. All children, regardless of gender, need these skills.

♡ Whenever possible in guiding young children, use suggestions more than commands. Young children respond more positively to suggestions.

10 to 12 months

Chalk Scribbling

SOCIAL

Child's Developmental Goals

✓ To play parallel to another child

✓ To engage in a conversation with another person

MATERIALS:

❑ 1 chalk set containing different colored pieces per child

❑ Nonbreakable container

PREPARATION:

♡ Select a section of the sidewalk out of the normal traffic path.

♡ Then place a container of chalk in the designated area. If other children join the activity, position them so there is working space.

NURTURING STRATEGIES:

1. To encourage chalk scribbling, sit by one of the containers. Your presence may gain the child's attention.

2. As the infant begins scribbling on the sidewalk, describe the child's actions. Comments to make include:
   "Isabel, you're making a long line with the red chalk."
   "Circles. You're drawing yellow circles."
   "Round and around your arm is going."

3. To engage the infant in conversation, ask questions. Your discussion may include events happening now, in the recent past, or in the near future. For example, say:
   "You like drawing."
   "You are making large markings."
   "We'll have a snack when we go inside. Would you like apples or oranges?"

4. Always provide the child with uninterrupted working time. Respond to vocalizations with positive nonverbal and verbal reinforcement. For example, nod your head and smile while saying:
   "Wow! I didn't know that. Tell me more."
   "Really! We'll have to make that snack."

5. If another child is present and joins the activity, provide a welcome by saying:
   "Would you like to draw with Isabel?"

6. Allow the children to work in silence together.

7. Comment on how the infants are using the same space and materials. Comments might include:
   "Isabel and Roslyn, you are both drawing with chalk. You are making a large picture."
   "Isabel is making big circles. Roslyn, you are making small circles. You're both drawing circles."

☀ Highlighting Development

First words tend to represent favorite people, objects that move, and familiar actions. Mostly children at this stage of development will use only one or two words to communicate. Later they will learn how to form sentences by forming a series of words. To understand the message they are communicating, observe their body language and listen to their vocalization.

VARIATION:

♡ This activity could be introduced indoors at a child–size table or coffee table. Cover the table with paper and provide the chalk.

ADDITIONAL INFORMATION:

♡ Your understanding of the conversation will depend on the infant's language skills. The social aspects of conversation are what is important rather than understanding the vocalizations.

10 to 12 months

Emotional Development

♡

TEN to TWELVE MONTHS

Coming in from Outside

Child's Developmental Goals

✓ To comply with a caregiver's request
✓ To assist in dressing self

MATERIALS:

❏ Children's clothing with large fasteners

PREPARATION:

♡ Dress the child with clothing containing large fasteners.

NURTURING STRATEGIES:

1. After coming in from outside, talk about what the infant needs to do before beginning to play. To illustrate, state:
   "Porter, you need to take off your coat. Then hang it up."
2. If necessary, assist the infant in unfastening the coat. Encourage the infant to help remove the coat by making comments such as:
   "Porter, pull them apart. Pull the snaps apart."
3. Reinforcing your words with actions may be necessary. If needed, open a snap and then encourage the infant to continue.
4. Provide positive reinforcement for attempts or accomplishments. To illustrate, say:
   "Thank you for helping, Porter."
   "What a helper! You opened your coat."
5. Once the coat is removed, say:
   "I am going to hang up your coat."

☀ Highlighting Development

Infants need lots of time to practice new skills. Being impatient or verbally pushing the child to work faster may result in the child refusing to help. Try fostering independence by being warm, nurturing, and patient when infants are learning or practicing these new skills. Always give the child the minimum amount of help, which will provide the maximum opportunity for independence.

VARIATION:

♡ Elicit the child's help when putting on the coat.

ADDITIONAL INFORMATION:

♡ Dressing can be a time-consuming and frustrating experience for an infant. Therefore, observe closely.
♡ If purchasing clothing for young children, select garments with fasteners that are large and, therefore, easy to manipulate.
♡ When the children's eye-hand and motor skills improve, they can use their fingers and hands to assist in dressing.

10 to 12 months

Pudding Time

Child's Developmental Goals

✓ To feed self using a spoon

✓ To express the emotion of excitement

MATERIALS:

☐ High chair or snack table

☐ Unbreakable bowls

☐ Spoon

☐ Bibs

PREPARATION:

♡ Prepare pudding from a mix or favorite recipe. Place the pudding in a small unbreakable bowl. Keep pudding refrigerated until snack time.

NURTURING STRATEGIES:

1. Before snack, warn the child that a transition is about to occur by saying:
   "It is almost snack time. We will need to wash our hands."

2. Before snack, bring out the pudding and place it out of reach.

3. Tell the child that it is time to go to the bathroom and wash hands. Assisting the child in this entire process will probably be necessary.

4. Help the child into a high chair or a seat at the snack table. To promote independence, offer the child a choice of two bibs. If needed, put the bib on the child.

5. Tell the children what is for snack by saying:
   "Today we have pudding for snack. You can eat it with a spoon."

6. Give the child a bowl and spoon.

7. Encourage the infant to use the spoon. Comments include:
   "Use your spoon."
   "Bring the pudding to your mouth with the spoon."

8. Providing positive reinforcement for attempts and accomplishments may result in the infant engaging in the behaviors again. For example, say:
   "Oh, it fell off. Try again."
   "You are working hard to use that spoon."

9. Comment on the infant's facial expressions, especially when the spoon reaches the mouth. To illustrate, say:
   "You are smiling. You must be excited about using the spoon."
   "You look excited. Is the pudding good?"

☀ Highlighting Development

At this stage, interest in self-feeding typically begins. Adults often have to assist the children in this process by helping them fill their spoon. Observe their manipulation of the eating tools. Because they lack coordination, they often turn the spoon before it reaches their mouths. Thus, the food on the spoon is dumped.

VARIATION:

♡ Other nutritious snacks such as applesauce or yogurt help the infant learn to use a spoon.

ADDITIONAL INFORMATION:

♡ Eating with a spoon can be a very frustrating experience. Often for infants, all the food falls off before it gets to the mouth! Therefore, encourage them to use the spoon but also discuss how using fingers can be efficient.

♡ Young children need to wear bibs because spilling occurs often.

 To avoid injuries caused by slipping, spilled food needs to be wiped up immediately.

10 to 12 months

Playing a Song

Child's Developmental Goals

✓ To express feelings through music

✓ To initiate play with an adult

MATERIALS:

❑ 2 to 3 empty oatmeal or similar containers with lids

PREPARATION:

♡ Clean oatmeal containers and lids. Clear an area and place the containers where the child can view them.

NURTURING STRATEGIES:

1. When an infant chooses a container, observe the behavior.
2. If the infant initiates play with you by babbling or gazing, position yourself beside the child.
3. Describe the child's actions with the container. To illustrate, say:
   "Zoë, you're hitting the lid with your fingers."
   "You're using your palms to make music."
4. If a song comes to mind, sing it while the infant hits the drum.
5. If the infant seems interested in continuing, join the activity.
6. Imitate the infant's behaviors with the drum while commenting:
   "Zoë, look at me. I'm doing what you're doing."

7. Provide positive reinforcement for expressing feelings through music. Comment on the child's feelings at the time. Examples of comments include:
   "Zoë, you are playing a happy tune."
   "You are angry. You're hitting the drums very hard."

☀ Highlighting Development

Music can be used to help infants express their emotions. The role of the adult includes labeling the child's emotional expressions. Words to use include *happy, sad, excited, frustrated,* and *angry.*

VARIATIONS:

♡ Use other food containers such as nonbreakable peanut or some coffee containers. Listen. You will find that the sound generally varies with the size of the container.

♡ Choose a song in advance to accompany the drum.

ADDITIONAL INFORMATION:

♡ Infants enjoy making noise. At this stage, they have learned the principle of cause and effect. Consequently, providing them with appropriate outlets promotes independent play.

10 to 12 months

Getting Dressed

Child's Developmental Goals

✓ To increase knowledge of self-help skills

✓ To express happiness through clapping

MATERIALS:

☐ Cardboard book about dressing, such as *My Clothes* by Sian Tucker

PREPARATION:

♡ Recognize the child's readiness and interest in learning self-help skills.

♡ Place the book in an area that is easily accessible.

NURTURING STRATEGIES:

1. Gain the infant's attention by stating that you have a special book to read. See if the infant is interested in sitting on your lap. To illustrate, say:
   "Timothy, I have a special book about getting dressed. Would you like to sit in my lap while I read it?"

2. Begin reading the book. While pointing to each article of clothing, name it. Ask the child to point to a corresponding article of clothing on his body. For example, ask:
   "Where is your shirt?"
   "Where are my shoes?"

3. Provide positive reinforcement for attempts and accomplishments. Comments include:
   "Timothy, yes. That is your shirt."
   "Excellent!"
   "You are very good at this!"
   In addition, model clapping behaviors to show your excitement.

4. Discuss the similarities and differences in colors and styles of the infant's and your clothing. To illustrate, comment by saying:
   "Timothy, your shirt has buttons and mine has a zipper."
   "Your shoes are brown and mine are blue."
   "They are just like the ones in the book. You both have brown shoes."

5. If the infant shows interest, read the book again.

☀ Highlighting Development

Creating a stimulating environment for the infant is important. However, constant adult-child interaction can cause overstimulation and, therefore, stress. Observe the infants' signals. When infants become irritated, reduce the level of interaction. Like adults, children also need time to themselves.

VARIATION:

♡ To foster turn-taking skills, after you verbally identify and point to an article of clothing, encourage the child to repeat your behavior.

ADDITIONAL INFORMATION:

♡ For children to engage in self-help skills, they need to develop a working vocabulary. You can promote this development by providing a language-rich environment.

♡ Children at this stage typically use their two hands together symmetrically while clapping. When this occurs, both sides of the body are working together making the same motion at the same time.

10 to 12 months

"I Know an Old Turtle"

EMOTIONAL

Child's Developmental Goals

✓ To laugh in response to something funny

✓ To initiate playing with an adult

MATERIALS:

❑ Index card

❑ Felt-tip marker

PREPARATION:

♡ If desired, write out the words to the finger play on the index card.

NURTURING STRATEGIES:

1. When the infant approaches you, respond to the child's verbal and nonverbal cues. For example, say:
   "Do you want to play, Rory?" or
   "Well, hello Rory. Let's play."

2. Invite the child to sing a finger play with you by commenting:
   "You liked the finger play we did yesterday. Let's do it again."

3. Sing the finger play while performing the motions:

   ♫ I know an old turtle (fist)

   ♫ Who lives in a box (place fist on palm of other hand)

   ♫ Who swam in the puddles (swim fingers)

   ♫ And climbed on the rocks. (climb fingers upward)

   ♫ She snapped at a minnow (clap hands)

   ♫ She snapped at a flea (clap hands)

   ♫ She snapped at a mosquito (clap hands)

   ♫ She snapped at me! (clap hands)

   ♫ She caught the minnow (clap hands with arms extended, bring toward body)

   ♫ She caught the flea (clap hands with arms extended, bring toward body)

   ♫ She caught the mosquito (clap hands with arms extended, bring toward body)

   ♫ But she didn't catch me! (smile while shaking head no)

4. Respond to the infant's reactions to the finger play by describing what you observed. Comments to make include:
   "What a laugh. You like this finger play."
   "You smiled while clapping your hands. I think you like this song."

5. If the child seems interested, sing the finger play again.

☀ Highlighting Development

With familiar people, one-year-old children typically are friendly and social. At this stage of development, you need to continue playing, cuddling, hugging, rocking, singing, and talking to them. Through these actions, you are teaching children that they are loved, valued, and respected.

VARIATIONS:

♡ Substitute people or family names for bugs in the song.

♡ Sing a favorite song.

ADDITIONAL INFORMATION:

♡ Infants will often initiate contact with you. It is often difficult to understand their intentions. Do they want something specific or just your attention? Be prepared by having some finger plays or songs memorized for these occasions.

10 to 12 months

Solving Problems

Child's Developmental Goals

✓ To express emotions, such as anger

✓ To follow a caregiver's request or suggestion

MATERIALS:

☐ Pull toy

PREPARATION:

♡ Place the pull toy on a flat, smooth surface outdoors.

NURTURING STRATEGIES:

1. Observe the child interacting with a pull toy. When the pull toy falls over, the child may continue pulling but become frustrated and cry.
2. Walk over to the child and describe what you see. To illustrate, say:
   "Len, you are having trouble with the pull toy. You are crying because it won't work."
3. Ask the child a question to assist with the problem solving. For example, ask:
   "Is the pull toy working?"
4. If the child responds "no," respond by saying:
   "Len, set the toy on its wheels."
   If the child responds by saying "yes," then say:
   "Len, try it on the sidewalk."
5. When the child successfully pulls the toy on the sidewalk, provide positive reinforcement. Comments include:
   "You did it! You solved the problem! Now the toy works."
   "You figured out how to make the pull toy work."

☀ Highlighting Development

Solving problems for infants fosters dependence rather than independence. Providing hints or suggestions allows them to discover the solution to the problems on their own, thereby promoting independence as well as positive self-esteem.

VARIATION:

♡ Note other sources of frustration for the child. Provide assistance and encouragement to allow the child to solve the problem.

ADDITIONAL INFORMATION:

♡ Observe the child and note when he is frustrated. Allow the infant time to experiment with possible solutions before offering assistance. This gives the child an opportunity to grow in independence.

♡ Provide the minimum amount of help to allow the infant the maximum learning experience.

♡ Pull toys are excellent for encouraging movement. They hold the child's attention while she is practicing walking. As they physically control a pull toy, children learn stop, go, and to change directions. Observe the child with the pull toy. With practice and experimentation, the child's interactions will become more refined.

10 to 12 months

Family Tree

Child's Developmental Goals

✓ To express excitement
✓ To clap when proud of self

MATERIALS:

❑ Pictures of the infant, the infant's family members, and pets
❑ Large sheet of paper

PREPARATION:

♡ Tape the pictures on a large piece of paper. Then tape the entire piece of paper onto a wall at the child's eye level. In a home environment, the pictures may be attached to the refrigerator or bulletin board, if desired.

NURTURING STRATEGIES:

1. When a child moves close to the pictures, join the infant.
2. Observe the infant looking at or touching the pictures. Typical behaviors include pointing, touching, and attempting to remove the pictures. This is normal behavior and should be encouraged.
3. Discuss the pictures with the infant. For example:
   "Janna, this is your picture. Look."
   "Here is your family."
4. Reinforce the infant's attempts and accomplishments. Say, for example:
   "You are excited! You're pointing to your grandma."
   "You did it! You pointed to your dog."

5. Model clapping as a way to show pride. For example, when the infant points to her family, clap while saying:
   "Janna, you should be proud. You found your daddy."

☀ Highlighting Development

At least two areas of development must be working at the same time for this experience to be successful. First, the infant must demonstrate the ability to retrieve information stored in her long-term memory by recognizing a familiar face. This recognition, then, results in an emotional reaction such as happiness.

VARIATIONS:

♡ To allow the infant repeated exposure, preserve the collage of pictures. Cover the entire paper in a clear, self-adhesive laminate so that the pictures can be touched but not damaged or removed.
♡ Extend the activity by cutting pictures from magazines, catalogs, and calendars of animals, transportation vehicles, and clothing to create concept pictures.

ADDITIONAL INFORMATION:

♡ Changing the pictures over time will create interest. Moreover, it depicts changes in the child's and family's development.

Promoting Optimal Development in Toddlers

THIRTEEN to EIGHTEEN MONTHS

NINETEEN to TWENTY-FOUR MONTHS

TWENTY-FIVE to THIRTY MONTHS

THIRTY-ONE to THIRTY-SIX MONTHS

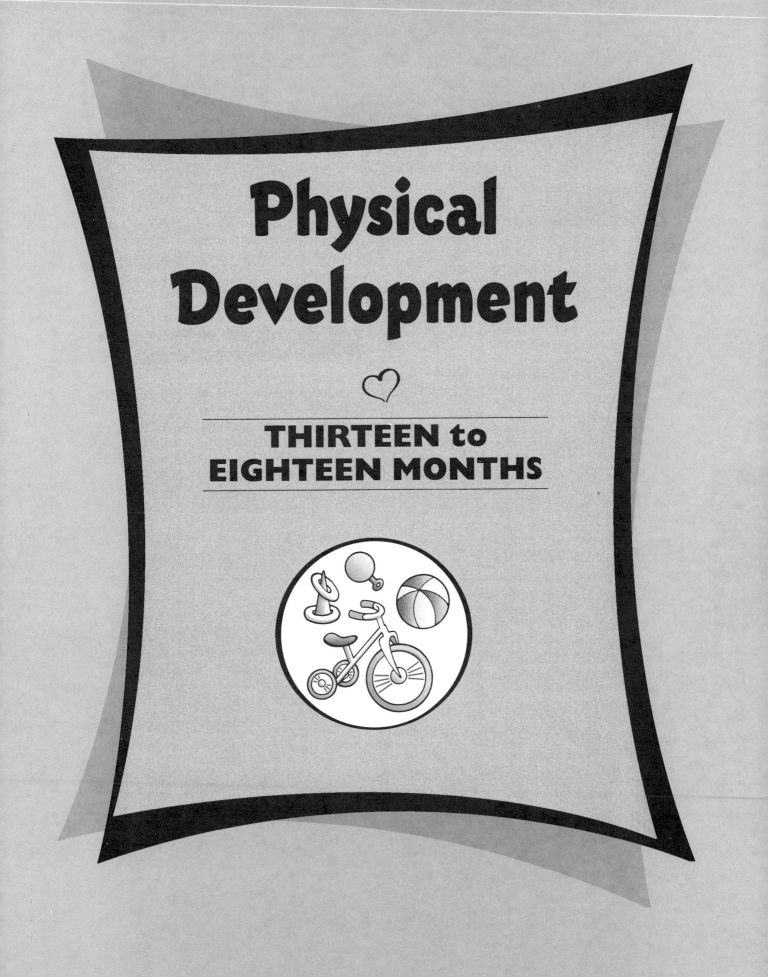

Physical Development

♡

___

THIRTEEN to EIGHTEEN MONTHS

Teddy Bear Push

PHYSICAL

Child's Developmental Goals

✓ To improve balancing skills

✓ To continue developing eye-hand coordination skills

MATERIALS:

❑ 2 eight-foot pieces of wool yarn

❑ 2 teddy bears

PREPARATION:

♡ Attach the teddy bear to a sturdy structure. To do so, tie one end of each piece of yarn around an arm of one teddy bear. Wrap the opposite ends of the yarn around the structure. Secure the yarn and adjust the height of the bear so that it can be easily reached by the toddler. Lay the other teddy bear on the ground near the structure.

NURTURING STRATEGIES:

1. When a child selects the activity, observe closely.
2. If the infant is pulling rather than pushing the bear, redirect the child's attention by saying:
   "Johannes, push it like a swing."
   "Move the teddy bear back and forth. Use your hands."
3. Talk about the skills this activity requires while the infant is working. Comments include:
   "Johannes, it is hard to keep your balance."
   "You are pushing with your hands while walking forward."
   "Move back so the teddy bear won't knock you off balance."
4. Providing positive reinforcement may help the toddler develop a positive self-identity. Comments include:
   "Johannes, you worked hard to push the teddy bear."
   "You are pushing the teddy bear high."
   "You are good at keeping your balance."

5. The toddler may wish to carry the teddy bear. If so, point out the other teddy bear and suggest playing with it. Comments to say include:
   "Johannes, here is a teddy bear that you can carry around."
   "I have another teddy bear over here. You can carry this one."

☀ Highlighting Development

The fundamental motor skills infants develop during the first year of life continue to be refined during the second year. Children use their eyes to provide feedback on the use of their hands. During this process, children monitor their movement. While this occurs, their brain sends messages for making adjustments to increase accuracy. Thus, their hand-eye coordination continues to improve.

VARIATION:

♡ For nonmobile children, lower the teddy bear so it may be reached from a sitting position.

ADDITIONAL INFORMATION:

♡ This activity will prove to be great fun for the child. Depending on the number of children, you may need to set up two teddy bear pushes to prevent problems that could arise from waiting or taking turns. Young toddlers have yet to master these skills.

Painting a Picture

Child's Developmental Goals

✓ To refine eye-hand coordination

✓ To practice motor coordination skills

MATERIALS:

❑ Easel

❑ Large sheets of easel paper

❑ Masking tape

❑ Newspaper

❑ Smock or painting shirt

❑ Drying rack

❑ Clothespins

❑ Short, thick paintbrushes

❑ Containers of red tempera paint

PREPARATION:

♡ Select a container and fill it one-third full with paint to prevent excessive cleanup. Place the brush inside the container.

♡ Cover the easel, if available, with newspapers and secure with masking tape.

♡ Attach the paper to the easel. If an easel is unavailable, tape the paper to a wall.

♡ Cover the floor with newspaper to make cleanup easier.

NURTURING STRATEGIES:

1. When a toddler chooses the area, assist with putting on a smock or paint shirt. Explain why you would like the covering worn. Comments include:
   "Devon, it will protect your clothes from the paint."
   "This will keep your clothes clean."
   However, avoid forcing the toddler to wear a smock.

2. Observe the child experimenting with the materials.

3. Guide the child to engage in appropriate behaviors by stating limits in a positive manner. To illustrate, say:
   "Devon, paint on the paper."
   "Use the paintbrush for painting."

4. Describe the toddler's actions in creating a picture. In other words, focus on the process of painting rather than the product. While pointing to the painting, say:
   "You are making long, red lines. They go from the top to the bottom."
   "You are making tiny, red dots."

☀ Highlighting Development

The child's fine motor skills are improving. Observe. The toddler now can pick up small objects between a forefinger and a thumb. As a result, the child's ability to pick up and examine toys and other objects has improved. Additionally, the child is beginning to gain control of tools such as a spoon, paintbrush, toothbrush, etc.

VARIATIONS:

♡ Paint at a child-size table or coffee table.

♡ Paint outdoors by attaching larger pieces of paper to a fence.

ADDITIONAL INFORMATION:

♡ When talking to the toddler, focus on the process rather than the product. This strategy will prevent the child from having to explain the artwork. At this stage, the child is interested in manipulating the tools and observing the reaction.

♡ Never force a child to wear a smock. Immediately change and rinse out the clothes if paint spills or splatters.

13 to 18 months

Stacking Blocks

PHYSICAL

Child's Developmental Goals

✓ To refine fine motor skills

✓ To improve eye-hand coordination skills

MATERIALS:

❑ Set of foam blocks

❑ Plastic container

PREPARATION:

♡ Separate the blocks so that you have two identical sets of blocks. Remove any blocks that are round. These blocks are too difficult to work with at first.

♡ Place the set of blocks in the container. Clear a spot on the floor and place the container there.

NURTURING STRATEGIES:

1. Observe the toddler's behavior when selecting the blocks.
2. Describe what the toddler is doing with the blocks. To illustrate, say:
   "Austin, you are lining up the squares."
   "You are filling up the container with the blocks."
3. Join the toddler by sitting on the floor. Position your body so that you can continue to observe any other children you may be supervising.
4. Continue conversing with the toddler regarding the interactions with the blocks.
5. In the meantime, model building a tower with the blocks.
6. Verbally describe what you did with the blocks. To illustrate, say:
   "Austin, I made a tower. I used three blocks."
   "I stacked two blocks on top of each other."

7. Encourage the toddler to stack the blocks in the same manner. Comments include:
   "Austin, stack your blocks like I did."
   "Can you do this? Stack the blocks."
8. Provide positive reinforcement for attempts or accomplishments. For example, say:
   "Austin, you did it! You stacked two blocks."
   "Oh, they fell over. Keep trying. You can do it."

☀ Highlighting Development

Although the toddler may use one hand more than the other, the child is developing skills using both. Now the toddler is beginning to enjoy activities such as stacking blocks that require the use of both hands. Typical behaviors include stacking the blocks into towers and then knocking them down. Observe the child's facial expression during this process. Some children revel in the delight of watching the blocks tumble.

VARIATION:

♡ Use small wooden blocks or just the square ones from a set of unit blocks.

ADDITIONAL INFORMATION:

♡ You must carefully select the blocks to give the children. Select square or rectangular blocks at first because they are easier to stack. Round blocks are too difficult to stack and should be added later. Therefore, removing the round blocks may prevent some frustration and promote a successful learning experience for toddlers.

13 to 18 months

Obstacle Course

Child's Developmental Goals

✓ To refine balancing skills

✓ To improve eye-foot coordination skills

MATERIALS:

❑ Ladder that can be laid flat

❑ Tunnel

PREPARATION:

♡ Select a flat, grassy area that can be constantly supervised. Clear this area of any movable equipment or debris. Place the tunnel and ladder in this area. Make sure that each piece of equipment is lying flat on the ground.

NURTURING STRATEGIES:

1. While preparing the child to go outside, talk about the new activity. To illustrate, say:
   "Zalika, you can crawl through a tunnel. Then, walk on a ladder."
   Use your voice as a tool for communicating enthusiasm.
2. Once outdoors, observe the toddler's behaviors with the equipment.
3. For safety reasons, only one child should be in the tunnel at a time. The number of children on the ladder will vary depending on its size. Clearly state and reinforce these limits as needed. Comments include:
   "One person at a time. The tunnel is made for one person."
   "Zalika, you can go next. Two people are already on the ladder."

4. If necessary, you may need to model walking between the rungs of the ladder. While modeling the behavior, reinforce your actions with words by saying, for example:
   "I'm walking on the grass between the ladder parts. This is tricky."
   "Walking between the ladder parts takes lots of balance."
5. Reinforce the toddler's attempts and accomplishments. Comments to make include:
   "You crawled through the tunnel."
   "What balance! You walked on the ladder."

☀ Highlighting Development

Children change physically as they grow. In the first 12 months of life, an infant increases in size by approximately 50 percent. To illustrate, a child who was 22 inches long at birth will be approximately 33 inches at one year. With increasing activity, toddlers' muscles are also becoming more developed. After walking for a few months, their stance changes. Their feet will begin pointing forward rather than being positioned outwardly to the sides of the body. However, even after beginning to walk, children may revert back to creeping when they need to get someplace quickly. Creeping is often faster for them.

VARIATION:

♡ If a tunnel is unavailable, drape a blanket over an object to create a tentlike structure.

 For safety purposes, carefully observe toddlers to make sure they walk on the grass between the rungs of the ladder. Walking directly on the ladder can cause toddlers to lose their balance or twist an ankle.

13 to 18 months

Fruit Puzzles

PHYSICAL

Child's Developmental Goals

✓ To reinforce the pincer grasp

✓ To continue developing fine muscle skills

MATERIALS:

❏ 2 wooden puzzles with knobs, if available

❏ Child-size table or coffee table

PREPARATION:

♡ Clean a child-size or coffee table and display the puzzles on it. Remove one piece from each puzzle and lay it on the table.

NURTURING STRATEGIES:

1. When a toddler is looking for an activity, direct the child to the table with the puzzles. Say, for example:
   "Paul, look at what is on the table. You can do a puzzle."

2. Show the toddler how to take out the pieces one by one. Discuss the puzzle pieces as the child removes them.

3. Replace the pieces and then encourage the child to repeat your actions. Use comments such as:
   "You are removing a piece of the puzzle."
   "Now you have taken out two pieces."

4. Verbally encourage the child when he is replacing the puzzle pieces. Comments include:
   "Paul, keep turning. That's where the piece goes."
   "That piece is round. Find the round place on the puzzle."

5. Providing positive reinforcement may help maintain the toddler's attention and may result in him spending more time with this activity. For example, comment:
   "Paul, that's it! Only one more piece. You are good at putting together puzzles."
   "All done! You are quick. Are you going to put together another puzzle?"

☀ Highlighting Development

As toddlers' hand-eye coordination skills improve, they are able to construct puzzles. In addition to promoting physical skills, puzzles can be used to promote language skills and concepts. For example, colors can be introduced and reviewed. In addition, spatial concepts such as above, below, in, and on can be taught.

VARIATIONS:

♡ Place the puzzles on the floor out of traffic paths.

♡ Introduce new puzzles for variety.

ADDITIONAL INFORMATION:

♡ Young toddlers need very simple puzzles that have knobs. They lack the fine muscle coordination skills to pick up puzzle pieces without knobs. In addition, children at this stage of development are most successful with three to five puzzle pieces. When children acquire the fine muscle skills, you can challenge them by providing puzzles with smaller knobs and more pieces.

Going Shopping

Child's Developmental Goals

✓ To refine balancing skills

✓ To improve coordination skills

MATERIALS:

❏ A child-size shopping cart, if available

❏ Multiethnic baby doll

❏ Construction paper

❏ Felt-tip marker

PREPARATION:

♡ Place a baby doll in the shopping cart. If introducing this activity in a center rather than a home setting, make a "cart return" sign.

♡ Hang the cart return sign on the wall and park the cart under it.

NURTURING STRATEGIES:

1. Observe the toddlers as they experiment with moving the cart.

2. You may need to set and reinforce limits specific to the use of a shopping cart. For example, you may need to remind the child to walk inside the area designated.

3. Encourage the child to take the baby shopping. Comments to make include:
   "Sasheen, your baby is crying. Do you need to buy some food?"
   "You are shopping with your baby. What are you going to buy at the toy store?"
   Note: Your comments should directly relate to the materials available in your area.

4. Reinforce the toddler's positive behaviors with the shopping carts by commenting:
   "You are slowly pushing your baby in the shopping cart."
   "Look at all you bought at the store. You've been busy."

5. When the toddler is finished with the shopping cart, encourage returning the cart to the "cart return" area. This will foster independence and respect for property. To illustrate, while pointing or moving toward that area, say:
   "The cart goes over here when you are done."
   "Help clean up the room. Put the shopping cart in the cart return area."

6. Thank the toddler for returning the cart.

☀ Highlighting Development

Activities that encourage large muscle exercise and refine whole-body coordination are of more interest to toddlers than activities that require small muscle coordination (Bukato & Daehler, 1992). Some activities of interest include pushing carts or cars; stacking or nesting large boxes; and, eventually, riding a toy or pulling a wagon.

VARIATION:

♡ Using the shopping cart outdoors will increase the challenge. Wheeled toys are difficult to push on grass, sand, or uneven surfaces.

ADDITIONAL INFORMATION:

♡ When stating limits, word them in a positive manner. In other words, highlight acceptable behaviors by saying:
   "Walk while pushing."
   "Push your cart slowly."

13 to 18 months

Building a Tower

PHYSICAL

Child's Developmental Goals

✓ To refine eye-hand coordination skills

✓ To continue developing large motor skills

MATERIALS:

❑ 4 to 5 boxes of similar size

PREPARATION:

♡ To prevent possible cutting or scratching, place tape over the edges and lid of the boxes. If desired, you can decorate the boxes by covering them with colored, self-adhesive paper.

♡ Clear and place the boxes in an open area where they will attract the toddler's attention.

NURTURING STRATEGIES:

1. Observe the toddler interacting and experimenting with the blocks.

2. Describe the toddler's actions. To illustrate, say:
   "Ismail, you are lining up the blocks."
   "You have stacked two blocks."

3. Encourage the toddler to build a tower. Suggestions include:
   "Can you put the blocks on top of each other?"
   "How tall can you build?"

4. Reinforcing your words with actions may be necessary. If so, while touching the block, say:
   "Ismail, put this block on top of this one."

5. Encourage the child to work with you to stack the blocks. Comment, for example:
   "Ismail, I can help. The box is heavy. Let's work together to move it."

6. Reinforce the toddler's efforts at building a tower and working with you. Comments to make include:
   "Ismail, you worked hard to build a tower! You used three boxes."
   "Your tower is three boxes high."

☀ Highlighting Development

Toddlers' bodies are top-heavy. As a result, they walk with their toes pointed outward and waddle from side to side. At the beginning of the process, they are slow in moving. Often they tumble over. However, balance improves as their bodies become less top-heavy. With maturity, their pace also increases.

VARIATION:

♡ Choose boxes of different sizes and shapes.

ADDITIONAL INFORMATION:

♡ Toddlers love to build and move things around. Providing lightweight boxes or containers may encourage such behaviors. Boxes from typing or copier paper are particularly effective for children this age because they are lightweight and sturdy. In addition, this activity fosters social skills by encouraging the child to interact with others.

Washing Hands

Child's Developmental Goals

✓ To learn to vigorously rub hands together

✓ To begin learning self-help skills for washing hands

MATERIALS:

❑ Liquid soap

❑ Disposable towels

❑ Poster with steps and pictures, if available or desired

❑ Sink

PREPARATION:

♡ If desired, make a poster with all of the steps for washing hands sequenced in the correct order. Include as many pictures or graphics as possible.

♡ Hang this poster at the toddler's eye level beside the sink.

♡ If you have more than one sink, make a poster for each.

♡ Review the handwashing steps:

1. Turn on water to a comfortable temperature.
2. Wet hands.
3. Apply liquid soap.
4. Vigorously rub hands together for at least 10 seconds.
5. Rinse the soap off the hands from the wrist to fingertips.
6. Dry hands.
7. Turn off water.

NURTURING STRATEGIES:

1. Take the toddler to the sink or bathroom.
2. Using the poster as a tool, verbally and physically guide the toddler through the steps. In other words, at each step, tell the toddler what to do. Begin by turning on the water. Reinforcing your words with actions may be necessary. If so, physically guide the toddler through the motion while verbally describing the action.

3. During the step of rubbing the hands together vigorously, sing the following song. Doing this may increase the time spent rubbing the hands together and, therefore, remove more germs.

   ♫ Wash, wash, wash your hands
   ♫ Wash them all day long
   ♫ Wash, wash, wash your hands
   ♫ While we sing this song.

4. Throughout the procedure, continue providing positive reinforcement. Comments include:
   "Sahara, you're really getting your hands clean."
   "What dry hands."

☀ Highlighting Development

Children need to develop the routine of washing their hands before eating and after having a diaper changed. During this stage of development, the coordination of their hands and fingers improves. This progress helps provide them with the necessary coordination needed to begin caring for their own bodies.

VARIATION:

♡ Make up your own song that varies with what steps the toddlers are doing such as "push, push, push the soap" while pushing the liquid soap dispenser down three times.

ADDITIONAL INFORMATION:

♡ Because toddlers are more stable when standing, they can now learn the proper procedures for washing their hands at a sink.

♡ Toddlers will be unable to follow all of these steps independently for some time but starting now will foster the development of positive skills and attitudes.

13 to 18 months

Climbing the Stairs

PHYSICAL

Child's Developmental Goals

✓ To practice walking up stairs
✓ To practice walking down stairs

MATERIALS:

❑ Commercially produced stairs with railing, if available
❑ Mat

PREPARATION:

♡ If a commercial staircase is available, select an area of the room that allows ease in supervision.

♡ Clear this area and spread out the mat. Place the stairs on the mat. This helps create a safe fall zone around the stairs. Without this equipment, stairs within a home can be used if carefully supervised.

NURTURING STRATEGIES:

1. When the toddler moves close to the stairs, join the child.

2. Observe the child working and provide physical assistance as necessary.

3. Provide positive reinforcement as often as possible while remaining honest about the toddler's abilities. Comments include:
   "Raj, you are holding on to the rail. That keeps you safe."
   "One foot, then the other foot. That's how you walk up stairs."

4. Set and maintain limits as necessary to protect the safety of the toddler. Say, for example:
   "Hold on to the railings. Hold on with both hands, Raj."
   If the child continues without holding on, it is time to state a logical consequence, such as:
   "No hold. No walk on stairs."
   If the child continues without holding on, physical removal from the stairs may be necessary. Enact the consequence while saying:
   "No hold. No walk on stairs."
   "No hold. No walk. You can try again later."

☼ Highlighting Development

Most children learn to walk at about one year of age. With their improved mobility, they are attracted to stairs; consequently, navigating stairs is an important skill. Note their mode of locomotion. First, children move one foot up to the step, and then they bring the second foot to the same step. Learning to walk up the stairs with alternating steps occurs later. Also, note that children learn walking up stairs before walking down.

VARIATION:

♡ Practice walking up and down real stairs having the child hold one of your hands while placing the other on the railing. This will encourage the child to use handrails. For safety purposes, provide lots of support and assistance.

ADDITIONAL INFORMATION:

♡ Due to developmental variations, some children will practice walking up the stairs while others practice creeping.

 For safety reasons, you should never leave a toddler unattended near the steps.

13 to 18 months

Table Painting

Child's Developmental Goals

✓ To continue developing fine muscle skills

✓ To learn through sensory exploration

✓ To experience cause and effect

MATERIALS:

❑ One color of nontoxic finger paint

❑ Child-size table or coffee table

❑ Spoon

❑ Paper towel

❑ Sponge

❑ Container

❑ Washable table covering, if needed

❑ Smocks, paint shirts, bibs, or aprons

PREPARATION:

♡ Clean and sanitize a child-size table or coffee table. If appropriate, place a spoonful of paint directly onto the table. Otherwise, lay down a washable table covering. Fill the container with lukewarm water and a sponge. Place the container so it is easily accessible.

NURTURING STRATEGIES:

1. Help the toddler put on a smock, paint shirt, apron, or bib. Then roll up the child's sleeves as necessary.

2. Help the toddler sit on a chair, if needed, and move it closer to the table. After this, introduce the activity by saying:
   "Chloe, you can paint on the table using your hands."
   "Move the paint around with your fingers."

3. Talk to the toddler about how the paint is being manipulated. Comments might include:
   "Chloe, you are painting."
   "You are pushing the paint with one finger."

4. To foster language development, introduce a new word that describes an action. You must know the toddler's vocabulary skills to do this. Repeat the

word several times while the child is working. For example, if the word is *squishing*, state:
"Chloe, you are squishing the paint. Squish, squish, squish. You are smiling. It must be fun to squish the paint."

5. Paint with the child. Discuss how each of you is using different and similar processes with the paint. For example, say:
   "Chloe, you are painting a picture. You are making circles while I am making lines."
   "We are friends. We are working together."

6. When the child is finished, wipe her hands with the paper towel. Then have the toddler finish washing off the paint at the sink.

☀ Highlighting Development

Finger painting is an activity that can stimulate the child's senses. It involves seeing and touching. In addition, the child experiences cause and effect. This occurs when the paint responds to movement of the fingers and hands, which work as application tools or brushes.

VARIATIONS:

♡ By placing a piece of paper over the paint on the table, you will create a reverse print. Display the toddler's work on the wall, refrigerator, or bulletin board.

♡ Place paint on the table only after child is ready to begin the activity.

♡ Substitute shaving cream for the paint.

ADDITIONAL INFORMATION:

♡ Keep a sponge handy for wiping up spills.

🚫 CAUTION Toddlers love to get messy and still place things in their mouths. Hence, close supervision is necessary to ensure that paint or shaven cream are not eaten or wiped into a child's eyes. Even if the paints are nontoxic, consuming the paint may cause an upset stomach.

13 to 18 months

Lining Up the Pins

PHYSICAL

Child's Developmental Goals

✓ To continue developing fine muscle coordination skills

✓ To refine pincer grasp

MATERIALS:

❑ Cardboard shoe box

❑ 10 peg clothespins

PREPARATION:

♡ Select and clear an area for this activity.

♡ If desired, cover the shoe box with self-adhesive paper. Place all but one clothespin in the box. Place the one remaining clothespin on the rim of the box. For the toddler, this will help by modeling the purpose of the activity.

NURTURING STRATEGIES:

1. Observe the toddler's behavior while engaging in the activity.

2. Position yourself near the child, allowing the toddler to work independently.

3. If the child initiates interaction, respond promptly. Likewise, respond promptly to sounds of distress with verbal support. Using your voice as a tool, communicate warmth and support. Comments might include:
   "Omar, the clothespin fell off. Put it back on."
   "You're working hard."

4. After the child has placed the clothespin on the rim of the box, model counting them while pointing to each pin. This not only connects your actions with words but also promotes the development of the mathematical concept of one- to-one correspondence.

5. Provide positive reinforcement when the child appears to be finishing up the activity. Comments include:
   "Omar, you worked hard at this activity."
   "You used all of the clothespins."

6. Encourage the toddler to return the materials to their original location. State, for example:
   "Place the box back on the table."

☀ Highlighting Development

Children need to learn responsibility for picking up their toys. Therefore, encourage them to clean up after they are finished playing. During this process, the children may need to be assisted both verbally and physically. Then, too, provide them with positive reinforcement so they develop responsibility and autonomy for continuing this behavior.

VARIATIONS:

♡ Use a round plastic container such as a gallon ice cream pail instead of the shoe box.

♡ When a toddler is ready for a new challenge, introduce the squeeze-type clothespins.

ADDITIONAL INFORMATION:

♡ Young toddlers lack the strength and fine muscle control to successfully manipulate the squeeze-type clothespins. In six to eight months, they may be able to master this skill.

13 to 18 months

Pushing the Activity Walker

Child's Developmental Goals

✓ To practice the locomotion skill of walking

✓ To continue practicing balance skills

MATERIALS:

❑ Activity walker

PREPARATION:

♡ Clear the floor of obstacles.

NURTURING STRATEGIES:

1. Observe the child's behavior with the activity walker. It may be necessary to set and maintain limits with this activity. To illustrate, say:
   "Hillary, walk while pushing the activity walker."
   "Walk around people."

2. If the activity walker gets blocked, help the toddler solve the problem. Comments include:
   "Hillary, pull the walker backward."
   "It is caught in the table. Walk backward."

3. Reinforcing your words with actions may be necessary. If so, while pulling the walker backward, say:
   "The walker is caught. Pulling it backward helps."

4. Provide positive reinforcement for using the toy properly. To illustrate, say:
   "Hillary, you are pushing the toy while walking."
   "Thank you for walking around the chair."

5. Encourage the toddler to return the walker to the wall when finished. For example, say:
   "Hillary, put the walker back by the wall."

☀ Highlighting Development

Shoes are unnecessary for babies who have not yet begun to walk. They can interfere with the growth of the feet and make balancing more difficult. Shoes reduce the ability of the children's toes to grip surfaces under their feet. However, children who are walking need comfortable, well-fitting shoes with nonskid soles to promote safety.

VARIATION:

♡ Use the walker in an outdoor area.

ADDITIONAL INFORMATION:

♡ This is a wonderful activity to use with children this age, who are enjoying their mobility skills. The activity provides them with confidence in their large muscle abilities and it also fosters their problem-solving skills.

13 to 18 months

"Open, Shut Them"

PHYSICAL

Child's Developmental Goals

✓ To coordinate hands in a clapping motion

✓ To imitate the adult's movements

MATERIALS:

❑ Poster board

❑ Felt-tip marker

PREPARATION:

♡ If you have the finger play memorized, no materials are needed. If you do not have the finger play memorized and are working with a group of children, make a poster with the words. This can serve as an effective teaching tool that adults can use for reinforcing this activity.

NURTURING STRATEGIES:

1. Slowly introduce the motions to "Open, Shut Them" two times. Notice who is imitating your motions.

   Open, shut them
   Open, shut them
   Open, shut them
   Give a little clap.

   Open, shut them
   Open, shut them
   Open, shut them
   Put them in your lap.

2. Introduce the finger play by saying:
   "Let's put some words to these actions."

3. Slowly recite the finger play. Share your enthusiasm by smiles, gestures, and the intonation of your voice.

4. Providing positive reinforcement may increase the toddler's desire to perform the actions. Comments include:
   "What a wonderful job! You learned a new finger play. I heard you clap!"

5. Repeat the finger play if the child seems interested.

☼ Highlighting Development

Clapping is a difficult skill for young children to master. Even though they may have been working on this skill for several months, they may be less than proficient. This skill requires not only eye-hand and bilateral coordination but also timing of movements.

VARIATION:

♡ As the children develop these motions, increase the number of verses. Refer to Appendix F for the entire finger play.

ADDITIONAL INFORMATION:

♡ If other children or siblings are present, encourage them to participate in the finger play activity.

♡ Observe the child to identify favorite finger plays and songs. Frequently repeat these.

13 to 18 months

Scooping Sand

Child's Developmental Goals

✓ To experience rough textures

✓ To refine fine muscle skills

MATERIALS:

❑ Plastic quilt box

❑ Clean sand

❑ Metal spoons

❑ 1-cup measuring cup

❑ ½-cup measuring cup

❑ Broom and dustpan or vacuum cleaner

PREPARATION:

♡ Place 1½ to 2 inches of sand in the quilt box. Place the spoons and measuring cups on the sand.

♡ Select an area that can be constantly supervised. Clear this space and lay out the vinyl tablecloth. Place the sandbox on the cloth.

♡ Keep a broom, dustpan, and vacuum cleaner in a convenient location.

NURTURING STRATEGIES:

1. When the child approaches the activity, state the basic limits. For example, say:
   "Jaron, the sand stays in the container."
   "Sand is for scooping."

2. Observe the toddler's handling of the tools.

3. If necessary, encourage the toddler to use the tools or handle them differently. Comments include:
   "Jaron, use the spoon to fill the cup.
   "Hold the cup by the handle. Use your thumb."

4. To promote both sensory awareness and language development, ask questions about how the sand feels. To illustrate, ask:
   "How does the sand feel?"

5. Continue the conversation by responding to the toddler's vocalizations and gestures. Use comments such as:
   "Jaron, that's right! The sand is rough."
   "The sand is bumpy."

6. Provide positive reinforcement to encourage the continuation of desirable behaviors. Comments include:
   "Jaron, you filled both cups. You used the spoon."
   "You are working hard. You've filled both cups."

☀ Highlighting Development

Young children find pleasure in sensory experiences such as sand or water play. These experiences encourage relaxation by the release of tension.

VARIATION:

♡ If the children are tall enough, place the container of sand on the top of a small table.

ADDITIONAL INFORMATION:

♡ Add a small amount of water to the sand. This makes the sand easier to handle and provides a new form of tactile stimulation.

13 to 18 months

Language and Communication Development

♡

THIRTEEN to EIGHTEEN MONTHS

Head and Shoulders

Child's Developmental Goals

✓ To increase receptive language skills

✓ To promote self-expression through spoken language

MATERIALS:

❑ Felt-tip marker

❑ Index card

PREPARATION:

♡ If needed, write the words to the action song on an index card and place it in your pocket.

NURTURING STRATEGIES:

1. Repeat this song spontaneously whenever a toddler appears to need a new experience.

2. Introduce the action song to the child by saying:
   "Jee-Eun, let's play a game. Show me where your head is."
   Pause. *"Great! Now show me where your knees are."*
   Help the toddler identify all the body parts in the song.

3. Begin singing the action song and modeling the actions. Touch each body part as you sing it:

   ♪ Head, shoulders, knees, and toes
   ♪ Knees and toes
   ♪ Eyes and ears and mouth and nose
   ♪ Head, shoulders, knees, and toes
   ♪ Knees and toes.

4. Encourage the child to join you in singing the action song. Comments include:
   "Jee-Eun, do it with me."
   "Let's do it together."

5. Provide positive reinforcement when the child verbally and physically joins you by participating in the song. To illustrate, say:
   "Jee-Eun, you were singing along! I heard you say the word 'toes'!"
   "You did all of the actions!"
   "Good for you."

6. Repeat the action song if the toddler seems interested.

☼ Highlighting Development

Most children start linking words to meaning by their first birthday. At this point, they build their vocabulary slowly. When they are about 18 months of age, the rate of acquiring words explodes (Cawley, 1997).

VARIATION:

♡ Repeat the action song, including other children or family members.

ADDITIONAL INFORMATION:

♡ When singing the song and modeling the actions, go very slowly, allowing the toddler to successfully participate.

♡ Increase the pace when the toddler is ready.

What Could It Be?

Child's Developmental Goals

✓ To associate sounds with the objects that make them

✓ To increase expressive language skills

MATERIALS:

❏ Tape recorder-player and blank cassette
❏ Photographs of objects that made sounds

PREPARATION:

♡ Record four or five communication sounds in the child's immediate environment such as the sound of a microwave buzzer. While recording, leave space between the sounds to allow time for the children to identify them. Then take photographs of the taped objects.

♡ If desired, mount the photographs on tagboard and cover with clear, self-adhesive paper to provide support and protection.

♡ Select an area for this activity that has a table and chairs. There also should be an electrical outlet nearby.

♡ To promote independent use of this center, label the play button with a green dot and the stop button with a red dot.

♡ Place the tape player and photographs on the table.

NURTURING STRATEGIES:

1. When a child appears interested in the activity, introduce it by saying, for example:
   "Akbar, we are going to play a game. Listen to the sounds. You can match the sound with the object in the photograph."

2. Assist the toddler in turning on the tape by saying:
   "Green means go. Press the green button."

3. Reinforcing your words with actions may be necessary. If so, press the green button while saying:
   "The tape is playing now."

4. After the first sound plays, ask the child:
   "Akbar, listen. What was that?"
   Direct the child's attention to the pictures on the table. To illustrate, say:
   "Which of these objects made the sound?"

5. If the next sound begins before the first sound is identified, stop the tape. Verbalize your actions. Comments include:
   "Akbar, I'm going to push the red button. That means stop. The tape will stop while you look for the source of the sound."

6. Assist the child by verbally labeling and describing the photographs. To illustrate, say:
   "This is the microwave. It heats our bottles. When it's done, it says 'beep, beep, beep.'"

7. Provide positive reinforcement if the toddler chooses the photograph that matches the sound on the tape. Use comments such as:
   "Akbar, you did it!"
   "Yes. The vacuum cleaner makes that noise!"

8. If the child does not identify the object, you need to continue with the game. To do this, suggest that the toddler turn on the tape.

☼ Highlighting Development

Children at this stage of development enjoy cause-and-effect relationships. Watch them. They enjoy turning the television or radio on and off. They also enjoy banging on objects to create sounds and splashing water. Therefore, the children may delight in identifying these taped sounds.

VARIATIONS:

♡ Repeat this activity with a small group of children.
♡ Increase the difficulty of the sounds when the child has identified the ones recorded on the first tape.

ADDITIONAL INFORMATION:

♡ Move out of the child's immediate environment by recording sounds such as a dog barking, a car horn, a train whistle, etc.

13 to 18 months

Our Families

Child's Developmental Goals

✓ To verbally identify family members

✓ To communicate excitement when identifying oneself in a photograph

MATERIALS:

❑ Family photographs
❑ Colored paper
❑ Yarn
❑ Marker

PREPARATION:

♡ Collect photographs of family members.

♡ Mount each photograph on a piece of colored paper. Write a caption for each photograph, being sure to include the names of all the people in the pictures. If desired, prepare a book of the pages by punching holes in the left-hand side of the paper and lacing with yarn or placing in a three-ring binder.

♡ Place the book in a convenient location for the child.

NURTURING STRATEGIES:

1. When a toddler selects the book, observe the child's behavior.

2. Ask the toddler questions about the pictures. Questions to ask include:
   "Sadie, who is in that picture?"
   "Porter is your brother. What is he doing in this photograph?"

3. Encourage the toddler to verbally respond to the questions rather than just using gestures. To illustrate, say:
   "Who is this?"
   "Sadie, what is your dog's name?"

4. Providing positive reinforcement may result in the toddler talking more about all of the photographs. Say, for example:
   "You've told me a lot by using your words."
   "Yes! That is your mama."

5. Describe the toddler's reaction to the book. Comments to make include:
   "Sadie, you were excited when you saw yourself in the photograph."
   "You are smiling. You must like this book."

6. Read the book again if the toddler desires.

☼ Highlighting Development

Although speech begins slowly, by 18 months of age most children's speaking ability begins to explode. Studies show the size of a toddler's vocabulary is dependent on how many times the child hears different words. Therefore, it is important that you provide language-rich experiences that are meaningful to the child.

VARIATIONS:

♡ Prepare similar books using magazine pictures of animals, foods, clothing, etc.

♡ Allow the toddler to read the book independently after you've read it together two or three times.

ADDITIONAL INFORMATION:

♡ Toddlers love to identify family members in photographs. Activities such as this one can be used not only for stimulating language development but also for emotional development. For example, if the child is experiencing separation anxiety, you can direct attention to the photograph.

♡ Toddlers at this stage of development understand more words than they can say. That is, they have better receptive than expressive language skills.

13 to 18 months

Toddler Talk

Child's Developmental Goals

✓ To expand expressive language skills

✓ To practice engaging in telegraphic speech

MATERIALS:

None

PREPARATION:

♡ To understand what the child is saying, observe for behavior cues.

NURTURING STRATEGIES:

1. Whenever working with a toddler, engage the child in conversation. During routine care times such as snack, this activity works especially well.

2. While he is eating snack, ask the child about activities in the recent past. For example, ask:
   "Jacques, what did you do outside?"
   "Did you have fun with the ball?"

3. Depending on the child's developmental level, the response will vary. Some children will engage in "jargon" talk. When this happens, you will probably be able to understand one word. Use that word to continue the conversation with the child. To illustrate:
   If the child says, "xyzgrstuv ball crput yrusd," respond by saying:
   "Yes, I remember you playing with the ball. You rolled it down the hill. Did you kick the ball?"
   If the child engages in telegraphic speech, you will want to use expansion. This involves expanding the toddler's telegraphic sentence into a more complete sentence. For example:
   If the toddler says, "Wash baby," respond by saying:
   "You washed a baby. Was that fun?"

4. If more than one toddler is present, encourage another child to join in the conversation. Begin by focusing on things the children did that were similar or that they did together. To follow one of the previous examples, say:
   "Marnie, I saw you rolling the ball down the hill also. Did you kick the ball?"
   You will need to connect the children's answers and then continue. To illustrate, state:
   "Neither of you kicked the balls. How did you get the balls to move?"

5. Continue engaging in the conversation as long as possible. When you sense that the topic is exhausted, move on to another.

☀ Highlighting Development

At about 15 months, toddlers become increasingly interested in learning language. They may want you to read to them more often, and they may even watch your mouth while you are talking. Therefore, this is a prime time to focus on language development. Provide the toddlers with pictures; books; tapes; puppets; and, most important, your own voice.

VARIATION:

♡ Describe the toddler's behavior while engaging in experiences. This provides language skills to use in later conversations.

ADDITIONAL INFORMATION:

♡ As an adult, you will need to frequently ask questions. However, you will often need to answer them yourself.

♡ More complex sentences can be introduced. Studies show that children who hear complex sentences are more inclined to use them.

13 to 18 months

"Where Is My...?"

Child's Developmental Goals

✓ To practice asking questions

✓ To use expressive language to receive desired object

MATERIALS:

None

PREPARATION:

♡ Observe the toddler's desire for interaction.

NURTURING STRATEGIES:

1. Respond to the toddler's cues for interaction. Such cues might include touching your body or repeating a word/phrase. If the toddler, for example, is saying the word "blankie," expand this by asking a question about the blanket such as:
   "Edo, where is your blanket?"
   "Have you lost your blanket?"

2. Help the child solve the problem. Ask, for example:
   "Where is your blanket?"
   "Did you leave it in your crib?"
   Verbally answer your own question. If the toddler doesn't respond, for example, say:
   "I saw you with your blanket in your crib. Let's look there."
   Then, move to look for the lost item.

3. Verbally describe what you are doing. To illustrate, say:
   "I'm looking for your blanket. I don't see it. Let's look somewhere else."

4. Provide positive reinforcement to the toddler when solving the problem. Comments to make include:
   "Edo, thank you for helping me locate your blanket."
   "I am happy we found it."

☀ Highlighting Development

Between 12 and 18 months, toddlers learn how to ask questions. They use intonations rather than words such as *where, why,* and *what* to indicate a question. Therefore, you must pay close attention to how things are being said to understand the child's meaning.

VARIATION:

♡ Repeat the activity, capitalizing on other words the child uses.

ADDITIONAL INFORMATION:

♡ Remember, using a higher-pitched voice when talking to infants and toddlers typically captures a child's attention.

♡ Parentese is useful when talking to toddlers. The simplified utterances and repetition serve to maintain their attention and foster language development.

13 to 18 months

Animal Sounds

Child's Developmental Goals

✓ To continue developing receptive language skills

✓ To verbally identify animals

MATERIALS:

❏ Book with animals such as *Moo, Baa, La La La!* by Sandra Boynton

PREPARATION:

♡ Place the book in an area that will attract the child's attention.

NURTURING STRATEGIES:

1. When a toddler selects the book, observe the child's behavior.
2. Ask the toddler if you can read the book together. Carefully observe the toddler's nonverbal cues to know what to do next. For example, if the toddler shakes her head "no" or doesn't make eye contact, say:
   "Maybe you would like to look at the book alone."
   On the other hand, if the child smiles at you or hands you the book, ask:
   "Jenisa, would you like to sit on my lap?"
3. Read the title of the story. Ask the toddler:
   "What do you think the story is about?"
   Always pause and provide the child time to think or respond.
4. Begin reading the story.
5. To promote language skills, make this experience interactive by asking questions. To illustrate, ask:
   "Jenisa, what sound does a cat make?"
   "What animal is this?" (while pointing to a picture).

6. Provide positive reinforcement for vocalizations or gestures. Comments might include:
   "Jenisa, you're pointing to the pig."
   "That's right. Cats say 'meow.'"
7. Read the story again if the toddler seems interested.

☀ Highlighting Development

Repeating children's utterances is an important technique for promoting language development. When you repeat an utterance, you are assuring them that they are understood. To illustrate, if the child says "car," recast this word into a full sentence. For example, you might say, "That's right! This is a car. This is a red car."

VARIATION:

♡ Create a book by cutting out pictures of animals, objects, or people from magazines.

ADDITIONAL INFORMATION:

♡ Children will grasp grammar more readily when short sentences are spoken to them. However, do not completely avoid complex sentences.

♡ Toddlers are slowly developing a sense of humor. This book may be particularly interesting because it mixes up the sounds a pig might say. Those who know the correct sound will find this humorous.

13 to 18 months

Label It

Child's Developmental Goals

✓ To continue developing expressive language skills

✓ To connect verbal labels to objects

MATERIALS:

None

PREPARATION:

♡ Have the child wash hands prior to coming to snack.

NURTURING STRATEGIES:

1. Engage the child in conversation about snack. To illustrate, say:
   "Raul, what are we eating for snack today?"
   "Where do bananas come from?"
2. While passing out snack, discuss any limits for the snack time. To illustrate, say:
   "Sit at the table while eating."
   "You can have three pieces of banana and two glasses of milk."
3. Encourage the toddler to verbally express desires. For example, when a toddler points to the milk container, say:
   "Raul, what do you want?"
4. Expand upon the child's responses to your question. For example, if a child says "more," respond:
   "Do you want more milk?"
   Extend your hand and say:
   "Please hand me your cup and I'll pour you more milk."

5. Provide positive reinforcement for verbal expressions. Comments include:
   "You used words to tell me what you needed."
   "Thank you for using words."

☀ Highlighting Development

Some letters are difficult for toddlers to pronounce such as *t* and *b*. For most children, these sounds will be added in time. Therefore, there is no need to push children to pronounce words correctly. For example, accept "wawa" for water and "nana" for banana while continuing to model the correct pronunciation.

VARIATION:

♡ Language interactions should occur continuously throughout the day.

ADDITIONAL INFORMATION:

♡ Communicate often throughout the day about real-life experiences. Repeating the children's utterances is important because it reassures them that they have been heard and that language is important.

13 to 18 months

Spotlighting Objects

Child's Developmental Goals

✓ To verbally label objects

✓ To continue developing expressive language skills

MATERIALS:

❏ 1 flashlight for each child

❏ Clear, heavy adhesive tape

PREPARATION:

♡ Tape the opening of each flashlight to prevent the batteries from being removed.

NURTURING STRATEGIES:

1. During free play exploration, introduce flashlights. To illustrate, you might say:
   "These are flashlights. Have you seen one before?" Pause to allow response. *"Flashlights give light. Watch me. I can turn the flashlight on. Then I'm going to place this rattle in the light. Now it is your turn. What can you put in the light?"*

2. Observe the children interacting with the lights.

3. Converse with the children about the focus in their "spotlight." To guide your behavior, use your knowledge of each of the toddlers. For example, if you know the toddler has a particular vocabulary word, encourage verbal labeling by asking:
   "Hannah, what is that?"
   "Tell me. What do you have your light on?"
   On the other hand, if you know the toddler is lacking a vocabulary word, say:
   "Hannah, you have your light on the doorknob."

4. After labeling an item, reinforce your words with actions while physically touching the object:
   "This is a doorknob."

5. When the toddler is familiar with the flashlight, begin to discuss ways to increase the brightness of the flashlights. One way to do this is to turn off the room lights.

6. Reinforce the toddler when objects are correctly labeled. Comments include:
   "Yes, that is a puppet."
   "What a tough word! It is a banana."

7. Continue this activity as long as the toddler remains interested.

☼ Highlighting Development

Social interaction is viewed as an important factor in language development. Adults are the main models of language for young children. Therefore, language-rich environments and interactions promote the development of both expressive and receptive language skills.

VARIATIONS:

♡ For an adult-directed activity, use the flashlight to spotlight unfamiliar objects to foster the development of expressive language skills.

♡ To reinforce the toddler's expressive language skills, use the flashlight to spotlight familiar objects.

ADDITIONAL INFORMATION:

♡ When you turn off the lights, keep the blinds or drapes open. This will permit some light into the room, thus reducing the possibility of fear of the dark.

 To promote safety, the batteries should not be handled by the toddler.

13 to 18 months

Texture Book

Developmental Goals

✓ To continue developing expressive language skills

✓ To associate a label with a sensory experience

MATERIALS:

❑ 3-by-3-inch squares of different textures of fabric such as satin, fur, flannel, or corduroy

❑ A 4-by-6-inch index card for each piece of fabric and 2 additional cards

❑ Hole punch

❑ Key ring

❑ Rubber cement

❑ Felt-tip marker

PREPARATION:

♡ Punch a hole in the top left corner of each index card.

♡ Attach each square of fabric to an index card using the rubber cement. Promote durability by securely adhering the corners of the fabric to the index card.

♡ Use the marker to write a title, such as "Our Feely Book," on one index card and write "The End" on another card.

♡ When everything is dry, stack the index cards in order from title card to end card. Secure the cards together by inserting the key ring through the hole in the top left corner of each index card.

NURTURING STRATEGIES:

1. When a toddler selects the book, observe the child's reaction to each fabric texture. Notice if there is a preference for one type of fabric over another.

2. Talk to the toddler about the book. Comments include:
   "Todd, this is very soft. Feel it. It reminds me of your blanket."
   "Feel the fabric. It feels bumpy."

3. Engage the child in conversation by asking questions such as:
   "How does this feel on your fingers?"
   "What else feels like this?"

4. Providing positive reinforcement may encourage the toddler to practice expressive language skills even more. To illustrate, say:
   "Yes, that is smooth."
   "It feels like my shirt."

☀ Highlighting Development

Toddlers learn words that are relevant to them. Consequently, introducing words that are out of context or not part of their environment will be meaningless, making the words difficult for them to remember. Therefore, focus on introducing and reinforcing words associated with their immediate environment.

VARIATION:

♡ Use real objects instead of pieces of fabric. For example, glue sand, pebbles, or sandpaper to the index cards. For safety reasons, spray each card with a light coat of clear varnish or cover with clear self-adhesive paper.

ADDITIONAL INFORMATION:

♡ Introduce or reinforce one descriptive word for each type of fabric. This will assist the toddler in associating the physical sensation with the verbal label. Use terms such as *rough, smooth, bumpy,* or *furry* depending on the fabric samples you have.

Touching Tour

Child's Developmental Goals

✓ To continue developing expressive language skills

✓ To verbally apply labels to objects

MATERIALS:

None

PREPARATION:

♡ Observe. When a toddler appears to need attention, pick up the child and begin this activity.

NURTURING STRATEGIES:

1. Walk around the room touching items. Encourage the toddler to verbally label the item you are touching by asking questions such as:
   "Meena, what is this?"
   "What am I touching?"

2. Pausing after asking a question may prompt the toddler to respond. If the child fails to respond, use your knowledge of the toddler to decide the next strategy to introduce. For example, if the toddler fails to identify the object, provide a verbal label while touching it. To illustrate, say:
   "This is the microwave. This heats your bottle."

3. Foster conversational skills by asking additional questions about familiar objects. For example, ask:
   "What do we do with a ball?"
   "Show me how to sort these shapes."

4. Providing positive reinforcement for responses may encourage the toddler to continue talking. Comments might include:
   "Tell me more about the ball."
   "Excellent, Meena! The block fits in the hole."

☼ Highlighting Development

Soon after their first birthday, young children begin producing two-word sentences. These sentences focus on meaning and express needs or ideas. Children make their wants known through speech. Examples include "me milk," "mama bye-bye," or "all done."

VARIATION:

♡ Repeat a similar tour of objects outdoors.

ADDITIONAL INFORMATION:

♡ Focus on common items within the toddler's environment.

13 to 18 months

Write-and-Wipe Board

Child's Developmental Goals

✓ To create markings on a piece of paper

✓ To communicate through art

MATERIALS:

❑ 1 large sheet of heavy tagboard

❑ 1 plastic container

❑ 1 damp sponge

❑ Transparent lamination or clear self-adhesive paper

❑ 1 set of washable, nontoxic felt-tip markers

❑ Smock

PREPARATION:

♡ Laminate the tagboard sheet to create a write-and-wipe board. Hang one write-and-wipe board on an easel, wall, or refrigerator.

♡ Place the markers in the container and set it next to the tagboard. Lay the damp sponge beside the markers.

♡ Hang or display the smock so the toddler knows your expectations for the experience.

NURTURING STRATEGIES:

1. When a toddler chooses the activity, observe the child's behavior.

2. If necessary, introduce the activity. Most likely, you will need to explain the use of the sponge. To illustrate, while marking a little mark and then erasing it, say:
   "Write with the markers on this special paper. Then erase it with the sponge."

3. As the child works, describe what you see. For example, say:
   "Tyrone, you're making a red circle."
   "Here are long green lines."
   "These go up and down. Up and down."

4. Encourage the child to discuss the work by asking open-ended questions or making statements such as:
   "Tyrone, would you like to tell me about your work?"
   "Tell me about your picture."

5. Discuss the cause or effect of the damp sponge on the markings. Comments to make include:
   "Tyrone, you erased that green mark."
   "Look. The red circle is all gone."

6. Elaborate on the emotional expressions of the toddler. Say, for example:
   "You're smiling. You like to write and then erase."
   "What a sad face. Did you erase too much? Use the markers again."

☀ Highlighting Development

During the second year of life, a child's vocabulary begins expanding rather quickly. Language development is promoted by the child's increasing mobility and experiences. Typically, the number of people, events, and objects in his life is increasing. As a result, growth is rapid. At 12 months, the child generally has a vocabulary of 3 words. By 15 months, the child's vocabulary has increased to 22 words. Around 18 months, the child's vocabulary usually increases to approximately 100 words (Snow, 1998).

VARIATIONS:

♡ Use finger paints instead of felt-tip markers on the tagboard sheet.

♡ Use chalk rather than markers.

ADDITIONAL INFORMATION:

♡ This activity promotes not only development of written communication skills but also emotional development. It gives toddlers a sense of self-efficacy because they can erase what they've written.

13 to 18 months

Cleaning Up after Snack

Child's Developmental Goals

✓ To follow simple directions

✓ To continue developing receptive language skills

MATERIALS:

❏ Serving tray

PREPARATION:

♡ Prepare and serve snack as usual. Place the tray for dirty snack dishes in the center of the table.

NURTURING STRATEGIES:

1. While you are eating snack with a toddler, discuss the tray in the center of the table. Foster divergent thinking by asking open-ended questions such as:
   "What is this tray for?"
   "Why is that tray there?"

2. Accept and discuss the toddler's answers. For example, if the child says "paint," you may respond:
   "We carry paint on trays? Do you see any paint?"

3. Whenever you are able, guide the conversation back to the relationship between snack and the tray. For example, ask:
   "How could we use the tray for snack?"

4. Responding to the toddler's comments may encourage continuation of the conversation.

5. As the toddler finishes with snack, explain the purpose of the tray. To illustrate, say:
   "This tray is for dirty dishes. Put your cup, bowl, and spoon on the tray when you are finished eating."

6. Remind the child to assist with cleaning after snack. Say, for example:
   "Rosario, put your cup on the tray. Then you need to wash your hands."

7. Reinforcing your words with actions may be necessary. If so, gently guide the toddler through each step while repeating the directions. For example, while helping the toddler put the cup on the tray, say:
   "Rosario, put the cup on the tray."

8. Providing positive reinforcement may encourage the toddler to complete the tasks independently. Comments include:
   "Rosario, you did a great job of cleaning up after snack."
   "What a good helper. All of the snack items are cleaned up."

☼ Highlighting Development

Listen to toddlers. Many of their words are overgeneralized. They may identify any four-legged animal, such as a cow or horse, as a being a dog. Initially, toddlers begin by having only one or two meanings for a word. Gradually, over a period of years, children add new meanings to words. Eventually, their definitions will correspond to an adult's definition.

VARIATION:

♡ Perform similar "following directions" activities throughout the day. These activities can be introduced during routine activities such as washing hands, picking up toys, or getting dressed for outdoor play.

ADDITIONAL INFORMATION:

♡ Young toddlers should be able to follow two to three simple directions given at the same time. However, if a toddler has difficulty doing this, provide only one instruction at a time. Slowly build up to two or three directions at once.

♡ Keep your commands as simple and direct as possible.

13 to 18 months

Putting Eggs in a Basket

Child's Developmental Goals

✓ To understand the meaning of the words *full* and *empty*

✓ To continue developing expressive language skills

MATERIALS:

❑ 5 or 6 plastic colored eggs
❑ 2 baskets for holding the eggs

PREPARATION:

♡ Place the eggs in one of the baskets; then set both baskets in an accessible location.

NURTURING STRATEGIES:

1. Observe the child's behavior with the eggs and basket.
2. If the toddler doesn't seem to know what to do, introduce the activity. To illustrate, say:
   "Kano, empty the basket . Dump out the eggs. Then fill it up again."
3. You may need to model emptying and filling by using the second basket.
4. Reinforce your actions with words by describing what you or the child is doing. Comments include:
   "Kano, your basket is full of eggs."
   "Show me how to dump it."
5. Check the child's understanding of the terms *full* and *empty* by asking the toddler questions. For example, say:
   "Can you empty your basket?"
   "How can you make your basket full?"
   "Is your basket full or empty?"
6. Providing positive reinforcement may increase the time spent at the activity. Comments include:
   "Kano, you did it! Your basket is now full."

Highlighting Development

Listen to the child's speech. The first words are generally nouns referring to things that are familiar or of interest. Among them typically are *cat, dog, no, go, ball,* and *car.* First words tend to end with "ie" such as *birdie, blankie,* and *doggie.* Moreover, new vocabulary words are likely to appear one at a time. Later the child will begin acquiring verbs, adjectives, adverbs, and prepositions (Snow, 1998).

VARIATIONS:

♡ Substitute favorite toys such as balls, blocks, or cars for the eggs.
♡ Use six plastic eggs and an egg carton instead of a basket.

ADDITIONAL INFORMATION:

♡ Toddlers love to fill and spill. Providing them with these types of activities reduces the occurrence of random dumping of other containers. Through these activities, they are learning the interrelationship of the size of objects.
♡ As the toddler becomes older and more experienced with this activity, add a new element. For example, count the number of objects in the basket or label the color of each object.

13 to 18 months

"Peas, Porridge Hot"

Child's Developmental Goals

✓ To develop a sense of rhythm

✓ To continue developing expressive language skills

MATERIALS:

❑ A large sheet of heavy tagboard

❑ Washable, felt-tip markers

❑ Transparent lamination or clear, self-adhesive paper

PREPARATION:

♡ Create a teaching aid by writing the nursery rhyme on the tagboard sheet:

Peas, porridge hot
Peas, porridge cold
Peas, porridge in the pot nine days old.
Some like it hot
Some like it cold
Some like it in the pot nine days old.

♡ Laminate or cover the tagboard with the transparent self-adhesive paper.

♡ Hang the poster in a convenient location.

NURTURING STRATEGIES:

1. Hold the toddler in your lap or sit in a position to visually connect with the child.
2. If necessary, position yourself to allow a view of the teaching aid.
3. Slowly recite the nursery rhyme while clapping to the rhythm.

4. Encourage the toddler to clap along with you. Say, for example:
   "Katelyn, clap when I do."
5. Provide positive reinforcement for attempts and accomplishments. Comments include:
   "Katelyn, we're clapping together."
   "What a big smile. You must enjoy clapping to the rhyme."
   "You're saying the words with me."
6. Continue to recite the nursery rhyme as long as the toddler seems interested.

☀ Highlighting Development

When toddlers can join two words to create a sentence, they are demonstrating their knowledge of language syntax. This important milestone is called telegraphic speech—like a telegram, only key words are included in the sentence. These words occur in an order that reflects an adult's language.

VARIATION:

♡ Recite and clap to the rhythm of other favorite nursery rhymes. See Appendix F for a list of other nursery rhymes.

ADDITIONAL INFORMATION:

♡ Favorite nursery rhymes should be repeated over and over. This repetition fosters the development of expressive language skills. The more times the toddler hears a word, the more likely it will be repeated.

13 to 18 months

Cognitive Development

♡

THIRTEEN to EIGHTEEN MONTHS

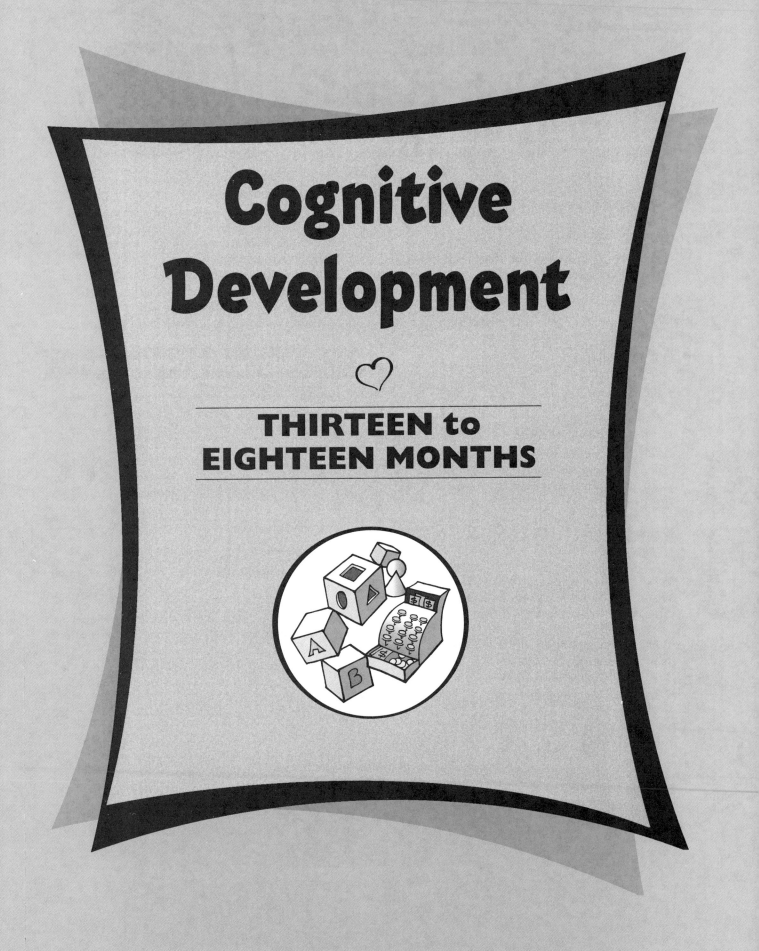

Which Hand Is It In?

COGNITIVE

Child's Developmental Goals

✓ To search for a hidden object

✓ To engage in problem solving using trial and error

MATERIALS:

❏ Toy that is small enough to fit inside your hand

PREPARATION:

♡ If the child appears to need a new activity, tell the toddler you have a game.

NURTURING STRATEGIES:

1. Introduce this game by saying:
   "Yuri, I'm going to hide this toy. See if you can find it."
   At the same time you are speaking, show the child the toy.
2. Put your hands behind your back. Shuffle the toy between your hands. Using your voice as a tool to communicate enthusiasm, ask:
   "Where do you think it is?"
3. Put the toy in one hand and make a fist to surround it. Show the toddler both fists and ask:
   "Yuri, where is the car? Point to the hand where you think it is hiding."
4. When a toddler points, verbally describe the actions. Comments include:
   "You think it is in my right hand."
   "You pointed to my left hand."

5. Open the hand that the toddler picked. If it was the correct choice, respond with enthusiasm and positive reinforcement. To illustrate, say:
   "Yuri, you found the car!"
   "You're good at this game."
   If the toddler chooses the empty hand, respond with disappointment while saying:
   "No, that is the empty hand. Try again."
6. Repeat the game as many times as the toddler desires.

☀ Highlighting Development

During this period, children recognize that a hidden object is somewhere. They will continue searching for an object long after it is out of sight. Moreover, they will gradually begin to remember where hidden objects are housed after leaving their sight. To illustrate, if you remove a toy and place it in your purse, toddlers usually will remember it. Moreover, they probably will begin searching for it.

VARIATION:

♡ Let the child hide the toy in a hand and you search for it.

Never leave the child unattended with the toy for this activity. If the toy easily hides in your hand, it can be a choking hazard for young toddlers. As a result, remove the toy from the area or from the toddler's reach as soon as you are finished with the game.

Separating Blocks

Child's Developmental Goals

✓ To focus on one dimension or shape

✓ To categorize objects by shape

MATERIALS:

❑ 10 round and 10 square blocks

❑ A round and a square unbreakable container

❑ Child-size table or coffee table

PREPARATION:

♡ Clear an area on a child-size or coffee table. Place the blocks and containers on the table.

NURTURING STRATEGIES:

1. When a toddler selects the activity, carefully observe the child's behavior. Ask yourself, "What is the child's response to the blocks?"

2. If the blocks are being used for building, encourage this behavior. Say, for example:
   "Esme, you've stacked three blocks. What a tall tower!"
   When the child is finished building, introduce the activity.

3. Discuss the shapes of the blocks. To illustrate, while pointing to the shapes, say:
   "There are two shapes here, a square and a circle."

4. Encourage the toddler to sort the blocks by shapes. Say, for example:
   "Let's put the square blocks in a pile."

5. Provide positive reinforcement while the toddler is sorting the blocks. Comments include:
   "Esme, look at this big pile of square blocks."
   "You've put all of the circles in one pile."

6. If the toddler has not discovered the round and square containers, show the child the containers and ask:
   "What could we do with these?"

7. While the child is putting the blocks into the containers, count the number of square and round blocks.

8. Continue the interaction as long as the toddler seems interested.

☼ Highlighting Development

Children need challenging materials and experiences. Therefore, making the match of appropriate play experiences and developmental abilities is important. When presented with materials and equipment that they were interested in at an earlier period, the toddlers may reject them. Likewise, if the materials are too advanced, chances are the children will not show an interest.

VARIATIONS:

♡ Introduce circle and square blocks that are different colors.

♡ To increase the challenge, use square and rectangular blocks.

ADDITIONAL INFORMATION:

♡ Toddlers often move from one activity to another quickly. However, their ability to attend to one activity for longer periods of time is increasing. When interested, toddlers can spend 5 to 10 minutes at one activity. Your presence will often increase their participation.

13 to 18 months

Goop

Child's Developmental Goals

✓ To explore materials through the senses

✓ To add information and modify existing cognitive structures

MATERIALS:

- ❏ Box of cornstarch
- ❏ Water
- ❏ ½-cup measuring cup
- ❏ Sensory table or plastic dishpan
- ❏ Smock

PREPARATION:

♡ Empty the box of cornstarch into the sensory table or plastic dishpan. Add small amounts of water and mix with a spoon or with fingers. The mixture will be the right consistency when it feels hard to the touch and molds in your hand.

♡ Place a smock close to the sensory table as a visual reminder.

NURTURING STRATEGIES:

1. When a toddler chooses the sensory activity, help the child put on a smock if necessary.

2. Discuss the material in the sensory table, including how it feels. You might say:
   "Wolf, we have goop to play with today. It feels funny! Sometimes it is hard and sometimes it is runny."

3. If the child seems hesitant, provide ample time for exploring the medium.

4. If the child remains hesitant, modeling ways to explore the goop may be helpful. For example, scoop some goop into your hand and let it run between your fingers. Then verbally describe the child's and your actions. To illustrate, say:
   "Look. I'm poking the goop with my fingers."
   "It feels hard."

5. If the toddler seems worried about getting dirty, demonstrate how easily the goop washes away with soap and water.

6. Providing positive reinforcement may result in extended exploration by the toddler. Use comments such as:
   "Wolf, you are really working hard."
   "Squish. Squish. You're squishing the goop in your hand."

☀ Highlighting Development

During this period, there are subtle changes in the children's ability to use their hands and fingers. Gradually, more control is developed. As a result, the children will engage in manipulating and exploring materials as well as objects. By using a multisensory approach, the children will gain cognitive information about the media: how it looks, feels, moves, responds, etc.

VARIATIONS:

♡ Have the child assist in preparing the goop by mixing the cornstarch and water together with his hands. What a unique sensory experience that is!

♡ Introduce other sensory materials such as sand or shaving cream.

ADDITIONAL INFORMATION:

♡ Goop can be kept for up to one week if covered and refrigerated when not in use. However, you may need to add a slight amount of water before using it again.

♡ If a child seems particularly hesitant to play in the goop, provide gloves or tools to use instead of just bare hands.

 This experience requires constant supervision to ensure that the shaving cream is not accidentally wiped into the children's eyes or ingested.

13 to 18 months

Sorting Shapes

Child's Developmental Goals

✓ To differentiate objects by shape

✓ To match individual shapes to forms and the sorter

MATERIALS:

❑ Shape sorter containing three different shapes
❑ Child-size table or coffee table

PREPARATION:

♡ Clear an area on a child-size or coffee table. Remove the shapes from the sorter. Then place them next to it.

NURTURING STRATEGIES:

1. When a toddler chooses the activity, observe the child's behavior.
2. Describe the shapes as the child picks them up. Comment, for example:
   "Tilda, you are holding a triangle. It has three sides."
   "This is a circle. It is round."
3. Verbally encourage the child to put the object into the shape sorter. Comments include:
   "Find the circle on the sorter. Put it through the circle form."
   "Match the triangles."
4. It may be necessary to reinforce your words with actions while modeling putting the triangle in the sorter. Say:
   "Match up the triangles."

5. Providing positive reinforcement may encourage the toddler to continue the activity for a longer period of time. To illustrate, say:
   "Tilda, you've matched up all the circles!"
   "You did it! You matched all of the shapes."
6. If the toddler demonstrates interest, allow the child to work independently with the shape sorter.

☀ Highlighting Development

At this stage of development, children may begin understanding positions in space. To promote this development, introduce words such as *up, down, in,* and *out* while the child is constructing puzzles, playing with shape sorters, or placing round pegs in holes.

VARIATIONS:

♡ When the child is ready, introduce a shape sorter with more than three shapes.
♡ Provide the child with simple puzzles containing knobs.

ADDITIONAL INFORMATION:

♡ Encourage the child by introducing and using words referring to spatial relationships. Refer to see the Highlighting Development box for this activity.

13 to 18 months

What's Inside the Bag?

Child's Developmental Goals

✓ To use an existing scheme to solve a problem

✓ To identify sounds

MATERIALS:

❑ Cloth bag such as a pillowcase

❑ Several rattles

PREPARATION:

♡ Place the rattles in a cloth bag. Then place the bag in a safe and easily accessible location.

NURTURING STRATEGIES:

1. When a toddler appears to be searching for a new activity, retrieve the cloth bag. Then introduce the activity. While shaking the bag to gain the toddler's attention, say:
   "Alfredo, what could be in the bag?"
2. Encourage the child to use expressive language skills by saying:
   "Guess. What could be in the bag?"
3. Provide positive reinforcement for vocalizations and gestures. Say, for example:
   "Alfredo, what a good guess."
4. Encourage the child to explore the contents of the bag by using the hands and fingers. To illustrate, say:
   "Let's use our hands to explore."
   "Can you guess what is in the bag?"
5. Again, provide positive reinforcement for vocalizations and gestures:
   "Alfredo, that's it! We'll take turns. We will take something from the bag with our hands."
6. Call the child by name and say:
   "Alfredo, choose something from the bag. Pull something from the bag with your hand."

7. Ask the child:
   "Alfredo, what did you find?"
8. If the child doesn't respond, label the item. Say, for example:
   "You found a red rattle."
9. If another child is present, encourage participation in the game by asking:
   "Did you find the same thing in the bag?"
10. Respond to whatever the child communicates.

☀ Highlighting Development

Children at this stage particularly enjoy hiding games. They also will begin communicating the role they expect you to play. To illustrate, a child may hand you a shaker. Then, looking directly at you, the child may pick one up and begin shaking it. With these actions, the toddler is trying to engage and direct your involvement in the play.

VARIATION:

♡ Put different types of objects in the bag such as balls, blocks, cars, etc.

ADDITIONAL INFORMATION:

♡ Toddlers may be better at labeling the objects taken from the bag than guessing what could be in the bag. This is due to their expressive language skills. Therefore, don't spend too long in the guessing part. As children become more skillful in speaking, the guessing part will naturally begin to take up more time.

Making Pudding

Child's Developmental Goals

✓ To observe a transformation
✓ To follow simple directions

MATERIALS:

❑ Recipe card including pictures and words
❑ Mixing bowl
❑ Eggbeater
❑ Small bowls
❑ Measuring cups
❑ Milk
❑ Instant pudding
❑ Individual and serving spoons

PREPARATION:

♡ If interested, prepare a recipe card.
♡ Gather all of the supplies and place them on a tray. Carry the tray to the table when you are ready to begin the activity.
♡ If working in a child care center, you may want to place a Hand Washing sign on a table. This serves as a visual reminder to encourage hand washing before the beginning of the activity.

NURTURING STRATEGIES:

1. Remind the child that hand washing is needed prior to preparing the pudding. Say, for example:
   "We need to wash our hands before cooking."
   "Keisha, please go into the bathroom. Wash your hands. Then we will make our pudding."
2. Introduce the activity by saying:
   "Today we are going to make pudding."
3. Respond to the child's comments. Discuss how pudding tastes and feels.
4. If prepared, introduce the recipe card. Explain that the card shows how to make the pudding. Read the recipe card to the child.

5. Assist the child in completing the tasks. Provide more verbal assistance than physical assistance whenever possible. For example, say:
   "Keisha, hold the measuring cup with both hands. There you go. You are doing it! You didn't spill a drop!"
6. Refer back to the recipe card often for guidance. Say:
   "Let's look at the recipe card to see what to do next."
7. Ask open-ended questions throughout the activity to spark a conversation with the toddler. For example, ask:
   "Keisha, what happened to the dry mix that we put in the bowl first?"
   "How can we get rid of the bumps in the pudding?"
   "What is your favorite flavor of pudding?"
8. Once the preparation of the pudding is completed, thank the child for assisting. Then have the child wash her hands.
9. Divide the pudding into the smaller bowls and place them in the refrigerator until snack time.

☀ Highlighting Development

Engaging children in cooking experiences teaches important development skills. Included are basic concepts such as color, shape, size, and number. Critical thinking skills are learned by exploring similarities and differences. In addition, children learn about transformations when observing the outcome of mixing dry and liquid ingredients.

VARIATION:

♡ Add bananas to vanilla or chocolate pudding.

ADDITIONAL INFORMATION:

♡ Toddlers are developing independence. You can foster this trait by introducing simple cooking activities. Preparing snack also seems to be a successful technique for encouraging picky eaters to sample different foods.

13 to 18 months

Feely Bag

Child's Developmental Goals

✓ To distinguish common objects through touching

✓ To associate a verbal label with an object

MATERIALS:

❑ Decorated paper gift bag

❑ 6 common objects such as balls, blocks, cars, etc.

PREPARATION:

♡ Place all six objects in the decorated bag. Then set the bag so that it is easily accessible for the child.

NURTURING STRATEGIES:

1. When a toddler selects the activity, observe the child's behavior.

2. Encourage the toddler to feel the objects without looking into the bag. Say, for example:
   "Waylon, put your hand in the bag. What do you feel?"
   "Use your fingers. Touch the objects."

3. Encourage guessing about what the toddler is touching before actually looking at the object. Comments include:
   "What object do you have in your hand? What does it feel like?"
   "Guess before you look."

4. Encourage the toddler to look at the object to verify the verbal label.

5. Provide positive reinforcement for attempts and accomplishments. To illustrate, say:
   "Waylon, it was a ball! You were right!"
   "It is fuzzy like a bear, but that is a duck."

6. If a toddler is having difficulty, change the game slightly by asking the child to "find the ball." As before, encourage the toddler to explore the objects by touching with fingers and hands.

7. Continue the game as long as the toddler seems interested.

☀ Highlighting Development

Cognitive and language development overlap. Learning labels for objects is one example of this overlap. Cognitively the child is developing and refining memory and classification skills. As for language, the child is learning to match labels with objects and communicate through expressive language skills.

VARIATION:

♡ Suggest that the toddler find objects to put inside a decorated bag.

ADDITIONAL INFORMATION:

♡ Encourage the child to slowly explore the object before labeling it.

♡ Carefully choose the items to place in the bag. At first, select only familiar objects. As the child becomes skilled at the game, try introducing one or two new items each time you play the game.

13 to 18 months

Matching Game

Child's Developmental Goals

✓ To match similar objects

✓ To develop visual discrimination skills

MATERIALS:

- ❏ 5 to 6 pictures of toys from magazines or catalogs
- ❏ Toys to match the pictures
- ❏ 2 baskets
- ❏ Glue
- ❏ Tagboard sheet
- ❏ Transparent self-adhesive paper
- ❏ Child-size table or coffee table

PREPARATION:

♡ Cut the tagboard sheet into pieces of equal size so that the largest pictures will fit on it. Mount each picture on a piece of tagboard. If desired, cover the pictures with transparent self-adhesive paper.

♡ Place the pictures in one of the baskets and the matching items in the other.

♡ Sit both baskets on a child-size table. Match one picture and item as an example.

NURTURING STRATEGIES:

1. When a toddler selects the activity, observe the child's behavior.

2. If necessary, introduce the activity to the toddler. To illustrate, say:
"Debbie, this is a matching game. Find the toy that is in the picture. Watch me. See how these two match? They are both cars."

3. If necessary, help the toddler find a match. To connect your words with actions, verbally describe your actions. To illustrate, say:
"Here is a picture of a ball. I'm going to look in the basket for a ball. Here it is! The ball was hidden! Now I have two balls."

4. Encourage the toddler to play the game. Say, for example:
"Debbie, it is your turn. You find a match."

5. As the child is working, provide assistance to promote visual discrimination skills by pointing out the similarities and differences between two items. For example, say:
"They are both green, but only one is a frog. Which one hops?"

☀ Highlighting Development

To promote the child's development, a technique called scaffolding can be used. This technique is used when the child is about to give up. It involves providing tutoring or prompting to assist the child in learning.

VARIATION:

♡ Match two identical magazine or catalog pictures.

ADDITIONAL INFORMATION:

♡ You will need to carefully select pictures for this matching game. The pictures need to be of familiar objects. At first, items should be fairly distinct such as a ball and rattle. After the child is familiar with the game, promote cognitive development by providing categories of items such as animals, transportation vehicles, foods, clothing, etc.

13 to 18 months

Comparing Apples

COGNITIVE

Child's Developmental Goals

✓ To identify similarities between objects
✓ To identify differences between objects

MATERIALS:

❑ 3 different colors of apples: green, red, and yellow
❑ Crackers
❑ Knife to slice apples
❑ Bowl
❑ Water
❑ Cup
❑ Napkins
❑ Tray

PREPARATION:

♡ Wash the apples.
♡ Fill a pitcher with water and place the crackers in the bowl.
♡ Put the first seven materials listed above on a tray for ease in transporting to a table for snack.

NURTURING STRATEGIES:

1. Sanitize the table for snacking.
2. Assist the toddler with hand washing and finding a seat at the snack table. Wash your own hands.
3. Carry the tray containing the snack to the table.
4. Show the child the apples. Then ask: *"What are these?"* Pause. *"Are these all the same color?"* *"Do you think they all taste the same?"*
5. Cut the apples into slices. Provide one color at a time for the child to taste.
6. Discuss how each type of apple tastes. Introduce words such as *sweet* or *tart*.
7. Ask the toddler if one type of apples is preferable. Discuss how some people like the same apples and some like different ones.
8. Provide crackers and water to balance the snack. Continue conversing about the apples throughout the remainder of the snack.

☀ Highlighting Development

The ability to perceive, store, recall, and use information is a key element in cognitive development. Observe the toddlers. At this stage of development, they concentrate on everything they do. If activities are developmentally appropriate, the toddlers will be interested. However, if handed a toy from an earlier period, they may be bored and move away.

VARIATION:

♡ To increase the challenge, introduce a variety of different fruits for the child to taste.

 Extreme caution must be taken to keep the knife out of the reach of children.

13 to 18 months

Stop Me From . . .

Child's Developmental Goals

✓ To identify body parts

✓ To associate body parts with function

MATERIALS:

None

PREPARATION:

♡ Observe the child's desire for interaction.

NURTURING STRATEGIES:

1. Share this activity with one child at a time. Position your body so that you can visually connect with the toddler and still supervise the other children, if present.

2. Introduce the experience to the toddler by saying:
   "Christopher, what do we talk with?" Pause. "What do we see with?" Pause.
   "In this game, I want you to gently use your hands to stop me from doing something."

3. Begin the game by asking the toddler to:
   "Stop me from seeing."
   "Stop me from talking."
   "Stop me from hearing."
   Continue the activity using other examples such as smiling, eating, walking, touching, kissing, hugging, and tickling.

4. Throughout the game, provide positive reinforcement to the child for gently covering the correct body part. Comments include:
   "Christopher, you covered my eyes! Now I can't see."
   "That's right. I can't smell with my nose covered."
   "You are playing so gently."

5. When necessary, give the toddler clues for locating the correct body part. For example, if the toddler is having difficulty with touching, you can say:
   "Christopher, I also use this part to eat a snack."

6. Continue this game as long as the toddler seems interested.

☀ Highlighting Development

Children are gathering information about themselves at this stage of development. Knowing the proper labels for body parts adds important information to their cognitive structures, including sense of themselves.

VARIATION:

♡ Reverse roles in the activity by having the toddler direct you to cover body parts.

ADDITIONAL INFORMATION:

♡ When older children are present, they may want to play the game with the toddler.

13 to 18 months

The Magical, Disappearing Toy

Child's Developmental Goals

✓ To refine the understanding of object permanence

✓ To find a hidden toy

MATERIALS:

❑ Tube from paper toweling

❑ 20-inch piece of string

❑ Toy that will fit inside the paper towel tube

PREPARATION:

♡ Thread a piece of strong string through a paper towel tube. Then tie both ends of the string to one of the toys, creating a loop. Test your knots by tugging on them to ensure the toy is secure.

NURTURING STRATEGIES:

1. When the toddler selects the toy, observe the child's interaction with the toy.

2. As the toy disappears into the tube, ask in an excited voice:
   "Sheila, where did the duck go? It was just here and now I don't see it! Where is it?"

3. Encourage the toddler to look for the toy. Say, for example:
   "Look for it. Where could it be?"

4. If the child seems confused, suggest a way to find the toy. You might suggest:
   "Pull the string. Pull it and see what happens."

5. Share in the toddler's excitement when the toy is found by providing positive reinforcement. Comments to say, while clapping, include:
   "Sheila, you did it! You found the duck."
   "Yes, you found it."

6. Allow the toddler to work independently with the toy. However, if the child seeks interaction, be a willing participant.

☀ Highlighting Development

There is a developmental progression to laughter. During the first year of life, infants laugh in response to loud sounds or from physical stimulation such as tickling. Now you will observe that children's laughter is based more on cognition. At this stage, they are beginning to laugh at things while participating. In this game, they burst into laughter when the toy emerges after pulling the string.

VARIATIONS:

♡ Hide a toy behind another object and see if the toddler can find it.

♡ Increase the challenge by hiding an object in another location.

ADDITIONAL INFORMATION:

♡ Typically, finding a disappearing toy is an easy task for children at this developmental level; however, an important part of learning is repetition.

13 to 18 months

Building with Blocks

Child's Developmental Goals

✓ To stack blocks either horizontally or vertically

✓ To sort blocks by size

MATERIALS:

❏ 10 blocks of similar shapes but of 2 different sizes

❏ Child-size shelf

PREPARATION:

♡ Place the blocks on a shelf, grouping by size.

NURTURING STRATEGIES:

1. When beginning to build, allow the child to work independently while you observe.

2. Describe the toddler's actions with the blocks. Comments might include:
   "Gabriel, you are carrying three blocks."
   "You've stacked four rectangle blocks in a row."

3. Model stacking the blocks vertically and horizontally. Comment on your behavior as well.

4. Encourage the toddler to use the blocks in a new way. For example, if the child is carrying the blocks, ask:
   "Gabriel, can you lay the blocks in a row?"
   "Can you help me build my tower?"

5. When it is time to clean up, focus on the size of the blocks by asking:
   "Which size are you going to pick up?"

6. Identify the size of the block by stating:
   "Gabriel, you're picking up the small blocks. Then I'll pick up the larger blocks."

7. Discuss where the blocks are to be placed on the shelf. To illustrate, say:
   "I'm putting the larger blocks together. See, they are all the same size."

8. Thank the toddler for cleaning up the area. Use comments such as:
   "Gabriel, thanks for your help with the blocks."
   "What a big helper. Now the blocks are ready for playing with later."

☀ Highlighting Development

Toddlers learn block building, like other skills, through imitation and practice. Therefore, you can assist them by demonstrating new ways to use their hands and materials. Observing, you will note that children enjoy manipulating objects at this stage of development. At 18 months, typically they are able to build a tower of four blocks. By 24 months of age, their skills will increase and they can build a tower of seven blocks.

VARIATION:

♡ Provide cars and trucks as accessories when stacking the blocks horizontally.

ADDITIONAL INFORMATION:

♡ The very first stage of block building is carrying the blocks to learn about things such as length and weight. Stacking blocks horizontally and vertically develops next.

13 to 18 months

Hidden Treasure

COGNITIVE

Child's Developmental Goals

✓ To use a variety of schemas to solve a problem

✓ To increase the understanding of object permanence

MATERIALS:

❑ Object for hiding such as a rattle

❑ 3 hand towels

❑ 20-inch piece of wool yarn

PREPARATION:

♡ Tie the wool yarn to the rattle. Lay three towels down on the table. Place the rattle under one towel, leaving the wool yarn exposed.

NURTURING STRATEGIES:

1. When the activity is selected, observe the toddler's behavior.

2. Ask questions or make statements to expand the toddler's level of play with the materials. For example, if the toddler reveals the rattle by lifting up the towel, while pointing to the string, ask:
   "Keren, what could this string be used for?"
   This may encourage the toddler to use a different scheme for locating the hidden toy.

3. Providing encouragement may result in the toddler extending the search for the hidden toy. Comments to make include:
   "Keren, keep looking. You'll find it."
   "You're looking so hard."
   "I know you'll find it."

4. Provide positive reinforcement when the toddler finds the hidden toy. Use comments such as:
   "Keren, you did it!"
   "You found the rattle."

5. Encourage the toddler to play independently by observing and commenting from 3 to 4 feet away.

☀ Highlighting Development

According to Piaget (1952, 1977), cognitive structures, or schemes, are created to organize or interpret our experiences. Cognitive structures, then, develop through the interaction of individuals with the environment. This perspective has come to be called constructivism because children actively create knowledge of the world or "construct reality" from their experiences.

VARIATION:

♡ Minimize the challenge of the game by partially hiding the toy.

ADDITIONAL INFORMATION:

♡ Toddlers enjoy repeating successful activities. Therefore, the same activity may be frequently repeated during a day, week, or even month.

Hidden Bear

Child's Developmental Goals

✓ To refine object permanence skills
✓ To search in a second place for a hidden object

MATERIALS:

❑ Small stuffed bear
❑ 3 hand towels

PREPARATION:

♡ Spread out the three hand towels on the table and place the bear under one of them.

NURTURING STRATEGIES:

1. If a toddler fails to choose the activity, extend an invitation for joining you in play.
2. Briefly introduce the activity. To illustrate, say:
   "Luther, I put down a bear. Now I can't find it. Could you help me find it?"
3. Provide positive reinforcement when the toddler finds the bear. Say, for example:
   "Luther, you found the bear!"
   "Way to go!"
4. Increase the challenge of the game for the toddler. Begin by hiding the toy in one place and then moving it to a second location. Make sure the toddler watches you move the bear to the second location.
5. Again, invite the toddler to find the bear.
6. Provide support and encouragement for finding the bear. Comments include:
   "Luther, you can do it."
   "Take your time. Think about where you last saw the bear."
   "Keep looking. I know you'll find it."

7. React with enthusiasm when the toddler finds the bear. You could, for example, smile, clap, and say: *"You did it, Luther. You found the bear."*
8. Continue the game as long as the toddler seems interested.

☀ Highlighting Development

The technique of matching the amount of assistance to the developmental needs of the child is called scaffolding. When first introducing a task, you may have to provide the child with more direct instruction. As the child begins to learn through practice, the amount of assistance you provide should be reduced. When this occurs, the child begins taking more responsibility for the task.

VARIATION:

♡ Hide the bear and another stuffed animal. Instruct the toddler to find a particular animal.

ADDITIONAL INFORMATION:

♡ Vary the activity depending upon the abilities of the child. Avoid creating excessive frustration. Some frustration leads to learning, but too much may decrease the child's desire to participate or show interest in the activity.

13 to 18 months

Social Development

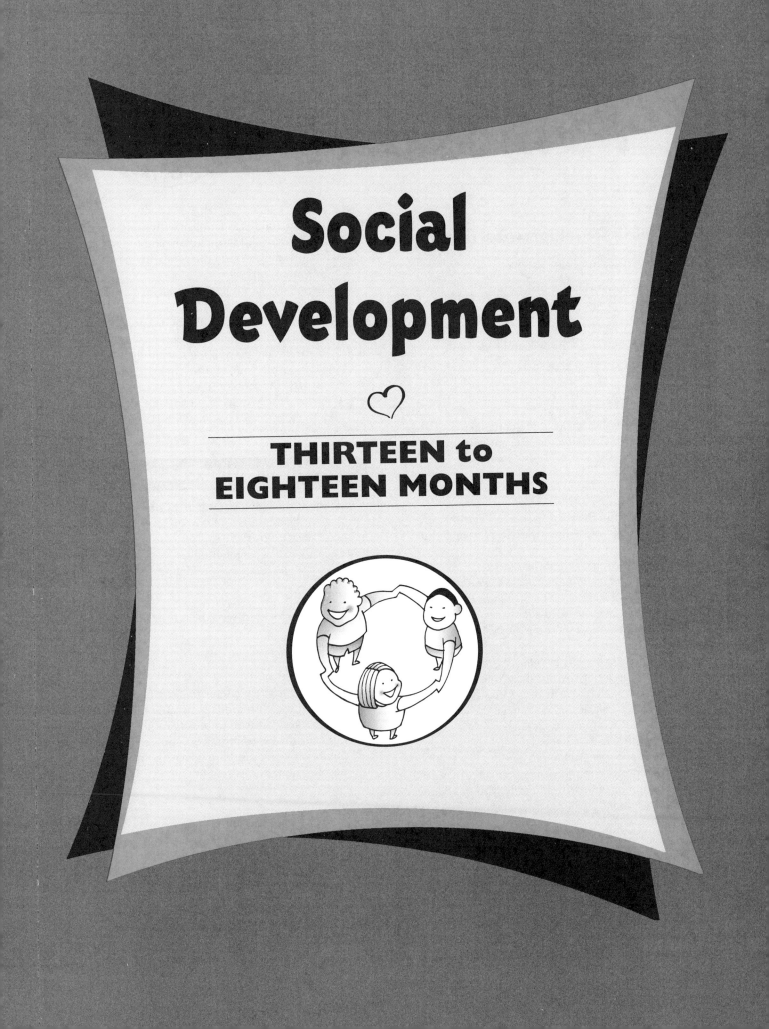

THIRTEEN to
EIGHTEEN MONTHS

Music Parade

SOCIAL

Child's Developmental Goals

✓ To participate in a joint activity

✓ To work with others to make music

MATERIALS:

❑ 1 set of rhythm sticks for each child and adult

❑ Container to hold rhythm sticks

PREPARATION:

♡ Place the rhythm sticks in the container.

♡ Introduce this activity with the child in a sitting position.

NURTURING STRATEGIES:

1. Show the child the rhythm sticks. Then verbally describe how to use the sticks. To illustrate, you might say:
   "Morgan, these are called rhythm sticks."
   "Watch me hit the sticks together to make music. Listen to the sounds I make when I hit the sticks together."

2. Before you give the child a set of rhythm sticks, it will be necessary to set some limits. For example, state:
   "Rhythm sticks are only for hitting together."

3. Pass out one set of rhythm sticks to each child if more than one child is in your care.

4. While she is still sitting, encourage the child to make music. Comments include:
   "Morgan, let's make music together."
   "You can play your instruments now."

5. Provide positive reinforcement for the behaviors you want continued. To illustrate, you might say:
   "We are working together to make music."
   "What beautiful music we are making."

6. When the toddler is familiar with using the rhythm sticks, ask the child to stand up and follow you while parading around the room. To gain the child's attention, say:
   "Morgan, let's have a parade! Stand up and follow me. Don't forget to make music."

7. Walk around the room making music. Continue as long as the toddler seems interested.

8. Stop the parade by walking toward the container and depositing your rhythm sticks. Likewise, encourage the toddler to repeat your behavior.

9. Conclude the activity by saying, for example:
   "Morgan, we worked hard together. We made beautiful music."

☀ Highlighting Development

Toddlers at this age love audiences and are in the process of distinguishing between themselves and others. They enjoy your applause when they are attempting to master new skills.

VARIATION:

♡ Use sand blocks or wrist bells instead of rhythm sticks.

ADDITIONAL INFORMATION:

♡ Rhythm sticks are one of the first musical instruments to use with toddlers because they are easy to use and very difficult to break. Young toddlers are typically unable to produce a consistent rhythm but practicing will assist with advancing this type of development.

13 to 18 months

Rocking in a Boat

Child's Developmental Goals

✓ To contribute to a group activity

✓ To engage in parallel play

MATERIALS:

❑ Wooden rocking boat

❑ Mat that is larger than the boat

PREPARATION:

♡ Select an area that can be constantly supervised. Clear this area for the mat. Then place the boat on top of the mat.

NURTURING STRATEGIES:

1. When a child selects the activity, position yourself in the area.

2. Help the child get into the boat. Typically, your role may focus on steadying the boat to prevent it from rocking while the child is stepping into it.

3. State any limits at this time. For example, say:
   "Thayer, rock gently."
   "Sit down while rocking the boat."
   "Hold on with both hands."

4. If the child is alone in the boat, suggest that a friend join the activity, if available. To illustrate, say:
   "Shaline, Thayer needs someone to rock with him. Would you like to rock in the boat?"

5. If a second child joins the activity, repeat steps 2 and 3.

6. While the children are rocking, comment on their behavior. To illustrate, say:
   "Shaline and Thayer are working together. You are rocking the boat together."
   "What fun it must be to rock with a friend. You are both smiling."

7. To foster language development, engage the toddlers in conversation while they are rocking. They may enjoy talking about fishing or riding in a real boat.

☀ Highlighting Development

During this developmental stage, toddlers are beginning to demonstrate an interest in others. Their increased mobility skills bring them in close proximity to other children. Watch them. You will notice they will share the space and materials. However, their preference is for interacting with you or other adults rather than each other.

VARIATION:

♡ Sing songs such as "Row, Row, Row Your Boat" while the children are rocking in the boat.

ADDITIONAL INFORMATION:

♡ At this age, toddlers more than likely will be engaging in parallel play rather than associative play.

 To prevent injuries, young children need to be constantly supervised while in or around the boat.

13 to 18 months

"Ring around the Rosie"

SOCIAL

Child's Developmental Goals

✓ To interact with an adult

✓ To participate in a small–group activity

MATERIALS:

None

PREPARATION:

♡ Memorize words to the song "Ring around the Rosie."

♡ Select either a soft, grassy outdoor or carpeted indoor area for conducting this activity.

NURTURING STRATEGIES:

1. Observe. When you see a toddler wandering around and appearing to have difficulty choosing an activity, invite the child to play a game with you. Comments to make include:
   "Tira, let's play 'Ring around the Rosie.' Do you know that game?"

2. Explain the activity if the toddler indicates the game is new. To illustrate, say:
   "We'll sing a song while walking in a circle. When the song says, we all fall down."

3. Sing the song while walking in a circle. Hold the toddler's hand while walking. Fall down when the song indicates while smiling and giggling. The words to the song are:

   ♫ Ring around the rosie
   ♫ Pocket full of posie
   ♫ Ashes, ashes
   ♫ We all fall down!

4. If other children are available, invite them to join in the game.

5. Provide positive reinforcement when the children interact with each other. Say, for example:
   "There are four of us playing this game."
   "Tira and Sidney are holding hands."

6. Continue this game as long as the children show signs of being interested.

☀ Highlighting Development

During the second year of life, toddlers are becoming interested in interacting with others around them. With your assistance, they can engage in brief interactions. To provide a positive experience with others, keep the number of people to a minimum.

VARIATION:

♡ Using a compact disc or cassette player, play music and instruct the child to fall down when the music stops.

ADDITIONAL INFORMATION:

♡ Children love this game! Eventually, the children will initiate the game with you instead of vice versa.

Water Wheels

Child's Developmental Goals

✓ To engage in parallel play
✓ To take ownership of toys

MATERIALS:

❑ 2 plastic quilt boxes
❑ Water
❑ 4 identical unbreakable cups
❑ 2 water wheels
❑ Smock
❑ Vinyl tablecloth
❑ Towel

PREPARATION:

♡ Spread out a vinyl tablecloth to protect the flooring and prevent slipping.
♡ Fill the quilt boxes with 1 or 2 inches of lukewarm water. Place two unbreakable cups and a water wheel in each quilt box. Place the quilt boxes on the tablecloth.
♡ Lay the smock adjacent to the box.

NURTURING STRATEGIES:

1. When a child chooses the area, help the toddler put on the smock. Explain to the toddler why the smock is needed:
   "Milos, wear a smock so your clothes stay dry."
2. Observe the child interacting with the materials. Suggest new ways to use the tools. To illustrate, say:
   "Milos, you can use the water to move the wheel."
   "Fill the cup with water."
3. If another toddler is available, extend an invitation to use the other wheel by saying:
   "Tanner, would you like to play with the water wheel?"
   Repeat steps 1 and 2 with this child.

4. Comment on how the children are working with the same types of materials by saying:
   "Milos and Tanner are both moving the water wheels."
   "Milos is using his hands to scoop the water. Tanner is using the cup."
   "Everyone is scooping the water with the cups."
5. If a child takes another's materials, discuss how their tools are identical by reinforcing who the tools "belong to." To illustrate, say:
   "This blue cup is Milos's. It was in his tub."
   "Tanner, this blue cup is yours. You both have blue cups to work with."

☀ Highlighting Development

Engaging in parallel play fosters identity as well as social development. Toddlers need to learn ownership—what is theirs as well as what belongs to others. They must learn this before they are able to engage in prosocial behaviors.

VARIATION:

♡ Use sand or dirt with the water wheels.

ADDITIONAL INFORMATION:

♡ Toddlers, in their quest for independence, begin to identify what materials belong to them. Sharing skills, you will note, are not developed. Therefore, it is very important that you provide identical materials so that more than one child can use the desired object.
♡ Toddlers can focus on only one aspect of an object such as color or shape.

13 to 18 months

Coloring Box

SOCIAL

Child's Developmental Goals

✓ To engage in parallel play

✓ To contribute to a group project

MATERIALS:

❏ 2 plastic containers to hold felt-tip markers

❏ 2 sets of nontoxic, washable felt-tip markers

❏ Large cardboard box

❏ White butcher paper to cover box

❏ Transparent tape

PREPARATION:

♡ Clear an area that can be constantly supervised.

♡ Cover the box by taping white butcher paper on it. Place the box in the cleared area.

♡ Check each felt-tip marker to make sure it contains fluid. Divide the markers so that one set is in each plastic container.

♡ Place the plastic containers on opposite corners of the cardboard box.

NURTURING STRATEGIES:

1. Invite a child to color the box by saying:
   "This box is for coloring. Look at all the markers you can use to decorate the box."

2. If necessary, help the toddler remove and replace the caps on the markers.

3. Observe the toddler's behavior with the markers.

4. Set limits as necessary. For example, to prevent the markers from leaving the area, say:
   "The markers go in the container when you're finished with them."

5. Describe the work being done by the toddler. Comments to say, while pointing, include:
   "Baraka, you're using red. You're making red circles."
   "You're making lines. Long lines and short lines."

6. Discuss how the child is working independently or with another child, when applicable. To illustrate, say:
   "Baraka and David are working at the same time. You both are coloring the box."
   "Baraka, you are working all by yourself."

7. As the child finishes coloring, print her name in the area next to her marks on the box. This will provide recognition of the toddler's contribution to the project.

8. Close the activity for each child or group of children by focusing on how everyone worked together to color the box. Say, for example:
   "You worked hard today. Everyone helped to color the box."
   "We did this together."

☀ Highlighting Development

During the second year of life, children begin showing a possessiveness of their toys and belongings. To illustrate, if another child picks up one of their marking tools or toys, there will be a reaction. The child may grab it out of the hand of the other child. When this occurs, remind the child who took the object that it is another's property. Tell the child, "You have David's toy. Give it back to him. Here is a blue crayon just like his. You can mark with it."

VARIATIONS:

♡ Prepare smaller paper-covered boxes for children to decorate individually.

♡ Decorate using crayons or washable tempera paint instead of markers.

♡ Crawl inside the box and decorate it with crayons or markers.

ADDITIONAL INFORMATION:

♡ When talking to toddlers about their art, be descriptive. Discuss what you see. Talk about color, shape, size, and the use of space. In other words, focus on the process rather than the product being made.

13 to 18 months

Guessing Game

Child's Developmental Goals

✓ To engage in a game with an adult

✓ To participate in a verbal conversation

MATERIALS:

❑ Adult-size sock

❑ Common items to hide such as a block, spoon, ball, and toy car

❑ Child-size table

PREPARATION:

♡ Place one item inside the sock and lay it on a child-size table. Place the other items beside the sock.

NURTURING STRATEGIES:

1. When a child chooses the activity, ask:
   "What's in the sock?"
2. Encourage the toddler to guess what is in the sock before looking.
3. Suggest that the toddler shake or feel the sock if he is having trouble guessing. In addition, you could provide the toddler with some verbal clues such as:
   "You can roll this, Dion"
   "It has wheels."

4. After the toddler guesses, either remove the item from the sock or encourage the toddler to do the task. During the process, provide positive reinforcement for attempts and accomplishments. Comments include:
   "Dion, you guessed it!"
   "Oh, it rolls like a ball but it is a car."
5. Continue the game by asking the toddler to look away while you are adding a new toy to the sock.

☀ Highlighting Development

Children at this stage of development love an audience. They enjoy repeating performances. They also enjoy sociability. Therefore, they continue enjoying hide-and-seek games and receiving applause from adults for their attempts as well as accomplishments.

VARIATION:

♡ Encourage the toddler to put an item in the sock for you to guess.

ADDITIONAL INFORMATION:

♡ Toddlers love guessing games. These types of games advance not only social development but also cognitive skills such as object permanence and language/communication skills.

13 to 18 months

Imitating Me

SOCIAL

Child's Developmental Goals

✓ To imitate an adult's behavior

✓ To experience participating in a small group activity

MATERIALS:

None

PREPARATION:

None

NURTURING STRATEGIES:

1. When a toddler needs something to do, introduce this activity. To illustrate, say:
   "Do what I do. Follow my lead."
2. Engage in the following types of behavior: clap hands, pat head, rub tummy, and tap toes. Go slowly so that the toddler has time to observe and repeat the behavior.
3. Provide positive reinforcement for attempts or accomplishments. Comments to make include:
   "Wow! You are skilled at patting your head."
   "What a loud clap."
4. If another toddler is present but hasn't voluntarily joined in the activity, invite the child to play. Say, for example:
   "Peta, would you like to play a game with Elle and me?"
   "Indira, Donah would like to play with you."

5. Discuss how the children are playing a game together by saying:
   "Peta and Elle are both tapping their toes."
   "Indira and Donah are imitating me."
   "You are both clapping your hands."
6. Continue this activity as long as the child remains interested.

☀ Highlighting Development

From the moment of birth, a child is a social being. Through social interaction with other people, the child is learning about human relationships and the values of the society. Consequently, as a caregiver, your behavior will either help or inhibit the child's social development (Kostelnik et al., 1998).

VARIATION:

♡ Reverse roles by having the toddler provide the leadership, with you following her lead.

ADDITIONAL INFORMATION:

♡ Carefully select the behaviors to model. Begin by introducing actions that you have observed the toddlers doing independently. Then introduce new behaviors.

13 to 18 months

SOCIAL

"I'll Touch"

Child's Developmental Goals

✓ To improve self-awareness

✓ To interact with an adult

MATERIALS:

❏ Unbreakable mirror for viewing the entire body

❏ Felt-tip marker

❏ Index card

PREPARATION:

♡ Place a mirror in the room so that there is space for you to work with child in front of it.

♡ Write words to "I'll Touch" on note card, if desired:

I'll touch my nose
My head, my lips.
I'll touch my toes.
And then my hips.
I'll touch my chin.
And I'll touch my knees.
Then you have seen most of me.

Refer to card as needed throughout the activity.

NURTURING STRATEGIES:

1. When a toddler is seeking an activity, tell the child you have a new rhyme. Then direct the child to the mirror.

2. Ask the toddler to point to the different body parts in the rhyme. Say, for example:
"Mareo, where is your hair?"
Encourage the toddler to view the behavior in the mirror.

3. Provide positive reinforcement for correctly identifying the parts. Comments include:
"Correct."
"Great job. I can see in the mirror that you are pointing to your hair."
"You are good at this, Mareo."

4. Begin saying the rhyme, repeating it slowly to allow the toddler to follow along.

5. Increase the pace of the song as the toddler gains familiarity.

6. Continue singing the song as long as the toddler seems interested.

☀ Highlighting Development

Touch is important for building and maintaining relationships. It can also be an effective tool for guiding young children. When children need guidance, use a caring approach. To illustrate, position yourself so you are at the child's eye level. Then communicate your interest in the child by leaning forward and maintaining a relaxed posture. To gain the child's attention, gently touch the child on the arm. Then provide the appropriate guidance.

VARIATION:

♡ Repeat just the movements of the song without saying the words. Observe to see if the child imitates your movements.

ADDITIONAL INFORMATION:

♡ Observe carefully while saying the rhyme. Alter your speed to allow time for the toddler to touch the identified body part.

13 to 18 months

Friendship Tree

SOCIAL

Child's Developmental Goals

✓ To contribute to a group project
✓ To interact with an adult

MATERIALS:

❑ Green butcher paper cut slightly larger than table
❑ Brown butcher paper cut in shape of tree trunk
❑ Damp sponge or towel
❑ Transparent tape
❑ 2 plastic containers
❑ Red tempera paint
❑ Liquid hand soap
❑ Smocks
❑ Child-size table

PREPARATION:

♡ Remove chairs from around a child-size table.
♡ Cover the table with green butcher paper and secure with tape.
♡ Mix the paint and liquid hand soap to desired thickness and divide into the plastic containers. Place one container on each side of the table.
♡ Lay smocks near the activity so the toddler knows to wear one.
♡ Tape the tree trunk to a wall.

NURTURING STRATEGIES:

1. When a toddler shows interest in the activity, assist the child with rolling up shirt sleeves and putting on a smock.
2. Introduce the activity to the toddler as needed. To illustrate, say:
   "We are making a friendship tree. Everyone will paint on this paper. You can paint with your hands. I'll hang the painting on the wall when we are done."
3. Observe while the toddler is working.
4. Comment on how the toddler is painting using the fingers or hands as tools. Comments include:
   "Rachael, you're spreading the paint with both hands."
   "You made two handprints."

5. Converse with the toddler about the friendship tree, being sure to point out that everyone is working together to make one picture.
6. Have a damp sponge or towel nearby to immediately clean up drips or spills.
7. When the toddler is finished, help wash the paint off her hands.
8. When everyone is finished or it is time to stop, lay the painting in a safe place to dry.
9. When the paint is dry, cut the paper into a treetop and tape it to the wall on top of the tree trunk.

☀ Highlighting Development

The beginnings of self-awareness continue during this stage of development. Children begin to distinguish between themselves and others. Often they may use the words *me* or *mine* when referring to tools, toys and materials. In fact, they may even claim other's belongings by hugging them and saying "mine." This behavior will continue because sharing toys is a difficult skill to learn. By 2½ to 3 years of age, children begin sharing their toys more. Meanwhile, adult support and supervision are vital.

VARIATION:

♡ Cut sponges into apple shapes as tools for applying the paint. Otherwise, purchase apple sponges from a craft store or early childhood catalog.

ADDITIONAL INFORMATION:

♡ This activity requires constant supervision to help minimize the spread of paint. However, the fact that it is messy is the real attraction for toddlers. They are exploring with the senses.
♡ Depending on the interest and the number of children you are working with, it may be necessary to limit the number of children at the activity. Likewise, the amount of time may have to be limited to allow everyone an opportunity to participate.

SOCIAL

Boogie Dancing

Child's Developmental Goals

✓ To participate in an activity with at least one other child

✓ To engage in parallel play

MATERIALS:

❑ Cassette tape or a compact disc of dancing music

❑ Tape or compact disc player

PREPARATION:

♡ Plug in the tape or compact disc player and place it out of the reach of children. Place the tape or compact disc in the player. Then select a song for dancing.

♡ Select and clear a large area for this activity.

NURTURING STRATEGIES:

1. Gather at least two children in the area you cleared. Introduce the activity by saying:
   "I have some special dancing music. We will listen to the music. Then we will dance."

2. Turn on the music and begin dancing.

3. Suggest different ways to dance. These may include squatting while bouncing to the beat, lying down while wiggling to the beat, sitting while clapping or bouncing the upper body to the beat, crawling to the beat, and walking while bouncing to the beat.

4. It may be necessary to connect your words with actions. If that is the case, state the behavior while modeling it at the same time.

5. Describe how the toddlers are moving to the beat.

6. Comment on how the children are dancing at the same time by saying:
   "Yancey and Lydia are dancing together."
   "There are four children dancing to the music."

7. If the children seem interested, dance to a second or third song.

☀ Highlighting Development

Moving to rhythm is a lifelong skill. Music is important for children this age. It is noted for promoting listening, language, and coordination skills. Observe. Children love hearing the same music over and over again. While you may become bored, the children gain a sense of comfort.

Make music experiences pleasurable by choosing developmentally appropriate music. If the tempo is too fast for moving, children at this stage of development will be unable to rhythmically move their bodies.

VARIATION:

♡ Repeat this activity when you observe toddlers dancing spontaneously to music.

ADDITIONAL INFORMATION:

♡ Dancing is an important skill for toddlers to practice because it exercises both sides of the brain simultaneously. Encourage the toddlers to dance often and experiment with various movements.

13 to 18 months

"Here We Go Round"

SOCIAL

Child's Developmental Goals

✓ To interact with another person
✓ To participate in singing an action song

MATERIALS:

None

PREPARATION:

None

NURTURING STRATEGIES:

1. If you see a toddler turning in circles or needing something to do, invite the child to play with you.
2. Sing the song while walking in a circle. The song is as follows:

   ♫ Here we go round the mulberry bush
   ♫ The mulberry bush, the mulberry bush
   ♫ Here we go round the mulberry bush
   ♫ On a cold and frosty morning.

3. Encourage other children, if present, to join in singing the song. Comments include:
   "April, Clayton needs a partner. Come sing with us."
   "Marcos, would you like to sing with us?"
4. As soon as possible, remove yourself from the interaction by saying:
   "I'm tired. I'll sing while you three play."
5. Provide positive reinforcement for playing together. Make comments such as:
   "April and Clayton are playing together."
   "I see three friends playing a game together."

☀ Highlighting Development

Brain development continues as young toddlers create pathways. These pathways develop through sensory motor experiences: seeing, hearing, touching, and experiencing body movements. Examples include singing, dancing, and acting out songs. These teach young children spatial relationships, cause and effect, and body awareness. Therefore, surrounding the children with these types of experiences advances their development.

VARIATION:

♡ Introduce other action songs. See Appendix G for a list.
♡ Bring in a mulberry bush for the children to look at, touch, and dance around, if available. This may help them to understand the song.

ADDITIONAL INFORMATION:

♡ After the introduction, usually you can physically withdraw while providing verbal assistance when necessary. For example, you may need to extend an invitation for a child to join the activity. If the child joins, comment to show you are aware of the child's developing abilities.

13 to 18 months

A Visit from a Musician

Child's Developmental Goals

✓ To reduce stranger anxiety

✓ To interact with a new adult

MATERIALS:

None

PREPARATION:

♡ Invite a musician to visit during a time the child or group of children is dry, fed, and well rested. Ask the musician to play an instrument while the toddlers sing. Provide the musician with a list of the children's favorite songs.

NURTURING STRATEGIES:

1. When the musician arrives, provide an introduction such as:
   "This is Yusuf. He is my friend. He wanted to visit today. Yusuf is going to play his instrument. Would you like to sing with Yusuf?"
2. Sing along with the music.
3. Provide positive reinforcement between songs. Comments to make include:
   "What a good singer. I heard your voice."
   "You were singing."
4. If time permits and the child is interested, ask for suggestions of songs to sing.
5. Thank the guest for playing the instrument.
6. Write a formal thank-you letter and encourage the child to decorate it.
7. Take a walk and mail the letter.

☼ Highlighting Development

Like separation anxiety, stranger anxiety represents social progress. Stranger anxiety is evident during this stage of development for most children. Observe and you will notice that there are differences. Not all strangers evoke the same reaction. For some children, female strangers tend to elicit less anxiety than those who are male. Then, too, strangers who are children tend to elicit less anxiety than adults.

VARIATION:

♡ Invite a friend who plays a different musical instrument or wants to read to the child to visit.

ADDITIONAL INFORMATION:

♡ Pay close attention to the child's reactions to the visitor. If a child appears to be upset, move closer and offer a hug or words for calming the child.

♡ Children pay close attention to our reactions to other people. Therefore, calm, relaxed interactions model that the individual is friendly.

13 to 18 months

Oil Pastel Drawings

Child's Developmental Goals

✓ To participate in a group project

✓ To share supplies with another child

MATERIALS:

❑ White butcher paper cut slightly larger than the child-size or coffee table

❑ Transparent tape

❑ Plastic container

❑ 1 set of oil pastels

❑ Smock, if desired

PREPARATION:

♡ Cover the table with the butcher paper and secure the edges with the tape.

♡ Select the bright colors from the set of oil pastels and place them in the container.

NURTURING STRATEGIES:

1. Observe the toddler using the oil pastels.
2. Describe the toddler's behavior. Say, for example:
   "Winona, you are making dark, red lines."
   "Look at all the colors you've used. I see red, blue, green, and orange."
3. If available and possible, encourage another child to join the experience. Then comment on how the children are working together to create a picture by saying:
   "Winona and Dylan are working on the picture at the same time."
4. Encourage the children to help each other by passing needed supplies. For example, if the container is placed near one child, ask that child to pass it to a friend.

5. Comment on how friends help each other by saying:
   "What a good helper. You passed the oil pastels to a friend."
   Whenever possible, write the toddlers' names near the area they worked.
6. After the activity, remove the paper from the table. Then hang the picture on the wall or bulletin board for everyone to see.

☀ Highlighting Development

Sharing is an important interpersonal skill that children need to learn. However, by nature, young children are egocentric and territorial. Thus, sharing is difficult. As children mature, sharing becomes more common and it is easier for them to relinquish items they are still playing with. However, children at this stage of development find it easier to share with an adult than with their peers or siblings. Therefore, adults can teach children the concept of sharing through on-the-spot instruction.

VARIATION:

♡ Use other tools for marking such as crayons or nontoxic markers.

ADDITIONAL INFORMATION:

♡ When working with more than one toddler, chances are some children may want to make their own picture. To accommodate this desire, have additional paper available.

"Old MacDonald"

Child's Developmental Goals

✓ To interact with another person

✓ To suggest an animal for the song

MATERIALS:

❑ Stuffed animals to correspond with the song

❑ Bag, box, or crate to house the stuffed animals

PREPARATION:

♡ Memorize the words to this nonsexist version of the popular children's song:

♫ Old MacDonald had a farm
♫ E-I-E-I-O
♫ And on that farm there was a cow
♫ E-I-E-I-O
♫ With a *moo, moo* here
♫ And a *moo, moo* there
♫ Here a *moo*, there a *moo*
♫ Everywhere a *moo, moo*
♫ Old MacDonald had a farm
♫ E-I-E-I-O.

Other verses: sheep (baa), pig (oink), dog (bow wow), horse (neigh), cat (meow), duck (quack), etc.

NURTURING STRATEGIES:

1. When a toddler needs a new experience, begin singing the song. Take out the stuffed animal that corresponds to the verse being sung.

2. If a child is hesitant to participate, provide a special invitation. To illustrate, say:
   "Ray, come sing with me."

3. After the first verse, ask the toddler for the next animal on the farm. Sing the song including the suggested animal. Encourage the toddler to hold the stuffed animal while singing.

4. Thank the toddler for a suggestion after singing verses.

5. If more than one child is participating, comment on how they are singing together. Comments to make include:
   "There are three of us singing."
   "Ray and Autumn both suggested we sing about a sheep."

6. Continue singing the song as long as the toddlers seem interested.

☼ Highlighting Development

Toddlers are becoming interested in classifying people as males and females. When singing songs, omit pronouns whenever possible. If omission is not possible, balance your presentation of pronouns. For example, the first time you sing a song, use "she" and the second time, use "he." Toddlers need to be exposed to the fact that males and females can engage in the same behaviors.

VARIATION:

♡ Cut animal shapes out of felt for the toddlers to place on a flannel board.

ADDITIONAL INFORMATION:

♡ As you may notice, the version of this traditional song printed above omits pronouns. The change is nonsexist, allowing both women and men to be land owners.

13 to 18 months

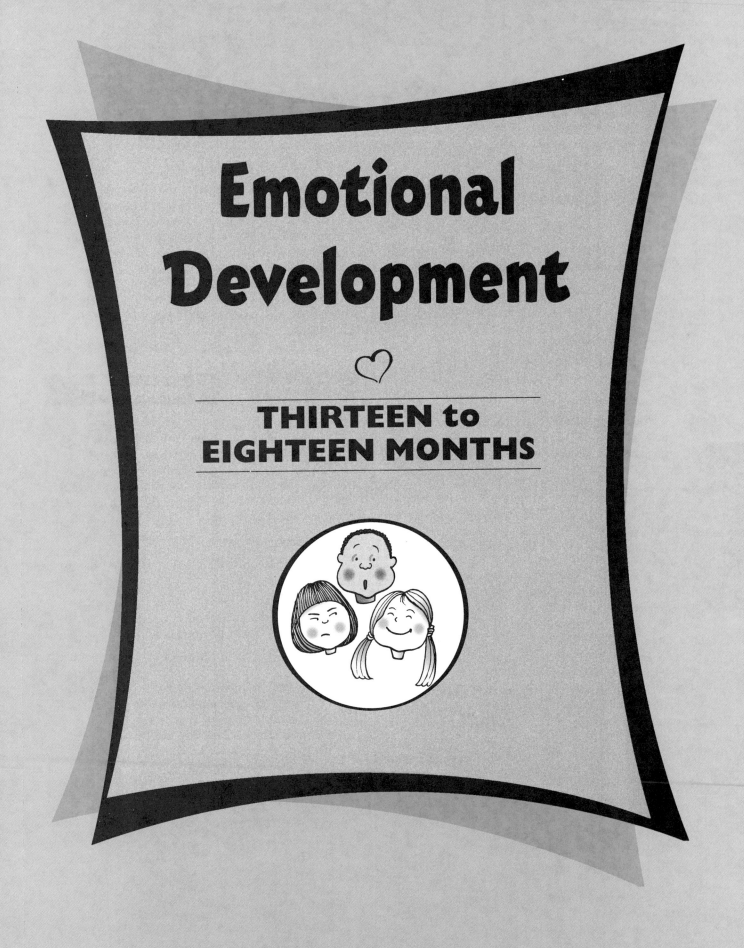

Emotional Development

♡

THIRTEEN to EIGHTEEN MONTHS

Tearing Paper

Child's Developmental Goals

✓ To express a sense of satisfaction when a task is completed

✓ To express emotions such as enjoyment or anger

MATERIALS:

❑ 2 plastic containers

❑ Lightweight colored paper for tearing

❑ Child-size table

PREPARATION:

♡ Set four pieces of paper on a child-size or coffee table in the place you want the child to sit. Place the plastic container next to the paper.

NURTURING STRATEGIES:

1. When a child chooses the activity, introduce it. To illustrate, say:
   "The paper is for tearing. How many pieces can you make? Let's count!"

2. To improve language skills, introduce descriptive words such as *tearing, ripping, small,* and *large* when appropriate.

3. Encourage the toddler to tear the paper. Comments include:
   "Sarah, use both of your hands to tear the paper."
   "How many pieces can you make?"

4. Comment on how the toddler is feeling while engaging in this activity by interpreting the child's nonverbal behavior, including facial expressions. To illustrate, say:
   "You are smiling. Do you like this tearing activity?"
   "What an angry look. Your nose is all crinkled."

5. Providing positive reinforcement may result in the continuation of the desired behavior. Comments include:
   "Sarah, you are tearing the paper."
   "You are working hard at this activity."
   "What a small piece of paper! It started out big and now it's small."
   "Thank you for putting the pieces in the plastic container."

6. To introduce the concept of one-to-one correspondence, count the number of pieces of paper. Given the age of the toddler, avoid counting beyond the numeral 4. You might say, for example:
   "One, two, three. You have three pieces of paper."
   "Look at all of these pieces of paper."

7. To conclude the activity, talk about how completing an activity feels. Comments include:
   "Sarah, you worked hard. You should be proud of your work."
   "Look at all the pieces. You worked hard today."

☀ Highlighting Development

Research tends to support the belief that females are more emotionally expressive than males. Girls cry and smile more than boys (Kostelnik, et al., 2002). Therefore, it is important that boys receive positive reinforcement for expressing emotions. They might even need more assistance in this developmental area.

VARIATION:

♡ Follow up this activity by using the torn paper to make a collage. Adhere the torn paper to clear self-adhesive paper.

ADDITIONAL INFORMATION:

♡ Some papers are more difficult to tear than others. Because toddlers lack the necessary strength to tear heavier-weight paper, select grades of paper that are developmentally appropriate.

♡ Toddlers typically enjoy tearing activities; therefore, you can expect an abundance of small pieces.

13 to 18 months

"If You're Happy . . ."

Child's Developmental Goals

✓ To connect labels of emotions with social behaviors

✓ To label emotions

MATERIALS:

❑ Index card

PREPARATION:

♡ If needed, prepare and place the index card in your pocket. Retrieve the card when you are ready to introduce the activity.

NURTURING STRATEGIES:

1. Sing this song with the child:

   ♬ If you're happy and you know it
   ♬ Clap your hands.   (clap two times)
   ♬ If you're happy and you know it
   ♬ Clap your hands.   (clap two times)
   ♬ If you're happy and you know it
   ♬ Then your face will surely show it   (smile)
   ♬ If you're happy and you know it
   ♬ Clap your hands.   (clap two times)

   Other verses:

   . . . sad . . . Say "boo hoo" or "wipe your tears"
   . . . angry . . . Say "I'm mad" or "scowl"
   . . . happy . . . Say "hurray" or "smile"

2. If a child is performing one of the behaviors in the song, begin with that verse. For example, if a child is scowling, begin with "If you're angry and you know it."

3. Discuss the connection between emotions and behavior. To illustrate, say:
   "What do you do when you're sad?"

4. Respond to the toddler's verbalizations or gestures.

5. Close the activity by stating:
   "We talked about three different feelings: happy, sad, and angry."

☀ Highlighting Development

Adults play an important role in connecting emotional labels to social experiences. First, the child's emotions appear. Then you will need to help the child connect the emotion's label to the social behavior by tutoring. This involves describing the child's emotional expressions.

VARIATION:

♡ Repeat this activity with more than one toddler as a group activity.

ADDITIONAL INFORMATION:

♡ This song presents a simplistic expression of emotions. Toddlers quickly learn that one emotion can result in several social behaviors.

13 to 18 months

Show Me

EMOTIONAL

Child's Developmental Goals

✓ To express a need or desire

✓ To find ways to get a need or desire met

MATERIALS:

None

PREPARATION:

None

NURTURING STRATEGIES:

1. Respond to a toddler's verbal or physical request for assistance.
2. Encourage elaboration of the toddler's needs so that you can better assist. Comments include:
   "Taj, what about your blanket?"
   "Show me. Take my hand and show me."
3. Work with the toddler to solve the problem.
4. Provide positive reinforcement when the need or desire is met. To illustrate, say:
   "You showed me what you needed. We solved your problem."
   "You used words to tell me what you needed. That was helpful, Taj."

Highlighting Development

Most children at this age are attached to soft objects such as teddy bears and blankets. Cuddly toys serve as a source of security. They help children manage the stress associated with separation. The need for security items occurs at a period when the toddlers are increasing their psychological separateness from their primary caregivers.

VARIATION:

♡ Pay close attention to the child's nonverbal cues. This may allow you to quickly respond, thereby meeting the child's emotional needs.

ADDITIONAL INFORMATION:

♡ The use of physical gestures will begin to decline as verbal communication skills increase. Providing children with the necessary words to communicate will facilitate this process.

13 to 18 months

Feeling Masks

Child's Developmental Goals

✓ To identify emotions

✓ To connect emotions with social behaviors

MATERIALS:

☐ 4 paper plates
☐ 4 popsicle sticks
☐ Multicultural colors of felt-tip markers or crayons
☐ Glue

PREPARATION:

♡ Draw faces on the paper plates to exemplify the following feelings: happy, sad, afraid, and surprised.

♡ Attach the popsicle stick to the bottom of the paper plate with the glue.

NURTURING STRATEGIES:

1. Introduce the activity to the toddler by saying:
   "Let's play a guessing game. Guess how I'm feeling."
2. Hold up a feeling mask.
3. Encourage the toddler to guess how you are feeling.
4. Reinforcing guesses may result in the toddler continuing the game. To illustrate, say:
   "Ashanti, look at my mask. How am I feeling?"
   "Yes. I was wearing a mask with a surprised look."
5. Discuss how people behave when they feel a particular way. For example, ask:
   "What do you do when you are surprised?"

6. Continue the conversation by expanding or elaborating on the toddler's verbal responses and gestures. For example, if the toddler begins jumping up and down, say:
   "Ashanti, when you are surprised, you jump up and down."
7. Use the masks as long as the toddlers appear interested.

☀ Highlighting Development

Children's emotional signals, such as smiling or crying, affect the behavior of other people in powerful ways. Similarly, emotional reactions of others regulate children's social behavior. In this experience, the toddlers will be able to alter their reaction based on the expression of the mask.

VARIATIONS:

♡ Encourage the child to imitate you by holding up a mask and behaving accordingly.

♡ Repeat this activity with a small group of children.

ADDITIONAL INFORMATION:

♡ Given toddlers' levels of cognitive development, they often express fear of masks. Reduce this anxiety by providing repeated exposure. Furthermore, hold the mask so that your face is always visible.

13 to 18 months

Labeling Emotions

EMOTIONAL

Child's Developmental Goals

✓ To practice labeling complex emotions

✓ To continue identifying emotions

MATERIALS:

None

PREPARATION:

None

NURTURING STRATEGIES:

1. When you observe a toddler displaying an emotion, label and explain it. For example, the toddler may be hiding behind your leg. When this occurs, say, for example:

   "Antonio, you are feeling shy today. You are hiding your face from me."

2. If the toddler is crying, label the child's emotion by saying:

   "You are crying. You must be feeling sad."

3. If the child is smiling, again label the emotion by saying:

   "Antonio, you are smiling. You must be feeling proud because you stacked the blocks."

4. If the child looks frustrated, label the emotion by saying:

   "You look frustrated. The puzzle piece won't fit."

☀ Highlighting Development

More complex emotions such as shame, embarrassment, guilt, shyness, and pride begin appearing in the second year of life. These are called self-conscious emotions because each involves injury or enhancement to the sense of self. Toddlers need complex emotions labeled and explained to understand them.

VARIATION:

♡ Continue introducing the labels for new emotions whenever the toddler displays them.

ADDITIONAL INFORMATION:

♡ By labeling young children's emotions, you are a role model. Eventually, they will imitate your labeling when interacting with their peers.

13 to 18 months

"I Love You"

Child's Developmental Goals

✓ To express the emotion of caring through a hug or kiss

✓ To feel loved and valued

MATERIALS:

None

PREPARATION:

♡ In preparation for nap time, dim the lights and put on quiet music.

NURTURING STRATEGIES:

1. After gathering a toddler's comfort items, have the child sit on your lap in a rocking chair.
2. Gently rock and sing the following chant:

> Kelly, Kelly, you are so sweet.
> Kelly, Kelly, you are so sweet.
> Kelly, Kelly, you are so sweet.
> I'll rock, rock, and rock you
> Till you fall asleep.

3. Use your voice as a tool for communicating a quiet, restful time.
4. When the child is relaxed, carry and place the toddler in a crib or on a cot. Remain nearby until the toddler is comfortable.

Highlighting Development

Expressing love for another is the basis for later prosocial or altruistic behavior. When children express love, they do so without the expectation of rewards for themselves. They may express their love through actions such as kissing, hugging, and even patting.

VARIATION:

♡ Sing this song again after the toddler wakes up from her nap. At this time, you can pick up the tempo and sing the song faster, communicating a more active time.

ADDITIONAL INFORMATION:

♡ If older children are present, encourage them to sing this song to or with the toddler.
♡ If caring for more than one child, ensure that you individualize the song for each child.
♡ If you are caring for other people's children, share the song with the parents or caregivers of those children.

13 to 18 months

How Am I Feeling?

EMOTIONAL

Child's Developmental Goals

✓ To label emotional expressions
✓ To connect emotional labels with social behaviors

MATERIALS:

None

PREPARATION:

None

NURTURING STRATEGIES:

1. When working one-on-one with a toddler, introduce the activity by saying:
   "Mekhi, let's play a guessing game. Guess how I am feeling. Look at my face."
2. Make a face to illustrate one of the following feelings: happy, sad, surprised, or angry.
3. Encourage the toddler to guess how you are feeling.
4. Reinforcing guesses may result in the toddler continuing the game. To illustrate, say:
   "Mekhi, you are good at this game!"
   "Yes, I was making an angry face."
5. Continue the game as long as the toddler demonstrates signs of interest.

☀ Highlighting Development

Children at this age are extremely lovable. Moreover, they are sociable and friendly. Because of their understanding of the connection between behaviors and emotions, they observe other people's faces for cues. If others are sad and crying, they may cry. Likewise, they will be joyful when others are happy.

VARIATION:

♡ When the toddler has identified the emotions listed above, ask the child to act them out.

ADDITIONAL INFORMATION:

♡ Toddlers should be able to easily identify the four emotions of happiness, sadness, surprise, and anger.

13 to 18 months

Beanbag Toss

Child's Developmental Goals

✓ To express the emotion of excitement

✓ To feel a sense of accomplishment

MATERIALS:

❑ 6 to 8 beanbags

❑ Laundry basket

PREPARATION:

♡ Select and clear an area that can be constantly supervised. Place three or four beanbags in the basket. Then place the basket in the area with the remaining beanbags lying alongside of it.

NURTURING STRATEGIES:

1. Introduce the activity if the toddler seems interested. To illustrate, say:
   "Yoko, today we have a beanbag toss game."
   Throw a beanbag into the basket and ask:
   "How many beanbags can you throw in the basket?"
2. Providing positive reinforcement for attempts and accomplishments helps the toddler to identify strengths. Make comments such as:
   "Yoko, you tossed one in the basket."
   "Look. You almost got the beanbag in the basket."
3. Encourage the toddler to keep working at the activity. Say, for example:
   "Keep trying. You almost got that one."
4. Modify the physical environment as necessary to increase the toddler's chance of success. This can be accomplished in one of two ways. Either move the basket closer to the toddler or verbally instruct the toddler to move closer to the basket.

5. Comment on emotional expressions displayed while playing this game. Comments include:
   "Yoko, what a big smile! You must be happy because you tossed the beanbag into the basket."
   "You have a sad face. Keep trying. I know you can do it."
   "You are jumping up and down. You are proud of yourself. You tossed in three beanbags."

☀ Highlighting Development

Toddlers learn to feel proud when adults provide them emotional instruction. In other words, adults define situations and reactions in terms of self-conscious emotions. Situations invoking pride vary considerably from culture to culture. For example, in some cultures, pride is associated with individual achievement, such as tossing a beanbag into a basket (Berk, 1997).

VARIATION:

♡ Cover boxes of assorted sizes with different colors of self-adhesive paper. Then provide directions to the child. To illustrate, you may encourage the toddler to throw the beanbag into the yellow box.

ADDITIONAL INFORMATION:

♡ Always arrange the environment and design activities to promote the child's success.

13 to 18 months

Pouring Water

Child's Developmental Goals

✓ To develop self-help skills as a means of independence

✓ To increase self-esteem

MATERIALS:

❑ Child-size pitcher

❑ 2 cups

❑ Sensory table, plastic tub, or quilt box

❑ Smock

PREPARATION:

♡ Fill the pitcher about halfway full of water and place it inside the sensory table, plastic tub, or quilt box. Sit the cups beside the pitcher. Then lay a smock where the child can see it and know it is needed for the activity. If more than one child is participating, increase the number of materials for the activity.

NURTURING STRATEGIES:

1. Observe the child's behavior after he chooses the activity.

2. If necessary, introduce the activity to the toddler. To illustrate, say:
   "Reed, you can practice pouring water. Pour the water into the cups."

3. Encourage the toddler to use both hands to hold the pitcher. This will increase the toddler's control and accuracy.

4. Provide assistance as necessary to help make this activity successful. For example, you may need to steady the cup while the child is pouring.

5. Provide positive reinforcement for pouring water into a cup. Say, for example:
   "Reed, look at you! You're pouring water into the cup."
   "You did it! You're good at pouring."

☀ Highlighting Development

According to Eriksen (1950), toddlers face a crisis of autonomy versus shame and doubt. During this crisis, healthy resolution is reached when toddlers are able to choose and decide things for themselves. Of course, autonomy is fostered when adults permit a reasonable choice of activities and avoid shaming the toddler for accidents or lack of accomplishment.

VARIATION:

♡ When the toddler is ready, encourage the child to pour water, juice, or milk during snack by providing child-size plastic pitchers. Assist as necessary.

ADDITIONAL INFORMATION:

♡ Toddlers love helping. However, they lack the necessary fine motor skills to be successful at some tasks. Therefore, be selective when choosing tasks for promoting their independence and self-esteem.

♡ Toddlers may want to drink the water in the sensory table. This interest may be magnified due to the snack cups being used as part of the activity.

CAUTION To promote the child's health, safety and maintain sanitary conditions, have drinking water available.

Assisting with Diapering

Child's Developmental Goals

✓ To assist in dressing
✓ To feel a sense of pride for an accomplishment

MATERIALS:

❏ Regular diapering supplies

PREPARATION:

♡ Arrange the supplies on or near the changing table.

NURTURING STRATEGIES:

1. While diapering the toddler, visually connect with the child.
2. Converse with the toddler about what you are doing. To illustrate, say:
   "Anita, I'm putting on my gloves now."
   "This wipe might be cold. I'm going to wash your bottom."
3. Enlist the child's assistance whenever possible during the diapering process. Given toddlers' large and fine muscle skills, they can easily and successfully participate in pulling up their pants after the clean diaper has been securely fastened. To assist the toddler, stand the child on the diapering table while securely holding her under the arms with both hands. Then encourage the toddler to assist by saying, for example:
   "Anita, pull up your pants."
   "Use both hands to grab your pants." Pause. *"Now pull."* Observe. The toddler will probably be able to pull up only the front of the pants.

4. Provide positive reinforcement for assisting. Comments to make include:
   "Anita, diapering goes faster when we work together."
   "What a good helper. You pulled up your pants."
5. Finish the diapering procedure.

☼ Highlighting Development

To assist children in dressing, demonstrating at the child's eye level usually is the most effective. For children at this stage of development, you may need to start an action and then allow the child to complete the process. For example, demonstrate to the child closing a zipper halfway. Then encourage the child to complete the task. Children take pride in developing self-help skills (Herr, 1998).

VARIATION:

♡ Encourage the toddler to assist in putting on her jacket or other clothing when getting ready to go outside, if needed.

ADDITIONAL INFORMATION:

♡ During the first year of life, diapering served as a way for the adult to build trust with the child. During the second year, the focus should shift to fostering the child's autonomy.

13 to 18 months

Scarf Dancing

Child's Developmental Goals

✓ To express emotions through movement

✓ To associate feelings with behaviors

MATERIALS:

❑ Cassette tape or compact disc of fast-paced classical or jazz music

❑ Cassette tape or compact disc player

❑ One scarf for each toddler and adult participating

❑ Bag, basket, or other container for holding scarves

PREPARATION:

♡ Plug in the tape or compact disc player and place it on a shelf out of the child's reach.

♡ Insert the cassette or compact disc of desired music into the player.

♡ Place the scarves in the container.

NURTURING STRATEGIES:

1. Introduce the activity by saying:
   "We are going to dance to music today. We have scarves for moving to the music. Let me give you one."

2. Turn on the music and begin dancing. Model how to move the scarf to the music.

3. Suggest different ways for moving the scarf such as high or low, fast or slow, in waves or in circles. In addition, discuss how the music makes you feel. For example, quick, light sounds might make you excited whereas long, heavy sounds might remind you of times when you were angry.

4. Use children as models by commenting on their movements with the scarves. If more than one child is present, you might say:
   "Look at how Jonathan is moving his scarf. It is floating to the ground."
   "Graeme, you're walking around your carpet piece."

5. Assist the toddlers in calming down after the music has stopped by encouraging slow movements with the scarves. Ask, for example:
   "Who can move the scarf the slowest?"

6. Tell the children to return their scarves to the bag or basket.

☀ Highlighting Development

Moving to music can be an important way of expressing emotions. It also fosters the development of the whole child: physical, emotional, social, cognitive, and language. For example, creative movement experiences promote spatial relationships, emotional expression, social interactions, cause-and-effect relationships, and receptive language skills.

VARIATION:

♡ Using streamers or bells instead of scarves, dance to the music.

ADDITIONAL INFORMATION:

♡ Toddlers should be introduced to a wide variety of music. However, you will need to carefully select pieces for individual activities to ensure the goals of the experience are met.

Painting with Shaving Cream

Child's Developmental Goals

✓ To express one's emotions through art

✓ To feel a sense of satisfaction when performing a task

MATERIALS:

❑ Can of unscented shaving cream

❑ Sponge

❑ Nonbreakable container of lukewarm water

❑ Damp towel

❑ Smock

PREPARATION:

♡ Fill the container with lukewarm water and place a sponge in it. Immerse the towel in the container of water and wring it out so that it is slightly damp. Then place the water and towel within easy reach of the high chair.

♡ If the room is warm, remove the toddler's clothing. If the room is drafty, roll up the toddler's sleeves and pant legs. Then encourage the child to put on a smock to prevent wet clothing.

NURTURING STRATEGIES:

1. While preparing the toddler for the activity, talk about it. To illustrate, you might say:
   "Nadia, we have shaving cream today. The shaving cream is smooth. You can use your fingers to paint. Paint the tray."

2. Secure the toddler in the high chair. Lock the tray in place.

3. Squirt a small amount of shaving cream on the tray.

4. Observe the toddler's behavior with the shaving cream. Whenever the toddler raises the hands toward the face, restate the limit:
   "Paint the tray."

5. Describe how the child is manipulating the shaving cream and reacting to the experience. Comments include:
   "Nadia, you're pushing the shaving cream with your fingers."
   "What a puzzled look. Do you need more shaving cream?"
   "You are smiling. You must be proud of your work."

6. Add more shaving cream if needed. Then continue the activity as long as the toddler remains interested.

7. When the toddler is finished with the experience, remove the tray. Wipe the child with the damp cloth to remove as much of the shaving cream as possible. Take the child to the bathroom to continue the cleaning process.

8. Clean the tray of the high chair with the sponge.

☀ Highlighting Development

Consensus is lacking on materials that are appropriate for sensory experiences. Some people suggest using food. This may be an acceptable solution to the problem of children's oral exploration; however, food activities can cause confusion. Playing with food teaches young children that sensory materials are edible. Thus, they learn to put sensory material in their mouths. You must take responsibility for helping children to distinguish between play materials and edible substances.

VARIATIONS:

♡ Have the toddlers finger paint on a child-size table while standing up.

♡ For interest, add a few drops of food coloring to the shaving cream.

ADDITIONAL INFORMATION:

♡ Young children experience their world orally by tasting. This can be problematic when planning and supervising activities. Therefore, careful observation is needed.

 This experience requires constant supervision to ensure that the shaving cream is not accidentally wiped into the child's eyes or ingested. To prevent safety hazards, use the sponge to clean up spills as soon as they occur.

13 to 18 months

Dressing for Fun

EMOTIONAL

Child's Developmental Goals

✓ To practice self-help skills by putting on simple articles of clothing

✓ To develop independence

MATERIALS:

❑ Hats and shoes for dress up

❑ Child-size shelf

❑ Shatterproof, full-length mirror

PREPARATION:

♡ Display the hats and shoes on the child-size shelf.

NURTURING STRATEGIES:

1. Observe the toddler dressing in the shoes and hats.
2. Provide verbal, as well as physical, assistance as needed. Comments include:
   "It may be easier to take off your shoes when you are sitting down."
   "Can I help to untie your shoes?"
3. Encourage the toddler to try on several different pairs of shoes and hats. Suggest viewing the outfit in the mirror.
4. Provide positive reinforcement for attempts and accomplishments. Make comments such as:
   "What a neat hat you have on."
   "Fancy shoes. Are they new?"
5. Encourage the child to act out different roles while dressed in the clothing. To illustrate, say:
   "That looks like a shopping outfit. What will you buy at the store?"
6. If appropriate, suggest that two or more children play together. For example, say:
   "Tyler is going shopping for shoes. Should Darby come along to get a new pair?"
7. Observe the child undressing and provide any needed assistance.

☀ Highlighting Development

Play is important for young children's development. Play is children's work. The first stage in dramatic play is functional. In other words, they will use the prop in the traditional manner. For example, when provided dress-up clothes, they will explore, manipulate, and dress in them, thereby improving their self-help skills. As they progress developmentally, their play will change, becoming more imaginative or creative. To illustrate, eventually they may dress up and pretend to take a bus ride to the library.

VARIATION:

♡ Provide purses, wallets, and play money as accessories. Add simple articles of clothing such as pants with elastic bands and pull-on shirts.

ADDITIONAL INFORMATION:

♡ This activity provides time to practice self-help skills in a fun atmosphere.

♡ Let the child play and explore the clothing. Be respectful attentive by observing and assisting only when necessary.

 CAUTION Carefully examine the shoes and hats before you put them out. Select low-heeled shoes that can easily be slipped on and off rather than being buckled or tied. Hats should be loose-fitting and without long strings. Check the hats to make sure there are no removable decorations that could pose a choking hazard.

Peanut Butter and Jelly

Child's Developmental Goals

✓ To improve self-help skills

✓ To feel a sense of pride when accomplishing a task

MATERIALS:

❑ Plastic knife for each person

❑ 2 teaspoons

❑ Creamy peanut butter

❑ Jelly

❑ Saltine crackers

❑ Pitcher of milk

❑ Cups and napkins

❑ 3 nonbreakable plastic bowls

PREPARATION:

♡ Spoon peanut butter and jelly into separate bowls, leaving the spoon in each of the bowls. Pour crackers into the third bowl. Place the bowls, cups, napkins, spoons, knives, and pitcher on a tray. Place the tray on the table.

♡ Clean and sanitize the snack table.

NURTURING STRATEGIES:

1. Assist the child in washing hands for snack. Then wash your own hands.

2. If more than one child is present, ask a toddler to assist in passing out cups, napkins, and knives. Work on one-to-one correspondence skills by providing one of each item to a child. To illustrate, say:
   "LaRonda, does everyone have a cup?"
   "Alex still needs a cup."

3. Pass around the bowl of crackers. Remind the toddlers of how many crackers can be taken at one time. Say, for example:
   "Two crackers. You may take two crackers. One for each hand."
   State how much food can be eaten by each person at this snack. For example, say:
   "You can have six crackers and two glasses of milk."

4. Offer the children peanut butter and jelly to spread on the crackers.

5. Encourage the toddlers to use a spoon to put peanut butter or jelly onto their cracker. Using the knife, spread the topping.

6. Provide positive reinforcement for spreading the topping. Comments might include:
   "LaRonda, excellent job spreading the jelly."
   "You spread out the peanut butter."
   "What a well-covered cracker."

7. Pour milk for the children to enjoy with the crackers.

☀ Highlighting Development

Toddlers' growing, active bodies need plenty of the healthy foods that form a balanced diet. By one year of age, diets should include all of the basic food groups. Toddlers' stomachs, however, are too small to consume the necessary nutrients at three main meals. Hence, they need to eat small amounts of food approximately every 2 to 2½ hours.

VARIATIONS:

♡ Make peanut butter and jelly sandwiches.

♡ Spread softened cream cheese or apple butter on graham crackers.

ADDITIONAL INFORMATION:

♡ Consider the serving size of the food provided for snack. You may need to limit the quantity consumed.

♡ A snack should be a small offering of food to sustain children between meals. It is important to avoid overeating at snack time because it reduces appetites at the next meal. If this occurs, the children may not consume a balanced diet.

♡ Check children's records to ensure there are no allergies to peanut butter.

♡ Informing the children of their limits at snack time is important. It teaches language, numerals and sharing.

CAUTION Peanut butter can be a choking hazard. To reduce the potential hazard, serve small quantities and provide plenty of fluids.

13 to 18 months

Physical Development

♡

NINETEEN to TWENTY-FOUR MONTHS

Jump, Frog, Jump

PHYSICAL

Child's Developmental Goals

✓ To practice jumping
✓ To improve balance skills

MATERIALS:

☐ Book, *Jump, Frog, Jump* by Robert Kalan

PREPARATION:

♡ Select and clear a large space for reading the book.

NURTURING STRATEGIES:

1. Gather the children in the selected area.
2. Read the book, *Jump, Frog, Jump.* This story contains repetitious phrases; therefore, read slowly so the toddler can join in, if desired.
3. Discuss how frogs move from one place to another.
4. Ask the children if they can move that way.
5. Remind the toddlers of any limits, such as jumping around their friends.
6. Let the jumping begin!
7. Using children as models may result in the other children imitating the behavior. Comments to make include:
   "What a safe jump. You waited until Dustin moved his body."
   "You're jumping up and down in place."
8. Assisting the children in calming down after the jumping is very important. Begin by encouraging the toddlers to jump slowly or to make small jumps. Use comments such as:
   "Who can move the slowest?"
   "What a tiny jump; you barely moved!"

☀ **Highlighting Development**

Toddlerhood is a time of rapid change. Large motor skills are continuing to develop. Likewise, improved balance skills and whole body coordination skills lead to the ability to jump in place. The first attempts at jumping occur at about 18 months of age. Observe them. Toddlers enjoy jumping off the bottom step of a staircase with assistance (Snow, 1998). At about 23 months of age, children are successful at jumping with a two-footed takeoff.

VARIATION:

♡ Play leapfrog by having the children jump over a teddy bear.

ADDITIONAL INFORMATION:

♡ Toddlers will attempt to jump for several months before they can master a two-footed takeoff and landing. Initially, the jumps look like a one-foot bouncing step.

CAUTION To promote safety, all attempts to jump from safe locations should be reinforced.

19 to 24 months

Driving a Car

Child's Developmental Goals

✓ To move a wheeled toy vehicle

✓ To improve eye-foot coordination skills

MATERIALS:

❑ Plastic toy car that can be pushed or self-propelled

❑ Helmet

PREPARATION:

♡ Sweep sidewalk or slab of concrete to remove loose stones or pebbles. Park the car in the "parking" area. Finally, place the helmet on the seat of the car.

NURTURING STRATEGIES:

1. When a child moves close to the car, provide a reminder that a helmet is needed and assist, if necessary.

2. Set any necessary limits while buckling the helmet. Comments to make include:
   "Shanta, walk while pushing the car."
   "Push the car on the cement."

3. Encourage imaginative play by asking questions such as:
   "Where are you going in your car?"
   "Are you taking a trip?"

4. Describe what the toddler is doing with the car. Comments include:
   "You are pushing the car up the hill."
   "Shanta, you're driving the car, turning the steering wheel, and pushing with your feet."

5. Providing reinforcement may result in the continuation of positive behavior. To illustrate, introduce comments such as:
   "Shanta, you're riding the car slowly."
   "You're wearing your helmet. You're keeping your head safe."

6. Encourage the toddler to return the car to the parking area and place the helmet on the seat.

☀ Highlighting Development

Toddlers are naturally somewhat unbalanced because their heads are one-quarter of their total height. With practice and maturation, children walk with more balance. Toddlers' knees are less flexed and their feet are positioned closer together. Moreover, toddlers' toes are pointed in the direction the body is moving. Previously, they used wheeled toys for support and balance. Now they can independently move wheeled toys, using them in a functional manner.

VARIATION:

♡ When pushing or pulling a wagon, enlist the toddler's help.

ADDITIONAL INFORMATION:

♡ Provide the minimum amount of assistance so the child has the maximum opportunity to grow in independence, thereby promoting an "I-can-do-it" attitude.

 For safety purposes, make sure that wheeled toys are well balanced and move easily.

19 to 24 months

A Balancing Act

PHYSICAL

Child's Developmental Goals

✓ To improve eye-foot coordination skills
✓ To practice balancing skills

MATERIALS:

❑ 5 feet of masking tape

PREPARATION:

♡ Select and clear a flat, smooth area that can be easily supervised. Apply the tape to the flooring or carpet in a straight line.

NURTURING STRATEGIES:

1. When a toddler chooses the activity, observe the child's behavior.
2. If the toddler doesn't seem to know what to do, introduce the activity. To illustrate, say:
   "Jordan, walk on the tape. Can you walk all the way to the end of the tape?"
3. Suggest holding the arms out to the side to assist in balancing.
4. If necessary, model walking on the line. Walk while holding out your arms.
5. Provide support and encouragement for attempts and accomplishments. Comments include:
   "Jordan, keep going. You're doing it. You're walking on the line."
   "You took two steps on the line."

☀ Highlighting Development

Running, jumping, and climbing are activities toddlers enjoy. In observing them, you will note that they cannot run with ease because they are still having difficulty balancing themselves. Therefore, to maintain balance, they will often take a few rapid steps.

VARIATION:

♡ Arrange tape in the shape of a square, rectangle, or circle.

ADDITIONAL INFORMATION:

♡ If possible, use masking tape that is 2 or 3 inches wide. This will be easier for the toddler to see and, therefore, visually track.
♡ Because toddlers spend much of their time practicing their locomotion skills, to promote their safety, provide them plenty of open space indoors and outdoors.

Ring Toss

Child's Developmental Goals

✓ To increase eye-hand coordination skills

✓ To refine fine motor skills

MATERIALS:

❏ Ring toss game

PREPARATION:

♡ If a ring toss game is unavailable, you can make your own game. Begin by collecting six to eight plastic container lids and one margarine container. Cut the center out of the lids. Then cut a hole the size of a paper towel roll in the bottom of the container. If necessary, cover sharp edges with masking tape. Insert the paper towel roll into the container. Test each ring to be sure it easily fits around the tube.

♡ Select an area in the room or outdoors that has sufficient space for this activity. Then set the ring toss game in this area.

NURTURING STRATEGIES:

1. When a toddler selects the activity, observe the child's behavior. Note the child's ability at the game.

2. Providing support and encouragement may result in the toddler engaging in the activity for a longer period of time. Make comments such as:
"Colette, almost. Try it again."
"You're working hard at this game."

3. Modify the environment as necessary to decrease or increase the challenge by asking the toddler to step closer to or farther away from the ring toss.

4. Incorporate math into the activity by counting the number of rings that encircle the tube.

5. Provide positive reinforcement by clapping or smiling when the toddler gets a ring on the tube.

☀ Highlighting Development

To promote the development of toddlers, consideration needs to be given to choosing appropriate toys and materials. Unlike younger children who are used to grasping, shaking, and mouthing objects, toddlers are beginning to move objects from container to container. They also enjoy stacking or tossing objects. Then, too, toddlers prefer realistic-looking toys that encourage involvement such as transportation toys, dolls, or puzzles where they can cause a reaction.

VARIATION:

♡ To increase the challenge, use large-mouth canning rings to toss onto the tube.

ADDITIONAL INFORMATION:

♡ Often, games can be made from common household items. Not only is this inexpensive, but it teaches children creativity and recycling.

19 to 24 months

Batting Practice

Child's Developmental Goals

✓ To improve eye-hand coordination skills

✓ To refine large muscle coordination skills

MATERIALS:

❑ 8-foot piece of wool yarn

❑ Masking tape

❑ Rubber or sponge ball at least 12 inches in diameter

❑ Tree or other structure

PREPARATION:

♡ Tie one end of the yarn piece to the ball and secure with masking tape as necessary. Tie the other end of the yarn to a low tree limb or structure so that the ball will be in reach of the child's hands.

NURTURING STRATEGIES:

1. Introduce the activity to the toddler by saying:
   "Ewan, the ball is for hitting. Hit it gently with your hand."

2. State additional limits as needed if other children are present. Comments include:
   "One person at a time" or "Stand still while hitting the ball."

3. Encourage the toddler to hit the ball with both hands by saying, for example:
   "Now use your other hand."

4. Discuss how the ball moves after being hit. To illustrate, say:
   "Ewan, look. The ball hit the tree trunk and bounced back."

5. Provide positive reinforcement for the child's behaviors. Use comments such as:
   "What a gentle hit."
   "Wow. The ball went higher that time."

6. If necessary, when other children are present, set a time limit for the child so that others can take a turn. An egg timer works great for this. Tell the child that when the timer rings it will be another's turn. Comments include:
   "Ewan, when the timer rings, it will be Bailey's turn. Bailey has been waiting for her turn."

☀ Highlighting Development

By six months, infants will begin to show a preference for handedness. Most of the time, infants will use their right hand. By two years of age, most toddlers show a preference for one hand. While 10 percent show a preference for their left hand, 90 percent prefer their right. To check children's handedness, observe their behavior in this activity. What hand are they repeatedly using to swipe at the ball? Some children at this stage will use both hands equally.

VARIATION:

♡ As the child's accuracy increases, reduce the size of the ball.

ADDITIONAL INFORMATION:

♡ Toddlers are more focused on ownership than sharing or taking turns. Therefore, you should always provide duplicate items to prevent conflicts. However, with this activity, it would be difficult to supervise two children at one time. As a result, helping the children to take turns will be necessary. Likewise, it is a starting point for learning the skills of sharing and problem solving.

19 to 24 months

Beach Ball Kick

Child's Developmental Goals

✔ To improve balancing skills

✔ To practice eye-foot movements

MATERIALS:

❑ 2 to 3 beach balls

PREPARATION:

♡ Inflate the beach balls. Clear an open area, grassy, if available, of any obstacles.

NURTURING STRATEGIES:

1. Observe the toddler's behavior with the beach balls.
2. Suggest different ways to use the balls. For example, if the toddler is pushing or hitting the ball with a hand, suggest kicking the ball with a foot.
3. Encourage the toddler to kick the ball with both feet.
4. If the child is having difficulty kicking the ball, provide plenty of time to practice that skill. Comments include:
   "Emily, oops. You lost your balance. Keep trying."
   "You're getting it! I saw the ball move."
   "It takes time to learn something new."
5. Make a game of kicking the ball by suggesting that the toddler kick it to you.
6. Model suggestions that would improve the toddler's kicking. Connect your actions to words by verbally describing your actions. If the toddler loses balance, model kicking the ball with your arms out to your side while saying:
   "Holding out my arms helps to keep me balanced."
   If, on the other hand, the toddler is trying to run and kick the ball, stand still and say:
   "I'm going to kick the ball while standing still. That works better for me."
7. Play the kicking game as long as the toddler seems interested.

Highlighting Development

Toddlers at this stage are typically showing a preference for one side of their body over the other. The child's handedness is related to the dominant side of the body. Observe. Right-handed people use their right hand and ear. Moreover, they kick using their right foot.

Toddlers like rolling, kicking, and tossing balls. To prevent injuries, choose a foam or soft rubber ball that is about the size of a volleyball. Because toddlers are passive in their first efforts to catch, throw the ball gently.

VARIATION:

♡ If caring for more than one child, encourage two toddlers to kick the ball back and forth.

ADDITIONAL INFORMATION:

♡ For success, children need large, lightweight balls to kick.

♡ At this stage, toddlers also enjoy playing roll-and-catch with an adult.

19 to 24 months

Exercising

PHYSICAL

Child's Developmental Goals

✓ To increase body awareness

✓ To exercise large muscles

✓ To develop healthy habits

MATERIALS:

❑ Rag doll

PREPARATION:

None

NURTURING STRATEGIES:

1. If more than one child is present, gather the children in a group.
2. Introduce your rag doll and the activity. To illustrate, say:

   "I brought a special friend with me today. His name is Yuji. Yuji likes to move his body. Let's see if you can do what he can do."
3. Move the rag doll while verbally describing the movement. Introduce actions such as jumping in place, touching your toes, nodding your head, moving your arms in circles, stretching to touch the sky, and turning in a circle.

4. If other children are present, use them as models by providing positive reinforcement for desirable behaviors. Comments to make include:

   "Yuji, look at how Lydia is jumping. Up and down."
   "Patrick, you're moving your arms in little circles."
5. Assist the children in calming down by introducing slow movements such as sitting on the floor, clapping hands, or tapping toes.
6. If the toddlers want to continue the activity, have other dolls available for them to manipulate.

☀ Highlighting Development

Obesity has been related to lack of regular exercise. Obese children have a higher incidence of health-related problems. Although toddlers should not be labeled as overweight, they should be taught skills for healthy living. You should model exercising and eating low-fat foods.

VARIATION:

♡ Exercise to music.

ADDITIONAL INFORMATION:

♡ If you model the importance of being physically fit, children will imitate you.

19 to 24 months

Pulling a Wagon

Child's Developmental Goals

✓ To improve eye-foot coordination skills

✓ To strengthen large muscles

MATERIALS:

❑ Toddler-size wagon

❑ 2 stuffed animals

PREPARATION:

♡ Place the stuffed animals in the wagon

NURTURING STRATEGIES:

1. When a toddler chooses the activity, observe the child's behavior.

2. If necessary, introduce the activity. To illustrate, say: *"Jacinta, the stuffed animals want to go riding. Pull the handle of the wagon and walk. Stay on the cement."*

3. Explain that the stuffed animals are riding today. Provide a choice for the toddler. Ask if the child wants to push or pull the wagon.

4. Describe the toddler's behavior with the wagon. For example, comment: *"Jacinta, you're pulling the wagon up the hill."*

5. Restate limits as necessary to protect the safety of the toddler.

6. Provide positive reinforcement for following the limits and, when applicable, working with another person. Use comments such as: *"You remembered to keep the wagon on the sidewalk." "Jacinta, you are taking the animals for a walk." "We are working together to give the animals a ride."*

☀ Highlighting Development

Toddlers are becoming increasingly independent. Because they are interested in pursuing their own purposes and enjoy movement, they lack the ability to make safe judgments. They love climbing into, on top of, or out of almost anything—a shelf, a wagon, or even a dresser. To protect them, you must constantly supervise them.

VARIATIONS:

♡ Provide infant strollers for pushing.

♡ Take the toddler for a ride in the wagon.

ADDITIONAL INFORMATION:

♡ Pulling wagons will help build the child's strength and endurance.

 Carefully observe toddlers to prevent potential accidents, especially when they are turning corners. They will often turn too sharply and dump the contents of the wagon.

19 to 24 months

Picking Up Cotton Balls

PHYSICAL

Child's Developmental Goals

✓ To improve eye-hand coordination skills

✓ To practice fine muscle skills

MATERIALS:

❑ 2 nonbreakable bowls

❑ Bag of cotton balls

❑ 2 pairs of tongs

❑ Child-size table or coffee table

PREPARATION:

♡ Clear an area on a child-size table. Place several cotton balls and a pair of tongs in each bowl. Scatter approximately 20 cotton balls on the table in front of the bowls.

NURTURING STRATEGIES:

1. When a toddler chooses the activity, observe.
2. If necessary, introduce the activity. To illustrate, say: *"Nigel, use the tongs to pick up the cotton balls. Then put the balls in the bowl."*
3. Suggest different ways, such as one hand versus two hands, to hold the tongs.
4. Model different ways to hold the tongs, if necessary. Reinforce your actions with words by saying, for example: *"I'm holding the tongs with both of my hands."*
5. Count the number of cotton balls the toddler puts in the bowls with the tongs.
6. Provide positive reinforcement for attempts and accomplishments. Comments include: *"Nigel, you're getting it. Keep trying."* *"You put nine cotton balls in the bowl. That is a lot of cotton balls."*
7. Encourage the toddler to work independently by saying: *"Come and get me if you need something."*

☀ Highlighting Development

Large muscle skills develop first. They are also easier to master than small muscle skills. Observe toddlers' developmental progression holding tools. At first, the children hold marking tools such as pencil, crayons, and chalk with their fists to scribble. Later, they will hold the tools with their thumb and finger. At this time, tongs can be introduced to continue strengthening and developing control of the hand and finger muscles.

VARIATION:

♡ Use different tools such as large spoons or pliers to pick up the cotton balls.

ADDITIONAL INFORMATION:

♡ When handing materials to toddlers, position them in either the right or left side of their body as opposed to the middle. This will encourage the children to rotate the body and cross their midline as they reach to obtain the materials.

 Closely supervise toddlers when they are working with tongs. Be prepared to quickly set limits for the proper use of tongs, if necessary. Say, for example, "Use the tongs to pick up the cotton balls."

19 to 24 months

Putting On and Taking Off Lids

Child's Developmental Goals

✓ To practice eye-hand coordination skills

✓ To improve fine muscle skills

MATERIALS:

❑ 4 to 5 plastic nonbreakable containers with snap-on lids
❑ Basket

PREPARATION:

♡ Clean the containers, checking each for sharp edges. If any sharp edges are discovered, cover them with masking tape.
♡ Put all containers in the basket and then place it in a convenient location for the child.

NURTURING STRATEGIES:

1. Observe the child's behavior with the materials.
2. If necessary, introduce the activity. To illustrate, say:
   "Zhu, find the lids that fit on the containers."
3. Provide support and encouragement as the toddler is working. Comments include:
   "Push with your fingers. It will fit."
   "Keep trying. The lid is almost on."
4. If the toddler is having difficulty finding a lid that fits, verbally assist by saying:
   "Zhu, try the red lid. It might fit."
   "The container is small. Look for a small lid. Let me help you."

5. Providing positive reinforcement may result in the toddler spending more time at the activity. Use statements such as:
   "Zhu, you've matched three lids and containers."
   "You're working hard at this activity."
6. Continue the activity as long as the toddler shows interest.

☀ Highlighting Development

Motor development continues to mature during this period as children master small muscle skills. Although there are variations among child-rearing practices in different cultures, the sequence of motor development proceeds at about the same rate and sequence. Milestones include making more controlled marks on paper. With their increased ability, children's accuracy in using nesting boxes, placing shapes in sorters, and placing lids on containers is also increasing.

VARIATION:

♡ Increase the challenge by using nonbreakable containers with screw-on lids.

ADDITIONAL INFORMATION:

♡ Toddlers revel in opening and closing containers, as well as filling and emptying them. Therefore, be sure to have objects available for filling and spilling.

19 to 24 months

Puddle Jumping

PHYSICAL

Child's Developmental Goals

✓ To improve balance skills
✓ To practice jumping

MATERIALS:

❑ Blue butcher paper
❑ Transparent adhesive tape
❑ Scissors

PREPARATION:

♡ Clear a large area on the floor.
♡ Cut six "puddles" from the butcher paper. Arrange the puddles on the floor, placing them approximately 8 to 12 inches apart. Tape the puddles to the floor.

NURTURING STRATEGIES:

1. Introduce the activity as a toddler chooses it. To illustrate, say:
   "Tyee, look here. These are pretend puddles. See if you can jump in all of them."
   "Watch me jump. Now show me how you can jump."
2. Encourage the toddler to jump to another puddle. Enthusiastically say, for example:
   "Jump. Jump. Jump to another puddle."
3. Describe how the toddler jumps. Comments include:
   "Tyee, you jumped with both feet."
   "You swung your arms while jumping."
4. Provide positive reinforcement while the toddler is engaged in the activity. Comments to make might include:
   "What a long jump. You landed right in the middle of the puddle."
   "Wow! You jumped high that time."

5. If present, invite another toddler to join in the activity.
6. If two or more toddlers are playing together, comment by saying:
   "Tyee and Oshima are puddle jumping together."

☀ Highlighting Development

Normal development assumes many different forms and proceeds at a pace appropriate to each child. Although you need to carefully observe for completion of developmental milestones, avoid creating a climate of comparison or competition (Greenman & Stonehouse, 1996).

VARIATIONS:

♡ Tape two different shapes such as squares or triangles on the floor. Encourage the toddlers to jump to the triangle or square. This activity could also be designed to include puddles of different colors.
♡ Provide plastic raincoats, hats, and galoshes to wear while jumping.

ADDITIONAL INFORMATION:

♡ Observe the child. Typically, toddlers thoroughly enjoy moving their bodies. When the child appears to particularly enjoy an activity, consider repeating it.

19 to 24 months

Follow the Footprints

Child's Developmental Goals

✓ To improve balancing skills

✓ To practice eye-foot coordination skills

MATERIALS:

❑ Several pairs of adult-size shoes

❑ Construction paper

❑ Scissors

❑ Transparent self-adhesive paper

❑ Bag

PREPARATION:

♡ Trace the shoes onto two or three pieces of construction paper. Cut out the footprints. Then cut rectangles that are larger than the footprints from the transparent, self-adhesive paper.

♡ Clear a path on the vinyl floor or carpet from one door to another. Lay the footprints on the floor about 6 inches apart in a stepping fashion. Adhere each footprint to the floor with the transparent self-adhesive paper.

♡ Put adult-size shoes in the bag and set them at the end of the footprints.

NURTURING STRATEGIES:

1. Observe the reactions to the footprints. Are they being noticed immediately? If so, are the footprints being followed?

2. Begin introducing the activity by saying:
   "Look, someone came into our room last night. They left tracks or footprints behind. What can we do with the footprints?"

3. Encourage creative thinking by asking open-ended questions such as:
   "Why do you think the person was here?"
   "Do you think the person left something for us?"

4. Suggest that the toddler follow the footprints from beginning to end.

5. Provide positive reinforcement for walking on the footprints. Comments to make include:
   "You're stepping on each footprint. Left, right, left, right."
   "You're using your arms for balance. You're holding them out to your sides."

6. If more than one child is participating, use a child as a model. For example, say:
   "Look at the way Junie is using her arms. She holds them that way for balance."

7. When you reach the end of the footprints, ask the toddlers if they can see anything new.

8. If necessary, provide clues to encourage the discovery of the bag of shoes.

9. Encourage each toddler to pick out a pair of shoes, put them on, and follow the footprints again.

10. Discuss whether moving in the adult-size shoes is harder or easier than walking in their own shoes.

☼ Highlighting Development

Gradually, children improve their balancing skills. Watch them. They enjoy imitating another person's walk in the sand or snow. You can foster balancing and eye-foot coordination skills by providing a path for the toddlers to track.

VARIATION:

♡ Cut out animal or dinosaur footprints to follow.

ADDITIONAL INFORMATION:

♡ This activity, although designed for physical development, emphasizes creative thinking. Asking open-ended questions with an activity can encourage toddlers to think about things in a variety of ways, even though they may lack the ability to clearly communicate what they are thinking.

19 to 24 months

Popping Bubbles

PHYSICAL

Child's Developmental Goals

✓ To practice jumping up and down

✓ To improve whole-body coordination skills

MATERIALS:

❑ 2-foot-square piece of bubble wrap

❑ Wide masking tape

PREPARATION:

♡ Clear a surface that can be easily supervised. If available, a carpeted area is preferred for safety purposes. Secure the bubble wrap to the floor with the masking tape.

NURTURING STRATEGIES:

1. Introduce the activity to the toddler. To illustrate, say:
   "Look, here is bubble wrap. These bubbles have air in them. They make noise when they are popped. How could we pop these bubbles?"

2. Converse with the toddler about his answers. If necessary, ask, for example:
   "Rashid, what would happen if we jumped on the bubbles?"

3. Encourage the toddler to jump on the bubble wrap and find out.

4. Act surprised when a bubble pops.

5. Encourage the toddler to join in the jumping. Carefully supervise the activity and set limits as needed.

6. If there is only one child jumping, you can join in the play. Begin by holding on to the toddler's hands while jumping. Swing your arms while jumping to promote the toddler's whole-body coordination.

7. Provide positive reinforcement for jumping. Comments include:
   "Rashid, you're jumping up and down in the same spot."
   "Listen. The bubbles are popping."

8. If present, invite another child to join in the jumping.

☼ Highlighting Development

Remember that norms represent the average performance of a group of children. Before children can jump off the floor, they walk backward and up stairs. Typically, they can perform a two-footed takeoff by about 23 months of age. Watch them. Once they have mastered this skill, they will enjoy repeating it over and over again.

VARIATION:

♡ Tape bubble wrap to serving trays and provide wooden hammers for popping the bubbles.

ADDITIONAL INFORMATION:

♡ This is a very noisy activity. Therefore, make it available only for short periods of time. If you can devise a safe way for introducing the activity outdoors, then do it outside. The noise level will be lower.

19 to 24 months

"Hokey Pokey"

Child's Developmental Goals

✓ To improve balancing skills

✓ To refine whole-body coordination skills

MATERIALS:

❏ Index card

❏ Pen

PREPARATION:

♡ Clear a large space on the carpet for this activity.

♡ Write the words to the song on the index card, if desired. Put the card in your pocket.

♪ You put your arm in   (arm in a circle)
♪ You put your arm out   (arm out of a circle)
♪ You put your arm in   (arm in and shake)
   and you shake it all about.

♪ You do the hokey pokey   (twist body)
♪ And you turn yourself   (walk in circle)
   about
♪ That's what it's all about.   (clap to beat)

♡ For additional verses, substitute the leg, elbow, hand, foot, head, and/or whole body.

NURTURING STRATEGIES:

1. Gather the toddlers and introduce the activity and model, if necessary. Begin by saying:
   "We are going to sing. Singing is fun. Stand up. Put your arms out to your side. For this song, we need plenty of space. If you touch someone, move your body. Good. Now everyone has enough space. Let's sing."

2. Begin to sing the song at a very slow pace, allowing the toddlers to join in.

3. Provide positive reinforcement throughout the activity. Comments to make include:
   "You're really good at singing this song."
   "This is fun!"
   "You are keeping your body safe."

4. Continue the activity as long as the toddlers seem interested.

☀ Highlighting Development

By the end of the second year, toddlers are able to control their bodies remarkably well. They enjoy jumping, running, and dancing. Additionally, they can identify body parts with ease. Therefore, activities that combine these skills may soon become favorites that are frequently repeated. Moreover, these activities are beneficial because they stimulate toddlers' sensory and motor systems.

VARIATION:

♡ Weather permitting, introduce this activity outdoors, preferably on a grassy area, if available.

 For safety purposes, if more than one toddler is participating, each toddler will need plenty of space. Therefore, you will need to assist the toddlers in positioning themselves a safe distance from their peers.

19 to 24 months

Driving a Car

Child's Developmental Goals

✓ To move a wheeled toy vehicle

✓ To improve eye-foot coordination skills

MATERIALS:

❑ Plastic toy car that can be pushed or self-propelled

❑ Helmet

PREPARATION:

♡ Sweep sidewalk or slab of concrete to remove loose stones or pebbles. Park the car in the "parking" area. Finally, place the helmet on the seat of the car.

NURTURING STRATEGIES:

1. When a child moves close to the car, provide a reminder that a helmet is needed and assist, if necessary.

2. Set any necessary limits while buckling the helmet. Comments to make include:
   "Shanta, walk while pushing the car."
   "Push the car on the cement."

3. Encourage imaginative play by asking questions such as:
   "Where are you going in your car?"
   "Are you taking a trip?"

4. Describe what the toddler is doing with the car. Comments include:
   "You are pushing the car up the hill."
   "Shanta, you're driving the car, turning the steering wheel, and pushing with your feet."

5. Providing reinforcement may result in the continuation of positive behavior. To illustrate, introduce comments such as:
   "Shanta, you're riding the car slowly."
   "You're wearing your helmet. You're keeping your head safe."

6. Encourage the toddler to return the car to the parking area and place the helmet on the seat.

☼ Highlighting Development

Toddlers are naturally somewhat unbalanced because their heads are one-quarter of their total height. With practice and maturation, children walk with more balance. Toddlers' knees are less flexed and their feet are positioned closer together. Moreover, toddlers' toes are pointed in the direction the body is moving. Previously, they used wheeled toys for support and balance. Now they can independently move wheeled toys, using them in a functional manner.

VARIATION:

♡ When pushing or pulling a wagon, enlist the toddler's help.

ADDITIONAL INFORMATION:

♡ Provide the minimum amount of assistance so the child has the maximum opportunity to grow in independence, thereby promoting an "I-can-do-it" attitude.

 For safety purposes, make sure that wheeled toys are well balanced and move easily.

19 to 24 months

A Balancing Act

PHYSICAL

Child's Developmental Goals

✓ To improve eye-foot coordination skills
✓ To practice balancing skills

MATERIALS:

❑ 5 feet of masking tape

PREPARATION:

♡ Select and clear a flat, smooth area that can be easily supervised. Apply the tape to the flooring or carpet in a straight line.

NURTURING STRATEGIES:

1. When a toddler chooses the activity, observe the child's behavior.
2. If the toddler doesn't seem to know what to do, introduce the activity. To illustrate, say:
   "Jordan, walk on the tape. Can you walk all the way to the end of the tape?"
3. Suggest holding the arms out to the side to assist in balancing.
4. If necessary, model walking on the line. Walk while holding out your arms.
5. Provide support and encouragement for attempts and accomplishments. Comments include:
   "Jordan, keep going. You're doing it. You're walking on the line."
   "You took two steps on the line."

Highlighting Development

Running, jumping, and climbing are activities toddlers enjoy. In observing them, you will note that they cannot run with ease because they are still having difficulty balancing themselves. Therefore, to maintain balance, they will often take a few rapid steps.

VARIATION:

♡ Arrange tape in the shape of a square, rectangle, or circle.

ADDITIONAL INFORMATION:

♡ If possible, use masking tape that is 2 or 3 inches wide. This will be easier for the toddler to see and, therefore, visually track.
♡ Because toddlers spend much of their time practicing their locomotion skills, to promote their safety, provide them plenty of open space indoors and outdoors.

19 to 24 mon

Language and Communication Development

♡

NINETEEN to TWENTY-FOUR MONTHS

Listening to a Story

Child's Developmental Goals

✓ To improve receptive language skills

✓ To practice reading along with a book

MATERIALS:

❑ Tape or compact disc player

❑ Headphones

❑ Tape or compact disc book set

PREPARATION:

♡ Select an area for this activity that has a child-size table and chairs and is near an electrical outlet.

♡ To promote independence, tape a green dot on the play button and a red dot on the stop button.

♡ Place the electronic device and headphones on the table.

♡ Insert the tape or compact disc into the player and lay a book next to it. To ensure it is working properly, test the player.

NURTURING STRATEGIES:

1. When a child selects the activity, introduce it by saying:
   "Eloise, this is a new way to read a book. You can listen to the words with the headphones. Turn the page when you hear a beep."

2. Help the toddler put on the headphones. Talk about how the headphones feel. Say, for example:
   "The headphones are heavy."

3. Demonstrate turning on the tape. While pointing to the green dot, say:
   "Green means go. Press the green button."

4. Reinforcing your words with actions may be necessary. If so, press the green button while saying:
   "Green means go. Push down on the button. Now the tape will play."

5. Observe the toddler "reading" the book. If the child is not turning the pages, put on a set of headphones and model this. Verbally describe your actions. Comments to make include:
   "Eloise, I turned the page because the tape beeped."
   "When the tape beeps, I turn the page."

6. When the toddler is finished with the listening activity, help the child remove the headphones. While doing so, talk about the activity by saying:
   "This is a new way to listen to stories. Do you like it?"

7. Encourage the toddler to repeat the activity later. To illustrate, say:
   "This player and book will be here. Come and listen to the story again."

☀ Highlighting Development

Language is the most important method of communication. When reading to a child, respond to any vocalizations that are made. Greet the child's language with a smile or nod or verbally acknowledge it by expanding the child's words into a sentence. These strategies will reinforce the value of language as well as encourage the child to repeat the words.

VARIATION:

♡ Read and tape the recordings of the children's favorite stories.

ADDITIONAL INFORMATION:

♡ Provide two or more headphones if several children are present.

♡ Some children will not like how the headphones feel. Encourage them to try the headphones on. However if they feel uncomfortable, allow the child to remove them.

♡ Stories on tape should be used to supplement reading stories to the child. They should never be used as a substitute for daily reading.

19 to 24 months

Locating "Spot"

Child's Developmental Goals

✓ To increase receptive language skills

✓ To demonstrate expressive language skills

MATERIALS:

❑ Book, *Where Is Spot?* by Eric Hill

❑ Felt-tip marker

❑ Buff-colored paper

❑ Dog stencil

PREPARATION:

♡ Trace and cut a dog shape for the toddler. If more children are present, prepare one shape for each child. Then prepare at least two extra dog shapes. Print the toddler's name on a dog shape.

NURTURING STRATEGIES:

1. Signal that it is time to pick up the toys by singing a cleanup song. See Appendix G for a list of songs.
2. Model cleanup skills by assisting the toddler in picking up toys.
3. Briefly introduce the book by saying:
   "I have a book about Spot. He is hiding. Let's see if we can find him."
4. Read the story. Ask the child to describe where Spot might be hiding. Look where the child suggests.
5. Provide positive reinforcement for guesses whether correct or not. Use comments such as:
   "Troy, what a thoughtful guess."
   "Good guess!"

6. When the story is complete, show the child a dog shape. When the child's eyes are closed, hide the dog someplace in the area where it will be visible.
7. Encourage the child to guess where the dog is hiding.
8. If the child remains interested, hide the dog again.
9. To end the activity, provide each child participating with a dog shape.

☀ Highlighting Development

New words are learned by young children through conversing and reading. Reading helps encourage an enjoyment of books and promotes the development of language skills. As in other developmental areas, growth in language is asynchronous. It has intermittent spurts, and these spurts vary with each individual child (Deiner, 1997). However, by 24 months, most children are using two-word phrases.

VARIATION:

♡ Play "Hide the Bone" game by providing a rubber bone, which can be purchased from a pet store.

ADDITIONAL INFORMATION:

♡ Depending on the child's understanding of object permanence, carefully select a location for hiding the toys. For some children, the dog will need to be visible positioned. For others, select a more challenging location.

19 to 24 months

Tickling a Teddy Bear

Child's Developmental Goals

✓ To interact with an adult

✓ To practice following directions

MATERIALS:

❑ 2 to 3 teddy bears

PREPARATION:

♡ Place teddy bears in an open area.

NURTURING STRATEGIES:

1. When a toddler is carrying a teddy bear, suggest playing a game with the toy.
2. Introduce the game by saying:
   "Aida, this is a tickle game. I'm going to tell you what to do. Then you do it to the teddy bear."
3. Recite areas for the toddler to tickle. Include toes, nose, eyes, mouth, chin, fingers, arm, leg, knee, ear, and tummy.
4. Periodically provide positive reinforcement for accuracy. Comments include:
   "Aida, you found the teddy bear's knee."
   "The teddy bear likes having its tummy tickled."
5. Converse with the toddler about being tickled. Start the conversation by asking, for example:
   "Aida, do you like to be tickled?"

6. Encourage the toddler to repeat the label for the area being tickled by asking questions such as:
   "What are you tickling now?"
7. Continue the game as long as the toddler remains interested.

☀ Highlighting Development

Children at this stage possess the necessary receptive language skills to follow a simple directive. It is necessary, however, to tailor your directions to the abilities of the child. To illustrate, you may tell one child to touch only a body part. You may tell another child, who is more advanced, to touch two body parts. Thus, you have made the activity developmentally appropriate for both children.

VARIATIONS:

♡ Repeat similar activities using a baby doll.
♡ Tickle a toddler's body area and encourage the child to name it.

ADDITIONAL INFORMATION:

♡ Toddlers enjoy moving items from one area of a room to another. This gives them power and control over their environment. Therefore, avoid discouraging this behavior until it is time to clean up.

19 to 24 months

Taking a Trip

Child's Developmental Goals

✓ To practice using expressive language skills

✓ To engage in functional play

MATERIALS:

❑ 1 small suitcase with flip latches or 1 child-size backpack per child

❑ 1 or more of the following items: shirts, hats, pairs of shoes, small dolls, or stuffed animals

PREPARATION:

♡ Arrange all materials neatly. In a child care center, place the items on a shelf or sturdy coat rack in the dramatic play area.

NURTURING STRATEGIES:

1. Observe the toddler. Ask yourself, "Is the child using the suitcase?"

2. If the toddler is not using the suitcase, think how it can be integrated into the child's current play. You may suggest that the child pack a suitcase for a visit to granny's house, if appropriate. If the suitcase doesn't fit into the play, return at a later time and see if it does.

3. When the child is packing the suitcase, to prevent distraction, engage in minimum dialog. Use comments such as:

    "Steve, here is a shirt. Do you need to pack a shirt?"

    "What do you have packed?"

    "Are you ready to leave on your trip?"

4. When the child gets to the destination, encourage unpacking the suitcase. Focus on promoting language skills while the child is unpacking. Assist the toddler in labeling unfamiliar items.

☀ Highlighting Development

Listen to the children. The words they use are the names of people, objects, or actions. Favorite words in their vocabulary refer to toys, people, animals, and food. Common mistakes during this period are underextension and overextension. To illustrate, an underextension is defining a word too narrowly. The child may use the word *bear* to refer only to a favorite teddy bear. The opposite problem, overextension, occurs when the child uses a word too broadly; for example, *kitty* may refer to all four-legged animals. As children refine their word meanings, underextensions and overextensions gradually will disappear.

VARIATION:

♡ Discuss real-life props that could be packed in a suitcase for a trip.

ADDITIONAL INFORMATION:

♡ Use language to extend, elaborate, or prompt play by following the toddler's cues.

♡ Toddlers tend to engage in functional play without interacting with others. Avoid forcing toddlers into interactions before they are developmentally ready.

19 to 24 months

Acting Out "Little Miss Muffet"

Child's Developmental Goals

✔ To combine actions and words
✔ To repeat a familiar nursery rhyme

MATERIALS:

❑ Spider puppet
❑ Small stool or pillow
❑ Tagboard
❑ Felt-tip markers
❑ Bowl and spoon

PREPARATION:

♡ Create a poster that contains the words to the nursery rhyme, if desired. See Appendix F for the words. Hang the poster where the child can view it at eye level.
♡ Clear an area to display the rest of the material.

NURTURING STRATEGIES:

1. When a toddler selects the activity, ask:
   "What could these be used for?"
   "Do you know a nursery rhyme that has a spider in it?"
2. Introduce the activity. To illustrate, say:
   "Jin, these are things for acting out 'Little Miss Muffet.' There is a spider, puppet, pillow, bowl, and a spoon."
   "Would you like to be Little Miss Muffet or the spider?"
3. Discuss the nursery rhyme and encourage the toddler to recite it with you. Ask, for example:
   "What did the spider do in the nursery rhyme?"

4. Begin to act out the nursery rhyme. Support the toddler's behavior. Use comments such as:
   "So Little Miss Muffet runs away at the end."
   "The spider moves quickly."
5. If present, invite another toddler to join in the activity. Then continue reciting the nursery rhyme.
6. Continue as long as the child seems interested.

☀ Highlighting Development

Children need to be exposed to a wide variety of language-stimulating activities beginning at birth. Remember: The first activity listed under Language and Communication for infants from birth to three months of age was "Reciting Nursery Rhymes." Listening and speaking skills can be encouraged through the use of nursery rhymes. By adding a new twist or variety to a familiar nursery rhyme, you will captivate the child's interest and encouraging active participation.

VARIATION:

♡ Act out other familiar nursery rhymes such as "Jack and Jill," "Humpty Dumpty," etc. Repeat nursery rhymes as often as the child desires.

ADDITIONAL INFORMATION:

♡ If more than one child is present, rotate the parts of the nursery rhyme so that each child wishing to participate has an opportunity. You may need to have more than one Little Miss Muffet to keep this activity running smoothly.

19 to 24 months

Calming Down to Rest

Child's Developmental Goals

✓ To use books for relaxation

✓ To look at a book independently

MATERIALS:

❑ Calm, soothing story such as *The Sleepy Little Lion* by Ylla

❑ Box of other "nap" books

PREPARATION:

♡ Review the nap books. These should be familiar stories that can be used independently by the toddlers. Be sure the books have good illustrations. See the criteria in Appendix A for choosing books for infants and toddlers.

NURTURING STRATEGIES:

1. Prepare the child for the transition to nap time by finishing diapering, brushing teeth, and drinking water. Make sure the child's security items are available.
2. Dim the lights in the room and begin moving at a slower pace.
3. While reading the story, use your voice as a tool for calming the child. Refrain from asking questions or engaging the child in the story.
4. Show your affection by hugging, kissing, or rubbing the child's back.
5. Encourage the child to rest quietly by choosing and looking at books in the "nap box."
6. Observe. If the child falls asleep, discontinue reading.

☀ Highlighting Development

When choosing books for children, consider content, illustrations, vocabulary, length, and durability. Children enjoy looking at books that repeat and add to their own experiences. For example, books related to potty training; messy eating; caring for pets; and separating from parents, grandparents, and siblings are all appealing at this stage of development.

VARIATION:

♡ Play soothing music instead of reading a story.

ADDITIONAL INFORMATION:

♡ If caring for children other than your own, discuss with each family how the toddler likes to relax and how the nap routine is handled at home. Following each routine as closely as possible will help reduce frustration for you and increase the length of nap time for the toddler.

♡ Toddlers like and need routines for predictability and consistency as much as they did when they were infants. Create a routine and stick to it as much as possible.

19 to 24 months

Puppet Show

Child's Developmental Goals

✓ To talk through a puppet

✓ To practice expressive language skills

MATERIALS:

❑ 6 multigender, multicultural hand puppets, if available

❑ Puppet stands: 6 cylindrical blocks or empty dish detergent bottles

PREPARATION:

♡ Clear an area for the puppets. Set each puppet on a stand.

NURTURING STRATEGIES:

1. Observe the behavior of a toddler after choosing a puppet.
2. Select a puppet and join the toddler in play sitting on the floor. If other children are present, placing your back toward a wall will enable supervision of the room.
3. Model the puppet talking to the toddler and yourself. For example, talk about what is happening. Address the toddler's puppet by asking a question.
4. Encourage the toddler to converse using the puppet.

5. Whenever necessary, state the limit such as: *"Pedro, talk with the puppet."*
6. Provide positive reinforcement when the toddler makes the puppet talk. Comments to make include:
   "You're making the puppet talk."
   "Your puppet is talking about the blocks."
7. If available, invite another toddler to play with the puppets.

☼ Highlighting Development

Puppets are wonderful tools for promoting language development. Using a puppet to tell a story adds variety. Puppets are beneficial for gaining children's attention and adding novelty. Puppets are useful for encouraging children to talk and retell their experiences and stories. Furthermore, puppets can be valuable tools for expressing emotions.

VARIATION:

♡ Use animal puppets.

 To eliminate a potential choking hazard, check the eyes on the puppet to ensure they are securely attached.

19 to 24 months

Who Said That?

Child's Developmental Goals

✓ To identify other people's voices

✓ To practice language skills by speaking into a microphone

MATERIALS:

❑ Blank cassette tape

❑ Cassette tape recorder that is powered by batteries

❑ Paper and pen

PREPARATION:

♡ Insert the tape into the recorder. Then run an audio test to ensure the recorder is working properly.

NURTURING STRATEGIES:

1. Carry the tape recorder and approach each toddler. Begin by introducing the activity. To illustrate, you may say:
   "I want you to talk. Then I can save your words on this machine. When you are finished, we will listen to your words."
2. Show the toddler how the machine works. For example, demonstrate that when the record button is pushed, the tape moves.
3. Ask the toddler a couple of questions to elicit speech such as:
   "What is your name?"
   "What do you like to play with?"
4. Rewind and play the tape of the toddler's voice.
5. Discuss how the child sounded on the tape.
6. If more than one child is participating, write the names of the children on the paper in the order that they were taped.

7. Then repeat the taping process with other children. If other children are not present, tape your own voice.
8. After everyone has had a chance to be taped, gather in one area and play the tape.
9. Encourage the children to guess who is speaking on the tape.
10. Provide positive reinforcement for attempts and accomplishments. Comments include:
    "You're right! That is Felicity talking on the tape."
    "Keep guessing. It wasn't Dorian that time."

☀ Highlighting Development

Auditory and visual discrimination are both continuing to rapidly develop during this stage. Children are learning to associate people by verbal and nonverbal cues. When recognizing a sound or voice, they become outwardly excited. Nonverbal cues may confuse them. For example, a child whose mother is a police officer may see another female uniformed officer and greet her by saying "mama."

VARIATION:

♡ Tape a toddler or group of children singing a favorite song. Play back the tape and sing along with it.

ADDITIONAL INFORMATION:

♡ Show the children how to stop and start the tape recorder using visual cues. To do this, cut a red circle and tape it onto the stop button. Likewise, cut a green circle and place it onto the start button.

19 to 24 months

Fruit Salad

Child's Developmental Goals

✓ To identify, compare, and contrast fruit according to shape and color

✓ To discuss how fruit tastes

MATERIALS:

❑ Fresh fruit such as pineapple, banana, apple, orange, and grapes

❑ Large, nonbreakable plastic bowl

❑ Knife

❑ Cutting board

❑ Tray

PREPARATION:

♡ Clean the fruit and place it with other supplies on a tray. Place the tray on the table.

♡ Then encourage the toddler to wash hands for snack.

NURTURING STRATEGIES:

1. Introduce the activity by saying:
   "Look at what we are having for snack. I'm going to cut some fruit. Watch me."
   "After I cut the fruit, we can taste it."

2. Set limits as necessary. Limits may include:
   "Only I can touch the knife."
   "Stay seated while the fruit is being cut."

3. Hold up a piece of fruit. Encourage the toddlers to identify the fruit by asking:
   "What is the name of this fruit?"

4. Discuss the appearance of the fruit. Talk about size, color, shape, etc.

5. Cut the piece of fruit and share some with the children. Encourage each of the children to taste each type of fruit.

6. Converse about how the fruit tastes.

7. Cut another type of fruit and repeat steps 3 through 6.

8. Encourage the toddlers to discuss the fruit they have tasted by asking:
   "Which fruit was crunchy?"
   "Which fruit was sweet?"
   "Which fruit was sour?"

9. Place the untouched pieces of fruit in the bowl. They can be enjoyed later as a fruit salad.

☀ Highlighting Development

A study shows that questioning is one effective method for teaching young children the meaning of words. Two groups of parents were compared. One group just read to their children and had the children listen. The other group of parents read the book and stopped after reading certain parts to ask "where" and "what" questions. When asked, the children responded with the targeted words. After the experience, the children who answered questions were more likely to reproduce the words contained in the story (Sénéchal, Thomas, & Monker, 1995; Kail, 1998). Therefore, when engaging in activities, ask questions to focus the children's attention and maintain their involvement.

VARIATIONS:

♡ Introduce new types of fruits such as kiwi or papaya.

♡ Cut vegetables for a salad and eat with lunch.

ADDITIONAL INFORMATION:

♡ Before making your selection, ensure that the child does not have an allergy to the fruit.

 To prevent choking, exercise caution by cutting the fruit into small pieces. Grapes present a particular choking hazard; therefore, cutting them in half or even smaller pieces is recommended.

19 to 24 months

"I'm a Little Teapot"

Child's Developmental Goals

✓ To continue developing expressive language skills

✓ To act out a song using nonverbal communication

MATERIALS:

❏ Index card

❏ Felt-tip marker

PREPARATION:

♡ Write the song's words on the index card, if desired. The words are:

♬ I'm a little teapot
♬ Short and stout
♬ Here is my handle   (put hand on hip)
♬ Here is my spout.   (bend arm and hand away from body)

♬ When I get all steamed up
♬ Hear me shout
♬ Just tip me over and
♬ Pour me out.   (lean over)

NURTURING STRATEGIES:

1. When a toddler needs something to do, invite the child to sing with you.
2. Introduce the activity to the toddler by saying, for example:
   "Brendan, I would like to teach you a new song. We can act it out while singing. Let's start with the motions."
3. Model each movement in sequence. Connect your actions with words by describing each movement. State, for example:
   "Here is my handle."
   "Tip me over."

4. When the toddler successfully completes the movements, begin to sing the song and perform the movements.
5. Sing the song slowly to encourage the toddler's participation.
6. Providing positive reinforcement may result in the child practicing the behaviors. To illustrate, say:
   "You're singing along with me. You know the words."
   "Brendan, you are acting like a teapot."
7. Repeat the song as long as the toddler appears interested.

☀ Highlighting Development

Children, like adults, communicate the majority of their messages nonverbally. Watch them. Toddlers will gesture while babbling or engaging in telegraphic speech. Music is another important form of communication. Use it to provide a background for playing. It can help enhance the child's expression of feelings. Furthermore, it can help the child build vocabulary, release pent-up feelings, and relax.

VARIATION:

♡ Tape the song using a cassette recorder and replay it for the child.

ADDITIONAL INFORMATION:

♡ Music experiences are beneficial to young children. Make music a natural part of daily experiences. As children participate in music, language skills build.

19 to 24 months

Animal Shadow Match

Child's Developmental Goals

✓ To provide labels for objects

✓ To continue developing expressive language skills

MATERIALS:

❑ Poster board
❑ Glue
❑ Magazines
❑ Black construction paper
❑ Scissors
❑ Clear adhesive paper

PREPARATION:

♡ Cut out pictures of animals from magazines. Trace around each animal on the black construction paper and cut out the shapes. Using glue, adhere the black animal shapes to the poster board. Then cover the poster board with clear adhesive paper. Finally, cover each of the individual animal pictures with adhesive paper and trim the excess.

♡ Clear a spot on the floor and lay out the poster board and animal pictures.

NURTURING STRATEGIES:

1. When a toddler selects the activity, provide time for exploring the materials. During this process, observe the child's behavior.

2. If necessary, introduce the activity using comments such as:
   "Krista, match the shapes. Which shape on the board looks like a bird?"

3. Ask the toddler to verbally label the animals by asking:
   "What animal is this?"

4. Assist the toddler with matching by describing the shapes:
   "This animal has four legs and a long tail. Look for a black shape with a long tail."

5. Provide positive reinforcement when a child makes a match. Smiling and clapping are ways to non-verbally reinforce the toddler. Verbally reinforce the child by saying, for example:
   "Krista, you did it! You matched the cow."

6. Encourage the toddler to converse about the animals. Questions to ask might include:
   "What do kittens drink?"
   "What do dogs like to eat?"

☀ Highlighting Development

Toddlers need a rich, stimulating environment to promote their cognitive, social, emotional, language, and physical development. Observe them. Staring is one of their most time-consuming activities. Take advantage of these opportunities for promoting language skills. Labeling and describing what they are looking at will develop their vocabulary.

VARIATION:

♡ Create shadow matches for different shapes such as eating utensils, forms of transportation, toys, etc.

ADDITIONAL INFORMATION:

♡ Choose animals that are familiar and often seen in the children's environment. This will increase the chances of the toddlers having the necessary language skills to successfully label the animals.

19 to 24 months

Acting like Dogs

Developmental Goals

✓ To act like animals

✓ To make animal sounds

MATERIALS:

☐ Headbands
☐ Brown paper
☐ Scissors
☐ Stapler or glue

PREPARATION:

♡ Cut "ears" from the brown paper and attach them to the headbands.

♡ Clear a large space on the floor to allow plenty of room for movement.

NURTURING STRATEGIES:

1. Gather the toddlers and introduce the activity by saying:
   "We are going to pretend to be dogs. What noise do dogs make?"

2. Converse with the toddlers about dogs. Talk about things such as how dogs look, feel, and act.

3. Put a pair of ears on your head. Then hand the children a pair of ears. Help put them on, if necessary.

4. Model acting like a dog. For example, crawl on the floor and bark.

5. Comment on the children's behavior. Comments include:
   "Shane, you're a fast-moving dog."
   "What a loud bark."

6. Provide positive reinforcement for acting and sounding like dogs. To illustrate, say:
   "You are barking like dogs."
   "Look at all the dogs moving on the carpet."

☀ Highlighting Development

Engaging in creative drama fosters the development of cognitive, imaginative, and language skills. Moreover, imitating animals in this activity involves the production of sounds, resulting in the children exercising and strengthening muscles in the tongue, mouth, and vocal chords.

VARIATION:

♡ Act like different animals such as a cow, pig, elephant, cat, pony, or monkey.

ADDITIONAL INFORMATION:

♡ When acting like animals, be sure to crawl on the floor.

♡ Children this age need props to help them pretend; hence, the ears will contribute to the success of this activity.

19 to 24 months

Tunnel Crawl

Child's Developmental Goals

✓ To continue increasing vocabulary skills
✓ To practice expressive language skills

MATERIALS:

❑ Duct tape
❑ Several large cardboard boxes

PREPARATION:

♡ Tape the boxes together to make a tunnel. Select and clear an area that can be easily supervised. Place the tunnel in the cleared area.

NURTURING STRATEGIES:

1. When a child chooses the activity, position your body to supervise the area. To view the child inside the tunnel, you will need to sit on the floor at one end.

2. Set limits to protect the safety of the child. For example, if a toddler is climbing on the outside of the boxes, tell the child to crawl inside the tunnel.

3. It may be necessary to reinforce your words with actions. If this occurs, pat the inside of the box while repeating,
   "Crawl inside the tunnel."

4. Use other children, if present, as models of appropriate behavior by saying:
   "Look at Tovah. She is crawling inside the tunnel."

5. Describe the child's behavior in and around the tunnel, focusing on three words: inside, outside, through. To illustrate, say:
   "You are crawling outside the tunnel."
   "Tovah crawled through the tunnel."

6. Converse with the toddler about the experience or about pretending during the experience. Ask, for example:
   "What did you see inside the tunnel?"

7. Providing positive reinforcement may result in the toddlers increasing the time engaged in the activity. Comments include:
   "You crawled through the tunnel with a friend."
   "You are crawling slowly. It took you a lot of time to crawl through the tunnel."

☀ Highlighting Development

The relationship between understanding and producing language is asymmetrical. By 24 months, toddlers typically understand approximately 300 words. In comparison, they can produce approximately 250 words. In the beginning, there is a five-month lag between comprehension and production. However, "fast mapping" virtually eliminates this time lag. With maturity, the child is able to connect a new word with an existing concept after a brief encounter (Berk, 1997; Santrock, 1993).

VARIATION:

♡ Create other obstacles for the toddler to move around and through. Use a clothesline, blanket, and clothespins to create a tent.

ADDITIONAL INFORMATION:

♡ The best way to introduce new vocabulary words is to create experiences and then describe the children's behavior. In other words, children more easily learn words that reflect or describe their lives.

♡ When using children as models, equally distribute your attention. Children can recognize adults' preferences at very young ages.

19 to 24 months

Story Quilt

Child's Developmental Goals

✓ To "read" a book independently

✓ To use a quilt as a relaxing area

MATERIALS:

❏ Quilt

❏ Container such as a crate, box, bag, or basket

❏ 6 to 8 books for toddlers; see Appendix A for a list of toddler books.

PREPARATION:

♡ Spread out the quilt in an open area. Lay the books on the quilt. Keep the container nearby for easily storing the books and quilt when finished.

NURTURING STRATEGIES:

1. Observe the toddler's behavior after choosing the activity.
2. Avoid interrupting the toddler while reading. However, when the toddler is finished reading, ask questions about the book. Questions to ask include:
   "Who was in the story you read?"
   "What was the story about?"
3. Encourage the toddler to read another story independently. But, if asked, read a story to the toddler.
4. If you notice that a toddler is becoming very excited and needs to relax or calm down, direct the child to the quilt.

5. Encourage the toddler to pick out a book for you to read. Sit on the quilt beside the toddler. Use your body and voice as tools for calming the toddler while reading the story.
6. Converse about the book during and after reading it.
7. Suggest that the toddler select another book to read. Excuse yourself and allow the child to read independently.

☀ Highlighting Development

Early experiences have an influence on children's literacy development. Children who are read to during the early years typically enjoy higher levels of success in learning to read than their peers who have not had these experiences. Evidence suggests that hearing and responding to stories read from books is probably the most important literacy experience for children. However, the importance of talking and conversing should not be overlooked (Rice, 1997).

VARIATION:

♡ Set up a story area inside a tent or tepee.

ADDITIONAL INFORMATION:

♡ You may need to set limits for using books while outdoors. For example, to prolong the life of the books, they must stay on the quilt.

19 to 24 months

Cognitive Development

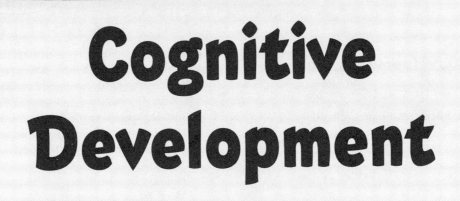

♡

NINETEEN to TWENTY-FOUR MONTHS

Sorting Socks

Child's Developmental Goals

✓ To match similar objects

✓ To discriminate between objects visually

MATERIALS:

❑ 6 pairs of different-colored socks such as white, red, and black

❑ Basket to hold socks

PREPARATION:

♡ Mix up the socks. Place the socks in the basket. Then set the basket on a table or place it on the floor where it is easily accessible to the child.

NURTURING STRATEGIES:

1. When a toddler selects the activity, observe the child's behavior. Note how the toddler is exploring or arranging the socks.

2. Comment on the child's behavior. Comments to make include:
    "Benito, you put the two green socks close together."
    "You're sorting the socks."

3. Use your knowledge of the child's skills to guide your behavior. If, for example, the toddler can correctly label some colors, point to a sock and ask:
    "What color is this sock?"
    If the child has not begun to label by colors, introduce them. Begin by labeling the color of the sock the child is touching or manipulating. Say, for example:
    "Benito, you are touching a black sock."
    "You have two socks in your hand. This one is brown and this one is green."

4. Encourage the toddler to match the socks by color. While holding up a sock, make comments such as:
    "Let's match up the socks. Find the other sock that looks like this."

5. Provide positive reinforcement when a match is made. Clapping or smiling indicates you are proud of the toddler's accomplishments. Additionally, you could say:
    "Benito, you made a match. Both socks are red."
    "You're fast at finding matches!"

6. If the toddler desires, mix up the socks and begin again.

☀ Highlighting Development

At this stage, children become more actively involved in developing classification skills by physically grouping objects into classes or categories based on one attribute: color, size, shape, function, or pattern. One form of classification is matching. This process involves putting together like objects. Toddlers are capable of simple matching activities. That is, they can put two identical objects together such as the socks in this activity (Herr, 1998).

VARIATION:

♡ Sort baby shoes, scarves, or shirts.

ADDITIONAL INFORMATION:

♡ Whenever possible, elicit the child's assistance when sorting laundry, nonbreakable dishes, groceries, blocks, etc.

Melting Ice

Child's Developmental Goals

✓ To observe and discuss transformations.

MATERIALS:

❑ Several plastic containers of varying sizes
❑ Water
❑ Water table or a minimum of two quilt boxes
❑ Smocks

PREPARATION:

♡ Fill each container with water and freeze to make large ice cubes.
♡ Lay towels on the floor to prevent slipping in splashed water.
♡ Sanitize water table and move to desired location. Fill with 2 to 3 inches of water.
♡ Remove ice from container when ready to use (this may require cutting the plastic) and place it in the water table.
♡ If working in a child care center, you may want to place a Hand Washing sign on the table. This serves as a visual reminder to encourage hand washing before the beginning of the activity.

NURTURING STRATEGIES:

1. Assist the toddler, as necessary, with washing hands.
2. As the toddler is putting on her smock, discuss the experience. To illustrate, say:
   "There are large blocks of something in the water. Can you guess what they are?"
   Pause to allow answer/discussion.
3. Encourage the toddler to test her hypothesis. Use comments such as:
   "Touch them, Bailey, and see if they are hard."
   "I don't know. Move them around to see if they roll like a ball."

4. When necessary, set limits on behavior. For example say:
   "Splash gently so the water stays on the table."
   "Use the towel to clean up the spill so no one slips and falls."
5. Encourage the toddler to talk about what is happening to the blocks of ice. During the discussion, introduce vocabulary words such as *melting, solid, liquid, changing,* and/or *transforming.* Connect with child's past experience whenever possible.

☀ Highlighting Development

Toddlers, like preschoolers, focus on beginning and ending states and tend to ignore any transformations in between (Berk, 1999). Furthermore, they often treat the initial and final states as unrelated. Providing toddlers with the opportunity to manipulate, observe, and discuss transformations assists them in reaching a higher level of understanding.

VARIATIONS:

♡ Add food coloring to the water before freezing.
♡ Do this activity outdoors on a warm day.
♡ Add small toys, such as a car or a golf ball, to the water before freezing.

ADDITIONAL INFORMATION:

♡ Most children are delighted with experiences related to water. It is a satisfying medium for young children that can promote the development of many science concepts. Through water play children learn that water makes objects wet, it takes many forms, and it can be held in a container.

 Using large chunks of ice is safer than using small ice cubes for very young children.

19 to 24 months

Color Search

Child's Developmental Goals

✓ To find similar colors in the environment

✓ To discriminate between objects visually

MATERIALS:

None

PREPARATION:

None

NURTURING STRATEGIES:

1. Invite a toddler who needs an activity to play this game with you. To illustrate, say:

   "Dan, let's play a game. It is a color matching game. I'll point to something. You then point to something different that is the same color. Here we go."

2. Point to an object in the room and verbally describe it, emphasizing the color. For example, say:

   "Dan, this is a yellow apple."

3. Remind the toddler of his part of the game by stating:

   "Now you look around the room. Find something else that is yellow."

4. Provide positive reinforcement when the toddler identifies another object of the same color. Comments might include:

   "The bus is yellow. Good match!"
   "You found a yellow plate. Good eye!"

5. Support and give encouragement to a toddler who is having difficulty finding a similar color. Use comments such as:

   "Blue is a hard color to find; keep looking."
   "Would you like to carry the red crayon to match to other items?"
   "Have you looked at the books?"

6. Repeat the game as long as the toddler is interested.

☀ Highlighting Development

Color matching is considered a mathematical activity. These experiences help children develop cognitively by refining their discrimination skills. Color matching experiences also help promote language development—children are generating a visual image with a name.

VARIATION:

♡ Provide the child with a piece of colored paper for matching.

ADDITIONAL INFORMATION:

♡ Use color searching to follow up after reading a story. Color searching can be practiced anywhere. It can be done while walking outside or waiting for your food in a restaurant.

♡ When playing this game, choose the color of your object carefully. Avoid shades of colors that would be difficult to match easily.

Making Pizzas

Child's Developmental Goals

✓ To follow simple directions

✓ To observe and discuss transformations

MATERIALS:

- ❏ 1 English muffin per person
- ❏ 1 jar of pizza sauce
- ❏ 1 bag of shredded mozzarella cheese
- ❏ ¼-cup measuring cup
- ❏ Metal or plastic mixing bowls
- ❏ Plates
- ❏ Napkins
- ❏ Masking tape
- ❏ Felt-tip markers
- ❏ Tagboard
- ❏ Toaster oven

PREPARATION:

♡ If desired, prepare a recipe board that uses pictures as well as words to outline step-by-step directions for making a pizza. Hang the recipe board in the area that you will be using to prepare the pizza.

♡ Plug in the toaster oven.

♡ Pour the pizza sauce into one of the mixing bowls and the cheese in the other. Put the ¼-cup measuring cup in the cheese. Gather all equipment and ingredients, including bowls, spoons, plates, English muffins, cheese, and napkins. Place them in the area that you will be working.

NURTURING STRATEGIES:

1. Assist the toddler, as necessary, with washing hands.
2. While pointing to the recipe board, introduce the activity by saying:
   "We are going to make pizzas for our snack. The recipe or directions are right here. What do you like on your pizza?"
3. Explain to the toddler how to make the pizza as you work. Refer to the recipe board as needed.
4. Discuss how the English muffins, pizza sauce, and cheese taste by themselves. Speculate on how they might taste together.
5. As you put on the cheese, describe what it looks like. Talk about what happens to cheese when it is heated. Introduce and explain the word *melts*.

6. When it is time to bake the pizza, set any limits related to the toaster oven. Comments include:
   "The oven is hot. Stand near this end of the table."
   "The oven could burn you. Sit in your chair."
7. Allow the pizzas to cool slightly before eating.
8. While eating the snack, discuss how the pizzas were made, how they taste, and how they look now. Do so by asking questions such as:
   "How did you make your pizza?"
   "What does the cheese look like now?"
   "What else could we put on our pizza?"

☀ Highlighting Development

Toddlers discover and learn through concrete, hands-on experiences. To do this, they need to be provided a rich environment with opportunities for examining, exploring, manipulating, and experimenting with objects. Hence, cooking activities are a method for facilitating toddlers' cognitive growth.

Toddlers, like preschoolers, fail to recognize transformations. They treat the initial and final states as completely unrelated, ignoring the dynamic transformation between them (Berk, 1997). Therefore, observing and discussing the transformation will help their cognitive and language development.

VARIATION:

♡ Prepare one large pizza for everyone to share.

 Use extreme caution once the toaster oven becomes hot. Never leaving it unattended as well as setting and following through on limits may prevent accidents. If necessary, have the child turn the chair with the back facing the heat source. Sitting on the chair in this position may prevent the child from reaching forward and possibly touching a hot appliance.

 For safety purposes, avoid using an extension cord, if possible. If that isn't possible, tape the extension cord to the floor to reduce the possibility of tripping.

19 to 24 months

Toddler Picture Match

Child's Developmental Goals

✓ To discriminate between objects visually

✓ To identify people in photographs

MATERIALS:

❑ Camera

❑ Tagboard

❑ Glue or tape

❑ Scissors

❑ Basket

PREPARATION:

♡ Take pictures of the toddlers working independently. When developing the film, request double prints.

♡ Cut the tagboard slightly larger than the pictures. Adhere one picture to each piece of tagboard by gluing or taping. Place sets of pictures in a basket and put it on a child-size table.

NURTURING STRATEGIES:

1. When a child selects the activity, observe the toddler's behavior.

2. If necessary, introduce the activity. To illustrate, say:
   "Look at these pictures of us. Match the pictures that are alike."

3. Providing verbal assistance may help the toddler to match the photographs. Comments include:
   "Tamara, here you are wearing a red shirt. Look for a red shirt."
   "Look for another picture with lots of books."

4. Encourage the toddler to identify other people in the photographs. Questions to ask include:
   "Who is in this picture?"
   "Where is the picture of Noel?"

5. Provide support and encouragement when a toddler is having difficulty finding a particular picture. Make comments such as:
   "Keep looking. You're working hard."
   "Who is that? What are they doing in this picture?"

6. Reinforce the toddler when he makes a match. To illustrate, say:
   "Tamara, those two pictures are identical!"
   "You found two pictures that match."

7. Encourage the toddler to continue playing the game independently. Check on the child periodically to provide support, encouragement, or reinforcement as necessary.

☀ Highlighting Development

The toddlers' ability to remember, although not efficient, continues to improve. Toddlers are able to recognize family members in photographs before they are able to recognize themselves. However, by age two, recognition of the self is well established (Berk, 1997). To facilitate the toddlers' recognition, provide mirrors and photographs.

VARIATION:

♡ If in a classroom setting, ask the parents or guardians for duplicate photographs of their family. Repeat the activity by matching the family photos.

ADDITIONAL INFORMATION:

♡ Toddlers delight in seeing themselves in photographs. Therefore, they probably will want to repeat the activity several times. Furthermore, they may want to carry their photographs for looking at and sharing with others.

19 to 24 months

Sorting Lids

Child's Developmental Goals

✓ To classify objects by color

✓ To discriminate between objects visually

MATERIALS:

❑ 1½ dozen egg carton

❑ 12 plastic milk jug lids, 6 of one color and 6 of another

PREPARATION:

♡ Place the lids in an egg carton. After this, set the carton in an easily accessible location.

NURTURING STRATEGIES:

1. When a child chooses the activity, observe the child's behavior.

2. Ask the toddler how the lids are being grouped. For example, you may comment by saying:
   "Tell me about the lids. How do you decide where to put them?"

3. If the child is using the lids in a different way, allow the toddler time to explore. After that, talk about the lids. Discuss, for example, the color of the lids. Comments include:
   "Chen, I see two colors of lids: red and green."
   "I see red lids and I see green lids."

4. If necessary, encourage the toddler to continue sorting the lids by asking:
   "How can you group the lids?"

5. Provide positive reinforcement for sorting the lids by color. Make comments such as:
   "Chen, you've sorted the lids by color."
   "I see two groups of lids: one group is red and the other group is green."

☀ Highlighting Development

Toddlers typically are able to follow simple directions, classify objects by color, and discriminate between objects visually. Notice how hard toddlers concentrate when playing. Likewise, notice how the children keep you informed of your role. For example, while sorting lids, a child may reverse the roles, assuming a leadership role by showing or telling you what to do. Reinforce the behavior by following the child's lead.

VARIATION:

♡ Sort objects, such as cars and airplanes, by color.

 Sometimes toddlers continue exploring their world orally. Therefore, it is necessary to verify that the objects you provide are not choking hazards.

19 to 24 months

Picture Puzzles

Child's Developmental Goals

✓ To connect parts to make a whole

✓ To match pictures

MATERIALS:

❑ 4 to 6 magazine or catalog pictures with a related theme such as animals, vehicles, or clothing

❑ Self-adhesive paper

❑ Tagboard or heavy cardboard

❑ Scissors

PREPARATION:

♡ Cut pictures from magazines or catalogs and mount them on tagboard or heavy cardboard. Then cover them with self-adhesive paper. Cut each picture in half.

♡ Shuffle the pictures and lay them out on a child-size table.

NURTURING STRATEGIES:

1. Invite a toddler to the table and point out the pictures. Introduce the activity by saying, for example:
   "Noelle, help me put these pictures together."
2. Observe the child working with the puzzle pieces.
3. Providing encouragement and support while the toddler is working may result in longer participation. Comments include:
   "Noelle, keep going. You've matched two pictures."
   "That is almost a match. Both of the animals are black, but they look different. Look for a long tail."

4. Assist the toddler as necessary with completing the puzzles. Comments to make include:
   "Here is a dog's head. Let's find a picture with a dog's tail."
   "This animal is brown. Look for a picture with brown in it."
5. Provide positive reinforcement when the toddler completes a puzzle. Clapping or smiling may reinforce the desired behavior. In addition, examples of verbal reinforcement include:
   "You did it! You put together all of the puzzles."
   "Noelle, what a hard worker. You've completed three puzzles."
6. Mix up the pictures and begin the experience again if the toddler shows interest.

☀ Highlighting Development

By the end of the second year of life, toddlers have made many cognitive advances. While playing now, children are able to draw on information already learned. To illustrate, body parts, objects, and familiar people can be recognized. Likewise, when the objects are named, children are able to point to them. Hence, the picture puzzle and other related puzzle activities will promote problem-solving skills.

VARIATION:

♡ Use store-bought puzzles with knobs.

ADDITIONAL INFORMATION:

♡ Mounting the pictures on tagboard makes them easier for the toddler to grasp and pick up.

What's under the Basket?

Child's Developmental Goals

✓ To refine object permanence skills

✓ To develop auditory memory skills by remembering and identifying a missing object

MATERIALS:

❑ Tightly woven basket

❑ 3 favorite identically colored objects that fit in the basket

PREPARATION:

♡ Place the three objects inside the basket. Then place the basket out of the child's reach.

NURTURING STRATEGIES:

1. When a toddler needs a new activity, get the basket and invite the child to play a game with you.
2. Introduce the activity to the toddler by saying: *"Look. I have three things here: a ball, a car, and a block. All of these are colored red. I'm going to hide one of them under the basket. Then you can guess which one is missing."*
3. Instruct the toddler that eyes need to be closed while you hide one item under the basket.
4. Ask the toddler to open his eyes and guess the missing item.

5. Provide support and reinforcement for guesses. Comments include:
   "The red ball is right here. What else could be in the basket?"
   "Good guessing! The red block was in the basket."
6. Continue the game as long as the toddler seems interested. Changing the objects being hidden may sustain the toddler's interest in the game.

☀ Highlighting Development

Children love the game of hide-and-seek. At this stage, they will remember where items are hidden. In fact, they may even want to reverse roles. They will hide the item and have you look for it.

VARIATION:

♡ Increase the challenge by placing one item inside the basket and keeping the other items out of sight. Provide hints, if necessary, to help the toddler guess which item is under the basket.

ADDITIONAL INFORMATION:

♡ Reinforce the child's efforts as well as accomplishments.

19 to 24 months

Making Play Dough

COGNITIVE

Child's Developmental Goals

✓ To observe transformations

✓ To discuss similarities and differences

MATERIALS:

❑ Play dough recipe

❑ Supplies for recipe

❑ High chair or child-size table

PREPARATION:

♡ Choose a noncooked play dough recipe from the list located in Appendix I. Then gather the necessary supplies. For this age group, it is preferable to premix the dry and liquid ingredients in separate containers so that the toddler mixes only two things together.

NURTURING STRATEGIES:

1. Assist the toddler, if necessary, in hand washing.
2. Sit the toddler in the high chair, securing the safety straps.
3. Introduce the activity. To illustrate, say:
   "Ginger, today we're going to make play dough. You can help. You can mix the play dough."
4. Discuss and elaborate on the toddler's responses.
5. Pour the dry ingredients onto the toddler's tray. Encourage the child to explore the ingredients using her fingers.
6. Introduce and reinforce the appropriate vocabulary words such as *bumpy, gritty,* and *dry.*
7. Pour the wet ingredients onto a corner of the tray. Again, encourage the toddler to explore the wet substances with her fingers.

8. Introduce and reinforce vocabulary words such as *wet, oily,* and *smooth.*
9. Suggest mixing the substances together. Discuss what happens to the dry ingredients when liquid is added. In addition, talk about how the dough now feels and looks.
10. Encourage the toddler to continue exploring the dough once it is mixed.

☀ Highlighting Development

Most children enjoy using play dough, which is material that can be formed, molded, and reshaped. They enjoy the tactile appeal and the response to touch. Typical behaviors include pushing, pulling, squeezing, and rolling. Observe them during this process. When they are ready, provide them with tools such as small rolling pins and cookie cutters to use with the play dough.

VARIATION:

♡ If more than one child is present, encourage the children to work together to prepare one recipe of play dough.

ADDITIONAL INFORMATION:

♡ Play dough typically is a messy activity. Control the mess by placing the high chair on a vinyl tablecloth and having damp towels available to wash the child's hands.

19 to 24 months

Tasting Bread

Child's Developmental Goals

✓ To use sensory stimulation to distinguish between objects by texture

✓ To compare and contrast objects

MATERIALS:

❑ Pita bread
❑ Yeast rolls
❑ Bagels
❑ Italian bread
❑ Cutting board and knife
❑ Napkins
❑ Cups
❑ Pitcher of milk or juice

PREPARATION:

♡ Clean and sanitize a child-size table. Gather the snack ingredients and place them on the tray.

NURTURING STRATEGIES:

1. Encourage the child to engage in hand washing. If necessary, provide assistance.
2. Carry the supplies to the table and ask the child to sit down.
3. Show the child one type of bread. Verbally label it and elicit descriptions by asking, for example:
   "What is this?"
   "What does this look like?"

4. Discuss the size, shape, and color of the bread.
5. Cut the bread and encourage the child to taste it.
6. Converse about how the bread feels and tastes.
7. Choose another type of bread and repeat steps 3 through 6.
8. Compare and contrast how the bread feels and tastes.
9. Continue with the rest of the breads.
10. Provide positive reinforcement for comparing and contrasting the breads. Comments to make include:
    "Yes, Lamar. The bagel and Italian bread are both chewy."
    "Good observation! The pita bread and yeast rolls both have holes."

☀ Highlighting Development

Tasting experiences are important because young children learn through their senses—feeling, smelling, seeing, hearing, and tasting. By observing and tasting the breads, children learn the color, texture, smell, feel, and taste of each. Moreover, you can assist in the development of cognitive skills such as comparing and contrasting by asking questions.

VARIATION:

♡ Make bread in a bread machine.
♡ Introduce other types of bread such as tortillas, waffles, pancakes, and crepes.

 Safety always comes first. As a result, set limits for using the knife.

19 to 24 months

Mixing Colors

Child's Developmental Goals

✓ To make a secondary color by mixing two primary colors

✓ To observe transformations

MATERIALS:

❑ Recipe for Rainbow Stew; see Appendix I for a list of recipes

❑ Red and blue food coloring

❑ Tray

❑ Resealable plastic bags

❑ Supplies and equipment needed to prepare the stew

PREPARATION:

♡ Prepare the Rainbow Stew. Allow it to cool to room temperature and then spoon it into the plastic bags. Place bags and food coloring onto a tray.

♡ Clean a child-size table and place the tray in the center.

NURTURING STRATEGIES:

1. When the child shows interest in the activity, move to the table.

2. Explain the experience by saying, for example:
   "This bag is for mixing colors. I'm going to put in blue and red food coloring. Help me. Hold the bag while I put in the food coloring."

3. Drop the food coloring into different sides of the bag.

4. Remove as much air from the bag as possible and seal it.

5. Encourage the toddler to talk about what is happening to the Rainbow Stew. Discuss, for example, the movement of the colors in the bag.

6. When a third color emerges, act surprised and say, for example:
   "What happened here? We added the colors red and blue. Look, now I see purple. What happened?"

7. Converse with the toddler about the transformation.

☀ Highlighting Development

Color is all around young children. Children can describe their world through naming colors. Many children by the age of two can also match a color to a sample. One approach for teaching children color concepts is to mix colors. Mix two primary colors to create a secondary color.

VARIATION:

♡ For an outdoor activity, place the Rainbow Stew in a wash tub or quilt box. Add food coloring and encourage mixing.

 Many toddlers continue exploring their world through their mouths. All of the materials used to make the Rainbow Stew, as well as the food coloring, are nontoxic. However, consuming large quantities may cause an upset stomach. Therefore, close supervision is recommended.

19 to 24 months

Sink or Float?

Child's Developmental Goals

✓ To understand the terms *sink* and *float*

✓ To create and test a hypothesis

MATERIALS:

❑ Bath towels

❑ Plastic container

❑ Basket

❑ Items to put in water such as cork, fishing bobber, wood, boat, plastic car, golf ball

❑ Smocks

PREPARATION:

♡ Clear off a child-size table. Spread out one towel and set the plastic container on it. Fill the container with 1 to 2 inches of water.

♡ Place the sink and float items in the basket. Then place the basket beside the container of water on the table. Lay the smocks on the corner of the table.

♡ Keep other towels handy in case of spills.

NURTURING STRATEGIES:

1. When a toddler selects the activity, move closer and observe the child's behavior. Note how the toddler is interacting with the available materials.

2. Discuss the items the toddler has placed in the water. Point out items that are floating and those that are sinking to the bottom. To illustrate, say: *"The cork and wood pieces are floating on top of the water. See how they stay on top? But look at the car. It sank to the bottom."*

3. When the toddler picks up another item from the basket, ask the child if the item will sink or float. Use comments such as:
"Katrina, do you think the golf ball will sink or float?"
"What will happen to the boat when it's put in the water? Will it sink or float?"

4. Repeat the toddler's guess and then encourage the child to test the hypothesis.

5. Provide support and reinforcement when the results are discovered. State, for example:
"Look. The ball sank. You thought it would."
"The boat floated. It stayed on top of the water."

6. Encourage the toddler to create and test hypotheses for the remaining items.

☼ Highlighting Development

Children at this age are anxious to explore their world using a hands-on approach. By exploring, they construct knowledge. Provide them a stimulating environment containing hands-on materials. When playing with the materials, they will observe and solve problems. Hence, complex science concepts can be introduced through simple activities such as Sink or Float.

VARIATION:

♡ Provide large rocks and boats in the water table. Discuss why some objects sink and others float.

ADDITIONAL INFORMATION:

♡ If the toddlers are more interested in just playing in the water, encourage this behavior by removing the sink and float items.

19 to 24 months

Matching Nuts and Bolts

Child's Developmental Goals

✓ To differentiate sizes
✓ To match objects

MATERIALS:

❑ 6 different sizes of plastic, color-coded nuts and bolts
❑ Basket

PREPARATION:

♡ Place the nuts and bolts in the basket and put it on a child-size shelf.

NURTURING STRATEGIES:

1. When a toddler selects the activity, observe the child's behavior.
2. If necessary, introduce the activity by saying and pointing to each:
   "Roberto, there is one nut for each bolt. See if you can match them up."
3. Providing verbal assistance may reduce the toddler's frustration with the activity. Comments include:
   "The bolt in your hand is very big. Let's look for the biggest nut and try it."
4. If necessary, assist the toddler with placing the nut on the bolt.
5. Encourage the toddler to match up all of the nuts and bolts.

6. Provide positive reinforcement for attempts and accomplishments. Make comments such as:
   "Roberto, you're working so hard at matching the nuts and bolts."
   "Two more matches to go. You've almost matched them all!"

☼ Highlighting Development

Even at this stage, children are learning math concepts. Math can be defined as the science of shapes and numbers. Children can learn shapes by playing with the color-coded plastic nuts and bolts. They also can practice sorting by colors while using these materials.

VARIATIONS:

♡ When developmentally ready, provide appropriate-size wrenches for working with the nuts and bolts.
♡ To focus on fine motor skills, provide nuts and bolts of the same size.

ADDITIONAL INFORMATION:

♡ Modify your interactional style to meet the individual needs of the toddlers. For example, one toddler may desire your physical presence only, while another toddler may desire verbal assistance as well.
♡ Supervise the activity to ensure that the child uses the nuts and bolts as intended.

Which One Is It Under?

Child's Developmental Goals

✓ To improve memory skills

✓ To find a hidden object

MATERIALS:

☐ 3 cans of different sizes

☐ 1 toy that will easily fit inside the smallest can but large enough not to be considered a choking hazard

☐ Masking tape

PREPARATION:

♡ Cover any sharp edges on the cans with masking tape. If desired, decorate the outside of the cans with self-adhesive paper, wrapping, or construction paper.

♡ Clear an area on a child-size table and place the cans there.

♡ Hide the toy under one can.

NURTURING STRATEGIES:

1. When the toddler selects the activity, ask:
   "Sioux, what are these cans for?"

2. Converse with the toddler about the purpose of the cans. While talking, lift up each can. Act surprised when the toy is uncovered as this may pique the child's interest.

3. Show the toddler what container you're hiding the toy under and then shuffle the cans.

4. Have the toddler guess which can the toy is under.

5. Provide support and reinforcement for guesses. Comments include:
   "Sioux, you found the toy. It was under the tall, skinny container."
   "Keep guessing. I know you'll find the toy."

6. Switch roles in the game by allowing the toddler to hide the toy, shuffle the cans, and have you guess where the toy is hidden.

☀ Highlighting Development

Between 18 and 24 months, growth spurts occur in cognitive development. This coincides with the increasing development of representational thought, memory, and language skills (Berk, 1997). Current research emphasizes the importance of a rich, supportive environment that promotes such development (Shore, 1997).

VARIATION:

♡ Hide two objects and have the toddler find a specific object to increase the challenge if the child is developmentally ready.

ADDITIONAL INFORMATION:

♡ When you switch roles, to promote the child's self-esteem, purposefully choose the container that does not contain the toy.

19 to 24 months

Social Development

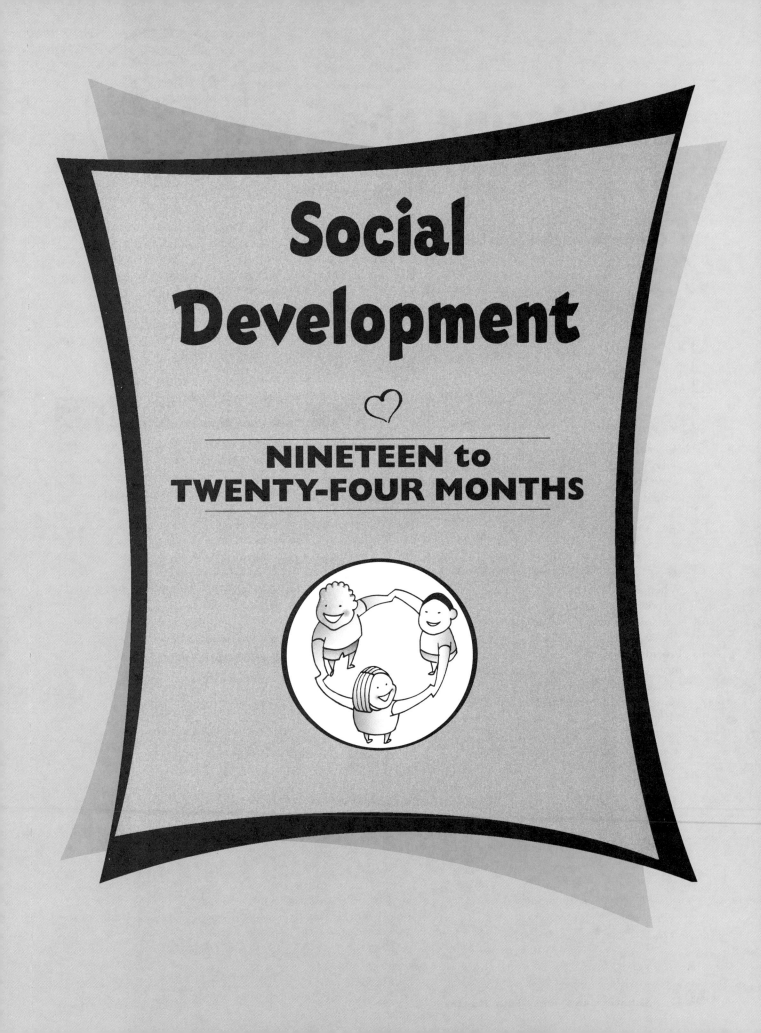

NINETEEN to
TWENTY-FOUR MONTHS

Passing the Beanbag

SOCIAL

Child's Developmental Goals

✓ To interact with others

✓ To participate in a group game

MATERIALS:

❑ 2 to 3 identical beanbags

❑ Tape or compact disc player

❑ Musical cassette or compact disc

PREPARATION:

♡ Select an area that has an electrical outlet for this activity. Plug in the tape or compact disc player. Then fast forward or rewind the tape to obtain the desired song.

♡ Place the beanbags on the floor in the selected area.

NURTURING STRATEGIES:

1. When a toddler selects the beanbags, discuss their purpose. Ask for example:
   "Andrew, what are these beanbags for?"
   "What can we do with these?"
2. Providing positive reinforcement may encourage more creative responses or divergent thinking. Comments include:
   "Good idea. I didn't think about taking them shopping."
   "Wow! You thought of four things to do with the beanbags."
3. If a child suggested the activity of passing the beanbag around, say:
   "Let's play what Andrew suggested. Let's pass the beanbag to each other."
4. Encourage and give suggestions for playing the game. Ask, for example, if the game should be played while standing up or sitting down.

5. Pass the beanbag back and forth to the child.
6. If available, invite other children to join in the game.
7. After the beanbag has been passed, suggest playing the game to music. Say, for example:
   "Let's turn on some music while we pass the beanbag."
8. Begin the game again. When not holding a beanbag, clap or dance to the beat of the music to express your enjoyment of the music.
9. Continue as long as the toddlers seem interested.

☀ Highlighting Development

During infancy, peer sociability begins emerging. In infancy, early social gestures are followed by peer-directed smiles and vocalizations. By two years of age, however, children are beginning to develop preferences for particular people and, as a result, seek them out (Spodek, 1993).

VARIATIONS:

♡ Use other items to pass such as a hand-size stuffed toy, block, or car.

♡ Play "freeze" while passing the beanbag to music.

ADDITIONAL INFORMATION:

♡ If working with more than one child, promote everyone's self-esteem by ensuring all children have an equal opportunity to participate.

 To promote safety, place the tape player out of the children's reach.

19 to 24 months

Spray Art

Child's Developmental Goals

✓ To participate in a group project

✓ To interact with others

MATERIALS:

☐ Large piece of white butcher paper

☐ Masking tape

☐ 4 small spray bottles set to a fine stream

☐ Food coloring and water

PREPARATION:

♡ Adhere the butcher paper to a fence or wall with the masking tape.

♡ Prepare the spray bottle by filling it half full with water and adding several drops of food coloring. Prepare two spray bottles with solutions of each color you choose. Adjusting the spray to a fine stream will prevent the paper from getting soggy.

NURTURING STRATEGIES:

1. When a child chooses the activity, introduce it. To illustrate, say:
   "This is a new way to make a picture. Squeeze the trigger while pointing at the paper. Colors will spray on the paper."

2. While speaking, reinforce your words with actions by showing the child how to squeeze the bottle. State limits positively and clearly. Say, for example:
   "Ada, spray the paper."

3. Describe the child's picture. Comments to make include:
   "You're using green."
   "You're spraying at the top of the page. Look, it is dripping down."

4. Restate limits when necessary. If the limit continues to be violated by a child, state a logical consequence for the behavior. State, for example:
   "Ada, spray on the paper. Otherwise, you will need to find another activity."
   Follow through with the consequence as necessary.

5. Providing positive reinforcement may result in the desired behavior being repeated. If several children are participating, comments might include:
   "Ada is spraying the paper to make a picture."
   "Squirt. Squirt. Squirt. Maria is squirting colors on the paper."

☀ Highlighting Development

Toddlers engage in solitary play—playing independently and alone—more than any other type of play. They also engage in parallel play such as the spray art activity. By observing them, you will note that they are engaged in the same activity but independently using the materials and equipment. To promote desirable social behaviors as well as minimize undesirable behaviors, adults need to provide duplicate materials.

VARIATION:

♡ If appropriate, repeat the activity during the winter by painting the snow with colored water.

ADDITIONAL INFORMATION:

♡ Children delight in spray art because they can see the immediate effect of their actions. Limits regarding spraying the paper must be consistently enforced. If limits are repeatedly violated, enact logical consequences such as taking the spray bottle away and finding a new activity.

19 to 24 months

Playground Picnic

SOCIAL

Child's Developmental Goals

✓ To engage in functional play

✓ To interact with an adult

MATERIALS:

☐ Blanket

☐ Picnic basket

☐ Stuffed animals

☐ Plastic plates and cups

☐ Assorted plastic food

PREPARATION:

♡ Select a flat area that is easy to supervise and spread out the blanket. Sit the stuffed animals on the blanket.

♡ Put the plates, cups, and food inside the picnic basket.

NURTURING STRATEGIES:

1. While preparing the children to go outside, show them the picnic basket. Ask, for example:
   "Tito, what is this for?"

2. Briefly discuss their answers. If necessary, state:
   "We're going to have a pretend picnic on the playground. Some friends are already waiting for us."

3. Enlist the help of the toddlers to carry out the picnic basket.

4. Encourage the toddlers to engage in functional play by asking questions such as:
   "Tito, what do people do on a picnic?"
   "What do people eat on a picnic?"
   "Do you think the bear is hungry?"

5. Verbally describe the children's actions. If more than one child is present, comments might include:
   "Tito, you're feeding the lion spaghetti."
   "Rosie, you stacked two pieces of bread together. You made a sandwich."

6. Whenever possible, focus on social interaction between the children. Discuss how two or more children are engaging in the same activity. Say, for example:
   "Tito and Rosie are feeding the animals."
   "There are four of us on a picnic right now."

☀ Highlighting Development

Toddlers are beginning to engage in functional play. They particularly enjoy imitating others' behaviors, which is part of their learning process. Watch. Their play behavior is changing. Previously, they may have played with a ring of keys by just shaking or manipulating them. Now they are beginning to use objects, such as the keys, for their intended use or function. To illustrate, now toddlers will try to insert the keys into a door lock or a pretend car.

VARIATION:

♡ Plan an indoor picnic on a rainy day by serving snack on a blanket.

ADDITIONAL INFORMATION:

♡ Functional play involves children using props for their intended purpose, such as feeding and dressing. As children continue developing socially and cognitively, their play begins involving toys such as dolls and animals. Therefore, you will want to have these props readily available.

 Whenever pillows or blankets are used, constant supervision is necessary to prevent the possibility of suffocation.

Animals in the Zoo

SOCIAL

Child's Developmental Goals

✓ To participate in a small group activity

✓ To sing a song with others

MATERIALS:

❑ Stuffed animals or plastic figurines that you want to sing about

❑ Bag

PREPARATION:

♡ Place the animals in the bag. When you are ready to introduce the activity, move the bag to the area where you want the children to interact with you.

NURTURING STRATEGIES:

1. Gather the toddlers and introduce the activity by saying:
   "Let's sing a song about animals that live in a zoo. This is a new song, so I'm going to sing part of it to you."

2. Remove the first animal from the bag and sing:

   ♪ The lions in the zoo
   ♪ Go roar, roar, roar
   ♪ The lions in the zoo
   ♪ Go roar, roar, roar
   ♪ All around their home.

   Additional verses include: snakes—hiss; monkeys—hee; parrots—swack; gorillas—hoo; donkeys—hee haw; bears—growl.

3. Encourage each child to remove one animal from the bag at a time. While singing the verse related to the animal, the child can stand beside you.

4. Provide positive reinforcement to the children at the end of the song. To illustrate, say:
   "Thank you for helping to sing the song. You helped by selecting an animal from the bag. We worked together to sing this song."

5. Leave the bag and animals in a place where the toddlers can continue exploring and singing the song, if desired.

☀ Highlighting Development

At this stage, toddlers are aware of themselves as being separate from caregivers, parents, siblings, and peers. Toddlers frequently are referred to as being egocentric or self-centered. From their standpoint, everyone thinks like they do. As a result, toddlers have difficulty interacting with others. To promote healthy interactions between two or more children, model by sharing or taking turns.

VARIATIONS:

♡ Sing about farm animals or pets.
♡ Add actions to the song.

ADDITIONAL INFORMATION:

♡ Toddlers are constantly gaining independence. Encouraging them to participate in related activities will foster a sense of pride and self-worth as well as independence. This occurs because they are able to perform the task on their own.

19 to 24 months

Nature Walk

SOCIAL

Child's Developmental Goals

✓ To explore the physical environment

✓ To hold a person's hand when walking

MATERIALS:

❑ Lunch-size paper bag for each child

❑ Felt-tip markers

❑ Field trip supplies such as tissues, first aid kit, and medical release form(s)

PREPARATION:

♡ Walk the route you will take to look for dangers. If possible, fix dangers; otherwise, alter your route as necessary.

♡ Write the child's name on a paper bag. If there is more than one child present, provide a bag for each.

♡ Gather all supplies needed for the field trip, including medical release form(s), a first aid kit, and tissues, and put them in one bag.

NURTURING STRATEGIES:

1. While transitioning to go outside, discuss the nature walk you will be taking. To illustrate, say: *"Today we are going to do something special. We are going to take a walk. We are going to a park with lots of trees. We need to hold hands."*

2. Assist the child in holding hands.

3. Begin walking. Conversing with the children may help improve their observation skills, especially when you are talking about things around them. Comments to make include:
"Mikko, what are you looking at?"
"Here comes a car. Look, it is red."
Focus on objects and people at the toddler's eye level.

4. Once you arrive at your destination, give each toddler a bag and explain its use. To illustrate, say: *"If you find something special that you want to keep, put it in your bag. We'll use these treasures tomorrow for art."*

5. Verbally label items being put into each bag, being as descriptive as possible. For example, say: *"What a shiny blue rock"* rather than *"You found a rock."*

6. On the trip back, talk about the objects observed or gathered.

7. If the children are tired of conversing, singing a favorite song may be effective.

☀ **Highlighting Development**

Because toddlers are curious by nature, they enjoy taking walks around their neighborhood. Watch them. They use their senses in an effort to understand their world.

VARIATION:

♡ Take a walk just to enjoy nature.

ADDITIONAL INFORMATION:

♡ As the toddlers fill their bags, encourage them to leave some items behind for others to enjoy.

♡ Follow up on your nature walk by using the items gathered in an art collage.

♡ Toddlers can tire easily, making the return trip challenging. Therefore, you may need to use strollers.

⊘ **CAUTION** Caution needs to be continuously exercised on walks. If toddlers observe some object or person that interests them, they typically lack judgment concerning safety hazards. Therefore, they need very careful supervision.

19 to 24 months

Reading to a Friend

Child's Developmental Goals

✓ To engage in imitating another's play

✓ To interact socially with a toy

MATERIALS:

❑ 2 stuffed animals

❑ Favorite books

PREPARATION:

♡ Place the books in an area that will attract the child's attention or display them neatly on a child-size shelf.

♡ Sit the stuffed animals on both sides of the books.

NURTURING STRATEGIES:

1. When a toddler chooses a book, observe the child's behavior.
2. If the child invites you to participate by handing you the book, read it.
3. While reading, move the stuffed animal closer or even on your lap. Reinforce your actions with words by saying, for example:
   "The teddy bear can't see the pictures. Teddy also wants to read the story."
4. When the story is completed, tell the toddler you must do something else and encourage reading another story. To illustrate, state:
   "I need to check the charts. Teddy still wants to read. What book are you going to read to your teddy bear?"

5. Periodically observe the toddler.
6. Provide positive reinforcement after the toddler finishes the activity. Use comments such as:
   "The teddy bear really enjoyed the story."
   "You read two stories."

☀ Highlighting Development

A growing tenderness toward toys will begin to emerge. Children at this stage of development often show a fondness for a particular stuffed toy, doll, etc. They will begin playing affectionately with it by hugging, smiling, and kissing it. When this occurs, it is a healthy sign. Children who have been properly nurtured have the capacity to demonstrate this behavior.

VARIATION:

♡ Encourage the toddler to look at books before napping.

ADDITIONAL INFORMATION:

♡ Reading to others serves to increase the toddlers' self-esteem and independence.

♡ Some toddlers enjoy having a book in their bed. They may look at the book before falling asleep or when they wake up.

19 to 24 months

The Freeze

Child's Developmental Goals

✓ To interact with others

✓ To control one's body

MATERIALS:

❑ Tape or compact disc player

❑ Tape or compact disc of favorite song

PREPARATION:

♡ Plug in the tape or compact disc player and place it on a shelf out of the children's reach. Fast-forward or rewind the tape or compact disc to the song you wish to dance to.

♡ Clear a space for dancing.

NURTURING STRATEGIES:

1. Direct the toddler to the open space.
2. Introduce the activity by saying:
   "We're going to dance to music. When there is no music, stop moving."
3. Turn on the tape or compact disc player. Model dancing to the music.
4. Set and enforce limits as necessary. If supervising more than one child, you may need to have the dancers remain in one area so that others can work undisturbed.
5. Turn off the music and stop dancing. You probably will need to gently remind the child to stop moving. If several children are participating, one way to do this is to use a child as a model by saying:
   "Hailey, you stopped moving as soon as the music stopped."

6. Turn the music on again and begin dancing. Express your enjoyment of the activity by smiling or laughing. This may encourage the toddler to express her feelings.

☼ Highlighting Development

With self-orientated motives, toddlers have difficulty acting in a prosocial manner. Adults need to help them develop an awareness and recognize when another person needs support or assistance. In addition, toddlers have difficulty understanding the intentions of others. Therefore, during this activity, you may need to explain why a behavior occurred. For example, if one child accidentally bumps into another, say, "That was an accident. Sometimes when we are dancing too close, we bump each other."

VARIATION:

♡ Vary the type of music for dancing by including fast, slow, jazz, country, or ethnic songs.

ADDITIONAL INFORMATION:

♡ The benefits of this activity include promoting social skills and fostering the development of large muscle skills. Toddlers are working on how to stop movements once started. Therefore, it will take them a few seconds to "freeze." In addition, they are learning to keep their balance. Hence, limit the "freeze" to only 10 to 15 seconds. Once the children demonstrate a readiness, slowly increase the time.

19 to 24 months

Color Hop

Child's Developmental Goals

✓ To engage in parallel play

✓ To initiate play

MATERIALS:

❑ Mat from Twister game, if available; otherwise, see the Variation section

❑ Clear, wide tape

PREPARATION:

♡ Select an area that can be easily supervised. Clear this area and lay down the mat. Securing the mat with tape may prevent falls.

NURTURING STRATEGIES:

1. When the toddler chooses the activity, observe the child's behavior.
2. Comment about the child choosing the activity by saying:
   "Elijah, you picked this activity. What do you do here?"
3. Converse about possible uses of the mat. If the child doesn't mention jumping from color to color, suggest this behavior.
4. Encourage the toddler to stand on a color on the mat and then jump to another circle. Describe the circles the child stood on. Comments include:
   "You jumped from a red to a green circle."
   "You jumped from one red to another red circle. You jumped to the same color."
5. Given your knowledge of the toddler's understanding of color concepts, you may want to encourage the child to jump to a particular color by saying:
   "Now jump to a green circle."

6. If more than one child is present, comment on how they are using the mat in similar or different ways. Statements to use include:
   "You're both jumping from color to color."
   "Elijah is on a red circle and Tangine is on a blue circle."
7. Providing positive reinforcement may result in the toddlers extending their parallel play. Use comments such as:
   "You two are having so much fun jumping on the mat."
   "Two friends are jumping and playing together."

☀ Highlighting Development

The three types of play typically seen during this stage are solitary, parallel, and associate. Solitary and parallel play dominate, while associate play is seen less frequently. In associate play, children interact by exchanging toys and/or commenting on one another's behavior. To illustrate, they may smile, talk, and offer each other toys.

VARIATION:

♡ Create a map by adhering circles of different colors to a piece of vinyl. Another approach would be to cut circles from construction paper and tape them on the floor.

ADDITIONAL INFORMATION:

♡ Check the distance the child is able to jump.

 Periodically check the mat to make sure it is securely taped to the floor. Given the toddlers' balance and full-body coordination, they are very likely to lose their balance and fall if the mat moves.

19 to 24 months

Cozy Quilt

Child's Developmental Goals

✓ To share a space with another child

✓ To read a book to a doll or an adult

MATERIALS:

☐ Large, fluffy quilt
☐ Pillows
☐ Dolls
☐ Books

PREPARATION:

♡ Spread out the quilt in an open area of the room. Place the pillows, dolls, and books on top of the quilt.

NURTURING STRATEGIES:

1. When a toddler shows interest in the activity, move closer to provide assistance.
2. Ask what the quilt is for. Expand upon the child's answer. For example, if the child says, "books," reply with *"Yes, this quilt is a place for reading books."*
3. Encourage the toddler to read a story to one of the dolls.
4. If other children are present and want to join the activity, discuss ways to share the space by saying: *"The quilt is large enough for three children. Where can Reina sit?"*

5. Assist the children in solving and implementing a solution to the problem of limited space.
6. If more than three children want to be on the quilt, make a waiting list and redirect the additional children to another activity. Reassure these children that you will call them when it is their turn.

☀ Highlighting Development

At this stage, toddlers are struggling between wanting independence and needing dependence. This struggle is evident in their behavioral incongruencies. At one moment toddlers will model independent behavior. At this time, it is important for them to do things independently. Then the next moment, the toddlers model dependent behavior and solicit your assistance.

VARIATION:

♡ Lay the quilt, dolls, and books outside for an outdoor activity.

ADDITIONAL INFORMATION:

♡ Toddlers need opportunities to explore materials before they are able to use them for the intended purpose.

 Whenever pillows or blankets are used, constant supervision is necessary to prevent the possibility of suffocation.

SOCIAL

Animal Prints

Child's Developmental Goals

✓ To engage in parallel play

✓ To interact with an adult

MATERIALS:

☐ Play dough recipe; see Appendix I for a list of dough recipes

☐ 4 place mats

☐ Identical plastic animal figures such as dinosaurs, monkeys, dogs

☐ Child-size table or coffee table

PREPARATION:

♡ Select a child-size table for the experience and lay out place mats. Divide the play dough equally and lay it on the place mats with two animal figures.

NURTURING STRATEGIES:

1. When a toddler chooses the activity, observe the child's behavior.
2. Encourage sensory exploration through the use of the fingers and hands.
3. Describe the toddler's actions with the dough. Comments include:
   "Goran, you're squishing the dough through your fingers."
   "You're poking the dough with your finger."
   "You're rolling the dough with your palms."
4. Suggest that the toddler incorporate the animals in playing by asking:
   "What are the animals for?"
5. If necessary, modeling imprinting the animal's feet in the dough may increase the child's level of play.

6. Invite another child, if present, to join the activity.
7. Comment on the similarities and differences of the children's work, if several are present. To illustrate, say:
   "Goran is making dinosaur prints, and Dale is flattening the dough with her fist."

☼ Highlighting Development

To promote a healthy self-concept, positive guidance is necessary. Guidance can be described as the direct or indirect actions used by adults to help children develop socially acceptable behavior. During parallel or associative play, children might invade others' physical space or take their property. When this occurs, you need to set and maintain limits. If necessary, you may need to enact a consequence for negative behavior. For example, if a child pretends his animal bites another, say, "Sarah doesn't like it when you are pretending to bite her. If you do that again, you will need to give me the animal."

VARIATION:

♡ Spread out a vinyl tablecloth on the floor for a working surface.

ADDITIONAL INFORMATION:

♡ Experiment with various play dough recipes because each has a slightly different texture. Compare and contrast the doughs.

♡ Use different animals, small rolling pins, or cookie cutters.

19 to 24 months

Follow the Leader

SOCIAL

Child's Developmental Goals

✓ To imitate another's behavior
✓ To participate in a game

MATERIALS:

None

PREPARATION:

None

NURTURING STRATEGIES:

1. When a toddler loses interest in an activity, suggest playing a game. To illustrate, say:
   "Amber, let's play a game. It is called 'Follow the Leader.' Listen and do what I say or do. Are you ready?"
2. Begin with something easy, such as clapping hands or rubbing your tummy. Alternate between doing the behavior and providing verbal instructions. Behaviors may include walking around the room, crawling under a table, jumping/hopping in place, stamping your feet, flapping your arms, wiggling your nose, or shaking your head.
3. Providing positive reinforcement may result in the toddler imitating or paying more attention. Comments might include:
   "Amber, excellent job listening to my words. You crawled under the table. This time walk around the table."
   "You're good at this game. You do everything that I do."

4. If the child is ready, increase the difficulty and silliness of the game by trying to do two things at once. Laugh at yourself for not being able to do both tasks. Discuss how silly you look, for example, when crawling and shaking your head.

☀ Highlighting Development

Toddlers are very skilled at observing and imitating people that surround and are important to them. Use this to your advantage. Demonstrating prosocial behaviors results in the toddlers imitating them. For example, when the child hands you something, respond by saying "thank you." Likewise, when asking the child to hand you an object, include the word "please." Gradually, they will incorporate these words into their vocabulary.

VARIATIONS:

♡ Follow the child's lead.

ADDITIONAL INFORMATION:

♡ As discussed earlier, encourage toddlers to crawl during activities like these. Crawling exercises both sides of the brain at once and should be encouraged often.
♡ Respect the child's attempts by laughing "with" and not "at" the child.

19 to 24 months

Bowling

Child's Developmental Goals

✓ To interact with at least one other person

✓ To participate in a game

MATERIALS:

❑ 6 two-liter bottles

❑ Lightweight, plastic ball

PREPARATION:

♡ Set up the six bottles in a triangle. Lay the ball several feet away on the sidewalk. If several children are present, set up a second bowling game and ball in a separate area.

NURTURING STRATEGIES:

1. When a toddler chooses the activity, observe the child's behavior.

2. Introduce the activity to the child by saying: *"This is a bowling game. Roll the ball and knock down the bottles. When you knock them down, set them back up. Then you can roll the ball again."*

3. Observe the toddler playing the game. If other children are present, invite them to join.

4. If more than one child is participating, assist the toddlers in working together. Comments to make include:
   "Cooper, you can roll the ball after Sania has a turn."
   "Set up the bottles so your friend can have a turn."

5. Provide positive reinforcement both for individual skills and working together. To illustrate, comment: *"Wow! You knocked down all six bottles."*
   "You're sharing the bowling game. Cooper goes and then Sania goes next."

☼ Highlighting Development

Toddlers often find transitions to or from another activity stressful. Observe. Transition frequently involves waiting. This is difficult for toddlers, who are used to being busy. Sometimes they test your limits. To illustrate, when told to pick up the game, toddlers may refuse to clean up, cry, or throw toys. To prevent this behavior, warn them several minutes before cleanup time. The warning will provide time to finish current activities and for mental preparation for the next transition. To reduce potential guidance problems, avoid a waiting time during a transition.

VARIATION:

♡ Play the game inside in a hallway or open area of a room.

ADDITIONAL INFORMATION:

♡ Depending on the number of children present and interested, you may need to set a limit of two to three children per bowling game.

Going Camping

SOCIAL

Child's Developmental Goals

✓ To share physical space with another person

✓ To engage in functional and/or pretend play

MATERIALS:

❑ Tent for two to four children

❑ Backpacks

❑ Adult-size flannel shirts

❑ Items to carry in backpacks

PREPARATION:

♡ Select and clear an area that can be constantly supervised. Set up the tent in this area. Place the flannel shirts, backpacks, and other items near the tent.

NURTURING STRATEGIES:

1. Introduce the activity to the toddler. To illustrate, say:
   "We are going to pretend to go camping. You can go inside the tent. There are backpacks for carrying supplies."
2. Observe the toddler exploring the available materials.
3. Assist with putting on shirts, zipping and unzipping backpacks, and putting on the backpacks. Encourage the toddler to assist in helping as much as possible. Comments to make include:
   "Push your arm through the sleeve."
   "I'll hold it while you pull the zipper."
4. Suggest that two toddlers, if present, get inside the tent.

5. Provide positive reinforcement for sharing the space. Use comments such as:
   "You are sharing the tent."
   "You two are inside the tent."
6. Encourage the toddler to engage in pretend play by asking questions related to camping. For example, say:
   "What are you taking camping?"
   "Where are you going camping?"

☀ Highlighting Development

Toddlers need to be responsible for caring for toys and maintaining the environment. Therefore, participating in cleanup activities is an important routine. Set expectations that are developmentally appropriate. For a child of this age, putting away two toys may be sufficient. As the toddler matures, expectations should be raised accordingly.

VARIATION:

♡ Set up an area outdoors for the camping activity.

ADDITIONAL INFORMATION:

♡ Toddlers enjoy private spaces such as those provided by tents.

♡ Tents are safe yet adventurous toys. To encourage participation in functional or pretend play, place accessories in the tent such as flashlights, portable radios, and sleeping bags.

Kicking the Ball

Child's Developmental Goals

✓ To engage in parallel play

✓ To interact with an adult

MATERIALS:

❏ 2 rubber balls

PREPARATION:

♡ Lay the balls in a grassy and/or open area outdoors.

NURTURING STRATEGIES:

1. Observe the toddler playing with the ball.
2. Suggest new ways to use the ball. For example, if the toddler is rolling the ball, suggest that the ball be kicked with the feet.
3. In addition, suggest that the child kick the ball to you. When you receive the ball, gently kick it back to the child.
4. Comment on how the child or group of children is playing with the ball. Comments include:
   "You are kicking the balls."
   "Shelby and Darby are chasing the balls."
5. Providing positive reinforcement may result in the toddler spending more time at the activity. To illustrate, say:
   "You kicked that ball to me."
   "What a good kick."
6. The toddlers may be uncoordinated in their initial attempts at kicking. Therefore, you will need to provide much support and encouragement.

☀ Highlighting Development

Selecting an appropriate ball is important to the success of this activity and, therefore, the children's view of themselves. Balls should be lightweight and approximately the size of volleyballs. If the ball is too small, the children may lack the necessary eye-foot coordination to successfully kick it when swinging their leg. Ensuring success is important because one way children evaluate themselves is in relationship to their physical abilities.

VARIATION:

♡ Encourage the toddler to kick the ball to another person.

ADDITIONAL INFORMATION:

♡ If several children are present, be sure to divide your time equally among them. It is important for all children to receive positive attention to make them feel valued as individuals.

19 to 24 months

Emotional Development

♡

NINETEEN to TWENTY-FOUR MONTHS

Paper Crunch

Child's Developmental Goals

✓ To express emotions such as anger or enjoyment

✓ To coordinate behaviors with emotions

MATERIALS:

❑ Used wrapping paper of different sizes and designs

PREPARATION:

♡ Cut large sheets of paper into smaller pieces, if necessary. Place the wrapping paper in the center of a child-size table.

NURTURING STRATEGIES:

1. When a toddler chooses the activity, observe the child's behavior.
2. If necessary, introduce the activity. To illustrate, say: *"Randall, this paper is for crumpling and crunching. You can wad it into a ball."*
3. Describe the emotions displayed by the child while working. Use comments such as: *"You are smiling. Crunching paper must make you happy."* *"You have a frightened look. Does the noise scare you?"*
4. Encouraging the toddler to express different emotions may result in a greater understanding of them. Say, for example: *"If you were mad, how would you crunch the paper?"*
5. Follow up by providing positive reinforcement that connects the child's behaviors with the displayed emotion. To illustrate, say: *"I can tell that you are mad. You are scrunching the paper hard. You are also scrunching your nose."*

6. If necessary, model crunching the paper to express different emotions such as happiness, fright, anger, or sadness. Ask the child to guess how you are feeling.
7. Continue the activity as long as the toddler seems interested.

☀ Highlighting Development

Toddlers display anger more frequently, with more intensity, and in more situations than do infants. This change is linked to growth in cognitive development. As they engage in more intentional behavior and are better at identifying the source of their blocked goals, their expressions of anger may be particularly intense (Berk, 1997).

VARIATION:

♡ Toss paper balls into a laundry basket to practice eye-hand coordination skills.

ADDITIONAL INFORMATION:

♡ Young toddlers delight in the cause and effect as well as the sounds created by crunching paper. Keeping paper available for this purpose will assist when redirecting the child's inappropriate behaviors with materials such as the daily paper or pages in a book.

19 to 24 months

Sad Little Spider

Child's Developmental Goals

✓ To associate emotions with behaviors

✓ To express emotions through a song

MATERIALS:

❑ Felt-tip pen
❑ Index card

PREPARATION:

♡ See Appendix G for the song, "The Itsy Bitsy Spider." If desired, copy the song on an index card.

NURTURING STRATEGIES:

1. When you notice a toddler wandering in search of an activity, extend an invitation for singing by saying:
   "I feel like singing. Would you like to sing with me?"
2. Sing the song, "The Itsy Bitsy Spider."
3. Tell the child that you'd like to sing the song about a sad spider.
4. Converse briefly about some things that make you and the toddler sad.
5. Ask the toddler to show you what she looks like when she is sad.
6. Describe the facial and bodily gestures made by the child. For example, say:
   "When you are sad, you stick out your bottom lip. You also look at the floor. Let's do those movements while singing about the spider."
7. Sing the song again, substituting the "sad little" instead of the "itsy bitsy" spider.
8. Provide positive reinforcement for singing and performing the movements of the song. Comments include:
   "Your spider was so sad."
   "You made all of the motions in the song."
   "You sang along with me."

☀ Highlighting Development

At this stage, toddlers experience a wide variety of emotions. To assist them, adults can provide verbal and nonverbal support when the child is experiencing success, frustration, or failure. Responding to a child's accomplishments with gestures such as smiling or nodding can convey an important emotional understanding. When the child is frustrated, try saying "Try it again. It is hard." Likewise, when the child is failing to complete a task such as inserting a puzzle piece, you may say, "Turn the piece around. Then it will fit."

VARIATIONS:

♡ Change words to reflect different emotions such as anger, happiness, or excitement.
♡ While singing the song, make facial expressions corresponding to the emotions being sung. Then ask the child to identify the emotion.

ADDITIONAL INFORMATION:

♡ Observe and assess the toddler's body language while singing. Is the child able to associate emotions with behaviors? If not, continue focusing on these skills. Otherwise, begin introducing more complex emotions.

19 to 24 months

Popping Popcorn

Child's Developmental Goals

✓ To develop self-control when excited

✓ To express emotions while singing

MATERIALS:

❑ Hot air popper

❑ Popcorn

❑ Metal or plastic mixing bowl

❑ Extension cord (if necessary)

PREPARATION:

♡ Gather all the necessary supplies and place them out of the children's reach.

♡ Clear a spot on the floor for popper and children.

♡ Gather all other supplies needed for snack and place in the snack area.

NURTURING STRATEGIES:

1. Introduce the activity to the children by saying:
   "Today we are going to make popcorn for snack. Have any of you eaten popcorn before?"
2. Discuss limits to prevent safety hazards. Comment, for example:
   "The machine gets hot. It could burn us. Stay sitting."
3. Plug in and turn on the popcorn machine. Then pour the popcorn into the appliance.
4. Talk about the sound of popping corn.
5. Sing the following chant and clap to the rhythm: (Tune: "Hot Dog Song")

   ♫ Three little kernels
   ♫ In the pan
   ♫ The air got hot
   ♫ And one went bam! (Continue until zero kernels: "The air got hot and the pan went bam!")

6. The children will become excited as the popcorn begins to pop.
7. Provide positive reinforcement for remaining seated. Comments to make include:
   "What a good listener."
   "You were safe because you followed the rules."
8. Wash hands and enjoy the snack.

 Highlighting Development

Children at this age are more skilled at imitating your actions. Observe them as you introduce this new chant. They may try clapping to the beat and repeating some of the words.

VARIATIONS:

♡ Act out what it would be like to be a kernel of corn.

♡ See Appendix F for other popcorn chants.

ADDITIONAL INFORMATION:

♡ Children enjoy eating foods they have participated in preparing. In some instances, they may even try new foods because of their involvement.

CAUTION Popcorn can be a choking hazard for children. Therefore, introduce this activity only if the toddlers are 24 months or older. Pay close attention to children who tend to not chew their food well because they might be at a higher risk for choking, even if they are over 24 months of age.

CAUTION Keep popcorn kernels out of the children's reach.

19 to 24 months

Painting the Playground

Child's Developmental Goals

✓ To express enjoyment during an activity

✓ To experience a sense of satisfaction

MATERIALS:

❑ Bucket for each child

❑ 2-inch paintbrush for each child

❑ Water

PREPARATION:

♡ Fill the bucket half full of water. Then place a brush in the bucket. Set the bucket on a sidewalk. Repeat the process as necessary for additional children.

NURTURING STRATEGIES:

1. Introduce the activity by saying:
   "Kiri, you can paint. Here is a brush and a bucket of water."
2. Observe the child's behavior.
3. Be prepared to redirect the toddler, if necessary. For example, if the child is painting the slide, suggest painting the fence.
4. Describing the child's behavior will assist in connecting actions with language. Comments include:
   "Kiri, stretching. You're stretching your body to reach the top of that pole."
   "You're painting side to side."
5. If two or more children are painting, comment on how they are working together. Say, for example:
   "Everyone is painting. You're working hard."
   "The fresh paint makes everything look so new."

6. Describe the emotions being displayed by the children. Use comments such as:
   "Kiri, you're smiling. You like painting."
   "Josiah, you're stopping. You must be finished."

☀ Highlighting Development

Children's view of themselves comprises two separate yet related components—self-worth and competence (Berk, 1997). Self-worth is the belief that you are important as a person (Herr, 1998). Competence, on the other hand, is the belief that you can do things well (Berk, 1997). Therefore, you need to consider both components when helping toddlers to develop a healthy view of themselves. It is too limiting to focus on just the children's evaluation of their self-worth. Creating developmentally appropriate experiences is one way to help toddlers view themselves as being competent individuals.

VARIATION:

♡ Providing brushes of different sizes may result in experimentation.

ADDITIONAL INFORMATION:

♡ This is a wonderful activity to do on warm summer days. Repeat the activity as long as it appeals to the child.

19 to 24 months

Brushing Teeth

EMOTIONAL

Child's Developmental Goals

✓ To practice self-help skills
✓ To develop healthy living habits and skills

MATERIALS:

☐ Sink
☐ Toothbrush and toothpaste
☐ Paper towels
☐ Basket

PREPARATION:

♡ Store the toddler's toothbrush and toothpaste on a child-size shelf or cabinet. In a child care center, you may want to clearly label the child's personal belongings.

NURTURING STRATEGIES:

1. After eating a meal or snack, direct the toddler to the sink to brush her teeth. Accompany the child to the sink and provide assistance, if needed.
2. Assist the child in selecting the basket holding the supplies. Say, for example:
   "Keiji, K, K, K—Where is Keiji's basket? Here it is."
   (while pointing to the label)
3. Ask the toddler to help you by holding the toothbrush while you squeeze out a small amount of toothpaste.
4. Instruct the toddler to begin brushing.
5. Sing the following song while the toddler brushes:

   ♫ Brush, brush, brush your teeth
   ♫ Until they're nice and strong
   ♫ Brush, brush, brush your teeth
   ♫ While we sing this song.

6. Provide positive reinforcement for brushing teeth. Comments include:
   "You cleaned your front and back teeth."
   "You cleaned the fronts and backs of your teeth."

7. Encourage the toddler to spit out the toothpaste rather than swallowing it. To do this, comment by saying:
   "Keiji, spit the toothpaste in the sink."
8. After rinsing the toothbrush, have the toddler return it to its proper place. To remove remaining toothpaste, wiping the face and hands with paper towels may be necessary.

☀ Highlighting Development

Children differ in their response to requests made by adults. Some children easily comply, while others resist. When resisting, children typically feel frustrated. The frustration may be expressed through a temper tantrum. This is the toddlers' way of communicating that they have had enough. Observe them. They may throw themselves on the floor, scream, and kick. When this occurs, simply ignoring the tantrum can be effective. Otherwise, distraction is one of the most effective techniques for diverting attention. Because these emotions need to be expressed, however, distraction should not be immediately introduced.

VARIATION:

♡ Encourage the child to wash his face after a meal by providing a warm, damp washcloth.

ADDITIONAL INFORMATION:

♡ Preventing tooth decay is necessary and important. Once the child's first tooth erupts, it should be brushed after meals or bottles. Until the infant/toddler is able to stand unassisted, you will need to do the brushing. Teaching lifelong habits for healthy living is a necessary role of adults.

19 to 24 months

EMOTIONAL

Happy and Sad

Child's Developmental Goals

✓ To label emotions

✓ To associate emotions with behaviors

MATERIALS:

❑ Masks with different expressions (if unavailable, make your own with paper plates and felt-tip markers)

PREPARATION:

♡ If using commercially manufactured masks, select a happy face and a sad face. If you wish to make your own, draw a happy face on one side of the paper plate and a sad face on the other side. Decorate the masks with the felt-tip markers so the faces are easy to see.

NURTURING STRATEGIES:

1. Gather the masks and introduce the activity by saying:
   "I have a story to tell you today. It is about two children. Sometimes the children are happy, and sometimes they are sad. Let's look and see how the children feel."
2. Begin telling your story. Parallel your story with the lives of the children in the audience. For example, discuss a recent incident in which a child had hurt feelings.
3. During the story, hold up a mask while describing an emotion.
4. Ask the children to label the emotion being described. Ask, for example:
   "How is Sonya feeling now?"
5. Close the activity by asking the children to describe something that makes them sad and happy.

☀ Highlighting Development

Toddlers learn emotional display rules, which are guidelines that specify when, where, and how it is culturally appropriate to express emotions, through both direct and indirect instruction. Toddlers may be told or encouraged, for example, to express anger in self-defense such as when a friend grabs their toy or hits them. Indirectly, children learn how to behave emotionally by watching others control or express their feelings (Kostelnik et al., 1998).

VARIATION:

♡ Cut out faces from magazines that represent different emotions such as surprised, scared, or angry. Mount the pictures on poster board and share them with the children.

ADDITIONAL INFORMATION:

♡ Toddlers are often frightened of masks because they lack a clear understanding of transformations. They fail to see the relationship between beginning and ending states. Therefore, avoid holding the mask directly in front of your face during this activity.

19 to 24 months

Helping with Lunch

EMOTIONAL

Child's Developmental Goals

✓ To experience a sense of self-satisfaction

✓ To improve self-help skills

MATERIALS:

☐ Fresh green beans

☐ Salt and pepper

☐ Basket

☐ Water

☐ Saucepan with lid

PREPARATION:

♡ Wash, drain, and place the green beans in the basket. Then place the basket on a child-size table. Finally, set the saucepan in the middle of the table.

NURTURING STRATEGIES:

1. Sit at the table and begin snapping the stems off the beans.

2. Invite a child to help you. To illustrate, say: *"Darrell, I'm snapping beans to cook for lunch. Would you help me? Wash your hands first."*

3. Discuss how and why you are breaking the stems from the beans. Comment, for example: *"The stems are tough. We need to take them off. Watch me. See how I am bending the end of the bean. The end will break off. I'm placing the stems in this pile."*

4. While handing the child a bean, encourage the toddler to join in the snapping by saying: *"Darrell, try snapping this bean."*

5. Provide positive reinforcement for attempts and accomplishments. Comments to make include: *"Darrell, you broke off the stem. You are helping me." "No stems here. You're working hard."*

6. Before putting the bean into the saucepan, model breaking each bean in half.

7. Talk about how the beans are easier to eat when smaller. That is why you are breaking them in smaller pieces.

8. Count the number of beans the toddler makes. Comment, for example: *"You now have two beans to put into the pan."*

9. Thank the child for snapping the beans.

10. Wash, season, and cook the beans. Serve for lunch or snack.

☀ Highlighting Development

Toddlers enjoy imitating and assisting adults. It is important that they participate in routine activities such as helping with lunch, eating, dressing, and caring for the environment. When these activities are first introduced, expect that they usually will be time intensive. With maturity and practice, children will become more proficient. In the meantime, they need time, instruction, encouragement, and praise.

VARIATIONS:

♡ Shell large peas or kidney beans.

♡ Plant a garden and, when the food ripens, prepare fresh salads.

ADDITIONAL INFORMATION:

♡ While eating the cooked beans, introduce raw beans for comparison tasting. Discuss the differences. Interject comments on how the toddler assisted in preparing the beans for lunch. To improve memory skills, recap the steps in snapping the beans.

19 to 24 months

I Need a Hug

Child's Developmental Goals

✓ To express caring emotions
✓ To learn ways for meeting needs

MATERIALS:

None

PREPARATION:

None

NURTURING STRATEGIES:

1. Observe a toddler at work, noticing how the child is feeling about the day.
2. If the child is feeling frustrated, sad, or tired, move closer and position yourself at the toddler's eye level.
3. Involve yourself in the toddler's play without disrupting it. For example, if the toddler is feeding a doll, begin feeding a doll of your own.
4. When that play episode is over, say to the toddler: *"Oksanna, I'm sad and need a hug. Can I have a hug?"*
5. While hugging, say, for example: *"Hugs always make me feel better."*
6. Thank the child for making you feel better. Comments include: *"Thank you, Oksanna. I feel much better now." "Thanks for the wonderful hug, Oksanna. You helped me to feel better."*
7. Converse with the toddler about ways of positively getting needs met. To illustrate, say: *"When I'm sad and need a hug, I ask someone. Do you ask others for hugs?"*
8. Comment on the toddler's answer and then encourage the child to practice asking for a hug. Respond by hugging the child.

☀ Highlighting Development

To direct their behavior, children at this stage often continue to rely on cues from others. They search for cues, such as facial expressions from parents, caregivers, siblings, and peers. This phenomenon is referred to as social referencing. To illustrate, when an adult appears afraid, the child will pick up on the nonverbal clues and move away from what the adult views as fearful. Likewise, chances are the child will also move closer to the adult for support.

VARIATIONS:

♡ Provide dolls or stuffed animals for hugging.
♡ If the child is feeling happy, offer a hug.

ADDITIONAL INFORMATION:

♡ Toddlers are battling the conflict between autonomy and dependence. On one hand, they want to do everything themselves and, on the other hand, they lack some of the necessary skills. Therefore, toddlers consistently need love and support.
♡ Be open and flexible in meeting the immediate needs of the child. If the child needs help, always try to provide assistance. Typically, tasks you are engaged in can temporarily wait.
♡ Show you care. Love and hugs are contagious. If a child feels loved, the child will hug others in return.

19 to 24 months

"Skinamarink"

Child's Developmental Goals

✓ To express caring to others

✓ To receive caring emotions from others

MATERIALS:

❑ Index card

❑ Felt-tip marker

PREPARATION:

♡ Write out the following words to the song on an index card, if preferred:

♫ Skinamarink, a rink, a dink (roll hands in circle)

♫ Skinamarink, a doo (roll hands in circle)

♫ I love you. (point to self, cross arms over chest, point to child or group)

♫ I love you in the morning and in the afternoon (roll hands in circle)

♫ I love you in the evening and underneath the moon. (roll hands in circle)

♫ Oh . . . (clap)

♫ Skinamarink, a rink, a dink (same as first verse)

♫ Skinamarink, a doo.

♫ I love you.

NURTURING STRATEGIES:

1. Introduce this song during a routine waiting time such as before mealtime. Begin by saying:
   "I have a new song for you. The song is about the feeling I have for you."
2. While rolling your hands in a circle, ask:
   "Can you do this?"
3. Provide positive reinforcement by commenting:
   "Good job."
   "Excellent. You can do it!"

4. Move on to the next movement but allow sufficient time for the child to imitate your actions.
5. After all movements have been introduced, say:
   "Let's put some words with the movements."
   Then begin to sing the song. Sing the song slowly the first couple of times. Ensure that the toddler can sing the song with you.
6. Repeat as time allows or introduce again throughout the day. Repetition will assist the toddler in learning the words and movements.

☀ Highlighting Development

The ways adults treat young children have been found to have a profound impact in the development of empathy. Adults who are nurturing and encouraging and show a sensitive, empathic concern have children who are more likely to react in a concerned way to the distress of others. Relatedly, harsh and punitive caregiving is related to disruptions in the development of empathy (Berk, 1997).

VARIATION:

♡ Sing the song to children when they are calming down prior to nap time.

ADDITIONAL INFORMATION:

♡ This song will quickly become a favorite for toddlers and teachers. The song has emotional appeal because it makes a person feel good. If working with children in a center, share the words in a printed form with parents and guardians.

19 to 24 months

Catching Bubbles

Child's Developmental Goals

✓ To associate emotions with behaviors

✓ To express emotions such as excitement

MATERIALS:

☐ Bottle of bubble solution or prepare own solution; see Appendix I for a list of recipes

☐ Bubble wands

☐ Paper towels

PREPARATION:

♡ If desired, prepare a bubble solution.

♡ Select a safe outdoor area for this activity.

♡ When planning an area to stage the activity, consideration needs to be given to the ground cover. Young children are developing balance and coordination skills. While chasing the bubbles, they may fall. Cement should be avoided; a soft grassy area would offer the most protection.

NURTURING STRATEGIES:

1. Observe the child playing. When a change of activity is apparent, get the bubble solution and wand.

2. The position of your body is important for this activity. Sit so you can see everyone you might be supervising. If the wind is blowing, position yourself so the wind carries the bubbles over the selected area.

3. Begin blowing the bubbles. Observe to see if the toddler notices. If so, continue. Otherwise, gain the attention of the toddler by using the child's name.

4. Often toddlers want to participate in blowing the bubbles. For safety purposes, encourage the child to chase the bubbles by saying:
   "Austin, go catch the bubbles. See how many you can get."

5. Describing the child's reactions to the activity may help in promoting understanding of emotions. Comments include:
   "You caught one. What a big smile. You must be proud!"
   "Oh, what a sad look. Are you disappointed because the bubble got away?"

6. Offering support and encouragement promotes participation. To illustrate, say:
   "Austin, almost. You almost got that one. Keep trying."
   "Here comes another bubble. Try to catch this one."

7. Providing positive reinforcement may result in the toddler chasing the bubbles longer and, therefore, allowing you to engage in more "emotion talk." Use comments such as:
   "Austin, you are working so hard to catch a bubble."
   "Wow! You've caught three bubbles now!"

☀ Highlighting Development

The beginnings of self-control emerge after the first birthday. At this time, children are aware that they must react to other people's demands. By two years of age, they have internalized some self-control. To illustrate, if the toddler is told not to touch something, the child may inhibit the desire. At this stage, the child may remember being told not to touch it. However, close supervision is always necessary because of lapses in memory and recall as well as the excitement of the moment.

VARIATIONS:

♡ Use a variety of tools such as a berry basket, large wand, or slotted kitchen spoon to create the bubbles.

♡ When children are skilled at blowing, encourage them to create their own bubbles.

 Exercise caution when playing with bubbles. The bubble solution can be irritating if it makes contact with the eyes. Therefore, encourage the children to stand away from the tool when you're actually blowing the bubbles. The children should also periodically wipe their hands with a paper towel, especially if they've caught several bubbles.

19 to 24 months

Nineteen to Twenty-Four Months **331**

How Does the Child Feel?

Child's Developmental Goals

✓ To associate emotions with behaviors

✓ To identify and label emotional expressions

MATERIALS:

❑ Pictures of children from books, magazines, or catalogs

❑ Transparent self-adhesive paper

❑ Basket

PREPARATION:

♡ Select and cut out pictures of people expressing different emotions from books, magazines, or catalogs. Covering each picture with transparent self-adhesive paper will help preserve it.

♡ Place the pictures in the basket and put it on a shelf out of the reach of the children.

NURTURING STRATEGIES:

1. When you notice a child needing a new activity, retrieve your basket. Then sit on the floor close to the child.

2. Introduce the activity by saying:
   "Cami, I have some pictures for us to play with today. Look. The children are making different faces. Let's see if you can tell how each child must be feeling."

3. Hold up the first picture and say, for example:
   "Let's take a good look at this child."
   Allow time for visually exploring the picture.

4. To promote labeling emotions, ask the toddler:
   "Cami, how is the child feeling?"

5. If the child says "angry," nod and ask:
   "Does the child look really mad?"

6. Next, ask the child to tell you how she knew the child was sad. Focusing on the association between behavior and emotions may increase the toddler's understanding.

7. Lastly, ask the child for possible reasons why the child might be happy. Questions to ask include:
   "Cami, why is the child happy?"
   "What could have made this child happy?"

8. Move on to a second picture. Continue as long as the toddler is interested.

☼ Highlighting Development

Emotions emerge throughout childhood. By nine months of age, infants have experienced all four core emotions—joy, anger, sadness, and fear. During the second year, five additional emotions are added, including pride, guilt, affection, jealousy, and defiance.

Observe. One task facing young children is emotional self-regulation. As toddlers mature, their emotional responses become more differentiated. The children's responses grow in complexity as well. They may cry, scream, pout, hit, grab, and shove when angry. Moreover, they move into or out of situations depending on their needs. As children continue developing cognitive and language abilities, they begin using words for expressing their emotions. Likewise, they recognize the emotions of others. They may say, "Mama happy," "Tommy sad," or "baby cry" (Kostelnik et al., 1998).

VARIATION:

♡ Repeat the activity while reading a picture book.

ADDITIONAL INFORMATION:

♡ Toddlers use telegraphic speech for several months. Continue expanding their language development by elaborating on their sentences. For example, if a toddler says, "Toy broke," you could expand it by saying, "The child was sad because her toy broke."

♡ Adults need to frequently ask questions. At times, they also need to provide the answers to these questions.

19 to 24 months

Coloring to Music

Child's Developmental Goals

✓ To express one's feelings through art

✓ To discuss feelings

MATERIALS:

❑ Tape or compact disc player

❑ Tape or compact disc containing instrumental music such as classical or jazz

❑ 8½ × 11–inch sheet of light-colored construction paper for each child

❑ Basket for each child

❑ Box of chubby crayons for each child

PREPARATION:

♡ Place one sheet of construction paper on a child-size table. Place a basket of chubby crayons beside each piece of paper. If there is more than one child, provide paper and crayons for each child.

♡ Plug in the tape or compact disc player and set it on a shelf beyond the toddler's reach. Insert the tape or compact disc you selected.

NURTURING STRATEGIES:

1. When a toddler chooses the activity, begin playing the music.

2. Observe the toddler's behavior.

3. If the toddler is coloring with the music, describe the child's behavior. Say, for example:
   "Amit, you are drawing quickly, just like the music."

4. If the toddler is ignoring the music, you may need to model. Begin by drawing scribbles in response to the music. Reinforce your actions with words by making comments such as:
   "Amit, the music is slow, so I'm slowly drawing a large circle."
   "Now the music is fast, so I'm drawing lots of short lines."

5. Allow the toddler to work in silence by minimizing conversation.

6. After the toddler is finished coloring, discuss the drawing. Describe what you see. Comments include:
   "Amit, you used lots of red."
   "Look at these long lines. They go from side to side."

7. Expand your conversation by commenting on how the song made the toddler and you feel. Elicit the child's feelings by asking, for example:
   "Amit, how did you feel when you heard that music?"

☼ Highlighting Development

During play, children display emotions. Depending on the circumstances, these emotions can be intense. As a result, children need appropriate self-expression skills. Often this requires adult assistance and guidance. For children to learn skills, adults need to set clear limits and enforce them as necessary. To illustrate, when a child throws a toy, adults need to intervene. They can respond by saying, "You are angry. I cannot let you hurt others." Adults need to reinforce the concept that the child's feelings are acceptable; however, their actions are unacceptable.

VARIATION:

♡ Experiment by providing different types of instrumental music.

ADDITIONAL INFORMATION:

♡ When modeling working with the music, avoid drawing objects. Toddlers will scribble. They lack the skills to create representational drawings.

19 to 24 months

Golf Ball Painting

EMOTIONAL

Child's Developmental Goals

✓ To associate behaviors with emotions

✓ To express one's feelings through art

MATERIALS:

❑ Unused pizza boxes
❑ Construction paper
❑ Masking tape
❑ Paint
❑ Damp sponge
❑ Golf ball for each child
❑ Nonbreakable paint container for each child
❑ Spoon for each child
❑ Smock for each child

PREPARATION:

♡ Cut construction paper to fit inside the top and bottom of the pizza box. Using two pieces of tape, secure the paper to the top and bottom of the pizza box.

♡ Mix the paint to the desired thickness by using liquid soap to help facilitate cleanup. Pour paint into the container. If more than one child is participating, divide the paint equally among containers. Then put a golf ball and a spoon in each container.

♡ Place one pizza box and container at a child-size table for each child. Lay a smock over the back of each chair.

NURTURING STRATEGIES:

1. When a child chooses the activity, introduce it while assisting the child with putting on the smock. To illustrate, say:
   "Mulan, roll the ball in the paint and then place it in the box." Pause and wait for the child to follow the directions. *"Now close the lid and shake the box. You will make two pictures at once. Try it!"*

2. Assist the toddler, if needed, with getting the golf ball into the box.

3. Encourage the toddler to shake the box using different motions such as from side to side, fast, and slow. Then ask the toddler to act out different feelings by asking questions such as:
   "How would you shake the box if you were happy?"
   "How might you shake the box if you were sad?"

4. Provide positive reinforcement for the toddler associating behaviors with emotions. Use comments such as:
   "Mulan, I can tell you are angry. Your forehead is crinkled and you're shaking the box hard."
   "You are smiling and shaking the box firmly. You look happy."

5. Use the sponge to wipe a spill or dirty hands.

☀ Highlighting Development

During this stage of development, toddlers are learning referential and expressive speech. Referential speech includes the child's objects, actions, and location. Basically, this speech describes what is occurring. Expressive speech, on the other hand, includes feelings, emotional content, and social experiences. During art activities, children who use an expressive style will talk about their feelings and needs. In contrast, those preferring referential speech may focus their language on the materials, tools, or outcomes.

VARIATIONS:

♡ Introduce other types of art activities such as sponge painting or cookie cutter prints.

♡ For an outdoor activity, line a refrigerator box with butcher paper. Provide large items such as basketballs, footballs, or baseballs coated with paint. Encourage two or more toddlers to work together to shake the box.

ADDITIONAL INFORMATION:

♡ Whenever using paint, keep a damp sponge near the activity. If paint spills, wipe it up immediately.

19 to 24 months

"You Are Special"

Child's Developmental Goals

✓ To feel pride in oneself

✓ To recognize oneself as someone special

MATERIALS:

❏ Index card

❏ Felt-tip marker

PREPARATION:

♡ Either memorize the words to the song or write the words on an index card. If recorded, the words can be carried in your pocket:
(Tune: "Where is Thumbkin?")

♬ I am special, I am special
♬ Yes I am, yes I am (nod head)
♬ I am very special, I am very special
♬ Because I'm me, (point to self) because I'm me.

(Or)
♬ You are special, you are special
♬ Yes you are, yes you are
♬ You are very special, you are very special
♬ Because you're you, because you're you.

NURTURING STRATEGIES:

1. Introduce the song before napping or during a quiet time.
2. This can be sung to the child using your voice as a tool to soothe and calm. If more than one child is in your care, sing the song individually to each.
3. Further assist the toddler in calming down by rubbing the stomach or back.
4. Repeat the song several times until the toddler is ready to rest.

☀ Highlighting Development

The development of self-conscious behavior emerges as a result of adult instruction. Among some cultures, pride is evoked by generosity, helpfulness, and sharing. Situations that may evoke pride in one culture, however, may evoke shame or embarrassment in another. Pride may be shown for achievements of an entire group in one culture. In another, individual accomplishments result in pride (Kail, 1998).

Self-conscious emotions play an important role in children's achievement-related and moral behavior later in life. Therefore, adults need to help children develop an understanding of these complex emotions early in life (Berk, 1997).

VARIATION:

♡ Talk about the specific traits that make the toddler special.

ADDITIONAL INFORMATION:

♡ Toddlers often have a difficult time calming down at nap time. Making modifications to the environment or transitions to nap time can greatly help to reduce problem behaviors.

♡ As with infants, toddlers need predictability and consistency. Therefore, routines are important for guiding their behavior.

19 to 24 months

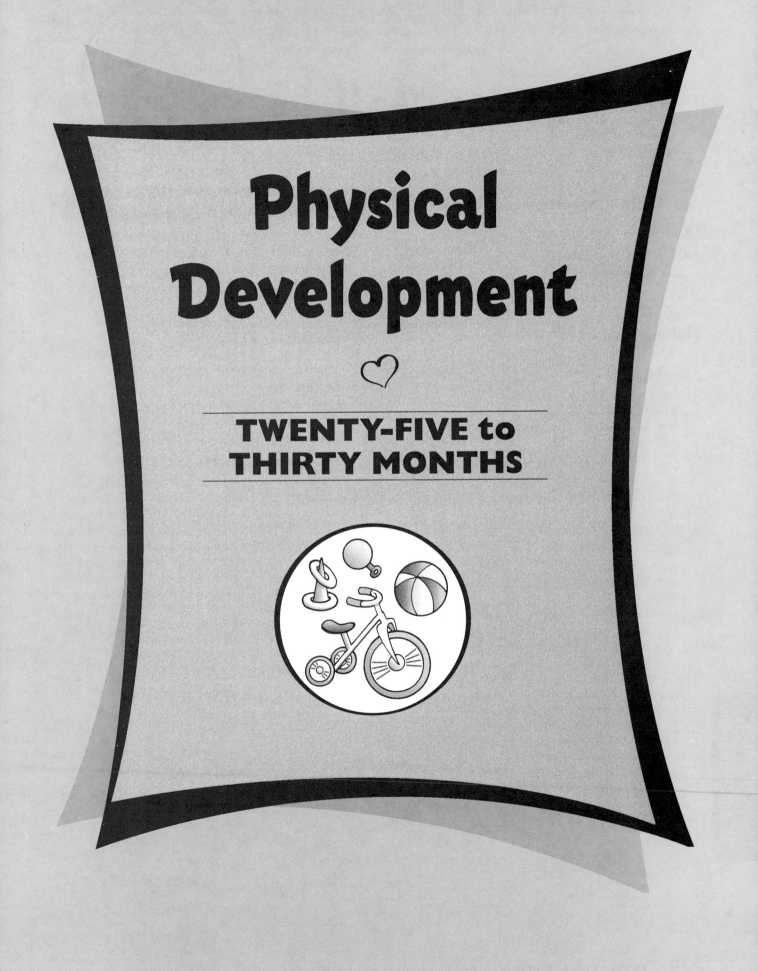

Physical Development

♡

TWENTY-FIVE to THIRTY MONTHS

Square Ball

Child's Developmental Goals

✓ To practice throwing a ball

✓ To improve eye-hand coordination

MATERIALS:

❑ Masking tape

❑ Balls, approximately 12 inches in diameter.

PREPARATION:

♡ Sweep and clean an area of sidewalk.

♡ Make a rectangle (4′ × 6′) on the sidewalk with the tape. Use another piece of tape to divide the rectangle in half.

♡ Place one ball in each square.

♡ Use tape to mark spots approximately 1 and 2 feet away from square.

NURTURING STRATEGIES:

1. When a child shows interest, introduce the experience. To illustrate, say:
   "Stand on this piece of tape and throw the ball into the square."
   While speaking, reinforce your words with actions by pointing to the tape and square.
2. Observe the child's performance. If the child consistently misses the ball, he may need to move even closer to the square. If, on the other hand, the child is consistently accurate, encourage the child to move to the second piece of tape farther away.
3. In any case, providing positive reinforcement may result in the child remaining at the experience for a longer period of time.

☀ Highlighting Development

During the toddler stage play continues to be the primary vehicle for learning. Toddlers are learning many ways to move their bodies. At this stage of development, they enjoy throwing and kicking balls. By now, they should be able to throw a ball at a target from approximately 2 feet with some accuracy (Charlesworth, 2000).

VARIATION:

♡ As the toddler's skill level increases, make the box smaller to provide a challenge.

ADDITIONAL INFORMATION:

♡ Toddlers frequently have their own agenda, so introducing activities to them can be challenging. Avoid pushing them too hard, and do not be surprised if they resist following directions. Frequently described as "the terrible twos," in the eyes of adults, toddlers' behavior can be contrary, demanding, and unreasonable. Allen and Marotz (1999) describe this behavior as an early step toward establishing independence.

25 to 30 months

Fill 'er Up

Child's Developmental Goals

✓ To improve eye-hand coordination

✓ To increase muscle strength

✓ To continue developing special awareness

MATERIALS:

❑ 2 medium boxes without lids

❑ Packing tape

❑ Thick rope, cut into two pieces

❑ Scissors

PREPARATION:

♡ Remove any flaps from box and cover edges with tape to prevent scratches.

♡ Punch two holes on same end of the box. Insert one end of the rope through each hole and tie on the inside of the box. Wrap knot with tape to secure.

♡ Repeat with second box.

♡ Place boxes in an eye-catching location.

NURTURING STRATEGIES:

1. Observe the toddlers' use of the boxes. They will probably immediately begin to put items from their immediate environment into the box . . . even their bodies!

2. If a toddler happens to fill the box so full that he cannot move it, encourage the toddler to problem solve.

3. To illustrate, identify the problem by saying: *"You found many blocks to put in your box. It seems too heavy for you to move now."*

4. Encourage the child to generate solutions by asking: *"What can you do so that your box can be moved?"*

5. If necessary, model generating solutions by asking: *"What if you asked Payton to help move the box?"* *"What if you took some of the (blocks) out of the box?"*

6. Help the child select one solution to try.

7. Assist the child as needed in following through with the selected solution. For example, say: *"I'll take the blocks out of the box. You can put them back on the shelf. There, now you can try and move the box."*

8. Provide positive reinforcement for solving the problem.

☀ Highlighting Development

Young children will concentrate for long periods of time when interested in an experience. An example for children of this stage of development is "filling and spilling" which offers many learning opportunities. By participating in this activity, children develop fine motor skills, visual perceptual skills, and gain an understanding of concepts such as full, empty, light, heavy, more, and less.

VARIATION:

♡ Increase or decrease size of box to alter size and number of objects that fit inside.

ADDITIONAL INFORMATION:

♡ Toddlers enjoy repetition. They may wish to repeat this experience many times. Moreover, they may modify the activity by changing the manipulatives they put into the box.

25 to 30 months

Screwing On a Lid

PHYSICAL

Child's Developmental Goals

✓ To practice eye-hand coordination skills

✓ To improve fine muscle skills in fingers and wrists

MATERIALS:

❑ Varying sizes of plastic containers with screw-on lids

❑ Basket

PREPARATION:

♡ Clean the containers, checking for sharp edges.

♡ If any sharp edges are discovered, cover them with masking tape.

♡ Put all lids and containers in the basket.

♡ Place the basket in a convenient location for the child.

NURTURING STRATEGIES:

1. When a toddler selects the materials, observe her behavior.

2. If necessary, provide a suggestion for using the materials. Say, for example, while pointing:
   "Kyra, can you find a lid that fits this container?"

3. If the toddler is having difficulty finding a lid that fits, verbally assist by saying:
   "The container in your hand is skinny. Look for the smallest lid."
   "Try the blue lid, Kyra. It might fit."

4. Encourage the toddler, if you notice the level of frustration rising. Comments to make include:
   "This is hard work. You can do it."
   "That is the right lid. Turn it a little more."

5. Continue the experience as long as the toddler shows interest.

☀ Highlighting Development

Toddlers' motor skills continue to develop during this period. Recall that by 24 months, they were successful at removing snap-on lids from containers. By 30 months, they are often proficient with screw-on lids. This means that they are also able to open doors by turning the knob (Berk, 1999). Hence, adults must be constantly alert if the toddler is tall enough to reach the door knob. Door knob safety covers can be installed to protect toddlers.

VARIATION:

♡ If necessary, decrease the challenge by providing snap-on lids (see the Putting On and Taking Off Lids activity on p. 267).

ADDITIONAL INFORMATION:

♡ Toddlers often modify an activity to fit their interests. So, do not be surprised if this activity turns into a fill and close, then open and empty exercise.

 Be sure to have available hazard-free objects that the child cannot choke on.

25 to 30 months

Kangaroo Jump

Child's Developmental Goals

✓ To practice jumping up and down

✓ To improve full-body coordination

MATERIALS:

❑ Compact disc player

❑ Compact disc, *The Ultimate Kids Collections: Favorite Sing-a-Longs Vol. 3* (2000). (Wonder Workshop, Inc., 2000)

PREPARATION:

♡ Select and clear an area that is large enough for full-body movements.

♡ Set the player in a safe and convenient place.

♡ Cue the compact disc to the song "The Numbers Jump."

NURTURING STRATEGIES:

1. Gather the toddlers and introduce the activity; model, if necessary. Begin by saying:
   "We are going to jump to music. Stand up. Put your arms out at your side. For this activity, we need plenty of space. If you touch someone, move your body. Good. Now everyone has enough space. Listen to the words, they will tell you how many times to jump."

2. Practice jumping up and down. Say a number and count while jumping.

3. Provide positive reinforcement throughout the activity. Comments to make include:
   "What a great song!"
   "This is fun!"
   "You are doing a great job of keeping your body safe."

4. Repeat the song as long as the toddlers seem interested.

☀ Highlighting Development

Older toddlers are quite skillful, especially when compared to their motor skills during the first two years of life. Gross motor skills often dominate their activities. Toddlers revel in repeating actions over and over again. Sometimes it seems as if they are practicing to master a skill. At the beginning, they have simple and separate leg-arm actions. Gradually, these actions develop into an integrated system of movement.

VARIATION:

♡ If the weather and facilities permit, perform this experience outdoors, preferably on a grassy area.

ADDITIONAL INFORMATION:

♡ Hopping is a fundamental motor skill that serves as a foundation for later skills. By age six or seven, children can integrate two or more separate skills into an action. For example, they can run, leap, and throw a ball at a hoop.

25 to 30 months

Drawing with Pencils

PHYSICAL

Child's Developmental Goals

✓ To refine grasping of tools with fingers and thumb

✓ To develop visual discrimination skills

MATERIALS:

❑ 8½ × 11–inch pieces of construction paper cut into 4¼ × 5½–inch rectangles

❑ Small and large diameter pencils

❑ Felt-tip, nontoxic, washable black pens

❑ Containers for holding marking tools

PREPARATION:

♡ Make sure all writing tools are in working condition.

♡ Arrange the tools in a container, and then place all materials so that they are easily accessible to the toddlers.

NURTURING STRATEGIES:

1. When a toddler selects the activity, observe the child's behavior.

2. Position yourself near the child, allowing the toddler to work independently.

3. If the child initiates interaction, respond promptly. Likewise, respond to sounds of distress with verbal support. Use your voice as a tool to communicate warmth and support. Comments to make include: *"Reizo, push hard. There! The caps are tough to put back on sometimes."*
"Your pencil lead broke. Let's go sharpen it."

4. Describe what you see in the child's artwork. Say, for example:
"You made a long curved line, Reizo. It stretches from one side to the other."

5. Encourage the child to talk about the artwork. Some questions to ask include:
"Would you like to tell me about your picture?"
"What were you thinking about while working on your picture?"
Write the child's response on back of the artwork or on another piece of paper.

6. To develop responsibility, encourage the toddler to return all pens and pencils to the container before selecting a new experience.

☀ Highlighting Development

Young children are able to grasp a crayon with their entire fist by 13 to 18 months. By 30 months, they are able to hold a large-diameter pencil in their hand. They are also using instruments to make straight and curved lines and circles. These marks may be either random or controlled scribbles (Charlesworth, 2000) at this time.

VARIATIONS:

♡ Slowly increase the size of paper while providing the same tools.

♡ Use other writing tools such as watercolor markers and/or chalk pieces.

ADDITIONAL INFORMATION:

♡ Children learn through repetition. They must have, and enjoy, opportunities for repeating experiences. Therefore, leave out the small paper for at least one week.

♡ Notice how the toddler's use of blank space changes after repeating this experience numerous times.

♡ Save examples of the child's work for his portfolio.

♡ Because two-year-olds do not hold the paper with one hand, it is likely to move. If the paper moves, it most likely will not bother them.

♡ Study the toddler's movements while marking. They are large, muscular, and random. At this stage, the child enjoys the feel of the marking tool in his hand. With milestones in physical and cognitive development, his work will gradually become more controlled (Herr, 2001).

Shape Run

Child's Developmental Goals

✓ To practice running skills
✓ To improve full-body coordination

MATERIALS:

❑ Colored construction paper
❑ Masking tape

PREPARATION:

♡ Draw one familiar shape (e.g., square, apple) on each piece of paper. Make these shapes large enough to be viewed from about 10 to 15 feet away.
♡ Tape the shapes at the children's eye level on different areas of the outside play area. For example, tape one shape to a tree and another on the fence.

NURTURING STRATEGIES:

1. If you notice a child wandering or otherwise appearing to need something to do, encourage her to run over and touch the square.
2. Provide positive verbal and nonverbal reinforcement when the first direction is followed. Say, for example, while smiling:
   "Isadora, you ran very fast to touch the square."
3. Suggest that the child run and touch another shape.
4. If the child easily accomplishes one direction at a time, increase the difficulty by giving two at once.
5. If possible, invite another child to join in the activity.
6. Continue the experience as long as the children seem interested.

7. Make a notation of the child's running and/or listening abilities on an anecdotal record (see Appendix L).

☀ Highlighting Development

Fogel (2001) uses the 4 *E*'s to describe toddlers, calling them energetic, expressive, experimental, and exploratory. Toddlers are in a constant state of motion. Their coordination and, therefore, their running ability is changing. They are now more adult-like, meaning that their arms swing in opposition to their legs. Furthermore, their knees are slightly bent and their feet actually lift off of the ground. As any adult who cares for toddlers knows, they are also increasing in speed.

VARIATIONS:

♡ Change the color of construction paper and shapes to promote the development of additional concepts.
♡ Perform this experience indoors on a rainy day.

ADDITIONAL INFORMATION:

♡ This experience also fosters listening and auditory memory skills.
♡ Remember that the rate of skill attainment varies from child to child. Each child has her own unique rate of development.

25 to 30 months

Chair Maze

Child's Developmental Goals

✔ To move around an obstacle

✔ To improve full-body coordination

MATERIALS:

❏ Child or adult size chairs

PREPARATION:

♡ Select and clear a carpeted area.

♡ Place chairs in a maze-like fashion in that area.

NURTURING STRATEGIES:

1. When a child selects the area, observe his behavior. Allow him to experiment and problem-solve the purpose of the chairs. If he seems confused, introduce the activity by saying:

    "The chairs are arranged in a maze. Walk around them and try not to bump anything."

2. Supervise the area carefully. It may be necessary to redirect the child's behavior. To illustrate, if he is attempting to jump off of the chair, take him to a safe place to jump.

3. Provide positive reinforcement when the toddler walks around the chairs without bumping. Say, for example:

    "Yahto, you walked very close to the chair but did not touch it."

4. Encourage the toddler to take a different route in the maze by rearranging the chairs.

☀ Highlighting Development

Avoiding obstacles in a pathway is a tricky maneuver that requires both cognitive processing and physical coordination. Toddlers must see the object, decide how to solve the "problem," and then actually perform a selected behavior. Because of the difficulty inherently involved in maneuvering around obstacles, it is best to minimize such challenges unless a soft floor or ground covering is available.

VARIATIONS:

♡ Encourage the toddlers to move in different ways around the chairs. You might suggest crawling or hopping.

♡ Do this experience outside. Use bales of hay if available and no one is allergic.

ADDITIONAL INFORMATION:

♡ Toddlers enjoy climbing on and off of adult-size chairs. As a result, they may decide to climb on the chairs instead of walking around them.

25 to 30 months

Taping the Day Away

Child's Developmental Goals

✓ To improve fine motor skills
✓ To enhance eye-hand coordination

MATERIALS:

❑ Scotch tape with dispenser for each child
❑ Pieces of construction paper
❑ "Beautiful junk" to tape to picture, such as cotton balls, bottle caps, yarn
❑ Containers

PREPARATION:

♡ Place a piece of paper and a tape dispenser at each workstation.
♡ Aesthetically arrange "beautiful junk" in containers and place in easy reach.

NURTURING STRATEGIES:

1. When a child selects the area, engage her in conversation about the materials.
2. Observe the child's use of the tape and the dispenser. How is she using the materials? Is any assistance needed? Use answers to these questions to guide your behavior.
3. Provide verbal and physical assistance as necessary. For example, say:
   "Bryn, it might help to have me hold down the tape dispenser."
4. Engage the toddler in conversation about the tape. Questions to ask include:
   "Why is one side of the tape sticky?"
   "Have you ever used tape before? What did you do with it?"
5. Provide encouragement to help the toddler persist when frustrated. Verbal support is often effective in such situations. Comment, for example:
   "That tape keeps sticking to your fingers. How annoying!"

6. When the toddler is finished, write her name on the artwork. Also, write any comments she might make about it, such as "for Mommy."

☀ Highlighting Development

Toddlers enjoy moving their bodies and working on gross motor skills. They also work on fine motor skills. Gradually they will use their hands with more precision as the coordination of the thumb and fingers improve. This lays a foundation for later skills such as cutting with scissors and writing. Young children need ample opportunities to strengthen and develop their fine motor movements.

VARIATIONS:

♡ Use self-adhesive stickers instead of tape to make a picture.
♡ Provide a wide variety of tape such as clear packing, duct, double-sided, and colored masking tape.

ADDITIONAL INFORMATION:

♡ The magical powers of tape seem to be lost on adults, but luckily not toddlers. Observe them and share their enjoyment!
♡ Maintain a container of beautiful junk for the children to use creatively. Include items such as different types of paper, toilet and paper towel rolls, small boxes, and pine cones (see Appendix D). It's amazing how toddlers will think of 100 ways to use a cereal box!

25 to 30 months

Jumping Hose

PHYSICAL

Child's Developmental Goals

✓ To jump over an object
✓ To practice full-body movements
✓ To practice using one's body in space

MATERIALS:

❑ Garden hose with the metal ends removed
❑ Camera
❑ Notepad and pencil

PREPARATION:

♡ Select and clear an area outdoors, if possible.
♡ Lay the garden hose on the ground in a curved design.
♡ Place the camera so that it is easily accessible.

NURTURING STRATEGIES:

1. Introduce the experience to the toddlers before going outside. For example, say:
    "I've noticed that many of you have been jumping off the bottom step of the staircase. I have put a hose in the yard for you to jump over. Let's go outside so you can go try it!"
2. Take pictures of the toddlers as they are jumping. Note picture number and reason for taking snapshot in notepad for later documentation purposes.
3. Comment on the children's performance and enthusiasm. Statements include:
    "You pushed off with both feet."
    "Jacob Wayne, you seem proud of your landing. You didn't use your hands that time."
4. If necessary, model jumping over the garden hose and describe your behavior while doing so.
5. After the pictures are developed, make a panel (Gandini and Goldhaber, 2001; Helm, Beneke, & Steinheimer, 1998) to document the children's learning and/or abilities displayed during the experience. Such documentation allows children to revisit the experience as well as to help their parents/guardians better understand their children's development.

☼ Highlighting Development

Jumping skills are practiced and then improve greatly during toddlerhood. In the early stages, toddlers propel their bodies off the ground using only their leg muscles. In time, they will begin to swing their arms, as well (Berk, 1999). In fact, toddlers seem to take every opportunity to jump on and down from things. Because toddlers lack good judgment based on experience, it is imperative that they are constantly supervised.

VARIATIONS:

♡ Perform this experience indoors by having the children jump over tape adhered to the floor.
♡ Encourage the children to try other movements, such as hopping or crawling, to get across the hose.

ADDITIONAL INFORMATION:

♡ By two years of age, the typical child can walk in a straight line and jump off of the floor. Within the next six to eight months, other gross motor skills will emerge. The child will be able to walk on his tiptoes; hop on one foot for two or more hops; walk up and down stairs with alternating feet; and jump from a bottom and second step (Turner & Hammer, 1994).
♡ The pictures taken should be displayed at eye level for the children. In a home setting, the pictures could be displayed, for example, low on a refrigerator door; in a child care program, they could be mounted on a bulletin board or wall. Such displays help promote language and communication skills, memory skills, and self-esteem.

25 to 30 months

Arranging Flowers

Child's Developmental Goals

✓ To improve eye-hand coordination
✓ To practice fine motor skills

MATERIALS:

❑ Floral foam or Styrofoam™ piece for each child
❑ Plastic flowers or natural items such as leaves, twigs, etc.

PREPARATION:

♡ Clean a child-size table.
♡ Arrange objects at the center of the table.
♡ Set a piece of floral foam on the table in front of each child.

NURTURING STRATEGIES:

1. When a toddler selects the area, discuss the materials. Say, for example,
   "Josy, these twigs are from our nature walk yesterday. Do you remember which items you found?"
2. Providing hints or clues may help the child remember better. Comments to make include:
   "You were walking with Jaffa by the water's edge."
   "Do you remember what we saw under the evergreen tree?"
3. While naturally continuing the conversation with the child, begin to stick objects into the foam. Describe your behavior by saying, for example:
   "Wow! The pinecone stays in the foam when I press hard. I'm making a sculpture."
4. If the child has not already joined in the work, invite her to do so.
5. Continue to work as long as she seems interested.

☀ Highlighting Development

Although it may seem like toddlers spend the majority of their time perfecting gross motor skills, they are also working to refine fine motor skills. Fine motor development is defined as the ability to coordinate small muscles. During this stage of development, toddlers progressively improve the coordination of their wrists, thumbs, and fingers. In addition, they are able to use their hands with more precision.

VARIATIONS:

♡ Encourage social interactions by using one larger piece of foam to create a group flower arrangement.
♡ Encourage the development of kindness by having the child give the flower arrangement to a family member or friend.

ADDITIONAL INFORMATION:

♡ Preserve work by taking photographs and posting them on a bulletin board. Encourage the children to revisit their work experience, thus improving visual and auditory memory as well as language skills.
♡ Capitalize on teachable moments. In a home setting, explain the value of the experience to older siblings or other adults. In a child care program, place the flower arrangements on a "Look at What We Did" table. To teach center visitors the value of the activity, create a sign that reads "Flower Arranging," and under the title, list the developmental goals for this activity.

 If working with a child who still explores objects orally, substitute play dough for floral foam.

25 to 30 months

Language and Communication Development

♡

TWENTY-FIVE to THIRTY MONTHS

Rhyming Books

Child's Developmental Goals

✓ To increase phonological awareness
✓ To hear rhyming words

MATERIALS:

❑ Cardboard book, *Hand, Hand, Finger, Thumb,* by Dr. Seuss

PREPARATION:

♡ Display the book on a child-size table or shelf to attract the toddler's attention.

NURTURING STRATEGIES:

1. When a toddler selects the book, observe his behavior. Notice book handling skills such as proper orientation of text (e.g., right side up, working front to back) and/or turning pages one at a time. Record observations in the form of an anecdotal record.
2. Ask the child for permission to join in reading the story. For example, ask:
   "May I sit down and read the story with you, Gian-Carlo?"
3. Respect the child's answer. For example, if the toddler says, "no," you may wish to reply, *"Maybe we can read together later."*
4. If, on the other hand, the child welcomes your involvement, make yourself comfortable and begin reading the book.
5. Use your voice as a tool to communicate delight in reading the story and its content.
6. Initiate a conversation about the rhyming words in the book. Comments to make include:
   "I noticed several words that sounded alike in the book. These rhyming words are fun to read. Which rhyming words did you like best?"
7. If the toddler is interested, read the book again.

Highlighting Development

The English language comprises 44 speech sounds, or phonemes. Young children must gain phonological knowledge, which includes the abilities to distinguish speech from other kinds of sounds, one phoneme from another, questions from statements, and so on (McGee & Richgils, 2000). Speaking and listening skills are acquired easily through many and varied experiences with adults. In contrast, phonological awareness is necessary for reading and writing. "This is a special kind of phonological knowledge that requires the ability to think and talk about . . . differences in speech sounds" (McGee & Richgils, 2000, p. 22). Children who have phonological awareness are able to decide if two words rhyme, for example.

VARIATIONS:

♡ Choose other rhyming books.
♡ Make up own rhymes or songs to describe the toddler's behavior.
♡ If possible, encourage another adult to read to the toddler while you record his behavior using a running record or a video camera.

ADDITIONAL INFORMATION:

♡ Toddlers enjoy a sound-rich environment. They like hearing songs, rhythms, and chants. Given enough experience with predictable rhymes, they may be able to supply a rhyming word when you pause to encourage such behavior. This will help them with acquiring spoken language.
♡ This experience also supports a print-rich environment, which is needed if toddlers are to develop early literacy skills.

25 to 30 months

Learning More about . . .

Child's Developmental Goals

✓ To gain information from a book

✓ To converse about a topic of interest

MATERIALS:

❑ Nonfiction book

PREPARATION:

♡ Select a nonfiction book with real photographs on a topic of interest to a child or small group of children.

NURTURING STRATEGIES:

1. When a toddler appears to need a new experience, gain the child's attention and introduce the book. To illustrate, say:
   "Eva, look what I have. I went to the library and checked out a new book on turtles. I know how much you enjoy watching the turtles at the pond. Let's sit and read this book together."

2. Get comfortable and snuggle close. This will allow the toddler to easily see the photographs and enjoy the physical contact.

3. Read the book to the toddler. Connect labels and descriptive words to the photographs by pointing at them while speaking.

4. Pause often to encourage the toddler to converse about the pictures.

5. Reinforce utterances, words, or phrases produced by the toddler; for example:
   "Wow, Eva, you really know a lot about turtles. They are a green color."

6. Provide new information or vocabulary in small amounts; connect to past experiences whenever possible. For example, state:
   "This is a red-eared slider turtle. It lives in a pond, just like the painted turtle we saw yesterday on our walk."

7. Continue to read the book as long as the toddler expresses interest.

Highlighting Development

Very young children enjoy being read to. They will come to value books for a variety of uses. "They discover that books can provide information, comfort, and joy in their lives" (Puckett & Black, 2001, p. 384). For example, toddlers enjoy reading about how other young children cope with being separated from important adults or learning about a favorite animal. At this age they are able to show empathy for characters. In fact, they may even pretend to cry or look sad if one of the characters in the book is upset or crying.

VARIATIONS:

♡ Provide nonfiction magazines on the topic.

♡ Create a picture file on the topic. If you laminate the pictures, toddlers will be able to "read" the photographs independently.

ADDITIONAL INFORMATION:

♡ Observe the toddlers closely to assess their interests as the basis for planning future experiences. To do this, ask yourself questions such as:

What are their topics of conversation?
What are their play themes?
What books do they select independently?

♡ It will be difficult to find a nonfiction book written for the toddler's language abilities. Selecting a book with photographs will provide the toddler with realistic representations of the topic of interest. You will need to read the text or picture captions so that you are accurately describing what everyone is viewing.

25 to 30 months

Dogs, Dogs, Dogs... and a Cat?

Child's Developmental Goals

✓ To practice expressive language skills by describing and labeling a photograph

✓ To practice using gestures as well as words to communicate

MATERIALS:

☐ Instant camera and film
☐ Poster board
☐ Pen
☐ Transparent packing tape
☐ Stapler
☐ Basket

PREPARATION:

♡ Take photographs of at least six different dogs and two different cats. If possible, select animals that are familiar to the child. Prepare the poster board by laying it horizontally in front of you. Cut a third of the bottom of the poster board off. Then, make a pocket by placing that piece on the bottom of the existing board and securing with the tape.

♡ Now divide the large pocket that is taped to the bottom of the sheet into six smaller pockets to accommodate the individual photographs. Measure the photographs to estimate the size of the pockets. Use the stapler to divide the six pockets in the bottom strip. Then, cover each staple on the back of the poster board with transparent tape to increase safety and security.

♡ Print the title "Dogs, dogs, and more dogs" on the poster board. After this, mount one photograph of a dog on the top of the poster board and place the rest of the photographs in a basket.

♡ Make the game accessible to the toddler by securing the poster board to the refrigerator, propping it against a wall, placing it on a bulletin board, or laying it flat on a child-size table or coffee table. Place the basket of photographs beside the poster board.

NURTURING STRATEGIES:

1. When the child selects the activity, observe his behavior. Try to determine how she is using the materials.

2. If this is primarily a fine motor activity, encourage this line of play to continue. Comment on the toddler's behavior by saying, for example: *"Dylan, you are putting the pictures in the pockets!"*

3. Eventually, engage the child in sorting the pictures and labeling his work. Asking questions, while pointing to the pictures, can facilitate such behaviors. For example, ask: *"Are all pictures in the pockets pictures of dogs?"* *"How did you decide which pictures to put in the pockets?"*

4. Expand on the toddler's words, if necessary, or verbally label his gestures.

5. Continue to sort the pictures as long as the toddler is interested.

☀ Highlighting Development

Toddlers are action categorizers during their play (Berk, 1999). By 18 months, toddlers spontaneously and correctly categorize objects into two classes such as dogs and cats or circles and squares. As discussed earlier, this is roughly the same time that toddlers show a language explosion, or a sharp increase in vocabulary, enabling them to label objects. Language development seems to facilitate as well as build on toddlers' ability to categorize a group of items (Berk, 1999).

VARIATIONS:

♡ Take two photographs of the same animal from different angles and see if the toddler can match the two perspectives.

♡ Increase the number of animals in the matching game to increase the challenge.

♡ To simplify the task, take six different pictures of the same dog for the toddler to sort.

♡ If animals are unavailable, cut pictures of them from magazines.

ADDITIONAL INFORMATION:

♡ Adults can help to facilitate language and categorizing skills by verbally describing and labeling objects. Another useful technique is to pause when describing an object, allowing the toddler to fill in the missing condition/label.

25 to 30 months

Lifting Flaps

Child's Developmental Goals

✓ To develop receptive language skills through reading

✓ To practice expressive language skills

✓ To build vocabulary

MATERIALS:

❑ Book, *The Cat in the Hat's Great Big Flap Book,* by Dr. Seuss

PREPARATION:

♡ Attractively display the book at the toddler's eye level.

NURTURING STRATEGIES:

1. When a toddler selects the book, observe the behaviors displayed.
2. Allow the toddler plenty of time to explore/read the book independently.
3. If the child initiates contact or asks you to do the reading, enthusiastically accept.
4. Make reading the story as interactive as possible by asking open-ended questions. Use this technique to draw on the toddler's past knowledge as well. Moreover, make sure the toddler, not you, lifts the book flaps.
5. Provide support and encouragement for language expressed by the toddler.

☀ Highlighting Development

Support for young children's understanding of reading and writing is important during the toddler years. During these early years, children learn many literacy-related concepts while being read to one-to-one or in a small group. Some of these concepts are:

♡ Books are pleasurable.
♡ Books are handled in particular ways.
♡ Pictures in books are symbols.
♡ Books and pictures communicate meaning (McGee & Richgils, 2000, pp. 34–35).

VARIATIONS:

♡ Provide other books with flaps.
♡ Make your own flap books about the toddler's day or favorite subject.

ADDITIONAL INFORMATION:

♡ Books with flaps are very popular with toddlers. Flap books appeal to their understanding of object permanence and their emerging sense of autonomy.
♡ This flap book is enjoyed best when the toddler has had experience with the Dr. Seuss stories referred to in the text. You may wish to introduce those stories first and/or make them available with the flap book.
♡ Reinforcing the flap with clear, strong tape (such as that used for packing) before giving the book to the toddlers will minimize ripping.

25 to 30 months

Secret Pocket

Child's Developmental Goals

✓ To increase receptive language skills

✓ To increase expressive language skills

MATERIALS:

❑ Several objects, small enough to fit inside your pocket

PREPARATION:

♡ Put one or two of the objects into your pocket. Place other items in a convenient location that the toddlers cannot reach.

NURTURING STRATEGIES:

1. If a toddler appears to be searching for a new experience, tell the child you have a game to play. Introduce the game by saying:
   "I have something in my pocket. What do you think it is? Let's see if you can guess what it is."

2. Provide a clue to help the toddler guess. Say, for example:
   "I'm going to give you a clue. Megan, the object in my pocket rolls. What could it be?"

3. Wait to encourage the toddler to guess. If the toddler does not guess after waiting 10 seconds, elaborate on the first clue or supply another clue. Whenever possible, connect your clue to experiences in the child's life. To illustrate, say:
   "I saw you rolling this in the grass when we were outdoors."

4. If the toddler guesses, provide feedback about the accuracy of the guess. Avoid labeling the answer as wrong; instead focus on the part that is correct. Comments include:
   "A car does roll. I have something else in my pocket that rolls."

5. If the toddler guesses the object, show her the item and enthusiastically say:
   "You did it! What a great guess! You used the hints to figure out what I hid."

6. Repeat the game as many times as the toddler desires.

☀ Highlighting Development

Between 18 months and 4 years, sentences produced by young children become longer and more complete or adult-like (Charlesworth, 2000). However, two-year-olds vary a great deal in their expressive capabilities. The developmental range varies from a holophrastic stage (one word represents an entire sentence or idea), to telegraphic speech (sentences only contain essential components), to adult-like speech (sentences contain subjects, verbs, prepositions, noun markers, etc.).

VARIATIONS:

♡ Sew a large pocket onto a child-size apron. Encourage the toddlers to hide objects and have you guess.

♡ Increase the challenge by selecting objects that are less familiar to the children, such as a large paper clip.

♡ Use large and small objects to reinforce these concepts.

♡ Because toddlers are typically able to match three to four colors, use objects of different colors.

🚫 **CAUTION** Never leave children unattended with the objects for this activity. If the object easily hides in your pocket, it could be a choking hazard for toddlers. Remove the toy from the area or from the toddlers' reach as soon as the game is finished.

25 to 30 months

Sequencing Pictures

Child's Developmental Goals

✓ To describe photographs

✓ To increase use of time words, such as *before* and *after*

MATERIALS:

❑ Camera and film
❑ Basket

PREPARATION:

♡ Obtain photographs of a daily routine (e.g., eating breakfast, getting dressed, or playing outdoors). Place them in the basket on a child-size table or coffee table.

NURTURING STRATEGIES:

1. When a toddler selects this activity, sit near the child, being as unobtrusive as possible. Note if he is speaking to himself. If he is, record the words as an anecdotal record.

2. After a while, involve the toddler in a natural conversation about his work. Do so by commenting:
   "It looks like you are lining up the pictures. How did you decide what order to put them in?"

3. Expanding on the toddler's words or gestures will help to motivate him, because young children talk more when they know others understand them. To illustrate, if the toddler says the word *eat,* while pointing to the photograph, you should expand his language by reframing the word and incorporating it into a complete sentence. For example, you could say:
   "Eat. You are eating breakfast cereal in this picture."

4. Ask questions to help the toddler think about the daily routine. Alter the level of directedness needed depending upon the toddler's behaviors/skills. For example, if the toddler is focusing exclusively on the content of the photographs, you may need to

encourage him to sequence them by asking:
"Deon, which picture shows you playing outdoors?"
[Pause.]
"That's right. I'm going to put that picture after the one of you eating breakfast. We always play outdoors after breakfast."
On the other hand, if the toddler is attempting to sequence the cards, say:
"You can do it. What do you do every day after lunch?"
[Pause.]
"That's right! You take a nap. Do you see a picture of your crib?"

5. When the toddler finishes with the photographs, encourage him to clean up by putting them back in the basket.

☀ Highlighting Development

Children often talk to themselves while working. Piaget and Vygotsky differ in their interpretations of this behavior. Piaget believed that the children are unaware that they can be heard, so the speech is egocentric and serves no real development function. Vygotsky, on the other hand, felt that children use private speech as a way to regulate or guide their own behavior. Thus, private speech is an important tool for thought (Charlesworth, 2000).

VARIATION:

♡ Use several photos that sequence one daily event, such as washing hands or going to the toilet.

ADDITIONAL INFORMATION:

♡ The toddlers will probably become very excited when they see themselves, friends, and/or significant others in the photographs.

♡ Increase or decrease the number of photographs for sequencing, depending on the toddlers' abilities.

25 to 30 months

Stroller Talk

Child's Developmental Goals

✓ To use expressive language to communicate thoughts

✓ To engage in a conversation

MATERIALS:

❑ Stroller

PREPARATION:

♡ Secure the toddler in the stroller using the safety restraints.

♡ If you will be traveling for more than 20 minutes, consider packing a small snack and beverage.

NURTURING STRATEGIES:

1. Begin pushing the stroller. Take clues for your behavior from the toddler. If she is excited and talking, join in the conversation. If, on the other hand, she is quiet and attentive to her surroundings, do the same.

2. After a while of enjoying the quiet, initiate a conversation with the toddler. A great question to begin with is:
   "Cynthia, you are really quiet. What are you thinking about?"

3. Elaborate on the toddler's response, if necessary. For example, if the child says "fish," reply:
   "Yes, Mr. Gross does have a fish sculpture in his flower garden."

4. Connect the conversation to the toddler's past experiences whenever possible. Allow the toddler to change the topic if something else of interest comes into view.

☀ Highlighting Development

A period of rapid language development occurs during early childhood. Children progress from uttering sounds to producing sentences containing compete thoughts. Researchers have found that young children can add new words to their vocabulary through a process called fast mapping (Berk, 1999). During fast mapping, toddlers connect a new word to an underlying concept after only a brief encounter. When a term is fast mapped, children have to work to refine their understanding of its exact meaning. Consequently, fast mapping does not capture all of the word's meanings. Rather, understanding the meanings of words happens over many years.

VARIATIONS:

♡ Increase the number of children on your walk.

♡ Take the children to a grocery store, bakery, or library for new things to look at and talk about.

ADDITIONAL INFORMATION:

♡ Overcorrecting young children's pronunciation or grammatical errors often discourages toddlers from trying out new words or creating new sentences; therefore, adults must exercise restraint (Berk, 1999).

 Check your planned route in advance for safety hazards, such as no sidewalk, and modify it as necessary.

 Make sure stroller is in good repair to protect the toddler's safety.

25 to 30 months

We're Off to See . . .

Child's Developmental Goals

✓ To build vocabulary

✓ To have a new experience

MATERIALS:

☐ The materials you select will depend on the outing you plan. For example, if your experience is outside during the summer, pack sunscreen and sunglasses.

PREPARATION:

♡ Make necessary arrangements for your outing. If the outing is part of an early childhood program, follow the stated protocol to protect the health and safety of the toddlers.

NURTURING STRATEGIES:

1. Explain to the toddler where you are going.
2. Engage in conversation to see what the toddler thinks you will do and see there. Gently clarify any misconceptions. Use this conversation to assess the toddler's prior knowledge of the subject.
3. Use this information to guide your conversations while on the outing. For example, reinforce what the toddler already knows and expand on it by introducing new information.
4. Encourage the toddler to engage in conversation while on the outing. Ask open-ended questions to facilitate this process.
5. Review what was learned after the outing.

☀ Highlighting Development

Adults promote and support language development by providing an environment rich in social and informational experiences (Charlesworth, 2000). This gives children many opportunities for both receptive and expressive language experiences. To make the most of these experiences, adults need to engage children in authentic dialog, that is, a dialog in which "children and adults talk to each other about interesting, relevant matters" (Trawick-Smith, 1994, p. 10).

VARIATION:

♡ Take photographs during the outing to review the event or to spark conversation afterwards.

ADDITIONAL INFORMATION:

♡ Toddlers are notoriously curious. They are interested in the world about them, particularly people and objects. Toddlers have had limited exposure to the greater world. At this stage, their understanding of the world comes primarily from their family, pictures, storybooks, and television. First-hand experiences in the neighborhood or community allow toddlers to gather information that helps them develop, clarify, and expand knowledge and concepts. During this process, they will be building their language skills as well.

25 to 30 months

Listening to a Book on Tape

Child's Developmental Goals

✓ To continue developing expressive language skills

✓ To hear native language patterns

MATERIALS:

❏ Blank cassette tape

❏ Cassette tape recorder that is powered by batteries

❏ Green and red circles

❏ Book, *Quick as a Cricket,* by Audrey Wood

❏ Canvas bag

PREPARATION:

♡ Place all materials in the canvas bag. Encourage adults, preferably the parents or guardians of the toddlers, to record their reading of the story. If necessary, show the adult how to use the cassette recorder. Pass the canvas bag around to a number of adults. Be sure to keep track of the name and language spoken in the order recorded on the tape.

♡ Once the recording is complete, punch out the tabs on the cassette so that it cannot be taped over. Adhere the red circle on the "stop" button and the green circle on the "play" button. Gather the tape player, cassette, and book.

NURTURING STRATEGIES:

1. Gather a small group of toddlers and introduce the experience. While holding up the book, say, for example:
   "This tape contains voices of people reading this story."
   "Pay close attention because all of the readings sound different. See if you can tell me how they are different."
2. Press "play" and turn the pages of the book to accompany the story.
3. To engage them in a brief conversation ask the toddlers:
   "Did you recognize who was reading that story?"
4. Direct their attention back to the tape by saying:
   "Let's listen to the story again."

5. Repeat steps 2 and 3.
6. Have the toddlers compare the two readings of the book by asking open-ended questions.
7. Tell them that you will leave the tape, book, and tape player out for them to use. Explain to the toddlers how to work the tape player. For example, say:
   "Push the green dot to start the tape player and the red dot to stop it."

☀ Highlighting Development

Children need to be immersed in their native language. Some children hear their native language spoken while at child care. Others hear their native language only in their home environment. In 1997, it was estimated that 6 million school-age children in America speak a language other than English at home. Studies indicate that providing experiences in both languages spoken by a child results in greater development in both languages. Furthermore, it shows children that their heritage is valued and respected (see, for example, Berk, 1999).

VARIATIONS:

♡ Have toddlers select their favorite books, then record adults reading the books.

♡ Tape the children's voices, then play them back.

ADDITIONAL INFORMATION:

♡ Tape recordings of stories should be used to supplement daily reading not replace it.

♡ Two-year-olds are gathering information about race, ethnicity, and linguistic patterns of themselves and others. Like adults, young children are sometimes uncomfortable around people who are different than them. This feeling might cause them to laugh at the voices on the tape. See *Anti-Biased Curriculum, Tools for Empowering Young Children* (Derman-Sparks & the A.B.C. Task Force, 1988) for suggestions on how to deal with this behavior.

Reading "Hickory, Dickory, Dock"

Child's Developmental Goals

✓ To develop expressive language skills

✓ To view written words

✓ To develop an appreciation for the printed word

✓ To develop visual memory skills

MATERIALS:

❑ Poster board

❑ Markers

❑ 18-inch to 20-inch strip of Velcro™, cut into 1-inch pieces

❑ Glue

PREPARATION:

♡ Write words to the nursery rhyme (see Appendix F) on poster board, leaving blanks for the time struck and the actions performed by the mouse.

♡ Adhere Velcro strips to the board in the blanks.

♡ Cut five small pieces of poster board for the numbers and five for the actions.

♡ Write each number and action on a separate piece of poster board.

♡ Adhere Velcro strips to the back of each.

NURTURING STRATEGIES:

1. Introduce the activity to the toddler. To illustrate, say: *"This board has the rhyme 'Hickory, Dickory, Dock' written on it, but some words are missing. Let's fill them in."*

2. Hand the number cards to the toddler. Encourage the toddler to stick a number to the board.

3. Recite the nursery rhyme verse that corresponds to the number provided by the toddler. Put up action card before you say the words.

4. Encourage the toddler to remove the number and action cards and select another number card.

5. Do not be concerned about progressing in order from 1 to 5 when reciting the nursery rhyme. Follow the child's lead as long as she is interested in participating.

☀ Highlighting Development

Just as young children need to be spoken to in order to learn to talk, they need to see and hear written language to develop ideas about how to read and write (Puckett & Black, 2001). Frequent and varied experiences with printed media foster literacy development.

VARIATION:

♡ Chant rhymes slowly as a way to help the children relax before naptime

ADDITIONAL INFORMATION:

♡ Listen to children. Toddlers' vocabulary skills are rapidly increasing. As a result, they need myriad opportunities to solidify their concepts (Seefeldt & Barbour, 1994). Toddlers need daily experience with literacy activities such as listening, speaking, reading, and writing.

25 to 30 months

Cognitive Development

♡

TWENTY-FIVE to THIRTY MONTHS

Math Blocks

Child's Developmental Goals

✓ To use blocks for measuring

✓ To count blocks

MATERIALS:

❑ Set of unit (wooden) blocks

❑ Shelf to store blocks

PREPARATION:

♡ Select an area that can be constantly supervised and that is large enough for block play.

♡ Clear this area and place shelf with unit blocks there.

NURTURING STRATEGIES:

1. When a toddler selects the block area, observe the child's behavior. Note how the toddler is using the blocks.

2. Engage the toddler in conversation about the structure, using open-ended questions.

3. During the conversation with the toddler, use mathematical terms such as *estimating* or *comparing*. For example, ask:

   "Porter, I noticed that you used two small blocks here and one larger block here. How did you know to use two small blocks?"

   "Oh, so you compared the lengths of the blocks. You had to use two to equal one."

4. When the child finishes working, assist him in deciding if the structure should be preserved. If yes, decide on the appropriate way to preserve it. For example, the toddler could sketch his work, take a photograph of it, or make a sign asking for it to be saved if space permits.

5. If the child does not wish to save his work, assist him with returning the blocks to the shelves. Focus the child's attention to counting the blocks. To illustrate, say:

   "You pick up the small blocks and hand them to me. I'll put them on the shelf. Hey, I have an idea. I'll count the blocks that you hand to me. I wonder how many you used in building your structure?"

   Count the blocks as the child hands them to you.

6. Thank the child for cleaning up the area. Comments include:

   "It is very responsible of you to clean up the toys you played with."

   "Thanks, now someone else can build with the blocks."

☼ Highlighting Development

Around two years of age, children generally understand that objects, people, and events possess certain characteristics and can hold complex images—or schemata—in their mind. These abilities set the stage for learning more advanced concepts about their world. In other words, the children are ready to transition from the sensorimotor stage of cognitive development to the preoperational stage (Puckett & Black, 2001).

VARIATION:

♡ Add items such as vehicles, road signs, or animals to encourage creative play.

ADDITIONAL INFORMATION:

♡ Toddlers need plenty of space for block play, because they tend to build large, horizontal structures. Sitting on the floor in the block area may result in the toddlers, especially females, spending a greater amount of time in the area.

♡ Blocks are important learning tools for young children. When playing with blocks toddlers are in constant motion: reaching, stretching, lifting, carrying, stacking, and changing body positions. As they interact with blocks they strengthen their muscles and improve their eye-hand coordination skills. They also develop balance, weight, and measurement concepts.

25 to 30 months

Grocery Shopping

Child's Developmental Goals

✓ To substitute one object for another

✓ To represent ideas through play

MATERIALS:

☐ Advertisements/coupons

☐ Shopping bags

☐ 2 shopping carts

☐ 2 cash registers

☐ Shelves and baskets for storing food

☐ Purses/wallets

☐ Dress-up clothes

☐ Many empty food containers (e.g., cardboard boxes, plastic containers, or frozen food bags stuffed with paper and taped shut)

☐ Plastic fruits and vegetables, if available.

PREPARATION:

♡ Create an entrance to the store with a sign, grocery carts, and weekly advertisements/coupons.

♡ Set up store area so that food is grouped like in a natural grocery store. Label several areas.

♡ Place the cash registers on a table or shelf to create checkout lanes.

♡ Create a home area where the toddlers can dress up and write grocery lists before going to the store.

NURTURING STRATEGIES:

1. When a toddler selects the experience, observe her from afar; allow time to explore the materials.

2. If the child is engaging in functional play (e.g., pushing an empty grocery cart), prompt make-believe play by asking a question, such as: *"Nerida, you have a shopping cart. What are you going to buy at the store?"*

3. If a toddler is engaging in make-believe play, provide support for the play. Be cautious not to disrupt the flow of play or to take over the play.

4. Encourage the toddler to engage in conversation while playing with the material by asking open-ended questions. This will allow you to better understand what the child is thinking.

5. Make cleaning up the area part of the play. For example, say: *"The grocer needs help restocking the shelves. Do you want to replenish the fruits or vegetables?"*

☀ Highlighting Development

Preoperational children continue to develop in their ability to use mental symbols. They use gestures and language, typically expressed through play, to represent their thoughts. They also use one object to represent another. For example, they can use a banana as a telephone. Thus, they need to be provided a variety of materials that can be used in multiple ways.

VARIATION:

♡ Take a field trip to a grocery. Then have children help set up the dramatic play area.

ADDITIONAL INFORMATION:

♡ Dramatic play themes/props should reflect the lives of the young children. They cannot yet act out or pretend about something if they lack personal experience.

♡ Communicating with families about frequent experiences such as a train ride to visit grandparents may help young children to select themes/props.

♡ Asking close–ended questions can be disruptive to make-believe play. Close–ended questions, or single-answer questions, are those that require few decision-making skills; most often they require a yes or no answer. For example, asking a child to verbally label an object or its color, or count a group of objects creates interference. Instead, ask an open-ended question such as: "What items are you going to buy at the store?"

CAUTION Make sure all of the food containers are clean by washing them in hot, soapy water.

25 to 30 months

Preparing Frozen Bananas

COGNITIVE

Child's Developmental Goals

✓ To experience transformations
✓ To follow directions

MATERIALS:

- ❑ Half banana for each child
- ❑ Popsicle™ sticks for each banana
- ❑ Corn syrup
- ❑ Knife
- ❑ Wheat germ
- ❑ Wax paper
- ❑ 3 metal pie pans
- ❑ Cookie sheet
- ❑ Finely chopped peanuts
- ❑ Permanent markers
- ❑ Recipe board including pictures and words

PREPARATION:

♡ Print the following recipe on a large piece of tag board. If desired, draw a picture of each of the five steps on the recipe chart. Hang the chart where the children can easily view it.

RECIPE

1. Remove the peel from the banana.
2. Insert stick into banana.
3. Dip the banana in corn syrup.
4. Roll the banana in wheat germ and/or nuts.
5. Place on cookie sheet.
6. Freeze.

♡ To prevent browning, cut each banana in half before peeling.
♡ Pour a small amount of corn syrup, wheat germ, and nuts in the bottom of the three different pie pans.
♡ Cover cookie sheet with wax paper.
♡ Clean and sanitize child-size table, then place all material there.
♡ Write each child's name on their Popsicle stick for easy identification later.

NURTURING STRATEGIES:

1. Assist each toddler, as necessary, with washing hands.
2. Introduce the experience by saying, for example: *"We love to eat bananas. I have found a new way to make and enjoy them. Have you ever eaten a frozen banana?"* Pause for response. Then say: *"I need your help to make frozen bananas. Here is the recipe for making them. Let's read it together."*
3. Assist the children in completing the tasks. To promote independence, provide more verbal assistance than hands-on assistance whenever possible. Further-

more, ask questions to prompt recall. For example, say: *"Dhani, what should you do with this Popsicle stick?" "What should you do next?"*
4. Refer to the recipe board for guidance.
5. Ask open-ended questions throughout the activity to spark conversation with the toddler. Questions include: *"Where did the banana go, Dhani? I can only see nuts."*
6. Once the banana is coated and placed on the tray, explain that the last step involves putting the banana in the freezer. Discuss how it will take a long time for the banana to freeze and that he won't be able to eat it until the afternoon snack. Then have the toddler wash his hands.
7. When frozen, serve the banana for snack. Explain that you will read the names written on the sticks to know who made the banana.

☼ Highlighting Development

Good nutrition and healthy eating habits that are developed during the toddler years build the foundation for future good health. A balanced diet ensures that nutritional needs for growth are met and aids in a child's ability to learn (Thompson, 1999). However, a healthy diet for toddlers is not the same as that for adults. Toddlers need to eat three meals with snacks in between because they have smaller stomachs. Furthermore, the amount of food required for each serving is about one-third to one-half of an adult serving.

VARIATIONS:

♡ Roll bananas in peanut butter that has been mixed with small amount of milk.
♡ Find other fruits to eat frozen on hot days, such as blueberries or grapes cut in half.

ADDITIONAL INFORMATION:

♡ Children who learn to make healthy food choices develop life-long habits. The Food Guide Pyramid for young children was developed by the U.S. Department of Agriculture (USDA) as a model for planning meals and snacks for children two to six years old. According to this guide, toddlers need six servings from the grain food group, three servings of vegetables, two servings of fruit, two servings of meat, and two servings of milk daily.

 Check children's records to ensure that there are no food allergies before introducing this experience.

25 to 30 months

COGNITIVE

Locating Something Bigger . . . Something Smaller

Child's Developmental Goals

✓ To increase understanding of size differences

✓ To create or modify schema for comparing objects

MATERIALS:

❑ Large object

❑ Small object (large enough so that it is not a choking hazard)

PREPARATION:

♡ Place chosen objects in a convenient and accessible location.

NURTURING STRATEGIES:

1. If you notice a toddler who is not engaged with materials, retrieve the two objects.
2. Gain the toddler's attention by saying her name and inviting her to play a game.
3. Explain the purpose of the game. While holding up the larger object, say:
   "Mackenzie, look at this teddy bear. Isn't it big? Can you find something in the room that is smaller than this bear? Go look."
4. Provide encouragement and support for this challenging task.
5. If necessary, model how to play the game. Describe your actions and thought processes. For example, say:
   "This block is kind of big. I'm going to compare it to the bear to see which is bigger. Yes! The bear is bigger."
6. If the toddler is still interested in the game after finding several items, show her the small item and encourage her to find bigger items.

☀ Highlighting Development

Toddlers spend a great deal of time creating schemas about how the world works. These schema allow them to compare and contrast items along one dimension. Observe toddlers as they seek to understand the concept of size. They are also adding other size concepts such as *big, small, large,* and *tiny* to their vocabulary.

VARIATIONS:

♡ While toileting or changing the toddler's diaper, play this as a word game.

♡ Increase the challenge by having the toddler find items that are smaller than the small object you chose.

ADDITIONAL INFORMATION:

♡ Toddlers at this stage of development can follow two-step directions. They can also provide answers to where questions or place questions that deal with familiar information related to their immediate environment.

♡ Early mathematical experiences should focus on exploration and discovery. Toddlers develop these concepts by using hands-on, minds-on materials and discovering their relationships such as in this activity. In addition to size, other basic mathematical concepts that can be introduced to toddlers include color, shape, classification, space, volume, time, and temperature.

25 to 30 months

Rocking Baby

Child's Developmental Goals

✓ To imitate an action viewed or experienced at an earlier time

✓ To represent understanding of a bedtime routine

MATERIALS:

☐ 2 large boot boxes
☐ 2 baby dolls
☐ 4 baby blankets
☐ 2 small pillows, if available

PREPARATION:

♡ Make a bed in the box for the baby.
♡ Fold one blanket as bedding, then place pillow on top.
♡ Place the baby doll in the bed and cover with other blanket. Repeat for second doll.
♡ Place both the dolls and beds in the dramatic play area.

NURTURING STRATEGIES:

1. When you see a toddler playing with the doll, observe his behavior. What do you notice?
2. Use your knowledge of the child, his family, and his behavior to guide your actions. Facilitate his play, if necessary, through the use of the second doll.
3. Model, for example, rocking and soothing the baby by gently patting the doll and singing a lullaby. Label your behaviors verbally. For example, say: *"What a sleepy baby. I'll rock you to sleep and sing your favorite song."*

4. Without interrupting the child's play, engage the child in conversation about his behavior. Comments include:
"What a beautiful song. It helped your baby fall right to sleep. Is this a song your grandfather sings to you at night?"
"You rock the baby gently. He'll be asleep in no time."

☀ Highlighting Development

Cognitive development is tied to social interactions. Young children learn from observing and imitating others. Research has found that learning can be enhanced when an adult labels an action while performing it (Hay, Murray, Cecire, & Nash, 1985). While hanging up a coat, an adult might say, "I'm putting the coat on the hook." This strategy of combining modeling with verbal cues, as opposed to using one strategy or another, appears to be more effective in supporting the recall and imitation of behaviors.

VARIATION:

♡ Encourage two children to play together.

ADDITIONAL INFORMATION:

♡ Young children are greatly influenced by other people. Through modeling, they learn new behaviors as well as a context for those behaviors (Fabkes & Martin, 2001).

What's for Snack?

Child's Developmental Goals

✓ To read the snack poster
✓ To practice following directions

MATERIALS:

❑ Poster board
❑ Marker
❑ Photographs or pictures of snack items
❑ All snack items on a tray

PREPARATION:

♡ Create a poster that depicts what will be served for snack. Use graphics from magazines, pictures, drawings, and photographs to assist the children with "reading."
♡ If the children are able to have more than one of a particular item, represent the amount they are able to have with the appropriate number of pictures.
♡ Display the poster in a prominent location near the eating area.

NURTURING STRATEGIES:

1. Just before snack time, sanitize a child-size table. Assist the toddlers as necessary with washing their hands.
2. Place tray of snack items on the table. Encourage the toddlers to help, as appropriate, with passing out snack materials such as cups and napkins.
3. Direct the toddlers' attention to the poster.
4. Encourage them to look at the pictures to assist them with reading and understanding the poster. Provide clues, if necessary.

5. Provide positive reinforcement for reading the snack poster. Comments include:
   "You read the poster to know what was for snack."
   "We counted the pictures to know how many crackers to take from the basket."
6. Provide encouragement and support for this challenging task.

☀ Highlighting Development

"The early childhood years—from birth through age eight—are the most important period for literacy development" (Neuman, Copple, & Bredekamp, 2000, p. 3). Adults can use specific strategies or approaches to support this type of learning. To enhance children's awareness that print conveys meaning, for example, comment on signs and notes in the environment by saying, "Look at the snack menu to see how may crackers you can have."

VARIATIONS:

♡ Make a menu for lunch.
♡ In dramatic play, encourage the children to make their own menus using photographs or pictures of favorite foods.

ADDITIONAL INFORMATION:

♡ With practice, the toddlers will eventually be able to independently serve themselves snack, thus promoting autonomy. To assist them in this process, provide unbreakable, lightweight serving dishes, pitchers, and glasses.

25 to 30 months

Ice Tubs

COGNITIVE

Child's Developmental Goals

✓ To show ownership of an object

✓ To discuss how the medium feels

MATERIALS:

❑ Large plastic container or quilt box for every two children

❑ Ice cubes or crushed ice

❑ ½-cup measuring cup for each child

❑ Small plastic bowl for each child

PREPARATION:

♡ Divide the ice between the plastic containers, if more than one is used. Place two measuring cups and two bowls in each container.

NURTURING STRATEGIES:

1. If two toddlers select the activity, encourage them to play in the same tub. Say, for example:
   "There are enough room and toys for both of you."

2. Assist the toddlers in equally dividing the toys in the tub to reduce potential conflict. Define the toys as being for one child or the other.

3. Encourage the toddlers to touch the ice. Talk about how the ice feels using words such as *cold, slippery,* or *hard.*

4. Describe the child's actions with the tools by saying:
   "You're using the measuring cup to fill up the bowl with ice."
   "You're scooping the ice with your hands."

5. Provide positive reinforcement for sharing the tools. Comments to make include:
   "Each of you has a measuring cup."
   "You're both playing in the ice."

☀ Highlighting Development

Children at this age lack an understanding of others' feelings, including those of their playmates, siblings, and pets. Often they become very physical and engage in hitting, grabbing, or pushing. You need to be to be aware of these behaviors and respond immediately to any physical aggressiveness. For example, you might say, "Your friend Johnny does not like to be hit. Touch him gently on the arm to get his attention."

VARIATION:

♡ Use tongs or large spoons to pick up the ice cubes.

ADDITIONAL INFORMATION:

♡ Toddlers have to be able to show and experience ownership of materials before they will be able to share them.

♡ Toddlers will often want to eat the ice. For sanitation purposes, provide additional crushed ice in cups that can be eaten.

 Observe carefully to reduce a potential choking hazard.

25 to 30 months

Measuring

Child's Developmental Goals

✓ To begin to understand part and whole relationships

✓ To count when filling a cup

MATERIALS:

❑ At least two of each of the following measuring cups: ¼-, ½-, and 1-cup

❑ Water table or quilt boxes

❑ Towels

❑ Smock for each child

PREPARATION:

♡ Sanitize water table, move to desired location and fill with 2 to 3 inches of water.

♡ Place towels on the floor to prevent slipping.

♡ Place measuring cups in the water.

NURTURING STRATEGIES:

1. Assist the toddler, if necessary, with washing hands.
2. As the toddler is putting on his smock, introduce the experience by saying, for example:
   "I noticed you measuring sand yesterday. Today, you can measure water with the different size cups."
3. Observe the child working. Note the toddler's use of materials.
4. Describe the toddler's behavior with the measuring cups. Statements include:
   "Diego, you are pouring the water from one cup to another. You are transferring the water."
   "It took four little cups of water to fill up the largest cup."
5. Encourage the toddler to count the number of cups of water that fit inside the largest measuring cup.
6. To spark thinking about quantity and whole-part relationships, ask the toddler to explain a problem he may be facing with the cups. Ask, for example:
   "Why does the little cup overflow every time you pour in water from the big cup?"

Highlighting Development

Through play, toddlers build understanding of concepts such as size, shape, number, classification, comparisons, space, parts and wholes, weight, length, temperature, and time (Charlesworth & Lind, 1999). To promote the development of these concepts, adults must provide a variety of materials and extended periods of time for active learning through exploration. This time of exploration is vital since active learning is the path that promotes optimal brain development (Shore, 1997).

VARIATION:

♡ Use various sizes of measuring spoons with smaller amounts of water.

ADDITIONAL INFORMATION:

♡ The number of measuring cups provided depends on the number of children who can easily engage in the experience at one time. It is best to provide one set of measuring cups for each child who can interact at the same time.

♡ Children acquire concepts through constructive play experiences that activate their senses and engage their minds (Cromwell, 2000).

 Constant supervision is needed to protect children from water hazards. No child should ever be left unattended at a water table or near a water source.

25 to 30 months

Watering Plants

COGNITIVE

Child's Developmental Goals

✓ To experience cause and effect

MATERIALS:

❏ Plastic milk jug for each child (gallon or half-gallon size)
❏ Hammer
❏ Nail
❏ Water source (spout or hose)

PREPARATION:

♡ To make a watering can, poke holes in the bottom of each milk jug using the hammer and nail.
♡ Place near water source.

NURTURING STRATEGIES:

1. When the children notice the "watering cans," fill them with water and introduce the activity. For example, you might say:
   "It hasn't rained in several days. Will you water the plants for me? They need water to be healthy."
2. Describe the children's behavior with the watering cans. Statements include:
   "The ground is soaking up all of the water."
   "You made a puddle in the flower bed."
3. Redirect the children's behavior to maintain a safe, outdoor play area. For example, suggest that the toddlers water the grass instead of the sidewalk because someone might slip on the wet concrete.
4. Refill the watering cans as often as necessary to sustain the toddlers' interest in the experience.

☼ Highlighting Development

Toddlers' thinking capacities reflect a movement toward reasonable and sometimes rational behavior. Their increased verbal abilities allow them not only to express their ideas better but also to understand situations and ideas better. By the middle of the third year of life, toddlers' behavior can be guided by capitalizing on their developing thought and language capabilities (White, 1995).

VARIATIONS:

♡ Teach the toddlers how to fill their own watering cans.
♡ Fill watering cans with sand and sift it through the holes by shaking.
♡ Provide the children with large paintbrushes and bucket of water. They will enjoy "painting" outdoor buildings and sidewalks.

ADDITIONAL INFORMATION:

♡ Plan to introduce this experience on a warm day.
♡ Experienced teachers recommend providing water and sand experiences, either indoors or outdoors, on a daily basis. Water and sand are nonstructured materials that children find satisfying. By sifting sand or water through their fingers or pouring it back and forth between containers, they release tension (Isenberg, 1993).

25 to 30 months

Counting Cars

Child's Developmental Goals

✓ To develop skills for counting a group of objects

✓ To develop an understanding of the use of numbers

MATERIALS:

❑ Basket

❑ 10 plastic cars

❑ Child-size table or coffee table

PREPARATION:

♡ Clear an area on the child-size table or coffee table.

♡ Place the cars in the basket on the table.

NURTURING STRATEGIES:

1. When a child engages with the materials, observe the toddler's behavior. Determine if the toddler is engaged in functional play.

2. Provide support and encouragement for the functional play. For example, state:
   "Phoebe, you are pushing the cars. They are going fast."

3. If appropriate, model counting the cars. However, take care not to disrupt the flow of play. To illustrate, say: "Five cars: 1, 2, 3, 4, 5 (touch each car while saying the number) are lined up waiting to go to the circus."

4. Note if the child spontaneously imitates your counting of the cars. If the toddler does this, you may consider documenting the behavior with an anecdotal record.

5. Encourage the toddler to count the cars while returning them to the basket at the end of the experience.

☀ Highlighting Development

When provided with frequent and varied experiences, young children begin to acquire a nominal sense of numbers; an understanding that numeral labels represent amounts. Hence, they can verbally apply a number label to an object or group of objects. This is the very beginning of mathematical understanding. At this point, children will use verbal labels inconsistently or in no apparent order.

VARIATIONS:

♡ Find other objects to count.

♡ Counting other objects during cleanup time is a natural thing to do.

ADDITIONAL INFORMATION:

♡ Avoid pushing the toddler to count items. Model applying labels, but encourage free exploration of the materials.

♡ Reciting finger plays, nursery rhymes, and singing counting songs all assist in this development as well (See Appendices F and G).

♡ There are two types of counting used by young children: rote and rational. Rote counting is the process of reciting numbers in order from memory; rational counting involves attaching a numeral to each object in a series or group, which is the type of learning supported in this experience. Listen. Often beginning learners make mistakes by either counting an object twice or failing to count one or more objects. Adults should consider this as normal behavior and need not correct the child. With repeated experiences, children will learn rational counting skills.

25 to 30 months

Social Development

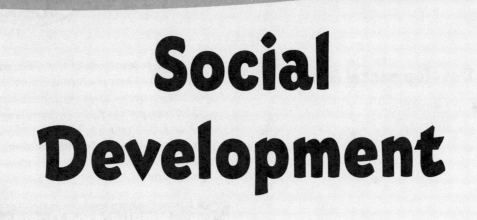

TWENTY-FIVE to THIRTY MONTHS

Bluebird

Child's Developmental Goals

✓ To participate in a small group activity

✓ To sing a song with others

MATERIALS:

None

PREPARATION:

♡ Write words to song on a note card for yourself or on a poster board for everyone to view if this song is unfamiliar.

♡ Clear a large floor space of any obstacles to prevent possible injury and allow for optimal movement.

NURTURING STRATEGIES:

1. Gather a small group of toddlers in the cleared space and introduce the activity. Explain that everyone who wants to fly like a bird in and out of a window will get a chance.

2. Have the children stand up, hold hands and take one or two steps backwards to make the circle bigger. Demonstrate and then assist one toddler with pretending to be a bird by "flying" and weaving between the other children.

3. Set a limit so that the toddler will know when his turn is over. State, for example:
   "Each person will get to fly while we sing two times. I will let you know when your turn is almost over."

4. Lead singing the song.

   Bluebird, bluebird
   In and out my window
   Bluebird, bluebird
   In and out my window
   Bluebird, bluebird
   Won't you fly with me?

5. After the first singing of the song, pause briefly to tell the child that his turn is almost over and then it will be someone else's turn. For example, say: *"Matthew, you can fly for one more song and then it will be Faith's turn."*

6. Encourage the toddlers to sing along with you.

7. Repeat the game for any children who want to participate.

☀ Highlighting Development

Group games are often too complicated for toddlers, because they lack the cognitive ability to understand rules or how to coordinate their actions with one another. However, they revel in playing games that allow them to practice and refine gross motor skills. Thus, the focus for children at this stage of development should remain on movement skills and sharing space rather than following a particular set of rules.

VARIATIONS:

♡ Sing other movement songs such as "London Bridge."

♡ Alter the color of the bird for a bit of variety.

ADDITIONAL INFORMATION:

♡ A child's capacity for developing pro-social behaviors, including turn-taking, increases with age. By three years of age, young children are less egocentric and territorial, thus more able to engage in simple games.

SOCIAL

Oops!

Child's Developmental Goals

✓ To begin to consider another's perspective

✓ To see the effect of their behavior on others

MATERIALS:

None

PREPARATION:

None

NURTURING STRATEGIES:

1. Carefully observe the toddlers and anticipate situations that might need your assistance. For example, one toddler is building with blocks in the middle of the carpet and another toddler is pushing a grocery cart.

2. When possible, be proactive rather than reactive in your guidance approach. In this situation, you may wish to redirect the toddler with the cart to avoid knocking over a block structure. It is much easier to push the cart elsewhere than to move the block structure. When redirecting the pushing behavior, focus on possible outcomes for both children. Comment, for example:

   "Jodelle, push your cart over here. You can go around the shoe store. Booker would be upset if you accidentally knocked over her block structure."

3. If an accident does occur, move to the children and stoop down to their level. Explain to Booker that it was an accident. Say, for example:

   "Jodelle did not mean to knock over your blocks. It was an accident. Let's tell her how you feel."

4. Gain the other toddler's attention and help the first child explain his feelings. Expand on Booker's comments whenever necessary.

5. In a warm and caring way, explain to Jodelle how she needs to use her toys carefully to keep from interrupting another child's work.

☀ Highlighting Development

A sense of morality grows out of social relationships (Damon, 1988). In the early years, adults externally control a child's morality by using positive guidance techniques that involve discussing the effects of the child's behavior on others. This technique has been shown to support moral development. On the other hand, punitive or guilt-inducing techniques tend to impede moral development (Berk, 1999).

VARIATION:

♡ Describe the child's reaction if she is unable to do so.

ADDITIONAL INFORMATION:

♡ If working in an early childhood setting, you may want to write newsletter articles for parents/guardians on the type of positive guidance strategies. Marion (1999) is an excellent resource for assisting you in this process.

♡ Utilizing positive guidance strategies contributes greatly to creating a caring community of learners (Bredekamp & Copple, 1997). Such an environment fosters consideration and contribution to each person's well-being in a group.

25 to 30 months

What Do You Do?

SOCIAL

Child's Developmental Goals

✓ To begin to understand that men and women can do similar jobs

✓ To continue developing their sense of gender identity

MATERIALS:

❑ Two photographs of familiar people, if possible, who have the same occupation but are different genders such as male and female firefighter

❑ Photo album or three-ring binder

❑ Colored paper

❑ Marker

PREPARATION:

♡ Mount each photograph on a piece of colored paper. Write a caption for each photograph being sure to highlight the name of the person in the picture and his/her occupation. Place the mounted pictures in the photo album or three-ring binder. Then, place the book in a convenient location for the toddlers.

NURTURING STRATEGIES:

1. Observe the toddler once the book is selected.
2. Engage the toddler in a conversation about the pictures by pointing to them and asking questions such as:
   "Who is in this picture?"
   "What job does Malcolm's mom do? Look at her uniform." Pause for a response.
3. Elaborate and/or recast the child's response, if necessary. For example, if the toddler says "policeman" say:
   "Yes, Malcolm's mom is a police officer. She keeps us safe."
4. Encourage the toddler to find the other gender police officer. When the second photograph is located, discuss similarities and differences between the photographs.

5. Continue as long as the toddler is interested.
6. Conclude the experience by commenting:
   "These pictures were fun to look at. We learned that men and women can have the same job."

☀ Highlighting Development

At this stage of development, toddlers are in search of a sense of self. By viewing themselves as separate and different from their primary caregiver, toddlers begin to develop gender identity. This process takes many years, and some argue that there is no end to this process. During toddlerhood, young children can identify themselves and others as boys or girls. To do this, they rely on visual clues. They can easily become confused by appearances such as males with longer hair. It is not until the end of the preschool period that children realize that gender is constant or nonchanging. Until that time, they believe, for example, that little boys can grow up to be mommies, if they want.

VARIATION:

♡ Use paper or wooden dolls that can "dress" in different unrelated uniforms.

ADDITIONAL INFORMATION:

♡ Adopt gender-neutral language when speaking with young children. Contrary to popular belief, they do not think male or female when they hear "fireman or policeman." In their concrete interpretation of the terms, they think "man." Words or phrases such as firefighter, police officer, mail carrier, flight attendant, and hair stylist eliminate such gender bias.

♡ By age two and a half, most children have learned basic stereotypes about the sexes. They think that girls cry a lot and have long hair. On the other hand, boys hit people more and are stronger than girls.

London Bridge

Child's Developmental Goals

✓ To participate in a game
✓ To sing a song with others

MATERIALS:

None

PREPARATION:

♡ Write words to sing on a note card for yourself or on a poster board for everyone to view if this is not a familiar song.
♡ Clear a large space of any obstacles.

NURTURING STRATEGIES:

1. Gather at least two toddlers who are good friends in the cleared space and introduce the activity. Explain that both of them will be able to be the bridge and both of them will be able to walk. Comment also about how they will be taking turns.
2. Sing the song through one time.

   London Bridge is falling down
   Falling down, falling down.
   London Bridge is falling down
   My fair lady.

   Take the key and lock her up
   Lock her up, lock her up.
   Take the key and lock her up,
   My fair lady.

3. Take the hands of one child and form the bridge. Encourage the other toddler to walk under the bridge while everyone sings.
4. When you get to the "lock her up" part, drop your arms around the walking toddler and gently rock back and forth.

5. Comment on the toddlers' enthusiasm and how fun the game is to play.
6. Switch roles and begin again. Encourage the toddlers to sing along.
7. Whenever possible, invite other interested toddlers to join the experience.

☀ Highlighting Development

Young children need time to form relationships with peers. Toddlers who are around age mates on a regular basis, such as at a play group, library story hour, or a child care program are more likely to build true peer relationships that are evidenced by reciprocal play and positive emotion (Ross, Conant, Cheyne, & Alevizos, 1992).

VARIATIONS:

♡ Sing other movement songs such as "Ring Around the Rosie" (see Appendix F).
♡ Have the toddlers be the bridge that you walk through.

ADDITIONAL INFORMATION:

♡ After infancy, there is a gradual shift in the importance of friendships. At this stage of development, toddlers' social relationships are broadening to include peers. However, the ability to form friendships is not innate. Toddlers must be taught to respect and act pro-socially by using positive behaviors. Gradually, they learn that acting in a positive manner elicits positive responses, and therefore, opportunities for friendships with others.

25 to 30 months

Save Some for . . .

SOCIAL

Child's Developmental Goals

✓ To develop concern for the welfare of others

✓ To act in a caring manner

MATERIALS:

❑ Snack items on a tray

PREPARATION:

♡ Clean a child-size table or coffee table.
♡ Place the snack tray on it.

NURTURING STRATEGIES:

1. Assist the toddlers as needed with washing hands.
2. Invite them to join you at the table and find a seat.
3. Enlist their help in distributing napkins, cups, etc.
4. Allow the children to serve themselves snack with guidance. For example, say:
   "Today we have cheese and crackers. You can have four crackers and two pieces of cheese to start with."
5. Engage the children in meaningful conversations. Topics might include discussing their day, either past events or ones to come shortly, or specific projects they worked on.
6. When the children want seconds of snack, involve them in problem solving. Say, for example:
   "Before we have seconds, we need to think about Evita. She is still asleep. What can we do to make sure she gets snack?"
7. Guide them to consider Evita's point of view. Label her possible emotional reactions to waking up hungry and not having any snack.
8. Encourage the toddlers to set aside a serving of snack.
9. Provide positive reinforcement for helping Evita.
10. Set new limits on serving size and repeat steps 4 and 5.

☀ Highlighting Development

According to Charlesworth (2000), toddlers are pre-moral: They are just beginning to learn about right and wrong. Figuring out which kinds of acts fall into each category is complex and takes much trial and error. Thus, it often appears that their values are specific to a situation. For example, just because they have learned to be nice to their sister does not mean they will be nice to a neighbor.

VARIATION:

♡ Encourage the toddlers to make get-well cards for a sick relative or friend.

ADDITIONAL INFORMATION:

♡ Toddlers learn the cognitive skills, values, and norms of their culture through active participation with others. This activity focuses on developing a moral consciousness that unfolds in stages. The initial sense of right and wrong at this stage is concrete with the child anticipating the personal consequences of her act. In other words, the child asks, "What will happen to me if I eat all of the cheesecake?" At a later stage, the child will learn to think of how another person will feel.

♡ Research has shown that toddlers respond emotionally and physically to moral transgressions but often pay little attention to conventional transgressions. Thus, even toddlers demonstrate concern when they or others are harmed or toys are taken without permission (Smetana, 1984, cited in Charlesworth, 2000).

SOCIAL

Singing on the Stage

Child's Developmental Goals

✓ To interact with other children
✓ To share a space with another child

MATERIALS:

❑ Large hollow blocks
❑ Transparent adhesive tape

PREPARATION:

♡ Clear a corner of the room.
♡ Build a platform out of the blocks and secure in place with the tape.

NURTURING STRATEGIES:

1. Observe the toddlers' behaviors after they select the stage. Note what they do spontaneously or without your guidance.
2. Prevent inappropriate behavior by suggesting they sing a song. Encourage the toddlers to select the song to be sung. To illustrate, say:
   "This is a stage. People sing from stages. What songs would you like to sing?"
3. Record the children's suggestions, if necessary, so that they do not forget a suggestion.
4. Singing along with the children will denote the value of this experience.
5. If necessary, redirect inappropriate behavior by providing alternative activities. Use comments such as:
   "It is not safe to jump from the stage. Too many friends are close-by. Someone might accidentally get hurt. You can jump over by the climber. That would be safer for everyone—including you!"
   Reinforce the last statement nonverbally with a smile and a gentle squeeze.

☀ Highlighting Development

Children's patterns of behavior have been related to the way in which they are treated by their parents. Baumrind (1967) classified parental control into three groups: authoritarian, authoritative, and permissive. Children of authoritative parents were more likely to be self-reliant, cheerful, cooperative with peers, and so on. Parents, like teachers, can learn positive guidance strategies, which parallel behaviors of the authoritative parenting style (see, for example, Marion, 1999).

VARIATION:

♡ Have the toddlers act out a favorite nursery rhyme or book on the stage.

ADDITIONAL INFORMATION:

♡ All areas of development are interrelated—physical, language and communication, cognitive, social, and emotional. Moreover, the primary focus of socialization in any culture is language. Therefore, it is important for children to develop competence in social communication, which is the ability to convey a message intended to others (Fabes & Martin, 2001). To promote this development, children need a supportive yet challenging environment with excellent role models.

 Construct the platform only one block high. Building higher may be a safety hazard, especially if a toddler would fall.

25 to 30 months

Eggs in a Basket

SOCIAL

Child's Developmental Goals

✓ To play a game with a friend
✓ To interact with another toddler

MATERIALS:

❑ Plastic eggs
❑ 2 or 3 baskets, depending on the number of toddlers

PREPARATION:

♡ Check the eggs to ensure that there are no cracks, which could pinch the children's fingers, scratch, or cut their skin.
♡ Hide the eggs in different locations in the outdoor area where they are easily accessible.

NURTURING STRATEGIES:

1. When a toddler selects a basket, introduce the activity enthusiastically by saying:
   "I saw a chicken out here earlier. I wonder if she left some eggs for us. Can you help me look?"
2. Explain the purpose of the basket, if necessary.
3. At your first opportunity, invite another child to join in the egg hunt. Select this child based on your knowledge of the children's friendships.
4. If a child is becoming frustrated and needs assistance with finding an egg to put in the basket, encourage the other toddler to help. Say, for example:
   "Nassef is frustrated because he cannot find an egg. Can you help him find one?"
5. Provide positive reinforcement for helping. Comments to make include:
   "Nicholas, you were a good friend to Nassef. You helped him to find an egg."
   "You helped Nassef feel better by showing him where to find an egg."
6. Discuss with the toddlers whether the eggs they found came from a real chicken. Clarify and/or reinforce their construction of the concept of make believe depending on the toddlers' current level of understanding.

☀ Highlighting Development

Although they lack the ability to verbally communicate the importance of friends or friendships, older toddlers clearly demonstrate this understanding through their behavior. Watch them. Toddlers will greet a friend with more excitement, engage in more laughter, and talk more to each other than do non-friends (Berk, 1999).

VARIATIONS:

♡ Hide other toys or objects for the toddlers to find.
♡ Encourage the toddlers to hide the eggs and then find them again.
♡ Play the game indoors.

ADDITIONAL INFORMATION:

♡ Increase or decrease the challenge for this experience by using your knowledge of the toddlers' level of understanding about object permanence.
♡ According to Fogel (2001), at this stage of development children are showing a tendency to engage in social play. In the past, they engaged in pretend sequences on their own. Now they are increasing their rates of verbalizations to their peers as well as social interactions.
♡ This activity builds on the "Putting Eggs in a Basket" activity (see p. 000) for two main reasons. First, this activity requires the children to pretend that the eggs are real. In other words, they use symbolic representation to have the plastic eggs stand for the real eggs. Moreover, this activity involves social play. The toddlers are now able to play a simple game with each other.

25 to 30 months

Sand Roads

Child's Developmental Goals

✓ To engage in parallel play

✓ To demonstrate interest in another child

MATERIALS:

❑ Water table

❑ 8 to 10 plastic cars

❑ Road signs

❑ Clean, sifted sand

❑ Water

PREPARATION:

♡ Clean the water table and fill with 3 to 4 inches of sand.

♡ Place cars and signs in the sand.

♡ If necessary, dampen the sand with water.

NURTURING STRATEGIES:

1. When a toddler selects the activity, observe his behavior noting how the toys are being used.

2. If necessary, invite another child to play in the sand table. To illustrate, say:
   "Ming-Na, would you like to play with the cars in the sand table? These are the cars you built yesterday."

3. When the two toddlers are working at the sand table, observe their behavior. Ask yourself if they are looking at each other and if they are imitating each other's behavior.

4. Comment on the fact that the toddlers are sharing the sand. If applicable, comment on sharing the signs and cars. State, for example:
   "Ming-Na and Caleb, you are both using the sand table. I see that each of you has two cars."

5. Encourage the toddlers to attend to each other's behavior. Comments to make include:
   "Caleb, look at how Ming-Na is making a road. The car drives better on a road."

☀ Highlighting Development

Toddlers are very interested in other children at this stage of development. Unfortunately, they lack important social skills such as the ability to coordinate their actions with another or to share materials. Observe them. Toddlers engage in parallel play. When this type of play occurs, the toddlers play independently but in the same area with similar materials. They will demonstrate interest in each other while playing by observing, making eye contact, and imitating the play behaviors of the children around them.

VARIATIONS:

♡ Use wet sand instead of dry sand to provide a new experience.

♡ Add people to further encourage pretend play.

ADDITIONAL INFORMATION:

♡ Adults play an important role in promoting children's play by showing respect and acting as a facilitator. They can stimulate the children's natural curiosity and active engagement by describing the children's actions or the properties of play objects and asking open-ended questions. In addition to verbally responding, adults can support play by observing and modifying the environment by adding or removing props as necessary.

25 to 30 months

Riding the Horsey

SOCIAL

Child's Developmental Goals

✓ To engage in pretend play

✓ To use a baby doll as the object of their play

MATERIALS:

❑ 2 or 3 baby dolls

❑ Rocking horse

PREPARATION:

♡ Clean an area for the rocking horses.

♡ Place the stuffed animals near the horses, but not too close to cause a safety hazard.

NURTURING STRATEGIES:

1. When a toddler selects a rocking horse, observe the child's abilities.

2. Model giving a baby doll a ride on the other horse. Connect your actions with words by saying:
   "Charlie likes to ride the horse. Hear him say 'whee'?"

3. If the child does not imitate your behavior, allow him time to rock for a while. Then, suggest giving one of the babies a ride. While pointing to the baby doll, say:
   "I think that Charlie would like to ride the horse too. Can he ride with you?" Whenever possible, encourage another toddler to give the doll a ride on the horse or offer for Charlie to share his horse with the toddler.

Highlighting Development

Given their ability to think using symbols, toddlers start to engage in pretend play. In the beginning, their pretend play is self-directed (Berk, 1999). For example, toddlers pretend to feed themselves, go to sleep, or even take a bath. After this stage, they will begin to incorporate pretend objects. To illustrate, instead of feeding themselves, they would feed a doll or stuffed animal. It is not until after toddlerhood that they, typically, become a "detached participant" who assists a doll with feeding itself or one doll with feeding another (Berk, 1999, p. 325).

VARIATION:

♡ Provide cars and stuffed animals.

ADDITIONAL INFORMATION:

♡ Children between 25 and 36 months of age can typically be expected to use a rocking horse for three minutes without falling off (Charlesworth, 2000).

♡ In dramatic play, children try out many roles drawn from daily life. They may be a mommy, daddy, or even baby. They may wash the car, cook dinner, go to a birthday party, or vacuum the rug. Through this type of play, concept development grows as the children engage in practicing their understanding of the world (Gonzalez-Mena, 2001).

25 to 30 months

Mailing Letters to . . .

Child's Developmental Goals

✓ To communicate with another child

✓ To increase understanding of the purpose of writing

✓ To begin developing an appreciation for print

MATERIALS:

❑ Box for each child (small boxes used by bakeries for cookies are perfect because the lid is attached and they are sturdy)

❑ Photo of each child

❑ Paper

❑ Washable, nontoxic, felt-tip markers

❑ Envelopes

PREPARATION:

♡ Label a box for each child with her or his photograph and printed name.

♡ Display the boxes so that toddlers can easily access them.

♡ Provide paper, markers, and envelopes in a writing area on a child-size table.

NURTURING STRATEGIES:

1. Introduce the mailboxes to the children. To illustrate, say:
   "These boxes are here to collect mail. If you want to write a letter to someone, write it. Then, place it in the box with her or his picture. That way your friend will get the letter you wrote."

2. Once a toddler has completed her letter, you may need to provide assistance in locating the appropriate mailbox. To do this, focus the child's attention on the photographs. When the correct mailbox has been selected, point out the written name also. To illustrate, say:
   "You found Tama's mailbox. Here is her photograph and here is her name. Look at the letters. Here is a T."

3. Keep an informal tabulation regarding who is sending and receiving mail. If a child has not received any mail from a friend, you can encourage someone to write him/her a letter or write a letter to the child yourself.

☀ Highlighting Development

A print-rich environment should be a part of a child's world from birth. However, awareness of print takes many years to develop. As young children experience people around them reading and writing, they come to understand that the printed word can be used for many purposes— to regulate actions, to communicate information, to interact with others, and to seek information— to name just a few (see McGee and Richgils, 2000).

VARIATION:

♡ Create real postcards and take a walking field trip to mail them to important others.

♡ Create a pen pal system with children in other classrooms within your building.

ADDITIONAL INFORMATION:

♡ Mailing and receiving latters can provide meaningful opportunities for literacy development. When writing or identifying a child's name, focus on the first letter.

♡ To encourage pre-writing, children need special space devoted to this purpose. The area should include a variety of tools and paper for exploration. To sustain their interest, this area must remain neat and orderly and contain properly functioning tools. Therefore, the children should assume responsibility for caring for the felt-tip markers to prevent them from drying out. Teach them how to replace the caps. When necessary, provide reminders.

25 to 30 months

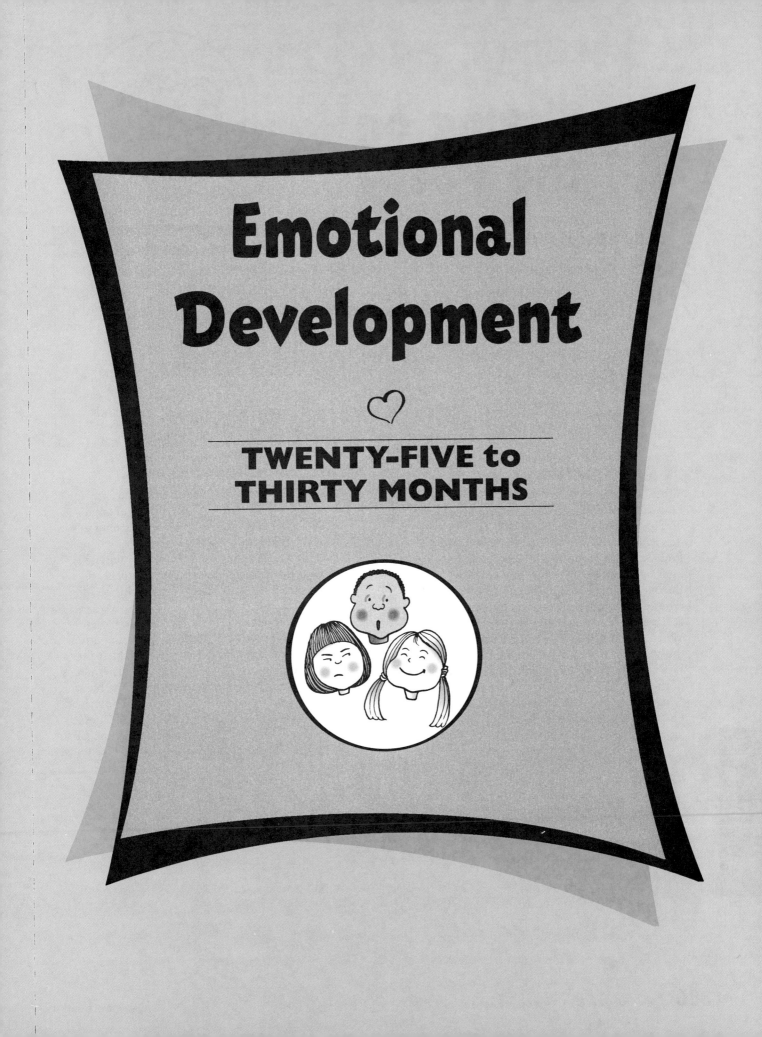

Emotional Development

♡

TWENTY-FIVE to THIRTY MONTHS

Sitting on the Potty

Child's Developmental Goals

✓ To experience a sense of satisfaction

✓ To gain a sense of accomplishment

✓ To practice self-help skills

MATERIALS:

❏ Regular diapering supplies

PREPARATION:

♡ Arrange supplies on or near the changing table.

NURTURING STRATEGIES:

1. When it is time to diaper the toddler, provide him with a warning about the upcoming change. To illustrate, say:
   "It will be your turn to sit on the potty next, Mac."
2. Provide verbal reminders, as necessary, of the steps in using the potty.
3. Encourage the toddler to pull down his pants and remove his diaper before sitting on the toilet.
4. Engage the toddler in conversation.
5. When the child is finished, move the toddler to the changing table and replace the diaper.
6. Provide support for completing the next two steps of the diapering routine. Say, for example:
   "Pull up your pants Mac. Then wash your hands."
7. Finish the diapering procedures.

VARIATION:

♡ If facilities are available, encourage two toddlers to use the restroom at the same time. Children can be models for each other, so pair a toddler who is almost toilet-trained with a child who is just beginning the process.

Highlighting Development

Learning to use the toilet independently is a complicated task. There are many steps to remember in a relatively set sequence. To promote autonomy and a sense of accomplishment, it is necessary to divide the task into small steps. Between 25 and 30 months of age, toddlers should be able to remove their pants and then pull them back up when finished. Likewise, they should also be able to wash their hands with minimal assistance.

ADDITIONAL INFORMATION:

♡ In a child care program, you may need to provide suggestions to parents or guardians about appropriate clothing for toddlers who are learning to use the toilet independently. Bib overalls, for example, are attractive, but they inhibit young children's ability to undress independently. Sweatpants or other pants with elastic waists are much easier for them to remove.

♡ According to Leach (1992), for young children, becoming clean is far easier than becoming dry. Typically, toddlers will follow a predictable pattern with toilet training. Bowel control usually emerges first followed by the daytime control of the bladder. Finally, nighttime control of the bladder is obtained.

♡ Carefully observe the toddler for toileting cues. Typically, a child will communicate using the same words or gestures whenever needing to use the toilet.

My Turn

Child's Developmental Goals

✓ To express emotions appropriately

✓ To take turns

MATERIALS:

❑ 2 toddler swings in outside play area

PREPARATION:

♡ Check that the swings are in good repair and free of any safety hazards.

NURTURING STRATEGIES:

1. When a toddler chooses to swing, provide assistance as needed.
2. Converse or sing with the toddler while pushing the swing.
3. If available, invite another toddler to swing. Involve that child in the conversation or singing.
4. When a third toddler asks to swing, tell him that he can have a turn next. For example, say:
   "Erica, you can swing when either Ida or Santiago is finished."
5. If the toddler becomes upset with having to wait, label the emotion she may be feeling. Use comments such as:
   "It is frustrating to have to wait."
   "You're sad because you wanted to swing."
6. Encourage the toddler to select another area in which to play until it is her turn. This is often a difficult task for toddlers. Therefore, be prepared for the toddler to remain in the area. Set any limits to keep the toddler safe. Say, for example:
   "Erica, please stand in the grass and sing with us. I don't want you to get hit with the swing."

7. If the child does choose another area, politely interrupt her play when it is her turn. Give her a choice of continuing her play or joining the others at the swings. This step is important in maintaining a trustful relationship with the toddler.

☀ Highlighting Development

Learning to express and regulate emotions appropriately has been found to be predictive of later development, whereas a lack of such skill has been associated with pathological disorders (Charlesworth, 2000). Carefully observe toddlers in your care. If you notice a lack of a particular skill, take the time to teach and promote further development. It will pay off in the long run.

VARIATION:

♡ Incorporate literacy skills by posting a notepad near the swings. When a child wants a turn, write the toddler's name on the waiting list.

ADDITIONAL INFORMATION:

♡ Learning to take turns is a high-level skill. Children must trust that you will follow through with what you say. Therefore, do not make promises you cannot keep, because outdoor play space must often be shared. Keep a close eye on the time before promising a child a turn. It may not be possible.

25 to 30 months

Serving Myself Juice

Child's Developmental Goals

✓ To experience sense of accomplishment

✓ To perform a task independently

MATERIALS:

❑ 2 to 3 small, child-size plastic pitchers

❑ Unbreakable glass for each toddler

❑ Snack items

❑ Tray

❑ Juice

PREPARATION:

♡ Pour approximately 4 inches of juice into each pitcher.

♡ Keep extra beverages handy to refill pitchers when necessary.

♡ Place all snack items on a tray.

NURTURING STRATEGIES:

1. Clean and sanitize the child-size table. Remind the toddlers to wash their hands before snack. Set tray with snack items on the table.

2. Assist the toddlers with passing out snack. Encourage them to pour their own juice. Comments might include: "Sydney Ray, please pour your juice and then pass the pitcher to Wade. He would like some juice also."

3. Provide physical and verbal assistance, as needed, with pouring the juice. The main assistance needed might be your holding the cup still while the toddler pours liquid into it.

4. Ask open-ended questions throughout the snack to spark conversations with the toddlers.

☼ Highlighting Development

By 30 months, toddlers should possess sufficient eye-hand coordination skills to pour water from one container to another with minimal spilling (Charlesworth, 2000). Thus, they should be given small pitchers of liquids from which to pour beverages at snack and mealtimes. Serving themselves will not only promote physical development but also their sense of autonomy.

VARIATIONS:

♡ Repeat the "Making Pudding" activity (see p. 215) encouraging the toddler to pour the milk into the measuring cup.

♡ On hot days, make ice water and cups accessible while playing outside. Encourage toddlers to serve themselves when thirsty. This will add to their sense of autonomy and help prevent dehydration.

ADDITIONAL INFORMATION:

♡ Children at this age are learning to coordinate their movements. With age and experience, they will become increasingly more efficient with self-help routines such as eating, dressing, and brushing teeth. Toddlers should possess sufficient skills so they no longer need spillproof cups. Help them pour small amounts of liquids into their cups to reduce cleanup if an accident occurs.

25 to 30 months

388 **Twenty-Five to Thirty Months**

Bye, Bye Window

Child's Developmental Goals

✓ To cope with separation distress

✓ To express feelings appropriately

MATERIALS:

❑ Large hollow blocks

❑ Strong, adhesive tape

PREPARATION:

♡ Arrange large hollow blocks into steps and a platform under a window, facing the parking lot.

♡ Measure to ensure that a toddler can easily see out of the window when standing on the blocks.

♡ Secure the blocks with tape to prevent movement.

NURTURING STRATEGIES:

1. When a toddler becomes upset with the departure of a significant other, provide support and comfort. Label the emotion being displayed by the toddler. Say, for example:
   "Ruby, you are mad that dad left. You wanted to leave with him."
   "What a sad face. You will miss mom while she's at work."
2. Encourage the toddler to go to the Bye, Bye Window and wave good-bye.
3. Accompany the toddler to the window, if she desires.
4. Provide positive reinforcement for using positive coping skills to deal with strong emotions. Comments to make include:
   "It hurts when dad leaves. Watching him from the window helped you to calm down."
   "You used the Bye, Bye Window to help you feel less sad."

Highlighting Development

Often toddlers still experience separation distress when a parent or significant adult leaves them. Such behavior can be expected to last up to three years of age. Children who receive a verbal explanation for the leave-taking tend to protest less and show less stress (Field, Gewirtz, Cohen, Garcia, Greenberg, & Collins, 1984). Hence, parents need to know the importance of saying good-bye and of the normalcy of such protests by toddlers.

VARIATIONS:

♡ If windows are low enough, arrange a few chairs for the children to sit in and wave good-bye.

♡ Encourage toddlers to help each other when coping with separation distress.

ADDITIONAL INFORMATION:

♡ Toddlers need to learn that others can be trusted. As a result, help create a positive environment by explaining to parents/guardians the importance of saying and waving good-bye to their toddlers as part of the separation process. Sneaking out of the room damages the child's confidence in the parents/guardians. It can also increase the children's anxiety and create a sense of abandonment.

 If the platform needs to be greater than two blocks high, consider having a carpenter build a sturdy platform with stairs and a railing to prevent falls.

25 to 30 months

Welcoming a New Friend

EMOTIONAL

Child's Developmental Goals

✓ To develop pro-social behaviors such as helping someone

✓ To begin considering someone else's perspective

MATERIALS:

None

PREPARATION:

None

NURTURING STRATEGIES:

1. Tell the toddler that a new child will be visiting your home or classroom, whichever the case may be.
2. Engage the toddler in a conversation about how it feels to visit someplace new. Utilize descriptive words such as *excited, scary, nervous, confused,* and so on. Whenever possible, connect your conversation to the toddler's past experiences.
3. Tell the toddler the visitor's name.
4. Encourage the toddler to consider things he could do to help the visitor feel better. Comments to make include:
   "Urian, could you show him your favorite toy?"
   "Maybe you should show him where the bathroom is."
5. When the visitor arrives, greet him by bending to his level and calling him by name. Provide the child time to take in his surroundings before introducing him to Urian.
6. After the visitor leaves, provide positive reinforcement about at least one thing the toddler did to help the visitor. Comment, for example:
   "Urian, I think that Zu-Wang felt much better after you showed him the slide."
   "Our visitor seemed less nervous after you shared animal crackers with him."

☀ Highlighting Development

Piaget's theory suggests that toddlers and young preschoolers are very egocentric, meaning they have difficulty taking another person's perspective. Research on emotional development, specifically pro-social behaviors, is causing this notion to be reconsidered. Toddlers spend a great deal of time studying other people's reactions (see, for example, "I Need a Hug," p. 329), which suggests they understand, to a limited degree, that others have feelings or reactions, which may differ from their own. In terms of friendships, they think primarily about their side of the relationship. That is, what others can do for them.

VARIATION:

♡ Help the toddler identify how it feels to meet someone new. Focus on his emotional reactions to the situation.

ADDITIONAL INFORMATION:

♡ Meeting new people and entering new environments can be scary for anyone—adults included. Discussing how you feel can be an important model for the toddlers.

♡ According to Kostelnik, et al. (2002), young children define friendship in terms of proximity. They call those peers with whom they play most often or engage in similar activities their friends. They will also value friendships for possessions. For example, a child might say, "He is my friend; he has a fire truck."

Recovering from a Tantrum

Child's Developmental Goals

✓ To regain control after a tantrum

✓ To use an adult for emotional support

MATERIALS:

None

PREPARATION:

None

NURTURING STRATEGIES:

1. When you see a child throwing a tantrum, clear the area as quickly as possible to prevent injuries.
2. Speak to the child in a calm and loving voice about what behaviors you are observing. State, for example:
   "Amy, I can see that you are very, very upset. You are crying and kicking your feet."
3. Avoid attempting to physically assist or restrain the toddler. This could result in injury to the child or yourself.
4. However, provide verbal support. Say, for example:
   "It is very upsetting to be so out of control. It can even be scary. I can help you calm down."
5. Discuss strategies such as deep breathing or counting to three as a way to regain self-control.
6. When the child begins to regain control, express your desire to provide physical comfort. Offer to hold the child on your lap and read a book or rock in a rocking chair.
7. After the "hot" emotional moment has passed and the child is calm, discuss the event focusing on teaching strategies for dealing with strong emotions.

☀ Highlighting Development

During the second and third year of life, toddlers become very skilled at throwing tantrums. The physical signs of these intense physical and emotional responses may include screaming, crying, and flinging the arms and/or legs. With adult guidance and support, they can also become skilled at recovering from them (Philadelphia Child Guidance Center, 1994). Toddlers dislike the feeling of having "lost control" that accompanies a tantrum. Oftentimes, tantrums are an outward expression of toddlers' struggle between dependence and independence.

VARIATION:

♡ Closely observe children who are prone to tantrums. Try to figure out what "sets them off." Then, work to prevent tantrums by helping the child to cope effectively with the triggering event(s).

ADDITIONAL INFORMATION:

♡ Never shame the toddler for having a tantrum, which is a natural part of toddlerhood for many children. Focus, however, on teaching skills for dealing with strong emotions to reduce the frequency of tantrums.

♡ Toddlers may have tantrums when they do not receive immediate gratification for their wants. According to Kostelnik, et al. (2002), there are four reasons why tantrums often occur:
1. The child may be fatigued.
2. The child may be subject to unrealistic adult demands.
3. The child received little attention for positive behavior.
4. The child is subject to unpredictable rule enforcement.

25 to 30 months

Helping with the Bags

Child's Developmental Goals

✓ To respond to another person's signal for help

✓ To demonstrate helpful behavior

MATERIALS:

❑ Grocery bags filled from a trip to the grocery store

PREPARATION:

None

NURTURING STRATEGIES:

1. Signal the toddlers to assist with carrying the bags of grocery to the kitchen. To illustrate, say:
   "Wow! Rosie bought lots of good food at the grocery store. I need to carry all of the bags to the kitchen. They sure look heavy. I don't know if I can do it myself."

2. If no one responds to your signal, be more direct and ask one or two toddlers for help. Try to pick toddlers who are not deeply engaged in play. Say, for example:
   "Hunter and Angat, please help carry these bags to the kitchen."

3. Comment on the toddlers' helping behaviors. Discuss, for example, if everyone is carrying separate bags ("We divided the task") or if some are working together to move one bag ("You are helping each other to finish the task").

4. Thank the children for their assistance. Avoid showering them with too much praise because it refocuses their internal motivation for helping on external rewards.

☼ Highlighting Development

When treated respectfully and caringly by adults, toddlers spontaneously show sympathy towards others. They will provide comfort and help those in pain or distress. Oftentimes, toddlers will offer their favorite comfort item, such as a blanket or stuffed animal, to another in distress. This gesture is representative of the sentiment, "It helps me feel better, so it will help you."

VARIATION:

♡ Enlist the children's help with rearranging the furniture in the room, moving boxes, or packing away toys at the end of the week.

ADDITIONAL INFORMATION:

♡ Children must learn their cultural display rules in order to be successfully integrated into society. Imitation, feedback, and direction are important teaching strategies that adults provide. Feedback is instrumental for toddlers to understand how, when, and where to express their emotions. This may be in the form of an adult tone serving as a social reward for appropriate behavior; likewise, it could be ignoring or frowning at inappropriate behavior. Adults can provide a social award for appropriate behavior by using supportive words with accompanying positive tone of voice. Examples include statements such as:
   "Look at Hunter. He is being helpful by carrying Jeffrey's coat."
   "Randy did a good job of hanging up his coat."
   "You should not laugh at children who fall down. It hurts their feelings."

♡ Avoid reinforcing gender stereotypes by requesting help from girls and boys.

Dealing with Anger

Child's Developmental Goals

✓ To build vocabulary associated with emotions

✓ To increase understanding of emotions

✓ To discuss nonaggressive strategies for expressing anger

MATERIALS:

❏ Book, *I Was So Mad,* by Mercer Mayer

PREPARATION:

♡ Review the book.

NURTURING STRATEGIES:

1. Gather either one toddler or a small group of toddlers in a comfortable location.
2. Introduce the book by showing the cover and reading the title, author, and illustration. Engage the children's attention by asking what they think the story might be about.
3. Read the story slowly while showing the illustrations to the toddlers.
4. Review the events in the story that made the character mad.
5. Provide positive reinforcement for remembering events. Comments to make include:
   "What a good memory. The frogs were on the first page of the book."
   "You were really paying attention to the story."
6. Discuss reasons for the main character being so angry in the story. Highlight, for example, the fact that he wasn't able to do what he wanted. Ask the toddlers how they feel when they are in that situation. Whenever possible, provide recent examples to help them recall their feelings.
7. Conclude the experience by asking the toddlers for other ways to deal with anger.

Highlighting Development

Young children feel emotions and express emotions; however, they have yet to reach a level of cognitive development where they understand emotions (Marion, 1997). Adults must devote a great deal of time and energy over many years (up through adolescence) to help children understand emotions. When working with young children, it is essential that adults recognize that this is a long road that often is marked by potholes and curves. The first step in dealing with anger is to acquaint toddlers with the vocabulary used to described this emotion.

VARIATIONS:

♡ Record, on large paper, things that make the toddlers angry.

♡ Find other stories to read about anger.

♡ Have the toddlers demonstrate how they act when angry.

ADDITIONAL INFORMATION:

♡ Books are an effective medium for communicating concepts related to emotional expression. Well-chosen books can convey societal and cultural rules regarding emotional expression. Print media can showcase particular situations and how emotions can be demonstrated, as well as what behaviors are acceptable or unacceptable in different situations.

25 to 30 months

Rainy Day Play

EMOTIONAL

Child's Developmental Goals

✓ To label feelings

✓ To counterbalance fear with feelings of self-efficacy

MATERIALS:

❑ Flashlight for each child

❑ Clear, heavy adhesive tape

PREPARATION:

♡ Tape the opening of each flashlight to prevent the batteries from being removed, for safety purposes.

NURTURING STRATEGIES:

1. During free play exploration, introduce the flashlights:
   "Flashlights provide light. They are useful on dark, rainy days like today. I'm going to turn off some of the big lights so that our flashlights are easier to see."

2. Turn off lights. Be sure to keep some blinds or curtains open. This will permit some natural light into the room, thus allowing toddlers to work on other projects.

3. Encourage the toddlers to explore the room using the flashlights.

4. Discuss how the flashlight can help you feel less afraid of the dark. Connect the discussion to other ways for reducing fear of the dark. For example, say:
   "I use a night light when I go to sleep at night. Do you?"
   Continue the activity as long as the toddlers remain interested.

☼ Highlighting Development

Young children live in a world that is far more frightening and emotionally challenging than adults can comprehend. It is important for healthy emotional development that their fears are dealt with in a compassionate and respectful manner. Avoid belittling, laughing, or dismissing a child's fear. Instead, help the child to talk about feelings and develop positive coping skills (Philadelphia Child Guidance Center, 1994).

VARIATIONS:

♡ Have children draw how they are feeling as a way to exercise self-control.

♡ Keep a flashlight accessible during naptime for a toddler who is fearful of the dark.

ADDITIONAL INFORMATION:

♡ Being calm and patient with a toddler experiencing a fearful reaction can have a soothing effect. Between the ages of 24 and 30 months, common fears include specific loud noises, flushing toilets, nightmares, darkness, changes in the environment (moved furniture), and bad weather.

25 to 30 months

Helping Out

Child's Developmental Goals

✓ To perform a task with minimal assistance

✓ To experience a sense of accomplishment

MATERIALS:

☐ Clear plastic container with a screw-on lid.
☐ Paper
☐ Scissors
☐ Tape
☐ Pen

PREPARATION:

♡ Create a Job Jar label and adhere it to container.
♡ Write simple tasks that often need to be completed throughout the day on slips of paper, then fold and place the slips inside the jar.

NURTURING STRATEGIES:

1. When you notice a child wandering and not engaged with an activity, encourage that child to select a job from the Job Jar.
2. Help the child by reading the card. Ask the child questions about the task. Use comments such as: *"Giselle, is the laundry folded? How do you know?"*
3. Make sure that the child understands the task before encouraging her to do it independently. When the child is ready, support her efforts by saying, for example:
   "Put all of the towels in the drawer."
4. Supervise from a distance, being sure to provide ample space and time for the child to complete the task.

5. Comment on the importance of the child's work to the functioning of the classroom. For instance, state: *"No one would know where the clean towels are if you hadn't put them in the drawer."*

☀ Highlighting Development

Erikson (1950) believed that the defining task for toddlers was to achieve autonomy. Even the language used by young children—"Me do it," "Mommy, me," "Mine"—reflects their need to be independent. However, toddlers vacillate between contradictory needs for dependence and independence. At one point, they want to do it all by themselves, and in the next moment they need the comfort and security of a trusted adult.

VARIATIONS:

♡ Put visual representations on the slips so the child can "read" the task card independently.
♡ Have a chart with words and pictures which shows the job assignment for the week.

ADDITIONAL INFORMATION:

♡ Teachers in early childhood programs need to encourage parents to create a Job Jar at home. Provide suggestions such as matching socks or stacking plastic cups that toddlers can accomplish.

25 to 30 months

Physical Development

♡

THIRTY-ONE to THIRTY-SIX MONTHS

Riding Trikes

PHYSICAL

Child's Developmental Goals

✓ To improve full-body coordination

✓ To practice steering the tricycle

MATERIALS:

❑ 2 or 3 tricycles

❑ Helmet for each tricycle

PREPARATION:

♡ Inspect the tricycles to make sure they are in good repair.

♡ Hang a helmet on the handlebars of each tricycle.

♡ Designate a "parking lot" and place the tricycles there.

NURTURING STRATEGIES:

1. When a toddler selects a tricycle, assist with securing the helmet.
2. Gently remind the toddler of any limits before he begins to ride.
3. Encourage the toddler to steer the tricycle, as well as peddle. Say, for example:

   "Use your hands to move the handle bars. Turn the handle bars so you stay in the path."
4. Reinforce the toddler's efforts at riding the tricycle. Comments to make include:

   "Jar, you practiced steering the tricycle today. You were able to stay on the path!"

   "You worked hard at steering and pedaling the tricycle."
5. Record your observations of the toddler's physical skills in the form of an anecdotal record. If more than one toddler is present, create a panel with photographs to document the learning.

☀ Highlighting Development

Most toddlers are able to successfully peddle a tricycle with their feet by three years of age (Berk, 1999). There is great variability in steering skills, however. Some toddlers are able to pedal and steer a tricycle with great coordination while others must concentrate exclusively on not falling off of the tricycle. Although most of these differing abilities can be explained by the individual toddler's gross motor skills, the types of toys provided must be examined. Some riding toys have steering wheels that serve no purpose in actually directing the toys' motion. Thus, toddlers learn that steering is not important. When presented with a tricycle, for example, that requires pedaling and steering, they must learn to coordinate both actions.

VARIATION:

♡ Provide other riding toys such as cars.

ADDITIONAL INFORMATION:

♡ When choosing a tricycle, carefully consider the design to prevent children from tipping over. The best-engineered tricycles have large wheels and are built low to the ground.

 To promote the safety of the children, carefully select a protective environment for using the tricycles. For example, make sure the tricycles are behind a fence away from traffic dangers. Then, set limits to guide behavior and require the toddlers to wear helmets. In addition, if more than one toddler is present, set limits on the direction toddlers should ride to prevent head-on collisions.

I'm a Real Sculptor

Child's Developmental Goals

✓ To increase strength of wrists, hands, and fingers

✓ To increase eye-hand coordination

✓ To increase visual perceptual skills

MATERIALS:

❑ Nontoxic potter's clay

❑ Slip

❑ Canvas or work board

❑ Wire for cutting clay

PREPARATION:

♡ Clear a child-size table and cover with canvas.

♡ Place clay and wire in the center of the table.

♡ Prepare slip in a bowl that can be easily passed between toddlers and set on table.

NURTURING STRATEGIES:

1. Introduce the concept of sculpting several days before providing the clay. Ways to do this include taking a field trip to a studio or inviting an artist to visit the toddlers.

2. When a toddler selects the activity, move the clay closer to the child. Assist her, as necessary, with using the wire to cut a piece of clay.

3. Communicate with the toddler about the texture and consistency of the clay. Questions to spark discussion include:

   "Emma, how does the clay feel in your hands?"

   "How can you flatten the clay since it is stiff?"

4. Allow the toddler uninterrupted time to explore the clay.

5. If the toddler attempts to adhere one piece of clay to another, remind her about the slip, while moving it closer to the toddler. Refer to your field trip or visitor, as appropriate. To illustrate, say:

   "Do you remember how the sculptor showed us to put two pieces of clay together?"

   Continue the discussion providing information as appropriate.

6. If more than one child is working, encourage them to pass the bowl of slip around the table. In addition, invite all toddlers to participate in the conversation. Whenever possible, prompt the toddlers to share information (instead of relying on you).

7. Provide positive reinforcement by focusing on the process the children are undertaking rather than the final product.

Highlighting Development

Remarkable advances in the development of fine motor skills occur during early childhood. Observe them. Toddlers gradually gain greater and greater control of their wrists, hands, and fingers. Moreover, they gradually gain muscular strength. As a result, they no longer have to exclusively use soft, homemade clay. Now, a firmer model clay that is used by older children or nontoxic sculpting clay used by adults can be introduced.

VARIATION:

♡ After the children are skilled at manipulating the clay, slowly introduce additional tools.

ADDITIONAL INFORMATION:

♡ You may need to spend time experimenting with the clay and slip in order to best assist/guide the toddlers. At first, the toddlers probably will lack the necessary strength and technique for cutting the clay with the wire. However, it will not take them long to acquire these skills.

♡ Children's reactions to play dough will vary by age. Typical responses of two-year-olds include feeling, squeezing, rolling, pounding, pinching, and tearing (Schirrmacher, 2001). For young children, working with clay is a multisensory experience. Clay has a distinct texture, smell, and color.

31 to 36 months

Balloon Toss

Child's Developmental Goals

✓ To practice catching skills

✓ To improve full-body coordination

✓ To improve eye-hand coordination skills

MATERIALS:

❏ 2 or 3 balloons, depending on the number of toddlers

PREPARATION:

♡ Blow up the balloons and firmly secure with a knot.

♡ Clear an open, outdoor, grassy area, if available, of any obstacles.

NURTURING STRATEGIES:

1. Observe the toddler's behavior with the balloons.
2. Suggest a different way to use the balloon. For example, if the toddler is kicking it, suggest he toss the balloon to you.
3. Encourage the toddler to catch it when you toss it back to him. Comment, for example:
   "My turn to toss. You catch it, Grant."
4. If the toddler is having difficulty with throwing or catching, provide plenty of time to practice those skills. In addition, provide verbal support. Use comments such as:
   "What a great attempt. You held out your arms to catch the ball, Grant."
   "Keep trying. You'll get it!"
5. Continue to throw and catch the balloon as long as the toddler seems interested.

☼ Highlighting Development

During early childhood, gender differences may become apparent in the development of the toddlers' physical skills. Biologically, there appears to be little support for these gender differences. Environmentally, these differences are often attributed to the way adults socialize them. Boys are usually encouraged to be more active, adventuresome, and participate in more rough-and-tumble play (Trawick-Smith, 2000). Thus, it is important to facilitate optimal physical development for children, regardless of gender.

VARIATIONS:

♡ To promote social development, encourage two toddlers to toss the balloon back and forth.

♡ Substitute other large, lightweight balls for the balloons.

ADDITIONAL INFORMATION:

♡ Gross motor development typically precedes fine motor development. Watch the children as they throw the balloons. At this stage, they move their whole body in a rather distorted posture. As the children continue developing, they will gradually be able to coordinate their bodies in a smooth sequence while throwing a balloon or other object.

 Broken balloons can be a serious choking hazard. Therefore, provide constant supervision when the children are engaged in the experience. Setting clear, positive limits about the use of the balloon can reduce hazards. State, for example,
   "The balloon is for tossing and catching."
   "Use your hands to hold the balloon."

Sketching

Child's Developmental Goals

✔ To refine fine motor skills in the wrist, hands, and fingers

✔ To develop eye-hand coordination skills

✔ To practice grasping a writing tool

✔ To practice making marks with a writing tool

MATERIALS:

❏ Small- and large-diameter pencils for every child

❏ Container for the pencils

❏ A clipboard for every child

❏ Typing or copier paper

PREPARATION:

♡ Put two to three pieces of paper on each clipboard.

NURTURING STRATEGIES:

1. Introduce the activity to a small group of toddlers. To illustrate, say:
   "We've been studying trees for three months now. I noticed the magnolia tree in the yard is blooming. Let's go outside and sketch it. I have a clipboard and pencil for each of you."
2. Accompany the children outside and find a comfortable place to sit to observe the tree.
3. Engage the children in conversation about the tree. Assist the toddlers in describing the tree's leaves, trunk, and so on.
4. Allow the children ample time to sketch uninterrupted. Reserve comments until a child initiates conversation with you.
5. When the children indicate they are finished, record any words they might use to describe their work.

Highlighting Development

Most children will be able to grip a small-diameter pencil in their hand by 36 months of age. There is controversy surrounding the type of pencil to provide children with at this age. It has often been assumed that very young children work best with large-diameter pencils or crayons. However, Carlson and Cunningham (1990) found that some children handle large-diameter pencils better while other children perform better with small-diameter pencils. Therefore, to encourage toddlers to write or draw provide a variety of different sizes and types of tools, thus allowing the children to select the tool they are most comfortable using.

VARIATION:

♡ Take a walk around the neighborhood and find interesting buildings, statues, and/or homes to sketch.

ADDITIONAL INFORMATION:

♡ Children are now becoming aware of colors and their preferences for certain ones. To minimize conflict, provide identically colored tools.

♡ Some children at this stage of development will hold the tool with an overhand grip. Other children will hold it like a hammer between the hands. Observe. When children hold the tools in this manner, you will find that neither the wrists nor fingers move (Herr, 2001).

♡ Children's first drawings are random scribbles. When they are able to hold drawing tools with their fingers, their scribbles will become smaller and more controlled.

Marble Painting

PHYSICAL

Child's Developmental Goals

✓ To refine small muscle skills

✓ To develop eye-hand coordination skills

MATERIALS:

- ❑ Construction paper
- ❑ Metal bread pans
- ❑ Masking tape
- ❑ 2 cans of paint
- ❑ Damp sponge
- ❑ Large marbles for each child
- ❑ Nonbreakable paint containers
- ❑ Spoon for each marble
- ❑ Smock for each child

PREPARATION:

♡ Cut construction paper to fit inside the bottom of the bread pans. Using masking tape, secure paper in place.

♡ Mix paint to desired thickness by using liquid soap to help facilitate cleanup.

♡ If more than one child is participating, divide each color of paint equally between containers for easy access.

♡ Place one bread pan for each child at a child-size table. Make sure both colors of paint are easily accessible.

♡ Put a smock over the back of each chair.

NURTURING STRATEGIES:

1. When a child chooses the activity, introduce it while the child is putting on the smock. To illustrate, say: *"Elita, do you remember when we painted with the golf balls? This time we're going to use marbles."*

2. If necessary, provide more details about how to use the spoon to scoop up the marble and place it on the paper.

3. Set clear, positive limits on behavior. State, for example: *"Place the spoon back in the paint container when you are finished with it." "Sit in the chair or stand by the table when making your picture."*

4. Describe the child's behavior when shaking the pan. Comments to make include: *"You are shaking the pan fast, Elita." "You are moving your entire body from side to side when shaking the pan."*

5. Encourage the toddler to use marbles dipped in both colors of paint. Share the toddler's enthusiasm when a new color is produced.

6. Assist the toddler with using the sponge to wipe a spill or dirty hands.

☀ Highlighting Development

Fine motor development is basic for the eventual mastery of handwriting skills. Some prerequisite skills include: thumb-finger coordination, eye-hand coordination, small muscle (wrist and fingers) development, ability to hold a writing tool, and the ability to make basic strokes (Lamme, 1979, cited in Charlesworth, 2000). None of these skills can be directly taught. Rather, they must be developed through play. The adult's role is to provide the necessary materials to foster the development of such skills.

VARIATION:

♡ Use other round objects to paint with such as a ping-pong ball or empty spool of thread.

ADDITIONAL INFORMATION:

♡ This experience builds on the "Golf Ball Painting" activity (see p. 334) for at least two reasons. First, the toddlers can immediately view the effects of their movements on the artwork. Second, the smaller objects require more refined small muscle skills to pick up with the spoon.

♡ Record the child's name in the upper left-hand corner or on the back of the artwork. Use numerals to record the date completed. Consider saving the artwork for the child's portfolio.

⊘ **CAUTION** Supervise this activity carefully. Moreover, do not introduce this experience if a toddler still has a tendency to put objects in her mouth.

Transferring Cards

Child's Developmental Goals

✓ To improve fine motor skills

✓ To enhance eye-hand coordination

MATERIALS:

❑ Deck of cards

❑ Plastic container (such as one for peanut butter)

PREPARATION:

♡ Select a jar with a mouth wide enough to insert the cards.

♡ Wash the jar carefully in hot, soapy water.

♡ Check the jar for sharp edges. If any sharp edges are discovered, either sand them smooth or cover them with masking tape.

♡ Place the deck of cards inside the jar and display the container on a child-size shelf.

NURTURING STRATEGIES:

1. When a child selects the materials, observe his behavior. Note what the child does with the cards.

2. Describe the child's behavior with the materials. Provide specific feedback on how the toddler is using his hands. Use comments such as:

   "Paco, you are picking up the cards with your finger and thumb."

   "What precision. You are laying the cards on top of each other."

3. If child does not see the connection between the materials, suggest a way to use both. For example, say:

   "Will the cards fit inside the container?"

4. Providing positive reinforcement while the toddler is working may increase the time the child spends at the activity.

5. Document the child's abilities in the form of an anecdotal record.

☀ Highlighting Development

By five years of age, girls tend to be ahead of boys in the development of fine motor skills (Berk, 1999). Close this gender gap by introducing, encouraging, and supporting boys in fine motor activities as much as, if not more than, girls. In play and activity, the fine motor skills developed at this stage are important. These skills provide the foundation for later skills necessary for cutting, writing, and so on.

VARIATION:

♡ Increase the challenge by having the toddler return the deck of cards to its original box.

ADDITIONAL INFORMATION:

♡ Set up the child's environment to promote the development of fine motor skills. Children at this age delight in exploring. They enjoy dumping, refilling, taking things apart, and putting them back together again. Provide toddlers with puzzles, peg boards, lacing cards, snap beads, and building blocks.

Up, Up, Up

PHYSICAL

Child's Developmental Goals

✓ To practice walking up stairs

✓ To practice walking down stairs

MATERIALS:

❑ Commercially produced stairs with railing, if available.

PREPARATION:

♡ If a commercial staircase is available, select an area of the room that can be easily supervised. Clear this area and put the staircase there. Without this equipment, carpeted stairs can be used if constantly supervised.

NURTURING STRATEGIES:

1. When a child selects the stairs, observe carefully.
2. If necessary, move closer to the child to provide physical assistance and/or guidance.
3. Verbally describe the toddler's abilities. Comments to make include:
   "Aisha, you are walking up the stairs with your left foot . . . now your right foot . . . now the left."
   "You're holding onto the rail. That helps to keep you safe."
4. Walking up steps tends to develop before walking down. Therefore, provide support and encouragement for walking down the steps. Set and maintain positive limits as necessary to promote safety. State, for example:
   "Jump from the bottom step."

☀ Highlighting Development

By the end of the third year, toddlers should be skilled at walking up small flights of stairs (Charlesworth, 2000). They will alternate feet so that one foot is on a step at a time. Of course, toddlers who have daily experience with walking up and down steps at home and/or school will typically be more skilled than children who do not have such opportunities.

VARIATION:

♡ Locate an interesting set of steps within the community and take a field trip to explore them.

ADDITIONAL INFORMATION:

♡ Major motor achievements occur during the third year of life. Watch. During this stage, children begin engaging in what is called exercise play. This involves playful locomotor movements such as running, chasing, and climbing. This play is vigorous and beneficial because it promotes skill, strength, fitness, and endurance.

 Never leave a child unattended on any stairs.

31 to 36 months

Trying a New Food

Child's Developmental Goals

✓ To try a new food
✓ To converse about healthy foods

MATERIALS:

❑ Lunch food and supplies

PREPARATION:

♡ Prepare a regular lunch.

NURTURING STRATEGIES:

1. Assist the toddlers with washing hands, as necessary.
2. Encourage the toddlers to help prepare the table for lunch by distributing cups, napkins, utensils, etc.
3. When the table is set, sit at the table with the children. Then begin serving the food "family style."
4. Discuss what is on the menu for today. Highlight the new food by saying, for example:
   "Today we are having burritos, salad, and beans. These are a new kind of bean. They are not mashed like the refried pinto beans we usually eat. These are called black beans."
5. Engage the children in meaningful conversation about the black beans. Ask, for example:
   "Has anyone eaten black beans before?"
6. Weave into the conversation, as naturally as possible, concepts about eating healthy. Discuss, for example, how healthy foods give us energy to run and play.
7. After the meal, encourage the toddlers to clean the table.

VARIATION:

♡ If in an early childhood program, involve the parents in preparing and serving foods that reflect their culture or heritage.

☀ Highlighting Development

It is important for adults to help young children to follow their internal guides for preferences, appetite, and satiation. Therefore, when a new food is introduced, encourage the toddler to try it, but if the child refuses or rejects it, do not force the issue (Gerber & Johnson, 1998). However, try introducing it again at another time. Offering new foods when the toddler is hungry, thirsty, or with others who enjoy the food might increase the child's willingness to try it. Toddlers are like adults. They will have days when their appetite wanes. When this happens, do not force them to eat. Rather, allow them to eat when they are hungry by providing healthy snacks.

ADDITIONAL INFORMATION:

♡ Eating family style is important for toddlers. Serving themselves not only promotes fine motor skills but it enhances autonomy.

♡ Setting the table is a routine that provides toddlers experiences in counting and spatial relationships. To assist them in learning to set the table, use a permanent, felt-tip marker to trace the position of eating utensils, plates, and cup onto a plastic placemat.

♡ Toddlers can also be expected to participate in cleanup after finishing a meal. To facilitate this process, place a utility cart and garbage can near the eating area. After the meal, the toddlers can throw their napkins and other disposable items directly into the trash. They should also be able to scrape food scraps from their plates into the garbage can and place their plates on the utility cart.

Putting the Cassette Inside

PHYSICAL

Child's Developmental Goals

✓ To improve fine motor coordination skills
✓ To continue developing eye-hand coordination skills

MATERIALS:

❑ Old audiocassette tapes
❑ Cassette holders
❑ Basket

PREPARATION:

♡ Remove all of the tape from the cassettes.
♡ Place all of the cassettes and holders in the basket.
♡ Place the basket where it is easily accessible.

NURTURING STRATEGIES:

1. If you notice a toddler needs something to do, direct his attention to the basket. Introduce the activity by saying, for example:
   "Samuel, can you match every tape with a plastic case?"
2. Observe the toddler's ability to complete this task. Although it seems easy for adults, it can be frustrating. Provide verbal assistance whenever possible. Refrain from providing physical assistance or modeling unless it is absolutely necessary.
3. Encourage the toddler to check his work. Questions or comments include:
   "Will the case close? Try it and see."
   "See if it is right. Test to see if the case will close."
4. Provide positive reinforcement for the process as well as the final outcome. To illustrate, say:
   "Samuel, you did a good job. You figured out. You needed to turn the tape a different direction."
   "You matched every tape with a case. You really worked hard."
5. When the toddler is finished, encourage him to return all of the cassettes and holders to the basket.

☀ Highlighting Development

During the first three years of life, infants and toddlers change their approach to playing with small objects. Infants and young toddlers focus on exploring objects with their hands and mouth to learn as much as possible about them. Older toddlers, in contrast, spend most of their time using objects for practicing simple skills. Older toddlers put objects through openings, manipulate simple locks, and build things up, just to knock them down and begin again (White, 1995).

VARIATION:

♡ Use videocassettes and plastic covers instead of the audiocassette tapes.

ADDITIONAL INFORMATION:

♡ Purchase cassettes at a garage sale or recycle ones you no longer listen to. However, after this activity be sure to keep out of reach the cassettes that you want to listen to. The toddlers might accidentally ruin the tape when playing.
♡ In order for young children to become motorically competent, they must be able to coordinate and integrate all body functions. Coordination of the hands and eyes is one of the most important (Weiser, 1991). Although caregivers cannot teach coordination, they can provide an interesting environment with many opportunities for exploration and practice.

CAUTION Remove the tape from the cassette before giving it to the toddlers to prevent strangulation and other safety hazards.

Follow the Leader

Child's Developmental Goals

✓ To imitate another child's physical movement

✓ To play a simple game with rules

✓ To improve visual-perceptual skills

MATERIALS:

None

PREPARATION:

None

NURTURING STRATEGIES:

1. If you notice two children performing similar behaviors, which often occurs naturally during play, describe the toddlers' behavior by saying, for example:

   "Kaya and Lisa appear to be playing a game. Whatever Kaya does, Lisa does the same. Kaya is the leader. I wonder what he'll do next."

2. If the toddler is having difficulty imitating the behaviors, assess to decide why. Vary your response accordingly. For example, if the follower is not as physically skilled, encourage the leader to slow down her behavior.

3. If necessary, encourage the toddlers to switch roles.

4. If possible, invite even more toddlers to join the game.

5. Provide positive reinforcement for both the physical skills demonstrated and the social skills it took to accomplish the task.

6. If in an early childhood program, take photographs to document the physical and social skills developed during simple games. Parents/guardians may not be aware of the benefits.

☀ Highlighting Development

Games that involve several children contain rules and are social in nature. Toddlers can typically play simple games that require few rules. They especially enjoy games that allow them to practice newly developed skills such as running and jumping. During the third year of life, toddlers are also able to enjoy simple games because of the emergence of the ability to lead and follow peers (White, 1995). Socially competent toddlers can easily and comfortably assume both roles and, thus, engage in true socializing with peers.

VARIATION:

♡ Have an adult lead the game at first.

ADDITIONAL INFORMATION:

♡ Gradually, as children develop social skills, they become interested in playing games. With toddlers, games usually involve simple turn taking. As children mature, games will become more complex.

Language and Communication Development

$\heartsuit$

THIRTY-ONE to THIRTY-SIX MONTHS

Once There Was a Toddler . . .

Child's Developmental Goals

✓ To increase receptive language skills

✓ To build vocabulary

MATERIALS:

None

PREPARATION:

None

NURTURING STRATEGIES:

1. When a toddler needs a new activity, invite him to listen to a story. To illustrate, say:
   "Ilya, I have a very special story to tell you. Let's sit together on the couch."
2. Get comfortable and snuggle close.
3. Give your stories a ritual beginning and ending. Begin your story by saying, for example:
   "Once there was a toddler . . ."
4. Speak in a natural voice. Trust yourself to use your voice as a tool to add inflection, drama, or suspense as necessary.
5. End your story using your ritual ending. For example, say:
   "And tomorrow will be a new day."

VARIATIONS:

♡ Encourage the toddlers to actively participate in the development of the story by asking questions or giving the children a choice between two outcomes.

♡ Tell a story when a toddler is relaxing for naptime or bedtime.

☀ Highlighting Development

Storytelling is an important activity for stimulating a lifelong love of literature. It supports cognitive development (imagination), language development (receptive language skills), social development (positive interactions with an important other), and emotional development (increases understanding about feelings; Philadelphia Child Guidance Center, 1994). Furthermore, it is good for the adult-child relationship because it allows time to focus exclusively on the child.

ADDITIONAL INFORMATION:

♡ Choosing the right topic for your story is important. Use your knowledge of the child's needs, interests, and abilities. For example, tell stories about your and your toddlers' days, even when you are separated, or about how another child deals with being afraid of the dark.

♡ Choose a good time for storytelling. Avoid telling a story if time is limited or rushed. A good story needs time to develop. Moreover, you want to maintain a positive atmosphere for storytelling.

♡ Adults often avoid storytelling because it makes them nervous. "What if I say a sentence wrong?" or "What if I use a word wrong?" are things they may worry about. Relax. Begin with a simple story about the toddler's day. Trust in your ability to use the right language.

Waking the Animals

Child's Developmental Goals

✓ To verbally label an object

✓ To actively participate in reading a book by identifying symbols

MATERIALS:

❑ Book, *Inside a Barn in the Country,* by Alyssa Satin Capucilli

PREPARATION:

♡ Place the book in library area with other reading materials.

NURTURING STRATEGIES:

1. When a toddler selects the book, allow her time to explore it independently.
2. Offer to read the story with the toddler.
3. Arrange yourself and the toddler so that there is close physical contact (e.g., have the toddler sit on your lap).
4. Read the title, author, and illustrator of the book. Ask the toddler to create a hypothesis about the content of the book, by saying, for example: *"Look at this picture. What do you think this story is about?"*
   Pause. Respond to comment by saying: *"Let's read the book and find out!"*
5. Begin reading the story. Pausing and pointing to the pictures in the text line may encourage the toddler to fill in the appropriate animal name. Also, encourage the child to make the animal sounds at the appropriate times.
6. Provide positive reinforcement either verbally or nonverbally for the toddler's participation when reading the story.

☀ Highlighting Development

Quality children's literature is a necessity for enhancing literacy development. Every toddler classroom and home should contain a library including picture books, predictable books, and big books (Cecil, 1999). Picture books use pictures, illustrations, and text to tell the story. A special type of picture book is the rebus book that provides pictures or symbols within the lines of texts. Young children feel especially empowered because they can read these books at very young ages.

VARIATIONS:

♡ Make available other rebus books for the toddlers to read independently.

♡ Read the story to a small group of toddlers, if possible.

ADDITIONAL INFORMATION:

♡ Utilize your local library as a resource. Librarians are knowledgeable professionals who can assist with selecting or suggesting books that reflect the children's needs and interests. See also Appendix B.

♡ Select the books based on your knowledge of the toddlers' interests and experiential backgrounds. Toddlers enjoy repetition and typically like to read favorite stories over and over again. Some books quickly become favorites. When you observe this, make sure they are available for a sustained period of time (days, weeks, and months, if necessary).

Finger Puppets

Child's Developmental Goals

✓ To practice using private speech to guide behavior
✓ To practice expressive language skills

MATERIALS:

❑ 2 commercially produced finger puppets for each toddler or adult-size, white cloth work gloves and markers
❑ Basket of plastic cars or wooden blocks

PREPARATION:

♡ If necessary, cut the fingers off of the glove and draw a face on each of the tips using a permanent, felt-tip marker.
♡ Place the finger puppets and basket of toys where they are easily accessible for the toddlers.

NURTURING STRATEGIES:

1. When a toddler selects the puppets or basket of toys, observe the child's behavior. Note how the toddler is using the materials and if he is using private speech.
2. Using the information gathered in Step 1 to direct your behavior, join the toddler with the materials.
3. Model private speech by describing what you are doing. For example, while placing the finger puppets on your fingers, say:
   "It is tough to get these on. I have to pull with my finger and thumb. There, I did it."
4. Have the finger puppets play with toys from the basket. After a few minutes, create a problem for them to solve. For example, have one puppet say to the other:
   "I was using that. Give it back."
   Then model a positive way for solving the problem.
5. Return to observing the toddler. Ask yourself if the toddler's behavior has changed and, if so, how.
6. Record your observations on an anecdotal record form.

Highlighting Development

According to Vygotsky, private speech serves an important developmental function: self-regulation of behavior. Private speech is the process of individuals speaking to themselves when problem solving. Gradually this process will become internalized as a means to help guide thinking. Adults can assist young children in problem solving by supplying the necessary vocabulary, phrases, and strategies that children can use during private speech. For example, you can help a child with matching markers with caps by saying "blue marker, blue cap, push together and snap." Later when the child is working independently to clean up the markers, do not be surprised to hear him echo your words.

VARIATION:

♡ Provide people puppets that cover the entire hand. Encourage the toddlers to involve the puppets in their make-believe play.

ADDITIONAL INFORMATION:

♡ Toddlers at this stage of development should easily be able to place a finger puppet on one finger. Once the puppet is placed on a pointer finger, it may be more challenging to put on the second puppet, as they are unable to use this finger. Consequently, you may have to help with this process.
♡ The word *puppet* comes from the Latin word that means "doll". Puppets are wonderful tools for toddlers. Listen. Puppets often encourage quiet children to talk. Through playing with puppets young children openly express their emotions. The puppets allow them to do or say things that they typically would not.

31 to 36 months

Singing "B-I-N-G-O"

Child's Developmental Goals

✓ To hear phonemes

✓ To practice expressive language skills

MATERIALS:

❑ Cardboard book, *Bingo,* by Rosemary Wells

PREPARATION:

None

NURTURING STRATEGIES:

1. Gather a small group of toddlers in a comfortable location.
2. Introduce the book to the children by showing the cover and reading the title and author's name. Encourage the toddlers to comment on what they think the book is about.
3. Read the story slowly while showing the illustrations.
4. The last page of text provides additional ways for singing the song (Ringo, Singo, etc.). Encourage the toddlers to sing along with you. Try the verses suggested by the author.
5. If the toddlers are interested in singing additional verses, choose different letters of the alphabet and continue!

☀ Highlighting Development

By their third birthdays, toddlers are skilled at using the individual sounds of the language or phonemes because they are fluent listeners and speakers by this age. However, knowledge of phonemes is unconscious. That is, toddlers use the sounds of the language without thinking about each individual phoneme or combination of phonemes to create words. Conscious awareness (or phonemic awareness) is essential in learning how to read and write (McGee and Richgils, 2000).

VARIATION:

♡ Sing the song while transitioning from one location to another.

ADDITIONAL INFORMATION:

♡ Few young children spontaneously acquire phonemic awareness. Adults must plan activities or interactions to their attention to phonemes (Neuman, Copple, & Bredekamp, 2000).

♡ Young children can learn from an environment in which they are surrounded by sounds of their native language. Reading and singing to young children will promote the development of spoken language. Through reading aloud, children also learn the connection between the spoken and written language.

Our Favorite Songs Book

Child's Developmental Goals

✓ To read illustrations in a book

✓ To sing a song

MATERIALS:

❑ Three-ring binder

❑ Plastic sleeves to hold the paper

❑ 8½ × 11–inch colored paper (typing or copier)

❑ Marker

PREPARATION:

♡ Print the words to a favorite song on each side of the paper. Begin by placing the title of the song at the top of the page. To assist with visual discrimination skills, place a picture that depicts the song beside the title.

♡ Place one piece of paper in each plastic sleeve and then place the sleeve in a three-ring binder.

♡ Decorate the front of the binder and title it "Our Favorite Songs." Display the book where it will attract the toddlers' attention.

NURTURING STRATEGIES:

1. When a toddler selects the book, observe her behavior.

2. If possible, make eye contact with the toddler and invite yourself to read the book by saying: *"Vina, may I read this book with you?"*

3. If the toddler indicates "no," either verbally or nonverbally, respect the child's desire. Then say: *"Maybe I can read it when you're finished."*

4. If the child says "yes" or indicates her approval through body language, say: *"Great! I've been waiting all morning to read this book."*

5. Make sure everyone is comfortable and snuggling close, if desired.

6. Read the title of the book and then encourage the toddler to read the book to you. For example, have her turn the pages and tell you about each song. Encourage her to "read" the pictures beside the title.

7. If necessary, provide hints about the song. Hints can be verbal or a quick humming of the tune.

8. Of course, sing the songs with great enthusiasm!

9. Discuss which song is the toddler's favorite and why.

☀ Highlighting Development

To become proficient at almost any skill, young children need multiple opportunities to practice. It is no different with early literacy skills. Toddlers need to listen, speak, read, and write in meaningful ways.

VARIATIONS:

♡ Instead of you picking the toddlers' favorite songs, have them choose. You will probably be surprised at the variety of songs they know and like.

♡ Make a "My Favorite Songs" book for each toddler. Encourage them to read each other's books and compare/contrast songs.

ADDITIONAL INFORMATION:

♡ With experience and maturity, toddlers' use and understanding of language becomes increasingly more sophisticated. Listen. Many now are using three or more words in their sentences. To convey meaning, their sentences are in an agent-action-recipient order (e.g., "I kiss Momma").

Retelling the Story: Goodnight Moon

Child's Developmental Goals

✓ To demonstrate auditory memory skills by retelling a story

✓ To continue developing expressive language skills

MATERIALS:

❏ Board book, *Goodnight Moon,* by Margaret Wise Brown

PREPARATION:

♡ Display the book so that it will attract the toddlers' attention.

NURTURING STRATEGIES:

1. When a toddler selects the book, observe the child's behavior.
2. Ask the toddler if he will read the book to you. If he appears hesitant, you could offer to read the story to him first. If that is the case, read the story following strategies outlined in Appendix A.
3. Pay close attention to the toddler's book-handling skills. Observe if the child is holding the book right side up, turning pages in the correct directions and one-by-one, and reading the pictures. Furthermore, note the child's knowledge of the text. For example, does he mention key components of the story, such as the moon, brush, or kittens?
4. Provide responses to the toddler's questions (or raised intonation) or comments when the toddler pauses. He is inviting you to participate in the experience just as you have done with him.
5. Thank the child for reading to you and provide positive reinforcement. Use comments such as: *"Wow, Josh, you read every page of the book. You are an excellent reader."* *"Thanks for reading to me."*
6. Record your anecdotal record of the toddler as soon as possible to minimize forgotten details.

☀ Highlighting Development

By the end of their third year of life, most toddlers use adverbs and adjectives frequently (approximately 17 percent of the time) during free speech (Charlesworth, 2000). They will naturally include in conversations words such as *small, large, happy, sad, hot, cold, soft, hard, fast,* and *slow.*

VARIATIONS:

♡ Provide props or a flannel board for retelling the story.

♡ Tell the story and encourage the child to listen and place the props on the flannel board in the sequence the story is told.

ADDITIONAL INFORMATION:

♡ Having children retell stories can be a way to assess their understanding (factual and comprehensive) of the text. It also helps you to assess their auditory memory skills and level of spoken language competence (McGee & Richgils, 2000). Children should have numerous opportunities to have the story read to them before being asked to retell it.

♡ Introduce a few new books every week, but be sure favorites are available to be read over and over again.

♡ Note that children at this stage of development talk about the characters and events in the storybooks and may relate them to their own experiences.

Lunch Count

Child's Developmental Goals

✓ To increase expressive language skills

✓ To connect a written label with a photograph

MATERIALS:

❑ Photograph of each toddler

❑ Velcro, cut in 1-inch pieces

❑ Sentence strip

❑ Poster board

❑ Lunch count form

PREPARATION:

♡ Mount each photograph on the poster board and label with the name of the classroom.

♡ Adhere one side of the Velcro to the poster board under each picture.

♡ Print each toddler's name on a piece of sentence strip. Then, adhere the other side of the Velcro to the back of each sentence strip.

♡ Display the poster board where it is easily accessible, such as on a low bulletin board.

♡ Put the sentence strips on a low shelf near the poster board.

NURTURING STRATEGIES:

1. Greet each child by squatting to the child's eye-level, saying the child's name, and then "hello," "good morning," or "I'm happy to see you today."

2. Assist the toddler with finding the sentence strip with her name on it. Discuss, for example, beginning sounds and letters.

3. Have the toddler place her sentence strip on the poster board, under her picture. Repeat this process for every child who is in your classroom.

4. After arrival time is complete, place any unclaimed sentence strips near the poster, but not on it.

5. During your morning meeting time, refer to the poster board and discuss who is present and who is absent. Assist the toddlers with counting each group. Then, record this information on the lunch count form so the kitchen staff will know how much food to provide at snacks and lunch.

6. Provide positive reinforcement for assisting with providing an accurate lunch count to the kitchen staff and for working together to accomplish a daily chore.

☀ Highlighting Development

Toddlers need an environment containing a variety of interesting materials that promote thinking, talking, drawing, reading, and writing. Furthermore, they need many opportunities to interact, talk, read, draw, and write with other children and adults. To produce the best outcomes, these opportunities must focus on meaningful topics that are worth knowing. In this activity, the goals focus on the promotion of language skills. The activity also focuses on creating a caring community of learners because children are assisting with a meaningful task and learning each other's names.

VARIATION:

♡ Match names and photographs as a class during circle or larger group time.

ADDITIONAL INFORMATION:

♡ Learning to read follows a developmental sequence. One of the first pre-reading tasks children need to learn is that symbols have meaning and make up words, such as their names. As a result, it is important that adults call attention to the printed word and provide a print-rich environment. Include the children's names to identify belongings, cubbies, and artwork. For many children, their first name is the first word they can "read."

I'm the . . . and You're the . . .

Child's Developmental Goals

✓ To communicate with another child

✓ To use expressive language skills to coordinate behaviors

MATERIALS:

❑ Props needed for dramatic play

PREPARATION:

♡ Display all materials in an attractive and inviting manner.

♡ Organize the props by function or purpose to assist the toddlers with cleaning up once finished.

NURTURING STRATEGIES:

1. If one toddler is in the dramatic play area, observe his behavior. Note how the toddler is using the materials.

2. Use this information to invite another toddler to play. Say, for example:
   "Kilian, would you like to help Nyle on his ranch? He needs some help feeding all of the horses."

3. Repeat the toddler's response. If he does not want to join the play, you can provide the needed assistance.

4. Follow the toddler's lead. Your presence in the area may encourage other toddlers to join the area. When this happens remove yourself from the play as soon as possible.

5. Remain in the area to provide guidance and assistance. For example, help the toddlers negotiate roles and responsibilities.

6. Assist also with maintaining the cleanliness of the area to protect the toddlers' safety and to invite new children to the area.

☀ Highlighting Development

Socio-dramatic play typically emerges around 30 months of age. During this type of play, older toddlers combine several complex schema and coordinate their behavior with peers (Berk, 1999). For example, a toddler cares for a baby while shopping in a shoe store. He then asks the salesperson for assistance with finding shoes and paying for the purchase. Toddlers need to be able to clearly articulate their wants, needs, or desires to another person to keep the play episode moving along.

VARIATION:

♡ To increase the challenge, begin to add props that are less realistic. The toddlers will use their imaginations and find uses for them.

ADDITIONAL INFORMATION:

♡ Adults learn to support and guide toddlers as they are learning to coordinate play with peers. Providing appropriate space, materials, and time for dramatic play, both indoors and out, are ways to show children you value this type of play. When guiding play, refrain from dominating or taking over. Rather, expand on the toddlers' behavior by making suggestions, modeling new behaviors, or asking open-ended questions (Miller, 1984). Adults can also help children substitute one object for another. In their play, children at this stage of development can substitute one object, but not two (Kostelnik, et al., 2002).

I'm a Little Teapot

Child's Developmental Goals

✓ To improve receptive language skills

✓ To demonstrate expressive language skills

MATERIALS:

❑ Book, *I'm a Little Teapot,* by Iza Trapani

PREPARATION:

♡ Place the book in an easily accessible location.

NURTURING STRATEGIES:

1. Signal that it is time to clean up the toys by singing a clean-up song. See Appendix G for a list of songs.
2. Model being a responsible member of the community of learners by assisting the toddlers with picking up toys.
3. Gather the children in a group and begin singing the song "I'm a Little Teapot" (see p. 478).
4. Show the cover of the book to the children. Ask them what they think the story will be about.
5. Read/sing the story. Encourage the toddlers to interact with the book by pausing for them to fill in words or by asking questions.
6. Review the story. Start the conversation by asking or stating, for example:
   "What was your favorite part of the story? Tell me about the places the teapot visited."
7. Encourage those who want to hear the story to remain while those not interested can choose something else.

☀ Highlighting Development

Receptive language develops ahead of expressive language even at this stage. By three years of age, children understand approximately 70 percent of the language that they will use in typical conversations throughout their lifetime (White, 1995). Typically, two-year-olds produce around 200 different words. By age six, they possess a vocabulary of around 10,000 words. A child must learn, on average, 5 new words a day to accomplish this (Berk, 1999).

VARIATION:

♡ Read the book, *The Itsy Bitsy Spider,* by Iza Trapani.

ADDITIONAL INFORMATION:

♡ Read/sing the book slowly, allowing the toddlers plenty of time to view the illustrations. They are fabulous!

♡ By this stage of development, children have learned to use language for many purposes. They learn language to tell about the past, solve problems, ask questions, direct the behavior of others, and protect their rights. Children at this age will elaborate on their ideas without being asked.

Name That Tune

Child's Developmental Goals

✓ To improve auditory discrimination skills

MATERIALS:

None

PREPARATION:

None

NURTURING STRATEGIES:

1. When transitioning the toddlers from one location to another, introduce the game by saying, for example: "Listen to this song. Can you guess its name?"
2. Hum or whistle the song.
3. If a child makes a guess, provide positive reinforcement. Say, for example:
   "What a good guess! You are really thinking about songs you know."
4. If necessary, hum or whistle the tune again.
5. When a toddler guesses the song, begin singing it. Encourage the toddlers to sing along with you.
6. If time permits, hum or whistle another song.

☼ Highlighting Development

During the first year of life, infants begin to analyze the internal structure of sentences and words (Berk, 1999). They focus on larger speech units to make sense of what they hear. Gradually, toddlers recognize familiar words when spoken. At this stage of development, they have yet to differentiate each individual sound in their native language. However, involvement with activities that promote auditory discrimination will gradually result in that ability.

VARIATION:

♡ If you play a musical instrument, use it to play the song.

ADDITIONAL INFORMATION:

♡ Choose songs that are very familiar to the toddlers. You want them to remain engaged in the activity while transitioning. Transitions can be very stressful for children and adults alike. Plan for them! Chant nursery rhymes or sing songs (see Appendices F and G) to further develop language skills.

Cognitive Development

♡

THIRTY-ONE to THIRTY-SIX MONTHS

A Balancing Act

Child's Developmental Goals

✓ To develop an understanding of the concepts heavy and light

✓ To practice balancing a scale

MATERIALS:

❑ Coat hanger
❑ Scissors
❑ String
❑ Objects to wiggle in baskets
❑ Hook
❑ 2 containers of identical size and weight

PREPARATION:

♡ Punch three holes in each of the containers at equal distance.
♡ Tie string through each hole and then secure the string to the clothes hanger to create the balance.
♡ Secure the hook slightly above the children's eye level and hang the balance in the hook.
♡ Place the container of objects near the balance.

NURTURING STRATEGIES:

1. When a toddler selects the activity, move closer and observe her behavior.
2. Ask questions to obtain an understanding of the child's knowledge base and thinking about the balance. Say, for example:
   "What are the containers for?"
   "What happens when you put the shoe in one container?"
3. Encourage the toddler to experiment with the balance.
4. Describe the results of the toddler's actions. Be sure to use the words *heavy* and *light* to assist the toddler in understanding these concepts. Comment, for example:
   "Amera, the mitten and spool are still lighter than the shoe. The shoe is very heavy."

5. Show your excitement both verbally and nonverbally when the toddler balances the scale. While smiling and clapping, say, for example:
   "You did it! It took lots of patience, but you balanced the weight of the shoe."
   "What a hard worker! You balanced the scale. The mitten weighs as much as three playing cards."

☀ Highlighting Development

According to information processing theory, cognitive growth is characterized by increasing ability to take in, store, use, and retrieve information. From infancy on, young children change in their abilities to organize and manipulate information by becoming more sophisticated in processing information (see, for example, Feldman, 2000). Mere exposure to information will not guarantee that it will be stored or retrieved. Young children often organize information in categories called concepts to help them with processing information and understanding their world. Concepts allow for the meaningful grouping of objects, events, or people that share common properties.

VARIATIONS:

♡ Use a commercial balance scale that can be placed on a child–size table.
♡ Have the toddlers select objects from the environment that are heavier or lighter.

ADDITIONAL INFORMATION:

♡ Understanding concepts such as heavy, light, big, and little occurs through play. Toddlers must be provided repeated opportunities to explore and experiment with a variety of objects in order to construct such knowledge.

Making Fruit Parfaits

Child's Developmental Goals

✓ To practice sequencing by following simple directions

✓ To practice "reading" the recipe board to develop left-to-right progression skills

✓ To associate spoken and written language

MATERIALS:

❑ Fruit such as strawberries, apples, blueberries, and bananas
❑ 4 ounces (half container) of vanilla yogurt for each toddler
❑ Poster board
❑ Marker
❑ Damp sponge
❑ Bowls
❑ Plastic parfait cups
❑ Plastic knife
❑ Napkins
❑ Spoons
❑ Tray

PREPARATION:

♡ Make and display recipe board using words and pictures/drawings.
♡ Wash your hands and prepare fruit by washing, hulling, peeling, and coring as necessary.
♡ Place each fruit in a separate bowl.
♡ Place all ingredients and tools on a tray.
♡ Clean and sanitize a child-size table or coffee table, then place the tray there.

NURTURING STRATEGIES:

1. Instruct the toddlers to wash their hands before the activity. Provide assistance as necessary.
2. Introduce the activity by enacting prior knowledge. To illustrate, say:
   "Does anyone remember what we had for breakfast yesterday?" [Pause.] *"That's right. We had a bagel and strawberry yogurt. Today, we are going to make a special treat with fruit and yogurt. Let's read the recipe board to see what we need."*
3. While reading the recipe board, point to the illustrations and to the real items to assist the toddlers with connecting words with objects.
4. Encourage each toddler to take a piece of fruit and cut it into smaller pieces to better fit in the parfait cup. Engage in meaningful conversation about the toddler's work.

5. Model the desired behaviors by preparing your own snack.
6. Refer to the recipe board as needed throughout the activity. Encourage the toddler to "read" it to you.
7. Enjoy eating this refreshing snack!

Highlighting Development

Toddlers often have to be reminded of rules or directions over and over again. According to information processing theory, this is because young children do not employ memory, associations, or other strategies to process information (Puckett & Black, 2001). To illustrate, they may not store the information for later retrieval or have a way for retrieving previously stored information. Consequently, they actually do not know the rules. Refer also to the "Making Rules" activity (p. 443).

VARIATIONS:

♡ Mix vanilla yogurt with fresh, squeezed orange juice and dip various types of fruit in it.
♡ Encourage the toddlers to try the yogurt. If they do not care for it, allow them to make the parfait without it.

ADDITIONAL INFORMATION:

♡ Some children will not like the taste of the vanilla yogurt or will prefer one fruit over the other. Encourage them to try everything but do not force them to eat. Allow them to provide suggestions for modifying the recipe to reflect their food preferences.
♡ First cooking experiences should revolve around simple recipes that can be served at snack time.

 For safety purposes, when using electric appliances, exercise extreme caution and continually supervise the activity.

 Carefully supervise the toddlers' use of the knives. Even plastic knives can cut if used improperly.

Shadow Fun

Child's Developmental Goals

✓ To investigate shadows

✓ To discuss shadows

MATERIALS:

❑ Thick, outdoor chalk—at least two different colors

PREPARATION:

♡ Select a sunny day to encourage this discussion.
♡ Place the chalk where it is easily accessible.

NURTURING STRATEGIES:

1. Introduce this experience to a toddler who has demonstrated an interest in shadows in the past or is doing so right now. To illustrate, in an excited voice say:
   "Hey, Seth, what is that following you on the ground?"
2. Discuss how the shadow moves. Encourage the toddler to locate the body parts of the shadow and attempt to move them. This helps them to begin connecting an object to a shadow.
3. Initiate a conversational topic about the different sizes of shadows. For example, compare your shadow to that of the toddler's. If available, compare another toddler's shadows. Using such words as *big, bigger,* or *biggest,* as appropriate, may assist with understanding this concept.
4. Encourage the toddler to think about shadows he has viewed in the past. How do they compare?
5. If possible, return to this conversation at a later time during the same day. Trace the toddler's shadow, using one color chalk.

6. Use the second color of chalk to trace the shadows again. Discuss how they have changed. Encourage the toddler to think about why they might by different.

☀ Highlighting Development

Toddlers are very aware of their surroundings. They notice things that we usually overlook. Shadows are intriguing and garner much attention and thought. Like other learning, toddlers must be actively engaged in conversations and exploration to gain a better understanding of shadows. Furthermore, toddlers begin their exploration by using their own bodies as tools for producing shadows.

VARIATIONS:

♡ Introduce objects that can be used for making shadows, such as a small plastic animal or a stick puppet.
♡ Provide a moveable light source such as a flashlight.

ADDITIONAL INFORMATION:

♡ Avoid trying to "teach" toddlers about shadows. The concepts behind shadows are complicated and will take many years to develop. Moreover, several variables need to be considered at one time. Instead, ask many open-ended questions that encourage the toddlers to explore further.
♡ Avoid doing this experience around noon, when the sun will be directly overhead because the shadows will be too small.

Today I'm Going to . . .

Child's Developmental Goals

✓ To create a plan for the day

✓ To select from a number of options

✓ To review the choice at a later time

MATERIALS:

❑ Photographs of favorite activities

❑ White construction paper

❑ Marker

❑ Glue

PREPARATION:

♡ Cut the construction paper about 1 inch larger than the photographs.

♡ Mount the pictures in the construction paper.

♡ Label each photograph with a short phrase, such as "riding my tricycle" or "building with blocks."

NURTURING STRATEGIES:

1. When it is time to begin the day, show the toddler the photographs. Begin by discussing each photograph and encouraging the toddler to describe what she sees. Point to the photograph to highlight the connection between the spoken and written language.

2. Ask the toddler to look at the pictures and select how she would like to begin her day. Say, for example: *"Mieko, look at the pictures. Pick the activity you'd like to do first today."*

3. Discuss the toddler's selection. Ask, for example: *"What do we need to do so you can ride your tricycle?"*

4. Set up the experience, as necessary, and enjoy it!

5. At a later time, such as lunch, ask the toddler about what she did on her tricycle.

☀ Highlighting Development

Language and cognitive development are intertwined. "As the toddler learns more language, there is more material to process when thinking, and as thought capabilities become more complex, language can be used in more complex ways" (Charlesworth, 2000, p. 298).

VARIATIONS:

♡ Have the toddler select her three favorite activities.

♡ Have the toddler sequence the things she did from the beginning until the end of the day.

ADDITIONAL INFORMATION:

♡ Only provide photographs that are options for the day. If, for example, it is raining, remove outdoor experiences.

♡ Reviewing the event at a later time serves three main functions. First, it promotes visual and auditory memory recall skills. Second, it fosters the development of expressive language skills. Finally, it assists with the development of language concepts, such as past, present, yesterday, today, and first.

Drawing a Flower Arrangement

COGNITIVE

Child's Developmental Goals

✓ To represent ideas using symbols

MATERIALS:
❑ Fine-tip, nontoxic pens
❑ Pencils
❑ White paper
❑ Containers for materials

PREPARATION:
♡ Ensure that all pens and pencils are in working order.
♡ Place all materials neatly in containers for easy access by the children.

NURTURING STRATEGIES:
1. As the child finishes the "Arranging Flowers" activity (see p. 347), suggest that he draw a picture of his arrangement.
2. If necessary, rearrange the sculpture so that it is at eye level in the child's working space.
3. Allow the child time to observe the flower arrangement and select tools.
4. Encourage the child to continue working by commenting on his work. To illustrate, say:
   "Diego, you are drawing the tall stick first."
   "What a detailed evergreen twig. I see lots of points."

☀ Highlighting Development

Drawing skills follow a predictable developmental sequence. First, children engage in random scribbling, that is, relatively uncontrolled movements of arms and shoulders and the resulting patterns on paper. Gradually, the movement becomes more controlled. In the second stage, controlled scribbling, children label their work (Charlesworth, 2000). For example, after finishing they may say, "It's a crocodile."

VARIATION:
♡ Provide real flowers in vases for the children to observe and draw or paint.

ADDITIONAL INFORMATION:
♡ Study the movements of a two-year-old using a drawing tool. They are large, muscular, and random. At this stage, the child enjoys the feeling of a marking tool in his hand. Children are universally similar in their artistic development. They begin with basic strokes such as circles, horizontal lines, and vertical lines. Gradually, using these basic forms they will be able to draw a person with three parts.

Move Like a . . .

Child's Developmental Goals

✓ To enhance mental representation skills

✓ To improve creativity

MATERIALS:

❑ Pictures of animals

PREPARATION:

♡ Clear a large area, preferably carpeted, of obstacles.
♡ Place pictures so they are easily accessible.

NURTURING STRATEGIES:

1. Gather the toddlers in the cleared space and introduce the activity. To begin, say:
   "We are going to move like animals today. I thought we'd do this because I noticed yesterday that Tyrienne was crawling on her belly. Do you know of any animals that crawl on their bellies?"

2. Discuss answers, allowing many to be correct. Remember that most any animal can drag its belly on the ground. However, introducing the idea of "most of the time" or "once in a while" might help the toddlers to distinguish the animals' movement patterns.

3. Set positive limits on behavior. State, for example:
   "In order to keep everyone safe, I need you to try very hard to remember to watch where you are going. This will help keep you and your friends safe."

4. Then, hold up the first picture of an animal. Have the toddlers label it and describe how it moves. Ask the toddlers to move their bodies in that way.

5. Move like the animal in the picture for a minute or so, then show another picture. Announce the change by saying:
   "Now, let's move like a penguin."
   Pause to encourage the toddlers to label the animal. Then, just begin moving. Trying to have a discussion at this point would probably be impossible because the toddlers are excited.

6. Repeat step 5 for each picture. Judge the number of pictures to show based on your observations of the toddlers.

7. End the activity by showing an animal that moves very slowly, such as a turtle or snail, to assist the toddlers with calming down for the next event of the day.

☀ Highlighting Development

Engaging in make-believe play not only requires certain developmental skills, such as the ability to represent objects, thoughts and actions symbolically, it also contributes to the development of cognitive, language, and social skills. Thus, adults should take particular steps to support make-believe play. Some suggestions include providing space, materials, and time for play, supporting play themes without controlling them, and providing many real-word experiences to inspire play (Berk, 1999).

VARIATIONS:

♡ Use a commercially produced song on a cassette or compact disc.
♡ Encourage the toddlers to move like a particular animal when moving from one location to another during transitions.

ADDITIONAL INFORMATION:

♡ To incorporate literacy, chart the toddlers' answers to your questions about types of movements.
♡ Creative movement, like that fostered in this activity, is a special type of make-believe play. The toddlers must pretend to be a particular animal and move in a way consistent with it. In this way, creative movement enriches intellectual development (Hughes, 1999).

Mirror, Mirror

Child's Developmental Goals

✓ To exercise visual–perceptual skills

MATERIALS:

❑ 2 nonbreakable, handheld mirrors

PREPARATION:

♡ If necessary, clean the mirrors before placing them in a convenient location.

NURTURING STRATEGIES:

1. Introduce this experience to a toddler when he lacks involvement with other activities. To illustrate, say:
   "I have two mirrors. Let's each look into one and talk about what we can see."
2. Ask the toddler to describe what he sees in the mirror.
3. Model looking beyond your own reflection to see objects or people in the background. Comment, for example:
   "Above my head I can see a flower pot."
4. Introduce the following rhyme:

   Mirror, mirror in my hand
   Find the clock
   So I can stand.

5. Encourage the toddler to use the mirror to find the object spoken of in the rhyme. Say, for example:
   "Franklin, see how I'm using the mirror? Look in the mirror to see the reflection of the clock."
6. Continue the activity as long as the toddler demonstrates interest.

☀ Highlighting Development

Infants are not born with the ability to see objects at the same distance or with the same acuity as adults. Visual acuity improves steadily throughout the first year of life. Once infants have near-adult capabilities, they must begin differentiating and categorizing what they are viewing to make sense of their world (Berk, 1999). Infants and toddlers must make finer and finer distinctions among stimuli. Visual-perceptual skills continue to improve over many years. These skills are necessary for recognizing and discriminating particular letters in order to successfully read and write in early elementary school.

VARIATION:

♡ Allow the toddler to lead the game by selecting items for you to locate with the mirror.

ADDITIONAL INFORMATION:

♡ This activity is best introduced to toddlers on a one-on-one basis.

♡ Select items to find and view with care. Begin with large items and gradually decrease in size. Also, begin with items easily viewed from the child's position. The toddler may lose interest if he has to continually reorient his body.

Moving Fast . . . Moving Slow

Child's Developmental Goals

✓ To create or modify a schema

MATERIALS:

❏ Drum

PREPARATION:

♡ Clear a large area, preferably carpeted, for this experience.

NURTURING STRATEGIES:

1. Stand in the cleared area. Gather the toddlers there by slowly and softly playing the drum. When a toddler joins you, avoid talking. Rather, begin moving your body to the music.
2. Whisper any directions to the toddlers. Say, softly, for example:
   "How else can we move our bodies to this music?"
3. Follow the toddlers' suggestions. If you are not sure what the toddler is suggesting, encourage the child to model for everyone.
4. Change the tempo to fast. Alter your behavior to better fit the music. Again, ask the toddlers for suggestions.
5. Alternate the tempo of the music between slow and fast.
6. Ending with a slow tempo will help the toddlers calm down after this activity.
7. Conclude the experience by briefly discussing the concepts of fast and slow. Encourage the toddlers to relate these terms to their previous actions.

☀ Highlighting Development

Toddlers still use the processes of assimilation and accommodation to modify their schemas. You might recall that a schema is an organized way of making sense of an experience. Sometimes, new information can be added to an existing schema (assimilation), whereas at other times schemas have to be adjusted or even created (accommodation) to understand it. Both of these processes require active, thoughtful exploration on the part of a child. Merely telling a child about a new concept is not enough. Toddlers often have to experience things to understand them.

VARIATION:

♡ Make your own or use a commercially prepared tape or compact disc instead of playing the drum.

ADDITIONAL INFORMATION:

♡ Physical movement and dancing activities are wonderful ways to foster the development of concepts such as fast, slow, loud, and soft, as well as spatial relationships. According to White (1995), well-developed toddlers can engage in elaborate, imaginative play, both alone and with others. Furthermore, through these experiences children can explore their bodies as they move.

Where Do I Belong?

Child's Developmental Goals

✓ To improve understanding of spatial symbols

✓ To match a part to a whole

MATERIALS:

❏ 2 sets of photographs of simple objects found in a house or classroom setting

❏ Photo album (commercially produced or homemade)

❏ Tape

❏ Resealable plastic bag

❏ Scissors

PREPARATION:

♡ Place one set of photographs in a photo album, making sure to place one photograph on each page.

♡ Cut one object from each photograph in the remaining set. The goal is for the toddler to match this object with the photograph containing it. Select the object to match carefully (see Additional Information).

♡ Tape the plastic bag to the last page or inside the back cover of the album. The bag will hold the matching objects when not in use.

♡ Place the photo album where it is easily accessible.

NURTURING STRATEGIES:

1. When a toddler selects the photo album, observe her behavior. If you notice a toddler needing a new activity, draw attention to the album.

2. If necessary, explain what the photo album is.

3. Engage the toddler in meaningful conversation about the photographs. Encourage the toddler to label and describe objects in the photographs. Ask open-ended questions such as:
   "What is your favorite thing to do in your bedroom?"
   "Leilani, what do you do with the letters on your refrigerator?"

4. Discuss the photographs at the toddler's pace. Stop and linger or skip pages depending on the toddler's interest level.

5. When the toddler discovers the plastic bag, encourage her to remove the objects from the bag.

6. Talk about the pictures. Draw her attention to the fact that you just saw these objects in other pictures.

7. Encourage the toddler to find the picture with the rocking chair in it. If necessary, suggest looking at the photographs in the picture album again.

8. Continue to match the objects to the photographs as long as the toddler is interested.

9. Encourage her to return the objects to the plastic bag before finding something else to do.

☀ Highlighting Development

Within each stage of development, there are new abilities and limitations. According to Piaget (1952), once in the preoperational stage of cognitive development, toddlers are able to solve problems by first thinking them through. Furthermore, they are able to extensively use symbolic representations. They also improve in their ability to understand spatial symbols such as photographs or simple maps. One limitation to preoperational thinking is called centration. This involves the child centering on one aspect of a problem and ignoring other relevant details.

VARIATIONS:

♡ Match photographs or pictures with real items.

♡ Encourage the toddlers to make maps or verbally describe their homes.

ADDITIONAL INFORMATION:

♡ In the beginning, select items for matching that are in the immediate environment. Gradually increase the challenge by selecting more difficult items. The toddler will have to use visual discrimination skills to find the exact match.

Planting and Tending a Garden

Child's Developmental Goals

✓ To begin to understand transformations
✓ To follow simple directions

MATERIALS:

❑ Flower bed or garden
❑ Handheld tools such as hoe, trowel, and rake
❑ Plants or seeds
❑ Watering can

PREPARATION:

♡ Clear the flowerbed or garden to get it ready for planting.
♡ Fill the watering can. Make sure the toddler is able to lift it.
♡ Gather the rest of the tools and items to be planted and place near the flowerbed or garden.

NURTURING STRATEGIES:

1. Before taking the toddler(s) outside, explain that you have a surprise. Using your voice as a tool to communicate enthusiasm, say:
   "I have a surprise! Do you remember what you had in your cereal for breakfast?"
   Pause to encourage answering.
   "It was strawberries. Because we love strawberries, I bought some strawberry plants. We can grow our own strawberries in the garden. Let's go read the directions on how to plant them."
2. Walk with the toddlers to the garden area. Read the directions to the toddlers and discuss the steps in planting the strawberry plants.
3. Assist the toddlers with completing the steps one at a time. However, if more than one toddler is present, encourage each toddler to move at his or her own pace. Avoid trying to have everyone do the same thing at the same time.
4. Provide positive reinforcement for following directions and/or behaving in a helpful manner.
   "Pierre, thank you for handing me the trowel. I needed it for digging a hole."
   "You remembered to pack down the dirt before watering the strawberry plant. Good memory."

5. Over the next weeks and months, periodically direct the toddlers' attention to the strawberry plants. Help them tend to the plants by pulling weeds or providing water, as necessary. Discuss how the plants are growing and changing.

☼ Highlighting Development

Preoperational children often have difficulty understanding transformations. They tend to treat the initial and final states as unrelated events; thus, ignoring the step or steps that occurred between them. For example, masks at Halloween often scare older toddlers. Watching a family member or friend put on the mask does not seem to help reduce the fear. They focus on the familiar face of the person and then the mask. They ignore, or are unable to use, their knowledge of the person under the mask.

VARIATIONS:

♡ Plant bulbs instead of plants or seeds.
♡ Plant a tree to celebrate a special occasion. Create a photo album of the toddlers. Find pictures of them at different ages. Discuss how the toddlers have changed.

ADDITIONAL INFORMATION:

♡ This experience will continue over many days, weeks, and months. Help the toddlers to recognize the change, or transformations, occurring in the seeds/plants by sketching or measuring them on a regular basis, such as once a week. If you measure the plants, display the results on a chart or graph.
♡ The planting activity may turn into a sensory experience. Set aside a special area for this in the beginning.
♡ This experience is probably best done one-on-one or in a small group. The toddlers will need assistance with following the steps in planting the seeds or plants. Moreover, make sure each toddler has the opportunity to plant several different plants.

CAUTION Before planting trees, shrubs, or flowers carefully research the varieties to make sure that they are nonpoisonous.

31 to 36 months

Social Development

♡

THIRTY-ONE to THIRTY-SIX MONTHS

Making Cards

SOCIAL

Child's Developmental Goals

✓ To develop an interest in the written form of communication

MATERIALS:

❑ Construction paper, folded in half
❑ Felt-tip, nontoxic, washable markers (fat and thin)
❑ Envelopes
❑ Container for writing tools

PREPARATION:

♡ Place all materials so they are attractive and easily accessible to the toddlers.

NURTURING STRATEGIES:

1. When a toddler selects the materials, observe. Ask yourself questions, such as:
   "Are tools being used? If so, how?"
   "What is the child writing about?"
   "Does the work seem to be for anyone else?"
2. If necessary, move closer to the child as she is working.
3. Gently begin a conversation by asking questions that reflect your observations. Ask, for example:
   "I see that you've put your paper inside the envelope. Naomi, are you going to give this card to someone special?"
4. Label the paper as a card. Ask the toddler if she has ever received a card before. Discuss the purpose of the card and how she felt about receiving it.
5. If appropriate, discuss a friend or relative who is celebrating a birthday in the near future. Suggest making a card for that person. Record the toddler's words about the card for the recipient.
6. When the card is completed, discuss how the child can get it to the other person. If the toddler does not seem to notice the envelope, direct the child's attention to it.
7. Conclude the experience by either mailing the card or getting it ready for someone else to mail.

☀ Highlighting Development

With exposure to print and written materials, toddlers begin to understand that written language is useful and powerful, and serves many different functions. For example, when eating at a restaurant, toddlers understand that a waitperson writes down something when you order and later produces a bill telling something else. They also learn that written language can create interactions with others. To illustrate, an invitation to a birthday party can result in a social event. Writing a letter or a note can also result in future interactions with the person (see, for example, McGee & Richgils, 2000).

VARIATIONS:

♡ In an early childhood program, encourage the toddlers to write a letter when they are sad that their parents/guardians are away.
♡ Have a toddler or group of toddlers send a thank you card to a visitor or leader of a field trip.

ADDITIONAL INFORMATION:

♡ Printing what a child tells you about her card/ illustrations assists with learning about the functions of written language.
♡ Encourage the toddlers to make a card for someone else. However, some toddlers are not ready for this because they are still working on ownership issues. This is developmentally appropriate.

SOCIAL

It's Mine

Child's Developmental Goals

✓ To discuss a problem and possible solutions

✓ To communicate a want or desire verbally

MATERIALS:

None

PREPARATION:

♡ During playtime, observe the toddlers for signs of conflict.

♡ Move quickly to provide guidance before the toddlers become too emotionally upset.

NURTURING STRATEGIES:

1. When you observe a situation that warrants your attention, move swiftly to the children's level.
2. Neutralize the object and identify the problem from your perspective and ask for confirmation from the toddlers. Say, for example:
   "Anoki and Victor, it looks to me like both of you want the red car. Is this the problem you are trying to solve?"
3. Listen to each toddler describe his version of the problem. To assist with perspective taking, encourage each toddler to listen to the other. Expand on the toddlers' statements, if necessary, to ensure that their needs are clearly defined.
4. Generate solutions to the problem. This step is a "brain-storming" step, so validate all suggestions. If necessary, provide possible solutions to model divergent thinking.
5. Select one solution that both toddlers can agree on.
6. Carry out the solution providing support and assistance, as needed.
7. Have the toddlers evaluate the effectiveness of the solution. If it is not working for one child, return to step 5 and select another solution.

☀ Highlighting Development

Researchers have studied children's abilities to solve problems with one solution (convergent problem solving) and with multiple solutions (divergent problem solving) (see Hughes, 1999). Young children who have many experiences with open-ended materials, such as blocks, sand, and dramatic play props, are more original and flexible in their problem-solving approaches when faced with both convergent and divergent problems (see Hughes, 1999, for a review of the literature). Thus, young children need many opportunities to discover that numerous approaches can be applied to any problem and that they have the power to solve problems.

VARIATION:

♡ Have two puppets have a conflict. Invite the toddlers to help them solve the problem.

ADDITIONAL INFORMATION:

♡ Using positive guidance strategies, such as the "no-lose" method of problem solving, assists the toddlers with learning nonviolent ways for resolving conflicts, as well as preserving their dignity (Marion, 1999).

♡ Toddlers are bombarded with messages about how to solve problems. Unfortunately, many of these messages model or discuss the use of violence, force, or other aggressive solutions. Such solutions are damaging to young children's senses of safety and the development of morality and pro-social behaviors.

31 to 36 months

Puppets Talk to Solve a Problem

SOCIAL

Child's Developmental Goals

✓ To solve a problem in a peaceful manner

✓ To increase perspective-taking skills

MATERIALS:

❑ 2 multicultural people puppets

❑ Basket of small toys

❑ 2 empty and sanitized liquid soap containers approximately the same size as the puppets

PREPARATION:

♡ Place the puppets over the top of the sanitized liquid soap containers to display them.

♡ Place the puppets and basket in a convenient location.

NURTURING STRATEGIES:

1. Tell the toddlers that a change in activities is coming by saying, for example:
   "Carmella, in two minutes we are going to clean up. Then we will gather on the rug."

2. After the two minutes have passed, begin singing a clean-up song (see Appendix G). Sing as long as it takes to pick up the toys.

3. Gather your materials and invite the toddlers to sit on the carpet with you.

4. Sing a song to welcome and identify everyone sitting on the carpet.

5. Then, introduce the activity using your voice as a tool to communicate excitement. To illustrate, say:
   "I have invited 2 special people to visit us today. Here come Sonia and Carlos now." Have the puppets greet the children and vice versa.

6. Have the puppets begin to play with the materials in the basket. Using your knowledge of the toddlers, create situations that pose challenges and conflicts. Examples include a block tower falling over because of its structural design; having to share toys, materials, or space; solving problems with violence; and failing to assist with cleanup.

7. Stop the puppets from playing and encourage the toddlers to help them solve the problem.

8. Set a rule that all solutions must be peaceful or nonviolent.

9. If the toddlers seem interested, pose another challenge or problem.

10. Provide positive reinforcement for the content or number of solutions generated.

☀ Highlighting Development

Toddlers tend to display instrumental aggression when a goal is blocked. This type of aggression results from wanting an object, privilege, or space and using aggressive strategies to get it. For example, a child sees another playing with a ball and pushes to gain ownership of the ball. Toddlers may also hit, bite, and shout to acquire a desired outcome. As verbal skills and social skills, such as the ability to compromise and share, increase, acts of instrumental aggression decrease.

VARIATION:

♡ In an early childhood program, make the puppets available for the toddlers' use during free choice time.

ADDITIONAL INFORMATION:

♡ Children who use violent methods of solving problems typically experience a stressful, conflict-ridden family atmosphere (see Berk, 1999). As a result, they lack the ability, when faced with a problem, to generate nonviolent solutions. Furthermore, toddlers in this situation tend to rely on using one or two solutions, regardless of the nature of the problem.

31 to 36 months

SOCIAL

Water Colors

Child's Developmental Goals

✓ To discuss artwork with another

✓ To engage in parallel play

MATERIALS:

☐ Red and blue individual watercolors and tray for each toddler
☐ Watercolor paintbrush for each toddler
☐ Small container for water
☐ Construction paper
☐ Damp sponge

PREPARATION:

♡ Set up workspaces on a child-size table or coffee table by arranging a watercolor tray, brush, water, and piece of paper for each child.

♡ Place a small amount of water on the watercolors so they are ready to use.

NURTURING STRATEGIES:

1. When a child selects the experience, observe his behavior. Note if the child seems to understand how to use this type of paint.

2. Use your observations to guide your behavior. If necessary, ask the toddler questions to guide his discovery of the water. If that does not seem to work, highlight another child's use of the materials. If further assistance is necessary, model the use of the materials while verbally describing your actions.

3. Discuss the process of making a picture. For example, describe the toddler's marks or use of space by saying: *"Radney, you are making red lines. The lines run clear across the page."* *"I see a blue circle in the center of the paper."*

4. When a toddler discovers the color purple, share in his excitement. Ask him how he made the color purple.

5. If more than one toddler is present, encourage the children to converse while working. However, if a toddler prefers to work in silence or concentrate on his work, be respectful of that desire.

6. Encourage the toddler to describe his work when it is finished. Print his name on the top left corner and then record the toddler's exact words.

7. If possible, discuss the similarities and differences between the toddlers' artwork. For example, say: *"Radney used red to make lines. Liang used red and blue."*

8. Save examples of the children's work to place in their portfolios.

☼ Highlighting Development

In *Picturing Learning,* Karen Ernst (1994) describes how art experiences can be used to assist children with making meaning. Ernst goes on to describe the need to include literature as part of artistic experiences, because painting and making pictures are true forms of expression. Through reading picture books, children learn how illustrations and written language work together to tell a story. Moreover, the children can use books to inspire their own work. Although an individual often creates works of art, many can enjoy them. Toddlers should engage in a sharing time in which they describe their work to an audience of peers or significant others. This time of sharing further connects early literacy, self-expression, and meaning making.

VARIATIONS:

♡ Make this activity a two-day experience. On the first day, provide crayons for drawing; on the second, provide watercolors. Encourage the toddlers to discuss how the two mediums work together.

♡ Read a story that is illustrated with watercolors, highlighting and discussing the pictures with the toddlers.

♡ Use one large piece of paper to make a group picture.

ADDITIONAL INFORMATION:

♡ Keep your expectations appropriate for the toddlers. At this stage of development, they are just beginning to label their work when it is complete. Dictating their descriptions about their artwork will assist in promoting the connections described in Highlighting Development.

31 to 36 months

Shape Game

SOCIAL

Child's Developmental Goals

✔ To play a simple game
✔ To share physical space with another child
✔ To recognize basic shapes

MATERIALS:

❑ 8½ × 11–inch sheets of red, green, blue, and yellow construction paper for each pair of toddlers
❑ Transparent, self-adhesive paper
❑ Scissors

PREPARATION:

♡ Cut the largest possible shapes (triangle, circle, and square) from the construction paper. Leave two colors of construction paper whole to represent rectangles. You should end up with two different colors of each shape. Add shapes, as necessary, so that no shape will have to be shared by more than two toddlers. Prepare one extra of each shape to use when introducing the activity.
♡ Cut sheets of transparent, self-adhesive paper that are larger than the shapes.
♡ Clear a large area of obstacles and lay the shapes on the floor about 2 feet apart. Adhere each shape to the floor with the self-adhesive paper.

NURTURING STRATEGIES:

1. Gather the toddlers in the cleared space and introduce the experience. To begin, say:
   "I have a game for us to play. This game involves shapes. Let's review. I'm going to hold up a shape and you can tell me what it is."
2. Hold up each shape, one by one. Label and discuss each shape.
3. Direct the toddlers' attention to the shape on the floor. Tell them they will be finding a shape to stand on during the game. Also, discuss the importance of having to share the shapes with someone else. Converse about safe ways to move and share the shapes.
4. Begin the game by singing:
   Go stand on a circle, on a circle,
   Go stand on a circle, on a circle,
   Go stand on a circle
   Oh, do it just for me
   Go stand on a circle, on a circle.

5. Repeat the song until you have substituted each shape.
6. Provide verbal and physical support, as necessary, for sharing the space.
7. Provide positive reinforcement on the toddlers' ability to share the shapes and/or to play the game. For example, say:
   "What a fun game. Everyone shared the shapes. Everyone kept their bodies safe while standing on the shapes. That made playing this game fun."

☼ Highlighting Development

Once children have acquired a sense of autonomy and feel secure about separating from parents/guardians, they are ready to tackle the next conflict of initiative versus guilt (Erikson, 1950). This transition often occurs around their third birthdays. Children who possess initiative are spiritual, enterprising, and ambitious. They have a sense of purpose and are eager to learn new skills, try new experiences, and join in activities with peers. Children who feel too much guilt are timid and approach the world in an overly fearful manner. Erikson believed that high levels of guilt result from excessive threatening, criticizing, and punishing by adults.

VARIATIONS:

♡ Play the game focusing on colors instead of shapes.
♡ Substitute other actions such as "pat your feet," "touch your elbow," or "pat your knees."

ADDITIONAL INFORMATION:

♡ Toddlers are not emotionally mature enough for games that have a strong acceptance-rejection theme (Philadelphia Child Guidance Center, 1994). Therefore, they should be encouraged to share and cooperate so that all players can stand on the shapes.
♡ Whereas some toddlers will be able to easily recognize the shapes, given their experiential backgrounds, other toddlers will lack this skill. Refrain from overcorrecting or attempting to "teach" shapes to the toddlers; rather, keep the game moving along.

Copy Cat

Child's Developmental Goals

✓ To engage in a social interaction

✓ To perform the role of a leader and the role of a follower

MATERIALS:

None

PREPARATION:

♡ If necessary, write the following words to the chart as an index card:

Copy Cat, Copy Cat
Name of the game
Whatever Jen does,
We'll do the same. (Slap thighs to beat while chanting)

♡ Clear an area, preferably carpeted, of obstacles.

NURTURING STRATEGIES:

1. Gather the toddlers in the cleared area and introduce the game. To illustrate, say:
   "I have a game for us to play today. Everyone will have a chance to be the leader. Whatever the leader does, we'll do also. Let's try it."

2. Begin the chant. Model being a leader and then encourage the toddlers to imitate your motions.

3. Play the game and monitor who has been a leader to ensure that every child has an opportunity.

4. Find at least one behavior that every child does, label it, and encourage the other toddlers to do it also. This is particularly important for children who are uncomfortable being in a leadership role. For example, if a child turns her head away from you to avoid eye contact, say:
   "Jen turned her head to look out the window. Let's do it also."

5. Provide positive reinforcement to the entire group of toddlers when the game is complete. Comment, for example:
   "What wonderful leaders. Everyone came up with actions for us to copy."

☀ Highlighting Development

Play, for very young children, is far from being asocial. As early as the first few months of life, infants show interest in each other and by the end of the third year, they are showing the ability to differentiate complementary roles (Hughes, 1999). Such social play involves the ability to communicate effectively with a peer so that one child leads the play and another child follows.

VARIATION:

♡ Play other simple games that allow a child to lead the play such as I Spy or Bee Bee Bumblebee.

ADDITIONAL INFORMATION:

♡ Toddlers gain much of their knowledge through daily interactions with adults who are much more skilled than themselves. Scaffolding is one successful teaching method that adults typically use. This is an informal teaching strategy that helps children extend their current skills to a higher level of competence. To illustrate, the adult may say, "Watch me do it," while demonstrating a new technique. Likewise, the adult might provide a cue by drawing attention to an object. For example, the caregiver may say to a child struggling with a puzzle, "Find the blue piece. The color matches the piece already in the puzzle."

Day 1: Making the Car Wash

SOCIAL

Child's Developmental Goals

✓ To cooperate with others
✓ To practice expressive language skills
✓ To improve perspective-taking skills

MATERIALS:

❑ Cardboard box large enough to drive a wheeled vehicle, such as a tricycle, through
❑ Nontoxic, washable, felt-tip markers
❑ Containers to hold markers

PREPARATION:

♡ Place the box and markers within easy access.

NURTURING STRATEGIES:

1. Observe the toddlers playing with the wheeled vehicles. When they appear to need something new, facilitate their play by suggesting the creation of a car wash. Comment, for example:
   "Your cars are dirty. They need a wash. What can you do about that? Why don't you make a car wash to clean them?"
2. Engage the toddlers in a conversation about how to make the car wash. When they begin to discuss the materials needed, tell them about what you have gathered. Avoid being too directive; this is their project. Gather additional materials as needed.
3. Verbally support the toddlers' work as necessary.
4. Provide assistance with problem solving, as necessary. Encourage the toddlers to use expressive language skills to communicate their needs and desires.
5. Assist the toddlers with planning ahead by conversing about how they are going to use the car wash once it is complete. If there is not enough time to play with the car wash immediately, discuss the reasons for this decision.

☀ Highlighting Development

Social construction play, that which results in a final product such as a block structure, requires cooperation and coordination, just like socio-dramatic play (see "Day 2: Washing the Car"). Children skilled in socio-dramatic play often demonstrate "group productivity," which is the ability to work with other children as a team to construct a specific object. Being a member of a team requires planning, cooperation, and the ability to avoid disagreements or, at least, resolve the conflicts nonaggressively (see Hughes, 1999).

VARIATION:

♡ Provide water, buckets, and towels for actually washing the vehicles.

ADDITIONAL INFORMATION:

♡ Toddlers need to continue play themes from one day to another. This provides the opportunity to begin to understand time concepts, such as yesterday, today, and tomorrow.
♡ Children benefit when they act pro-socially. Helping, sharing, comforting, giving, and cooperating are all examples of pro-social behaviors. These are all acts of kindness and affection that help others and promote friendships.

Day 2: Washing the Cars

Child's Developmental Goals

✓ To engage in socio-dramatic play
✓ To practice expressive language skills
✓ To improve perspective-taking skills

MATERIALS:

❏ Car wash, constructed the previous day (see "Day 1: Making the Car Wash")
❏ Wheeled vehicles, such as cars or tricycles
❏ Helmets for each vehicle

PREPARATION:

♡ Place the car wash where it is easily accessible to the toddlers.
♡ Inspect the wheeled vehicles to ensure they are in good repair.

NURTURING STRATEGIES:

1. When the toddlers select the tricycles or wheeled vehicles, assist with putting on helmets, as necessary.
2. Remind the toddlers of their conversation about how they wanted to use the car wash. Discuss if this is still their plan or if they have thought of something new.
3. Provide plenty of uninterrupted time for playing with the car wash.
4. Monitor the toddlers' play theme and provide guidance, as necessary, to promote problem-solving and perspective-taking skills.
5. Document this experience and the learning occurring during it by taking photographs of the children while playing.

☀ Highlighting Development

Up to this point, toddlers have engaged in solitary or parallel make-believe play. Now, however, socio-dramatic play is evident. This is organized make-believe play within a social setting that follows rules designed by the children. Socio-dramatic play is the most social form of play and, therefore, has the greatest impact on the social development of young children. In order for young children to engage in this type of play, they must cooperate and coordinate their own behavior with the behavior of others. Thus, young children must verbally communicate their thoughts to others, as well as listen to and take the perspective of their play partners.

VARIATION:

♡ Create a "garage" where the toddlers can repair "broken" tricycles or other wheeled vehicles.

ADDITIONAL INFORMATION:

♡ Planning, doing, and then reviewing are teaching techniques that promote thoughtful and meaningful play by the toddlers. This process also assists with the development of cognitive skills.
♡ Toddlers' play becomes more complex with advances in cognition and expressive language skills. At this stage, they can represent thought with the use of symbols such as words, toys, make-believe actions, and scribbles (Trawick-Smith, 2000).

Bouncing Babies

Child's Developmental Goals

✓ To interact in a caring manner

✓ To engage in pretend play with a doll

MATERIALS:

❑ Baby doll

PREPARATION:

♡ Dress the doll, if necessary, and sit in a location that will attract the toddler's attention.

♡ Write the following words to the song on an index card.

This is the way the baby rides,
The baby rides, the baby rides,
This is the way the baby rides,
So early in the morning.

NURTURING STRATEGIES:

1. When a toddler selects the baby doll, observe his behavior.
2. Join the toddler at his level and discuss what he is doing with the baby. State, for example:
   "You're feeding the baby cabbage. She must be very hungry."
3. If the toddler appears to need a new idea to sustain his play, say:
   "Gosh, your baby is still crying. Maybe she'd like to play a game with you. I know a song that you really liked when you were a baby."
4. Pick up another baby doll, if available, and model singing the song while bouncing the baby on your knee.

5. Encourage the toddler to join in the singing and bouncing.
6. Comment on how singing the song stopped the baby from crying.

☀ Highlighting Development

Research suggests that the availability of play materials early in life is related to later intellectual development. Play materials serve as an incentive for social interactions with adults and other children through functional, constructive, or pretend play. Thus, the structure and makeup of the physical environment seems to be important in supporting cognitive growth. This relationship holds true even when the quality of parent-child interactions is considered (see Hughes, 1999, for a review of this literature).

VARIATIONS:

♡ Substitute the child's name, "mommy," "daddy," and a friend's name, and use a different way to bounce for each new person.

ADDITIONAL INFORMATION:

♡ Children's abilities for developing pro-social behaviors are influenced by the adults in their lives. These adults can create a positive atmosphere by continuously modeling prosocial behaviors, helping children to develop pro-social skills, and providing positive reinforcement for their efforts.

Making Rules

Child's Developmental Goals

✓ To participate in a group discussion

✓ To assist with creating rules

MATERIALS:

❑ Marker

❑ Easel paper

❑ Easel

PREPARATION:

♡ Clear an area, preferably carpeted, that is large enough for the children to sit comfortably.

♡ Place the materials there.

NURTURING STRATEGIES:

1. Gather a small group of toddlers in the selected area. Tell them that a new piece of equipment such as a climber has been installed outdoors.

2. If possible, view the equipment from a window or provide a photograph of it.

3. Ask the toddlers what rules should be set to keep everyone safe when playing on the new climber.

4. Record the toddlers' answers exactly as spoken.

5. Review the list produced as a way to provide positive reinforcement for their suggestions. Say, for example:

   "Nahima thought we should not jump from the climber and Quentin thought we shouldn't run on the climber."

6. Assist the toddlers with framing the limits in a positive manner. Ask questions to elicit even more responses. Refer the children to the equipment or photograph to answer the questions, as necessary. For example, ask:

   "Nahima, where can we jump from?"

7. Post the completed list of rules outdoors, so the toddlers can easily view them.

8. Review the list of rules after a few days to see how they are working. Adjust as needed.

Highlighting Development

The cognitive development perspective of morality regards children as active thinkers about social rules (Berk, 1999). In order for young children to understand and follow rules, they must actively make sense of their experiences in moral situations. When adults highlight that moral rules are important for the protection of the rights and welfare of people, young children begin to believe this as well. However, children need repeated experiences to support this development. Young children need opportunities to work out their ideas about justice and fairness.

VARIATION:

♡ Discussing existing rules and their importance can assist toddlers with actively thinking about them and, hopefully, following them.

ADDITIONAL INFORMATION:

♡ Before forming rules, study child development norms to learn what behaviors and understanding can be expected of toddlers. Toddlers need as few rules as possible to maximize their ability to follow them. Rules should be introduced for the protection of the health and safety of the children. In addition, they should protect property and psychological well-being of others.

♡ Morality is a set of principles or values that helps children to distinguish between right and wrong. As children develop relationships with others, morality becomes an important part of their lives (Fabes & Martin, 2001).

31 to 36 months

Emotional Development

♡

THIRTY-ONE to THIRTY-SIX MONTHS

Falling Asleep

Child's Developmental Goals

✓ To follow a routine to calm down
✓ To rest or sleep

MATERIALS:

☐ Napping and resting materials for each toddler, such as cot, blanket, and any necessary security items
☐ Materials needed for transition such as tape and tape player

PREPARATION:

♡ Begin the transition to napping by turning down the lights and making cots available.
♡ Turn on soft, soothing music.

NURTURING STRATEGIES:

1. When the toddlers have used the toilet, washed hands, brushed their teeth, and had a drink of water encourage them to gather their special nap items from their cubbies.
2. Help each toddler get comfortable on a cot. Demonstrate respect by following the toddler's preferences for getting comfortable. Some toddlers like to have their backs rubbed while others prefer to be tucked in, kissed "good nap," and left alone.
3. Use your voice as a tool for calming the child. Speak slowly and softly.
4. Avoid power struggles or long discussions about naptime with toddlers. These only serve to increase anxiety and the amount of time needed to calm down.
5. If a child is not ready to sleep, encourage the toddler to rest quietly by choosing and looking at books in the "nap box" (see "Calming Down to Rest," p. 279).

☀ Highlighting Development

Because of their level of physical activity, toddlers need regular sleep and napping patterns to replenish their energy. However, this is often easier to say than do. Toddlers are so busy exploring, playing, and learning that they frequently resist stopping to sleep. Creating naptime and bedtime routines can be very helpful in signaling the child that a transition from waking to sleeping will occur soon (Lindsay, 1998). Observe and listen. To create a successful routine, following the expressed interests of the toddler is important.

VARIATIONS:

♡ Sing each child short lullabies that use the toddler's name.
♡ Read a story about sleeping.
♡ Play soft music or lullabies to help calm the children during naptime.

ADDITIONAL INFORMATION:

♡ Children at this stage sleep from 9 to 13 hours a day. Most toddlers take a nap. Some toddlers may resist falling asleep. Accept this behavior and provide them a quiet space and quiet materials, such as books, for resting. Resting approximately 30 minutes should help them feel and act rested. However, if in an early childhood program be sure to carefully read and follow any state or local guidelines for naptime.
♡ In an early childhood program, enlist the help of parents/guardians to better understand each toddler's naptime preferences.
♡ Whenever possible, schedule quiet activities before naptime, such as listening to a story.

Our Daily Routine

Child's Developmental Goals

✓ To practice predicting the daily schedule

✓ To develop a feeling of security

MATERIALS:

❑ Poster board
❑ Photographs
❑ Basket
❑ Markers
❑ Velcro, cut in 1-inch pieces

PREPARATION:

♡ Take photographs of the toddlers engaging in daily routines, such as playing indoors and outdoors, eating, napping, separating and reuniting with parents/guardians, and/or participating in circle time, classroom meetings, or large groups.

♡ Label the poster board with a title, such as "Our Daily Routine."

♡ Adhere four strips of Velcro to the poster board. Next, place a piece of Velcro on the back of each photograph and put them in the basket.

♡ Prop the poster board against a wall or secure to a refrigerator or bulletin board at the toddlers' eye level.

♡ Set the basket of photographs nearby.

NURTURING STRATEGIES:

1. When a toddler selects the activity, join him by sitting at his level. Observe his behavior.

2. Describe the toddler's behavior. State, for example:
   "Romig, you are sticking the pictures to this board."

3. Engage the toddler in a conversation about his work. Comments to make include:
   "Tell me how you decided which photographs to put on the board."
   "Are these pictures in any order?"

4. Prompt the toddler to think about his day by discussing what he does first, second, etc. Then, connect his words to the photographs by saying:
   "You said we eat breakfast first. Here is the picture of you eating pancakes."

5. Encourage the toddler to put the first picture on the first piece of Velcro on the left-hand side.

6. When the board is completed, "read" the daily schedule back to the toddler. While pointing, say:
   "Romig, let's read the daily schedule you made. First, you eat breakfast, then you play outdoors, third, you nap, and finally your grandma comes to pick you up."

7. Encourage the toddler to make any changes to the schedule.

☀ Highlighting Development

According to Erikson (1950), each developmental crisis, such as trust versus mistrust, autonomy versus shame and doubt, or irritation versus guilt, must be successfully resolved or it impacts the resolution of future crises. Toddlers, like infants, need routines and rituals to help them feel secure. This sense of security assists toddlers with exploring their environment more freely and, later on, willingly attempting new tasks. In other words, children's early experiences can influence their later lives.

VARIATIONS:

♡ To decrease the challenge, use fewer pieces of Velcro on the poster board.

♡ Increase the challenge by providing more than four photographs, thus allowing for different yet equally correct daily routines. This will encourage problem-solving behaviors and increase flexibility of thinking.

ADDITIONAL INFORMATION:

♡ To provide additional protection to the photographs, mount them on pieces of construction paper and laminate before adhering the Velcro.

♡ Sequencing is a challenging but achievable task if the toddlers are asked to order familiar events.

31 to 36 months

My Place Mat

EMOTIONAL

Child's Developmental Goals

✓ To express one's feelings through art

✓ To discuss healthy living habits

MATERIALS:

❑ Construction paper

❑ Transparent lamination or clear self-adhesive paper

❑ Oil pastels

❑ Containers to hold oil pastels

❑ Permanent markers

PREPARATION:

♡ Set up workspaces on a child-size table or coffee table by placing construction paper and oil pastels there.

NURTURING STRATEGIES:

1. When a toddler selects the activity, observe her behavior.

2. Engage in a natural conversation about the toddler's work. Describe, for example, the lines and colors you see.

3. Discuss what this artwork is for. To illustrate, say: *"I noticed that we need to have place mats to protect the table at lunch. I would like to save this artwork. Later, I will make it into a place mat."*

4. Discuss, if the toddler is interested, the steps in making the place mat.

5. Continue the conversation to discuss what you will be having for lunch. You can extend the topic to include favorite foods and reasons for healthy eating.

☀ Highlighting Development

During this stage of development, toddlers need to feel independent. They learn new skills best when adults realize what they can do and scaffold their learning by adding small steps. Take putting on shoes, for example. If the toddler can locate the shoes, then the next step might be having her untie them. You can help match the shoes to the correct feet and have the toddler put her feet inside, and so on. Encouraging toddlers to be independent by doing what they can do for themselves builds their self-confidence. Toddlers who are confident in their ability to learn are more willing to make choices and are pro-active. They will make things happen in their lives rather than waiting for things to happen to them (Van der Zande, 1995).

VARIATION:

♡ Make place mats that provide outlines of where to place the eating utensils, plates, and cups. That way, the toddlers can set the table independently.

ADDITIONAL INFORMATION:

♡ Children need to acquire a sense of independence and an "I can do it" attitude. To acquire these traits, they need to have adults in their lives who provide predictability and encourage them to create and take risks, as well as to engage in lively and imaginative play with peers (Trawick-Smith, 2000).

Door Painting

Child's Developmental Goals

✔ To express feelings through art

✔ To cope with feelings of frustration in a positive manner

✔ To express feelings in a socially acceptable manner

MATERIALS:

❏ Used storm door made of Plexiglas™

❏ 2 colors of liquid tempera paint

❏ 4 paintbrushes

❏ 2 containers

❏ Damp sponge

❏ Smocks for the maximum number of children who can paint at once.

PREPARATION:

♡ Pour paint into the containers.
♡ Prop the storm door up against a fence or building.
♡ Place paint containers and brushes nearby. Also, keep sponge handy for wiping hands at end of activity.

NURTURING STRATEGIES:

1. Before going outdoors introduce the activity. To illustrate, say:
   "I noticed Rex and Lorenzo were making handprints on the door yesterday. When they touched the glass, it left a mark. I found an old storm door for you to paint on today."

2. Set any limits necessary to protect the children or materials at this time. Use comments such as:
   "Please leave the storm door right where it is."
   "Everyone needs to wear a smock."
   "You may paint the storm door window with your hands or with the paintbrushes."

3. When a toddler selects the experience, provide verbal and/or physical assistance with putting on a smock.

4. Expect that conflict might arise around sharing the two containers of paint. When you see a toddler becoming frustrated, talk the child through the emotion. Comment, for example:
   "Lorenzo, it is frustrating to have to wait. Does Rex know that you want to use the green paint?"
   Pause, and then continue by saying:
   "You need to tell him then."

5. Encouraging the toddlers to problem solve and label their feelings will increase their perspective-taking skills.

☀ Highlighting Development

Toddlers at this stage are continuing to learn about display rules for emotions. These rules help them to learn how, when, and where to display emotions. Display rules also help toddlers to learn more about socially accepted methods of expressing emotions. For example, sensitive adults help children learn display rules for all emotions. Adults, who label and explain emotions, have toddlers who will gradually learn to do the same.

VARIATION:

♡ Use a variety of media on the screen door, such as fingerpaint, mud, shaving cream, or markers.

ADDITIONAL INFORMATION:

♡ Painting outdoors often reduces tension between adults and children because the worry about being messy is greatly reduced.

 To protect the safety of the toddlers, select a storm door made of Plexiglas™. The door will be lightweight and the glass will not shatter, if it was to break.

I Have to Go

EMOTIONAL

Child's Developmental Goals

✓ To communicate when needing to use the toilet

✓ To practice self-help skills

MATERIALS:

None

PREPARATION:

None

NURTURING STRATEGIES:

1. Carefully track the time when a toddler was last reminded to use the toilet and whether the child eliminated.

2. Create a routine for toileting, just as you did for diapering. Always encourage the toddler to use the toilet, but do not attempt to force her because that will usually cause the toddler to resist even more.

3. Discuss with the toddler how to recognize bodily cues.

4. Encourage the toddler to tell you when she needs to eliminate. When the child signals, move quickly as there probably will be little time to spare.

5. Encourage the toddler to assist with the process as much as possible. For example, have the toddler tear off a piece of toilet paper for you, flush the toilet, and then pull up her clothing.

6. Provide verbal and nonverbal reinforcement for becoming more independent. For example, smile while saying:

   "Karmele, thank you for telling me that you had to go potty. You've stayed dry all morning!"

☼ Highlighting Development

One of the major developmental milestones for toddlers is the ability to use a toilet. Controlling elimination depends on muscular maturation, cognitive abilities such as recognizing bodily signals and remembering instructions, emotional readiness, and desire. On average, boys tend to be ready for toileting slightly later than girls. However, most children are able to accomplish staying dry during the day by age three.

ADDITIONAL INFORMATION:

♡ In an early childhood program, frequent communication with parents or guardians is a must when helping toddlers learn to use the toilet. To support learning, all adults must use a consistent approach. Families and cultures differ in what they believe is the "right" way. Open communication can help reduce misunderstanding and increase consistency.

♡ There are several signs to indicate that children are ready to be toilet trained. First, bowel movements occur on a somewhat predictable schedule. Through facial expressions, actions, or comments, the child is signaling that he is ready to have a bowel movement. Then too, during diaper checks, dryness communicates that the child's bladder is capable of storing urine.

"Feelings"

Child's Developmental Goals

✓ To discuss different emotions

✓ To connect behaviors with emotions

MATERIALS:

❑ Felt-tip markers
❑ Poster board
❑ Easel with clean sheet of paper

PREPARATION:

♡ See Appendix G for the song, "Feelings." Print the words to the song on the poster board.
♡ Place the easel in the area where the toddlers will gather.
♡ Clip the poster board to the easel and then a piece of clean paper on top of it.
♡ Place the markers in tray of easel.

NURTURING STRATEGIES:

1. Signal that it is time to pick up the toys by singing a cleanup song. See Appendix G for a list of songs.
2. Model cleanup skills by assisting the toddlers in picking up toys.
3. Gather the children in one area and introduce the topic of emotions. Say, for example:
   "I noticed this morning that some children were happy to come to school while others appeared sad. I was thinking about how people can feel many different emotions."
4. Provide clues to help the toddlers identify different emotions, if necessary. Connect your clue to the toddlers' past experiences whenever possible. To connect feelings with behaviors, discuss how others might know what emotion you are feeling.
5. When the list is complete, uncover the poster board and introduce the song.

6. Slowly sing the song a number of times so that the toddlers can sing along as well as perform the actions.

☀ Highlighting Development

Toddlers can experience many emotions within a very short period of time. One moment they are telling you how much they like you, and the next how much they dislike you. Instead of becoming upset or angry, reassure the toddler that you care for him and that you are sorry that he is feeling upset (Lindsay, 1998). Encourage the toddler to talk about his feelings. Label the emotions and discuss appropriate ways for coping with them.

VARIATION:

♡ Locate other songs to sing about emotions.

ADDITIONAL INFORMATION:

♡ Children's social competence is directly affected by the way they understand their own emotions as well those of others. By nature, the behavior of two-year-olds includes ups and downs and mood swings. Their emotional responses change rapidly. One moment they may appear happy and cheerful and the next they may be angry. Even though they can experience many emotions at a time, they are struggling to understand individual emotions. With maturity, the children learn to understand the succession of emotions that they and others experience.

Decorating a Flower Pot

EMOTIONAL

Child's Developmental Goals

✓ To feel proud about an accomplishment

✓ To add information to their sense of self

MATERIALS:

❏ Glue

❏ Leaves, flower petals

❏ Clay flowerpot for each toddler

❏ Thin paintbrushes

❏ 2 small containers

❏ Newspaper

❏ Masking tape

❏ Damp sponge

PREPARATION:

♡ Cover a child-size table or coffee table with the newspaper and secure it with the tape.

♡ Pour glue into the two containers, place two brushes in each container, and set these on the table.

♡ Place the items for gluing around the table.

♡ Set a flowerpot upside down at each chair or workstation.

NURTURING STRATEGIES:

1. Observe the toddler when the activity is selected.

2. Introduce the experience, if necessary, by saying: *"We needed some new flowerpots to hold the flowers. I thought you could help decorate them by gluing these flower petals and leaves on them."*

3. To decrease the level of difficulty, you may want to suggest that the toddler apply the glue as if it were paint. Moreover, laying the pot on its side may help as well.

4. Allow the toddler time to work uninterrupted.

5. Before the toddler leaves the area, thank her for decorating the flowerpot. Discuss how her behavior is important to the whole community of learners. Say, for example: *"Matsuko, thank you for decorating this pot. It will look wonderful in the room. Everyone will enjoy looking at it. It will really help make this room beautiful!"*

☀ Highlighting Development

During early toddlerhood, young children firmly establish separateness from others. Listen to them and you'll hear them using words such as *me, mine,* or even their own name. This language allows the toddlers to talk about the "I self"—their own subjective experience of being (Harter, 1998). The next stage in the development of the self is called the "me-self," which is the recognition and evaluation of the self's characteristics (Berk, 1999). Young children, at this stage, begin to develop a sense of who they are—their attributes, abilities, preferences, attitudes, and values. This will be reflected in their language. Listen. They will label themselves and others on the basis of age (*baby, kid*), physical characteristics (*big, strong*), and accomplishments ("I did it").

VARIATION:

♡ After the glue dries, encourage the toddlers to use tempera paint to add another layer of decoration.

ADDITIONAL INFORMATION:

♡ Adults play an important role in helping young children to understand their emotions, develop a sensitivity to the feelings of others, and develop effective ways to cope with the emotions they experience (Kostelnik, et al., 2002).

Lost Basket

Child's Developmental Goals

✓ To develop strategies for coping with strong emotions

✓ To experience a sense of accomplishment

MATERIALS:

❑ Letter
❑ Envelope
❑ Basket

PREPARATION:

♡ Write a letter to a friend and place it inside the envelope.
♡ Place the envelope in the basket.
♡ Put the basket in a convenient location.

NURTURING STRATEGIES:

1. If you notice a toddler who needs an activity, show the child the basket and introduce the experience. To illustrate, say:
   "I have a basket that I'm using to carry a letter to the post office. See, here is the letter I want to mail to a friend. Let's walk to the post office."

2. Begin walking around the room or outdoor area. While walking, sing:
   "A tisket, a tasket, a very pretty basket, I wrote a letter to my friend [hide basket] *and on the way I lost it."*

3. Using your voice as a tool, communicate concern about the lost basket. Encourage the toddler to find the basket.

4. Assist the toddler in dealing with strong emotions, if necessary. If a toddler is upset because he can't find the basket, say, for example:
   "You can do it, Lev. Keep looking. Don't forget to look behind things."
   If the toddler is so excited that he can't concentrate, say, for example:
   "Slow down, Titus. Walk so you can search well for the basket."

5. When the basket is discovered, congratulate the child on the discovery and read the letter to the toddler. Vary your reading of the letter to individualize it for the toddler.

☀ Highlighting Development

Humans have two minds: the emotional mind and the rational mind, or one that feels and one that thinks, respectively. Although thought to be two separate minds, it is now clearer that emotions are crucial, or even indispensable, to effective thought (Goleman, 1995). Having a high emotional IQ means that one can recognize one's own emotions, manage emotions, motivate oneself, recognize the emotions of others, and handle relationships with others. These tasks are well beyond the capabilities of toddlers at this stage, yet the foundations for these skills should be laid.

VARIATIONS:

♡ Have the toddler "write" a letter to put in the basket.
♡ Encourage two toddlers to play the game.

ADDITIONAL INFORMATION:

♡ Emotional awareness is associated with cooperative and friendly behavior. Children who have greater emotional knowledge also have an increased ability to get along with others and, therefore, are inclined to experience success in their social relationships. Consequently, it is important that adults help and support children's development of these emotional skills.

Whispering

Child's Developmental Goals

✔ To use self-talk to control impulsive behavior

✔ To increase perspective-taking skills

MATERIALS:

None

PREPARATION:

None

NURTURING STRATEGIES:

1. When you see a child becoming very excited, move closer to the toddler.

2. State brief, positive limits for the toddler. Say, for example:

   "Inside voice. Please use your inside voice."

3. Encourage the toddler to repeat the limit, and then explain that she can say those words to herself to help remember it.

4. Observe the toddler to see if she is using private speech to guide her behavior. If yes, move away and allow her to resume playing. If no, provide a reminder. If this does not work, attempt a new strategy such as joining in the play and modeling whispering to the child.

5. After the play episode, discuss with the toddler the need to talk softly indoors. Include in your discussion how it hurts others' ears or disrupts their play.

6. Provide positive reinforcement for using an inside voice. Note how this is beneficial to others in the room by saying, for example:

   "Shari, thank you for talking softly. It helped me and Valerie concentrate on the book we were reading."

☀ Highlighting Development

In order to display self-control—the ability to resist the impulse to engage in a socially disapproved behavior—toddlers must be able to think of themselves as separate, autonomous beings who can make decisions (Berk, 1999). This ability develops gradually during early childhood. Research suggests that toddlers with more advanced language skills are more able to control themselves (see Berk, 1999, for a review). These toddlers are able to use strategies such as distraction or self-talk to guide their behavior. For example, they will sing a song to avoid touching a desired object.

VARIATIONS:

♡ Whisper to the children during transitions because it tends to attract the toddlers' attention.

♡ If reasonable for your situation, provide choices such as whispering indoors or playing outdoors.

ADDITIONAL INFORMATION:

♡ Adults play a significant role in the development of toddlers' self-control. Using positive guidance strategies, such as giving advance notice when the toddler needs to stop an enjoyable activity, assists with both self-control and emotional control.

I Hear Thunder

Child's Developmental Goals

✓ To learn coping skills for dealing with the emotion of fear

✓ To express fear appropriately

✓ To talk about fears

MATERIALS:

❏ Poster board

❏ Markers

PREPARATION:

♡ Write the following song lyrics on the poster board.

"I Hear Thunder" (to the tune of "Frere Jacques")
I hear thunder, I hear thunder   (stomp feet)
Listen now, listen now   (put hand to ear)
Pitter-patter raindrops,   (wiggle fingers in air)
Pitter-patter raindrops,
Now it's through, now it's through   (smile)

I see lightning, I see lightning
See it now, see it now   (point)
Pitter-patter raindrops,   (wiggle fingers in air)
Pitter-patter raindrops,
Now it's through, now it's through   (smile)

♡ Display the song at the children's eye level in the area where you will be working.

NURTURING STRATEGIES:

1. When a child expresses anxiety about thunder, lightning, or storms in general, discuss his fear.
2. To improve vocabulary skills, label his reactions with words such as *nervous, anxious,* or *afraid.*
3. In addition, talk about degrees of these feelings. For example, discuss whether storms make him a little anxious or a lot anxious. Encourage the toddler to compare his feelings about storms with another time when he felt anxious. Comment, for example,
   "Salim, are you a little bit anxious or a lot anxious about the storm outside?"
   Pause for an answer, and then continue:

"Do you remember meeting our new neighbors yesterday? That seemed to make you anxious also. Are you more or less anxious now about the storm?"

4. Continue the conversation as long as the toddler wants to talk. Then, introduce the song by saying, for example:
   "I have a new song we can sing about thunder and lightning. Sing along with me when you're ready."
5. Sing the song slowly to help the toddler learn the words and join in. Add the motions during the second singing.
6. Repeat the song at least one more time.
7. Bring closure to the experience by encouraging the toddler to sing the song the next time he is frightened by thunder and lightning.

☀ Highlighting Development

When immersed in emotionally rich environments, toddlers also engage in an expressive style of language usage (Berk, 1999). In other words, toddlers use language for the primary goal of talking about feelings and needs of themselves and others. In such an environment, toddlers seek to communicate how they are feeling with specific words (Philadelphia Child Guidance Center, 1994).

VARIATION:

♡ Sing songs about other fears, such as separation anxiety.

ADDITIONAL INFORMATION:

♡ Emotional development for infants and toddlers occurs in developmental stages. First, there are the four core emotions, including joy, anger, sadness, and fear. In the beginning, these emotions are extremely intense. That is why infants and toddlers typically have strong reactions and outbursts (Kostelnik, et al., 2002). Gradually, they begin to use language to express their emotions. For example, they may say, "I'm mad at you."

Abrams, B. W., & Kaufman, N. A. (1990). *Toys for early childhood development.* West Nyack, NY: The Center for Applied Research in Education.

Allen, K. E., & Marotz, L. (1999). *Developmental profiles: Pre-birth through eight* (3rd ed.). Albany, NY: Delmar.

Baillargeon, R. (1994). How do infants learn about the physical world? *Current Directions in Psychological Science,* 133–140.

Baron, N. S. (1992). *Growing up with language: How children learn to talk.* Reading, MA: Addison-Wesley.

Bates, E. (1979). *The emergence of symbols: Cognition and communication in infancy.* New York: Academic Press.

Baumrind, D. (1967). Child care practices anteceding three patterns of preschool behavior. *Genetic Psychology Monograph, 4* (1, Pt. 2).

Beaty, J. (1994). *Picture book story telling.* Fort Worth, TX: Harcourt, Brace.

Bentzen, W. R. (2001). *Seeing young children: A guide to observing and recording behavior* (4th ed.). Albany, NY: Delmar.

Berk, L. E. (1997). *Child development* (4th ed.). Boston: Allyn & Bacon.

Berk, L. E. (1999). *Infants, children, and adolescents* (3rd ed.). Boston: Allyn & Bacon.

Black, J. K., & Puckett, M. B. (1996). *The young child: Development from prebirth through age eight* (2nd ed.). Englewood Cliffs, NJ: Prentice Hall.

Bredekamp, S., & Copple, C. (Eds.). (1997). *Developmentally appropriate practice in early childhood programs* (Rev. ed.). Washington, DC: National Association for the Education of Young Children.

Bukato, D., & Daehler, M. W. (1992). *Child development: A topical approach.* Boston: Houghton Mifflin.

Bukato, D., & Daehler, M. W. (1995). *Child development: A thematic approach.* Boston: Houghton Mifflin.

Butterworth, G. (1997). Starting point. *Natural History, 106* (4), 14–16.

Carlson, K., & Cunningham, J. L. (1990). Effect of pencil diameter on the graphomotor skill of preschoolers. *Early Childhood Research Quarterly, 5,* 279–293.

Cassidy, J., Scolton, K. L., Kirsh, S. J., & Parke, R. D. (1996). Attachment and representations of peer relationships. *Developmental Psychology, 32,* 892–904.

Caulfield, R. (2001). *Infants and toddlers.* Upper Saddle River, NJ: Prentice Hall.

Cecil, N. L. (1999). *Striking a balance—Positive practices for early literacy.* Scottsdale, AZ: Holcomb Hathaway.

Charlesworth, R. (2000). *Understanding child development* (5th ed.). Albany, NY: Delmar.

Charlesworth, R. & Lind, K. K. (1999). *Math and science for young children* (3rd ed.). Albany, NY: Delmar.

Cobb, N. (2001). *The child: Infants and toddlers.* Mountain View, CA: Mayfield.

Cowley, G., & Foote, D. (1997). The language explosion. *Newsweek,* 16–17.

Cromwell, E. (2000). *Early childhood education.* Needham Heights, MA: Allyn & Bacon.

Damon, W. (1988). *The moral child: Nurturing children's natural moral growth.* New York: Free Press.

Deiner, P. L. (1997). *Infants and toddlers: Development and program planning.* Albany, NY: Delmar.

Derman-Sparks, L., & the A.B.C. Task Force. (1989). *Anti-bias curriculum: Tools for empowering young children.* Washington, DC: National Association for the Education of Young Children.

Eriksen, E. H. (1950). *Childhood and society.* New York: Norton.

Ernst, K. (1994). *Picturing Learning: Artists and writers in the classroom.* Portsmouth, NH: Heinemann.

Fabes, R. & Martin, C. (2001). *Exploring development through childhood.* Boston: Allyn & Bacon.

Feldman, R. S. (1998). *Child Development.* Upper Saddle River, NJ: Prentice Hall.

Feldman, R. S. (2000). *Development across the life span* (2nd ed.). Upper Saddle River, NJ: Prentice Hall.

Fenson, L., Dale, P. S., Reznick, J. S., Bates, E., Thal, D. J., & Pethick, S. J. (1994). Variability in early communication development. *Monographs of the Society for Research in Child Development, 59* (5, Serial No. 242).

Field, T., Gewirtz, J. L., Cohen, D., Garcia, R., Greenberg, R., & Collins, K. (1984). Leave-taking and reunions of infants, toddlers, preschoolers, and their parents. *Child Development, 55,* 628–635.

Fogel, A. (2001). *Infancy* (2nd ed.). Belmont, CA: Wadsworth.

Gandini, L., & Goldhaber, J. (2001). Two reflections about documentation. In L. Gandini and C. Pope Edwards (Eds.), *Bambini: The Italian approach to infant/toddler care* (pp. 124–145). New York: Teachers College Press.

Gandini, L., & Pope Edwards, C. (Eds.). (2001). *Bambini: The Italian approach to infant/toddler care.* New York: Teachers College Press.

Gerber, M., & Johnson, A. (1998). *Your self-confident baby: How to encourage your child's natural abilities—From the very start.* New York: Wiley.

Goleman, D. (1995). *Emotional Intelligence: Why it can matter more than IQ.* New York: Bantam.

Gonzalez-Mena, J. (2001). *Foundations: Early childhood education in a diverse society* (2nd ed.). Mountain View, CA: Mayfield.

Greenman, J., & Stonehouse, A. (1996). *Prime times: A handbook for excellence in infant and toddler programs.* St. Paul, MN: Redleaf Press.

Greenspan, S. (1999). *Building healthy minds.* Saddle River, NJ: Perseus.

Harter, S. (1998). The development of self-representation. In N. Eisenberg (Ed.), *Handbook of child psychology: Vol. 3, Social, emotional, and personality development* (5th ed., pp. 553–618). New York: Wiley.

Hay, D. F., Murray, P., Cecire, S., & Nash, A. (1985). Social learning of social behavior in early life. *Child Development, 56,* 43–57.

Helm, J. H., Beneke, S., & Steinheimer, K. (1998). *Windows on learning: Documenting young children's work*. New York: Teachers College Press.

Herr, J. (1998). *Working with young children*. Homewood, IL: Goodheart-Wilcox.

Herr, J. (2000). *Creative resources for the early childhood classroom* (3rd ed.). Albany, NY: Delmar.

Herr, J. (2001). *Creative learning activities for young children*. Albany, NY: Delmar.

Herr, J. (2002). *Working with young children* (4th ed.). Tinley Park, IL: Goodheart-Wilcox.

Herr, J., & Libby, Y. (1998). *Creative resources for the early childhood classroom* (3rd ed.). Albany, NY: Delmar.

Hughes, F. P. (1999). *Chlidren, play, and development* (3rd ed.). Boston: Allyn & Bacon.

Isenberg, J., & Jalongo, M. (1993). *Creative expression and play in early childhood education*. New York: Merrill.

Izard, C. E. (1991). *The psychology of emotions*. New York: Plenum.

Junn, E., & Boyatzis, C. J. (1998). *Child growth and development*. Guilford, CT: Dushken/McGraw Hill.

Kail, R. U. (1998). *Children and their development*. Upper Saddle River, NJ: Prentice Hall.

Kostelnik, M., Stein, L., Wheren, A. P., Soderman, A. K., & Gregory, K. (2002). *Guiding children's social development*. Albany, NY: Delmar.

Kratcoski, A. M., & Katz, K. B. (1998). Conversing with young language learners in the classroom. *Young Children, 53*(3), 30–33.

Lamme, L. L. (1979). Handwriting in early childhood curriculum. *Young Children, 35,* 20–27.

Leach, P. (1992). *Your baby and child: From birth to age five*. New York: Alfred A. Knopf.

Lindsay, J. W. (1998). *The challenge of toddlers* (Rev. ed.). Buena Park, CA: Morning Glory.

Marion, M. (1997). Research in review: Guiding young children's understanding and management of anger. *Young Children, 52,* 62–67.

Marion, M. (1999). *Guidance of young children* (5th ed.). Upper Saddle River, NJ: Merrill.

McGee, L. A., & Richgils, D. J. (2000). *Literacy's beginnings: Supporting young readers and writers* (3rd ed.). Boston: Allyn & Bacon.

Miller, K. (1984). *More things to do with toddlers and twos*. Chelsea, MA: TelShare Publishing.

Morrison, G. S. (1996). *Early childhood education today*. Upper Saddle River, NJ: Merrill.

Neuman, S. B., Copple, C., & Bredekamp, S. (2000). *Learning to read and write: Developmentally appropriate practices for young children*. Washington, DC: National Association for the Education of Young Children.

Nilsen, B. (2001). *Week by week: Plans for observing and recording young children* (2nd ed.). Albany, NY: Delmar.

Park, K. A., & Waters, E. (1989). Security of attachment and preschool friendships. *Child Development, 60,* 1076–1081.

Philadelphia Child Guidance Center. (1994). *Your child's emotional health: The early years*. New York: Macmillan.

Piaget, J. (1952). *The origins of intelligence in children*. New York: International Universities Press.

Piaget, J. (1977). The role of action in the development of thinking. In W. F. Overton & J. M. Gallagher (Eds.), *Knowledge and development* (Vol. 1). New York: Plenum.

Pope Edwards, C., Gandini, L., & Forman, G. (Eds.). (1993). *The hundred languages of children*. Norwood, NJ: Ablex.

Puckett, M. B., & Black, J. K. (2001). *The young child: Development from prebirth through age eight* (3rd ed.). Upper Saddle River, NJ: Merrill-Prentice Hall.

Rice, F. P. (1997). *Child and adolescent development*. Upper Saddle River, NJ: Prentice Hall.

Ross, H. S., Conant, C., Cheyne, J. A., & Alevizos, E. (1992). Relationships and alliances in the social interactions of kibbutz toddlers. *Social Development, 1,* 1–17.

Santrock, J. W. (1993). *Children* (3rd ed.). Madison, WI: Brown and Benchmark.

Schirrmacher, R. (2001). *Art and creative development for young children* (4th ed.). Albany, NY: Delmar.

Seefeldt, C., & Barbour, N. (1994). *Early childhood education*. New York: Macmillan.

Sénéchal, M., Thomas, E., & Monker, J. (1995). Children's acquisition of vocabulary during storybook reading. *Journal of Educational Psychology, 87,* 218–229.

Shore, R. (1997). *Rethinking the brain: New insights into early development*. New York: Families and Work Institute.

Snow, C. W. (1998). *Infant development* (2nd ed.). Upper Saddle River, NJ: Prentice Hall.

Spodek, B. (Ed.). (1993). *Handbook of research on the education of young children*. New York: Macmillan.

Thompson, J. (1999). *Toddler care day-by-day*. New York: HarperPerennial.

Trawick-Smith, J. (1994). Authentic dialogue with children: A sociolinguistic perspective on language learning. *Dimensions of Early Childhood, 22,* 9–16.

Trawick-Smith, J. (2000). *Early childhood development* (2nd ed.). Upper Saddle River, NJ: Merrill-Prentice Hall.

Turner, B., & Hammer, T. (1994). *Child development and early education*. Needham Heights, MA: Allyn & Bacon.

Van der Zande, I. (1995). *1, 2, 3 . . . The toddlers years*. Santa Cruz, CA: Santa Cruz Toddler Care Center.

Vygotsky, L. S. (1978). *Mind in society: The development of higher mental processes*. Cambridge, MA: Harvard University Press. (Original works published 1930, 1933, and 1935)

Warren, J., & Spewock, T. S. (1995). *A year of fun just for ones*. Everett, WA: Warren Publishing.

Weiser, M. (1991). *Infant/toddler care and education*. New York: Macmillan Publishing Company.

White, B. L. (1995). *The new first three years of life*. New York: Fireside.

Zigler, E., & Stevenson, M. F. (1993). *Children in a changing world: Development and social issues* (2nd ed.). Pacific Grove, CA: Brooks/Cole.

Books for Infants and Toddlers

Young children need to be immersed in a literacy-rich environment. A foundation for reading success begins as early as the first few months of life. Exposure to books and caring adults nourishes literacy development. Books and oral language are tools to help infants and toddlers become familiar with language. Young children enjoy handling books and listening to stories. Infants and toddlers enjoy the visual and auditory stimulation of having books read to them over and over again.

Books help very young children by:

♡ Developing visual discrimination skills
♡ Developing visual memory skills
♡ Developing listening skills
♡ Developing auditory memory skills
♡ Presenting new and interesting information
♡ Introducing new vocabulary
♡ Stimulating new thoughts and ideas
♡ Helping children learn book-handling skills such as turning pages and reading text versus pictures

Books that are developmentally appropriate for infants and toddlers are abundant. Some of the best examples feature various physical formats combined with clearly developed concepts or a simple story and distinctive art or photographic work.

Features of books for babies and infants include a scaled-down size appropriate for manipulation with small hands and for lap reading. Pages are either soft for safety or thick for sturdiness and ease of turning. Many books have a wipe-clean finish and rounded corners for safety. Formats include cloth, vinyl, and floatable bathtub books in chunky sizes. The content is concept-oriented with clear pictures or photographs, usually including babies or objects relating to a baby's life.

Books for toddlers also feature the scaled-down size and sturdiness. Other features may include interactivity such as touch-and-feel, lift-the-flaps, and detachable or cling-on pieces. Concept development remains paramount, and simple stories predominate. Recently, several picture book stories have been redone in board book format, greatly expanding the availability of quality literature for toddlers.

SELECTING BOOKS

Careful consideration should be given to selecting age-appropriate books for young children. When choosing books, begin by looking for award winners. You can ask the librarian at your local library to give you a list of award-winning picture books; likewise, do not hesitate to ask the salesperson at a local bookstore to provide this information. Chances are they will have a list of these award-winning books or can complete a computer search to obtain this information for you. On-line merchants should also be able to provide you this information.

You should also review the illustrations for size and quality before selecting a picture book. Study them carefully. You will notice a wide variety of illustration types in books for infants and toddlers. There are photographs, watercolors, line drawings, and collages. As you review books, remember that infants and toddlers need to have large, realistic illustrations. Realistic illustrations serve two purposes: They help the young children maintain their interest in the book and they help develop concept formation.

Other questions beside award-winning status and quality of illustrations to ask yourself while evaluating books for infants and young toddlers include:

♡ Is the book developmentally appropriate for the child or group of children?
♡ Does the book have visual appeal?
♡ Are the pages thick, durable, and easy to clean?
♡ Are the illustrations large and brightly colored?
♡ Do the illustrations contain pictures of familiar objects, routines, or people?
♡ Does the story reflect the children's own experiences?
♡ Is the vocabulary appropriate?

For older toddlers, ask yourself the following questions:

♡ Is the story simple and easy to follow?
♡ Does the book contain rhyming or repetitive phrases to entice toddlers to join in the reading?
♡ Does the book accurately depict children and/or people of different races, cultures, and abilities?

TRANSITIONING TO PAPER BOOKS

Older toddlers may be ready to transition to paper books. At first, provide paper copies only when you can constantly supervise their use. Toddlers' fine motor skills can still be somewhat jerky, resulting in torn pages. In addition, until they have been taught how to appropriately handle paper pages, toddlers tend to treat paper books in the same manner as they would cardboard books. With your guidance, they can learn to read a paper book "just like a big kid."

SUGGESTIONS FOR READING TO INFANTS AND TODDLERS

There are seven steps to making reading an enjoyable and educational experience for infants and toddlers.

♡ Get comfortable! Sit on a couch, in a rocking chair, or on the floor with your back against a wall. Hold the child in your lap or snuggle close to a small group of children.

♡ Read slowly, allowing plenty of time for children to look at the illustrations. This increases the pleasure and enjoyment derived from books for *everyone* involved.

♡ Ask questions to engage children in conversation. The experience should be as much about speaking skills as listening skills for young children.

♡ Pause to encourage children to read along with you. You will find that infants will coo or babble and toddlers will supply words or phrases. These experiences also serve to reinforce the development of turn-taking skills.

♡ Follow their lead. For example, encourage children to turn the pages. Do not worry if pages are skipped. It is highly likely that whatever you miss now will be covered in future readings of the book.

♡ Encourage children to read the story to you.

♡ Read for as long as children enjoy it. Forcing young children to remain in a situation when they are finished only serves to diminish their "love of books."

♡ Share your enthusiasm for the book through your voice and facial expressions. Children learn to love books when an adult shares their own enjoyment.

CLOTH BOOKS

Animal Play. Dorling Kindersley, 1996.
Briggs, Raymond. *The Snowman.* Random House, 1993.
Cousins, Lucy. My First Cloth Book series. Candlewick Press.
　Flower in the Garden. 1992.
　Hen on the Farm. 1992.
　Kite in the Park. 1992.
　Teddy in the House. 1992.
Harte, Cheryl. *Bunny Rattle.* Random House, 1989. (Has a rattle in it)
　Ducky Squeak. Random House, 1989. (Has a squeaker in it)
Hill, Eric. *Clothes-Spot Cloth Book.* Putnam, 1993.
　Play-Spot Cloth Book. Putnam, 1993.
My First Notebook. Eden International Ltd. (Has a rattle inside and plastic spiral rings.)
Pienkowski, Jan. Jan Pienkowski's First Cloth Book series. Little Simon.
　Animals. 1995.

Friends. 1995.
Fun. 1996.
Play. 1995.
Pienkowski, Jan. *Bronto's Brunch.* Dutton Books, 1995. (Has detachable pieces. Ages 3+)
　Good Night, Moo. Dutton Books, 1995. (Has detachable pieces. Ages 3+)
Potter, Beatrix. Beatrix Potter Cloth Books. Frederick Warne & Co.
　My Peter Rabbit Cloth Book. 1994.
　My Tom Kitten Cloth Book. 1994.
Pudgy Pillow Books. Grosset & Dunlap.
　Baby's Animal Sounds. 1989.
　Baby's Little Engine That Could. 1989.
　Barbaresi, Nina. *Baby's Mother Goose.* 1989.
　Ulrich, George. *Baby's Peek A Boo.* 1989.
Tong, Willabel L. Cuddly Cloth Books. Andrews & McMeel.
　Farm Faces. 1996.
　My Pets. 1997.
　My Toys. 1997.
　Zoo Faces. 1997.
Tucker, Sian. My First Cloth Book series. Simon & Schuster.
　Quack, Quack. 1994.
　Rat-A-Tat-Tat. 1994.
　Toot Toot. 1994.
　Yum Yum. 1994.

VINYL COVER AND BATH BOOKS

Bracken, Carolyn. *Baby's First Rattle: A Busy Bubble Book.* Simon & Schuster, 1984.
De Brunhoff, Laurent. *Babar's Bath Book.* Random House, 1992.
Hill, Eric. *Spot's Friends.* Putnam, 1984.
　Spot's Toys. Putnam, 1984.
　Sweet Dreams, Spot. Putnam, 1984.
Hoban, Tana. *Tana Hoban's Red, Blue, Yellow Shoe.* Greenwillow Books, 1994.
　Tana Hoban's What Is It? Greenwillow Books, 1994.
I. M. Tubby. *I'm a Little Airplane.* Simon & Schuster, 1982. (Shape book)
　I'm a Little Choo Choo. Simon & Schuster, 1982. (Shape book)
　I'm a Little Fish. Simon & Schuster, 1981. (Shape book)
My First Duck. Dutton, 1996. (Playskool shape book)
Nicklaus, Carol. *Grover's Tubby.* Random House/ Children's Television Workshop, 1992.
Potter, Beatrix. Beatrix Potter Bath Books series. Frederick Warne & Co.
　Benjamin Bunny. 1994.
　Jemima Puddle-Duck. 1988.
　Mr. Jeremy Fisher. 1989.
　Peter Rabbit. 1989.
　Tom Kitten, Mittens, and Moppet. 1989.
Reichmeier, Betty. *Potty Time.* Random House, 1988.

Smollin, Michael J. *Ernie's Bath Book.* Random House/ Children's Television Workshop, 1982.

Tucker, Sian. Sian Tucker Bath Books series. Simon & Schuster.
 Animal Splash. 1995.
 Splish Splash. 1995.

TOUCH AND FEEL BOOKS

Carter, David A. *Feely Bugs.* Little Simon, 1995.

Chang, Cindy. *Good Morning Puppy.* Price Stern Sloan, 1994.
 Good Night Kitty! Price Stern Sloan, 1994.

Demi, Hitz. *Downy Duckling.* Grosset & Dunlap, 1988.
 Fluffy Bunny. Grosset & Dunlap, 1987.

Hanna, Jack. *Let's Go to the Petting Zoo with Jungle Jack.* Doubleday, 1992.

Hill, Eric. *Spot's Touch and Feel Day.* Putnam, 1997.

Kunhardt, Dorothy. *Pat the Bunny.* Western Publishing, 1968.

Kunhardt, Dorothy & Edith. *Pat the Cat.* Western Publishing, 1984.
 Pat the Puppy. Western Publishing, 1993.

Lodge, J. *Patch and His Favorite Things.* Harcourt Brace, 1996.
 Patch in the Garden. Harcourt Brace, 1996.

Offerman, Lynn. *Puppy Dog's Special Friends.* Joshua Morris Publishing, 1998.

Scarry, Richard. *Richard Scarry's Egg in the Hole Book.* Golden Books, 1997.

Witte, Pat & Eve. *The Touch Me Book.* Golden Books, 1946.

CHUNKY AND CHUBBY BOOKS

Barton, Byron. Chunky Board Book series. HarperCollins.
 Boats. 1994.
 Planes. 1994.
 Trains. 1994.

Bond, Michael. *Paddington at the Seashore.* HarperCollins, 1992.

Brown, Marc. Chunky Flap Book series. Random House.
 Arthur Counts. 1998.
 Arthur's Farm Tales. 1998.
 D.W.'s Color Book. 1997.
 Where Is My Frog? 1991.
 Where's Arthur's Gerbil? 1997.
 Where's My Sneaker? 1991.

Cowley, Rich. *Snap! Snap! Buzz Buzz.* Firefly Books, 1996.

Dunn, Phoebe. *Baby's Animal Friends.* Random House, 1988.
 Farm Animals. Random House, 1984.

Freeman, Don. *Corduroy's Toys.* Viking, 1985.

Fujikawa, Gyo. *Good Night, Sleep Tight! Shhh . . .* Random House, 1990. (Chunky shape)

Hill, Eric. Spot Block Book series. Putnam.
 Spot's Favorite Baby Animals. 1997.
 Spot's Favorite Numbers. 1997.
 Spot's Favorite Words. 1997.

Hirashima, Jean. *ABC.* Random House, 1994. (Chunky shape)

Ingle, Annie. *Zoo Animals.* Random House, 1992.

Loehr, Mallory. *Trucks.* Random House, 1992. (Chunky shape)

Marzollo, Jean. *Do You Know New?* HarperCollins, 1997.

McCue, Lisa. *Little Fuzzytail.* Random House, 1995. (Chunky Peek a Board Book)

Miller, Margaret. Super Chubby Book series. Simon & Schuster.
 At the Shore. 1996.
 Family Time. 1996.
 Happy Days. 1996.
 Let's Play. 1997.
 My Best Friends. 1996.
 Water Play. 1996.
 Wheels Go Round. 1997.

Oxenbury, Helen. *Helen Oxenbury's Little Baby Books.* Candlewick Press, 1996.
 Boxed set includes: *I Can; I Hear; I See; I Touch.*

Pienkowski, Jan. Nursery Board Book series. Simon & Schuster.

Colors. 1987.	*Sizes.* 1991.
Faces. 1991.	*Stop Go.* 1992.
Food. 1991.	*Time.* 1991.
Homes. 1990.	*Yes No.* 1992.

Ricklen, Neil. Super Chubby Book series. Simon & Schuster.

Baby Outside. 1996.	*Baby's Good Night.* 1992.
Baby's 123. 1990.	*Baby's Neighborhood.* 1994.
Baby's ABC. 1997.	*Baby's Playtime.* 1994.
Baby's Big & Little. 1996.	*Baby's Toys.* 1997.
Baby's Clothes. 1997.	*Baby's Zoo.* 1992.
Baby's Friends. 1997.	*Daddy and Me.* 1997.
Baby's Home. 1997.	*Mommy and Me.* 1997.
Baby's Good Morning. 1992.	

Ross, Anna. *Knock Knock, Who's There?* Random House/Children's Television Workshop, 1994. (Chunky flap)

Ross, Katharine. *The Little Quiet Book.* Random House, 1989.

Santoro, Christopher. *Open the Barn Door.* Random House, 1993. (Chunky flap)

Scarry, Richard. *Richard Scarry's Lowly Worm Word Book.* Random House, 1981.
 Richard Scarry's Cars and Trucks from A–Z. Random House, 1990. (Chunky shape)

Shappie, Trisha Lee. *Where Is Your Nose?* Scholastic, 1997.

Smollin, Michael. *In & Out, Up & Down.* Random House, Children's Television Network, 1982.
 Ernie & Bert Can . . . Can You? Random House, Children's Television Network, 1982.

Snapshot Chubby Book series. Dorling Kindersley.
  ABC. 1994.
  Colors. 1994.
  My Home. 1995.
  My Toys. 1995.
  Shapes. 1994.
Van Fleet, Matthew. *Fuzzy Yellow Ducklings.* Dial Books, 1995.
Wik, Lars. *Baby's First Words.* Random House, 1985.

BOARD BOOKS

Alborough, Jez. *Ice Cream Bear.* Candlewick Press, 1997.
  It's the Bear. 1994.
  My Friend Bear. 1998.
  Bare Bear. Random House, 1984.
  Running Bear. 1985.
Bang, Molly. *Ten, Nine, Eight.* First Tupelo Board Book edition. Tupelo Books, 1998.
Boynton, Sandra. Boynton Board Book series. Simon & Schuster.
  But Not the Hippopotamus. 1995.
  Blue Hat, Green Hat. 1995.
  Doggies, A Counting and Barking Book. 1995.
  Going to Bed Book. 1995.
  Moo, Baa, La La La. 1995.
  Opposites. 1995.
  Hey! Wake Up! Workman Publishing, 2000.
Brett, Jan. *The Mitten: A Ukrainian Folktale.* Putnam, 1996. (Board book)
Brown, Margaret Wise. First Board Book editions. HarperCollins.
  Child's Good Night Book. Pictures by Jean Charlot. 1996.
  Goodnight Moon. Pictures by Clement Hurd. 1991.
  Runaway Bunny. Pictures by Clement Hurd, 1991.
Carle, Eric. First Board Book editions. HarperCollins.
  Do You Want to Be My Friend? 1995.
  The Mixed-Up Chameleon. 1998.
  The Secret Birthday Message. 1998.
  The Very Quiet Cricket. Putnam, 1997.
  Have You Seen My Cat? First Little Simon Board Book edition. Simon & Schuster, 1996.
  The Very Hungry Caterpillar. First Board Book edition. Philomel Books, 1994.
Carle, Eric. Play-and-Read Books. Cartwheel Books.
  Catch the Ball. 1998.
  Let's Paint a Rainbow. 1998.
  What's for Lunch? 1998.
Carlstrom, Nancy White. Illus. by Bruce Degen. Simon & Schuster. (Board book)
  Bizz Buzz Chug-A-Chug: Jesse Bear's Sounds. 1997.
  Hooray for Blue: Jesse Bear's Colors. 1997.
  I Love You, Mama, Any Time of Year. Jesse Bear Board Book. 1997.
  I Love You, Papa, In All Kinds of Weather. Jesse Bear Board Book. 1997.
  Jesse Bear, What Will You Wear? 1996.

Choosing Colors. Photos by Sandra Lousada. Dutton Children's Books/Playskool, 1995. (Board book)
Cohen, Miriam. *Backpack Baby.* Star Bright Books, 1999.
  Say Hi, Backpack Baby: A Backpack Baby Story. 2000.
Cousins, Lucy. Dutton Children's Books. (Board book)
  Humpty Dumpty and Other Nursery Rhymes. 1996.
  Jack & Jill and Other Nursery Rhymes. 1996.
  Little Miss Muffet and Other Nursery Rhymes. 1997.
  Wee Willie Winkie and Other Nursery Rhymes. 1997.
Day, Alexandra. *Good Dog, Carl.* First Little Simon Board Book edition. Simon & Schuster, 1996.
Degen, Bruce. *Jamberry.* First Board Book edition. HarperCollins, 1995.
dePaola, Tomie. *Strega Nona.* First Little Simon Board Book edition. Simon & Schuster, 1997.
Ehlert, Lois. *Color Farm.* First Board Book edition. HarperCollins, 1997.
  Color Zoo. First Board Book edition. HarperCollins, 1997.
  Eating the Alphabet. First Red Wagon Books. Harcourt Brace, 1996.
Fleming, Denise. *Count!* First Board Book edition. Henry Holt, 1997.
  Mama Cat Has Three Kittens. 1998.
  The Everything Book. 2000.
Hoban, Tana. *Black on White.* Greenwillow Books, 1993.
  Red, Blue, Yellow Shoe. 1986.
  What Is It? 1985.
  White on Black. 1993.
Hooker, Yvonne. Illus. by Carlo A. Michelini. Poke and Look books. Grosset & Dunlap.
  One Green Frog. 1989.
  Wheels Go Round. 1989.
Hopp, Lisa. *Circus of Colors.* Illus. by Chiara Bordoni. Poke and Look book. Grosset & Dunlap, 1997.
Isadora, Rachel. *I Touch.* Greenwillow Books, 1991. (Board book)
Keats, Ezra Jack. *The Snowy Day.* Viking, 1996. (Board book)
Kirk, David. *Miss Spider's Tea Party: The Counting Book.* First Board Book edition. Callaway & Kirk/Scholastic Press, 1997.
Lewison, Wendy. *Nighty Night.* Illus. by Giulia Orecchia. Poke and Look book. Grosset & Dunlap, 1992.
Lundell, Margaretta. *Land of Colors.* Illus. by Nadia Pazzaglia. Poke and Look book. Grosset & Dunlap, 1989.
Lundell, Margo. *What Does Baby See?* Illus. by Roberta Pagnoni. Poke and Look book. Putnam & Grosset, 1990.
Martin, Bill. Illus. by Eric Carle. First Board Book editions. Henry Holt.
  Brown Bear, Brown Bear, What Do You See? 1996.
  Polar Bear, Polar Bear, What Do You Hear? 1997.
Martin, Bill, & Archambault, John. *Chicka Chicka ABC.* Illus. by Lois Ehlert. First Little Simon Board Book edition. Simon & Schuster, 1993.

Marzollo, Jean. *I Spy Little Book.* Illus. by Walter Wick. Scholastic, 1997. (Board book)

I Spy Little Animals. Photos by Walter Wick. 1998. (Board book)

Do You Know New? HarperCollins, 1997.

Mama, Mama. HarperFestival, 1999.

Papa, Papa. 2000.

Pretend You're a Cat. Dial Books, 1990.

McBratney, Sam. *Guess How Much I Love You.* First Board Book edition. Candlewick Press, 1996.

McMullan, Kate. *If You Were My Bunny.* Illus. by David McPhail. First Board Book edition. Cartwheel Books, 1998.

Miller, Margaret. *Baby Faces.* Little Simon, 1998.

What's On My Head? 1998.

Miller, Virginia. *Be Gentle!* Candlewick Press, 1997.

Eat Your Dinner! 1992.

Go to Bed! 1993.

In a Minute! 2000.

On Your Potty! 1998.

Ogden, Betina, illus. *Busy Farmyard.* So Tall board book. Grosset & Dunlap, 1995.

Omerod, Jan. *101 Things to Do With a Baby.* Mulberry Books, 1993.

Opie, Iona Archibald. Illus. by Rosemary Wells. Mother Goose Board Book series. Candlewick Press.

Pussycat, Pussycat and Other Rhymes. 1997.

Humpty Dumpty and Other Rhymes. 1997.

Little Boy Blue and Other Rhymes. 1997.

Wee Willie Winkie and Other Rhymes. 1997.

Oxenbury, Helen. Baby Board Books. Wanderer Books.

Dressing. 1981.

Family. 1981.

Friends. 1981.

Playing. 1981.

Working. 1981.

Pfister, Marcus. Board book. North-South Books.

Hopper. 1998.

Hopper Hunts for Spring. 1998.

The Rainbow Fish. 1996.

Rainbow Fish to the Rescue. 1998.

Pinkney, Andrea & Brian. *Pretty Brown Face.* Harcourt Brace, 1997.

Piper, Watty. *The Little Engine That Could.* Illus. by Christina Ong. Platt & Munk, 1991.

Potter, Beatrix. *The Tale of Peter Rabbit.* Illus. by Florence Graham. Pudgy Pal Board Book. Grosset & Dunlap, 1996.

Pragoff, Fiona. Fiona Pragoff Board Books. Simon & Schuster.

Baby Days. 1995.

Baby Plays. 1995.

Baby Ways. 1994.

It's Fun to Be One. 1994.

It's Fun to Be Two. 1994.

Raffi. First Board Book editions. Crown Publishers.

Baby Beluga. Illus. by Ashley Wolff. 1997.

Wheels on the Bus. Illus. by Sylvie Kantorovitz Wickstrom. 1998.

Rathmann, Peggy. *Good Night, Gorilla.* Board book. Putnam, 1996.

Reasoner, Charles, & Hardt, Vicky. *Alphabite! A Funny Feast from A to Z.* Board book. Price Stern Sloan, 1989.

Rey, H. A. & Margret. Board books. Houghton Mifflin, 1998.

Curious George and the Bunny. 1998.

Curious George's ABC's. 1998.

Curious George's Are You Curious? 1998.

Curious George's Opposites. 1998.

Rosen, Michael. *We're Going on a Bear Hunt.* Illus. by Helen Oxenbury. First Little Simon Board Book edition. Simon & Schuster, 1997.

Seuss, Dr. Bright and Early Board Book series. Random House.

Dr. Seuss's ABC. 1996.

The Foot Book. 1997.

Mr. Brown Can Moo, Can You? 1996.

The Shape of Me and Other Stuff. 1997.

There's a Wocket in My Pocket. 1996.

Snapshot Board Book series. Dorling Kindersley.

All about Baby by Stephen Shott. 1994.

Baby and Friends by Paul Bricknell. 1994.

Good Morning, Baby by Jo Foord, et al. 1994.

Good Night, Baby by Mike Good & Stephen Shott. 1994.

Waddell, Martin. *Owl Babies.* Illus. by Patrick Benson. First Board Book edition. Candlewick Press, 1992.

Wells, Rosemary. *Max's Birthday.* Max Board Book. Dial Books for Young Readers, 1998.

Old MacDonald. Bunny Reads Back Board Book. Scholastic, 1998.

Wilkes, Angela. *My First Word Board Book.* Dorling Kindersley, 1997.

Williams, Sue. *I Went Walking.* Illus. by Julie Vivas. First Red Wagon Books edition. Harcourt Brace, 1996.

Williams, Vera B. *More, More, More Said the Baby.* First Tupelo Board Book edition. William Morrow, 1997.

Wood, Jakki. *Moo Moo, Brown Cow.* Illus. by Rog Bonner. First Red Wagon Board book. Harcourt Brace, 1996.

Ziefert, Harriet. Board Book. Dorling Kindersley.

Food! 1996.

Let's Get Dressed. Illus. by Susan Baum. 1997.

My Clothes. 1996.

Books for Two-Year-Olds

POP-UP BOOKS

Capucilli, Alyssa Satin. *Peekaboo Bunny: Friends in the Snow.* Scholastic, 1995.

Cousins, Lucy. *Maisy's ABC.* Candlewick Press, 1994.

Demarest, Chris L. *Honk!* Bell Books, 1998.

Doyle, Malachy. *Well, a Crocodile Can.* Millbrook Press, 2000.

Leslie, Amanda. *Flappy, Waggy, Wiggly.* Dutton, 1999.

Nagy, Krisztina (Illus.). *Fuzzy Bear's Bedtime.* Piggy Toes Press, 1999.

Nobles, Kristen. *Drive This Book.* Chronicle Books, 2001.
  Kiss This Book. Chronicle Books, 2001.

Rowe, Jeanette. *Whose Feet?* Little, Brown, 1998.

MOVEABLE BOOKS

Alexander, Harry. Mop Top Books series. Reader's Digest.
  Blue Rabbit. 2000.
  Red Dog. 2000.
  Yellow Bird. 2000.
  Green Cat. 2000.

Cousins, Lucy. *Maisy at the Farm.* Candlewick Press, 1998.

Davenport, Andrew. *Teletubbies: Po's Magic Watering Can.* Scholastic, 2000.

Davis, Billy (Illus.). *Tap the Tambourine!* Scholastic, 2000.

Dr. Seuss. *The Cat In The Hat's Great Big Flap Book.* Random House, 1999.

Maloney, Joan. *Teletubbies: The Boom-Boom Dance.* Scholastic, 2000.

Murphy, Chuck. *Slide 'n Seek Colors.* Simon & Schuster, 2001.

Regan, Dana. *Wheels on the Bus.* Scholastic, 1996.

Touch and Feel Farm. DK Publishing, 1998.

Touch and Feel Home. DK Publishing, 1998.

Watt, Fiona. *That's Not My Bunny.* Usborne, 2000.
  That's Not My Kitten. 2000.
  That's Not My Teddy. 1999.
  That's Not My Train. 2000.

Wells, Rosemary. *Goodnight, Max.* Penguin Putnam, 2000.

CLOTH BOOKS

Cousins, Lucy. *Flower in the Garden.* Candlewick Press, 1992.

Milne, A. A. *Hello, Eeyore.* Dutton Children's Books, 2000.
  Hello, Piget. 2000.
  Hello, Pooh. 1998.
  Hello, Tigger. 1998.

Ross, Anna. Furry Faces series. Random House.
  Big Bird. 1999.
  Cookie Monster. 1999.
  Elmo. 1999.
  Ernie. 1999.
  Grover. 1999.
  Oscar. 1999.

Warne, Frederick. *My Peter Rabbit Cloth Book.* Penguin Books, 1994.

BOARD BOOKS

Albee, Sarah. *Budgie and Pippa Count to Ten.* Simon & Schuster, 1996.
  Oreo Cookie Counting Book. 2000.

Alborough, Jed. *Hug.* Candlewick Press, 2000.

Awdry, Rev. W. *Thomas' Busy Day.* Random House, 2000.

Bailey, Debbie. *Hats.* Annick Press, 1991.

Boynton, Sandra. *Moo, Baa, La La.* Simon & Schuster, 1995.

Brown, Margaret Wise. *Goodnight Moon.* Harper & Row, 1947.

Carlstrom, Nancy White. *Jesse Bear's Tra-la Lub.* Alladin, 1994.
  Jesse Bear's Tum-tum Tickle. 1994.

dePaola, Tomie. *Tomie's Little Mother Goose.* Putnam & Grosset, 1985.

Dadko, Mary Ann. *Barney's Color Surprise.* Barney Publishing, 1993.

Degen, Bruce. *Jamberry.* Harper & Row, 1983.

Eastman, P. D. *Go Dogs, Go.* Random House, 1961.

Endersby, Frank. *Baby Sitter.* Child's Play, 1986.

Freeman, Don. *Courduroy Goes to the Doctor.* Viking, 1987.
  Courduroy's Busy Street. Viking, 1987.
  Courduroy's Party. Viking, 1985.

Geddes, Anne. *1-2-3.* Especially Kids, 1995.
  Colors. 1995.
  Dress Ups. 1995.
  Faces. 1995.

George, Emma. *Hop and Play.* Joshua Morris Publishing, 1989.

Greenfield, Eloise. *Honey, I Love.* Crowell, 1978.
  Kia Tanisha. HarperCollins, 1997.

Hayward, Linda. *Mine!* Random House, 1988.

Hines, Anna. *What Can You Do in the Rain?* Greenwillow, 1999.
  What Can You Do in the Snow? 1999.
  What Can You Do in the Sun? 1999.
  What Can You Do in the Wind? 1999.

Hughes, Shirley. *Being Together.* Candlewick Press, 1997.

Inkpen, Mick. *Wibbly Pig Likes Bananas.* Penguin Putnam, 1995.

Kenyon, Tony. *Pat-a-cake.* Candlewick Press, 1994.

Martin, Bill. *Polar Bear, Polar Bear.* Henry Holt, 1991.

Martin, Bill Jr. & Archambault, John. *Here Are My Hands.* H. Holt, 1998.

Marzollo, Jean. *Mama, Mama.* HarperCollins, 2000.
Papa, Papa. 2000.

McGrath, Barbara B. *M & M's Counting Board Book.* Charlesbridge, 1997.

Miller, Virginia. *Go to Bed.* Candlewick Press, 1993.
On Your Potty. 1994.

Opie, Iona. *Humpty Dumpty and Other Rhymes.* Candlewick Press, 1996.
Little Boy Blue. 1996.

Oxenbury, Helen. *Tom and Pippa.* Simon & Schuster, 1988.

Pandell, Karen. *Around the House.* DK Publishing, 1993.
In the Yard. DK Publishing, 1993.
I Love You, Sun, I Love You, Moon. G. P. Putnam's, 1994.

Pfister, Marcus. *Where Is My Friend?* NorthSouth Books, 1986.

Pinkney, Andrea & Brian. *Pretty Brown Face.* Harcourt Brace, 1997.

Tafuri, Nancy. *This Is the Farmer.* Greenwillow Books, 1994.

Tangvald, Christine & Rondi. *My Two Feet.* Chariot, 1990.
My Two Hands. 1990.

Waddell, Martin. *Owl Babies.* Candlewick Press, 1992.

Wellington, Monica. *Baby at Home.* Dutton Children's Books, 1997.
Baby Goes Shopping. 1997.
Bunny's Rainbow Day. 1999.

Wells, Rosemary. *Bear Went over the Mountain.* Scholastic, 1998.
BINGO. 1999.
Itsy Bitsy Spider. 1998.
Old MacDonald. 1998.
Max's Bath. Dial Books for Young Readers, 1985.

Williams, Sue. *I Went Walking.* Harcourt Brace, 1989.

Wolff, Ashley (Illus.). *Baby Beluga.* Crown, 1990.

Worth, Bonnie. *Bye-bye, Blankie.* Western Publishing, 1992.

VINYL BOOKS

Hoban, Tana. *Red, Blue, Yellow Shoe.* Greenwillow, 1994.

Warne, Frederick. *Benjamin Bunny.* Penguin Books, 1994.
Tom Kitten, Mittens, and Moppet. 1989.

Yablonsky, Buster. *Where Is Slippery Soap?* Nikelodeon, 2001.

SCRATCH AND SNIFF

DK Publishing.
Garden. 1999.
Food. 1999.
Party. 1999.

HARDCOVER PICTURE BOOKS

Brandenberg, Alexa. *I Am Me!* Red Wagon Books, 1996.

Burningham, John. *First Steps.* Candlewick Press, 1985.

Capucilli, A. S. *Inside a Barn in the Country.* Scholastic, 1995.

Carlson, Nancy. *I Like Me.* Puffin, 1988.

Carlstrom, Nancy White. *Jesse Bear, What Will You Wear?* Macmillan, 1986.

Cousins, Lucy. *Maisy* (series). Candlewick Press, 2001.

Crews, Donald. *Flying.* Greenwillow, 1986.

Davis, Katie. *Who Hoots?* Harcourt Brace, 2000.

Day, Alexandra. *Carl* (series). Farrar Straus Giroux, 1995.

Falwell, Cathryn. *We Have a Baby.* Clarion, 1993.

Florian, Douglas. *Vegetable Garden.* Voyager, 1991.

Ford, Miela. *Follow the Leader.* Greenwillow, 1996.
Little Elephant. 1994.

Fox, Mem. *Zoo Looking.* Mondo, 1996.

Frankel, Alona. *Once Upon a Potty* (His/hers versions). Barron's, 1984.

French, Vivian. *Not Again, Anna!* Levinson, 1998.
Oh No, Anna! Peachtree, 1997.

Gardiner, Lindsey. *Here Come Poppy and Max.* Little, Brown, 2000.

Geddes, Anne. *Down in the Garden (Alphabet Book).* Cedco, 1997.
Down in the Garden (Counting Book). 1997.

Ginsburg, Mirra. *Asleep, Asleep.* Greenwillow, 1992.

Hubbell, Patricia. *Pots and Pans.* Harper, 1998.
Bouncing Time. Harper, 2000.

Jay, Allison. *Picture This.* Dutton, 1999.

Krauss, Ruth. *Carrot Seed.* HarperTrophy, 1945.

LaCome, Julie. *I'm a Jolly Farmer.* Candlewick Press, 1994.

Lavis, Steve. *Cock-a-doodle-doo.* Lodestar Books, 1996.

Lewis, Kevin. *Chugga-chugga Choo-choo.* Hyperion, 1999.

Maccarone, Grace. *Cars! Cars! Cars!* Scholastic, 1995.
Oink, Moo! How Do You Do? Scholastic, 1995.

Mayer, M. *I was so mad.* A Golden Book, 1983.
Me Too! 1983.
When I Get Bigger. 1983.

Paul, Ann W. *Hello Toes! Hello Feet!* DK Ink, 1998.

Rau, Dana Meachen. *A Box Can Be Many Things.* Children's Press, 1997.

Reid, Rob. *Wave Goodbye.* Lee & Low, 1996.

Siddals, Mary McKenna. *I'll Play With You.* Clarion, 2000.

Sis, Peter. *Fire Truck.* Greenwillow, 1998.
Trucks, Trucks, Trucks. 1999.

Trapani, I. *I'm A Little Teapot.* Whispering Coyote Press, 1996.
The Itsy Bitsy Spider. 1993.

Whitman, Candace. *Now It Is Morning.* Farrar Straus Giroux, 1999.

Williams, Sue. *I Went Walking.* Harcourt Brace, 1989.

Criteria for Selecting Materials and Equipment for Children

Even though most materials and equipment appear safe, you will find that infants have an uncanny ability to find and remove parts. This may pose a threat. Therefore, to reduce safety hazards, you must constantly check and observe. When purchasing or choosing materials and equipment to use with infants, carefully determine if the items promote safety and development by using the following checklist.

SAFETY	Yes	No
A. Is it unbreakable?		
B. Is it durable?		
C. Is it washable?		
D. Is it too large to be swallowed?		
E. Is it free of removable parts?		
F. Is it free of sharp edges?		
G. Is it constructed from nontoxic materials?		
H. Is it free of pinching cracks?		
I. Is it suitable for the available space?		
PROMOTES DEVELOPMENT		
A. Is it developmentally appropriate?		
B. Does it challenge the child's development?		
C. Does it complement existing materials or equipment?		
D. Does it teach multiple skills?		
E. Does it involve the child?		
F. Is it nongender biased?		
G. Does it promote a multicultural perspective?		
H. Does it promote nonviolent play?		

Materials and Equipment for Promoting Optimal Development

Materials and equipment play a major role in promoting an infant's or toddler's development, as well as provide enjoyment.

Materials and Equipment to Promote Development for Infants

animal, toy
baby lotion
balls
bells
blanket or mat
blocks for building, lightweight
books (black & white and picture books—cardboard, cloth, and/or vinyl)
carpet pieces
cars, large toy
cassettes or compact discs, a variety of music: jazz, lullabies, classical, etc.
couch or sturdy furniture
crayons, large
diaper-changing table
dishes, nonbreakable (e.g., cups, spoons, plates)
doll accessories: blanket, bed, clothes

dolls, multiethnic
doughs and clays
elastic bands
fill and dump toys
glider
high chair
household items (e.g., pots, pans, wooden spoons, metal or plastic bowls, laundry baskets)
infant seat
infant stroller
large beads to string
mirrors (unbreakable)
mobile
musical instruments, child-size
nesting cups
pacifier
pails and shovels
paintbrushes
pictures of infants
pillows

pop-up toys
props to accompany finger plays
puppets
puzzles with large pieces
push and pull toys
rattles, different sizes, shapes, weights, and textures
riding toys
rocking chair
rubber toys
squeeze toys
stacking rings
stroller
stuffed animals
sun catchers
tape or compact disc recorder
teething rings
towels
toy telephones
wheeled toys
wind chimes

Materials and Equipment to Promote Development for Toddlers

all of the infant toys just listed plus . . .
blocks
cardboard boxes
dramatic play items: pots, pans, dishes
dress-up clothes: hats, shoes, scarves, jewelry, purse
drum

hammer and peg toy
masks
nuts and bolts
pencils and washable felt-tip markers
ring toss game
sand toys: scoops, shovels, cans, sifters
simple puzzles

simple shape sorters
snap beads
transportation toys: cars, trucks, boats, trains, airplanes
tricycles
wagon
wheelbarrow
wheeled push toys

Movement Activities for Children from Thirteen to Thirty-Six Months

Movement activities, like music, are valuable for young children. Movement is an important tool for young children to express themselves. They can move to verbal directions or music. For example, you may ask the children to lumber along like an elephant or hop like a bunny. Remember children's responses to movement will vary depending on age.

Through movement activities children can:

♡ Learn vocabulary words such as fast, slow, soft, and loud

♡ Explore their bodies as they move

♡ Practice combining rhythm and movements

♡ Learn how movement is related to space

♡ Express their imaginations (Herr 2001, p. 140)

This appendix contains movement activities designed for young children. To introduce these activities, you should demonstrate the actions for the children, while simultaneously giving the directions.

LISTEN TO THE DRUM

Fast.
Slow.
Heavy.
Soft.
Big.
Small.

MOVING SHAPES

Try to move like something huge and heavy—
an elephant.
Try to move like something small and heavy—
a fat frog.
Try to move like something big and light—
a beach ball.
Try to move like something small and light—
a butterfly.

PRESENT PANTOMIME

You're going to get a present.
What is the shape of the box?
How big is the box? Feel the box.
Hold it. Unwrap the present.
Take it out. Now put it back.

OCCUPATION PANTOMIME

Show me how a clown acts.
Show me how a truck driver acts.
Show me how a baby acts.
Show me how a mama acts.
Show me how a daddy acts.
Show me how a bus driver acts.

PANTOMIME FEELINGS

Show me how you look when you are happy.
Show me how you feel when you are tired.
Show me how you feel when you get up in the morning.
Show me how you feel when you are sad.
Show me how you feel when you are mad.

TO BECOME AWARE OF SPACE

Place your leg in front of you.
Place your leg in back of you.
Lift your leg in front of you.
Reach up high to the ceiling.
Touch the floor.

TO BECOME AWARE OF TIME

Run very fast.
Walk very slowly.
Jump up and down.
Jump slowly.
Jump fast.
Sit down on the floor slowly.
Slowly curl up on the floor as small as possible.

Favorite Finger Plays, Nursery Rhymes, and Chants

Finger plays, nursery rhymes, and chants help infants and toddlers to develop social interaction skills, listening and auditory memory skills, expressive language skills, and concept formation. They also help infants and toddlers become aware of their body parts and see themselves as persons who can do things.

Finger plays use a variety of actions and words together; some involve whole body actions. An example is the finger play "This Little Piggy," which is a favorite for infants. The younger the child, the shorter and simpler the rhyme and the body action need to be. For these children, larger body parts are more suitable. The young child will join you visually and participate in the actions before learning the words. Typically, after repeated exposure, the toddlers will gradually learn some of the words while others may learn the entire finger play. This appendix contains examples of finger plays, nursery rhymes, and chants that children may enjoy. Note that finger plays can be an important technique for teaching "Who am I?"; young children particularly enjoy these activities when their names are included.

ANIMALS

Can you hop like a rabbit?
  (*suit actions to words*)
Can you jump like a frog?
Can you walk like a duck?
Can you run like a dog?
Can you fly like a bird?
Can you swim like a fish?
And be still like a good child?
As still as this?

BODY TALK

When I smile, I tell you that I'm happy.
  (*point to the mouth*)
When I frown I tell you that I am sad.
  (*pull down corners of the mouth*)
When I raise my shoulders and tilt my head I tell you,
  "I don't know."
  (*raise shoulders, tilt head, raise hands, and shake head*)

BRUSHING TEETH

I move the toothbrush back and forth.
  (*pretend to brush teeth*)
I brush all of my teeth.
I swish the water to rinse them and then
  (*puff out cheeks to swish*)
I look at myself and smile.
  (*smile at one another*)

THE CHIMNEY

Here is the chimney,
  (*make hand into a fist with thumb inside*)
Here is the top.
  (*place other hand on top of fist*)

Open the lid.
  (*remove top hand*)
Out Santa will pop.
  (*pop up thumb*)

A CIRCLE

Around in a circle we will go.
Little tiny baby steps make us go very slow.
And then we'll take some great giant steps,
As big as they can be.
Then in a circle we'll stand quietly.

CIRCUS CLOWN

I'd like to be a circus clown
And make a funny face,
  (*make a funny face*)
And have all the people laugh at me
As I jump around the place.
  (*act silly and jump around*)

CLAP YOUR HANDS 1

Clap your hands 1, 2, 3.
  (*suit actions to words*)
Clap your hands just like me.
Roll your hands 1, 2, 3.
Roll your hands just like me.

CLAP YOUR HANDS 2

Clap, clap, clap your hands,
As slowly as you can.
Clap, clap, clap your hands,
As fast as you can.

CLOCKS

(rest elbows on hips; extend forearms and index fingers up
  and move arms sideways slowly and rhythmically)
Big clocks make a sound like
Tick, Tock, Tick, Tock.
  (speak slowly)
Small clocks make a sound like
  (move arms faster)
Tick, tock, tick, tock.
And the very tiny clocks make a sound
  (move still faster)
Like tick, tick, tock, tock.
Tick, tock, tick, tock, tick, tock.

FIVE LITTLE PUMPKINS

(hold up five fingers and bend them down one
  at a time as verse progresses)
Five little pumpkins sitting on a gate;
The first one said, "My it's getting late."
The second one said, "There are witches in the air."
The third one said, "But we don't care."
The fourth one said, "Let's run, let's run."
The fifth one said, "It's Halloween fun."
"Wooooooo" went the wind,
  (sway hand through the air)
And out went the lights.
  (loud clap)
These five little pumpkins ran fast out of sight.
  (place hands behind back)

FRIENDS

I like my friends,
So when we are at play,
I try to be very kind
And nice in every way.

GOBBLE, GOBBLE

A turkey is a funny bird,
His head goes wobble, wobble.
  (place hands together and move back and forth)
And he knows just one word,
Gobble, gobble, gobble.

GRANDMA'S SPECTACLES

(bring index finger and thumb together and place against face
  as if wearing glasses)
These are Grandma's spectacles.
This is Grandma's hat.
  (bring fingertips together in a peak over head)
This is the way she folds her hands,
  (clasp hands together)
And lays them in her lap.
  (lay hands in lap)

HERE IS A BALL

Here is a ball,
  (touch fingers of both hands to form a ball)
Here is a bigger ball,
  (bow the arms with fingers touching to form a second ball)
And here is the biggest ball of all.
  (extend arms and do not touch fingers)
Now let us count the balls we made:
  One,
  Two,
  Three
  (repeat making the balls to reinforce the concepts by
  showing the increasing size)

HICKORY, DICKORY, DOCK

Hickory, dickory, dock.
The mouse ran up the clock.
The clock struck one, the mouse ran down,
Hickory, dickory, dock.

I LOOKED INSIDE MY MIRROR

I looked inside my mirror
To see what I could see.
It looks like I am happy today,
Because that smiling face is me.

I LOVE MY FAMILY

Some families are large.
  (spread arms out wide)
Some families are small.
  (bring arms close together)
But I love my family
  (cross arms over chest)
Best of all!

JACK AND JILL

Jack and Jill went up a hill
To fetch a pail of water.
Jack fell down and broke his crown
And Jill fell tumbling after.

JACK-IN-THE-BOX

Jack-in-the-box
Sit so still
  (squat or stoop down, placing hands over head as a cover)
Won't you come out?
Yes, I will!
  (open hands and jump up)

LITTLE JACK HORNER

Little Jack Horner
Sat in a corner
Eating a Christmas pie.
 (*pretend you're eating*)
He put in his thumb,
 (*point thumb down*)
And pulled out a plum
 (*point thumb up*)
And said, "What a good boy am I!"
 (*say out loud*)

LITTLE MISS MUFFET

Little Miss Muffet
Sat on a tuffet
Eating her curds and whey.
Along came a spider
And sat down beside her
And frightened Miss Muffet away!

RING AROUND THE ROSIE

(*teacher and children hold hands and walk around
 in a circle*)
Ring around the rosie,
A pocket full of posies,
Ashes, ashes,
We all fall down.
 (*everyone falls to the ground*)

THE MONKEY

The monkey claps, claps, claps his hands.
 (*clap hands*)
The monkey claps, claps his hands.
 (*clap hands*)
Monkey see, monkey do,
The monkey does the same as you.
 (*use pointer finger*)

The monkey pats his arm, pats his arm.
 (*pat arm*)
The monkey pats his arm, pats his arm.
 (*pat arm*)
Monkey see, monkey do,
The monkey does the same as you.
 (*use pointer finger*)

The monkey touches his head, touches his head.
 (*touch head*)
The monkey touches his head, touches his head.
 (*touch head*)
Monkey see, monkey do,
The monkey does the same as you.
 (*use pointer finger*)

The monkey gives a big smile, gives a big smile.
 (*smile big*)
The monkey gives a big smile, gives a big smile.
 (*smile big*)

Monkey see, monkey do,
The monkey does the same as you.
 (*use pointer finger*)

The monkey crawls all around, crawls all around.
 (*get down on hands and knees and crawl*)
The monkey crawls all around, crawls all around.
 (*get down on hands and knees and crawl*)
Monkey see, monkey do,
The monkey does the same as you.
 (*use pointer finger*)

THE MUFFIN MAN

Oh, do you know the muffin man,
The muffin man, the muffin man?
Oh, do you know the muffin man
Who lives on Drury Lane?
Yes, I know the muffin man,
The muffin man, the muffin man.
Oh, yes, I know the muffin man
Who lives on Drury Lane.

THE MULBERRY BUSH

(*Since this is a lengthy finger play, begin with just a verse or
two and then gradually individually add the remaining verses
as the toddlers gain proficiency.*)

Here we go 'round the mulberry bush,
The mulberry bush, the mulberry bush.
Here we go 'round the mulberry bush,
So early in the morning.

This is the way we wash our clothes,
Wash our clothes, wash our clothes.
This is the way we wash our clothes,
So early Monday morning.

This is the way we iron our clothes,
Iron our clothes, iron our clothes.
This is the way we iron our clothes,
So early Tuesday morning.

This is the way we scrub our clothes,
Scrub our clothes, scrub our clothes.
This is the way we scrub our clothes,
So early Wednesday morning.

This is the way we mend our clothes,
Mend our clothes, mend our clothes.
This is the way we mend our clothes,
So early Thursday morning.

This is the way we sweep the house,
Sweep the house, sweep the house.
This is the way we sweep the house,
So early Friday morning.

This is the way we bake our bread,
Bake our bread, bake our bread.
This is the way we bake our bread,
So early Saturday morning.

This is the way we go to church,
Go to church, go to church.
This is the way we go to church,
So early Sunday morning.

(The children can join hands with you and skip around in a circle. They can act out the words of the song beginning with the second verse. If church is inappropriate for Sunday, another activity can be substituted such as barbeque, play ball, mow the lawn, etc.)

MY PUPPY

I like to pet my puppy.
  (pet puppy)
He has such nice soft fur.
  (pet puppy)
And if I don't pull his tail
  (pull tail)
He won't say, "Grr!"
  (make face)

MY RABBIT

My rabbit has two big ears
  (hold up index and middle fingers for ears)
And a funny little nose.
  (join the other fingers for a nose)
He likes to nibble carrots
  (separate thumb from other two fingers)
And he hops wherever he goes.
  (move whole hand jerkily)

MY TOOTHBRUSH

I have a little toothbrush.
  (use pointer finger)
I hold it very tight.
  (make hand into fist.)
I brush my teeth each morning,
And then again at night.
  (use pointer finger and pretend to brush)

MY TURTLE

This is my turtle.
  (make fist; extend thumb)
He lives in a shell.
  (hide thumb in fist)
He likes his home very well.
He pokes his head out when he wants to eat.
  (extend thumb)
And pulls it back when he wants to sleep.
  (hide thumb in fist)

OLD KING COLE

Old King Cole was a merry old soul
  (lift elbows up and down)
And a merry old soul was he.
  (nod head)

He called for his pipe.
  (clap two times)
He called for his bowl.
  (clap two times)
And he called for his fiddlers three.
  (clap two times then pretend to play violin)

ONE, TWO, BUCKLE MY SHOE

One, two, buckle my shoe.
  (count on fingers as verse progresses)
Three, four, shut the door.
  (suit actions to words)
Five, six, pick up sticks.
Seven, eight, lay them straight.
Nine, ten, a big tall hen.

OPEN, SHUT THEM

Open, shut them.
  (suit actions to words)
Open, shut them.
Open, shut them.
Give a little clap.
Open, shut them.
Open, shut them.
Open, shut them.
Put them in your lap.
Creep them, creep them
Right up to your chin.
Open up your little mouth,
But do not put them in.
Open, shut them.
Open, shut them.
Open, shut them.
To your shoulders fly,
Then like little birdies
Let them flutter to the sky.
Falling, falling almost to the ground,
Quickly pick them up again and turn
Them round and round.
Faster, faster, faster.
Slower, slower, slower.
  (repeat first verse)

PAT-A-CAKE

Pat-a-cake, pat-a-cake, baker's man.
Bake me a cake as fast as you can!
  (clap hands together lightly)
Roll it
  (roll hands)
And pat it
  (touch hands together lightly)
And mark it with a *B*
  (write B in the air)
And put it in the oven for baby and me.
  (point to baby and yourself)

POPCORN CHANT 1

Popcorn, popcorn
Hot, hot, hot
Popcorn, popcorn
Pop, pop, pop.

POPCORN CHANT 2

Popcorn, popcorn
In a pot
What'll happen when you get hot?
Boom! Pop. Boom! Pop. Pop.
That's what happens when you get hot!

POPCORN CHANT 3

Popcorn, popcorn
In a dish
How many pieces do you wish?
1, 2, 3, 4
Eat those up and have some more!

RAINDROPS

Rain is falling down.
Rain is falling down.
   (*raise arm, flutter fingers to the ground, tapping the floor*)
Pitter-patter
Pitter-patter
Rain is falling down.

READY NOW, LET'S GO

I am a little kitty,
I have to tippy toe.
Come and do it with me.
Ready now, let's go.
   (*take tiny steps*)

I am a little rabbit.
I love to hop, hop, hop.
Come and do it with me.
It's fun we will never stop.
   (*hop around*)

I am a big bird.
I love to fly around using my wings.
Come and do it with me.
Ready now? Let's go.
   (*use arms as wings to fly*)

I am a great big elephant.
I take big steps so slow.
I'd love to have you join me.
Ready now? Let's go
   (*take slow, big steps*)

I am a little puppy.
I love to run and run.
Come and do it with me.
We will have such fun.
   (*run like a puppy*)

RIGHT HAND, LEFT HAND

This is my right hand,
I'll raise it up high.
   (*raise the right hand up high*)
This is my left hand.
I'll touch the sky.
   (*raise the left hand up high*)
Right hand,
   (*show right palm*)
Left hand,
   (*show left palm*)
Roll them around
   (*roll hands over and over*)
Left hand,
   (*show palm*)
Right hand,
   (*show palm*)
Pound, pound, pound.
   (*hit fists together*)

SEE, SEE, SEE

See, see, see
   (*shade eyes with hands*)
Three birds are in a tree.
   (*hold up three fingers*)
One can chirp
   (*point to thumb*)
And one can sing
   (*point to index finger*)
One is just a tiny thing.
   (*point to middle finger, then rock baby bird in arms*)
See, see, see
Three birds are in a tree.
   (*hold up three fingers*)

STAND UP TALL

Stand up tall
Hands in the air.
Now sit down
In your chair.
Clap your hands
And make a frown.
Smile and smile.
Hop like a clown.

TEAPOT

I'm a little teapot,
> (*place right hand on hip, extend left, palm out*)

Short and stout.
Here's my handle.
And here's my spout.
When I get all steamed up, I just shout:
"Tip me over, and pour me out."
> (*bend to left*)

I can change my handle
> (*place left hand on hip and extend right hand out*)

And my spout.
"Tip me over, and pour me out."
> (*bend to the right*)

TEDDY BEAR

Teddy bear, teddy bear, turn around.
Teddy bear, teddy bear, touch the ground.
Teddy bear, teddy bear, climb the stairs.
Teddy bear, teddy bear, jump into bed.
Teddy bear, teddy bear, turn out the lights.
Teddy bear, teddy bear, blow a kiss.
Teddy bear, teddy bear, say goodnight.
Goodnight.

TEN LITTLE DUCKS

Ten little ducks swimming in the lake.
> (*move ten fingers as if swimming*)

Quack! Quack!
> (*snap fingers twice*)

They give their heads a shake.
> (*shake fingers*)

Glunk! Glunk! Go go little frogs.
> (*two claps of hands*)

And away to their mothers,
The ten ducks run.
> (*move hands in running motion from front to back*)

TEN LITTLE FINGERS

I have ten little fingers and ten little toes.
> (*children point to portions of body as they repeat words*)

Two little arms and one little nose.
One little mouth and two little ears.
Two little eyes for smiles and tears.
One little head and two little feet.
One little chin, that makes _____ complete.

THIS LITTLE PIGGY

This little piggy went to market.
> (*point to one finger at a time*)

This little piggy stayed home.
This little piggy had roast beef.
This little piggy had none.
This little piggy cried, "Wee, wee, wee."
And ran all the way home.

THREE FROGS

Three little frogs
> (*hold up three fingers of left hand*)

Asleep in the sun.
> (*fold them over*)

We'll creep up and wake them.
> (*make creeping motion with fingers of right hand*)

Then we will run.
> (*hold up three fingers while right hand runs away*)

THREE LITTLE DUCKIES

Three little duckies
> (*hold up three fingers*)

Swimming in the lake.
> (*make swimming motions*)

The first ducky said,
> (*hold up one finger*)

"Watch the waves I make."
> (*make wave motions*)

The second ducky said,
> (*hold up two fingers*)

"Swimming is such fun."
> (*smile*)

The third ducky said,
> (*hold up three fingers*)

"I'd rather sit in the sun."
> (*turn face to sun*)

Then along came a motorboat.
With a Pop! Pop! Pop!
> (*clap three times*)

And three little duckies
Swam away from the spot.
> (*put three fingers behind back*)

THREE LITTLE MONKEYS

Three little monkeys jumping on the bed.
> (*hold up three fingers*)

One fell off and bumped his head.
Mama called the doctor and the doctor said,
No more monkeys jumping on the bed.
> (*shake pointer finger as if scolding*)

Two little monkeys jumping on the bed,
> (*hold up two fingers*)

One fell off and bumped his head.
Mama called the doctor and the doctor said,
No more monkeys jumping on the bed.
> (*shake pointer finger as if scolding*)

One little monkey jumping on the bed.
> (*hold up one finger*)

He fell off and bumped his head.
Mama called the doctor and the doctor said,
No more jumping on the bed.
> (*shake pointer finger as if scolding*)

TWO LITTLE APPLES

(*hold hands above head, form circles with thumb
    and forefinger of each hand*)
Away up high in the apple tree,
Two red apples smiled at me.
    (*smile*)
I shook that tree as hard as I could.
    (*put hands out as if on tree—shake*)
And down they came.
    (*hands above head and lower to ground*)
And ummmmm were they good!
    (*rub tummy*)

TWO LITTLE BLACKBIRDS

Two little blackbirds sitting on a hill.
    (*show two fingers*)
One named Jack.
    (*hold up one finger on right hand*)
One named Jill.
    (*hold up one finger on the left hand*)
Fly away Jack.
    (*move right hand behind back*)
Fly away Jill.
    (*move the left hand behind back*)
Come back Jack.
    (*return right hand*)
Come back Jill.
    (*return left hand*)
(Children's names can be substituted for Jack and Jill in
    this finger play.)

TWO LITTLE KITTENS

(*hold up two fingers, cup hands together to form a ball*)
Two little kittens found a ball of yarn
As they were playing near a barn.
    (*bring hands together pointed upward for barn*)
One little kitten jumped in the hay,
    (*hold up one finger, make jumping then wiggling motion*)
The other little kitten ran away.
    (*make running motion with other hand*)

ZOO ANIMALS

This is the way the elephant goes.
    (*clasp hands together, extend arms, move back and forth*)
With a curly trunk instead of a nose.
The buffalo, all shaggy and fat.
Has two sharp horns in place of a hat.
    (*point to forehead*)
The hippo with his mouth so wide
Let's see what's inside.
    (*hands together and open wide and close them*)
The wiggly snake upon the ground
Crawls along without a sound.
    (*weave hands back and forth*)
But monkey see and monkey do is the
funniest animal in the zoo.
    (*place thumbs in ears and wiggle fingers*)

Songs

Music is a universal language and a natural form of expression for children of all ages. Infants and toddlers need to have a wide variety of music experiences that are casual and spontaneous. They enjoy lullabies that are slow, soft, and soothing. In addition to lullabies, classical, folk and music from different ethnic and cultural groups should all be included. Children like songs about animals and familiar objects, which tell a story and contain frequent repetition. Choose simple songs with a strong melody that represent their age, abilities, and interests. Chances are children will more easily remember these songs. While singing, remember to convey enthusiasm.

Music is a valuable experience for young children. They enjoy listening to music while engaged in activities and napping. Music promotes the development of listening skills and builds vocabulary. It is a tool that provides an opportunity for learning new concepts such as up/down, fast/slow, heavy/light, and loud/soft. Music releases tension, stimulates the imagination, and promotes the development of auditory memory skills.

ALL ABOUT ME

Brushing Teeth
(Tune: "Mulberry Bush")
This is the way we brush our teeth,
Brush our teeth, brush our teeth.
This is the way we brush our teeth,
So early in the morning.

Good Morning
Good morning to you.
Good morning to you.
We're all in our places,
With bright shining faces,
Good morning to you.

ANIMALS

The Animals on the Farm
(Tune: "The Wheels on the Bus")
The cows on the farm go moo, moo, moo,
Moo, moo, moo, moo, moo, moo.
The cows on the farm go moo, moo, moo,
All day long.

The horses on the farm go nay, nay, nay,
Nay, nay, nay, nay, nay, nay.
The horses on the farm go nay, nay, nay,
All day long.

OTHER VERSES:
Pigs—oink
Sheep—baa
Chicken—cluck
Turkeys—gobble

The Ants Go Marching One by One
The ants go marching one by one.
Hurrah! Hurrah!
The ants go marching one by one.
Hurrah! Hurrah!
The ants go marching one by one.

The little one stops to suck her thumb
And they all go marching,
Down in the ground
To get out of the rain.
Boom Boom Boom

OTHER VERSES:
Two by two
The little one stops to tie his shoe
Three by three
The little one stops to scratch her knee
Four by four
The little one stops to shut the door
Five by five
The little one stops to wave goodbye.

Circus
(Tune: "Did You Ever See a Lassie")
Let's pretend that we are clowns, are clowns, are clowns.
Let's pretend that we are clowns.
We'll have so much fun.
We'll put on our makeup and make people laugh hard.
Let's pretend that we are clowns.
We'll have so much fun.

Let's pretend that we are elephants, are elephants, are elephants.
Let's pretend that we are elephants.
We'll have so much fun.
We'll sway back and forth and stand on just two legs.
Let's pretend that we are elephants.
We'll have so much fun.

Let's pretend that we are on a trapeze, a trapeze, a trapeze.
Let's pretend that we are on a trapeze.
We'll have so much fun.
We'll swing high and swoop low and make people shout "oh"!
Let's pretend that we are on a trapeze.
We'll have so much fun!

Easter Bunny
(Tune: "Ten Little Indians")
Where, oh, where is the Easter Bunny,
Where, oh, where is the Easter Bunny,
Where, oh, where is the Easter Bunny,
Early Easter morning?

Find all the eggs and put them in a basket,
Find all the eggs and put them in a basket,
Find all the eggs and put them in a basket,
Early Easter morning.

Itsy Bitsy Spider
The itsy bitsy spider went up the water spout
Down came the rain and washed the spider out
Out came the sun and dried up all the rain
And the itsy bitsy spider went up the spout again.
(This is also a popular finger play.)

Kitty
(Tune: "Bingo")
I have a cat. She's very shy.
But she comes when I call Kitty
K-I-T-T-Y
K-I-T-T-Y
K-I-T-T-Y
and Kitty is her name-o.

(Variation: Let children think of other names.)

Old MacDonald Had a Farm
Old MacDonald had a farm,
E-I-E-I-O.
And on his farm he had some cows,
E-I-E-I-O.
With a moo, moo here and a moo, moo there,
Here a moo, there a moo, everywhere a moo, moo.
Old MacDonald had a farm,
E-I-E-I-O.

OTHER VERSES:
Sheep—baa, baa
Pigs—oink, oink
Ducks—quack, quack
Chickens—chick, chick

Two Little Black Bears
(Tune: "Two Little Blackbirds")
Two little black bears sitting on a hill
One named Jack, one named Jill.
Run away Jack
Run away Jill.
Come back Jack
Come back Jill.
Two little black bears sitting on a hill
One named Jack, one named Jill.

CLEANUP SONGS

Cleanup Time 1
(Tune: "London Bridge")
Cleanup time is already here,
Already here, already here.
Cleanup time is already here,
Already here.

Cleanup Time 2
(Tune: "Hot Cross Buns")
Cleanup time.
Cleanup time.
Put all of the toys away.
It's cleanup time.

Do You Know What Time It Is?
(Tune: "The Muffin Man")
Oh, do you know what time it is,
What time it is, what time it is?
Oh, do you know what time it is?
It's almost cleanup time.
  (Or, it's time to clean up.)

A Helper I Will Be
(Tune: "The Farmer in the Dell")
A helper I will be.
A helper I will be.
I'll pick up the toys and put them away.
A helper I will be.

It's Cleanup Time
(Tune: "Looby Loo")
It's cleanup time at the preschool.
It's time for boys and girls
To stop what they are doing.
And put away their toys.

Oh, It's Cleanup Time
(Tune: "Oh, My Darling Clementine")
Oh, it's cleanup time,
Oh, it's cleanup time,
Oh, it's cleanup time right now.
It's time to put the toys away,
It is cleanup time right now.

Passing Around
(Tune: "Skip to My Loo")
Brad, take a napkin and pass them to Sara.
Sara, take a napkin and pass them to Tina.
Tina, take a napkin and pass them to Eric.
Passing around the napkins.

(Fill in the appropriate child's name and substitute for "napkin" any object that needs to be passed at mealtime.)

Put Your Coat On
(Tune: "Oh, My Darling Clementine")
Put your coat on.
Put your coat on.
Put your winter coat on now.
We are going to play outside.
Put your coat on right now.
(Change "coat" to any article of clothing.)

This Is the Way
(Tune: "Mulberry Bush")
This is the way we pick up our toys,
Pick up our toys, pick up our toys.
This is the way we pick up our toys,
At cleanup time each day.
(Substituting "before bedtime" opposed to "cleanup time" could modify this song.)

Time to Clean up
(Tune: "Are You Sleeping?")
Time to clean up.
Time to clean up.
Everybody help.
Everybody help.
Put the toys away, put the toys away.
Then sit down. *(Or, then come here.)*
(Specific toys can be mentioned in place of "toys.")

We're Cleaning Up Our Room
(Tune: "The Farmer in the Dell")
We're cleaning up our room.
We're cleaning up our room.
We're putting all the toys away.
We're cleaning up our room.

FAVORITES

London Bridge
London Bridge is falling down,
Falling down, falling down.
London Bridge is falling down.
My fair lady.

Twinkle, Twinkle, Little Star
Twinkle, twinkle, little star,
How I wonder what you are!
Up above the world so high,
Like a diamond in the sky.
Twinkle, twinkle, little star,
How I wonder what you are!

Where Is Thumbkin?
Where is thumbkin?
Where is thumbkin?
Here I am,
Here I am.
How are you today, sir?
Very well, I thank you.
Fly away, fly away.

OTHER VERSES:
Pointer
Tall man
Ring man
Pinky

FEELINGS

Feelings
(Tune: "Twinkle, Twinkle, Little Star")
I have feelings.
You do, too.
Let's all sing about a few.
I am happy. *(smile)*
I am sad. *(frown)*
I get scared. *(wrap arms around self)*
I get mad. *(sneer and wrinkle nose)*
I am proud of being me. *(hands on hips)*
That's a feeling, too, you see.
I have feelings. *(point to self)*
You do, too. *(point to someone else)*
We just sang about a few.

If You're Happy and You Know It
If you're happy and you know it
Clap your hands.
    (clap twice)
If you're happy and you know it
Clap your hands.
    (clap twice)
If you're happy and you know it
Then your face will surely show it.
If you're happy and you know it
Clap your hands.
    (clap twice)

If you're sad and you know it
Say boo-hoo.
    (rub your eyes)
If you're sad and you know it
Say boo-hoo.
    (rub your eyes)
If you're sad and you know it
Then your face will surely show it.
If you're sad and you know it
Say boo-hoo.
    (rub your eyes)

If you're mad and you know it
Wrinkle your nose.
    (wrinkle nose)
If you're mad and you know it
Wrinkle your nose.
    (wrinkle nose)
If you're mad and you know it
Then your face will surely show it.
If you're mad and you know it
Wrinkle your nose.
    (wrinkle nose)

PEOPLE

Are You Sleeping?
Are you sleeping?
Are you sleeping?
Brother John, brother John,
Morning bells are ringing,
Morning bells are ringing.
Ding, ding, dong!
Ding, ding, dong!

Do You Know This Friend of Mine?
(Tune: "The Muffin Man")
Do you know this friend of mine,
This friend of mine,
This friend of mine?
Do you know this friend of mine?
Her name is _____.
Yes, we know this friend of yours,
This friend of yours,
This friend of yours.
Yes, we know this friend of yours.
Her name is _____.

The Muffin Man
Oh, do you know the muffin man,
The muffin man, the muffin man?
Oh, do you know the muffin man,
Who lives on Drury Lane?

Oh, yes we know the muffin man,
The muffin man, the muffin man.
Oh, yes we know the muffin man,
Who lives on Drury Lane.

Oh, how do you know the muffin man,
The muffin man, the muffin man?
Oh, how do you know the muffin man,
Who lives on Drury Lane.

Cause [Papaw] is the muffin man,
The muffin man, the muffin man.
[Pawpaw] is the muffin man,
Who lives on Drury Lane.

(Substitute names of other males who are important in the child's life, such as Daddy or Uncle Todd.)

This Old Man
This old man
He played one
He played knick knack on a drum
With a knick knack, paddy whack
Give the dog a bone
This old man came rolling home.

OTHER VERSES:
He played two
He played knick knack on my shoe.
He played three
He played knick knack on a tree
He played four
He played knick knack at my door
He played five
He played knick knack on a hive.

TRANSPORTATION

Row, Row, Row, Your Boat
Row, row, row your boat.
Gently down the stream.
Merrily, merrily, merrily, merrily,
Life is but a dream.

The Wheels on the Bus
The wheels on the bus go round and round.
Round and round, round and round.
The wheels on the bus go round and round.
All around the town.

OTHER VERSES:
The wipers on the bus go swish, swish, swish.
The doors on the bus go open and shut.
The horn on the bus goes beep, beep, beep.
The driver on the bus says, "Move on back."
The people on the bus go up and down.

Rhythm Instruments

Using rhythm instruments is a method of teaching young children to express themselves. Rhythm instruments can be common household objects or purchased through school supply stores or catalogs. Examples include:

Commercially Purchased	Household Items
Drums	Pots
Jingle sticks	Pans
Cymbals	Lids
Rattles	Wooden spoons
Wrist bells	Aluminum pie pans
Shakers	Metal whisks
Maracas	Plastic bowls
Sandpaper blocks	

You can also improvise and construct these instruments—save cans, cardboard tubes that have plastic lids from nuts, chips, and coffee. These items can be used as drums. If you place noise-making objects inside the cans or tubes, they can be used as shakers. However, make sure that you secure the lid using a high-quality adhesive tape that children cannot remove.

Recipes

Play dough and clay are satisfying materials for toddlers. Play dough is softer than clay and is usually preferred by the young toddler because it is pliable and easy to manipulate. When provided a handful of play dough, without encouragement, a child will begin to poke, push, roll, pinch, tear, squeeze, and pound it. Clay, on the other hand, is a firmer or stiffer medium, which requires more refined muscular development to successfully manipulate. As a result, clay typically is more appropriate for older toddlers and children.

Modeling materials such as play dough and clay are valuable tools for the young child. Play dough and play dough accessories provide young children with an opportunity to:

- explore materials using their senses
- represent their thoughts and ideas
- learn the physical nature of materials
- develop the ability to make choices
- learn to appreciate the value of tools in the human hands

- heighten perceptual powers
- develop small muscle coordination skills
- develop hand-eye coordination skills
- express their feelings, explore, and experiment

Colors can be added to play dough to increase interest. Food coloring is the preferred medium to add color to the dough because it will not rub off on a child's hands. Food coloring can be added directly to the liquids required in the recipe. Otherwise, colored tempera can be added to the flour. With this method, the dough requires kneading. A gallon-size, self-sealing plastic bag is a convenient way to mix and knead dough colored with tempera paint.

Give each child a piece of play dough the size of an orange or small grapefruit. Unless using Formica™, Corian™, or granite surface, cover the children's work area with a washable or disposable cover. Establish rules for playing with dough. Such rules might include the following: (1) dough should only be used at the table or other place you designate; (2) children should not be allowed to interfere with other children's use of dough; and (3) after using any modeling medium, children must wash their hands. While using play dough, toddlers need to be constantly supervised. Although nontoxic, play dough should not be consumed as it can upset a child's stomach.

Recipes for Doughs and Clays

Clay Dough

3 cups flour
3 cups salt
3 tablespoons alum

Combine ingredients and slowly add water, a little at a time. Mix well with spoon. As mixture thickens, continue mixing with your hands until it has the feel of clay. If it feels too dry, add more water. If it is too sticky, add equal parts of flour and salt.

Play Dough

2 cups flour
1 cup salt
1 cup hot water
2 tablespoons cooking oil
4 teaspoons cream of tartar
food coloring

Mix well. Knead until smooth. This dough may be kept in a plastic bag or covered container and used again. If it gets sticky, more flour may be added.

Favorite Play Dough

Combine and boil until dissolved:
2 cups water
½ cup salt
food coloring or tempera paint
Mix in while very hot:
2 tablespoons cooking oil
2 tablespoons alum
2 cups flour

Knead (approximately 5 minutes) until smooth. Store in covered airtight containers.

Cornstarch and Soda Play Dough

2 cups cornstarch
4 cups baking soda
2½ cups water
food coloring, if desired

In a pan, combine the baking soda, cornstarch, and water. Cook over a medium heat, while stirring constantly. When the mixture thickens and forms a ball, remove from the heat. Knead when cool and, if desired, add the food coloring. Note: If you are preparing the play dough for only one child, divide the recipe in half.

Cornstarch Play Dough

½ cup salt
¼ cup water
½ cup cornstarch
food coloring

Mix all ingredients thoroughly and cook over low heat, stirring constantly until the dough forms a ball. Add food coloring in desired color.

Laundry Modeling Dough

1½ cups laundry lint
1 cup warm water
⅓ cup flour
1 drop cinnamon or clove oil

Place lint and water in saucepan and stir. The lint will absorb most of the water. Add flour, stirring constantly. Add oil and cook over medium heat. When small peaks form, remove to a heatproof working surface and cool for ten minutes. (Note: This dough does not keep well, so use it immediately.)

Microwave Play Dough

2 cups flour
½ cup cornstarch
2 cups water
1 cup salt
1 tablespoon alum
1 tablespoon cooking oil
food coloring

Combine flour, salt, cornstarch, and alum in a 2-quart bowl. Mix the water, oil, and food coloring. Pour over dry ingredients and stir. Microwave 4½ to 5 minutes until thick, stirring every minute. Cool mixture. If desired, knead in color.

Sand Dough

4 cups sand
3 cups flour
¼ cup cornstarch
¼ cup oil
1 cup water

In bowl, mix sand and flour together. Add cornstarch, oil, and water. If needed, add more water for desired texture.

Baker's Clay #1

1 cup cornstarch
2 cups baking soda
1½ cups cold water

Combine ingredients. Stir until smooth. Cook over medium heat, stirring constantly until mixture reaches the consistency of slightly dry mashed potatoes.

Turn out onto plate or bowl, covering with damp cloth. When cool enough to handle, knead thoroughly until smooth and pliable on cornstarch-covered surface.

Store in tightly closed plastic bag or covered container.

Baker's Clay #2

4 cups flour
1½ cups water
1 cup salt

Combine ingredients. Mix well. Knead 5 to 10 minutes. Roll out to ¼-inch thickness. Cut with decorative cookie cutters or with a knife. Make a hole at the top.

Bake at 250 degrees for 2 hours or until hard. When cool, paint with tempera paint and spray with clear varnish or paint with acrylic paint.

Cloud Dough

3 cups flour
1 cup oil
scent (oil of peppermint, wintergreen, lemon, etc.)
food coloring

Combine ingredients. Add water until easily manipulated (about ½ cup).

Sawdust Dough

2 cups sawdust
3 cups flour
1 cup salt

Combine ingredients. Add water as needed. This dough becomes very hard and is not easily broken. It is good to use for making objects and figures that one desires to keep.

Cooked Clay Dough

1 cup flour
½ cup cornstarch
4 cups water
1 cup salt
3 or 4 pounds flour
coloring if desired

Stir slowly and be patient with this recipe. Blend the flour and cornstarch with cold water. Add salt to the water and boil. Pour the boiling salt and water solution into the flour and cornstarch paste and cook over hot water until clear. Add the flour and coloring to the cooked solution and knead. After the clay has been in use, if too moist, add flour; if dry, add water. Keep in covered container. Wrap dough with damp cloth or towel. This dough has a very nice texture and is very popular with all age groups. May be kept 2 or 3 weeks.

Salt Dough

4 cups salt
1 cup cornstarch

Combine with sufficient water to form a paste. Cook over medium heat, stirring constantly.

Play Dough

5 cups flour
2 cups salt
4 tablespoons cooking oil
add water to right consistency

Powdered tempera may be added in with flour or food coloring may be added to finished dough. This dough may be kept in plastic bag or covered container for approximately 2 to 4 weeks. It is better used as play dough rather than leaving objects to harden.

Soap and Sawdust

1 cup whipped soap
1 cup sawdust

Mix well together. This gives a very different feel and appearance. It is quite easily molded into different shapes by all age groups. May be used for 2 to 3 days if stored in tight plastic bag.

Used Coffee Grounds

2 cups used coffee grounds
½ cup salt
1½ cups oatmeal

Combine ingredients and add enough water to moisten. Children like to roll, pack, and pat this mixture. It has a very different feel and look, but it's not good for finished products. It has a very nice texture.

Soap Modeling

2 cups soap flakes

Add enough water to moisten, and whip until consistency to mold. Use soap such as Ivory Flakes, Dreft, Lux, etc. Mixture will have very slight flaky appearance when it can be molded. It is very enjoyable for all age groups and is easy to work with. Also, the texture is very different from other materials ordinarily used for molding. It may be put up to dry, but articles are very slow to dry.

Fingerpaint Recipes

Liquid Starch Method

liquid starch (put in squeeze bottles)
dry tempera paint in shakers

Put about 1 tablespoon of liquid starch on the surface to be painted. Let the child shake the paint onto the starch. Mix and blend the paint. Note: If this paint becomes too thick, simply sprinkle a few drops of water onto the painting.

Soap Flake Method

Mix in a small bowl:
soap flakes
a small amount of water

Beat until stiff with an eggbeater. Use white soap on dark paper, or add food coloring to the soap and use it on light-colored paper. This gives a slight three-dimensional effect.

Uncooked Laundry Starch

A mixture of 1 cup laundry/liquid starch, 1 cup cold water, and 3 cups soap flakes will provide a quick fingerpaint.

Flour and Salt I

1 cup flour
1½ cups salt
¾ cup water
coloring

Combine flour and salt. Add water. This has a grainy quality, unlike the other fingerpaints, providing a different sensory experience. Some children enjoy the different touch sensation when 1½ cup salt is added to the other recipes.

Flour and Salt II

2 cups flour
2 teaspoons salt
3 cups cold water
2 cups hot water
food coloring

Add salt to flour, then pour in cold water gradually and beat mixture with eggbeater until it is smooth. Add hot water and boil until it becomes clear. Beat until smooth, then mix in coloring. Use ¼ cup food coloring to 8 to 9 ounces of paint for strong colors.

Instantized Flour, Uncooked Method

1 pint water (2 cups)
1½ cups instantized flour
    (the kind used to thicken gravy)

Put the water in the bowl and stir the flour into the water. Add color. Regular flour may be lumpy.

Cooked Starch Method

1 cup laundry starch dissolved in a
    small amount of cold water
5 cups boiling water added slowly
    to dissolve starch
1 tablespoon glycerine (optional)

Cook the mixture until it is thick and glossy. Add 1 cup mild soap flakes. Add color in separate containers. Cool before using.

Cornstarch Method

Gradually add 2 quarts water to 1 cup cornstarch. Cook until clear and add ½ cup soap flakes. A few drops of glycerine or oil of wintergreen may be added.

Flour Method

Mix 1 cup flour and 1 cup cold water. Add 3 cups boiling water and bring all to a boil, stirring constantly. Add 1 tablespoon alum and coloring. Paintings from this recipe dry flat and do not need to be ironed.

Rainbow Stew

1 cup cornstarch
4 cups water
½ cup sugar
food coloring (if desired)

Cook water, cornstarch, and sugar until thick. Mixture will be clear and glossy. Add food color to desired boldness.

Tips:

Be sure you have running water and towels nearby or provide a large basin of water where children can rinse off.

Fingerpaint on a smooth table, oil cloth, or cafeteria tray. Some children prefer to start fingerpainting with shaving cream on a sheet of oil cloth.

Food coloring or powdered paint may be added to the mixture before using, or allow children to choose the colors they want sprinkled on top of paint.

Sometimes reluctant children are more easily attracted to the paint table if the fingerpaints are already colored.

Bubble Solutions

Bubble Solution #1

1 cup of water
2 tablespoons of liquid detergent
1 tablespoon glycerine
½ teaspoon sugar

Bubble Solution #2

⅔ cup liquid dish detergent
1 gallon of water
1 tablespoon glycerine (optional)

Allow solution to sit in an open container for at least a day before use.

Bubble Solution #3

3 cups water
2 cups Joy liquid detergent
½ cup Karo syrup

Source: Herr, J. (2000). *Creative resources for the early childhood classroom* (3rd ed.). Albany, NY: Delmar.

Resources Related to Infants and Toddlers

The authors and Delmar make every effort to ensure that all Internet resources are accurate at the time of printing. However, due to the fluid, time-sensitive nature of the Internet, we cannot guarantee that all URLs and Web site addresses will remain current for the duration of this edition.

The American Montessori Society Bulletin
American Montessori Society (AMS)
281 Park Avenue South, 6th Floor
New York, NY 10010-6102
(212) 358-1250; (212) 358-1256 FAX
www.amshq.org

Babybug
Cricket Magazine Group
PO Box 7437
Red Oak, IA 51591-2437
(800) 827-0227
www.babybugmag.com

The Black Child Advocate
National Black Child Development Institute
(NBCDI)
1101 15th Street NW, Suite 900
Washington, DC 20005
(202) 833-2220; (202) 833-8222 FAX
www.nbcdi.org

Child and Youth Quarterly
Human Sciences Press
233 Spring Street, Floor 5
New York, NY 10013-1522
(212) 620-8000

Child Development and Child Development Abstracts and Bibliography
Society for Research in Child Development
University of Michigan
505 East Huron, Suite 301
Ann Arbor, MI 48104-1567
(734) 998-6578; (734) 998-6569 FAX
www.srcd.org

Child Health Alert
PO Box 610228
Newton Highlands, MA 02161
(781) 239-1762
ericps.ed.uiuc.edu/npin/nls/chalert.html

Childhood Education; Journal of Research in Early Childhood Education
Association for Childhood Education
International (ACEI)
17904 Georgia Avenue; Suite 215
Olney, MD 20832
(301) 570-2111; (301) 570-2212 FAX
www.udel.edu/bateman/acei

Child Welfare
Child Welfare League of America (CWLA)
440 First Street NW, 3rd Floor
Washington, DC 20001-2085
(202) 638-2952; (202) 638-4004 FAX
www.cwla.org

Children Today
Superintendent of Documents
U.S. Government Printing Office
Washington, DC 20402
www.access.gpo.gov

Early Childhood Education Journal
Human Sciences Press
233 Spring Street, Floor 5
New York, NY 10013-1522
(212) 620-8000
www.wkap.nl/journalhome.htm/1082-3301

Developmental Psychology
American Psychological Association
750 First Street NE
Washington, DC 20002-4242
(202) 336-5500
www.apa.org

Dimensions of Early Childhood
Southern Association for Children Under Six
Box 56130 Brady Station
Little Rock, AR 72215
(800) 305-7322; (501) 227-5297 FAX

Early Child Development and Care
Gordon and Breach Publishing
Box 32160
Newark, NJ 07102
(800) 545-8398
www.gbhap.com

Earlychildhood NEWS
Earlychildhood.com
2 Lower Ragsdale, Suite 125
Monterey, CA 93940
(831) 333-5501; (800) 627-2829;
(831) 333-5510 FAX
www.earlychildhood.com

Early Childhood Research Quarterly
National Association for the Education of Young
Children (NAEYC)
1509 16th Street NW
Washington, DC 20036-1426
(202) 232-8777; (202) 328-1846 FAX
www.naeyc.org

Educational Leadership
Association for Supervision and Curriculum
Development (ASCD)
1703 North Beauregard Street
Alexandria, VA 22311-1714
(703) 578-9600; (800) 933-ASCD;
(703) 575-5400 FAX
www.ascd.org

Educational Researcher
American Educational Research Association
(AERA)
1230 17th Street NW
Washington, DC 20036
(202) 223-9485; (202) 775-1824 FAX
www.aera.net

ERIC/EECE
University of Illinois
Children's Research Center
51 Gerty Drive
Champaign, IL 61820-7469
http://ericps.ed.uiuc.edu/eece

Exceptional Children
Council for Exceptional Children
1110 North Glebe Road, Suite 300
Arlington, VA 22201-5704
(703) 620-3660; (888) CEC-SPED;
(703) 264-9494 FAX
www.cec.sped.org

Gifted Child Quarterly
National Association for Gifted Children
1707 L Street NW, Suite 550
Washington, DC 20036
(202) 785-4268
www.nagc.org

Instructor
Scholastic, Inc.
555 Broadway
New York, NY 10012
www.scholastic.com/instructor

Journal of Family and Consumer Sciences
American Association of Family and Consumer
Services (AAFCS)
1555 King Street
Alexandria, VA 22314
(703) 706-4600; (703) 706-4663 FAX
www.aafcs.org

Young Children
National Association for the Education of Young
Children (NAEYC)
1509 16th Street NW
Washington, DC 20036-1426
(202) 232-8777; (202) 328-1846 FAX
www.naeyc.org

Other information may be obtained through various
professional organizations.

The following groups may be able to provide you with
other resources:

American Association for Gifted Children
Box 90270
Durham, NC 27708-0270
www.aagc.org

*American Association of Family and Consumer Services
(AAFCS)*
1555 King Street
Alexandria, VA 22314
(703) 706-4600; (703) 706-4663 FAX
www.aafcs.org

American Montessori Association (AMS)
281 Park Avenue South, 6th Floor
New York, NY 10010
(212) 358-1250; (212) 358-1256 FAX
www.amshq.org

*Association for Childhood Education International
(ACEI)*
17904 Georgia Avenue, Suite 215
Olney, MD 20832
(301) 570-2111; (800) 423-3563;
(301) 570-2212 FAX
www.udel.edu/bateman/acei

Association for Supervision and Curriculum Development (ASCD)
1703 North Beauregard Street
Alexandria, VA 22311-1714
(703) 578-9600; (800) 933-ASCD;
(703) 575-5400 FAX
www.ascd.org

Canadian Association for the Education of Young Children (CAYC)
612 West 23rd Street
Vancouver, BC V7M 2C3
www.cayc.ca

Children's Defense Fund
25 E Street NW
Washington, DC 20001
(202) 628-8787
www.childrensdefense.org

Child Welfare League of America
440 First Street NW, 3rd Floor
Washington, DC 20001-2085
(202) 638-2952; (202) 638-4004 FAX
www.cwla.org

Council for Exceptional Children
1110 North Glebe Road, Suite 300
Arlington, VA 22201-5704
(703) 620-3660; (888) CEC-SPED;
(703) 264-9494 FAX
www.cec.sped.org

International Reading Association
800 Barksdale Road
PO Box 8139
Newark, DE 19714-8139
(302) 731-1600; (302) 731-1057 FAX
www.reading.org

National Association for the Education of Young Children (NAEYC)
1509 16th Street NW
Washington, DC 20036-1426
(202) 232-8777; (202) 328-1846 FAX
www.naeyc.org

National Association for Gifted Children
1707 L Street NW, Suite 550
Washington, DC 20036
(202) 785-4268
www.nagc.org

National Black Child Development Institute (NBCDI)
1101 15th Street NW, Suite 900
Washington, DC 20005
(202) 833-2220; (202) 833-8222 FAX
www.nbcdi.org

National Committee to Prevent Child Abuse
2950 Tennyson Street
Denver, CO 80212
(303) 433-2451; (303) 433-9701 FAX
www.childabuse.org

National Education Association (NEA)
1201 16th Street NW
Washington, DC 20036
(202) 833-4000
www.nea.org

Society for Research in Child Development
University of Michigan
505 East Huron, Suite 301
Ann Arbor, MI 48104-1567
(734) 998-6578; (734) 998-6569 FAX
www.srcd.org

Developmental Checklist

Child's Name: _____

Observer's Name: _____

Observation Date: _____

PHYSICAL DEVELOPMENT	OBSERVED	
Birth to Three Months	Date	Comments
Acts reflexively—sucking, stepping, rooting		
Swipes at objects in front of body, uncoordinated		
Holds head erect and steady when lying on stomach		
Lifts head and shoulders		
Rolls from side to back		
Follows moving objects with eyes		
Four to Six Months		
Holds cube in hand		
Reaches for objects with one hand		
Rolls from back to side		
Reaches for objects in front of body, coordinated		
Sits with support		
Transfers objects from hand to hand		
Grabs objects with either hand		
Sits in tripod position using arms for support		
Seven to Nine Months		
Sits independently		
Stepping reflex returns, so that child bounces when held on a surface in a standing position		
Leans over and reaches when in a sitting position		
Gets on hands and knees but may fall forward		
Crawls		
Pulls to standing position		
Claps hands together		
Stands with adult's assistance		
Learns pincer grasp, using thumb with forefinger to pick up objects		
Uses finger and thumb to pick up objects		
Brings objects together with banging noises		

The developmental milestones listed are based on universal patterns of when various traits emerge. Because each child is unique certain traits may develop at an earlier or later age.

PHYSICAL DEVELOPMENT (continued)	OBSERVED	
Ten to Twelve Months	Date	Comments
Supports entire body weight on legs		
Walks when hands are held		
Cruises along furniture or steady objects		
Stands independently		
Walks independently		
Crawls up stairs or steps		
Voluntarily releases objects held in hands		
Has good balance when sitting; can shift positions without falling		
Takes off shoes and socks		
Thirteen to Eighteen Months		
Builds tower of two cubes		
Turns the pages of a cardboard book two or three at a time		
Scribbles vigorously		
Walks proficiently		
Walks while carrying or pulling a toy		
Walks up stairs with assistance		
Nineteen to Twenty-Four Months		
Walks up stairs independently, one step at a time		
Jumps in place		
Kicks a ball		
Runs in a modified fashion		
Shows a decided preference for one hand		
Completes a three-piece puzzle with knobs		
Builds a tower of six cubes		
Twenty-Five to Thirty-Six Months		
Maneuvers around obstacles in a pathway		
Runs in a more adult-like fashion; knees are slightly bent, arms move in the opposite direction		
Walks down stairs independently		
Marches to music		
Uses feet to propel wheeled riding toys		
Rides a tricycle		
Usually uses whole arm movements to paint or color		
Throws a ball forward, where intended		
Builds tower using eight or more blocks		
Imitates drawing circles and vertical and horizontal lines		
Turns pages in book one by one		
Fingers work together to scoop up small objects		
Strings large beads on a shoelace		

Additional Observations for Physical Development

The developmental milestones listed are based on universal patterns of when various traits emerge. Because each child is unique certain traits may develop at an earlier or later age.

LANGUAGE AND COMMUNICATION DEVELOPMENT	OBSERVED	
	Date	Comments
Birth to Three Months		
Communicates with cries, grunts, and facial expressions		
Prefers human voices		
Coos		
Laughs		
Smiles and coos to initiate and sustain interactions with caregiver		
Four to Six Months		
Babbles spontaneously		
Acquires sounds of native language in babble		
Canonical, systematic consonant-vowel pairings; babbling occurs		
Participates in interactive games initiated by adults		
Takes turns while interacting		
Seven to Nine Months		
Varies babble in loudness, pitch, and rhythm		
Adds *d, t, n,* and *w* to repertoire of babbling sounds		
Produces gestures to communicate often by pointing		
May say *mama* or *dada* but does not connect words with parents		
Ten to Twelve Months		
Uses preverbal gestures to influence the behavior of others		
Demonstrates word comprehension skills		
Waves good-bye		
Speaks recognizable first word		
Initiates familiar games with adults		
Thirteen to Eighteen Months		
Has expressive vocabulary of 10 to 20 words		
Engages in "jargon talk"		
Engages in telegraphic speech by combining two words together		
Experiences a burst of language development		
Comprehends approximately 50 words		
Nineteen to Twenty-Four Months		
Continues using telegraphic speech		
Able to combine three words		
Talks, 25 percent of words being understandable		
Refers to self by name		

The developmental milestones listed are based on universal patterns of when various traits emerge. Because each child is unique certain traits may develop at an earlier or later age.

LANGUAGE AND COMMUNICATION DEVELOPMENT (continued)	OBSERVED	
Nineteen to Twenty-Four Months (continued)	Date	Comments
Joins three or four words into a sentence		
Comprehends approximately 300 words		
Expressive language includes a vocabulary of approximately 250 words		
Twenty-Five to Thirty-Six Months		
Continues using telegraphic speech combining three or four words		
Speaks in complete sentences following word order of native language		
Displays effective conversational skills		
Refers to self as *me* or *I* rather than by name		
Talks about objects and events not immediately present		
Uses grammatical markers and some plurals		
Vocabulary increases rapidly, up to 300 words		
Enjoys being read to if allowed to participate by pointing, talking, and turning pages		

Additional Observations for Language and Communication Development

COGNITIVE DEVELOPMENT	OBSERVED	
Birth to Three Months	Date	Comments
Cries for assistance		
Acts reflexively		
Prefers to look at patterned objects, bull's-eye, horizontal stripes, and the human face		
Imitates adults' facial expressions		
Searches with eyes for sources of sounds		
Begins to recognize familiar people at a distance		
Discovers and repeats bodily actions such as sucking, swiping, and grasping		
Discovers hands and feet as extension of self		

The developmental milestones listed are based on universal patterns of when various traits emerge. Because each child is unique certain traits may develop at an earlier or later age.

Four to Six Months	Date	Comments
Recognizes people by their voice		
Enjoys repeating acts, such as shaking a rattle, that produce results in the external world		
Searches with eyes for source of sounds		
Enjoys watching hands and feet		
Searches for a partially hidden object		
Uses toys in a purposeful manner		
Imitates simple actions		
Explores toys using existing schemas such as sucking, banging, grasping, shaking, etc.		
Seven to Nine Months		
Enjoys looking at books with familiar objects		
Distinguishes familiar from unfamiliar faces		
Engages in goal-directed behavior		
Anticipates events		
Finds objects that are totally hidden		
Imitates behaviors that are slightly different than those usually performed		
Begins to show interest in filling and dumping containers		
Ten to Twelve Months		
Solves sensorimotor problems by deliberately using schemas, such as shaking a container to empty its contents		
Points to body parts upon request		
Drops toys intentionally and repeatedly looks in the direction of the fallen object		
Waves good-bye		
Shows evidence of stronger memory capabilities		
Follows simple, one-step directions		
Categorizes objects by appearance		
Looks for objects hidden in a second location		
Thirteen to Eighteen Months		
Explores properties of objects by acting on them in novel ways		
Solves problems through trial and error		
Experiments with cause-and-effect relationships such as turning on televisions, banging on drums, etc.		
Plays body identification games		
Imitates novel behaviors of others		
Identifies family members in photographs		

The developmental milestones listed are based on universal patterns of when various traits emerge. Because each child is unique certain traits may develop at an earlier or later age.

COGNITIVE DEVELOPMENT (continued)	OBSERVED	
Nineteen to Twenty-Four Months	**Date**	**Comments**
Points to and identifies objects on request, such as when reading a book, touring, etc.		
Sorts by shapes and colors		
Recognizes self in photographs and mirror		
Demonstrates deferred imitation		
Engages in functional play		
Finds objects that have been moved while out of sight		
Solves problems with internal representation		
Categorizes self and others by gender, race, hair color, etc.		
Twenty-Five to Thirty-Six Months		
Uses objects for purposes other than intended		
Uses private speech while working		
Classifies objects based on one dimension, such as toy cars versus blocks		
Follows two-step directions		
Concentrates or attends to self-selected activities for longer periods of time		
Points to and labels objects spontaneously, such as when reading a book		
Coordinates pretend play with other children		
Gains a nominal sense of numbers through counting and labeling objects in a set		
Begins developing concepts about opposites such as big and small, tall and short, in and out		
Begins eveloping concepts about time such as today, tomorrow, and yesterday		

Additional Observations for Cognitive Development

The developmental milestones listed are based on universal patterns of when various traits emerge. Because each child is unique certain traits may develop at an earlier or later age.

SOCIAL DEVELOPMENT	OBSERVED	
Birth to Three Months	Date	Comments
Turns head toward a speaking voice		
Recognizes primary caregiver		
Bonds to primary caregiver		
Finds comfort in the human face		
Displays a social smile		
Is quieted by a voice		
Begins to differentiate self from caregiver		
Four to Six Months		
Seeks out adults for play by crying, cooing, or smiling		
Responds with entire body to familiar face by looking at a person, smiling, kicking legs, and waving arms		
Participates actively in interactions with others by vocalizing in response to adult speech		
Smiles at familiar faces and stares solemnly at strangers		
Distinguishes between familiar and nonfamiliar adults and surroundings		
Seven to Nine Months		
Becomes upset when separated from a favorite adult		
Acts deliberately to maintain the presence of a favorite adult by clinging or crying		
Uses adults as a base for exploration, typically		
Looks to others who are exhibiting signs of distress		
Enjoys observing and interacting briefly with other children		
Likes to play and responds to games such as patty-cake and peekaboo		
Engages in solitary play		
Develops preferences for particular people and objects		
Shows distress when in the presence of a stranger		
Ten to Twelve Months		
Shows a decided preference for one or two caregivers		
Plays parallel to other children		
Enjoys playing with siblings		
Begins asserting self		
Begins developing a sense of humor		
Develops a sense of self-identity through the identification of body parts		
Begins distinguishing boys from girls		

The developmental milestones listed are based on universal patterns of when various traits emerge. Because each child is unique certain traits may develop at an earlier or later age.

SOCIAL DEVELOPMENT (continued)		OBSERVED
Thirteen to Eighteen Months	Date	Comments
Demands personal attention		
Imitates behaviors of others		
Becoming increasingly aware of the self as a separate being		
Shares affection with people other than primary caregiver		
Shows ownership of possessions		
Begins developing a view of self as autonomous when completing tasks independently		
Nineteen to Twenty-Four Months		
Shows enthusiasm for company of others		
Views the world only from own, egocentric perspective		
Plays contentedly alone or near adults		
Engages in functional play		
Defends possessions		
Recognizes self in photographs or mirrors		
Refers to self with pronouns such as *I* or *me*		
Categorizes people by using salient characteristics such as race or hair color		
Shows less fear of strangers		
Twenty-five to Thirty-Six Months		
Observes others to see how they do things		
Engages primarily in solitary or parallel play		
Sometimes offers toys to other children		
Begins to play cooperatively with other children		
Engages in sociodramatic play		
Wants to do things independently		
Asserts independence by using "no" a lot		
Develops a rudimentary awareness that others have wants or feelings that may be different than their own		
Makes demands of or "bosses" parents, guardians, and caregivers		
Uses physical aggression less and uses words to solve problems		
Engages in gender stereotypical behavior		

Additional Observations for Social Development

The developmental milestones listed are based on universal patterns of when various traits emerge. Because each child is unique certain traits may develop at an earlier or later age.

EMOTIONAL DEVELOPMENT	OBSERVED	
Birth to Three Months	Date	Comments
Feels and expresses three basic emotions: interest, distress, and disgust		
Cries to signal a need		
Quiets in response to being held, typically		
Feels and expresses enjoyment		
Shares a social smile		
Reads and distinguishes adults' facial expressions		
Begins to self-regulate emotional expressions		
Laughs aloud		
Quiets self by using techniques such as sucking a thumb or pacifier		
Four to Six Months		
Expresses delight		
Responds to the emotions of caregivers		
Begins to distinguish familiar from unfamiliar people		
Shows a preference for being held by a familiar person		
Begins to assist with holding a bottle		
Expresses happiness selectively by laughing and smiling more with familiar people		
Seven to Nine Months		
Responds to social events by using the face, gaze, voice, and posture to form coherent emotional patterns		
Expresses fear and anger more often		
Begins to regulate emotions through moving into or out of experiences		
Begins to detect the meaning of others' emotional expressions		
Looks to others for clues on how to react		
Shows fear of strangers		
Ten to Twelve Months		
Continues to exhibit delight, happiness, discomfort, anger, and sadness		
Expresses anger when goals are blocked		
Expresses anger at the source of frustration		
Begins to show compliance to caregivers' requests		
Often objects to having playtime stopped		
Begins eating with a spoon		
Assists in dressing and undressing		
Acts in loving, caring ways toward dolls or stuffed animals, typically		
Feeds self a complete meal when served finger foods		
Claps when successfully completing a task		

The developmental milestones listed are based on universal patterns of when various traits emerge. Because each child is unique certain traits may develop at an earlier or later age.

EMOTIONAL DEVELOPMENT (continued)	OBSERVED	
Thirteen to Eighteen Months	Date	Comments
Exhibits autonomy by frequently saying "no"		
Labels several emotions		
Connects feelings with social behaviors		
Begins to understand complicated patterns of behavior		
Demonstrates the ability to communicate needs		
May say "no" to something they want		
May lose emotional control and have temper tantrums		
Shows self-conscious emotions such as shame, guilt, and shyness		
Becomes frustrated easily		
Nineteen to Twenty-Four Months		
Expresses affection to others spontaneously		
Acts to comfort others in distress		
Shows the emotions of pride and embarrassment		
Uses emotion words spontaneously in conversations or play		
Begins to show sympathy to another child or adult		
Becomes easily hurt by criticism		
Experiences a temper tantrum when goals are blocked, on occasion		
Associates facial expressions with simple emotional labels		
Twenty-Five to Thirty-Six Months		
Experiences increase in number of fears		
Begins to understand the consequences of basic emotions		
Learns skills for coping with strong emotions		
Seeks to communicate more feelings with specific words		
Shows signs of empathy and caring		
Loses control of emotions and throws temper tantrums		
Able to recover from temper tantrums		
Enjoys helping with chores such as cleaning up toys or carrying grocery bags		
Begins to show signs of readiness for toileting		
Desires that routines be carried out exactly as has been done in the past		

Additional Observations for Emotional Development

The developmental milestones listed are based on universal patterns of when various traits emerge. Because each child is unique certain traits may develop at an earlier or later age.

Anecdotal Record

SAMPLE ANECDOTAL RECORD

Child's name: ___Reyshawn___ Date of birth:___5/13_____

Observer's name: ___Chris___ Observation date:___3/31_____

Behavioral description of observation:

During diapering, Reyshawn took the clean diaper and covered his face. He then removed the diaper and began smiling and laughing.

Interpretation of observation:

Reyshawn was initiating a favorite game that we have played during diapering in the past. He is beginning to demonstrate advancements in his language and communication as well as his social skills.

SAMPLE ANECDOTAL RECORD

Child's name: _____ Date of birth:_____

Observer's name: _____ Observation date:_____

Behavioral description of observation:

Interpretation of observation:

Sample Running Record

Child's name:_____

Date of birth:_____

Location:_____

Date and time:_____

Observer's name:_____

Behavioral Description of Observations:	**Interpretations of/Reflections on Observations:**

Sample Running Record

Child's name: _____Christina R._____

Date of birth: _____2-10-96_____

Location: _____Inside, before and during snack_____

Date and time: _____March 2, 2xxx_____2:00–2:25 p.m.___

Observer's name: ___Jane U._____

Behavioral Description of Observations:	**Interpretations of/Reflections on Observations:**
Christina is playing with a toy truck. She says, "Katy, can I keep it?" She repeats this two times until a teacher responds, "No, the toys are for all the children to use at school." She drops the truck on the floor and walks over to the shelf. She picks up a guitar and plays it while walking around the room looking at the other children. The teacher says, "It's snack time. Wash your hands, Christina." Christina says to the boy beside her, "It's snack time." She walks to the snack table and sits down.	Working on ownership issues. Social development: Helping classmate to follow routine of classroom.
Christina sits in a hunched position between a boy and a girl. She says, "Look, bananas" in an excited voice while reaching for the plate. She grabs the plate and takes two bananas. The teacher says, "Start with one banana. If you eat the first one, you can have one more." Christina peels the banana using her thumb and fore-finger on her right hand. She puts the entire banana in her mouth and grabs for a second banana. The teacher says, "Chew up your banana. I don't want you to choke. Thank you for sitting while you are chewing." Christina smiles and takes a second banana and peels it in the same manner as before. She takes a large bite of the banana, eating half of it at once. She grabs her glass of milk with both hands and takes a large gulp. She burps loudly. The teacher says, "Excuse you." Christina leaves the table and dumps the uneaten part of the banana in the waste can. She uses a rag (the teacher gave her) to wash each finger individually and then wipes her face.	She didn't wash her hands, and the teacher didn't catch it! Okay with this limit. Continues eating snack. Good fine motor skills to peel own banana. She seems very hungry—when did she last eat? Receptive to positive reinforcement by teacher, seemed pleased with own behavior. In the process of learning manners. She didn't repeat the statement, though. Good self-help skills.
She walks in a stiff legged motion to another area of the classroom.	Always on the move!!

Panel Documentation

A panel is a two-dimensional display to communicate with others the learning that occurred during an activity. Panels present the learning of a group of children; thus, different children and their work must be featured. For ease of reading, you should neatly handwrite or type your message. Then, adhere all sections mentioned in the following list on a foam board, poster board, or trifold board.

A panel should contain the following information:

♡ Title of the activity
♡ A record of the children's *actual* words while engaging with the materials or interacting with peers
♡ Artifacts to document representations of the children's thinking—drawings paintings, writings, and/or graphs—or photographs of the children's work on sculptures, creative drama/movements, or roles during dramatic play
♡ A narrative that highlights and explains what learning and interactions occurred

To fulfill the goal of communicating with others, the panel will need to be displayed in a prominent location. Invite others to look at and converse about the children's work. Include the children as part of the audience by reviewing their work as a way to promote language, cognitive, and social development. Also, build on the experience during future activities.

For additional resources on making panels, see:

Gandini, L., & Pope Edwards, C. (Eds.). (2001). *Bambini: The Italian approach to infant/toddler care.* New York: Teachers College Press.

Helm, J. H., Beneke, S., & Steinheimer, K. (1998). *Windows on learning: Documenting young children's work.* New York: Teachers College Press.

Pope Edwards, C., Gandini, L., & Forman, G. (Eds.). (1993). *The hundred languages of children.* Norwood, NJ: Ablex.

Lesson Plan

Name: _____ Date: _____

Developmental area: _____

Child's developmental goals:

Materials:

Preparation:

Nurturing strategies:

Variations:

Infant Daily Communication: Home to Center

Infant's name: _____ Parent's name: _____

Day/date: _____ Time of arrival: _____ Time of departure: _____

FILLED IN BY PARENT:

Infant seems:
[ ] Normal, typical
[ ] Bit fussy
[ ] Not acting like usual

Infant slept:
[ ] Soundly
[ ] Woke up several times
[ ] Did not sleep well

Infant ate:
[ ] Meal before coming _____
[ ] Bottle or nursed before coming
[ ] Snack before coming
[ ] Nothing

Infant changed:
[ ] Bowel movement   Time _____
[ ] Wet   Time _____

SPECIAL INSTRUCTIONS FOR TODAY:

_____

_____

_____

_____

Parent's signature: _____

Caregiver's signature: _____

Adapted with permission from New Horizon Child Care, Inc.

Infant Daily Communication: Center to Home

Date: _____ Check-in time: _____

Read infant's daily communication: Home to center _____

_____

FILLED IN BY CAREGIVER:

Infant slept: Asleep _____ Awake _____

Asleep _____ Awake _____

Infant ate: Time _____ What _____ Amount _____

Time _____ What _____ Amount _____

Time _____ What _____ Amount _____

Infant changed: Time _____ Wet _____ Bowel movement _____

Time _____ Wet _____ Bowel movement _____

Time _____ Wet _____ Bowel movement _____

INTERACTIONS/ACTIVITIES: *(Description of adult interaction, developmental tasks, and activities that sustained child's interest)*

_____

_____

_____

_____

NOTES TO PARENTS:

_____

_____

_____

Caregiver's signature: _____

Parent's signature: _____

We need: [ ] Diapers   [ ] Wipes   [ ] Formula   [ ] Baby food

[ ] Change of clothing   [ ] Blankets   [ ] Other: _____

Adapted with permission from New Horizon Child Care, Inc.